D1405306

Children
Readings in Behavior and Development

Edited by

ELLIS D. EVANS
University of Washington

Holt, Rinehart and Winston, Inc.
New York Chicago San Francisco Atlanta Dallas
Montreal Toronto London

A Word of Thanks

The success of a project such as a book of readings is directly contingent upon the generous permission of its contributors. The editor wishes to express his deep gratitude to the authors and publishers whose works are included herein. Royalties from the sale of this volume are consigned to the March of Dimes; therefore, all authors are making possible a venture committed to the improvement of childhood disorders.

Library of Congress Catalog Card Number: 68–17851

03-068995-3

Printed in the United States of America

90123 22 98765432

Foreword

One of my most distinctive professional and personal pleasures during the five and one-half years preceding the writing of this preface has been the opportunity to know Ellis D. Evans, first as a student and now as a full-fledged professional worker and scholar in the field of developmental psychology.

He provides a distinct service in giving auxiliary breadth and depth to *Children: Behavior and Development*. His *Readings* should serve other general treatments of child development equally well.

I was impressed with his scholarly acuity as we discussed his plans for *Readings*. My reaction to seeing his set of final choices was indeed positive. In the press of time, I had not read some of the papers he had selected, but every one of such articles that he had chosen I found on an urgent (but often neglected) list I keep, entitled *Must read at once.*

Dr. Evans' reputation as an outstanding teacher has spread from Seattle to Atlanta through the rather reliable grapevine that professors have established and which they maintain in good working order. His selection of entries for his *Readings* is simply one more evidence of his interest in effective teaching and of his scholarly efficiency. One purpose of any course is that students, upon completing it, look at the field it represents not only with more knowledge, but also with more critical discrimination. *Children* attempts this; but a textbook cannot provide the exercise in depth reading which comes from recourse to original sources, when these original sources are wisely chosen. All Dr. Evans' choices are timely, and some of them will probably become classics in the field. A selective appreciation of their relevance and their strong and weak points will make any student of child development a stronger student. Yet, presentation of "readings" articles in isolation, with no editorial role aimed toward synthesizing, showing relevance, and pointing toward evaluation is likely to leave all but the most sophisticated students wondering exactly where they have been when they have finished reading. Many books of readings suffer from undereditorializing, while in a few the editor has literally predigested his inclusions, much in the manner of a mother pigeon feeding her young. Dr. Evans seems to me to fall at the Golden Mean. He supplies "reading organizers," as it were, that put the student reader in the ball park, yet are subtle enough to leave him free to play the game according to his own ingenuity and motivation. One cannot ask for more from an editor. In other words, Dr. Evans' contribution consists not only of canny choices of content, but moreover of sagacious use of guiding and integrating editorship. This is indeed a difficult, but worthwhile, original contribution to the field.

A book of readings such as the present volume also serves a very practical purpose: few libraries are equipped with enough copies of journals to accommodate assigned original source reading for any but a very small class. The professor who makes such readings often incurs the wrath of librarians. The journals in which the readings appear may be at the bindery, and there may be a long delay while students with money in their pockets wait to have offprints made (a process of dubious legality). Occasionally the entire issue of the journal may be permanently "borrowed" from the library—and even from the personal libraries of one's fellow professors. None of these things makes a professor socially comfortable on his campus.

A good book of readings minimizes these problems, particularly when it is as timely as the present volume.

To summarize, I appreciate the care and intelligence Professor Evans has brought to bear on the present book of readings and regard it as a valuable addition to the child-development field as well as to the book: *Children: Behavior and Development.*

Atlanta, Georgia
January 1968

Boyd R. McCandless

Preface

Introduction

Research and theory provide the stuff of which a scientific discipline is made, and the literature concerned with the scientific study of child behavior and development is, like that of other disciplines, proliferating at a rapid rate. This proliferation makes it increasingly difficult for a student of child development to maintain a perspective upon all avenues of research and theory development. Therefore, from time to time a compilation of papers reflecting various facets of the child-development literature proves very helpful in familiarizing students with major research problems and trends. This volume represents just such a compilation and has as a basic purpose to provide to students a convenient source of original papers that illustrate scholarly endeavor in the field of child development. The 38 papers included here, while not a reflection of all trends of significance in the literature, do provide a rich sample of data useful for survey and other educational purposes.

Criteria for Selection of the Papers

The selectivity exercised by an editor in the process of compiling a volume such as this reflects, inevitably, his own biases. Nevertheless, several objective criteria have been utilized for the execution of this project. These criteria include relevancy to standard textbooks on child development, variety, recency, and readability.

Relevance Many instructors and their students find a book of readings a useful adjunct to teaching and learning. Therefore, the selections in this volume have been made on the basis of their relevance to topics appearing with great frequency in most current child-development texts. As the chapter titles indicate, this volume is most closely integrated with its companion text, *Children: Behavior and Development* (second edition), by Boyd R. McCandless and published by Holt, Rinehart and Winston, Inc. (1967). Several of the readings have served as basic reference material for portions of the McCandless text, for example, the Frank (1.6) and Lowe (3.5) papers. Most of the other readings extend features of McCandless' discussion of certain issues, and a few introduce new concepts not specifically embodied in his textbook. Many provocative relationships among selections are suggested within the context of the orientation statement preceding each individual paper.

Variety Child behavior and development is studied in many different ways and with varying degrees of specificity. In this volume the student will encounter various types of studies, including cross-cultural comparisons, as illustrated by Barry, Child, and Bacon (1.3), and the experimental method, as illustrated by Bandura, Ross, and Ross (2.7). Bronson (2.1) supplies an empirical analysis of longitudinal data framed within the critical periods hypothesis. The Zigler and Kanzer study (2.5) involves the manipulation of experimental variables while Maurer (5.5) illustrates the cross-sectional approach to child study. Ames and Ilg (6.2) provide a prediction study founded upon correlational data, and Lipsitt (3.3) describes a relationship between two organismic variables, the self concept and anxiety. These are but a few of many empirically based studies to be found in this volume, studies that seek to answer different kinds of questions about different aspects of children's behavior and development. Students may find a classificatory system described in Chapter 2 (pp. 59–64) of the McCandless text useful in conceptualizing the types of studies represented in this book of readings.

Another major category in this volume encompasses papers such as those by Marshall (2.8) and Golann (4.4), which are both reviews of research related to a particular topic, and those of Stott and Ball (4.1) and of Hunt (6.3), which are high-level theoretical analyses of issues in child development. A third category circumscribes papers that are more philosophical and speculative in nature. Examples of such papers, often labeled "wisdom" articles in contrast to direct reports of research, include the work of Silverman (6.5) and Ausubel (6.6).

Recency Publications from the literature of the past decade provide the nucleus of this book. Many selections have appeared in journals within the past three years. This enables one to sense the flavor of current literature and to become familiar with new research findings and theoretical concepts. The recency criterion does not intend to imply that recent studies are necessarily better than their predecessors, although this is sometimes true inasmuch as research techniques are continually being improved. Space has not permitted the inclusion of classic studies of the 1930s and 1940s which have given impetus to many research trends apparent in this decade. Collections of earlier research are available for reference purposes, however, and interested students are encouraged to utilize these freely.*

Readability With few exceptions, skill in interpreting complex statistical data is not a prerequisite to understanding these selections. For the most part, highly technical, specific, and abstruse papers have been avoided, primarily out of regard for the beginning student who has

*For example: Seidman, Jerome (Ed.) *The Child: A Book of Readings.* New York: Holt, Rinehart and Winston, 1958. Baller, Warren (Ed.) *Readings in the Psychology of Human Growth and Development.* New York: Holt, Rinehart and Winston, 1962.

not yet developed competencies in statistical analysis. Nevertheless, since data from the empirical studies mentioned earlier may, in some cases, convey little meaning to a student completely unacquainted with descriptive statistics—especially correlation coefficients—and inferential statistics based upon probability, thorough study of the passage on "Statistical and Measurement Considerations" in the McCandless text (pp. 75–84) is recommended.

Organization of the Book

The content of many papers reproduced in this book is such that a variety of combinations are possible. Rarely are child-development research activities designed so that their themes are mutually exclusive, in any absolute sense. For example, many papers, while devoted to problems of social development and emotional behavior, carry implications for children's learning and motivation. The same may be said for research concerned with child-rearing practices. The organization portrayed in this book is only one of many alternative approaches that might be justified.

As was indicated earlier, the arrangement of topics in this book closely follows the format of Boyd R. McCandless' *Children: Behavior and Development* (second edition). Chapter 1 leads off with an analysis of historical developments in child rearing. This provides a point of departure for contemporary studies and analyses of broad cultural and social effects upon child-rearing practices and children's development. The issue of familial influences on the development of psychopathology in children and a lucid commentary on current socialization trends in our society conclude Chapter 1.

Chapters 2 and 3 are addressed to the foundations of development: learning and motivation. Chapter 2 embraces position papers on the optimal characteristics of the learning environment for the young child, the concept of reinforcement, and the effects of punishment on children's learning. Two papers are addressed to the motivational implications of critical periods in development. Further, the phenomena of learning by imitation, dependency behavior, and the effects of differential classes of verbal reinforcers on children's learning are examined. Chapter 3 extends the study of learning and motivation to such special factors as locus of control, intellectual-achievement responsibility in children, and the self concept.

Cognitive functioning, its development and measurement, provides the substance of Chapter 4. This chapter opens with an overview of the changes that have taken place in psychologists' conceptualizations of the construct intelligence. An original paper by Jean Piaget conveys this influential theorist's views on the development of basic cognitive processes, and the concept cognitive style is central to Irving Sigel's analysis of the limitations entailed in assessing intelligence by conventional techniques.

The extremely popular, yet problematic, study of creativity is dissected and critiqued in Chapter 4, after which follows a study of the relationships of cognitive style to certain anatomical characteristics of children. Closely related to the latter study is the terminal paper in Chapter 4, which deals with motor response inhibition and intellectual behavior.

A wide spectrum of topics related to social and emotional development constitutes Chapter 5. The opening paper, which focuses upon broad principles applicable to social development during the period of infancy, is followed by three selections that share an interest in the concept of identification. The last of this trilogy, a paper by Winfred F. Hill (5.4), draws heavily upon concepts from learning theory and thus is intimately related to Chapter 2 as well as to its "home" chapter. Aspects of children's fears and aggressive behavior are discussed in the last two studies of Chapter 5.

The application of data yielded by a scientific study of child behavior and development to problems of the socialization of children, including formal education, is a foremost concern of many psychologists. Chapter 6 opens with an analysis of several issues involved in bridging the gap between pure science and applied science with respect to data from developmental psychology. Other topics considered in this chapter are the use of specific procedures to assess developmental status and predict school-relevant behavior, and the apparent influence of test anxiety on children's intellectual behavior. The timely subject of education for the socially disadvantaged is represented in Chapter 6 by a thoughtful analysis of the psychological foundations of educational movements such as the Head Start Program. Finally, the issues of discipline and mental health, sources of controversy and perplexity to virtually all psychologists and educators, are examined. These last papers have been included chiefly to provoke thoughtful discussion among students who utilize this book during their formal study of child development.

Additional Features of This Book

Each selection is preceded by a brief orientation statement, the purpose of which is threefold: first, to provide some background to the basic theme(s) reflected in each selection; second, to suggest some relationships among the selections; and third, to clarify some issues for students to consider in the process of interpreting each selection.

In addition to the orientation to each paper, a brief list of related studies and position papers is provided for reference. The editor would have preferred to include the full text of many of these references in the present volume, but space and cost were limiting factors. These practical problems also made it impossible to include detailed material from all facets of contemporary dimensions of child-development research, notably early infancy and children's language development. For a broad sampling of research in these areas, two recently published collections will be of value to readers. These are:

Brackbill, Yvonne, and Thompson, George G. (Eds.) *Behavior in Infancy and Early Childhood*. New York: The Free Press, 1967.

DeCecco, John P. (Ed.) *The Psychology of Language, Thought, and Instruction*. New York: Holt, Rinehart and Winston, 1967.

Seattle, Washington E.D.E
January 1968

Contents

CROSS-REFERENCE CHART FOR USE WITH BOYD R. MCCANDLESS,
Children: Behavior and Development

McCandless Chapters	*Readings Chapters*
1. Culture and the Human Organism 3. Child-Rearing Practices	1. Culture, Child-Rearing Practices, and Child Development
4. Learning and Motivation	2. Motivation and Learning
5. Special Factors in Human Learning 6. The Self-Concept	3. Special Factors in Learning: Expectancies and the Self Concept
7. Intelligence: Measurement and Educational Practices 8. Sources of Variation in Measured Intelligence	4. Cognitive Functioning
10. Social and Emotional Development 11. Sex-Typing, Identification, and Moral Development	5. Social Development, Identification, and Emotional Behavior
13. Child Development and Childhood Education 14. The Middle-Class Teacher and the Every-Class Child	6. Child Development and Childhood Education

Current Texts in Child Development Cross-referenced to Evans Text in the chart on pp. xvi–xviii

Baldwin, Alfred L. *Theories of Child Development.* New York: John Wiley, 1967, 618 pp.

Bernard, Harold W. *Human Development in Western Culture.* (2d ed.) Boston: Allyn and Bacon, 1966, 552 pp.

Dinkmeyer, Don C. *Child Development: The Emerging Self.* Englewood Cliffs, N.J.: Prentice-Hall, 1965, 434 pp.

Garrison, Karl C., Albert J. Kingston, and Harold W. Bernard. *The Psychology of Childhood.* New York: Scribner's, 1967, 457 pp.

Hurlock, Elizabeth B. *Child Development* (4th ed.) New York: McGraw-Hill, 1964, 776 pp.

Johnson, Ronald C., and Gene R. Medinnus. *Child Psychology: Behavior and Development.* New York: Wiley, 1965, 556 pp.

McCandless, Boyd R. *Children: Behavior and Development* (2d ed.) New York: Holt, Rinehart and Winston, 1967, 671 pp.

Meyer, William J. *Developmental Psychology.* New York: Center for Applied Research in Education, 1964, 116 pp.

Munn, Norman L. *The Evolution and Growth of Human Behavior* (2d ed.) Boston: Houghton Mifflin, 1965, 594 pp.

Mussen, Paul H., John J. Conger, and Jerome Kagan. *Child Development and Personality* (2d ed.) New York: Harper and Row, 1963, 625 pp.

Mussen, Paul H. *The Psychological Development of the Child.* Englewood Cliffs, N.J.: Prentice-Hall, 1963, 109 pp.

Smart, Mollie S., and Russell C. Smart. *Children: Development and Relationships.* New York: Macmillan, 1967, 582 pp.

Stott, Leland H. *Child Development.* New York: Holt, Rinehart and Winston, 1967, 513 pp.

Thompson, George G. *Child Psychology* (2d ed.) Boston: Houghton Mifflin, 1962, 714 pp.

Watson, Robert I. *Psychology of the Child* (2d ed.) New York: Wiley, 1965, 635 pp.

Chart Cross-referencing Evans' text with Some Current Textbooks in Child Development (Double Numbers Refer to Readings in Evans)

Chap. Numbers in Texts Listed on p. xvi	*Baldwin (1967)*	*Bernard (rev. 1967)*	*Dinkmeyer (1965)*	*Garrison (1967)*	*Hurlock (rev. 1964)*
1					6.1
2					
3		6.1		2.1, 2.3, 2.6	
4		3.1			4.5, 4.6
5	4.2, 4.3	4.1, 4.2, 4.3, 4.4	2.2, 2.4, 2.5, 2.8, 3.1, 3.2		
6		2.1, 2.2, 5.1	1.2, 1.3, 1.4, 5.1		
7		2.1, 2.2, 4.6, 6.2	3.3, 3.4, 3.5	4.1, 4.2, 4.3, 4.4	2.6, 2.7, 5.5, 5.6
8		2.3	4.1, 4.2, 4.3, 4.4	2.7, 5.5, 5.8	5.1
9			2.6, 2.7, 5.5, 5.6	5.2, 5.3, 5.4	6.5, 6.6
10			2.1, 2.3, 6.5	2.2, 3.3, 3.4, 3.5, 5.1	
11	5.6		5.2, 5.3, 5.4	1.1, 1.5, 1.6, 1.7	4.1, 4.2, 4.3, 4.4
12	2.1	1.1, 1.4, 1.5, 1.7, 5.2, 5.3	3.2, 6.1, 6.2, 6.3, 6.4	Chap. 6	5.2, 5.3, 5.4
13		3.2, 6.3, 6.4, 6.5, 6.6	1.5, 1.6, 1.7		
14	2.4, 2.5				1.1, 1.5, 1.6, 1.7, 2.2
15	1.2, 1.3, 1.4, 2.6, 2.7, 5.2, 5.3, 5.4	1.6			2.1, 2.3, and Chap. 3
16		3.3, 3.4			

Chap. Numbers in Text	*Johnson, Medinnus (1965)*	*McCandless (rev. 1967)*	*Meyer (1964)*	*Mussen, Conger, Kagan (rev. 1963)*	*Munn (rev. 1965)*
1		1.1, 1.2, 1.3, 1.4	2.1, 2.3	1.1	
2					
3		1.5, 1.6, 1.7	4.1, 4.3, 4.4, 6.3		
4	Chap. 2	Chap. 2			
5		3.1, 3.2	3.1, 3.2, 4.2, 4.5, 4.6	2.4, 2.5, 2.6, 2.8	2.2
6	4.1, 4.2, 4.3, 4.4	3.3, 3.4, 3.5	3.3, 3.4, 3.5, 5.5, 5.6, 6.4	5.1	
7	1.1, 1.2, 1.3, 1.4, 1.7	4.1, 4.2, 4.3, 4.4	2.2, 2.6, 2.7, 5.1, 5.2, 5.3, 5.4, and Chap. 1	2.1	2.1, 2.3, 2.4, 4.6
8		4.5, 4.6		2.2, 4.6, 6.3	
9	2.1, 5.1			5.2, 5.3	
10	5.2, 5.3	5.1, 5.5, 5.6		2.7	
11		5.2, 5.3, 5.4		1.4	4.2 and Chap. 3
12	Chap. 6	6.1, 6.2, 6.4, 6.5		2.3, 4.1, 4.3, 6.1, 6.2, 6.4	
13		6.3, 6.6			4.1, 4.3, 4.4, 6.3
14					2.7, 5.5, 5.6, 6.4
15	4.5, 4.6, 5.4, 5.6, and Chap. 3			5.4	5.1
16	1.6				Chap. 1, 5.2, 5.3, 5.4

Chap. Numbers in Text	*Mussen (1963)*	*Smart, Smart (1967)*	*Stott (1967)*	*Thompson (rev. 1962)*	*Watson (rev. 1965)*
1		2.1	1.1		1.1
2	2.1, 2.2, 2.4, 6.1				
3	4.5, 4.6		4.5		
4	4.1, 4.2, 4.3, 4.4, 6.3	2.2		2.1, 2.3	Chap. 1 and 3.1
5	Chap. 1, 2.6, 2.7, 5.2, 5.3, 5.4, 5.6	1.2, 1.3, 1.6, 1.7, 5.1	4.6	Chap. 2	2.4
6	5.1		4.1, 4.3, 4.4	6.4	
7		4.2	2.1, 2.3, 3.2		
8		6.3	2.2, 2.4, 2.5, 2.7, 2.8	2.7, 5.5, 5.6	2.2
9		1.5, 2.6, 2.7, 3.3, 3.4		4.2	5.1
10		4.5	4.2		
11		4.1, 4.3, 4.4	2.5, 2.6	4.1, 4.3, 4.4, 6.3	4.1, 4.3, 4.6
12		2.3, 3.1, 3.2, 6.1, 6.2	5.2, 5.3, 5.4	5.1	
13		1.4, 5.6	1.5, 1.7, 3.1	5.4	2.7, 3.4
14			1.2, 1.3, 1.4, 1.6	1.6	5.2, 5.3, 5.4
15				1.5, 1.7	3.2
16				1.2, 1.3, 1.4, 3.1	3.3, 5.6
17					6.1, 6.2

Children
Readings in Behavior and Development

chapter one

Culture, Child-Rearing Practices, and Child Development

1.1 Orientation

Perhaps the most appropriate way to inaugurate a study of child development is to examine child-rearing practices in historical perspective. Robert Sunley is one of the very few authors who have attempted a synthesis of nineteenth-century literature on child rearing. His sources of information include parent-education literature, medical and religious books, popular journals, children's literature, advertisements, and artifacts such as children's toys and games. Sunley does not attempt to reconstruct parental and child behavior from this material, for this was not his objective. One is prompted to question if the parent-education literature evaluated here is a valid reflection of the practices of the time and did, in fact, influence the nature of socialization practices. Three criteria utilized by Sunley for his analysis tend to support an affirmative response to this question. One criterion he has used is the analysis of content in terms of the *frequency* with which certain topics were treated; another is the *consensus* of attitudes and theories reflected by various publications; a third is the *extent* to which materials were *circulated* throughout the society of that time.

Several penetrating features characterize the Sunley paper. One is his explanation of what was apparently a substantial increase in the amount of child-rearing literature during the middle 1800s. A second is his organization of the literature by topics that are of as much concern to parents today as they were to parents in the 1800s. A third feature is Sunley's description of the broad cultural influences, especially religious doctrine, upon socialization practices. Striking variations in the beliefs adults held about the basic nature of the child and his development are clarified and are shown to be rooted in the general concepts of human nature popular at that time. Vestiges of these concepts can be observed today. For example, Calvinistic interpretations of the nature of human nature are apparent in certain religious literature. However, as Kessen (1963) has indicated, one of the most dramatic changes in the child-development literature in this century relates to the beliefs held by the "experts" about the basic nature of childhood.

Readers are strongly encouraged to compare Sunley's analysis of past literature with Bronfenbrenner's contemporary review of socialization practices, which appears at the end of this chapter.

RECOMMENDED READING

Aries, Phillipe. *Centuries of Childhood: A Social History of Family Life.* New York: Vintage Books, Random House, 1965.

Kessen, William. "Research in the psychological development of infants: An overview." *Merrill-Palmer Quart. Behav. and Develpm.*, **9** (1963), 83–94.

Kessen, William (Ed.) *The Child.* New York: Wiley, 1965.

1.1 Early Nineteenth-Century American Literature on Child Rearing

Robert Sunley

In a changing culture like ours, ideas on how to bring up children undergo many transformations through time. If we look at the ideas prevailing on this subject a hundred years ago, we find, together with the beginnings of

---

Reprinted from *Childhood in Contemporary Cultures,* Margaret Mead and Martha Wolfenstein (Eds.) University of Chicago Press, 1955. By permission of the author and The University of Chicago Press.

many current developments in child rearing, concepts which seem remote, alien, and repugnant to us. However, the attitudes of past generations may retain more of a hold on us than we realize. Ideas we are not conscious of may continue to exert influence on the levels of less conscious feeling, transmitted from one generation to another through child rearing itself, as well as through literature. Thus a study of child-rearing ideas of the past century has a practical as well as a theoretical significance. It is a contribution to cultural history. It also can help to make us aware of precedents which remain dynamically related to our own work in the upbringing and education of children.

Between 1820 and 1860, the period which I have chosen for analysis here, the American public showed a markedly increasing interest in the importance of children and in child-rearing problems. For the first time in the United States, a substantial body of literature appeared on the subject, ranging from practical advice on infant care to elaborate theories on the moral training of children. The child-rearing literature suggests some of the reasons for this increased concern over the upbringing of children: an increasing emphasis on the child as the extension of parental ambitions and as the representative of the parents' status in society; a growing belief in man's power to control the environment and direct the future, including the molding of the child; a new need for personal direction, as established patterns of living and child rearing were being disrupted in the rapid shift to industrialization and urbanization. Child rearing, in the literature, was considered a rational process, certain results flowing forth if certain methods were followed. Particularly in the child-rearing theory based on Calvinism, methods were consciously related to the type of adult desired: a moral, honest, religious, independent individual who would take his proper place in society.

IMPORTANCE OF THE MOTHER

The mother's role in child rearing was generally considered paramount. She was regarded as the child's best instructor, the principal person in forming the child's character, a process which was considered to take place largely during the first six years or so of life.[1] "Especially the mother cannot act without leaving an impression on the child . . . by the mother's forming hand it receives its shape to a great extent, for all its future existence." [2] Thus the mother, according to Lydia Child in the 1830's, had to govern her own feelings and keep her heart and innocence pure.[3] Lydia Sigourney, a woman writer of advanced views, spoke of the "immensity of the mother's trust in raising a child" and "infancy [as] the only period of

[1] Fowler, 1847, p. 132; Searle, 1834, p. 260.

[2] Allen, 1848, p. 97.

[3] Child, 1831, p. 4.

a mother's perfect enjoyment." The mother, she writes, is "to nurture the infant . . . as a germ quickened by Spring, it opens the folding doors of its little heart . . . like timid tendrils, seeking where to twine." [4]

Some authors placed the entire burden of the child's well-being in this life and the next upon the mother: "Yes, mothers, in a certain sense, the destiny of a redeemed world is put into your hands; it is for you to say, whether your children shall be respectable and happy here and prepared for a glorious immortality, or whether they shall dishonor you, and perhaps bring your grey hairs in sorrow to the grave, and sink down themselves at last to eternal despair!" [5] Mothers were charged also with a larger responsibility than that for their individual children, as the following example indicates: "You hold the sceptre in your souls in which, more than in the laws of a legislature, now repose the futurity of the nation, the world, and the destinies of the human race." [6]

The mother represented also the force which protected her children after they had left home. Mother's voice was ever with the child: "In foreign climes the power of the tempter has been dispelled by some word of counsel." [7] An apt motto for these times in which grown-up children were likely to move away to the cities was "A happy childhood is a boy's best safeguard." [8] To insure such results in the adult, however, the mother had to exercise discipline as well as love. One writer inveighs against those who "love their own ease too well to employ that constant care and exertion, which is necessary to restrain children . . . they cannot bear to correct them, or put them to pain, not because they love their children, but because they love themselves, and are unwilling to endure the pain of inflicting punishment and of seeing their children suffer." [9]

The role of the father received little attention, in contrast to the great emphasis placed upon the role of the mother. In many households, especially in the cities and towns, the mother often was seen as devoting herself to the infant, to the neglect of the older children and the father. One writer attributed this shift in wifely and maternal affection to the woman's disappointment in marriage, in failing to receive the love and gratification she had expected.[10] The father in such families, whether from prior disposition or as a result of his wife's absorption in motherhood, then became more occupied with his work. Writers often mention how many fathers spent most of their time away from home and had little to do with their

[4] Sigourney, 1838, pp. 29, vii, viii.
[5] Hall, 1849, p. 27.
[6] Howard, 1849, p. 100.
[7] Canfield, 1849, p. 123.
[8] Bigelow, 1844, p. 28.
[9] Allen, 1849, pp. 128–29.
[10] Calhoun, 1917, p. 133.

children. The father gave such reasons as the need to frequent bars after working hours in order to make business connections.[11] While some writers on the subject still tried to give the father the position of the instructor of the children, even this function seems to have been declining. The mother not only was taking over the teaching of the young child but also was handling the daily disciplinary problems rather than waiting for the father's presence in the evening. Daily religious observances, previously conducted by the father as head of the family, were less and less practiced, and the mother tended to take over what was left of this function.[12]

Corporal punishment was widespread at this time, although many writers opposed it or felt it was best used as a last resort. Accounts indicate that at home it was most often the father who administered corporal punishment. In the school system, such punishment was universal at the beginning of the period 1820–60. At this time teachers were predominantly male. By 1860, an intensive campaign headed by Lyman Cobb had greatly lessened the use of corporal punishment in schools; and at the same time, the great majority of schoolteachers were now women rather than men.[13]

A similar shift thus seems to have occurred inside and outside the home, with discipline placed in the hands of women and with physical punishment apparently abandoned in favor of other forms of discipline to be administered by the mother or woman teacher.

FEEDING AND THE DANGERS OF STUFFING AND DRUGGING

During this period American mothers could, for the first time, turn for detailed, practical advice on infant care to a fairly large body of literature which was not, as earlier, imported from England. This literature generally urged mothers to breast-feed their children, refuting the current objections that breast feeding would spoil the figure, that it would tie the mother down at home, that mothers were too "nervous" to breast-feed. Doctors did recognize that breast feeding was not desirable for some women for health reasons but, in general, claimed that it was best for baby and mother, both physically and emotionally. Literature directed to fashionable women, however, conceded a point by giving advice on artificial or bottle feeding, although condemning the practice.

Writers on infant feeding generally advised leaving it up to the baby to establish a routine as to time and frequency of breast feedings. Guides on feeding were given for babies of various ages, though with some disagreement among the various writers, but with little insistence upon rigid adherence to a regular schedule.[14] There is insufficient evidence to indicate

[11] Beste, 1855, I, 127; Marryat, 1839, II, 115; Abbott, 1842, p. 148.

[12] Kuhn, 1947, pp. 9, 102–3, and 171–72; Sproat, 1819, p. 16.

[13] Cobb, 1847; Branch, 1934, p. 54.

[14] Kuhn, 1947, p. 138.

definitely what the actual practices were, beyond the doctors' advice and the implications as to practice. In general, it appears that the middle and upper economic groups were the ones to use bottle feeding and wet nurses as the alternatives to breast feeding. These same groups entertained the belief that the poor generally nursed their own babies with a plentiful supply of milk for many months. It was also believed that the children of the poor were often fretful as the result of the influence of the mother's ill-governed passions transmitted through the milk.

Medical books, with few exceptions, advocated gradual weaning to preserve the child's temper. However, weaning was to take place within a period of a week or two instead of being dragged out for months. For the completion of weaning it was often considered advisable for the mother to absent herself, to avoid the danger of her yielding to the infant's entreaties. The optimum age for weaning was set variously from eight to twelve months, with no particular change discernible in this time range during the 1820–60 period. The age depended upon other factors also, such as the appearance of teeth, which was a definite signal to begin weaning. Another factor, considered local to the United States, was the season of the year, as weaning in the warm weather was thought to expose the child to "cholera infantum" and other intestinal diseases. Consequently, the time of weaning might be advanced or delayed to avoid the warm weather.[15]

Bottle feeding, known also as "artificial feeding," "raising a baby by hand," or "dry nursing," seems to have been popular first in Continental Europe, then in England, and in the United States only by the beginning of this period, although not unknown before then.[16] Nursing bottles could be purchased inexpensively at drugstores in cities and towns.[17] Many formulas were devised, though it was not until about 1860 that the first good formula, "Liebig's," came into use.[18] Inventors were constantly at work improving the bottle, as evidenced by the steady flow of patents granted; the rubber nipple, for example, was patented in 1845 and was in increasing use from then on.[19]

Wet nurses were drawn primarily from the poor class, and a considerable number appear to have been unmarried mothers. Newspapers in the cities carried listings of wet nurses, even long past Civil War days. Wet nurses, all the books cautioned, should be carefully selected to avoid two dangers: that of the mother losing the baby's love and that of adverse influences on the baby from the wet nurse. Accordingly, the nurse should resemble the mother as closely as possible physically, as well as be in good health, be

[15] Combe, 1840, p. 43; Dewees, 1826, pp. 187–88; Donne, 1859, p. 154.

[16] Combe, 1840, p. 43.

[17] Ireland, 1820, p. 38.

[18] Warren, 1865, p. 10.

[19] Drake, 1948.

calm, reliable, and of good morals. Some felt that wet nursing beyond six months tended to attach the baby too firmly to the nurse.

Overfeeding, before and after weaning, was widely observed by travelers from abroad and was soundly condemned by the authors of the child-rearing literature. Babies on the bottle or those receiving supplementary feeding were often given candy, cake, and other food, as well as "pap," which consisted of moistened meal or bread served in bowls resembling modern gravy boats. Sweets were also given to elicit the baby's pleased response, which some parents took as an evidence of "love." [20] The primary reason for overfeeding, as noted by observers, was to quiet the baby, and there was a belief that servants were the most frequent offenders. Observers also commented that some mothers seemed to believe that an infant would starve if it were not crammed with food from birth. Overfeeding continued throughout childhood in some families; and doctors frequently warned against "piecing," that is, eating between meals.[21] Feedings were apparently somewhat irregular, only an occasional writer suggesting that regular feeding hours be instituted as early as possible, for the mother's comfort and convenience as well as the child's.[22]

Drugs were given to infants to stop their crying and put them to sleep. In the form of patent medicines, drugs were given to remedy a variety of illnesses, major and minor, including gripes, flatulence, and irregular bowels. The use of drugs is described by a contemporary writer: "The bane of infants and young children is laudanum [a form of opium] . . . which is the basis of all quack medicine and given almost indiscriminately in this country to infants, from the moment they are born—till—I may say—the day of their death." [23] Another writer comments, regarding a patent medicine based on laudanum: "If improper food has slain its hundreds, Godfrey's Cordial has slain its thousands." [24]

Alcohol was similarly used to quiet a child both in home-made and in patent medicines. Servants, it was believed, often resorted to such drugging to be quit for a time of a troublesome infant or to make sure the child slept while the servant took time off. Laudanum was used by some working mothers to make sure their children slept while they were away, but evidence indicates that mothers of the upper classes also used such drugs.[25] So often is this practice mentioned and so often condemned by medical writers that it may be inferred that the practice was widespread. A number of infant deaths were officially attributed to opium. In 1837–38, for example, in-

[20] Graves, 1844, p. 96.

[21] Fowler, 1847, p. 178; "Overfeeding of Children," 1839; Hough, 1849, p. 166.

[22] Dwight, 1834, p. 27.

[23] Ireland, 1820, p. 5.

[24] Searle, 1834, p. 212; Chavasse, 1862, p. 46.

[25] Wilson, 1940, p. 35.

quests showed that fifty-two infants were included in the total of one hundred and eighty-six deaths due to opium.[26]

MOTOR DEVELOPMENT AND INDEPENDENCE

The child-rearing literature of this period favored freedom of movement for the infant. The child was to be helped to gain voluntary control of his activity rather than be the passive subject of adult manipulation. Medical advice favored loose, light clothing and condemned the tight clothing and bands to which many infants were subjected.[27] However, babies generally seem to have been overclothed with layers of flannel and wool. Swaddling seems to have been customary in some regions of the country, possibly depending on the national origins of the inhabitants, but evidence is insufficient to indicate how prevalent swaddling was or in precisely which areas.[28] Modifications of swaddling, however, appear to have been widespread; and, in additon to the heavy clothing, the ends of the garments were often tied to prevent movement of hands and feet.[29] The reason given by parents and nurses for such tight clothing was that it gave the baby a proper shape, made it look nice and feel firm, and kept it warm, "like in the womb."[30]

Babies slept in cradles for the most part and were rocked a great deal. One British observer attributed the restlessness of the American adult to violent rocking in infancy.[31] Some mothers also took their infants to sleep with them, a practice which the child-rearing literature warned against as having two dangers. First, the infant sleeping with its mother was likely to be breast-fed too often. Second, there was the danger of "overlaying," which referred to the mother's rolling over and smothering the baby to death during the night.

Parents apparently often forced infants and young children to perform beyond their physical or mental level. Babies were sometimes required to sit upright before being able to do so. Some babies were not permitted to go through the crawling stage (perhaps to prevent dirtiness), and walkers and leading strings were used to get the baby to walk as soon as possible.[32] Mental precociousness was much admired, children being taught lessons far beyond their years, so that they could be shown off before company.

Encouragement of the child's independent activity was found also in many families where babies were permitted to feed themselves from a cup from a very early age; and at ten to fifteen months they would already be

[26] Chavasse, 1862, p. 124.
[27] Dewees, 1826, p. 65; Barwell, 1844, p. 40.
[28] Barwell, 1844, p. 41; Kuhn, 1947, p. 141.
[29] "Improper Clothing," 1838; Wilson, 1940, p. 128.
[30] Alcott, 1836, p. 49; Dewees, 1826, p. 65.
[31] Bishop, 1856, p. 122.
[32] Wilson, 1940, pp. 105, 109.

at the family dinner tables in high chairs, the center of attention. Travelers from abroad often considered this practice repellent because of the baby's noise and grabbing for food.[33]

The crying baby was, as always, a problem for parents. During this period the general attitude seems to have been, "Let the baby cry," rather than to rush at once to its side. One school of thought advised the parent to go to the baby, but not immediately; a certain amount of crying was good exercise for the baby, strengthening its lungs.[34] Too prompt attention to the baby might get it into the habit of making constant demands, which if met, would lead to the baby's becoming the ruler of the family. The other general attitude found in the literature held that the baby should be allowed to cry until it stopped: in this way its "will" would be broken.[35] This second attitude is part of the Calvinist theory on child rearing, of which more will be said in the section on "Moral Development." The use of drugs to halt crying has already been mentioned in the section on "Feeding."

Educational activities for the child up to school age were advocated, to encourage its independent gaining of control. Some authors advised trying to interest the young child in its environment, arousing its curiosity, displaying objects to it, urging close observation, and encouraging nature study and nature collections.[36]

TOILET TRAINING, CLEANLINESS, AND VIRTUE

The child-rearing literature tended to recommend early toilet training, though seldom specifying the exact age when the training was to start or be completed. Early training was advised as a means of establishing "habits of cleanliness and delicacy." One doctor cited with approval the example of a mother who "trained" her child at one month, and he urged other mothers to strive for this ideal.[37] While no specific age was indicated, disgust and disapproval of wetness and lack of control are evident throughout the literature. Training was to be accomplished through frequent changes of the child's clothing, by placing the child on the "chair," and by the example of older children. Some mothers expressed the feeling that success in early toilet training was to the credit of the child and themselves.

Some emphasis is placed in the literature on regularity; failure to "duly" discharge the bowels led to the retention of poisonous matter in the body.[38] Reabsorption would ensue, with dire consequences. Several means to relieve

[33] Gallaudet, 1839; Duncan, 1852, p. 78; Thomson, 1842, p. 31.

[34] Dewees, 1826, p. 115.

[35] "What Manner of Child Shall This Be?" 1843.

[36] Abbott, 1855; Holbrook, 1838.

[37] Dewees, 1826, p. 237.

[38] Warren, 1865, p. 15.

constipation and insure regularity, such as enemas, suppositories, and cathartics, were used with great frequency and for the most part were sanctioned in the literature. One doctor did warn against the "habit" which might be formed by too frequent use of such means, without specifying the precise danger.[39]

Playing with dirt was to be discouraged, according to some writers, as being neither cleanly nor useful; but digging and raking were permissible because they involved learning useful skills. There was much emphasis on cleanliness; soiled clothes should be promptly removed from children, washing should be frequent, and the mother should conduct a daily inspection of the children. Extreme neatness, cleanliness, and orderliness in children met with resounding approval from adults—at least in the literature and in some accounts written by mothers. Cleanliness had a moral counterpart: "For dirt and indelicacy are frequent companions, and a disregard for the decencies of life is a step toward indifference toward its virtues."[40]

Standards of cleanliness for adults, according to observers, were apparently high in regard to care of the person. Americans appeared to several travelers as the cleanest people in the world—not only the prosperous but also the ordinary tradesmen, mechanics, and police always wore clean clothing and even had clean fingernails.[41] An interesting counterpart to this personal cleanliness was the untidy, unkempt appearance of the gardens, yards, streets, and sidewalks.

DANGERS OF SEXUALITY

Masturbation presented a serious problem to the parents of the period. Books warned of the "ruin" consequent upon the child's masturbating—leading to disease, insanity, and even death. It was recognized that the danger applied to younger as well as older children. European doctors whose books were reprinted or read in this country were apparently the originators of such warnings, at least in the literature.[42] Juvenile books, especially the semi-illicit ones, were blamed for exciting children and suggesting possibilities to them.[43] The genitals, some writers advised, should be touched only for strictly hygienic purposes.

Among the more prosperous groups it seems to have been widely believed that children did not discover masturbation by themselves or through spontaneous sexual play with other children of their own class but had to be

[39] Donne, 1859, p. 170.

[40] Barwell, 1844, p. 53.

[41] Beste, 1855, p. 112; Thompson, 1842, p. 16; Baxter, 1855, p. 30.

[42] The European works referred to by American writers were by Tissot, Hufeland, and Lallmand, all of whom wrote between 1760 and 1836.

[43] Ray, 1849, p. 280.

inducted or seduced into such practices by servants, slaves, or depraved school children (presumably of the lower classes). One writer commented: "The coarse hugging, kissing, etc. which the children are sure to receive in great abundance from ignorant and low-minded domestics are certain to develop a blind precocious sexualism of feeling and action, which tends directly to all the evils I have mentioned, on the maturity of those offspring, and sometimes in sudden disease and death to little ones." [44] Catherine Beecher, a sister of Harriet Beecher Stowe, explained that the difficulties of bringing up children properly "are often heightened by the low and depraved character of a great portion of those who act as nurses for young people. One single vulgar, or deceitful, or licentious domestic may in a single month mar the careful and anxious training of years." [45] One of the leading doctors and advisers on children, Dr. Dewees, gave the following warning on spontaneous autoeroticism: "Children should not be permitted to indulge in bed long after daylight; as its warmth, the accumulation of urine and faeces, and the exercise of the imagination, but too often leads to the precocious development of the sexual instinct." [46]

Those who adhered to the Calvinist doctrine of "infant depravity," which held that the infant was destined to commit sins unless given thorough guidance by parents, also believed in "external corruption" of their children. These religious groups favored solitary prayer and solitary Bible reading by young children. An incident related by a mother suggests that one reason such solitary activity was favored was to counteract the child's desire to masturbate. The mother entered her little girl's bedroom precipitately one day, and saw the child hastily change her position. The child refused to answer her mother's question as to what she had been doing. The mother said, "But little children who do not like to tell what they are doing, are in great danger of doing something they are ashamed of." Whereupon the child, wounded, answered, "Oh no, mother, I was only going to pray a little while." [47] Parents and nurses were warned to be suspicious of their children's engaging in masturbation or sexual play with other children. At the same time, adults had to be careful not to be suggestive in their own words or behavior. One writer warns: "A nurse cannot be too guarded in what she says or does in the presence of children, nor must she fancy that they are always infants, or less alive than herself, to what passes before them. At the same time, the precautions taken should be perceived as little as possible, for she will defeat her end, if she excite curiosity, by giving them the idea that there is something to be concealed." [48]

[44] Hough, 1849, p. 160.
[45] Beecher, 1846, p. 13.
[46] Dewees, 1826, p. 251.
[47] "Little Ellen," 1840.
[48] Searle, 1834, p. 269.

MORAL DEVELOPMENT: "INFANT DEPRAVITY" AND "INFANT CONVERSION"

Religious doctrine played an important part in the moral training of the child, not only in the obvious form of religious training, but even more importantly as the ideological basis for child-raising theory and practice. Foremost among these doctrines during this period was the Calvinist theory, which was adhered to not only by the New England Puritans but also by many of the other Protestant sects, such as the Presbyterians, Methodists, and Congregationalists. The keystone of Calvinist doctrine regarding child rearing was "infant depravity," which, leaving theological subtleties aside, consisted in the belief that the infant was born "totally depraved" and doomed to depravity throughout life unless given careful and strict guidance by the parents and, ultimately, saved through Grace.[49] "No child," wrote one New Englander, "has ever been known since the earliest period of the world, destitute of an evil disposition—however sweet it appears."[50]

Complete obedience and submission were thus requisite if the child was to be kept from sin and evil. The parents were considered responsible and so had to exact such obedience in order to carry out their duty. As a corollary, the safety and health of the child depended upon complete submission. Parents were fond of relating how their child's life was saved because the child obeyed at a crucial moment—by taking medicine upon command, for example. Submission was necessary also so that the child would accept unquestioningly the positive virtues and the truth of religion at an age when it was not considered capable of arriving at such truths through its own reasoning.

Submission was obtained by "breaking the will" of the child—a concept not restricted, however, to those actually members of Calvinist religious groups. "Will" was seen as any defiance of the parents' wishes, at any age. "The very infant in your arms will sometimes redden and strike, and throw back its head, and stiffen its little rebellious will."[51] The child was not to have what it wanted, for its desires were sinful, "depraved." The techniques to be used for breaking the will were widely discussed during the period, especially among groups of mothers belonging to the more numerous Protestant-Calvinist sects. Beginning shortly before 1820, these mothers formed discussion groups to talk over child-rearing problems. The groups, known as "Maternal Associations," were spontaneously organized over much of the country, even on the frontier, and in foreign lands by wives of missionaries. Several magazines, either published by or involving these "asso-

[49] Hyde, 1830.

[50] Dwight, 1834, p. 31.

[51] Humphrey, 1840, p. 127.

ciations," gained a very large circulation for those times.[52] The members of the groups belonged generally to the middle-income class. Among the many topics discussed, "breaking the will" and "infant conversion" (referring to a child who became converted to and professed religion as an adult would) were perhaps foremost. In general, breaking of the will or training in obedience was begun by teaching the child to obey every command quickly and completely. Some felt that for the first three months of life, or even the first year, the infant should be tenderly cared for and its wishes granted. But then, "Establish your will, as the law," wrote one woman on the subject, for this would keep the child from experiencing "all those conflicts of feeling of those doubtful as to their guide." She pointed out that George Washington had been trained in this way.[53]

Sooner or later the child would refuse to obey a command, and the issue of "will" was at hand.[54] It was considered fatal to let the child win out. One mother, writing in the *Mother's Magazine* in 1834, described how her sixteen-month-old girl refused to say "dear mama" upon the father's order. She was led into a room alone, where she screamed wildly for ten minutes; then she was commanded again, and again refused. She was then whipped, and asked again. This was kept up for four hours until the child finally obeyed.[55] Parents commonly reported that after one such trial the child became permanently submissive. But not all parents resorted to beatings to gain this end. One mother spoke of "constant though gentle drilling," which consisted partly of refusing to give the child an object just out of its reach, however much it cried.[56] Another mother taught submission and self-denial at one and the same time by taking objects away from the child. Strictness in diet and daily routine was apparently frequently an accompaniment to obedience training. However, many mothers seemed to find it hard to follow out such prescriptions, and the *Mother's Magazine* carried many exhortations to mothers to do their duty toward their children.

"Infant conversion" was considered highly desirable, for it meant that the child had reached the point of accepting on its own the truths of religion and hence was well on the road to being saved from depravity. There were many signs of such conversion—quick conversion not being considered as sound as the more gradual—among which signs were the practices of solitary prayer and Bible reading already mentioned.[57] Little girls were apparently more often converted than boys, and the pages of the magazines

[52] *Mother's Magazine,* 1832–76; *Mother's Assistant,* 1841–63; *Parents' Magazine,* 1840–50.

[53] Sigourney, 1838, p. 35.

[54] Searle, 1834, p. 247.

[55] "To Mothers of Young Families," 1834.

[56] Warren, 1865, p. 39.

[57] Gallaudet, 1838.

contain quite a few melancholy stories of such children who became devoutly religious, submissive, seemingly drained of vitality and desires, and met an early death, often by the age of ten. Such children were held up as models of piety for the others, and a considerable number of children were quoted by their parents as having as a favorite book one of the classic stories of such "infant conversion" and early death.

For the parents of this group, "indulgence" was to be shunned. Presumably, indulgence was more or less equivalent to "spoiling" but carried with it a religious meaning related to "depravity," rather than the merely secular danger of having a troublesome, spoiled child. One writer in the *Mother's Magazine* commented, "Men are made monsters in life by indulgence in infancy."[58] Indulgence abetted natural depravity and jeopardized the child's future. Such a child was likely to become unreasonable in its demands and end up tyrannizing the family.

Somewhat distinct from the Calvinist theory of child rearing, which emphasized the innate tendency toward evil within the child, was a second general theory centered around "hardening" the child and fostering "naturalness" of behavior.[59] This theory, stemming from Locke and to some extent from Rousseau and not rooted in religion, implied that it was the external environment of civilization which was dangerous to the child. Children should become strong, vigorous, unspoiled men, like those in the early days of the country. Cold baths and cold plunges, for example, were considered necessary, in the manner of the Indians. While Locke's writings were apparently rather influential—quotations were printed even in the almanacs and calendars which entered many homes—it is not possible to estimate how widespread this attitude was, though it seemed focused primarily in the East.

A third general theory and body of practice in child rearing can be discerned, apparently widespread, though probably not so prevalent as the Calvinist. This theory advocated gentle treatment of the child and had its roots in English and European movements already afoot.[60] The child was to be led, not driven; persuaded to the right, not commanded. Consistency and firmness were counseled, but with understanding and justice to the child. Encouragements and rewards should be offered; beatings, reproaches, slaps, dark closets, and shaming were to be avoided. Punishment and reward were to be administered not according to the consequences of the child's act but according to the motives. In regard to consistency, one writer even

[58] "Hints for Maternal Education," 1834, p. 115.

[59] Dewees, 1826, p. 131; Edgeworth, 1815; Humphrey, 1840, p. 64; Wilson, 1940, pp. 71, 132; Kuhn, 1947, pp. 54, 162.

[60] De Saussure, 1835; Ackerley, 1836; Bushnell, 1867; Mann, 1863; Barwell, 1844; Cobb, 1847; and Kuhn, 1947, who, in particular, describes the development of this theory in the United States in some detail.

cautioned parents against "the secret smile," in which superficial disapproval of the child's behavior was undone by the tacit approval of the parent in smiling or giving other subtle signs.[61]

Corporal punishment was undesirable, partly because it did not bring about the desired results, partly because the child was felt to be too tender for such treatment. The child was likened to "an immortal bud just commencing to unfold its spotless leaves . . . a beautiful flower opening to the sunshine."[62] The child was ignorant of right rather than bent to wrong. Consequently, the fear of indulging the child and of being dominated by it was not marked, nor was it imperative to "break the will." A firm stand by the parent eliminated obedience problems.

There were also modifications of the Calvinist attitude which approached this third theory. Lydia Child, writing in the early part of the period, denied infant depravity but pointed out the need for a good environment for the child, to keep the child's "bad propensities" down until he was old enough to resist by himself. "Evil is within and without."[63] Other writers did not see corporal punishment as undesirable in itself but felt it should be withheld whenever possible and administered not in anger and the heat of the moment, but dispassionately and with deliberation. By 1844 even the *Mother's Magazine* had begun to admit some moderation of the strict obedience training. Articles appeared encouraging the parents to mingle more with the children, to understand and enter into their feelings. This would not, the writers claimed, result in lessened obedience from the children, nor did it amount to surrendering parental authority.[64]

The main ideas about child rearing in the American literature on this subject in the mid-nineteenth century can be summed up as follows: The mother at this time was expected to take over almost entirely the upbringing of the child, the role of the father declining markedly. Concurrently, the education of the child came more under the direction of women teachers in the schools.[65] With the mother taking over more of the disciplinary functions, it would seem that a major sanction became that of making her love conditional upon the child's obedience and conformity to her standards.[66] This sanction tended to replace, in principle if not in practice, corporal

[61] Hoare, 1829, p. 86.

[62] Taylor, 1849, p. 24; Briggs, 1849, p. 97.

[63] Child, 1831, p. 8.

[64] Abbott, 1844, p. 119.

[65] Geoffrey Gorer in *The American People* (1948) has interpreted the extensive significance for American character of the predominant role of women in the raising and education of children.

[66] Margaret Meade in *And Keep Your Powder Dry* (1942) has stressed the importance of "conditional love" in American mother-child relations.

punishment (associated with fathers and male teachers), which was increasingly frowned upon. The exclusive role of the mother was further enforced by a growing suspicion about nurses, who were regarded in particular as seducers of children.

The activity of the child was to be fostered and encouraged from earliest years. In the interests of this activity, writers inveighed against the overfeeding and soporific drugs which made the child stuporous and inert. Similarly, it was urged that loose clothing for the infant replace tight wrapping, so that he might have greater freedom of movement. The moral counterpart to this approved activity was the early internalization by the child of religious and moral principles. It was not considered desirable for the child to remain protractedly dependent on adult authority. Rather he was to become at an early age a self-maintaining moral being. The highly praised "infant conversion" was a striking instance of such achievement. Until such moral independence could be attained, however, the parents bore a total responsibility for the child's moral and spiritual well-being. The world was fraught with extreme moral hazards, and it was the parents' task to guard the child from "evil within and without."

Concepts of the child's nature varied. According to the Calvinist view, the child was born depraved: "No child has ever been known since the earliest period of the world, destitute of an evil disposition—however sweet it appears." [67] It followed that parents must vigilantly guard children against the tendency of their depraved impulses; enforcing absolute obedience to adult demands could alone secure the child's salvation. Breaking the child's will meant freeing him from the hold of his evil nature.

The second general theory, that of the "hardening" school, deriving from Locke and Rousseau, emphasized the importance of bringing out the manly virtues against the weakening effect of civilization. While the danger to the child was here quite differently defined as compared with the Calvinists, some of the recommendations, such as forcing on the child things that were hard for him to take, were similar.

The third school of thought, advocating "gentle treatment," saw the child as having certain needs and potentialities which the parents were not to frustrate or control, but rather were to help fulfill and encourage into full development. The child's sexual and aggressive drives, which were explicitly recognized and handled by the Calvinists, under this theory were minimized as being not basic or strong but rather elicited as the result of erroneous upbringing by the parents. The child was a tender creature who could be harmed by the lack of nurture, kindly care, and gentle discipline. This latter view would seem to be the one most favored in child-rearing literature today, though without the qualification of the child's fragility.

[67] Dwight, 1834, p. 31.

REFERENCES

Abbott, Jacob. 1844. "The Importance of sympathy between the mother and child." *Mother's Magazine,* **12,** no. 4, 111–119.

Abbott, Jacob. 1857. *Learning To Talk.* New York: Harper & Bros.

Abbott, John S. C. 1842. "Paternal neglect," *Parents' Magazine,* **3,** no. 3, 148.

Ackerley, G. 1836. *On the Management of Children.* New York.

Alcott, William A. 1836. *The Young Mother.* Boston: Light & Stearns.

Allen, Rev. Ralph W. 1848. "A mother's influence." *Mother's Assistant,* **13,** no. 5, 97–100.

Allen, Rev. Ralph W. 1849. "Family government." *ibid.,* **15,** no. 6, 126–129.

Barwell, Mrs. 1844. *Infant Treatment. . . .* (1st Amer. ed. with supplement for the U.S.). Boston: James Mowatt.

Baxter, W. E. 1855. *America and the Americans.* London: Routledge.

Beecher, C. E. 1846. *The Evils Suffered by American Women and Children.* New York: Harper & Bros.

Berger, Max. 1943. *The British Traveller in America, 1836–60.* London: King & Staples, Ltd.

Beste, J. Richard. 1855. *The Wabash.* (2 vols.) London: Hurst & Blackett.

Bigelow, Eliza. 1844. "Make home a happy place." *Mother's Assistant,* **4,** no. 2, 26–28.

Bishop, Isabella L. 1856. *Englishwoman in America.* London: John Murray.

Branch, E. Douglas. 1934. *The Sentimental Years, 1836–60.* New York: D. Appleton-Century Co.

Briggs, Caroline A. 1849. "Intellect of children." *Mother's Assistant,* **14,** no. 5, 97–101.

Bushnell, Horace. 184—. *Christian Nurture.* Reprinted in 1867. New York: Charles Scribner's Sons.

Calhoun, Arthur. 1917–1919. *A Social History of the American Family from Colonial Times to the Present.* (3 vols.) Ceveland: Clark.

Canfield, Charles H. 1849. "Never enter a theatre." *Mother's Assistant,* **15,** no. 6, 121–124.

Chavasse, P. H. 1860. *Advice to a Mother.* (5th London ed.; 1st Amer. ed., 1862.) London: Balliere.

Child, Lydia. 1831. *The Mother's Book.* (2d ed.) Boston: Carter & Hendee.

Chown, Stanley. 1936. "Some notes on the history of infant feeding." *Manitoba Med. Assn. Rev.,* **16,** no. 9, 177–184.

Cobb, Lyman. 1847 *Tendencies of Corporal Punishment as a Means of Moral Discipline in Families and Schools.* New York: Newman & Co.

Combe, Andrew. 1840. *Treatise on the Physiological and Moral Management of Infancy.* Philadelphia: Carey & Hart.

Dewees, William P. 1826. *Treatise on the Physical and Medical Treatment of Children.* Philadelphia: Carey & Lea.

Donne, Alfred. 1859. *Mothers and Infants, Nurses and Nursing.* Boston: Phillips, Sampson & Co.

Drake, T. G. H. 1948. "American infant feeding bottles as disclosed by U.S. patent specifications, 1841–1946." *J. History of Med. and Allied Sci.,* **3,** no. 2, 507–24.

Duncan, Mary. 1852. *America as I Found It.* New York: Robert Carter & Bros.

Dwight, Theodore. 1834. *The Father's Book.* Springfield, Mass.: G. & C. Merriam.

Edgeworth, Maria and Richard. 1815. *On Practical Education.* (2d Amer. ed.) Boston: Wait.

Fleming, Sandford. 1933. *Children and Puritanism.* New Haven: Yale Univ. Press.

Fowler, Orson S. 1847. *Self Culture and Perfection of Character, Including Management of Youth.* New York: Fowler & Wells.

Gallaudet, T. H. 1838. "On the evidence of early piety." *Mother's Magazine,* **6,** no. 11, 241–245.

Gallaudet, T. 1839. "Domestic education at the table." *Mother's Maagzine,* **7,** no. 4, 73–76.

Gorer, Geoffrey. 1948. *The American People.* New York: Norton.

Graves, Mrs. A. J. 1844. *Girlhood and Womanhood.* Boston: Carter & Mussey.

Hall, Mrs. Elizabeth. 1849. "A mother's influence." *Mother's Assistant,* **14,** no. 2, 25–29.

"Hints for maternal education." 1834. *Mother's Magazine,* **2,** no. 8, 113–115.

Hoare, Mrs. Louisa. 1829. *Hints for the Improvement of Early Education and Nursery Discipline.* (Reprinted from the 5th London ed.) Salem: Buffum.

Holbrook, Josiah. 1838. "Domestic education." *Mother's Magazine,* **6,** no. 8, 188–192.

Hough, Lewis S. 1849. *The Science of Man.* Boston: Bela Marsh.

Howard, Rev. Orin B. 1849. "The mother, an educator." *Mother's Assistant* **15,** no. 5, 97–100.

Humphrey, Heman. 1840. "Restraining and governing children's appetites and passions." *Mother's Magazine,* **8,** no. 6, 124–130.

Humphrey, Heman. 1840. *Domestic Education.* Amherst: Adams.

Hyde, Rev. Alvan. 1830. *Essay on the State of Infants.* New York: C. Davis.

"Improper clothing." 1838. *Mother's Magazine,* **6,** no. 9, 214–215.

Ireland, W. M. 1820. *Advice to Mothers on the Management of Infants and Young Children.* New York: B. Young.

Kiefer, Monica. 1948. *American Children through Their Books, 1700–1835.* Philadelphia: Univ. Penna. Press.

Kuhn, Anne L. 1947. *Mother's Role in Childhood Education: New England Concepts, 1830–60.* ("Yale Studies in Religious Education," vol. **29.**) New Haven: Yale Univ. Press.

"Little Ellen." 1840. *Mother's Magazine,* **8,** no. 1, 6–14.

Mann, Mrs. Horace, and Elizabeth Peabody. 1863. *Moral Culture of Infancy and Kindergarten Guide.* Boston: Burnham.

Marryat, Frederick. 1839. *A Diary in America.* (2 vols.) Philadelphia: Carey & Hart.

Mead, Margaret. 1942. *And Keep Your Powder Dry.* New York: Morrow.

Mott, Frank L. 1930. *A History of American Magazines, 1741–1850.* New York: Appleton.
Mother's Assistant. 1841–1863. Boston.
Mother's Magazine. 1832–1876. New York.
"Overfeeding of children." 1839. In *Lady's Annual Register,* ed. Caroline Gilman. Boston: T. H. Carter, p. 60.
Parents' Magazine. 1840–1850. Gilmanton and Concord, N.H.
Ray, Isaac. 1863. *Mental Hygiene.* Boston: Tichnor & Fields.
Saussure, Mme Necker de. 1835. *Progressive Education.* Notes, Appendix, and translation by Emma Willard and Almira Phelps. Boston: Tichnor.
Searle, Rev. Thomas. 1834. *Companion to Seasons of Maternal Solicitude.* New York: Moore & Payne, Clinton Hall.
Sigourney, Lydia H. 1838. *Letters to Mothers.* Hartford: Hudson & Skinner.
Sproat, Mrs. Nancy. 1819. *Family Lectures.* Boston: Armstrong.
Taylor, Catherine L. 1849. "Education." *Mother's Assistant,* **15,** no. 4, 73–80.
Thomson, William. 1842. *A Tradesman's Travels in the United States.* Edinburgh: Oliver & Boyd.
"To mothers of young families." 1834. *Mother's Magazine,* **2,** no. 4, 53–55.
Warren, Eliza. 1865. *How I Managed My Children. . . .* Boston: Loring.
"What manner of child shall this be?" 1843. *Mother's Magazine,* **11,** no. 3, 52–54.
Wilson, Elizabeth A. 1940. "Hygienic care and management of the child in the American family prior to 1860." Unpubl. master's thesis. Duke Univ., Durham, N.C.

1.2 Orientation

One fascinating pathway of research in child development is the investigation of the relation of culture to concepts of personality. As research evidence has accumulated, it has become increasingly apparent that variations in personality development are associated with culturally based variations in child rearing. One objective of cross-cultural research has involved the attempt to ferret out the various ecological factors that may produce, or which at least are related to, observed variations in child-rearing patterns. The following example of this approach specifically examines the relationship of beliefs held about deities in various societies to the infant and child care practices executed in those societies.

The interpretation of data yielded by cross-cultural research such as the Lambert, Triandis, and Wolf study, has frequently been complicated by the "chicken-egg" phenomenon. For example, do beliefs about the supernatural motivate certain child-rearing practices? Or does the way in which a child is handled by his parents influence his beliefs about the supernatural? With this in mind the reader may consider the proferred interpretation in this study especially provocative. Further, portions of this study are concerned with data relative to self-reliance and independence training and to an analysis that draws upon such concepts as nurturance, imitation, identification, and anxiety, all of which are phenomena of central importance to child psychologists. These phenomena provide the substance for many papers that follow in this volume.

RECOMMENDED READING

Elonen, A. S. "The effect of childrearing on behavior in different cultures." *Amer. J. Orthopsychiat.*, **31** (1961), 505–512.

Mead, Margaret and Martha Wolfenstein (Eds.) *Childhood in Contemporary Cultures.* Chicago: Univ. of Chicago Press, 1955.

Whiting, Beatrice (Ed.) *Six Cultures: Studies in Child Rearing.* New York: Wiley, 1963.

Whiting, J. M. W. and I. L. Child. *Child Training and Personality.* New Haven, Conn.: Yale Univ. Press, 1953.

1.2 Some Correlates of Beliefs in the Malevolence and Benevolence of Supernatural Beings: A Cross-societal Study

William W. Lambert, CORNELL UNIVERSITY
Leigh Minturn Triandis, UNIVERSITY OF COLORADO, BOULDER
Margery Wolf, CORNELL UNIVERSITY

A study of some of the social psychological functions of "primitive" religious beliefs, this paper tests cross-societally some hypotheses about how general anticipations of pain develop in children, and the relation of these to aspects of the formal belief systems of a society. The major hypothesis was that beliefs in the *malevolence* of the supernatural world reflect punitive practices in infant and child rearing, while beliefs in the *benevolence* of the supernatural world reflect nurturant practices in infant and child

Reprinted from *Journal of Abnormal and Social Psychology,* **58** (1959), 162–169. By permission of the authors and the American Psychological Association, Inc. [Footnotes 1, 3, 5, and part of footnote 4 of the original article have been omitted from this reprinting by the kind permission of the authors and the American Psychological Association, Inc.]

training. The research program in which the present study is included investigated antecedents of aggression by means both of direct field study (8) (not reported here) and of ratings derived from ethnographic reports of 62 societies.

METHOD

The societies rated for the present paper include a wide range of geographic settings. Thirty-one of Murdock's[1] 61 world culture areas are represented by at least one society. Our sources were necessarily limited to those affording adequate descriptions of child training practices. Most of the ethnographic sources were selected from the bibliography of Heinicke and Whiting (5). The geographical distribution of our "sample" is shown in Table 1. None of the tables of results includes all these cultures because in each case the available sources provided inadequate information for some of the ratings. Table 2 lists most of the societies studied. We attempted ratings that would reflect the *general* benevolence and aggressiveness of the supernatural belief system, on the assumption that there is some basic coherence in the "traits" underlying the various representations that the gods and spirits may take within the belief systems of a culture. The raters had therefore to consider the ethnographer's report of all situations in adult life in which the supernatural appears in any form; and specific beliefs in supernatural intervention in formal religion, ritual, witchcraft, and sorcery were thus all of some importance in making the judgments.

TABLE 1. Geographical Distribution of Societies in Sample

Polynesia	Micronesia	Melanesia	Indonesia
6	3	7	7
Africa	**Eurasia**	**North Amer.**	**South Amer.**
11	5	17	6

The ratings on socialization practices and on beliefs about gods were made independently, the former under the direction of Irvin Child at Yale University and the latter by members of a research seminar under the direction of Lambert and Triandis at Cornell. A recent analysis of the Yale data has been presented in two papers by Child et al. (3) and Barry et al. (1).

[1] Murdock, G. P. *World Ethnographic Sample* (mimeographed paper).

TABLE 2. Relation Between Absence of Pain from Nurturing Agent in Infancy and Properties of the Supernaturals [a]

High Pain (Low Absence of Pain)	Low Pain (High Absence of Pain)
Supernaturals—Mainly Aggressive	
Alor	Andaman
Aymara	Bena
BaVenda	Lepcha
Chagga	Lesu
Chirricahua Apache	Manus
Dahomey	Wogeo
Kurtachi	Yagua
Kwakiutl	
Kwoma	
Maori	
Navaho	
Ojibwa	
Lovedo	
Siriono	
Tenetehara	
Tepotztlan	
Thonga	
Supernaturals—Mainly Benevolent	
Arapesh	Ashanti
Chamorro	Chenchu
Klamath	Cheyenne
Ontong-Java	Comanche
Ovimbundu	Fiji
Puka Puka	Hopi
Tallensi	Papago
	Samoa
	Teton
	Tikopia
	Winnebago
	Zuni

[a] $p = .05$. 95 percent confidence limits for the relative frequency $(29/14 = .68) = .51 - .81$ (4; 66–69).

Socialization Scales[2]

Independent ratings of socialization measures were made by two judges on a 7-point scale, the sum of the two ratings being the score.

[2] In this study, only the infancy and childhood ratings related to boys are used.

Infancy Ratings were made on several variables covering the first year of a child's life and as long thereafter as the treatment of the infant remains approximately constant. The nine scales used were: *protection from environmental discomforts, absence of pain inflicted by nurturant agent, over-all indulgence, diffusion of nurturance, display of affection, consistency of drive reduction, immediacy of drive reduction, degree of drive reduction,* and *constancy of presence of nurturing agent.* The scale on over-all indulgence covers all the data on which the other infancy scales were rated, except diffusion of nurturance, in addition to other general statements on the topic made by the ethnographer. In regard to the scale of environmental discomforts, raters considered the extent to which these were not experienced, were usually prevented, or were quickly eliminated. Pain inflicted by nurturant agent included such things as cold baths, depilation, and so on, as well as physical punishment. In considering diffusion of nurturance, raters judged the degree to which nurturance is shared by others than the mother, who was thus used as reference point.

Childhood Ratings were made for the period between infancy and puberty (roughly 5–12 years). Scales for six behavior areas were rated: *nurturance, responsibility, self-reliance, achievement, obedience,* and *general independence.* For each of the scales, ratings were made on the basis of "positive training" (both reward for presence and punishment for absence of the behavior), punishment for nonperformance only, punishment for performance, and frequency of performance. In scoring "positive training," raters considered frequency, degree, consistency, and immediacy of reward for performance and of punishment for nonperformance. Examples of rewards are adult approval, approval of contemporaries, status gain, basic drive reduction, material gain, and anxiety avoidance. In scoring punishment, raters considered severity and frequency. Examples of punishments are corporal punishment, disapproval, deprivation (of freedom, food, etc.), threats, and natural consequences (such as curtailed freedom, food, etc.).

Scales on Properties of the Deities

A god or spirit was defined as any supernatural being who was capable in principle of responding to the actions of tribal members. The definition was designed to include diverse kinds of gods and spirits and to exclude such impersonal life forces as *mana.* In scoring aggressive behavior by the gods, judges were instructed to consider the frequency with which gods were considered responsible for such occurrences as famines, plagues, weather disturbances, personal mishaps, etc. Examples of benevolent behavior ascribed to the gods include protection from enemies, granting personal favors, curing, growing good crops, good hunting, etc. The bad things and good things that happen to people in a primitive society are much the same everywhere—sickness, death, love, birth, good hunting, or good crops cover most of the instances, and in terms of frequency the weight probably lies with the first four. Our procedure amounted to asking what proportion of these good or bad "things" are referred to the supernatural.

Two ratings were made of benevolence and aggressiveness with regard both to frequency of benevolent or aggressive action and to itensity of the modal action. The frequency scales were stated as the proportion of all the acts of the gods which were aggressive or benevolent. Any act could be considered as benevolent or aggressive, as both benevolent and aggressive, or as neither benevolent nor aggressive. The intensity measures were an over-all rating of the intensity of the gods' benevolent or aggressive actions. A culture was termed either "mainly aggressive" or "mainly benevolent" on the basis of the arithmetic relation between the two frequency scales, with the intensity scales being used to determine ties. Seven-point scales were used. If the ratings obtained independently by two raters diverged by more than two points, the raters conferred on the evidence involved in their judgments, and where agreement was not reached the score was omitted. Ratings with a disagreement of two points or less were averaged. In 85% of all the cases, the independent original ratings differed from each other by two points or less.

We report the following socialization data, knowing that the various measures of both infancy and childhood treatment are statistically and sometimes definitionally related. Our argument outlines one way of explaining some of the common variance.

RESULTS

Infancy

A clear relationship between absence of pain from nurturing agent in infancy and properties of the supernaturals is shown in Table 2. This relationship is significant at the .05 level.

The relationship of other infancy variables to the aggressive or benevolent properties of the deities is displayed in Table 3. Although none of these additional relationships emerges as significant, all of them are similar in direction in the sense that the children in societies with predominantly aggressive gods and spirits are less cosseted. The only exception to this generalization is that the nurturant agent tends to be more constantly present in the societies with aggressive deities. Even when only those societies are considered where little pain is inflicted by the nurturant agent, there is still a tendency for the nurturant agent to be present less often in benevolent cultures. This result may perhaps mean that what is

TABLE 3. RELATIONSHIPS BETWEEN INFANCY TREATMENT VARIABLES AND THE AGGRESSIVENESS AND BENEVOLENCE OF THE SUPERNATURALS

Infancy Training Variable	Supernaturals Predominantly:		Significance Tests [a]
	Aggressive	*Benevolent*	
High protection from environmental discomforts	36% (8/22)[b]	61% (11/18)	NS
High absence of pain inflicted by nurturant agent	29% (7/24)	63% (12/19)	$p = <.05$; c.l. for 29/43 = .51–.81
High over-all indulgence	39% (11/28)	60% (12/20)	NS
High diffusion of nurturance	44% (12/27)	68% (13/19)	NS
High display of affection	33% (8/24)	50% (10/20)	NS
High consistency of drive reduction	39% (9/23)	53% (10/19)	NS
High immediacy of drive reduction	35% (8/23)	47% (9/19)	NS
High degree of drive reduction	37% (10/27)	44% (8/18)	NS
High constancy of presence of nurturing agent	52% (14/27)	37% (7/19)	NS

[a] We report significance level by χ^2 test, usually as .05 level with no further refinement. We also report 95 percent confidence limits for either the proportion of "successful" cases or of "unsuccessful" cases.

[b] The figures in parentheses show the numbers on which the percentages are based. The numerator is the number of tribes showing the characteristic at the left out of the number of tribes classified as having either predominantly aggressive or benevolent gods (the denominator).

done to the child by caretakers is more closely related to the properties of the deities than is the mere fact of the presence of the caretaker.

If we combine the diffusion of nurturance ratings with the over-all indulgence ratings, the pattern of low diffusion—low indulgence characterizes the societies with aggressive deities to at least the .04 point of significance, employing the exact χ^2 solution.

In summary, there is a general tendency for less indulgent treatment in infancy to be related to predominantly aggressive deities in the cultural belief system, and for more indulgent treatment to be related to benevolent deities. The clearest relationship has to do with pain caused by the nurturing agents.

Childhood

The relations between the ratings of childhood variables and those of the supernaturals are examined in Table 4, which lists first "positive training" for the various systems of behavior, then punishments for failure to behave, then the reported actual frequency of children's behavior in the various systems. These relationships are followed by some compound indices of "pressure" (which combine the ratings of "positive training" and punishment for failure) and an index of "rigidity" of childhood training (the total score for punishment for nonperformance of all these behaviors).

The table shows that high self-reliance and independence training are related to the aggressiveness of the deities. This relationship holds for positive training, for punishment for nonperformance, for pressure, and for frequency of actual behavior. Despite an empirical relationship between the systems of self-reliance and independence training, we have retained them as separate because of differences in meanings of the ratings.

The nurturance behavior system appears generally to be positively related to the benevolence of the supernaturals. This relationship is significant at beyond the .05 level for frequency of actual behavior, and the trend is maintained at levels short of statistical significance for positive training and punishment for nonperformance.

There appears to be more positive training for responsibility behavior in societies with benevolent deities and more punishment for nonperformance in societies with aggressive deities, although neither of these relationships quite reaches statistical significance. There is also a suggestive trend for the frequency of responsibility behavior to be somewhat higher in societies with aggressive deities. Thus responsibility training through reward may characterize societies with benevolent deities, and responsibility training through threat of punishment, those with aggressive deities. The obedience behavior system follows the same pattern as that for responsibility, except that the frequency of children's performance of obedience behavior tends (nonsignificantly) to be greater in societies with benevolent deities.

The achievement behavior system appears to be least related of any of the systems to these properties of the deities. In no case is there any discernible trend.

There is a tendency for societies with benevolent deities to be higher in positive training for four of the behavior systems, but with a very strong reversal on the remaining two—self-reliance and independence. The

TABLE 4. RELATIONSHIPS BETWEEN CHILDHOOD TRAINING VARIABLES AND THE AGGRESSIVENESS AND BENEVOLENCE OF THE SUPERNATURAL

Childhood Training Variables	Supernaturals Predominantly:		Significance Tests[a]
	Aggressive	*Benevolent*	
High positive training for self-reliance	62% (16/26)[b]	16% (3/19)	$p = < .05$; c.l. for 32/45 = .54–.83
High positive training for independence	61% (17/28)	20% (4/20)	$p = < .05$; c.l. for 33/48 = .55–.82
High positive training for nurturance	40% (8/20)	73% (11/15)	NS
High positive training for responsibility	46% (12/26)	65% (13/20)	NS
High positive training for obedience	33% (8/24)	44% (8/18)	NS
High positive training for achievement	50% (11/22)	53% (8/15)	NS
High punishment for nonperf. self-reliance	73% (19/26)	31% (6/19)	$p = < .05$; c.l. for 32/45 = .54–.83
High punishment for nonperf. independence	57% (16/28)	20% (4/20)	$p = < .05$; c.l. for 32/48 = .52–.80
High punishment for nonperf. nurturance	60% (12/20)	71% (10/14)	NS
High punishment for nonperf. responsibility	63% (15/24)	30% (6/20)	$p = < .10$; c.l. for 29/44 = .51–.80
High punishment for nonperf. obedience	60% (15/25)	50% (9/18)	NS
High punishment for nonperf. achievement	48% (10/21)	47% (7/15)	NS
High frequency of child's self-reliance	67% (18/27)	26% (5/19)	$p = < .05$; c.l. for 32/46 = .53–.82
High frequency of child's independence	64% (18/28)	30% (6/20)	$p = < .05$; c.l. for 32/48 = .50–.59
High frequency of child's nurturance	24% (5/21)	67% (10/15)	$p = < .02$; c.l. for 25/36 = .54–.85
High frequency of child's responsibility	54% (13/24)	45% (9/20)	NS
High frequency of child's obedience	44% (11/25)	56% (10/18)	NS
High frequency of achievement behavior	45% (10/22)	44% (7/16)	NS

[a] We report significance level by χ^2 test, usually as .05 level with no further refinement. We also report 95 percent confidence limits for either the proportion of "successful" cases or of "unsuccessful" cases.

[b] The figures in parentheses show the numbers on which the percentages are based. The numerator is the number of tribes showing the characteristic at the left out of the number of tribes classified as having either predominantly aggressive or benevolent gods (the denominator). All "high-low" breaks reported in this paper are the closest possible to the median.

Childhood Training Variables	Supernaturals Predominantly:		Significance Tests[a]
	Aggresive	*Benevolent*	
High pressure for self-reliance	73% (19/26)	32% (6/19)	$p = < .05$; c.l. for 32/45 = .54–.83
High pressure for independence	71% (20/28)	35% (7/20)	$p = < .05$; c.l. for 33/48 = .55–.82
High pressure for achievement	58% (11/19)	57% (8/14)	NS
High rigidity score	71% (12/17)	18% (2/11)	$p = < .01$; c.l. for 21/28 = .55–.89

societies with aggressive deities, however, tend to use relatively more punishment for failure to perform in all but one of the systems—nurturance. This tendency in societies with aggressive deities toward control of behavior of children through punishment is most clearly highlighted in the rigidity score. Despite the general characterization of societies with aggressive deities as ones that make more use of punishment and less use of reward in socialization, it must be kept in mind that typical practices with respect to the various behavioral systems do differ. Societies with aggressive deities do reward self-reliance and independence (although this may be accompanied by some neglect), and societies with benevolent deities do tend to punish lapses from nurturance (although not significantly more than in the other kind of culture). To be ready to punish lapses does not necessarily betoken less attentiveness to children—it may require even more.

As far as children's actual performance of behavior in these systems is concerned, it appears to be clearly related to the properties of the supernaturals in three of the six systems. Children in societies with aggressive deities are more self-reliant, more independent, and less nurturant than those in societies with benevolent deities. The other directional tendencies in children's behavior have already been noted.

DISCUSSION

The relationships that have been presented are useful in evaluating theories of the culture-personality relationship but are not decisive with regard to any of the major causal assumptions that such theory may take. One may, like McClelland (7), view the religious belief system as the independent factor, or one may see it as a projection of parental behavior. Another approach would view both the religious system and the child training system as controlled by some other aspect of the culture or personality of the people. And one may also see these relationships as specific historical accidents of no theoretical interest.

Our own interpretation of these data draws upon conditioning theory, reinforcement theory, and conflict theory (2). Let us trace in these terms the interrelations between the factual, psychological, and belief levels in societies with predominantly aggressive deities and those with predominantly benevolent deities. In societies with predominantly aggressive deities, we begin with the facts of hurt and pain in infancy, along with some nurture. On the psychological level, these facts should lead to anxiety in the child, because of his conflicting anticipations of hurt and of nurture. The resulting conflict, and attendant conflict drive, is reduced by a conception of the deity as more angry than kind and thus consonant with human anticipations of hurt. Concurrently with this resolution, we find on the psychological level a reduction in the tension of ambivalence in the child's anticipations and, in addition, a vicarious anxiety on the part of the parent for the child's welfare in a hurtful world. Returning to the factual level, we find the parent reinforcing independent and self-reliant behavior in his child to prepare him for the adult world, thus reducing the parent's own anxiety for the child.

Our interpretation of socialization in societies with predominantly benevolent deities starts in much the same way. We begin in infancy with the fact of considerable nurture, along with some hurt. The psychological conflict between anticipations of nurture and of hurt is resolved here in the notion of a deity more kind than angry. Along with this belief we find, on the psychological level, a reduction in the tension arising from the ambivalence of the child's anticipations, and, in addition, vicarious anticipations in the parent of a probably pleasant future life for the child. On the factual level we find no pressures by the parent toward any particular behavior systems in the child but we do find considerable use of reward in child training, and we find the child, through identification or imitation, taking on such nurturant behavior.

An additional relationship that seems to require a different interpretation, though one not inconsistent with the foregoing, concerns the "capriciousness" of the gods. We assume that in societies with aggressive deities, the infant would not be able, particularly at the preverbal level, to understand or to predict the occasions of his receiving pain, and a property of capriciousness would thus accrue to the agent bestowing pain and nurture. A conception of the deities as capricious would therefore be seen as resolving the human anxiety deriving from inability to predict or foresee one's pains and woes. In another study, our raters were asked to judge whether a theme of "capriciousness" was present in the religious beliefs of a number of the same cultures as those analyzed in this study. A strong but nonsignificant tendency was found for the capricious deities to be the same as the aggressive ones, a relationship that becomes clearly significant when the variable of pain in infancy is controlled. Societies with predominantly aggressive deities and with high pain in the treatment of infants have capricious gods and spirits in six out of seven cases, and the societies with predominantly benevolent deities and with low pain in infant treatment lack capricious gods and spirits in seven out of seven cases ($p = < .004$).

We have considered two radically different interpretations of our data. The first of these would view the factual level of parents' training behavior toward infant and child as stemming from the religious belief system. That is, societies characterized by beliefs in predominantly aggressive deities would regulate their infant and child training practices along compatibly aggressive lines. This view does not seem to us as fruitful of testable consequences as the interpretation proposed above, and there seems to be little evidence for or against it. We were able to make a minor check on it concerning the possibility that the pain involved in infant care would be explained or rationalized in the culture along explicitly religious lines. In none of the six societies with preponderantly aggressive deities for which data were easily available was the hurting of infants reported as done for religious purposes. This result is, of course, not conclusive, nor does it bear on the possibility of a "latent" religious theme as the psychological mediator of the practice of inflicting pain in infant care.

A second major interpretation would have its causal base in what we might call "nature." The aggressiveness of the deity, the amount of pain inflicted during infant care, and the emphasis or lack of emphasis in child training on particular behavior systems would all derive from the physical setting of the society. Unfortunately no satisfactory index is available that combines for each society the relevant aspects of climate, diet, energy and work levels, natural hazards, frequency of natural "calamities," etc. Lacking such an index that would permit a more definitive test, we used Horton's data (5) in a preliminary test of the hypothesis that both the aggressive properties of the supernaturals and the infancy and child training practices arise from the low subsistence level of a society. A small number of our societies also fall in Horton's sample, and his categorization of the level of subsistence "insecurity" is available for these cultures. There was no apparent relationship between subsistence insecurity and the properties of the deities. Another partial test employed some indices of aspects of natural phenomena in a number of our cultures provided by Whiting.[3] One might entertain the possibility that belief in aggressive supernaturals is in part an outcome of extreme cold or of extreme heat conditions. No analyses that we have made to date show any clear relationships of this kind. The only trend is a weak directional one in which low mean temperatures (30°–75°) go with aggressive supernaturals in seven out of ten cases, whereas high mean temperatures (81° and up) tend to go with benevolent supernaturals in six out of eight cases. Temperature *variation*

[3] Whiting, J. W. M. *Personal communication.*

appears to have no trend of relationship with our data on the properties of the supernaturals.

Still additional explanatory hypotheses have been explored without appreciable support. According to one such hypothesis, mothers visit pain upon children as a displaced aggressive arising from the frustrations of particulary low status. In a different study, our raters judged the status of women on such dimensions as ownership of property, inheritance of status, control of arrangements for love affairs and marriage, exercise of family authority, and so on. None of these, nor these in combination, predict the position of the societies on the variable of pain in infancy. The only suggestive trend is a tendency for the nurturant agent to inflict less pain on the infant in societies where the property is owned by women.

SUMMARY

The belief systems concerning supernatural beings of 62 societies with a wide geographic spread were characterized as being mainly aggressive or hurtful, or mainly benevolent. Other, often interrelated, factors in the socialization of the infant (approximately to a year and a half) or child (up to ten years) were related to the benevolence of the supernatural.

Societies with beliefs in aggressive supernaturals were significantly more likely than those with beliefs in benevolent gods and spirits to be described as having generally punitive or hurtful practices in treating infants. At levels short of statistical significance, such cultures had fewer nurturant agents, protected the infant less from environmental discomforts, showed him less affection, were more inconsistent in caring for his needs, and took less care of his needs. Societies with beliefs in aggressive supernaturals also tended to see their supernaturals as "capricious" in hurting people.

In regard to childhood, parents in societies with beliefs in aggressive supernaturals were found to be more likely to reward their children for self-reliance and independence and to punish them for absence of these behaviors. They are generally more "rigid" in their training in the sense of depending more heavily on punishments than on rewards. Beliefs in benevolent gods and spirits are significantly related to the rated frequency of nurturant behavior shown by children in these cultures.

Several hypotheses according to which the obtained relationships might be explained were considered. The interpretation favored is derived from conditioning theory, reinforcement theory, and conflict theory. According to this view, the frequent hurt and pain in infancy in societies with aggressive deities causes anxiety in the child because of his conflicting anticipations of hurt and of nurture. His conflict is reduced by a conception of the deity as aggressive and thus compatible with human anticipations of hurt. The resulting reduction in the tension of ambivalence in the child's anticipations is accompanied by vicarious anxiety on the part of the parent concerning the child's future. The parent's anxiety is in turn reduced by following practices that reinforce independent and self-reliant behavior in his child to prepare him for the hurtful world he will encounter as an adult. In societies with benevolent deities there are no specific pressures toward training the child in particular behavior systems, but there is considerable reward used in child training. In result the child takes on such nurturant behavior through identification or imitation.

REFERENCES

1. Barry, H., Margaret K. Bacon, and I. L. Child. "A cross-cultural survey of some sex differences in socialization." *J. abnorm. soc. Psychol.*, **55** (1957), 327–332.
2. Berlyne, D. E. "Uncertainty and conflict: A point of contact between information theory and behavior theory." *Psychol. Rev.*, **64** (1957), 329–389.
3. Child, I. L., T. Storm, and J. Veroff. "An analysis of folk tales in relation to socialization practices." In *Motives in Fantasy, Action, and Society: A Method of Assessment and Study*, J. Atkinson (Ed.) Princeton, N.J.: Van Nostrand, 1958.
4. Hald, A. *Statistical Tables and Formulas.* New York: Wiley, 1952.
5. Heinicke, C., and B. B. Whiting. *Bibliographies on Personality and Social Development of the Child.* New York: Social Sci. Res. Council, 1953 (pamphlet 10).
6. Horton, D. "The functions of alcohol in primitive societies." *Quart. J. Study Alcohol.*, **4** (1943), 292–303.
7. McClelland, D. C. Some social consequences of achievement motivation. In *Nebraska Symposium on Motivation,* M. Jones (Ed.) Lincoln: Univ. Nebraska Press, 1955.
8. Whiting, J. W. M., I. L. Child, W. W. Lambert, *et al. Field Guide for a Study of Socialization in Five Societies.* Lab. of Human Develpm., 1955 (mimeo).

1.3 Orientation

Although all cultures share many of the same socialization problems, such as elimination training and sex and modesty training, cross-cultural research reveals variations in the broad goals of socialization. These goals, in turn, are associated with variations in the methods of socialization. The preceding paper has demonstrated one possible source of socialization differences. Another kind of question has been asked by Barry, Child, and Bacon in a second example of cross-cultural research: Are patterns of child rearing in a given society related to the way parents earn a living? The authors have built a rationale to support the hypothesis that child training is related to subsistence economy adaptation. Their interpretation of the data obtained for 104 societies culminates in the identification of a common variable underlying the relationship between subsistence economy and socialization practices, namely, the method of accumulating food resources.

The adaptation hypothesis provides an interesting confirmation of ideas advanced several decades ago by Max Weber (1930). Weber argued that a society strives, through its methods of socialization, to develop in its members the type of adult characteristics essential for the continued support and functioning of that society. Such concepts as "basic personality type," and "national character," are implicit in this position. Culturally patterned child-rearing practices are seen as the primary factor in the development of socially appropriate adult behavior. Research based upon this point of view has not, however, been limited to comparisons of nonindustrial, nonurban societies. For example, Miller and Swanson (1958) have examined the child-rearing practices of parents in the United States who differ on a basic subsistence criterion, specifically *occupational orientation* (entrepreneurial versus bureaucratic). These two broad orientations are distinguished by the degree of risk-taking involved in an occupation. Specifically, an entrepreneurial occupation is one in which a person typically is self-employed or works on a direct commission basis, the success of which is highly dependent on his personal initiative. Such occupations require self-reliance and usually involve a comparatively high degree of risk. Examples might be a contract fruit picker, a door-to-door salesman on a direct commission, and the operator of a small, independent business. A bureaucratic occupation is typically accompanied by a regular salary and carries a much higher degree of job security. Examples include the civil service, public school teaching, the military, and many industrial and corporation-based occupations. Miller and Swanson report that training children for independence and self-reliance is stressed more among entrepreneurial than bureaucratic parents who, in contrast, tend to emphasize social adjustment. Readers should find a study of the Miller and Swanson data extremely relevant to the Barry, Child, and Bacon paper.

RECOMMENDED READING

Miller, D. R., and G. E. Swanson. *The Changing American Parent.* New York: Wiley, 1958.

Weber, Max. *The Protestant Ethic and the Spirit of Capitalism.* London: G. Allen, 1930.

1.3 The Relation of Child Training to Subsistence Economy

Herbert Barry, III, UNIVERSITY OF PITTSBURGH
Irvin L. Child, YALE UNIVERSITY
Margaret K. Bacon, PRINCETON JUNCTION, NEW JERSEY

Cross-cultural research on child training has generally grown out of an interest in how the typical personality of a people is brought into being. The customary child-training practices of a group are thought to be one important set of influences responsible for the typical personality, and hence an important clue in tracing its causal background. But the typical personality may also be viewed as an existing set of conditions which may exert an influence on later child-training practices. Indeed, any present feature of culture may influence future child-training practices, either directly or through an influence on typical personality. Thus child training may just as well, and with equal interest of another sort, be viewed as effect in a series of cultural events, rather than as cause (being in fact, we presume, both at once). Moreover, even while considering child training as a cause of the typical personality of a people, one is led to inquire: Why does a particular society select child-training practices which will tend to produce this particular kind of typical personality? Is it because this kind of typical personality is functional for the adult life of the society, and training methods which will produce it are thus also functional?

By a variety of routes, then, the student of child training is led to inquire into the relation of child training to the basic patterns of social life—to those aspects of culture, whatever they be, which set the scene for the rest of culture. Among the features likely to hold this sort of dominant or controlling position is the general nature of the subsistence economy, and it is to this aspect of culture that we will here relate child-training practices.

Our research was built around certain variables of child training. Only after preliminary exploration of their relation to economy did we arrive at a notion of what kind of economic variable might be especially relevant. For ease of communication, however, we will begin with the eoonomic variable at which we eventually arrived.

Reprinted from *American Anthropologist,* **61** (1959), 51–63. By permission of the authors and the American Anthropological Association.

AN HYPOTHESIS ABOUT ECONOMIC ROLE AND TYPE OF SUBSISTENCE

Earlier anthropological writers classified economies in accordance with a notion of uniform sequences in cultural development from primitive to civilized. As a result of further research, this attempt has given way to more objective bases of classification. One such objective classification is that of Forde (1934). While stressing the limited usefulness of any classificatory scheme, in view of the great overlap between categories and the variation of economic practices within any one category, Forde does propose the following categories for dominant economy of a society: collecting, hunting, fishing, cultivation, and stock-raising. The usefulness of these categories has been affirmed by Herskovits (1952:86) and Murdock (1957).

Recent attempts to relate such a classification to more general aspects of adult behavior seem to have been principally concerned with their relevance to the complexity of society. Thus Steward (1955:28) states as a proposition universally accepted, that farming and herding are "preconditions of 'civilization,' which is broadly characterized by dense and stable populations, metallurgy, intellectual achievements, social heterogeneity and internal specialization, and other features." Oberg (1955) stresses the importance of food surplus as a condition for the development of such complexities. Agriculture appears on the whole more likely to permit food surplus than do hunting, fishing and gathering, though Oberg notes that this is not uniformly true.

In considering the relation of economy to adult role, and hence to child training, we felt that perhaps a variable of great significance is the extent to which food is accumulated and must be cared for. At one extreme is dependence mainly upon animal husbandry, where the meat that will be eaten in coming months and years, and the animals that will produce the future milk, are present on the hoof. In this type of society, future food supply seems to be best assured by faithful adherence to routines designed to maintain the good health of the herd. Agriculture perhaps imposes only slightly less pressure toward the same pattern of behavior. Social rules prescribe the best known way to bring the growing plants to successful harvest, and to protect the stored produce for gradual consumption until the next harvest. Carelessness in performance of routine duties leads to a threat of hunger, not for the day of carelessness itself but for many months to come. Individual initiative in attempts to improve techniques may be feared because no one can tell immediately whether the changes will lead to a greater harvest or to disastrous failure. Under these conditions, there might well be a premium on obedience to the older and wiser, and on responsibility in faithful performance of the routine laid down by custom for one's economic role.

At an opposite extreme is subsistence primarily through hunting or fishing, with no means for extended storing of the catch. Here individual initiative and development of high individual skill seem to be at a premium. Where each day's food comes from that day's catch, variations in the energy and skill exerted in food-getting lead to immediate reward or punishment. Innovation, moreover, seems unlikely to be so generally feared. If a competent hunter tries out some change in technique, and it fails, he may still have time to revert to the established procedures to get his catch. If the change is a good one, it may lead to immediate reward.

We recognize, of course, that there will not be a perfect correlation between the dominant type of food-getting and such aspects of the economic role. Agricultural and herding societies may produce a sufficient food surplus to allow some individuals to experiment with new techniques. Some hunting and fishing societies have means of preserving their catch, and this should increase the pressure for conformity to rules for ensuring preservation. Hunting and fishing may be done by teamwork, so that success depends partly upon responsible performance of the special duties assigned to each member. Some societies regard their hunting lands as a resource which must be protected by rigid conformity to conservation rules. A better picture of the relation of economy to socialization could surely be obtained through an analysis of such details of economic activity. But we feel that a useful initial exploration of this relation may be based on the expectation that, on the average, the dominant type of food-getting will exert on the adult economic rule the kind of influence we have portrayed. Thus in this paper our data on economy have to do simply with what general types of food-getting are predominant; our interpretation, however, hypothesizes that the degree of accumulation of food resources is the underlying variable likely to be of special importance for the understanding of our results. In our usage, "accumulation" is not necessarily related to whether there is a food surplus or shortage; it simply means the degree to which the food resources (however abundant or meager) are characteristically present in advance to be cared for or stored prior to being used, as against being consumed as soon as procured.

ECONOMY AND CHILD TRAINING

We have outlined above an hypothesis about economic behavior as an adaptation to the general type of subsistence economy. If economic role tends to be generalized to the rest of behavior, predictions might be made about the typical character or personality of adults in societies with different subsistence economies. In societies with low accumulation of food resources, adults should tend to be individualistic, assertive, and venturesome. By parallel reasoning, adults should tend to be conscientious, compliant, and conservative in societies with high accumulation of food resources.

If economic role and general personality tend to be appropriate for the type of subsistence economy, we may expect the training of children to foreshadow these adaptations. The kinds of adult behavior useful to the society is likely to be taught to some extent to the children, in order to assure the appearance of this behavior at the time it is needed. Hence we may predict that the emphases in child training will be toward the development of kinds of behavior especially useful for the adult economy.

As a method for testing the hypothesis of adaptation to subsistence economy, societies with different types of economy may be compared in adult economic roles, general adult personality, and child training. In the present paper, societies which differ in economy are compared in child training, not in adult economic role or adult personality. In comparing societies with different types of economy we might be less confident of finding appropriate differences in child training than in adult economic role and adult personality, because child training seems to have the most indirect connection with economy. If appropriate differences in child training are found, we may infer that the adaptation to economy includes a wide sphere of social behavior.

PROCEDURE

In the preliminary version of a recent article, Murdock (1957) classified the subsistence economy of societies into six categories, designated by the letters A, F, G, H, P, and R. We have considered societies as likely to be extremely high in accumulation of food resources, by our definition, if they were classified by Murdock as predominantly pastoral (P) or as agricultural with animal husbandry also important (A). Societies were considered likely to be extremely low in accumulation if Murdock designated them as predominantly hunting (H) or fishing (F).

Societies were considered intermediate in accumulation if Murdock designated them as predominantly agricultural, with either grain (G) or root (R) crops, with animal husbandry not important. The grain and root societies were for our purposes placed together, but were then subdivided according to another analysis with which Murdock provided us, of the degree of subsidiary importance of hunting and fishing in these predominantly agricultural societies. We averaged the rating of the importance of hunting and of fishing, and then divided this average rating at the median. Societies above the median in importance of hunting and fishing were then classified as intermediately low in accumulation of food resources. Societies below the median in importance of hunting and fishing were classified as intermediately high in accumulation.

Several other cultural variables, to be used somewhat incidentally later in the paper, were also taken from Murdock's analyses (1957, and preliminary unpublished version).

The authors of the present paper obtained ratings on several aspects of child training practices by their own analysis of ethnographic documents. The methods used are described in detail in Barry, Bacon and Child (1957). Societies were rated separately for boys and for girls with respect to six aspects of training.

1. Obedience training
2. Responsibility training, which usually was on the basis of participation in the subsistence or household tasks
3. Nurturance training, i.e., training the child to be nurturant or helpful toward younger siblings and other dependent people
4. Achievement training, which was usually on the basis of competition, or imposition of standards of excellence in performance
5. Self-reliance training, defined as training to take care of oneself, to be independent of the assistance of other people in supplying one's needs and wants
6. General independence training. This was defined more generally than self-reliance training, to include training not only to satisfy one's own needs but also toward all kinds of freedom from control, domination, and supervision. Ratings of general independence training were highly correlated with ratings of self-reliance training, but were not identical to them

For each of these six aspects of training, societies were rated on strength of socialization, which was defined as the combined positive pressure (rewards for the behavior) plus negative pressure (punishments for lack of the behavior). The ratings were for the stage of childhood, from age 4 or 5 years until shortly before puberty. Each rating was made by two separate judges, working independently, and the sum of their two judgments was used.

For each society, separately for boys and for girls, the ratings of the six aspects of strength of socialization were ranked, so that the score for each aspect depended not on its absolute rating but on its rank in comparison with the ratings of the other aspects for the same society. This device was used because in this paper we are interested in the relative stress a society places on one rather than another aspect of socialization. Tied ratings were given the same rank. A society was included on this measure only if it had been rated on at least five of the six aspects. Each rating, at the time it was made, was classified as confident or doubtful. In order to have a sizable number of cases, we decided to use all instances where both analysts made a rating, regardless of whether it was confident or doubtful, despite the inevitable lowering of reliability.

The ethnographic descriptions of child training practices from which these ratings were made inevitably contained some descriptions of economy; thus the raters may usually have been aware of the type of economy when they made ratings on socialization, and in many instances they certainly were. However, the nature of the adult economy was not used as a criterion for ratings and no information on it was sought. The classification of economy made by Murdock was unknown to the raters, and could not always have been dependably guessed from the portions of the ethnographies read in analyzing socialization. Moreover, the raters did not have in mind any such hypothesis as is presented here about the effects of adult economy on socialization practices; this hypothesis was developed after the analysis of socialization had been completed.

The results to be reported are on 104 societies which are included in two separate samples: Murdock's sample of over 500 societies classified on economy and social organization, and 110 societies rated on socialization by Bacon and Barry. Most of these 104 societies are nonliterate, and they are distributed all over the world. Many cultures were omitted from some of the ratings because of insufficient information; such omissions are much more frequent for the socialization variables than for Murdock's variables.

RESULTS

Economy and Specific Variables of Socialization

First let us consider the groups of societies at the extremes in accumulation of food resources: extremely high (animal husbandry important) and extremely low (hunting or fishing dominant). The upper half of Figure 1 shows the average ranking of our six socialization variables for these two groups of societies. Societies with extremely high accumulation, compared to those with extremely low accumulation, tend to show higher pressure toward responsibility and obedience and lower pressure toward achievement, self-reliance and independence. Nurturance is the only child training variable which has approximately the same average ranking in both groups of societies. The association of each variable with accumulation is in the same direction for boys and girls.

The lower half of Figure 1 shows the comparison between societies with intermediately high and intermediately low accumulation of food resources. The same general results are found for this comparison as for the comparison of the extremes.

It is apparent from these two graphs that child training practices are correlated with amount of accumulation of food resources. For example, strong pressure toward responsibility (i.e., high ranking) tends to occur more frequently in societies which have high accumulation of food resources. If this correlation were perfect, so that societies high in responsibility were always high in accumulation and vice versa, the coefficient of association would be +1.00. If societies high in responsibility, and those low in responsibility, were each divided equally between high and low accumulation, the association coefficient would be zero (0.00). If the correlation were in the reverse direction, so that societies high in responsibility were always low in accumulation, the association coefficient would

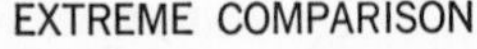

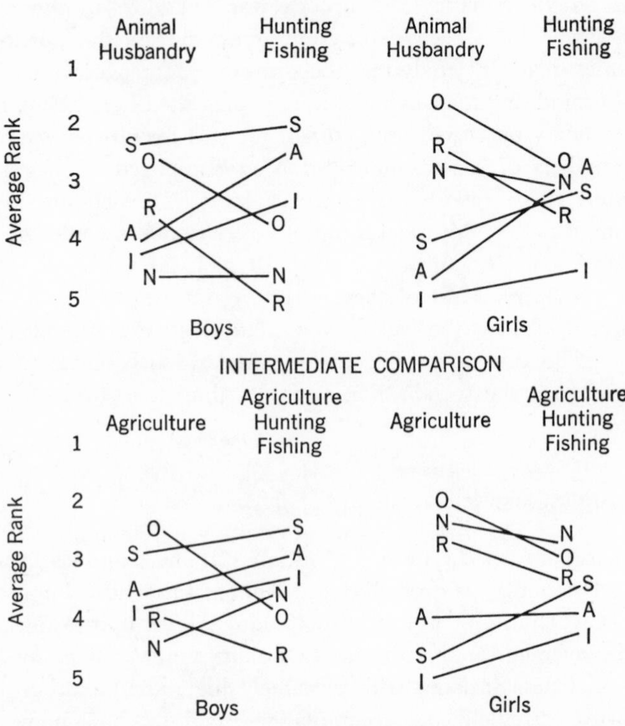

FIGURE 1. The average rank of each sociable socialization value, for groups distinguished by economy. Key: R = responsibility, O = obedience, N = nurturance, A = achievement, S = self-reliance, I = independence.

be negative but again of maximum size (−1.00). Thus the size of the association coefficient gives a measure of the consistency of the relationship between two variables; the plus or minus sign shows the direction of the relationship.

The results portrayed in Figure 1 have been expressed in coefficients of association in Table 1. As Table 1 shows, responsibility and obedience are positively correlated with accumulation of food resources; achievement, self-reliance, and independence are negatively correlated with accumulation. Nurturance shows inconsistent results, generally of small magnitude and in no instance statistically significant. The results are in the same direction both for the extreme and for the intermediate comparisons of economy, and as we might expect, the correlations are generally higher for the extreme comparison. The tests of statistical significance ($p < .05$ or $p < .01$) also give evidence that the results are more consistent for the extreme comparisons.

TABLE 1. Relation of Child Training Practices to Accumulation of Food Resources (Expressed as Coefficients of Association)

	Extremes in accumulation		Intermediate in accumulation	
	Boys	*Girls*	*Boys*	*Girls*
Responsibility	+.74 [a]	+.62 [a]	+.33	+.37
Obedience	+.50 [a]	+.59 [a]	+.66 [a]	+.45
Nurturance	−.01	+.10	−.26	+.11
Achievement	−.60 [a]	−.62 [a]	−.32	−.12
Self-reliance	−.21	−.46 [b]	−.19	−.53 [b]
Independence	−.41 [b]	−.11	−.21	−.42

[a] $p < .01$ } Two-tail tests, based on the Mann-Whitney *U* (Siegel 1956:116–127).
[b] $p < .05$ }

These results are all substantially alike for the training of the two sexes. The correlations between economy and child training are in the same direction for boys and girls for all the variables except nurturance. There seems to be no consistent difference between the sexes in sizes of the correlations. However, it is worth noting in Figure 1 that the variables which ranked higher in societies with high accumulation of food resources (obedience and responsibility) were emphasized more strongly in the training of girls than boys, whereas the variables which ranked higher in societies with low accumulation of food resources (achievement, self-reliance and independence) were emphasized more strongly in the training of boys than girls. A further description of sex differences for the same group of societies may be found in a recent paper by Barry, Bacon and Child (1957).

There remains the question of whether the information used in making the child training ratings was largely information about training in economic behavior, so that our results may not genuinely pertain to any more general variables of child training. The only way to answer this question with complete confidence would be to edit the material on socialization, removing all information about economic training, and then have other judges make the ratings again from the remaining information. It is not feasible for us to undertake this very expensive additional project. As a substitute, however, we have looked back at our notes on child training (made in the course of arriving at ratings) for the 20 societies showing the most extreme results in confirmation of the relationship reported in this paper. Our conclusion is that the information about the training of children in the predominant economy of the society played a much smaller role in determining the ratings than we might have supposed. For girls there was rarely any information about training in the predominant economy. For boys there was often (though not always) information about training in the predominant economy. This often played an important role in the judgments of responsibility, but seemed almost always to be accompanied by important relevant information about noneconomic aspects of training. For other aspects of training (nurturance, obedience, self-reliance, and achievement), information about economic training rarely seemed to play an important role in determining ratings even for boys. Our review of these cases leaves us convinced that the associations we find between economy and socialization apply not simply to direct training in economic functions but also to much more general aspects of child training.

Economy and a General Variable of Socialization

In their relation to economy, the socialization variables (if we omit nurturance) fall into two distinct groups. This fact suggests that a single more general variable might be extracted for presentation of data on individual societies and for further exploration of results. We have called this variable pressure toward compliance vs. assertion. It is based on the separate socialization variables, and was derived in the following way: The sum of the rankings of responsibility and obedience training, for both boys and girls, was subtracted from the sum of the rankings of achievement and self-reliance, for both boys and girls. A plus score meant that responsibility and obedience were ranked higher (i.e., were assigned lower numbers) than achievement and self-reliance, and for purposes of calculating a coefficient of association any plus score was designated as predominant pressure toward compliance. A zero or minus score was designated as predominant pressure toward assertion. We dealt with cases of missing information as follows: In the several societies in which the achievement rating was not made, general independence was substituted for it in deriving this general measure of pressure toward compliance vs. assertion. In the two societies where the obedience rating was not made, the responsibility rating was substituted for it. Eleven societies were omitted because some or all of the ratings had been made only for one sex.

Table 2 presents a list of societies, divided according to predominant economy and arranged in order of their score on relative predominance of compliance vs. assertion in child training pressures. The correlation portrayed in this table is very consistent. Societies with high accumulation of food resources almost always had predominant pressure toward compliance, whereas societies with low accumulation almost always had predominant pressure toward assertion. For the extreme comparison, 39 societies conformed to this result and only seven had high accumulation with assertion or low accumulation with compliance. The association coefficient for this relationship is .94. For the intermediate comparison, 26 societies conformed to this result and only seven were exceptions. The association coefficient is .93.

These results both show a high degree of statistical significance, which we

TABLE 2. Relation of Subsistence Economy to General Pressure toward Compliance vs. Assertion in Child Training [a]

Extremes in Accumulation		Intermediate in Accumulation	
High (Animal Husbandry)	*Low (Hunting, Fishing)*	*High (Agriculture Only)*	*Low (Agriculture, Hunting, Fishing)*
Aymara (+13½)			
Tepoztlan (+13½)			
Lepcha (+11½)			
Swazi (+8½)			
Tswana (+8½)			
Nyakyusa (+8)			
Sotho (+8)		Hopi (+10½)	
Nuer (+7)		Azande (+8)	
Tallensi (+7)		Ifaluk (+6)	
Lovedu (+6½)		Wogeo (+6)	
Mbundu (+6½)		Samoans (+5)	
Venda (+6½)		Yoruba (+5)	
Kikuyu (+6)		Navaho (+4½)	
Zulu (+6)		Arapesh (+4)	
Pondo (+4½)		Wichita (+4)	Vanua Levu (+11½)
Chagga (+4)		Zuni (+4)	Lesu (+10)
Ganda (+3)		Papago (+3½)	Lau Fijians (+6)
Chamorro (+2½)	Teton (+4)	Ulithians (+3)	Yagua (+6)
Masai (+2½)	Yahgan (+1)	Ashanti (+1½)	Malaitan (+2)
Chukchee (+1)	Hupa (+½)	Nauruans (+1)	Tikopia (+½)
Tanala (0)	Chiricahua (0)	Alorese (−6)	Camayura (0)
Thonga (−2½)	Murngin (0)		Cuna (0)
Araucanian (−3)	Paiute (0)		Omaha (−1½)
Balinese (−3)	Arapaho (−2)		Kwoma (−3½)
	Kwakiutl (−2)		Mandan (−3½)
	Cheyenne (−2½)		Jivaro (−4)
	Kaska (−2½)		Trukese (−5)
	Klamath (−2½)		Winnebago (−5)
	Ojibwa (−2½)		Marquesans (−9)
	Ona (−3)		Ifugao (−9½)
	Aleut (−4)		Pukapukans (−12)
	Jicarilla (−6½)		Maori (−13)
	Western Apache (−10)		
	Siriono (−10½)		

[a] The societies are grouped in columns on the basis of economy and are listed within each column in descending order of degree of pressure toward compliance as compared with pressure toward assertion. The number in parentheses after each society indicates the degree of preponderance of compliance (plus scores) or of assertion (minus scores).

Extremes in Accumulation		Intermediate in Accumulation	
High (Animal Husbandry)	*Low (Hunting, Fishing)*	*High (Agriculture Only)*	*Low (Agriculture, Hunting, Fishing)*
	West Greenland Eskimo (−11)		
	Aranda (−12)		
	Comanche (−12)		
	Crow (−13½)		
	Manus (−15)		

have measured by the Mann-Whitney *U* Test (Siegel 1956:116–127). The separate comparisons differ more in this respect than in their absolute value; for the extreme comparison, p is less than .001, and for the intermediate comparison p is less than .02.

It is not surprising, of course, that economy shows a higher correlation with the combined measure of socialization pressures than with any of the separate child training measures from which it is derived. The magnitude of the correlation is, however, surprising. We may conclude that a knowledge of the economy alone would enable one to predict with considerable accuracy whether a society's socialization pressures were primarily toward compliance or assertion.

Relation to Other Cultural Variables

We have suggested that child training practices are shaped by the behavioral requirements of the adult economic roles. This implies a fairly direct causal relation between economy and child training. It is quite possible, however, that the causal connection might be much more indirect. The subsistence economy may have a pervasive influence on many other aspects of culture, and some of these other aspects of culture may be more directly responsible for influencing child training practices. As a first check on this possibility, we decided to explore the relation of pressure toward compliance vs. assertion, and of subsistence economy, to nine other major cultural variables for which Murdock (1957, supplemented by personal communication) has prepared analyses from the ethnographic literature for these same societies.

For five of these variables, it was possible to treat Murdock's categories as falling along an ordered scale: these are the first five variables listed in Table 3. For three additional variables (the rest of those appearing in Table 3), Murdock's categories were divided into two groups to form a reasonable dichotomy. Clearly these eight variables show some consistency in their relation both to our economic measure and to pressure toward compliance vs. assertion. For our purposes, there seem to be two main conclusions to be drawn from the results reported in Table 3.

TABLE 3. RELATION OF OTHER CULTURAL VARIABLES TO PRESSURE TOWARD COMPLIANCE VERSUS ASSERTION, AND TO ACCUMULATION OF FOOD RESOURCES, SEPARATELY FOR TWO GROUPS OF SOCIETIES

Cultural Variable	For Societies in Extreme Comparison of Food Accumulation		For Societies in Intermediate Comparison of Food Accumulation	
	Relation to Accumulation	*Relation to Pressure toward Compliance*	*Relation to Accumulation*	*Relation to Pressure toward Compliance*
Size of permanent settlement unit	+.52	+.43	+.22	+.32
Degree of political integration	+.76	+.63	+.03	−.12
Complexity of social stratification	+.74	+.56	+.10	−.10
Greater participation by women in predominant subsistence activity	+.60	+.48	−.23	−.22
Extent of approach to general polygyny	+.25	−.08	+.18	+.25
Presence of bride-price or bride-service	+.84	+.86	−.26	−.46
Unilinearity of descent	+.83	+.49	−.02	+.50
Residence fixed or neolocal, rather than shifting or bilocal	+.32	+.35	+.89	+.77

The measure given here is the index of order association, for which see Wallis and Roberts, 1956:282–284; where both variables are dichotomous, this measure reduces to the more familiar coefficient of association. Pressure toward compliance, and accumulation of food resources, have been treated here as dichotomous variables; the other variables have from two to seven ordered categories. A plus or minus sign indicates whether the variables are positively or negatively related to high accumulation and high pressure toward compliance.

1. Pressure toward compliance vs. assertion shows higher correlations with accumulation of food resources (.94 and .93 for the extreme and intermediate comparisons) than with any of the other cultural variables. These other cultural variables are mostly related more closely to accumulation than to compliance vs. assertion (the only sizable exception is for unilinearity of descent, for the intermediate comparison only). Therefore it is plausible that the relation of compliance vs. assertion to the variables listed in Table 3 is principally due to their common relation to accumulation of food resources.

2. There is clearly a difference here between the extreme comparison and the intermediate comparison. For the extreme comparison, accumulation of

food resources shows consistent and often large positive correlations with the other cultural variables, and pressure toward compliance shows only one negative correlation with these variables. For the intermediate comparison, all but one of the correlations with accumulation are smaller than for the extreme comparison, and the correlations with compliance vs. assertion are equally divided between positive and negative. If only the extreme comparison were available, we might suspect that the societies with animal husbandry differ from the hunting and fishing societies in the other social variables because of their extreme difference in accumulation of food resources. However, the agricultural societies with different degrees of subsidiary reliance upon hunting or fishing, which also differ in accumulation (the intermediate comparison) do not show corresponding differences in the other social variables. An economy based on animal husbandry differs from one based on hunting or fishing in other respects besides accumulation, and it is likely that one or more of these other aspects of difference explains the correlation of economy with the other social variables. The identification of these aspects is a problem of great interest but not obviously related to the topic of this paper.

The important fact for our present purpose is that the extreme and intermediate comparisons of accumulation of food resources, which have conflicting relations to other social variables, show high and consistent correlations with pressure toward compliance vs. assertion. Therefore accumulation of food resources is indicated as a probable underlying variable responsible for the relationship found between socialization and subsistence economy.

DISCUSSION

Some readers may feel that our main results are obvious, to the extent of being therefore trivial. We believe that this is not the case, that we have instead obtained strong evidence for one hypothesis where some other quite different hypothesis might to some people seem more obvious in advance. For example, let us start the other way around and think of child training as the basic given. Pressure toward self-reliance and achievement should produce strongly independent people who hate to be dependent on others. This character tendency should render very rewarding all features of economic behavior that make it easier to avoid being dependent on others. Among such features, one of the most conspicuous might be the possession by each individual or family of an accumulated food supply (such as herd or crop), which ensures that an unlucky hunt will not leave one dependent upon the neighbor's catch. Hence child training pressure toward assertion should motivate (perhaps unconsciously) the quest for high accumulation techniques of subsistence. But according to our findings, it evidently does not. If any such process operates to a slight degree, it appears to be completely obscured by the much more important process to which our results point.

Our findings then are consistent with the suggestion that child training tends to be a suitable adaptation to subsistence economy. Pressure toward obedience and responsibility should tend to make children into the obedient and responsible adults who can best ensure the continuing welfare of a society with a high-accumulation economy, whose food supply must be protected and developed gradually throughout the year. Pressure toward self-reliance and achievement should shape children into the venturesome, independent adults who can take initiative in wresting food daily from nature, and thus ensure survival in societies with a low-accumulation economy.

REFERENCES

Barry, Herbert III, Margaret K. Bacon, and Irvin L. Child. "A cross-cultural survey of some sex differences in socialization." *J. abnorm. soc. Psychol.,* **55** (1957), 327–332.

Forde, C. Daryll. *Habitat, Economy and Society.* London: Methuen, 1934.

Herskovits, Melville, J. *Economic Anthropology.* New York: Knopf, 1952.

Murdock, George Peter. "World ethnographic sample." *Amer. Anthropologist,* **59** (1957), 664–687.

Oberg, Kalervo. "Types of social structure among the lowland tribes of South and Central America." *Amer. Anthropologist,* **57** (1955), 472–487.

Siegel, Sidney. *Nonparametric Statistics for the Behavioral Sciences.* New York: McGraw-Hill, 1956.

Steward, Julian H. *Theory of Culture Change.* Urbana: Univ. Ill. Press, 1955.

Wallis, W. Allen, and Harry V. Roberts. *Statistics, a New Approach.* Glencoe, Ill.: Free Press, 1956.

1.4 Orientation

Ample data suggest that industrialization, urbanization, and changes in adults' thinking about the nature of childhood have influenced socialization practices in our society. The theme implicit in the rationale developed by Boehm for her comparative study of American and Swiss children concerns the nature of the relationships between parents and children in these two cultures. Equipped with cues from the sociology of childhood and the developmental psychology of Jean Piaget (Chapter 5), Boehm has employed the *methode clinique* to gain insight into children's interpersonal relationships and their concepts of morality. Boehm's paper, therefore, anticipates several related studies, particularly those to be found in Chapter 5. The Boehm study is included here because of its comparative nature and its predominantly sociological rationale.

Aside from its involvement with Piagetian concepts and the development of independence (see the Bartlett and Smith and Bronfenbrenner papers in this chapter), Boehm's study reflects two research problems faced by all psychological researchers: the method utilized to obtain data and the sampling of children studied. With regard to methodology, it is clear that the responses to the questions asked by Boehm are a function of how well the children understand her questions. A necessary assumption is that their responses are reliable. Despite its limitations, direct questioning based upon contrived situations is often the only way to obtain certain kinds of information. Readers may wish to speculate on alternative possibilities. The second problem, sampling, involves the number and nature of the children available for study and how such children are selected. This is extremely important, for the generality of a study is contingent upon the sample of children utilized. Completely unbiased, or random, samples of children are rarely available to researchers for a variety of reasons, the most usual being problems of accessibility. The fact that Boehm's study is selective does not, however, negate its value as an exploration into children's concepts of independence.

RECOMMENDED READING

Karr, C., and F. Wesley. "Comparison of German and U.S. child-rearing practices." *Child Develpm.*, **37** (1966), 715–724.

Medinnus, G. R. (Ed.) *Readings in the Psychology of Parent-Child Relations.* New York: Wiley, 1967. (See Section VI, "Cultural Factors," pp. 323–365.)

Seagoe, M. V. "Children's play as an indicator of cross-cultural and intracultural differences." *J. educ. Sociol.*, **35** (1962), 278–283.

1.4 The Development of Independence: A Comparative Study

Leonore Boehm, BROOKLYN COLLEGE

THE PROBLEM

The European who comes to the United States is surprised to find a more rapid social development in American children than he has been used to see-

Reprinted from *Child Development,* **28** (1957), 85–92. By permission of the author and The Society for Research in Child Development, Inc.

ing in European children. In thought and action American children become independent of their elders at an earlier age than do European children. Not only do they depend less on adult guidance and judgment, but their consciences seem to mature earlier also.

Stendler (7) has indicated that the American mother unwittingly transfers some of the child's dependency from herself to his peer group at the preschool age, while the Parisian mother still thinks of him as *"bebé,"* constantly needing her to teach him which kind of behavior she approves and which she disapproves. The American child learns to find satisfaction in the approval of his young playmates and strives to avoid their disapproval. Through parent interviews Stendler uncovered certain significant differences in educational goals between Parisian and American middle class mothers. The younger Parisian child is encouraged to be gentle, quiet, self-controlled; in other words, well-mannered and civilized; the older one to be self-sufficient, well-integrated and an individualistic thinker, which prepares him to become a typical Frenchman (7). Middle class American parents attempt to bring up children who will be independent of their parents, who will be accepted, practicing members of their own peer groups. [Note that this is achieved by substituting peer dependency for parent dependency (2).] Riesman (6) explains this difference: In all "inner-directed societies" as in Europe's "old middle class," parents try to bring about, through education, the internalization in their children of the parents' values and goals. The smaller child is pushed until he learns to "push himself to the limits of his talents and beyond," regardless of the possible conflict that his achievements might raise for him in his efforts to relate to his peers. Throughout childhood the parent remains the source of guidance. The child is brought up to believe in and respect the authority of his parents, teachers, and other surrounding adults who, as such, are held to be superior to him. The European parent remains omnipotent and omniscient. Thus Piaget (5) received many answers from Swiss children who believed that it was their father or grandfather who had created the world, the rivers, the mountains. European parents think it is wrong to let children realize that they—the parents—do not know everything.

In all "other-directed societies," to which the upper middle class of our large cities belongs according to Riesman, parents are no longer sure of their own values and standards. Due to the rate of change of our society, to social mobility, to immigration, the new generation no longer follows in its parents' footsteps. On the contrary, children are supposed to surpass their parents. As Mead reminds us, many a mother dreams of her son's becoming President of the United States. No longer can the parent feel superior to the child, but suffering from a lack of self-assurance, he does not wish to face the responsibility of directing the child. He believes that the child's contemporaries can advise better than his parents, that they know better what standards are important, what ideals and goals a youngster should have.

Thus it is the peer group that has become the individual's source of direction, whose reactions have become important, whose approval must be obtained. Being popular with one's age group is a primary value. It is even more to be sought after than fame achieved through competitive activity. Social security has become one aim of education. The child, of course, senses the lack of self-confidence in his parents, he senses that the parents see in him at least a potential equal, if not a future superior. He realizes that the parents' knowledge is limited and that they, too, make mistakes. As a matter of fact, American parents, teachers, and other authorities feel that this realization is necessary for the sake of the children's feelings of security and early adult independence. Instead of learning to obey blindly, without questioning the adult's judgment, as one does in Europe, the child here is encouraged to use critical thinking in the hopes that his reasoning will become "autonomous" or "interiorized" as Piaget (4) calls this quality of objective, independent thinking.

Many an incident could be told by a person who has lived both in Europe and in the United States to give evidence of the differences in child development and behavior resulting from the respective differences in objectives and modes of training. A European child is a guest of his parents: a permanent guest, it is true, but one who will be asked to leave the dinner table if his behavior is not quiet and respectful. A European school child told this investigator that his father made the best pancakes when the fact was that the father, a scholar who was all thumbs in the kitchen or shop, would have difficulty boiling water. Contrast this with the American father who said that he believed he should treat his child as a potential equal (if not superior), and that their home belonged to children and parents together; or the director of a Congregational church school in Illinois, who, when asked by his five-year-old son if there was a God, though a firm believer himself, answered that some people believed in God, while others did not. He wanted his boy to decide independently in all matters possible, rather than to assume that his father was always right.

Good preschools in this country are geared toward an education for independent thinking as well as for group living. Perhaps because of the marked difference in educational aims, there are but few preschools in Europe. There the *"bebé"* is expected to look to his mother for guidance. It is held that he does not need to start his social education at such an early age. In our preschools children are encouraged to find their own solutions whenever they are able to, even if these are not as perfect as adults'. At a young age this is possible mainly in concrete, practical matters, be it in regards to their work or to social living. In most preschools there are fewer rules and regulations for the older than for the younger group. The older ones are supposed to make their own decisions. To give an example: There is usually a rule for the younger group, that rubbers or boots have to be worn outdoors on days when there are puddles on the playground. There often is no such rule for the older children. They have become old enough to realize that they must put boots on only if they want to play in puddles. They may choose to play where it is wet or where it is dry. Thus they may decide whether to wear boots or not.

Whereas the European school is concerned mostly with academic learning and little with cooperation or "character education"—the latter being the home's responsibility—a principal at an elementary school in Winnetka, Illinois, stated to the author that the school's primary functions are to teach children independent thinking and the skills necessary for living together. The teacher's role in this country is then, according to this informant, different from that of the European teacher. His obligation is to make the children realize that they are his potential equals. Children owe less respect merely to the teacher's role. They should be discerning enough to respect only a person who merits respect. Children should be made aware of the fact that their teachers sometimes err, and that their teacher's judgment is not always better than their own. Quite in contrast to the powerful European teacher, the more informal American teacher does not need to be feared and hated. He has become, in Riesman's words, a "peer-group facilitator and mediator."

Many observations in European and American schools give evidence of an earlier cooperation among children here. In Europe the child is often told to work individually; here, the children are encouraged to help each other, be it directly or by constructive suggestions and criticism. At an age when the European kindergartner uses "egocentric" speech, according to Piaget (3), the American one needs speech mainly for real peer communication.

A question which comes to the fore when studying differing rates of social development is whether, in a culture which values cooperation among children more than dependence upon adults, *social conscience* matures earlier due to stress on skills necessary for group life. Does the child's conscience remain "egocentric" longer in an inner-directed society than it does in an other-directed society? It is quite possible that the relatively early independence of the American child causes his conscience to develop not only from identification and interiorization of the ethical values of his parents, but also from the values of those of his peers to whom he has, in part, transferred his dependence. Is this "inner-directed child" older than his "other-directed" opposite number before he stops basing his moral judgments on the outcome of the subject's actions alone? As Piaget states, the young child is anxious to "expier par sanction" (to unburden his conscience of its sense of guilt by undergoing punishment). This atonement is relevant to his own needs only and is entirely unconnected with those of the victim. It is a childish expiation chosen in order to re-establish the offender's inner balance because his deed has "destroyed the equilibrium of the world." The worse the deed then, even though it be an accident and possibly due to excellent intentions, the more disagreeable must the punishment be to absolve the child's conscience. The question which we are raising here would also suggest that an "inner-directed child" must be older than an "other-directed child" before he bases his moral judgments not only on the effects of the deed but also on the feelings of the victim and on the offender's intentions.

One wonders whether these findings of Piaget are true for all children in the civilized world. There might be a difference in the rate of formation of the conscience as well as in its content when one compares children in the United States with those in Calvinist Switzerland. One might expect a different type of conscience here where education is directed outwardly rather than inwardly, where ideals, goals, and values are geared primarily toward social adjustment and not toward character improvement or toward perfection of the soul for the sake of salvation. Possibly the values of an outer-directed conscience are easier for a human being to achieve than are those of an inner-directed conscience. Perhaps this is another reason why the American child's conscience may become autonomous earlier. It requires less introspection. It is less inwardly turned in its self-evaluation, less self-concerned, less perfectionistic. Thus it becomes less destructive to his self-confidence, less guilt- and shame-ridden than in the conscience of the Swiss child who has been taught to struggle continually against his own tendencies toward wrongdoing. According to Riesman, however, Americans replace the inner-directed person's specific guilt feelings with diffuse anxiety, which he maintains is necessary to build up in the individual that emotional sensitivity to the feelings of others which will serve as a much needed facilitator of social adjustment.

PROCEDURE

This investigation grew out of an earlier study of the author's in which we used Piaget's "méthode clinique"—talking to individual children, telling stories, and asking questions designed to reveal their reasoning at different age levels. The original purpose of the research was quite different in nature from the study reported in this paper. At no time during the original investigation was it meant to be a comparative one. When the European data were gathered the author knew very little about the United States, its people, its culture, and its education. However, when gathering the American data in Winnetka, it became clear that significant comparisons could be made between children of the two cultures. The investigator has interviewed 261 children from kindergarten through high school, 80 Europeans and 181 Americans. In all, 12 stories have been used. This paper, however, reports on just two stories, used in elementary schools only.

Subjects

Europe: Twenty-nine French-speaking Swiss children, attending elementary school, which goes to tenth grade, in a rather run-down neighborhood in Geneva. United States: Forty American children, attending elementary school in Winnetka, a well-to-do suburb of Chicago.

One might wonder whether the results of this study were influenced by the difference in socioeconomic background between the children living in the United States and those in Geneva. However, results obtained, with the same stories, from 10 upper middle class German children living in Berlin were quite similar to those obtained from the Swiss children. This would seem to indicate that the phenomenon we are studying here is due more to the cultural structure of the society in which a child grows than it is to his socioeconomic class.

First Story—The Scoutleader's Birthday Party

"A group of children X years old (the subject's own age)" want to give a surprise birthday party to their scoutleader. One boy has accepted the responsibility of decorating the room. He wonders whom he could ask for advice." (The questions which follow are illustrative of the type used. Actually, in the "méthode clinique," the investigator probes and probes, formulating each question on the basis of the answer the subject has given to the preceding one; thus a uniform questionnaire is not employed. In the course of this probing the experimenter asks a large number of questions. The few here quoted are deemed sufficient to indicate the nature of the questions used.)

1. "Whom do you think he might ask?"
2. "He had thought of asking his home-room teacher, a whiz in English, history, and arithmetic, who knows nothing of art, or to ask another student who is so artistic that he has won a scholarship to the museum's art classes. Whom do you think he decided to ask?"
3. "He did ask both, and their advice differed. Whose advice do you think he followed?"
4. "He thought both ideas were equally good. Which one do you think he followed?"
5. "If he chooses the student's idea, will he be very embarrassed toward the teacher whose advice he did not follow?"

Second Story—Fight

"Two boys had a fight before school to see who was stronger. Louis hit Marc's nose which started bleeding profusely."

1. "How do you think Louis felt about it?"

2. "Louis felt guilty and wanted to get rid of his bad conscience. He knew that if he asked his teacher what to do the teacher would tell him to write one hundred times: 'I should not fight before school,' whereas another friend would advise him to give his favorite toy to Marc. Do you think he asked the teacher or the friend?"

3. "Why?"

4. "Louis went to Marc and Marc told him to forget the incident: 'In a fight one child is apt to get hurt,' he said, 'I might have hurt you just as easily.' When do you think that Louis no longer felt guilty, when Marc had told him that he had forgiven him, when he had written the pages for the teacher, or when he had given his toy to Marc?"

RESULTS

First Story

Sixteen (or 69.5 per cent) of the 23 Swiss children, with whom the story was used in the above given form, all of them at least 10.3 years old, insisted that teachers and parents always give the best advice, even in matters of talent. Upon further insistence by the experimenter that it is the child who has the training particularly helpful for the scout, the Swiss children explained that adults know better because they have more experience. In the United States only three out of 40 children (7.5 per cent) preferred the teacher's advice to that of the gifted child and all three of these were six years of age. Whereas all but two Swiss children (91 per cent) imagined that the teacher would be angry if his advice was not followed, only six children in the United States (15 per cent) believed so —three were six years, two were seven and one was nine years of age. Most American children felt certain that the teacher would want the scout to follow the best advice, not necessarily the teacher's. The answers seem to show that Swiss children have less confidence in their peers than do children in America, that Swiss children continue, until a later age, to believe in the omniscience of adult authorities and to rely on their judgment, and that they are afraid of their teachers.

Second Story

Only seven out of the 40 American children (17.5 per cent) showed "egocentricity" of conscience as compared to 20 out of 29 Swiss children (69 per cent). Whereas in America only two six-year-olds (5 per cent) at first thought about their expiation through punishment (though afterwards they did consider the whole situation), there were 13 Swiss children (45 per cent), distributed through the whole range of age, who remained solely concerned about their own atonement; another seven (24 per cent) were in a stage of transition. For many Swiss children the teacher's punishment alone re-established the equilibrium of the world, which was destroyed by their deed. In contrast to children in America, most Swiss children do not doubt the wisdom of their teacher's choice of punishment. When the investigator put these children on "the spot," questioning the teacher's judgment, a number of them became ill at ease and rationalized the teacher's action, finding some reason to justify his advice.

Rather than give up his favorite toy one American boy (2.5 per cent) and seven Swiss children (24 per cent) chose the written work. Others hated writing so much that they preferred giving away the toy. Thirteen Swiss children (45 per cent) wanted to undergo both punishments or at least the one they disliked the most to be sure of expiation. Several of these children were 14 years of age or older. In contrast, not a single American child expressed such a wish. Many Swiss children were of the conviction that some adult ought to be told of the accident even though the boys could take care of it very well themselves. One American boy thought that Louis should feel guilty, because he had not reported his misbehavior.

Being told that Marc has forgiven Louis hardly changed the Swiss children's position on needing punishment to be relieved from guilt feelings. These children again thought of the accident only from the point of view of their own expiation. None of the American children saw a need for punishment in this case.

Obviously the American children show an earlier independence from the teacher and his judgment than do the Swiss children; rather than assent to his wisdom they see the accident with more objectivity and accept the idea either that Marc is right and no guilt feelings are necessary, or that relief from guilt should come by giving pleasure to the child whom they have hurt. Thus they can conform with peer judgment. Their conscience becomes interiorized and autonomous at an earlier age than does that of the Swiss children. It is also a different type of conscience as pointed out before.

SUMMARY AND CONCLUSIONS

Twenty-nine Swiss children and 40 American children from 6 to 15 years of age were studied by the "méthode clinique" to determine the differences in rate of social development and in content of conscience. The study appears to have uncovered evidence that, in certain areas of social development, the American child matures earlier than does the Swiss child. The American child seems to transfer his parent dependence to a peer dependence at an earlier age. One result of this earlier transferring appears to be that the American child's conscience becomes less egocentric and interiorizes earlier than does that of the Swiss child. There is, however, some indication that the content of conscience differs in these two types of societies. Whereas the American child's conscience is turned, primarily, toward social adjustment, the Swiss child's is geared toward character improvement.

Within the age range studied, this study seems to support the following conclusions: [1] American children are emancipated from their own adults at an earlier age than are their Swiss counterparts. [2] They are less subjugated to adults. [3] They are, rather, more dependent on their peers. [4] They enjoy freedom of thought and independence of judgment at an earlier age. [5] They develop earlier a more highly autonomous, though less complex, conscience.

REFERENCES

1. Gillespie, T., and G. Allport. *Youth's Outlook on the Future.* New York: Doubleday, 1955.
2. Mead, Margaret. Social change and cultural surrogates. In *Personality in Nature, Society, and Culture,* C. Kluckhohn, and H. A. Murray (Eds.) (2d ed.) New York: Knopf, 1954, pp. 651–662.
3. Piaget, J. *The Moral Judgment of the Child.* New York: Harcourt, Brace, 1924.
4. Piaget, J. *The Language and Thought of the Child.* New York: Harcourt, Brace, 1926.
5. Piaget, J. *The Child's Conception of the World.* New York: Harcourt, Brace, 1929.
6. Riesman, D., N. Glazer, and R. Denney. *The Lonely Crowd.* New Haven, Conn.: Yale Univ. Press, 1950.
7. Stendler, Celia B. "The learning of certain secondary drives by Parisian and American middle class children." *Marriage Fam. Living,* **16** (1954), 195–200.

1.5 Orientation

An interesting phenomenon in the psychological literature is for some studies to become research classics and to enjoy widespread presentation in almost all textbook treatments. One example of this phenomenon is the famous Lewin, Lippitt, and White (1939) study which compared the effects of authoritarian, democratic, and *laissez-faire* leadership upon children's group productivity and social behavior. Another example is the study originating at the Institute of Child Welfare, Berkeley, which examined the relationship of maturation rate and self concept among adolescent boys (Mussen and Jones, 1957). Occasionally such studies, often based upon small or biased samples, are replicated using larger numbers of subjects. More often, however, they are not. The absence of replication data does not necessarily destroy the generality of research findings, but psychologists would feel more confident if such data were available.

The Bartlett and Smith study which follows is one that replicates, at least partially, a popular study by Marian Winterbottom (1958) on the relationship between children's achievement motivation and their experiences with independence training. Winterbottom disclosed a strong relationship between early independence training and the achievement motive among children. Since the Bartlett and Smith findings are at variance with the Winterbottom data, the reader may find an examination of Winterbottom's original study helpful, particularly to determine the validity of the claims made by Bartlett and Smith. The primary differences between the procedure followed by Bartlett and Smith and that followed by Winterbottom, however, are carefully explained below.

The Bartlett and Smith study is revealing in other ways. For example, the research procedure calls for mothers to supply data concerning their child-rearing practices at a time when the data are largely retrospective. A necessary assumption is that the responses given by these mothers are valid. This approach is common in the study of child-rearing practices and gives rise to legitimate criticism. Bartlett and Smith are careful to point out the limitations of this methodology, as a statement of methodological limitations is essential for any study claiming to be scientific.

Interested readers will want to consider these researchers' comments on achievement motivation and test anxiety with those of Sontag and Kagan (Chapter 2) and McCoy (Chapter 6).

RECOMMENDED READING

Lewin, Kurt, Ronald Lippitt, and R. K. White. "Patterns of aggressive behavior in experimentally created 'social climates'." *J. soc. Psychol.,* **10** (1939), 271–299.

Mussen, P. H., and M. C. Jones. "Self-conceptions, motivations, and interpersonal attitudes of late- and early-maturing boys." *Child Develpm.,* **28** (1957), 243–256.

Rosen, B. C., and Roy D'Andrade. "The psychosocial origins of achievement motivation." *Sociometry,* **22** (1959), 185–218.

Warren, J. R. "Birth order and social behavior." *Psychol. Bull.,* **65** (1966), 38–49. (A critical review of research on the "effects" of birth order.)

Winterbottom, Marian. The relation of need for achievement in learning experiences in independence and mastery. In *Motives in Fantasy, Action and Society,* John Atkinson (Ed.) Princeton, N.J.: Van Nostrand, 1958.

1.5 Child-Rearing Practices, Birth Order, and the Development of Achievement-Related Motives[1]

Edward W. Bartlett, YALE UNIVERSITY SCHOOL OF MEDICINE
Charles P. Smith, BROOKLYN COLLEGE

The present study concerns the relationship of parental child-rearing practices and birth order to the strength of the child's Need for Achievement (*n* Ach) and test anxiety. The introductory section of this paper reviews the background of theory and research concerning the development of achievement motivation and test anxiety.

Concerning the origin of the achievement motive, McClelland and his colleagues state: "All motives are learned, . . . they develop out of repeated affective experiences connected with certain types of situations and types of behavior. In the case of achievement motivation, the situations should involve 'standards of excellence,' . . . and the behavior should involve either 'competition' with those standards of excellence or attempts to meet them which, if successful, produce positive effect, or if unsuccessful, negative effect" (McClelland, *et al.,* 1953, p. 275). In an early study designed to test this theory, Winterbottom (1958) found that earliness of parental demands for independence and mastery was related to the development of high *n* Ach and that mothers of boys with high *n* Ach gave more effective rewards for their sons' accomplishments than mothers of boys with low *n* Ach. In her questionnaire, Winterbottom did not distinguish between demands for achievement and for independence. For example, one item asked the age at which the mother expected her son "To do well in school [achievement] on his own" [independence]. Later studies by Child, Storm, and Veroff (1958) and by Rosen and D'Andrade (1959) indicate that achievement training (setting standards of excellence) is more closely related to the child's *n* Ach than independence training

[1] This study is based, in part, on research conducted by E. W. Bartlett for an unpublished senior thesis at Princeton University. The latter phase of the research was supported by Public Health Service Research Grant No. MH 08065 to C. P. Smith from the National Institutes of Health. The authors are indebted to Roald Buhler for his advice concerning computer methods of data analysis. This work made use of computer facilities supported in part by National Science Foundation Grant NSF–GP 579.

Reprinted with permission of author and publisher: Bartlett, E. W. and Smith, C. P. Childrearing practices, birth order and the development of achievement-related motives. *Psych. Rep.* (1966), **18,** 1207–1216.

(emphasis on self-reliance and autonomy). Furthermore, studies by McClelland (1961) and Moss and Kagan (1961) suggest that the relationship between the age at which parental demands are made and strength of *n* Ach may be curvilinear rather than linear, with very early and very late demands producing low *n* Ach and intermediate demands producing high *n* Ach.

In view of the qualifications of Winterbottom's findings made by later studies and in view of the frequent reliance on the Winterbottom study in discussions of motivational development (cf. Berkowitz, 1964; McClelland, 1961) it was decided to undertake the present investigation, using essentially the same procedures as Winterbottom, but with distinctions between achievement and independence training.

Attention was also given to birth order as a variable with potentially important implications for the development of achievement-related motives. For example, a number of studies (cf. Altus, 1966; Sampson, 1962) indicate that first-born children have higher achievement motivation.

Research on the origins of test anxiety by Sarason, *et al.* (1960) suggests that high test anxiety results from parental practices involving (a) critical evaluations of the child's performance, (b) love contingent on success, and (c) encouragement of dependent behavior. The present study is also designed to obtain further information concerning these relationships.

METHOD

Subjects

*S*s were 31 8- to 10-yr.-old boys and their mothers. The children were third and fourth graders at a private preparatory school (non-Catholic) in a large Midwestern city. The fathers of the children were business and professional men with upper-middle or upper class socio-economic status as indicated by their occupations: 19 business executives, 7 doctors, 3 lawyers, 1 teacher (1 deceased). Letters were sent to 48 mothers and 31 agreed to complete the questionnaires. Because of partially incomplete data for two mothers and two children, the *N* varies between 29 and 31 for different analyses.

Procedure

Assessment of child-rearing practices The mothers were asked to fill out a revised version of Winterbottom's (1958) questionnaire. In part I they were asked to check, on a list of 22 possible behaviors, those behaviors which they desired in their sons and to write in the age by which they thought their sons should have learned the behavior. The original Winterbottom items were revised to represent demands for either achievement or independence but not both. For example, the original item "To do well in school on his own" was revised to read "To do well in studies" and was considered an achievement item. The revised items are presented in Table 1.

TABLE 1. ACHIEVEMENT AND INDEPENDENCE DEMANDS TO BE CHECKED BY MOTHERS

Achievement Subscale

[a] To be active and energetic in climbing, jumping and sports.
To do well in activities such as creative writing, painting, and drawing or music.
To stick with a task which is within his capabilities until he masters it.
To try hard to come out on top in games and sports.
[a] To do well in studies.
[a] To do well in competition with other children.
[a] To show pride in his own ability to do things well.
To develop many talents.
To try hard in everything he does.

Independence Subscale

[a] To know his way around his part of the city so that he can play where he wants without getting lost.
[a] To entertain himself when his parents are too busy to be with him.
[a] To try new things on his own without asking for help.
[a] To earn his own spending money.
[a] To have interests and hobbies of his own choosing.
[a] To make his own friends among children his own age.
[a] To make decisions like choosing his clothes or deciding how to spend his money by himself.
[a] To do things on his own initiative without asking for help.
[a] To be able to stay home alone during the day.
[a] To eat alone without help in cutting and handling food.

Additional Unclassified Items

[a] To lead other children and assert himself in children's groups.
To persist at a task that is very difficult even if it is not likely that he will master it.
To entertain himself by watching television.

[a] Items taken verbatim from or adapted from Winterbottom's (1958) questionnaire.

The second section of the questionnaire asked about family size, birth order of the child, and the father's occupation. In the last section, the mothers were asked to check the rewards and punishments they used in achievement situations. Winterbottom's items were supplemented by several additional items such as: "Tell him how much you love him" as a possible reward for the son's doing what the mother wanted. It was hoped that this item would, to some extent, assess the use of "conditional love" as a reward for successful behavior. The list of rewards and punishments used in the present study is presented in Table 2.

TABLE 2. Rewards and Punishments To Be Checked by Mothers

Rewards

If your son did something you wanted him to do, you would:
[a] Kiss or hug him to show how pleased you are.
Tell him how much you love him.
Tell him that he should be very proud of himself.
Tell him how proud you are of him.
[a] Give him a special treat or privilege.
[a] Do nothing at all to make it seem special.
[a] Show him you expected it of him.
[a] Show him how he could have done better.
Tell him if he keeps doing this well he will have many friends.
[a] Tell him what a good boy he is. Praise him for being good.

Punishments

If your son did something that you didn't want him to do, you would:
[a] Spank him for doing it.
Tell him he is not making his parents proud of him.
Pretend that you don't love him as much as you did before.
Turn cold on him.
[a] Don't show any feeling about it.
Encourage him to keep trying.
[a] Point out how he should have behaved.
[a] Deprive him of something he likes or expects, like a special treat or privilege.
Tell him he can't expect to be liked if he doesn't do better.
[a] Show him you are disappointed in him.
[a] Just wait until he does what you want.

[a] Items taken verbatim from or adapted from Winterbottom's (1958) questionnaire.

Assessment of need for achievement and test anxiety *E* (E. W. B.) interviewed each child individually to obtain projective stories and to administer the Test Anxiety Scale for Children (Sarason, *et al.,* 1960). He said he was interested in storytelling and would give the child some topics to tell stories about. After telling a "practice story" the child told six more stories to the following word cues: (1) "A boy who has just left his house." (2) "Two men standing by a machine. One is older." (3) "A young man sitting at a desk." (4) "A father and son talking about something important." (5) "A group of children playing. One is a little ahead." (6) "A boy at home is building something. He runs into a problem." The instructions and most of the word cues were adapted from the study by Winterbottom (1958). No time limit was imposed, but children were interrupted if the story became too lengthy. Since the correlation between the number of words in *S*'s stories and his *n* Ach score was not significant ($r = .22$, $N = 31$, n.s.), no attempt was made to correct *n* Ach scores for story length in the analyses which follow. All stories were scored independently by the two authors using the McClelland, *et al.* (1953) scoring manual. Inter-judge reliability was .83 (rank-difference correlation). *S*s were divided at the median of their scores to form groups high and low in *n* Ach and in test anxiety. Table 3 presents the means and standard deviations of the *n* Ach, test anxiety, and intelligence scores.

TABLE 3. MEANS, STANDARD DEVIATIONS AND RANGES OF *n* ACH, TEST ANXIETY, AND KUHLMANN-ANDERSON IQ

Variable	*N*	*M*	*SD*	Range
n Ach	31	5.74	6.20	−4 to 16
Test Anxiety	31	10.74	5.12	3 to 27
IQ	31	125.48	11.03	104 to 148

Intelligence, grades, rated dependence From the school records the grade average of each child and his Kuhlmann-Anderson IQ were obtained. In addition, the teachers were asked to rate each child on the following three questions which inquired about his dependence: (1) How is he about doing things in school on his own? (2) Generally how would you rate his over-all independence? (3) How would you rate his need for emotional support? For each question there were five answer-categories indicating different degrees of dependence. Scores for the three items were summed for each child, with the highest dependency score being 15 and the lowest 3.

RESULTS

Demands for Achievement and Independence and Strength of Achievement-Related Motives [2]

From the items checked by each mother, the average age for achievement demands and for independence demands was calculated separately. Table 4 shows correlations between these indexes of the earliness of demands and the strength of achievement-related motives. The correlations are small and non-significant, providing no evidence of a linear relationship between *n* Ach or test anxiety and the earliness of reported demands or restrictions pertaining to independence and achievement. The data also revealed no significant curvilinear relationships between the variables.

[2] Tabled data have been filed as Document No. 9163 with the ADI Auxiliary Publications Project, Photoduplication Service, Library of Congress, Washington, D. C. 20540. Remit $1.25 for photocopies or 35-mm microfilm.

TABLE 4. CORRELATIONS AMONG VARIABLES

Variable	N	n Ach	TASC [a]	IQ [b]
TASC	31	−.22		
IQ	31	.17	−.47 [c]	
Avg. age ach demands	31	.19	.04	−.11
Avg. age ind demands	31	.11	.07	−.15
Birth order	31	−.47 [c]	.38 [d]	−.32
Dependence (teacher ratings)	31	−.09	.42 [d]	−.43 [d]
Grade average	29	.12	−.38 [d]	.68 [c]

[a] Test Anxiety Scale for Children.
[b] Kuhlman-Anderson IQs.
[c] $p < .01$, two-tailed test.
[d] $p < .05$, two-tailed test.

It is interesting to note that intelligence appears to be related to the earliness of parental demands. Child's IQ is correlated .33 ($N = 31$, $p. < .10$, two-tailed test) with the number of independence demands made through age seven (an index of earliness of demands suggested by Winterbottom). In other words, there is a tendency for mothers of children with high intelligence to report making demands of their children at an earlier age than mothers of children with low intelligence.

Contrary to expectation, mothers of children with low n Ach checked significantly *more* demands for achievement and independence than mothers of children with high n Ach (chi square with Yates' correction = 393, $p < .05$). Some possible interpretations of this finding will be suggested in the discussion section below.

There are no significant correlations between test anxiety and the average age of demands for achievement or independence (see Table 4) but there is a near-significant correlation between test anxiety and the number of independence demands made through age seven ($r = -.27$, $p < .10$, one-tailed test). This correlation is in the direction expected from the hypothesis that encouragement of dependent behavior is associated with the development of high test anxiety.

Rewards, Punishments and Strength of Achievement-Related Motives

The number of mothers of children with high and low n Ach checking each reward item differed only on the item: "Tell him how much you love him." This item was checked significantly more often by mothers of children with low n Ach (chi-square with Yates' correction = 4.16, $p < .05$). Although the interpretation of this finding is not clear, it is possible that this indicates a greater use of "conditional love" by mothers of children with low n Ach.

Of the punishment items, the item "Show him you are disappointed in him" was checked by all 14 mothers of children with high *n* Ach and by 9 of the 15 mothers of children with low *n* Ach ($p < .03$, Fisher's exact test, two-tailed). This result may indicate a method by which the mothers of children with high *n* Ach hold up standards for their sons.

Mothers of children with high and low test anxiety did not give significantly different responses to any of the reward and punishment items.

Teacher Ratings of Dependence and Strength of Achievement-Related Motives

There is a significant positive relationship between test anxiety scores and rated dependence ($r = .42$, $p < .05$, two-tailed test) as would be expected on the basis of the hypothesis concerning the origins of test anxiety (see Table 4). There is no significant relationship between *n* Ach scores and rated dependence ($r = -.09$, n.s.).

Since intelligence is also related to ratings of dependence ($r = -.43$, $p < .05$, two-tailed test), it may be asked to what extent test anxiety is related to dependence when intelligence is not a contributing factor. The partial correlation between test anxiety and rated dependence with IQ constant is .27 ($N = 31$, $p < .10$, one-tailed test). It may not be appropriate to partial out intelligence, however, since decrements in performance on intelligence tests and manifestations of dependence may both be attributable to test anxiety.

Birth Order and Strength of Achievement-Related Motives

The variable discriminating most effectively between children with high and low *n* Ach in the present study is birth order. There is a strong correlation indicating that the earlier the birth order, the higher the *n* Ach ($r = -.47$, $p < .01$, two-tailed test). Of the 15 boys with high *n* Ach, 11 were first-born, while only 2 of the 16 children with low *n* Ach were eldest sons (chi-square with Yates' correction = 9.40, $p < .005$).

There is also a statistically significant relationship in the opposite direction between test anxiety and birth order ($r = .38$, $p < .05$, two-tailed test). That is, the later the birth order, the higher the test anxiety. Finally, there is a significant relationship between birth order and age of independence training ($r = .36$, $p < .05$, two-tailed test), indicating that early birth order goes with early independence training.

DISCUSSION

Origins of Achievement Motivation

Although highly similar techniques were employed, the results of the present study did not replicate the findings of the Winterbottom study.

There were no relationships between the strength of children's achievement motivation and the reported ages at which maternal demands for independence and achievement were made. In contrast to expectation, mothers of boys with low *n* Ach report making more demands for achievement and independence than mothers of boys with high *n* Ach ($p < .05$). This result may mean that frequent demands, particularly if they are unrealistic, produce unpleasant associations with achievement situations. Or, it may simply be that mothers of boys with low *n* Ach are giving what they think are the socially acceptable answers to the questionnaire.

There were no differences between mothers of children with high and low *n* Ach with respect to the use of the rewards for achievement included in the Winterbottom questionnaire. The only reaction to the child's success which differentiated between the two groups of mothers was the item added in the present study, "Tell him how much you love him," which was checked significantly more often by the mothers of children with low *n* Ach. Seemingly more consistent with the McClelland, *et al.* (1953) proposals is the finding that mothers of sons with high *n* Ach, as compared with mothers of sons with low *n* Ach, more often tell their sons they are disappointed when their children do not live up to their expectations ($p < .03$). This appears to be a way of holding up standards for the child's performances. While findings for this high socio-economic, high intelligence population are important in their own right, it should be noted that it is difficult to generalize the results because the obtained relationships may characterize the restricted portion of the continuum but do not necessarily hold for the entire population. At the same time, it is also possible that the correlations, being based on a restricted range, underestimate the relationships obtaining in the total population.

Two reservations may be noted concerning the procedure of asking for recall of training ages in a questionnaire. First of all, parental recall of the ages at which different events occurred in the lives of their children has been shown to be quite inaccurate (Robbins, 1963). Second, the parent may not be able to differentiate between making a "demand" *prior* to a child's demonstrating the behavior and coming to expect the behavior *after* the child has already begun to manifest it. The tendency for reported early training to be associated with higher intelligence shown in the present study ($p < .10$) and in a similar study by Siss (1962) suggests the possibility that more intelligent children may be ready for achievement training sooner. The mother in turn may come to expect achievement behavior at an early age, not because she tends to make particularly early demands but because the child is ready for the demands. It is difficult to determine the direction of causality. It may be that children of high intelligence prompt parents to make early demands because they are ready for them, or it may be that early demands produce higher intelligence. Another possibility is that children with higher intelligence have mothers with higher intelligence and that such mothers may make earlier demands than mothers with lower intelligence. These considerations suggest that the relationship between intelligence (of both mother and child) and age of training should be investigated in future studies of motivational development.

A further difficulty with even the revised Winterbottom items is their ambiguity. Parents frequently ask which of several quite different meanings an item has. A more effective procedure for obtaining information is clearly needed such as longitudinal observation or having the mothers keep a "current practices checklist" on which they record what they are doing, not what they recall having done some years earlier. Finally, it is difficult to get parents to admit to the use of socially undesirable forms of reward and punishment. The family interaction interview employed by Rosen and D'Andrade (1959) is an important contribution in this regard. In view of the foregoing problems in replication and interpretation, it appears that the findings of Winterbottom (1958) should be cited with greater caution and reservation than is common.

The most clear-cut difference between boys with high and low *n* Ach is the difference in birth order. First-born children have higher *n* Ach than later children, a finding also reported by Sampson (1962) for a combined group of males and females. Rosen (1961) pointed out that family size and social class influence the relationship between birth order and achievement motivation. In a review of studies dealing with birth order and accomplishment, Altus (1966) summarizes a great deal of evidence indicating that first-born children are more highly represented among the ranks of the eminent than later-born children. It seems likely to the present authors that the achievement tendencies of first-born children are due to such things as the relatively greater involvement, encouragement, and urging of their parents. It may be relevant also to note that more expectant mothers report anticipating their first child with pleasure than later children (Sears, Maccoby, & Levin, 1957). It is also true, of course, that the first child has his parents as models while later children have older children as well as parents. These and other possible determinants associated with birth order should be investigated in future research.

Origins of Test Anxiety

Although there is no evidence in the present data that mothers of boys with high test anxiety are especially critical of their children, they did tend to check less frequently than mothers of boys with low test anxiety the reward item "Praise him for being good" ($p < .09$, Fisher's exact test, two-tailed). The results concerning dependency are also consistent with the theory of the origin of test anxiety. Boys with high test anxiety were rated as more dependent by their teachers than boys with low test anxiety, and there is a tendency for mothers of boys with high test anxiety to report making fewer demands for independence through age seven than mothers of boys with low test anxiety ($p < .10$). The latter finding is similar to one reported by Feld (1959) who found that high test anxiety in adolescent boys was associated with relatively late maternal demands for independence while low test anxiety was associated with relatively early independence training. Test anxiety scores are negatively related, as expected, to intelligence and grades. The correlation of −.22 (n.s.) between test anxiety and *n* Ach is of about the same magnitude as has been reported between the two measures in groups of college students (e.g., Atkinson & Litwin, 1960). Although it may seem at first that the negative correlation between the two motives should be considerably stronger, it is possible to conceive of parents who hold high standards for the child and reward his successes but who also punish his failures and encourage dependent behavior. Under such conditions a child might be expected to develop strong motives of both kinds. In short, the various possible combinations of childrearing practices suggest that the two motives should be essentially uncorrelated rather than strongly correlated.

SUMMARY

The influence of parental demands and sanctions on the achievement-related motives of 31 boys (ages 8 to 10) is examined. The findings of an earlier study by Winterbottom were not replicated. However, boys with high as compared with low Need for Achievement were more often first-born ($p < .005$); their mothers more often expressed disappointment with unsatisfactory behavior ($p < .03$), less often told them how much they loved them as a reward ($p < .05$), and reported making fewer demands for achievement and independence ($p < .05$). Age of demands was unrelated to Need for Achievement. Boys with high as compared with low test anxiety had lower IQs ($p < .01$), lower grades ($p < .05$), later birth order ($p < .05$), and higher teacher-ratings of dependence ($p < .05$). Their mothers tended to make later demands for independence ($p < .10$) and to praise their sons' behavior less often ($p < .10$).

REFERENCES

Altus, W. D. "Birth order and its sequelae." *Science,* 1966, **151,** 44–49.

Atkinson, J. W., and G. H. Litwin. "Achievement motive and test anxiety conceived as motive to approach success and motive to avoid failure." *J. abnorm. soc. Psychol.,* 1960, **60,** 52–63.

Berkowitz, L. *The Development of Motives and Values in the Child.* New York: Basic Books, 1964.

Child, I. L., T. Storm, and J. Veroff. Achievement themes in folk tales related to socialization practice. In J. W. Atkinson (Ed.), *Motives in Fantasy, Action, and Society*. Princeton: Van Nostrand, 1958. Chap. 34.

Feld, S. Studies in the origins of achievement strivings. Unpubl. doctoral dissertation, Univ. of Michigan, 1959.

McClelland, D. C. *The Achieving Society*. Princeton: Van Nostrand, 1961.

McClelland, D. C., J. W. Atkinson, R. A. Clark, and E. L. Lowell. *The Achievement Motive*. New York: Appleton-Century-Crofts, 1953.

Moss, H. A., and J. Kagan. "Stability of achievement and recognition seeking behaviors from early childhood through adulthood." *J. abnorm. soc. Psychol.,* 1961, **62,** 504–513.

Robbins, L. C. "The accuracy of parental recall of aspects of child development and of child rearing practices." *J. abnorm. soc. Psychol.,* 1963, **66,** 261–270.

Rosen, B. C. Family structure and achievement motivation. *Amer. soc. Rev.,* 1961, **26,** 274–285.

Rosen, B. C., and R. G. D'Andrade. "The psychosocial origins of achievement motivation." *Sociometry,* 1959, **22,** 185–218.

Sampson, E. E. "Birth order, need achievement, and conformity." *J. abnorm. soc. Psychol.,* 1962, **64,** 155–159.

Sarason, S. B., K. S. Davidson, F. F. Lighthall, R. R. Waite, and B. K. Ruebush, *Anxiety in Elementary School Children*. New York: Wiley, 1960.

Sears, R. R., E. E. Maccoby, and H. Levin. *Patterns of Child Rearing*. Evanston, Ill.: Row, Peterson, 1957.

Siss, R. Expectations of mothers and teachers for independence and reading and their influence upon reading achievement and personality attributes of third grade boys. Unpubl. doctoral dissertation, Rutgers Univer., 1962.

Winterbottom, M. R. The relation of need for achievement to learning experiences in independence and mastery. In J. W. Atkinson (Ed.), *Motives in Fantasy, Action and Society*. Princeton: Van Nostrand, 1958. Pp. 453–478.

1.6 Orientation

One common research strategy in psychology is to examine the polar extremes in children's behavior for a clearer understanding of those variables influencing development. For example, hyperaggressive children may be compared to extremely passive age-mates on such criteria as activity level, attitudes toward child rearing held by parents, family size, birth order, and so on. By contrasting personal characteristics and family background factors related to such extremes it is generally thought that relevant antecedents may be detected. So it has been with much research on the etiology of psychopathology in children. Children with deviant behavioral patterns, such as schizophrenia, are often compared with normally functioning peers on criteria thought to be etiologically relevant. If differences are disclosed by such comparisons causation is frequently inferred, although it is difficult to indicate just which differences are responsible for the behavior in question.

The following paper by Frank represents a critical review of research into familial influences on the development of personality pathology among children. A large body of research on schizophrenia* and a smaller number of studies concerning neurosis and behavior disorders are summarized. The studies reviewed are categorized by method employed; that is, whether the data were derived from case histories, interviews, psychometric techniques (instruments for the measurement of psychological characteristics), direct observation, and the like.

At least three values can be found in Frank's critical view. One concerns the conclusions from his synthesis of the research selected for review and the explanation of these findings. A second is his relevant commentary on the function of data collection—specifically, measurement techniques in studying complex behavior patterns such as schizophrenia. A third value is his discussion of mediating variables that may confound the single cause-effect relationship often assumed to exist between parental treatment and children's personality development. Perhaps the central question for the reader to consider after a study of this paper is this: Does Frank's review invalidate the hypothesis that events in the parent-child relationship influence the course of the child's personality development?

RECOMMENDED READING

Kessler, Jane. *Psychopathology of Childhood.* Englewood Cliffs, N.J.: Prentice-Hall, 1966.

* Schizophrenia is a clinical term that subsumes several types of psychotic disorders. The most general characteristics of schizophrenia include an inability or unwillingness to relate to others in meaningful, emotional ways, distortions in thinking to the point of irrationality, and a loss of contact with reality. Schizophrenia is frequently accompanied by delusions (false beliefs about the self and others) and hallucinations (false sensory experiences) which illustrate the elaborate fantasy life of the psychotic person.

1.6 The Role of the Family in the Development of Psychopathology

George H. Frank

As psychopathology came to be viewed as the consequence of the emotional experiences to which the individual was exposed, interest was focused on the earliest of such experiences, those that occur in the family. The human infant is born incapable of sustaining its own life for a considerable length of time following birth, and is, in consequence, dependent upon the mother or a mother substitute for its very existence. There is no wonder, therefore, that the mother-child relationship is a close one and is expected to be influential with regard to the psychological development of the child. Some explanations for the development of psychopathology have therefore focused on this particular relationship as the major etiological factor. Levy (1931, 1932, 1937, 1943) has described a pattern centering around "maternal overprotection," involving a constellation of attitudes which he felt contributed to the development of neurotic disorders, and Despert (1938) focused on a kind of mother-child relationship which seemed to her to be closely associated with the development of schizophrenia, a pattern which has come to be termed the "schizophrenogenic mother."

The hypothesis that the emotional climate of the interpersonal relationships within the family—and between the child and its mother in particular—has a decisive part in the development of the personality of the child would seem to have face validity. In part, support for this hypothesis may be gleaned from the data demonstrating the devastating effects of being brought up in the extreme interpersonal isolation that comes from *not* having a family (Beres & Obers, 1950; Brodbeck & Irwin, 1946; Goldfarb, 1943a, 1943b, 1943c, 1945a, 1945b; Lowrey, 1940; Spitz, 1945) or extreme social isolation within a family (Bartmeier, 1952; Davis, 1940). Moreover, it has been demonstrated that various specific emotional behaviors of the child seem to be correlated causally with factors in the home. For example, children who could be described as emotionally immature, who are dependent, fearful, negativistic, emotionally labile, etc., have had mothers described as worriers (Pearson, 1931), overattentive (Hattwick, 1936; Hattwick & Stowell, 1936), or punitive (McCord, McCord, & Howard, 1961; Sears, Whiting, Nowlis, & Sears, 1953; Watson, 1934). Children who were described as being overly aggressive were described as having come from homes where mothers were seen as over-

Reprinted from *Psychological Bulletin,* **64** (1965), no. 3, 191–205. By permission of the author and the American Psychological Association, Inc.

controlling (Bishop, 1951) or punitive (McCord et al., 1961; Sears, 1961).

The evidence thus far suggests that there is, in fact, a correlation between events in the parent-child relationship and resultant personality *traits*. The question arises as to whether there is evidence which supports the hypothesis that there is a correlation between events in the parent-child relationship and the resultant complex patterns of behavior which have been termed personality. More specifically, in light of the theories which relate personality development to social (i.e., interpersonal) learning, the question is raised as to whether there is any consistent relationship between the emotional experience the child may have in the home and the development of personality pathology, that is, schizophrenia, neurosis, and behavior disorders. Towards this end, the findings of the research that has explored the psychological characteristics of the parents of these people will be analyzed in order to isolate those consistent characteristics of the parents that may emerge from study to study. The analysis will be done with regard to each major type of psychopathology as a group. Moreover, because psychological test data might yield different information than case history analysis, or direct observation of familial interaction as compared to attitudes as elicited by questionnaire, an attempt will be made to analyze the information gleaned from the studies in terms of the method of data collection within the specific psychopathological groupings.

SCHIZOPHRENIA

Case History

One of the classical methods of data collection in the study of psychiatric illness is the case history, the information for which has generally been gathered by other professionals. The individual conducting a piece of research notes the material in the folders and draws conclusions from the collation of these observations.

In so doing, Despert (1938) observed that approximately 50% of the mothers of a sample of schizophrenic children, generally between the ages of 7 and 13, had been described as aggressive, overanxious, and oversolicitious and were considered to be the dominant parent. Clardy (1951) noted that 50% of the 30 cases of children between the ages of 3 and 12 diagnosed as schizophrenic had families characterized as overprotective and yet basically rejecting. Frazee (1953) noted the presence of this constellation particularly when the families of schizophrenics were compared with the families of children diagnosed as behavior disorders. Canavan and Clark (1923) and Lampron (1933) noted that 30% of the children of psychotics were themselves emotionally disturbed. Huschka (1941) and Lidz and Lidz (1949) noted that over 40% of their sample of schizophrenics had parents who were psychotic or neurotic. Bender (1936, 1937) and Frazee (1953) noted the high incidence of psychopathology in the children of psychotic parents. Preston and Antin (1932), on the other hand, found no significant differences in the incidence of psychosis and neurosis as a function of parents who were psychotic as compared to parents who were "normal," and Fanning, Lehr, Sherwin, and Wilson (1938) found that 43% of the children of mothers who were psychotic were observed to be making an adequate social and personal adjustment, with only 11% of that sample classified as maladjusted.

Lidz and Lidz (1949) found that 40% of their sample of schizophrenic patients were deprived of one parent by divorce or separation before they were 19. Plank (1953) found that 63% of his sample of schizophrenics had families where one parent was absent either due to death or marital separation. Wahl (1954, 1956) found that there was a greater incidence of parental loss and rejection early in life for schizophrenics as compared to normals, and Barry (1936) found that from the case histories of 30 rulers adjudged, post facto, insane, 80% of them had lost one of their parents by the time they were 18. However, Barry and Bousfield (1937) found that the incidence of orphanhood in a psychiatric population (19 out of 26) was not much different from the incidence of orphanhood in a normal population (19 out of 24). Moreover, Oltman, McGarry, and Friedman (1952) found that the incidence of broken homes and parental deprivation in the families of schizophrenics (34%) was not very different from that found in the families of hospital employees (32%), alcoholics (31%), and manic-depressives (34%); indeed, in their sampling, neurotics (49%) and psychopaths (48%) showed a greater incidence. Other studies have found that the incidence of broken homes in the history of neurotics is between 20% (Brown and Moore, 1944) and 30% (Madow and Hardy, 1947; Wallace, 1935), and Gerard and Siegel (1950) found no particular incidence of broken homes in the family history of their sample of schizophrenics.

Psychiatric Interview

Another classical method of obtaining information regarding the individual with whom patients have been living is by having interviews with them directly. The quality of the mother-child relationship is then inferred from what the interviewee says. From this research, an overwhelming number of studies (Despert, 1951; Gerard and Siegel, 1950; Guertin, 1961; Hajdu-Gimes, 1940; Kasanin, Knight, and Sage, 1934; Lidz, Cornelison, Fleck, and Terry, 1957a, 1957b, 1957c; Lidz, Cornelison, Terry, and Fleck, 1958; Lidz and Lidz, 1949; Lidz, Parker, and Cornelison, 1956; Tietze, 1949; Walters, 1938) describe a familial pattern characterized by a dominant, overprotective, but basically rejecting mother and a passive, ineffectual father. Yet the data in the study by Schofield and Balian (1959) reflected similarity rather than differences in the families of schizophrenic and nonpsychiatric (general medical) patients, and the data of Gerard and Siegel (1950) indicated that the schizophrenics in their study, according to interpretation of the data gleaned from the interviews, received adequate breast feeding, had no history of particularly difficult toilet training or of obvious feeding problems, did not come from broken homes, and apparently were not unduly rejected or punished. Another factor which seems to emerge from the studies is that a dominant characteristic of the family life of schizophrenics is a quality of inappropriateness of thinking and behaving which seems to infiltrate the entire atmosphere (Fleck, Lidz, and Cornelison, 1963; Lidz et al., 1957b, 1957c; Stringer, 1962). Meyers and Goldfarb (1962), however, found that only 28% of the mothers of 45 children diagnosed as schizophrenic and only 12% of the fathers were themselves manifestly schizophrenic.

Psychological Evaluation

Attitude questionnaires One of the most widely used questionnaires in this area of research has been the Shoben (1949) Parent-Child Attitude Survey. The Shoben scale consists of 148 items which measure the dimensions of parental rejection, possessiveness, and domination. From the administration of this attitude survey, Mark (1953) and Freeman and Grayson (1955) reported significant differences in attitudes toward child rearing between mothers of schizophrenics and mothers of normal children. In comparison with the mothers of the control subjects, the mothers of schizophrenic patients (Mark, 1953) were revealed as inconsistent in their methods of control. They described themselves as being, at times, overrestrictive and controlling of behavior, but in some instances lax. They frowned on sex play and tended to keep information regarding sex from their children; they also seemed to frown on friends for their children. Their relationship to their children appeared inconsistent; they described what could be interpreted as excessive devotion and interest in the child's activities while at the same time revealing a notable degree of "cool detachment." Freeman and Grayson (1955) found that in comparison to mothers of students in an undergraduate course, mothers of 50 hospitalized schizophrenics (ages 20 to 35) tended to reveal themselves to be somewhat more possessive, but inherently rejecting of their children, and particularly disturbed about sexual behavior in their children. However, according to these same data, the mothers of schizophrenic patients did not reveal themselves to be more dominant, dogmatic, or inconsistent in their attitude than the controls. But most important was the fact that item analysis of these data revealed that the attitudes of the mothers of the schizophrenics and of the controls were distinguished on only 14 of the items, and then, in general, there was so much overlap that even on these items the statistical significance was contributed by a small percentage of each group. Freeman, Simmons, and Bergen (1959) included four items from the Shoben scale among a larger sample of questions posed to parents. These items had been derived from a previous study (Freeman and Simmons, 1958) and were included in the second study because they were the only ones in the first study which were found to discriminate between the attitudes of mothers of schizophrenic patients and those of mothers of normals. The items are:

1. Parents should sacrifice everything for their children.
2. A child should feel a deep sense of obligation always to act in accord with the wishes of his parents.
3. Children who are gentlemanly or ladylike are preferable to those who are tomboys or "regular guys."
4. It is better for children to play at home than to visit other children.

Freeman et al. (1959) found no capacity for these items to differentiate the attitudes of the mothers of schizophrenics from those of other individuals with severe functional disorders.

Zuckerman, Oltean, and Monashkin (1958) utilized another attitude scale, the Parental Attitude Research Inventory (PARI, developed by Schaefer and Bell in their work at the Psychology Laboratory at NIMH). The PARI was administered to mothers of schizophrenics, and it was found that only one item distinguished between their attitudes and those of mothers of normal children. The mothers of schizophrenics tended to describe themselves as being stricter than did the mothers of nonschizophrenic children.

The minimal discrimination value of the several attitude scales should be noted. This would seem to reflect either minimal capacity of the scales to make such distinctions or little in the way of measurable differences between the groups. In either case, it is very difficult to evaluate the meaning of these data since the attitudes of the mothers of schizophrenics seemed to be distinguished from the attitudes of the mothers of neurotics on only a few items (the obtained number of differences did not even exceed that expected by chance alone).

Projective tests Several studies presented Rorschach data on the mothers of schizophrenic patients (Baxter, Becker, and Hooks, 1963; Prout and White, 1950; Winder and Kantor, 1958). In comparison to those of the mothers of normals, the Rorschach protocols of the mothers of the schizophrenic patients were undistinguished as regards the general degree of immaturity (Winder and Kantor, 1958) and the use of defences which are essentially reality distorting, namely, denial and projection (Baxter et al., 1963).[1] However, Prout and White did find more pure color without

[1] The conclusion that the Rorschach protocols of the mothers of schizophrenics were undistinguished from the Rorschach protocols of the mothers of normals (as in the research by Winder & Kantor, 1958, Baxter et al., 1963) is an interpretation of the results made by the present author. In fact, in both of these

form and less human and animal movement and shading responses in the Rorschach protocols of mothers of schizophrenic boys as compared to the mothers of a comparable group of boys randomly selected from the community. Perr (1958) found that the parents of schizophrenic children gave responses to the Thematic Apperception Test (TAT) little distinguished from those of parents of normal children, and Fisher, Boyd, Walker, and Sheer (1959) found that the TAT and Rorschach protocols of the parents of schizophrenic patients were measurably different from those of the parents of nonpsychiatric (general medical) patients, but they were not distinguishable from the protocols of the parents of neurotic patients. The mothers of the schizophrenics revealed a higher degree of perceptual rigidity, greater incidence of indicators of maladjustment on the Rorschach, and less definitely conceived parental images on the TAT than the mothers of the normals.

Direct observation of interpersonal behavior Attempts have been made to study the interpersonal behavior of families of schizophrenics *in vivo;* some investigators have gone into the home, others have brought the family into a hospital setting and observed the interaction between family members for an hour or so at a time, others have brought the family into a laboratory setting (National Institute of Mental Health) where the family lives under actual but known conditions for months at a time.

In the study of the interpersonal relationships in the actual home setting, Behrens and Goldfarb (1958) observed that the personality of the mother seemed to set the tone of the family milieu and that there seemed to be a direct relationship between the degree of pathology that could be seen in the family setting and the degree of psychopathology demonstrated by the child. The homes they observed appeared physically deteriorated and crowded. There was a basic isolation between the mother and father, and the fathers were basically passive. Confusion and disorganization characterized the family atmosphere, with the family dem-

articles, the authors conclude that there *are* significant differences. However, in the article by Winder and Kantor, the mean rating of the degree of maturity of personality development for the mothers of the schizophrenics was 2.89, for the mothers of the normals, 2.43. In the article by Baxter et al., the means of the ratings of the degree of utilization of psychologically immature defenses on the Rorschach by the parents of poor premorbid schizophrenics, good premorbid schizophrenics, and neurotics are, respectively, 19.43, 19.62, and 19.49. Though in both of these investigations valid statistical significance was demonstrated between the obtained means, the actual means, in both researches, are so similar to each other that the interpretation of *psychologically* significant differences between groups on the basis of the obtained *statistically* significant differences seemed a highly doubtful conclusion.

onstrating inadequate mechanisms to handle emotional flareups. The intensive observation of one mother-child interaction (Karon and Rosberg, 1958) yielded the observation that the mother was unempathic. She blocked verbalizations of emotions and tended to live vicariously through the child, but her relationship to the child appeared to involve a basic, though unconscious, hostility and rejection. The mother was an obsessive-compulsive personality, dominated the home, and was unable to accept herself as a woman. The intensive observation of 51 families (Donnelly, 1960) tends to confirm this finding. Observing the mother-child interaction in the home, utilizing the Fels Parent Behavior Scales, Donnelly found that mothers treated a psychotic child differently than their other nonpsychotic children. To the psychotic child, the mother was generally less warm, less accepting, less empathic, more punitive, more controlling, and more overprotective. The father was passive, but more rational than the mother in relation to the child. Psychotic children tended to come from homes characterized as less well adjusted, full of discord, and low in sociability. However, in comparing the family interaction of schizophrenic patients with those of normal controls, both Perr (1958) and Meyers and Goldfarb (1961) found little that could stand as a valid measure of distinction between the two groups of families. Perr found that the parents of schizophrenics tended to show more self-deception and to describe themselves as being more hostile. Meyers and Goldfarb found that the mothers of schizophrenic children appeared less capable of formulating a consistent definition of the world for the child.

A method of directly assessing the interpersonal behavior of husband and wife was introduced by Strodtbeck (1951). He posed questions to each parent individually, then he brought them together and had them discuss those points where their attitudes differed. Farina and his associates (Bell, Garmezy, Farina, and Rodnick, 1960; Farina, 1960; Farina and Dunham, 1963) utilized this method to study the families of schizophrenic patients. The questionnaire they used was the PARI. They found that they could distinguish the interpersonal behavior of schizophrenics otherwise described as having good or poor premorbid adjustment. In these studies, mother dominance was discerned in the families of the poor premorbid group only, with interpersonal conflict greatest in that group. In comparing the family interaction of the schizophrenic patient with those of normal controls, Bell et al. (1960) found that in the family constellation of normals, authority tended to be shared by both parents, and parental conflict was at a minimum, although even here there was a trend towards maternal dominance.

Bishop (1951) reported a method of studying the mother-child interaction under live, yet controlled, conditions. The mother and child were brought into a play room where the interpersonal behavior was observed directly. In 1954, Bowen introduced the principle of this technique to the study of families of schizophrenics. Families were brought into what came to be known as the Family Study Section of NIMH (National Institute of Mental Health), and there they were observed living under actual but known conditions for long periods of time (6 months–2 years). Observations based on families living under these conditions revealed that the mothers of schizophrenics showed extremely domineering, smothering, close relationships with the child (Dworin and Wyant, 1957), with the mothers utilizing threat of deprivation to control the child. Bowen, Dysinger, and Basamanie (1959) observed the presence of marked emotional distance and intense conflict between the parents. The fathers were emotionally immature and unable to define their role in the family and unable to make decisions; the mothers were usually the dominant ones, affecting a close relationship with the child to the exclusion of the father. Brodey (1959) found that the behavior of the families of schizophrenics was characterized by a selective utilization of reality, particularly the use of externalization, and that the interpersonal relationships were highly narcissistic.

Perception of parental behavior by patients Several studies have indicated that schizophrenics tend to have experienced their mother as having been rejecting (Bolles, Metzger, and Pitts, 1941; Lane and Singer, 1959; Singer, 1954), and dominant, demanding, and overprotective (Garmezy, Clarke, and Stockner, 1961; Heilbrun, 1960; Kohn and Clausen, 1956; McKeown, 1950; Reichard and Tillman, 1950; Schofield and Balian, 1959). However, when one compares the perception of their mothers by normals (Garmezy et al., 1961; Heilbrun, 1960; Lane and Singer, 1959; Singer, 1954) the uniqueness of these attitudes toward the mothers of schizophrenics disappears. Recollections of dominance and overprotectiveness are common for both schizophrenics and normals. Although Heilbrun, Garmezy et al., and Bolles et al. report data which have shown that there is a greater incidence of a feeling of having been rejected on the part of a group of psychiatric patients when compared to medical-surgical controls, the actual incidence of this even in the psychiatric group was only 15% as compared to 1% in the controls. Moreover, Singer and Lane and Singer found that perception of parental relationships during childhood was more a function of the subjects' socioeconomic level than was psychopathology, paralleling a finding by Opler (1957) that familial patterns (parental dominance and attitudes) are a function of cultural factors (Italian versus Irish origin) rather than of psychopathology.

NEUROSIS

As compared to the research in the area of schizophrenia, investigations of the dynamics of the family life of neurotics are few and generally restricted to data gleaned from case histories. From these studies it appears that the neurotic behavior of the child is a direct function of the neurotic behavior of the mother (e.g., Fisher and Mendell, 1956; Ingham, 1949; Sperling, 1949, 1951; Zimmerman, 1930). Neurotic behavior in children has been seen to have been related to maternal overprotection (Holloway, 1931; Jacobsen, 1947; Zimmerman, 1930), maternal domination (Mueller, 1945), maternal rejection (Ingham, 1949; Newell, 1934, 1936; Silberpfennig, 1941), separation from the mother during the first 3 years of life (Bowlby, 1940; Ribble, 1941), and oral deprivation (Childers and Hamil, 1932). Neurotic involvement with the mother, where the mother needs the child for the satisfaction of her own needs and discourages the development of emotional separation between the child and herself, has been associated with the development in the child of psychosomatic disorders (Miller and Baruch, 1950; Sperling, 1949) and school phobia (e.g., Davidson, 1961; Eisenberg, 1958; Estes, Haylett, and Johnson, 1956; Goldberg, 1953; Johnson, Falstein, and Suzurek, 1941; Suttenfield, 1954; Talbot, 1957; van Houten, 1948; Waldfogel, Hahn, and Gardner, 1954; Wilson, 1955).

Neurosis in children has also been associated with such factors in the home as poverty (Brown and Moore, 1944; Holloway, 1931) and broken homes (Ingham, 1949; Madow and Hardy, 1947; Wallace, 1935). Silverman (1935), however, found that 75% of the children from broken homes were essentially "normal"; 16% were described as conduct disorders, and only 9% were classifiable as personality problems.

Of the studies that did not use the case history method of data collection, McKeown (1950) found that neurotic children perceive their mothers as demanding, antagonistic, and setting inordinately high standards for them to meet. Stein (1944) found that neurotics tended to perceive themselves as having been rejected, particularly as compared to the perception of their family life held by normals (Bolles et al., 1941). Although Kundert (1947) found that whether justified by experience or not (e.g., separation due to hospitalization of mother or child), emotionally disturbed children, in general, fear being deserted by their mothers and cling to them compulsively. The Rorschach protocols of mothers of neurotics reveal that they tend to utilize psychological mechanisms which abrogate reality, for example, denial and projection (Baxter et al., 1963).

BEHAVIOR DISORDER

The research on the family background of individuals whose personality problems take the form of antisocial behavior is scanty. Shaw and McKay (1932) found no differences in the incidence of broken homes from cases referred to Cook County Juvenile Court (36%) as compared to a random sample of children in the Chicago public school system (42%). Behavior disorders in children have been seen to have been related to neurotic behavior in their parents (Field, 1940; Huschka, 1941), primarily involving maternal rejection, overt and covert. In line with a social learning hypothesis, another interesting finding is that a correlation has been found between antisocial behavior in children and the children's perception of parents' antisocial behavior (Bender, 1937; K. Friedlander, 1945; Williams, 1932).

DISCUSSION

Let us now summarize what conclusions can be drawn from these data which illuminate the role of the family in the development of psychopathology. As regards the families of schizophrenics, from an overview of the research which has investigated the pattern of parent-child interaction of this pathological group considered without reference to any other pathological or control group, several factors emerge which seem to characterize this group, regardless of the method of data collection, that is, whether by case history, interview, psychological test, or direct observation. Families of schizophrenics seem to be characterized by mothers who are dominant, fathers who are passive, and considerable family disharmony. The mother is overprotective, overpossessive, and overcontrolling, yet basically, albeit unconsciously, rejecting. These mothers frown on sex, are inconsistent in their methods of discipline, and introduce modes of thinking, feeling, and behaving which are not reality oriented. In light of the fact that these patterns emerge as a function of almost all methods of data collection, these results seem very impressive. Had our review of these data stopped here, we would have had apparent verification of the thesis that certain kinds of mother-child relationships and family atmospheres indeed account for the development of schizophrenia in the offspring. However, when each of these parental characteristics is compared with those which emerge from the analysis of the family situation of the normal (apparently nonpsychiatrically-involved) individual, each characteristic that is found to be typical of the families of schizophrenics is found to exist in the families of the controls as well. Furthermore, research which has attempted to make direct comparisons between the families of children in different categories of psychopathology (e.g., Baxter et al., 1963; Fisher et al., 1959; Frazee, 1953; Freeman et al., 1959; D. Friedlander, 1945; Inlow, 1933; McKeown, 1950; Oltman et al., 1952; Pollack and Malzberg, 1940; Pollack, Malzberg, and Fuller, 1936) reveals no significant or consistent differences in the psychological structure of the families.

The results are the same with regard to the families of the neurotics as well. At first glance, it appears that the mother's neurotic involvement with the child is causally associated with the neurotic behavior of the child. However, the essential characteristics of this involvement—maternal overprotectiveness, maternal domination, maternal rejection, deprivation and frustration, and the mothers fostering an almost symbiotic relationship between themselves and their children—are basically the same as those found in the families of schizophrenics and of children with behavior disorders. Moreover, in many respects, it would be hard, on blind analysis, to distinguish the family which produced an emotionally disturbed child from that which produced the so-called normal or well-adjusted child.

It seems apparent that the major conclusion that can be drawn from these data is that there is no such thing as a schizophrenogenic or a neurotogenic mother or family. At least these data do not permit of the description of a particular constellation of psychological events within the home and, in particular, between mother and child that can be isolated as a unique factor in the development of one or the other kind of personality disorder. If one is looking for *the* factor to account for the development of neurosis or schizophrenia, that one factor does not appear to exist as a clear cut finding in the research.

It is incumbent upon us to wonder why the research literature does not permit support of a hypothesis regarding parental influence on the psychological development of children in the manner we hypothesized. One of the major problems with which we must contend is that human behavior is a very complicated event, determined by many factors, and not clearly understood out of the context in which it occurs, and, in this regard, not everyone reacts in a like manner to similar life experiences. For example, strict discipline is reacted to differently when this occurs in a "warm" or "cold" home atmosphere (Sears, 1961); maternal rejection is reacted to differently where the father is accepting and warm (McCord et al., 1961) as well as where the father can be a buffer between the child and the overprotective mother (Witmer, 1933). Emphasizing the multivariate aspect of the determinants of behavior, one notes that Madow and Hardy (1947) reported that of the soldiers who broke down with neurotic reactions there was a high incidence of those coming from broken homes. Amongst those soldiers who did not break down, the incidence of coming from a broken home was 11–15%; the incidence of broken homes in the history of soldiers who did break down was 36%. Statistically, there is a significant difference between these percentages; however, even the 36% datum leaves 64% of the soldiers who broke down *not* coming from a broken home. Huschka (1941) reported that the incidence of neurotic mothers of problem children is high (42%); however, this leaves 58% of the group *not* accounted for by this factor. Brown and Moore (1944) commented that the incidence of excessive poverty, drunkenness, and family conflict in soldiers who broke down was significant, but this accounted for only 20% of the cases. Although between 30% (Canavan and Clark, 1923; Lampron, 1933) and 40% (Huschka, 1941; Lidz and Lidz, 1949) of the children born to mothers who are psychotic become psychotic themselves, these percentages do not account for the majority of children born to these mothers. Indeed,

Fanning et al. (1938) found that 43% of the children born to mothers who were psychotic were observed to be making an adequate social and personal adjustment; only 11% of that sample of children was not. It should be noted that only half of the samples of mothers studied by Despert (1938) and Clardy (1951) resembled the traditional pattern of what has come to be known as the "schizophrenogenic mother." Finally, Beres and Obers (1950) observed that there is a wide reaction to an experience of emotional deprivation (in this instance, institutionalization) ranging from the development of a schizoid personality to schizophrenia itself, and including neurotic reactions and character disorders. Indeed, 25% of their sample of children who were brought up in institutions appeared to be making a satisfactory adjustment in spite of this ostensibly devastating experience.

Over and above the complexity of human behavior contributing to the inconclusiveness of the results, one must look at the way in which these data have been collected. It might be that the criterion measure, that is, the diagnosis, did not provide the investigator with meaningful groupings of subjects so that consistent findings *could* be obtained. As regards the method of data collection: Case histories may be inadequate in providing basic data; information can be gross and/or inaccurate; the informant has to rely on memory, and this memory might be consciously or unconsciously selective, or the informant might not be aware of the import of or feel shame in giving certain data. Yet, despite the many limitations of this mode of data collection, some of the primary research in schizophrenia has utilized this method, and almost all of the data with respect to the family life of neurotics and behavior disorders were gathered in this way. These same limitations apply to data that are gathered when the informant is asked to fill out an attitude questionnaire. Surely the data on parents elicited from the children are susceptible to distortion even when given by normal children, no less those who already tend to consciously or unconsciously confound their perception of reality with fantasy. The psychiatric interview is a much more sensitive procedure than the case history or attitude questionnaire. Either structured or open-ended interviews enable the interviewer to follow up leads and possibly detect where information is being omitted for one reason or another. The problem here, however, is that there is always the possibility that distorted or inaccurate data are gathered by the interviewer, either through the kinds of questions asked, or the perception of the answer or of the individual being interviewed. For example, it is interesting to note that although the majority of psychiatric interviewers experienced the mothers of schizophrenics as matching the model of the schizophrenogenic mother—the dominant, overprotective, but basically rejecting mother who induces inappropriateness of thinking in her children—the psychological test evaluation of mothers of schizophrenics failed to confirm these findings. One explanation for this is that the interviewer, already acquainted with the literature regarding the mother of schizophrenics, anticipating to experience the mothers in terms of the ideas about schizophrenogenic mothers, did, indeed, experience them in that way, whereas a more objective evaluation of the patterns of thinking and feeling of these mothers did not confirm the more subjective impression.

In order to try and avoid the pitfalls inherent in data gleaned through case history or interview, investigators hypothesized that direct observation of the mother-child interaction might yield more valid information. Unfortunately, here, too, limitations inherent in the mode of data collection become apparent. Observations of the mother-child interaction in the home or in an observation room in a hospital or clinic are generally restricted to a limited time segment, for example, 1 hour once a week. This factor, in and of itself, limits the observations to a fairly restricted aspect of the spectrum of the interaction between mother and child. Here, too, the behavior to which the observer is exposed may be influenced by the conscious or unconscious attitudes and motives of the parent being observed. It is not too difficult for the parent to present only that behavior which, for one reason or another, she feels it safe to display and to control the presence of other behaviors. Direct observation of the family for extensive periods of time, that is, months, and under controlled but as natural as possible living conditions (as in the Family Study Section of NIMH) avoids the restrictiveness and overcomes, to one degree or another, the artificiality of the relatively brief observation. However, the family is still aware that they are being observed and may, to one degree or another, be unable to act "natural." Moreover, unless the observations are independently made by several people whose reliability of observation has already been established, they may also be influenced by the *Zeitgeist* and perceive the family as being "schizophrenogenic" whether it is or not, mutually reinforcing each other's expectations. A more pressing consideration in evaluating the validity of these kinds of observations is the fact that the interaction, no matter how natural, takes place after the development of the psychopathology. It is quite possible that the aspects of the interpersonal relationship within the family, or between the mother and child in particular, that eventuated in the development of the patterns of thinking, feeling, and behaving characteristic of the schizophrenic or the neurotic, are no longer present; they may have occurred at a time of the child's life long since past and/or under conditions of intimacy not even accessible to the observer. There is no reason to assume that the etiological factors are still functioning or that they will be available to the trained observer even over the course of 6 months. Of course, it might be that whatever differentiates the psychological existence of the schizophrenic from that of the neurotic or of the normal might be so subtle that it is imperceptible to the participants themselves or even the trained observer and, hence, escape notice. Here, one is reminded of Freud's comment that "the years of childhood of those who are later neurotic need not necessarily differ from those who are later normal except in intensity and distinctness [Freud, 1938 (Orig. publ. 1910), p. 583]."

Theorizing about the etiology of psychopathology has characteristically been of the either/or variety. Nineteenth century scientists sought explanations for neurotic and psychotic disorders in the hereditary background of their patients, working from the assumption that many directly inherited the neurotic or psychotic "illness." On the other hand, the scientist of the twentieth century has sought explanations for psychopathology in the experiential aspect of man's life, in his emotional and interpersonal learning. As with most events in our life, the truth is probably somewhere in between these two positions. Indeed, in spite of the emphasis that is placed on the role of experience in the development of personality in psychoanalysis, Freud did not think, at least as regards the etiology of psychopathology, in such categorically black and white terms. He was able to bridge the gap between the nature-nurture extremes:

> We divide the causes of neurotic disease into those which the individual himself brings with him into life, and those which life bring[s] to him—that is to say, into constitutional and accidental. It is the interaction of these as a rule first gives rise to illness [Freud, 1950b (Orig. publ. 1913), p. 122].

> Let us bear clearly in mind that every human being has acquired, by the combined operation of inherent disposition and of external influences of childhood, a special individuality in the exercise of his capacity to love—that is, in the conditions which he sets up for loving, in the impulses he gratifies by it, and in the aims he sets out to achieve in it. . . . We will here provide against misconceptions and reproaches to the effect that we have denied the importance of the inborn (constitutional) factor because we have emphasized the importance of infantile impressions. Such an accusation arises out of the narrowness with which mankind looks for causes, inasmuch as one single causal factor satisfies him, in spite of the many commonly underlying the face of reality. Psycho-Analysis has said much about the "accidental" component in aetiology and little about the constitutional, but only because it could throw new light upon the former, whereas of the latter it knows no more so far than is already known. We deprecate the assumption of an essential opposition between the two series of aetiological factors; we presume rather a perpetual interchange of both in producing the results observed [Freud, 1950a (Orig. publ. 1912), p. 312].

Other psychoanalysts have followed Freud in the presumption of an inherent, predetermined characteristic functioning of the nervous system of the human organism which determines reactions to stimuli pre- and postnatally (e.g., Greenacre, 1941).

Augmenting the clinical observations of psychoanalysis, one must juxtapose the experimental evidence in psychology which indicates that (1) individuals reflect characteristic patterns of autonomic activity which are stable and which are typical of them as individuals (Grossman and Greenberg, 1957; Lacey, 1950; Richmond and Lustman, 1955; Wenger, 1941), (2) the characteristic patterns of neural activity are identifiable prenatally and are consistent with the patterns of activity observable postnatally (Richards and Newbery, 1938, (3) these characteristic patterns of autonomic activity consistently emerge in a factor of lability and balance in which specific personality factors are consistently highly loaded (Darling, 1940; Eysenck, 1956; Eysenck and Prell, 1951; Theron, 1948; van der Merwe, 1948; van der Merwe and Theron, 1947), (4) there is greater similarity of autonomic reactivity between identical twins than fraternal twins or ordinary siblings (Eysenck, 1956; Eysenck and Prell, 1951; Jost and Sontag, 1944), and (5) there is a selective influence on personality functioning due to the sex of the individual per se. For example, generally boys outnumber girls 2–1 in being referred for psychological help (Bender, 1937; Wile and Jones, 1937). Sears (1961) found a significant difference in the basic mode of self-reported expression of aggression between boys and girls: Girls appeared higher in socially acceptable forms of aggression and high in anxiety regarding hostility, while boys were significantly higher in aggression that was directed against social control. Sears also found that the more punitive the mother is, the more dependent the son becomes but the less dependent the daughter becomes. Newell (1936) found that maternal rejection affected males more than females: Marked increase in aggressive behavior was noted in the boys who experienced rejection, not so with the females. Baruch and Wilcox (1944) noted that interparental tensions lead to different reactions in boys as compared to girls; in boys, it led to ascendance-submission problems, in girls, to an experience of lack of affection.

We end this survey by concluding that we have not been able to find any unique factors in the family of the schizophrenic which distinguishes it from the family of the neurotic or from the family of controls, who are ostensibly free from evidence of patterns of gross psychopathology. In short, we end by stating that the assumption that the family is *the* factor in the development of personality has not been validated. It is interesting to note that Orlansky (1949), in his review of the literature exploring the relationship between certain childhood experiences, for example, feeding, toilet training, thumb-sucking, the degree of tactile stimulation by the mother, etc., upon the development of personality characteristics, was also forced to conclude that the data failed to confirm an invariant relationship between the experience in infancy and the resultant personality. Of course, it might well be that the reality of the family is not the important dimension in determining the child's reactions; rather, it might be the perception of the family members, and this might often have little or no relation to the people as they really are. This would mean, then, that in many instances the important variables in the development of psychopathology might be factors which the child brings to the family, the functioning of the nervous and metabolic systems and the cognitive capacity to integrate stimuli into meaningful perceptual and conceptual schema. Indeed, we are left to wonder, as do the psychoanalysts, whether the proclivity towards fantasy distortion of reality might not be *the* factor in the development of psychopathology, and this proclivity might not always be determined by the child's experiences per se.

Obviously, questions regarding the etiology of patterns of personality behavior which are regarded as pathological, unadaptive, or unadjusted cannot be met with simple answers. Apparently, the factors which play a part in the development of behavior in humans are so complex that it would appear that they almost defy being investigated scientifically and defy one's attempts to draw meaningful generalizations from the exploration which has already been done. It is, of course, conceivable that human behavior is so complex that it cannot be reduced to simple terms or be expected to yield unalterable patterns of occurrences. It might also be that what produces psychopathological reactions in one individual does not in another. All this would be understandable in light of the complexity that is the human being, neurologically as well as socially, but it is unfortunate as regards research endeavors. In 1926, Freud wrote:

> Anxiety is the reaction to danger. One cannot, after all, help suspecting that the reason why the affect of anxiety occupies a unique position in the economy of the mind has something to do with the essential nature of danger. Yet dangers are the common lot of humanity; they are the same for everyone. What we need and cannot lay our fingers on is some factor which will explain why some people are able to subject the affect of anxiety, in spite of its peculiar quality, to the normal workings of the mind, or which decides who is doomed to come to grief over the task [Freud, 1936, p. 64].

We end this review of forty years of research without being able to feel that we are any closer to an answer than was Freud.

SUMMARY

Psychologists generally make the assumption that the experiences to which the individual is exposed over a period of time lead to the development of learned patterns of behavior. From this, psychologists have reasoned that the experiences the individual has in his early life at home, with his family, in general, and his mother, in particular, are major determinants in the learning of the constellation of behaviors subsumed under the rubric, personality, and in particular, the development of psychopathology. A review of the research of the past 40 years failed to support this assumption. No factors were found in the parent-child interaction of schizophrenics, neurotics, or those with behavior disorders which could be identified as unique to them or which could distinguish one group from the other, or any of the groups from the families of the controls.

REFERENCES

Ayer, Mary E., and R. G. Bernreuter. "A study of the relationship between discipline and personality traits in little children." *J. genet. Psychol.,* 1937, **50,** 165–170.

Barry, H. "Orphanhood as a factor in psychoses." *J. abnorm. soc. Psychol.,* 1936, **30,** 431–438.

Barry, H., and W. A. Bousfield. "Incidence of orphanhood among fifteen hundred psychotic patients." *J. Genet. Psychol.,* 1937, **50,** 198–202.

Bartmeier, L. H. "Deprivations during infancy and their effects upon personality development." *Amer. J. ment. Deficiency,* 1952, **56,** 708–711.

Baruch, Dorothy W., and J. Annie Wilcox. "A study of sex differences in preschool children's adjustment coexistent with inter-parental tensions." *J. genet.* Psychol., 1944, **64,** 281–303.

Baxter, J. C., J. Becker, and W. Hooks. "Defensive style in the families of schizophrenics and controls." *J. abnorm. soc. Psychol.,* 1963, **66,** 512–518.

Behrens, Marjorie L. and W. Goldfarb. "A study of patterns of interaction of families of schizophrenic children in residential treatment." *Amer. J. Orthopsychiat.,* 1958, **28,** 300–312.

Bell, R. Q., N. Garmezy, A. Farina, and E. H. Rodnick. "Direct study of parent-child interaction." *Amer. J. Orthopsychiat.,* 1960, **30,** 445–452.

Bender, Lauretta. "Reactive psychosis in response to mental disease in the family." *J. nervous and ment. Disease,* 1936, **83,** 143–289.

Bender, Lauretta. "Behavior problems in the children of psychotic and criminal parents." *Genet. Psychol. Monogr.,* 1937, **19,** 229–339.

Beres, D., and S. J. Obers. "The effects of extreme deprivation in infancy on psychic structure in adolescence: A study in ego development." *Psychoanal. Study of the Child,* 1950, **5,** 212–235.

Bishop, Barbara M. "Mother-child interaction and the social behavior of children." *Psychol. Monogr.,* 1951, **65** (11, whole no. 328).

Bolles, Marjorie M., Harriet F. Metzger, and Marjorie W. Pitts. "Early home background and personal adjustment." *Amer. J. Orthopsychiat.,* 1941, **11,** 530–534.

Bowen, M., R. H. Dysinger, and Betty Basamanie. "The role of the father in families with a schizophrenic patient." *Amer. J. Psychiat.,* 1959, **115,** 1017–1020.

Bowlby, J. "The influence of early environment in the development of neurosis and neurotic character." *International J. Psychoanalysis,* 1940, **21,** 154–178.

Brodbeck, A. J., and O. C. Irwin. "The speech behavior of infants without families." *Child Develpm.,* 1946, **17,** 145–156.

Brodey, W. M. "Some family operations in schizophrenia." *Arch. Gen. Psychiat.,* 1959, **1,** 379–402.

Brown, W. T., and M. Moore. "Soldiers who break down—family background and past history." *Military Surgeon,* 1944, **94,** 160–163.

Canavan, Myrtelle M., and Rosamond Clark. "The mental health of 463 children from dementiapraecox stock." *Ment. Hygiene,* 1923, **7,** 137–148.

Childers, A. T., and B. M. Hamil. "Emotional problems in children as related to the duration of breast feeding in infancy." *Amer. J. Orthopsychiat.*, 1932, **2,** 134–142.

Clardy, E. R. "A study of the development and course of schizophrenic children." *Psychiat. Quart.*, 1951, **25,** 81–90.

Darling, R. P. "Autonomic action in relation to personality traits of children." *J. abnorm. soc. Psychol.*, 1940, **35,** 246–260.

Davidson, Susannah. "School phobia as a manifestation of family disturbance: Its structure and treatment." *J. of Child Psychol. and Psychiat.*, 1961, **1,** 270–287.

Davis, K. "Extreme social isolation of a child." *Amer. J. Sociol.*, 1940, **45,** 554–565.

Despert, Louise J. "Schizophrenia in children." *Psychiat. Quart.*, 1938, **12,** 366–371.

Despert, Louise J. "Some considerations relating to the genesis of autistic behavior in children." *Amer. J. Orthopsychiat.*, 1951, **21,** 335–350.

Donnelly, Ellen M. "The quantitative analysis of parent behavior toward psychotic children and their siblings." *Genet. Psychol. Monogr.*, 1960, **62,** 331–376.

Dworin, J. and O. Wyant. "Authoritarian patterns in mothers of schizophrenics." *J. Clin. Psychol.*, 1957, **13,** 332–338.

Eisenberg, L. "School phobia: A study in the communication of anxiety." *Amer. J. Psychiat.*, 1958, **114,** 712–718.

Estes, H. R., Clarice H. Haylett, and Adelaide M. Johnson. "Separation anxiety." *Amer. J. Psychother.*, 1956, **10,** 682–695.

Eysenck, H. J. "The inheritance of extraversion-introversion." *Acta Psychologica*, 1956, **12,** 95–110.

Eysenck, H. J., and D. B. Prell. "The inheritance of neuroticism: An experimental study." *J. ment. Science*, 1951, **97,** 441–465.

Fanning, Aneita, Sara Lehr, Roberta Sherwin, and Marjorie Wilson. "The mental health of children of psychotic mothers." *Smith College Studies in Social Work*, 1938, **8,** 291–343.

Farina, A. "Patterns of role dominance and conflict in parents of schizophrenic patients." *J. abnorm. soc. Psychol.*, 1960, **61,** 31–38.

Farina, A., and R. M. Dunham. "Measurement of family relationships and their effects." *Arch. gen. Psychiat.*, 1963, **9,** 64–73.

Field, Minna A. "Maternal attitudes found in twenty-five cases of children with primary behavior disorders." *Amer. J. Orthopsychiat.*, 1940, **10,** 293–311.

Fisher, S., Ina Boyd, D. Walker, and Diane Sheer. "Parents of schizophrenics, neurotics, and normals." *Arch. Gen. Psychiat.*, 1959, **1,** 149–166.

Fisher, S., and D. Mendell. "The communication of neurotic patterns over two and three generations." *Psychiat.* 1956, **19,** 41–46.

Fleck, S., T. Lidz, and Alice Cornelison. "Comparison of parent-child relationships of male and female schizophrenic patients." *Arch. gen. Psychiat.*, 1963, **8,** 1–7.

Frazee, Helen E. "Children who later became schizophrenic." *Smith College Studies in Social Work*, 1953, **23,** 125–149.

Freeman, R. V., and H. M. Grayson. "Maternal attitudes in schizophrenia." *J. abnorm. soc. Psychol.*, 1955, **50,** 45–52.

Freeman, H. E., and O. G. Simmons. "Mental patients in the community: Family settings and performance levels." *Amer. Sociol. Rev.*, 1958, **23,** 147–154.

Freeman, H. E., O. G. Simmons, and B. J. Bergen. "Possessiveness as a characteristic of mothers of schizophrenics." *J. abnorm. soc. Psychol.*, 1959, **58,** 271–273.

Freud, S. *Inhibitions, Symptoms, and Anxiety.* London: Hogarth, 1936.

Freud, S. Three contributions to the theory of sex. In A. A. Brill (Ed.), *The Basic Writings of Sigmund Freud.* (Orig. Publ. 1910) New York: Modern Library, 1938, p. 583.

Freud, S. The dynamics of the transference. (Orig. publ. 1912) In, *Collected Papers.* Vol. 2. London: Hogarth, 1950, pp. 312–322 (a).

Freud, S. The predisposition to obsessional neurosis. (Orig. publ. 1913) In, *Collected Papers.* Vol. 2. London: Hogarth, 1950, pp. 122–132 (b).

Friedlander, D. Personality development of twenty-seven children who later became psychotic. *J. abnorm. soc. Psychol.*, 1945, **40,** 330–335.

Friedlander, Kate. "Formation of the antisocial character." *Psychoanalytic Study of the Child,* 1945, **1,** 189–203.

Garmezy, N., A. R. Clarke, and Carol Stockner. "Child rearing attitudes of mothers and fathers as reported by schizophrenic and normal patients." *J. abnorm. soc. Psychol.*, 1961, **63,** 176–182.

Gerard, D. L., and L. Siegal. "The family background of schizophrenia. *Psychiatric Quarterly,* 1950, **24,** 47–73.

Goldberg, Thelma B. Factors in the development of school phobia. *Smith College Studies in Social Work,* 1953, **23,** 277–248.

Goldfarb, W. "The effects of early institutional care on adolescent personality (graphic Rorschach data)." *Child Develpm.*, 1943, **14,** 213–223 (a).

Goldfarb, W. "Infant rearing and problem behavior." *Amer. J. Orthopsychiat.*, 1943, **13,** 249–266 (b).

Goldfarb, W. The effects of early institutional care on adolescent personality. *J. exp. Educ.*, 1943, **12,** 106–129 (c).

Goldfarb, W. Psychological deprivation in infancy. *Amer. J. Psychiat.*, 1945, **102,** 19–33 (a).

Goldfarb, W. "Psychological privation in infancy and subsequent adjustment." *Amer. J. Orthopsychiat.*, 1945, **15,** 247–255 (b).

Greenacre, Phyllis. "The predisposition to anxiety." *Psychoanal. Quarterly,* 1941, **10,** 66–94.

Grossman, H. J., and N. H. Greenberg. "Psychosomatic differentiation in infancy. I. Autonomic activity in the newborn." *Psychosom. Med.*, 1957, **19,** 293–306.

Guertin, W. H. "Are differences in schizophrenic symptoms related to the mother's avowed attitudes toward child rearing?" *J. abnorm. soc. Psychol.*, 1961, **63,** 440–442.

Hajdu-Grimes, Lilly. "Contributions to the etiology of schizophrenia." *Psychoanal. Rev.*, 1940, **27,** 421–438.

Hattwick, Berta W. "Interrelations between the preschool child's behavior and certain factors in the home." *Child Develpm.*, 1936, **7,** 200–226.

Hattwick, Berta W., and Margaret Stowell. "The relation of parental over-attentiveness to children's work habits and social adjustment in kindergarten and the first six grades of school." *J. educ. Res.,* 1936, **30,** 169–176.

Heilbrun, A. B. "Perception of maternal childbearing attitudes in schizophrenics." *J. Consult. Psychol.,* 1960, **24,** 169–173.

Holloway, Edith. "A study of fifty-eight problem children, with emphasis upon the home situation as a causative factor in producing conflict." *Smith College Studies in Social Work,* 1931, **1,** 403.

Huschka, Mabel. "Psychopathological disorders in the mother." *J. nervous and ment. Disease,* 1941, **94,** 76–83.

Ingham, H. V. "A statistical study of family relationships in psychoneurosis." *Amer. J. Psychiat.,* 1949, **106,** 91–98.

Inlow, Ruby S. The home as a factor in the development of the psychosis. *Smith College Studies in Social Work,* 1933, **4,** 153–154.

Jacobsen, Virginia. Influential factors in the outcome of treatment of school phobia. *Smith College Studies in Social Work,* 1947, **19,** 181–202.

Johnson, Adelaide M., E. I. Falstein, S. A. Szurek, and Margaret Svendsen. "School phobia." *Amer. J. Orthopsychiat.,* 1941, **11,** 702–711.

Jost, H., and L. W. Sontag. "The genetic factor in autonomic nervous system function." *Psychosom. Med.,* 1944, **6,** 308–310.

Karon, B. P., and J. Rosberg. "Study of the mother-child relationship in a case of paranoid schizophrenia." *Amer. J. Psychother.,* 1958, **12,** 522–533.

Kasanin, J., Elizabeth Knight, and Priscilla Sage. "The parent-child relationship in schizophrenia." *J. nervous and ment. Disease,* 1934, **79,** 249–263.

Kohn, M. L., and J. A. Clausen. "Parental authority behavior and schizophrenia." *Amer. J. Orthopsychiat.,* 1956, **26,** 297–313.

Kundert, Elizabeth. "Fear of desertion by mother." *Amer. J. Orthopsychiat.,* 1947, **17,** 326–336.

Lacey, J. I. "Individual differences in somatic response patterns." *J. comp. physiol. Psychol.,* 1950, **43,** 338–350.

Lampron, Edna M. "Children of schizophrenic parents." *Ment. Hygiene,* 1933, **17,** 82–91.

Lane, R. C., and J. L. Singer. "Familial attitudes in paranoid schizophrenics and normals from two socioeconomic classes." *J. abnorm. soc. Psychol.,* 1959, **59,** 328–339.

Levy, D. M. "Maternal overprotection and rejection." *Arch. Neurology and Psychiat.,* 1931, **25,** 886–889.

Levy, D. M. "On the problem of delinquency." *Amer. J. Orthopsychiat.,* 1932, **2,** 197–211.

Levy, D. M. "Primary affect hunger." *Amer. J. Psychiat.,* 1937, **94,** 643–652.

Levy, D. M. *Maternal Overprotection.* New York: Columbia Univ. Press, 1943.

Lidz, T., Alice R. Cornelison, S. Fleck, and Dorothy Terry. "The intrafamilial environment of the schizophrenic patient: I. The father." *Psychiat.,* 1957, **20,** 329–342 (a).

Lidz, T., Alice R. Cornelison, S. Fleck, and Dorothy Terry. "The intrafamilial environment of schizophrenic patients: II. Marital schism and marital skew." *Amer. J. Psychiat.,* 1957, **114,** 241–248 (b).

Lidz, T., Alice R. Cornelison, S. Fleck, and Dorothy Terry. "The intrafamilial environment of the schizophrenic patient." *Psychiat.*, 1957, **20,** 329–342 (c).

Lidz, T., Alice Cornelison, Dorothy Terry, and S. Fleck. "Intrafamilial environment of the schizophrenic patient: VI. The transmission of irrationality." *Arch. Neurology and Psychiat.*, 1948, **79,** 305–316.

Lidz, Ruth W., and T. Lidz. "The family environment of schizophrenic patients." *Amer. J. Psychiat.*, 1949, **106,** 332–345.

Lidz, T., Neulah Parker, and Alice Cornelison. "The role of the father in the family environment of the schizophrenic patient." *Amer. J. Psychiat.*, 1956, **113,** 126–137.

Lowrey, L. G. "Personality distortion and early institutional care." *Amer. J. Orthopsychiat.*, 1940, **10,** 576–585.

Madow, L., and S. E. Hardy. "Incidence and analysis of the broken family in the background of neurosis." *Amer. J. Orthopsychiat.*, 1947, **17,** 521–528.

Mark, J. C. "The attitudes of the mothers of male schizophrenics toward child behavior." *J. abnorm. soc. Psychol.*, 1953, **48,** 185–189.

McCord, W., Joan McCord, and A. Howard. "Familial correlates of aggression in nondelinquent male children." *J. abnorm. soc. Psychol.*, 1961, **62,** 79–93.

McKeown, J. E. "The behavior of parents of schizophrenic, neurotic, and normal children." *Amer. J. Sociology*, 1950, **56,** 175–179.

Meyers, D. I., and W. Goldfarb. "Studies of perplexity in mothers of schizophrenic children." *Amer. J. Orthopsychiat.*, 1961, **31,** 551–564.

Meyers, D., and W. Goldfarb. "Psychiatric appraisals of parents and siblings of schizophrenic children." *Amer. J. Psychiat.*, 1962, **118,** 902–908.

Miller, H., and D. Baruch. "A study of hostility in allergic children." *Amer. J. Orthopsychiat.*, 1950, **20,** 506–519.

Mueller, Dorothy D. "Paternal domination: Its influence on child guidance results." *Smith College Studies in Social Work*, 1945, **15,** 184–215.

Newell, H. W. "The psycho-dynamics of maternal rejection." *Amer. J. Ortho-*psychiat., 1934, **4,** 387–401.

Newell, H. W. "A further study of maternal rejection." *Amer. J. Orthopsychiat.*, 1936, **6,** 576–589.

Oltman, Jane E., J. J. McGarry, and S. Friedman. "Parental deprivation and the "broken home" in dementia praecox and other mental disorders." *Amer. Psychiat.*, 1952, **108,** 685–694.

Opler, M. K. "Schizophrenia and culture." *Scientific Amer.*, 1957, **197,** 103–110.

Orlansky, H. Infant care and personality. *Psychol. Bull.*, 1949, **46,** 1–48.

Pearson, G. H. "Some early factors in the formation of personality." *Amer. J. Orthopsychiat.*, 1931, **1,** 284–291.

Perr, H. M. "Criteria distinguishing parents of schizophrenic and normal children." *Arch. Neurology and Psychiat.*, 1958, **79,** 217–224.

Plank, R. The family constellation of a group of schizophrenic patients. *Amer. J. Orthopsychiat.*, 1953, **23,** 817–825.

Pollock, H. M., and B. Malzberg. "Hereditary and environmental factors in the causation of manic-depressive psychoses and dementia praecox." *Amer. J. Psychiat.*, 1940, **96,** 1227–1244.

Pollock, H. M., B. Malzberg, and N. G. Fuller. "Hereditary and environmental factors in the causation of dementia praecox and manic-depressive psychoses." *Psychiat. Quart.,* 1936, **10,** 495–509.

Preston, G. H., and Rosemary Antin. "A study of children of psychotic parents." *Amer. J. Orthopsychiat.,* 1932, **2,** 231–241.

Prout, C. T., and Mary A. White. "A controlled study of personality relationships in mothers of schizophrenic male patients." *Amer. J. Psychiat.,* 1950, **107,** 251–256.

Reichard, Suzanne, and C. Tillman. "Patterns of parent-child relationships in schizophrenia." *Psychiat.,* 1950, **13,** 247–257.

Ribble, Margarethe A. "Disorganizing factors of infant personality." *Amer. J. Psychiat.,* 1941, **98,** 459–463.

Richards, T. W., and Helen Newbery. "Studies in fetal behavior: III. Can performance on test items at six months postnatally be predicted on the basis of fetal activity?" *Child Develpm.,* 1938, **9,** 79–86.

Richmond, J. B., and S. L. Lustman. "Autonomic function in the neonate: I. Implications for psychosomatic theory." *Psychosom. Med.,* 1955, **17,** 269–275.

Schofield, W., and L. Balian. "A comparative study of the personal histories of schizophrenic and nonpsychiatric patients." *J. abnorm. soc. Psychol.,* 1959, **59,** 216–225.

Sears, R. R. "Relation of early socialization experiences to aggression in middle childhood." *J. abnorm. soc. Psychol.,* 1961, **63,** 466–492.

Sears, R. R., J. W. M. Whiting, V. Nowlis, and Pauline S. Sears. "Some child-rearing antecedents of aggression and dependency in young children." *Genet. Psychol. Monogr.,* 1953, **47,** 133–234.

Shaw, C. R., and H. D. McKay. "Are broken homes a causative factor in juvenile delinquency? *Soc. Forces,* 1932, **10,** 514–524.

Shoben, E. J. "The assessment of parental attitudes in relation to child adjustment. *Genet. Psychol. Monogr.,* 1949, **39,** 101–148.

Silberpfennig, Judith. "Mother types encountered in child guidance clinics." *Amer. J. Orthopsychiat.,* 1941, **11,** 475–484.

Silverman, B. "The behavior of children from broken homes." *Amer. J. Orthopsychiat.,* 1935, **5,** 11–18.

Singer, J. L. "Projected familial attitudes as a function of socioeconomic status and psychopathology." *J. consult. Psychol.,* 1954, **18,** 99–104.

Sperling, Melitta. "The role of the mother in psychosomatic disorders in children." *Psychosom. Med.,* 1949, **11,** 377–385.

Sperling, Melitta. "The neurotic child and his mother: A psychoanalytic study." *Amer. J. Orthopsychiat.,* 1951, **21,** 351–362.

Spitz, R. A. "Hospitalism: An inquiry into the genesis of psychiatric conditions in early childhood." *Psychoanal. Study of the Child,* 1945, **1,** 53–74.

Stein, Lucille H. A study of over-inhibited and unsocialized-aggressive children. *Smith College Studies in Social Work,* 1944, **15,** 124–125.

Stringer, Joyce R. Case studies of the families of schizophrenics. *Smith College Studies in Social Work,* 1962, **32,** 118–148.

Strodtbeck, F. L. "Husband-wife interaction over revealed differences." *Amer. Sociol. Rev.,* 1951, **16,** 468–473.

Suttenfield, Virginia. "School phobia: A study of five cases." *Amer. J. Orthopsychiat.,* 1954, **24,** 368–380.

Talbot, Mira. "School Phobia: A workshop: I. Panic in school phobia." *Amer. J. Orthopsychiat.,* 1957, **27,** 286–295.

Theron, P. A. "Peripheral vasomotor reaction as indices of basic emotional tension and lability." *Psychosom. Med.,* 1948, **10,** 335–346.

Tietze, Trude. "A study of mothers of schizophrenic patients." *Psychiat.,* 1949, **12,** 55–65.

van der Merwe, A. B. "The diagnostic value of peripheral vasomotor reactions in the psychoneuroses." *Psychosom. Med.,* 1948, 10, 347–354.

van der Merwe, A. B., and P. A. Theron. "A new method of measuring emotional stability." *J. gen. Psychol.,* 1947, **37,** 109–124.

van Houten, Janny. Mother-child relationships in twelve cases of school phobia. *Smith College Studies in Social Work,* 1948, **18,** 161–180.

Wahl, C. W. "Some antecedent factors in the family histories of 392 schizophrenics." *Amer. J. Psychiat.,* 1954, **110,** 668–676.

Wahl, C. W. "Some antecedent factors in the family histories of 568 male schizophrenics of the United States Navy." *Amer. J. Psychiat.,* 1956, **113,** 201–210.

Waldfogel, S., Pauline B. Hahn, and G. E. Gardner. "A study of school phobia in children." *J. nervous and ment. Disease,* 1954, **120,** 399.

Wallace, Ramona. "A study of the relationship between emotional tone of the home and adjustment status in cases referred to a travelling child guidance clinc." *J. juv. Res.,* 1935, **19,** 205–220.

Walters, Jean H. A study of the family relationships of schizophrenic patients. *Smith College Studies in Social Work,* 1939, **9,** 189–191.

Watson, G. A. "A comparison of the effects of lax versus strict home training." *J. soc. Psychol.,* 1934, **5,** 102–105.

Wenger, M. A. "The measurement of individual differences in autonomic balance." *Psychosom. Med.,* 1941, **3,** 427 434.

Wile, I. S., and Ann B. Jones. "Ordinal position and the behavior disorders of young children." *J. Genet. Psychol.,* 1937, **51,** 61–93.

Williams, H. D. "Causes of social maladjustment in children." *Psychol. Monogr.,* 1932, **43** (1, whole no. 194).

Wilson, Margaret J. Grandmother, mother, and daughter in cases of school phobia. *Smith College Studies in Social Work,* 1955, **25,** 56–57.

Winder, C. L., and R. E. Kantor. "Rorschach maturity scores of the mothers of schizophrenics." *J. consult. Psychol.,* 1958, **22,** 438–440.

Witmer, Helen L. "Parental behavior as an index to the probable outcome of treatment in a child guidance clinic." *Amer. J. Orthopsychiat.,* 1933, **3,** 431–444.

Zimmerman, Anna C. Parental adjustments and attitudes in relation to the problems of five- and six-year-old children. *Smith College Studies in Social Work,* 1930, **1,** 406–407.

Zuckerman, M., Mary Oltean, and I. Monashkin. "The parental attitudes of mothers of schizophrenics." *J. consult. Psychol.,* 1958, **22,** 307–310.

1.7 Orientation

Chapter 1 concludes with a summary of the effects on children of changing patterns of child rearing as seen by Urie Bronfenbrenner to be taking place in our society. The author draws upon pertinent research of the past several decades to suggest the emergence of changes in patterns of parental behavior, socialization techniques applied by parents to their children's behavior, social class differences, and family structure. Also examined is the differential distribution of various parental behaviors according to the sex of the child.

Judging from the frequency with which this speculative analysis has been reprinted in books of readings such as this, one could say the insights offered by Bronfenbrenner are highly regarded by his colleagues. At the very least, his paper conveys a lucid commentary on trends in child rearing as reflected by current research. Of course, the analysis assumes that the research is valid and representative of phenomena actually occurring throughout our society. Bronfenbrenner's identification of the apparent importance currently placed upon intellectual achievement by parents in rearing their children suggests one reason for the mushrooming of research on children's cognitive development, achievement motivation, and early childhood education.

As an impetus to classroom discussion, a comparison of Bronfenbrenner's analysis of socialization practices to the Sunley and Boehm papers appearing earlier in this chapter is recommended.

RECOMMENDED READING

Wolfenstein, Martha. "The emergence of fun morality." *J. soc. Issues,* **7** (1951), 15–25.

Rodman, Hyman. "Talcott Parson's view of the changing American family." *Merrill-Palmer Quart.,* **11** (1965), 209–228.

1.7 The Changing American Child— A Speculative Analysis

Urie Bronfenbrenner, CORNELL UNIVERSITY

A QUESTION OF MOMENT

It is now a matter of scientific record that patterns of child rearing in the United States have changed appreciably over the past twenty-five years

Reprinted from the *Journal of Social Issues,* **17** (1961), 6–18. By permission of the author and The Society for Psychological Study of Social Issues.

(Bronfenbrenner, 1958). Middle class parents especially have moved away from the more rigid and strict styles of care and discipline advocated in the early Twenties and Thirties toward modes of response involving greater tolerance of the child's impulses and desires, freer expression of affection, and increased reliance on "psychological" methods of discipline, such as reasoning and appeals to guilt, as distinguished from more direct techniques like physical punishment. At the same time, the gap between the social classes in their goals and methods of child rearing appears to be narrowing, with working class parents beginning to adopt both the values and techniques of the middle class. Finally, there is dramatic correspondence between these observed shifts in parental values and behavior and the changing character of the attitudes and practices advocated in successive editions of such widely read manuals as the Children's Bureau bulletin on *Infant Care* and Spock's *Baby and Child Care*. Such correspondence should not be taken to mean that the expert has now become the principal instigator and instrument of social change, since the ideas of scientists and professional workers themselves reflect in part the operation of deep-rooted cultural processes. Nevertheless, the fact remains that changes in values and practices advocated by prestigeful professional figures can be substantially accelerated by rapid and widespread dissemination through the press, mass media of communication, and public discussion.

Given these facts, it becomes especially important to gauge the effect of the changes that are advocated and adopted. Nowhere is this issue more significant, both scientifically and socially, than in the sphere of familial values and behavior. It is certainly no trivial matter to ask whether the changes that have occurred in the attitudes and actions of parents over the past twenty-five years have been such as to affect the personality development of their children, so that the boys and girls of today are somewhat different in character structure from those of a decade or more ago. Or, to put the question more succinctly: has the changing American parent produced a changing American child?

A STRATEGY OF INFERENCE

Do we have any basis for answering this intriguing question? To begin with, do we have any evidence of changes in the behavior of children in successive decades analogous to those we have already been able to find for parents? If so, we could take an important first step toward a solution of the problem. Unfortunately, in contrast to his gratifying experience in seeking and finding appropriate data on parents, the present writer has, to date, been unable to locate enough instances in which comparable methods of behavioral assessment have been employed with different groups of children of similar ages over an extended period of time. Although the absence of such material precludes any direct and unequivocal approach to the question at hand, it is nevertheless possible, through a series of inferences from facts already known, to arrive at some estimate of what the answer might be. Specifically, although as yet we have no comparable data on the relation between parental and child behavior for different families at successive points in time, we do have facts on the influence of parental treatment on child behavior at a given point in time; that is, we know that certain variations in parental behavior tend to be accompanied by systematic differences in the personality characteristics of children. If we are willing to assume that these same relationships obtained not only at a given moment but across different points in time, we are in a position to infer the possible effects on children of changing patterns of child rearing over the years. It is this strategy that we propose to follow.

THE CHANGING AMERICAN PARENT

We have already noted the major changes in parental behavior discerned in a recent analysis of data reported over a twenty-five year period. These secular trends may be summarized as follows:

1. Greater permissiveness toward the child's spontaneous desires
2. Freer expression of affection
3. Increased reliance on indirect "psychological" techniques of discipline (such as reasoning or appeals to guilt) vs. direct methods (like physical punishment, scolding, or threats)
4. In consequence of the above shifts in the direction of what are predominantly middle class values and techniques, a narrowing of the gap between social classes in their patterns of child rearing.

Since the above analysis was published, a new study has documented an additional trend. Bronson, Katten, and Livson (1959) have compared patterns of paternal and maternal authority and affection in two generations of families from the California Guidance Study. Unfortunately, the time span surveyed overlaps only partially with the twenty-five year period covered in our own analysis, the first California generation having been raised in the early 1900's, and the second in the late '20's and early '30's. Accordingly, if we are to consider the California results along with the others cited above, we must make the somewhat risky assumption that a trend discerned in the first three decades of the century has continued in the same direction through the early 1950's. With this important qualification, an examination of the data cited by Bronson et al. (1959) points to still another, secular trend—a shift over the years in the pattern of parental role differentiation within the family. Specifically:

5. In succeeding generations the relative position of the father vis-à-vis the mother is shifting with the former becoming increasingly more affectionate and less authoritarian, and the latter becoming relatively more important as the agent of discipline, especially for boys.

"PSYCHOLOGICAL" TECHNIQUES OF DISCIPLINE AND THEIR EFFECTS

In pursuing our analytic strategy, we next seek evidence of the effects on the behavior of children of variations in parental treatment of the type noted in our inventory. We may begin by noting that the variables involved in the first three secular trends constitute a complex that has received considerable attention in recent research in parent-child relationships. Within the last three years, two sets of investigators, working independently, have called attention to the greater efficacy of "love-oriented" or "psychological" techniques in bringing about desired behavior in the child (Sears, Maccoby, and Levin, 1957; Miller and Swanson, 1958, 1960). The present writer, noting that such methods are especially favored by middle class parents, offered the following analysis of the nature of these techniques and the reasons for their effectiveness.

Such parents are, in the first place, more likely to overlook offenses, and when they do punish, they are less likely to ridicule or inflict physical pain. Instead, they reason with the youngster, isolate him, appeal to guilt, show disappointment—in short, convey in a variety of ways, on the one hand, the kind of behavior that is expected of the child; on the other, the realization that transgression means the interruption of a mutually valued relationship. . . .

These findings [of greater efficacy] mean that middle class parents, though in one sense more lenient in their discipline techniques, are using methods that are actually more compelling. Moreover, the compelling power of these practices is probably enhanced by the more permissive treatment accorded to middle class children in the early years of life. The successful use of withdrawal of love as a discipline technique implies the prior existence of a gratifying relationship; the more love present in the first instance, the greater the threat implied in its withdrawal (Bronfenbrenner, 1958).

It is now a well established fact that children from middle class families tend to excel those from lower class in many characteristics ordinarily regarded as desirable, such as self-control, achievement, responsibility, leadership, popularity, and adjustment in general.[1] If, as seems plausible, such differences in behavior are attributable at least in part to class-linked variations in parental treatment, the strategy of inference we have adopted would appear on first blush to lead to a rather optimistic conclusion. Since, over the years, increasing numbers of parents have been adopting

[1] For a summary of findings on social class differences in children's behavior and personality characteristics, see Mussen, P. H., and J. J. Conger, *Child Development and Personality*. New York: Harper, 1956.

the more effective socialization techniques typically employed by the middle class, does it not follow that successive generations of children should show gains in the development of effective behavior and desirable personality characteristics?

Unfortunately, this welcome conclusion, however logical, is premature, for it fails to take into account all of the available facts.

SEX, SOCIALIZATION, AND SOCIAL CLASS

To begin with, the parental behaviors we have been discussing are differentially distributed not only by socio-economic status but also by sex. As we have pointed out elsewhere (Bronfenbrenner, 1961), girls are exposed to more affection and less punishment than boys, but at the same time are more likely to be subjected to "love-oriented" discipline of the type which encourages the development of internalized controls. And, consistent with our line of reasoning, girls are found repeatedly to be "more obedient, cooperative, and in general better socialized than boys at comparable age levels." But this is not the whole story.

. . . At the same time, the research results indicate that girls tend to be more anxious, timid, dependent, and sensitive to rejection. If these differences are a function of differential treatment by parents, then it would seem that the more "efficient" methods of child rearing employed with girls involve some risk of what might be called "over-socialization" (Bronfenbrenner, 1961).

One could argue, of course, that the contrasting behaviors of boys and girls have less to do with differential parental treatment than with genetically-based maturational influences. Nevertheless, two independent lines of evidence suggest that socialization techniques do contribute to individual differences, *within the same sex,* precisely in the types of personality characteristics noted above. In the first place, variations in child behavior and parental treatment strikingly similar to those we have cited for the two sexes are reported in a recent conprehensive study of differences between first and later born children (Schachter, 1959). Like girls, first children receive more attention, are more likely to be exposed to "psychological" discipline, and end up more anxious and dependent, whereas later children, like boys, are more aggressive and self-confident.

A second line of evidence comes from our own current research. We have been concerned with the role of parents in the development of such "constructive" personality characteristics as responsibility and leadership among adolescent boys and girls. Our findings reveal not only the usual differences in adolescents' and parents' behaviors associated with the sex of the child, but also a striking contrast in the relationship between parental and child behaviors for the two sexes. To start on firm and familiar ground, girls are rated by their teachers as more responsible than boys, whereas the latter obtain higher scores on leadership. Expected differences similarly appear in the realm of parental behavior: girls receive more affection, praise, and companionship; boys are subjected to more physical punishment and achievement demands. Quite unanticipated, however, at least by us, was the finding that both parental affection and discipline appeared to facilitate effective psychological functioning in boys, but to impede the development of such constructive behavior in girls. Closer examination of our data indicated that both extremes of either affection or discipline were deleterious for all children, but that the process of socialization entailed somewhat different risks for the two sexes. Girls were especially susceptible to the detrimental influence of overprotection; boys to the ill effects of insufficient parental discipline and support. Or, to put it in more colloquial terms: boys suffered more often from too little taming, girls from too much.

In an attempt to account for this contrasting pattern of relationships, we proposed the notion of differential optimal levels of affection and authority for the two sexes.

The qualities of independence, initiative, and self-sufficiency, which are especially valued for boys in our culture, apparently require for their development a somewhat different balance of authority and affection than is found in the "love-oriented" strategy characteristically applied with girls. While an affectional context is important for the socialization of boys, it must evidently be accompanied by and be compatible with a strong component of parental discipline. Otherwise, the boy finds himself in the same situation as the girl, who, having received greater affection, is more sensitive to its withdrawal, with the result that a little discipline goes a long way and strong authority is constricting rather than constructive (Bronfenbrenner, 1960).

What is more, available data suggest that this very process may already be operating for boys from upper middle class homes. To begin with, differential treatment of the sexes is at a minimum for these families. Contrasting parental attitudes and behaviors toward boys and girls are pronounced only at lower class levels, and decrease as one moves up the socio-economic scale (Kohn, 1959; Bronfenbrenner, 1960). Thus our own results show that it is primarily at lower middle class levels that boys get more punishment than girls, and the latter receive greater warmth and attention. With an increase in the family's social position, direct discipline drops off, especially for boys, and indulgence and protectiveness decrease for girls. As a result, patterns of parental treatment for the two sexes begin to converge. In like manner, we find that the differential effects of parental behavior on the two sexes are marked only in the lower middle class. It is here that girls especially risk being over-protected and boys not receiving sufficient discipline and support. In upper middle class the picture changes. Girls are not as readily debilitated by parental affection and power; nor is parental discipline as effective in fostering the development of responsibility and leadership in boys.

All these trends point to the conclusion that the "risks" experienced by each sex during the process of socialization tend to be somewhat different at different social class levels. Thus the danger of overprotection for girls is especially great in lower class families, but lower in upper middle class because of the decreased likelihood of overprotection. Analogously, boys are in greater danger of suffering from inadequate discipline and support in lower middle than in upper middle class. But the upper middle class boy, unlike the girl, exchanges one hazard for another. Since at this upper level the more potent "psychological" techniques of discipline are likely to be employed with both sexes, the boy presumably now too runs the risk of being "oversocialized," of losing some of his capacity for independent aggressive accomplishment.

Accordingly, if our line of reasoning is correct, we should expect a changing pattern of sex differences at successive socio-economic levels. Specifically, aspects of effective psychological functioning favoring girls should be most pronounced in the upper middle class; those favoring boys in the lower middle. A recent analysis of some of our data bears out this expectation. Girls excel boys on such variables as *responsibility* and *social acceptance* primarily at the higher socio-economic levels. In contrast, boys surpass girls on such traits as *leadership, level of aspiration,* and *competitiveness* almost exclusively in lower middle class. Indeed, with a rise in a family's social position, the differences tend to reverse themselves with girls now excelling boys.[2]

TRENDS IN PERSONALITY DEVELOPMENT: A FIRST APPROXIMATION

The implications for our original line of inquiry are clear. We are suggesting that the "love-oriented" socialization techniques, which over the past twenty-five years have been employed in increasing degree by American middle class families, may have negative as well as constructive aspects. While fostering the internalization of adult standards and the development of socialized behavior, they may also have the effect of undermining capacities for initiative and independence, particularly in boys. Males exposed to this "modern" pattern of child rearing might be expected to differ from their counterparts of a quarter century ago in being somewhat more conforming and anxious, less enterprising and self-

[2] These shifts in sex difference with a rise in class status are significant at the 5 percent level of confidence (one-tailed test).

sufficient, and, in general, possessing more of the virtues and liabilities commonly associated with feminine character structure.[3]

At long last, then, our strategy of inference has led us to a first major conclusion. The term "major" is appropriate since the conclusion takes as its points of departure and return four of the secular trends which served as the impetus for our inquiry. Specifically, through a series of empirical links and theoretical extrapolations, we have arrived at an estimate of the effects on children of the tendency of successive generations of parents to become progressively more permissive, to express affection more freely, to utilize "psychological" techniques of discipline, and, by moving in these directions to narrow the gap between the social classes in their patterns of child rearing.

FAMILY STRUCTURE AND PERSONALITY DEVELOPMENT

But one other secular trend remains to be considered: what of the changing pattern of parental role differentiation during the first three decades of the century? If our extrapolation is correct, the balance of power within the family has continued to shift with fathers yielding parental authority to mothers and taking on some of the nurturant and affectional functions traditionally associated with the maternal role. Again we have no direct evidence of the effects of such secular changes on successive generations of children, and must look for leads to analogous data on contemporaneous relationships.

We may begin by considering the contribution of each parent to the socialization processes we have examined thus far. Our data indicate that it is primarily mothers who tend to employ "love-oriented" techniques of discipline and fathers who rely on more direct methods like physical punishment. The above statement must be qualified, however, by reference to the sex of the child, for it is only in relation to boys that fathers use direct punishment more than mothers. More generally, . . . the results reveal a tendency for each parent to be somewhat more active, firm, and demanding with a child of the same sex, more lenient and indulgent with a child of the opposite sex. . . . The reversal is most complete with respect to discipline, with fathers being stricter with boys, mothers with girls. In the spheres of affection and protectiveness, there is no actual shift in preference, but the tendency to be especially warm and solicitous with girls is much more pronounced among fathers than among mothers. In fact, generally speaking, it is the father who is more

[3] Strikingly similar conclusions were reached almost fifteen years ago in a provocative essay by Arnold Green ("The middle class male child and neurosis," *American Sociol. Rev.,* (1946), **11,** 31–41). With little to go on beyond scattered clinical observations and impressions, Green was able to detect many of the same trends which we have begun to discern in more recent systematic empirical data.

likely to treat children of the two sexes differently (Bronfenbrenner, 1960).

Consistent with this pattern of results, it is primarily the behavior of fathers that accounts for the differential effects of parental behavior on the two sexes and for the individual differences within each sex. In other words, it is paternal authority and affection that tend especially to be salutary for sons but detrimental for daughters. But as might be anticipated from what we already know, these trends are pronounced only in the lower middle class; with a rise in the family's social status, both parents tend to have similar effects on their children, both within and across sexes. Such a trend is entirely to be expected since parental role differentiation tends to decrease markedly as one ascends the socio-economic ladder. It is almost exclusively in lower middle class homes that fathers are more strict with boys and mothers with girls. To the extent that direct discipline is employed in upper middle class families, it tends to be exercised by both parents equally. Here again we see a parallelism between shifts in parental behavior across time and social class in the direction of forms (in this instance of family structure) favored by the upper middle class group.

What kinds of children, then, can we expect to develop in families in which the father plays a predominantly affectionate role, and a relatively low level of discipline is exercised equally by both parents? A tentative answer to this question is supplied by a preliminary analysis of our data in which the relation between parental role structure and adolescent behavior was examined with controls for the family's social class position. The results of this analysis are summarized as follows: . . . Both responsibility and leadership are fostered by the relatively greater salience of the parent of the same sex . . . Boys tend to be more responsible when the father rather than the mother is the principal disciplinarian; girls are more dependable when the mother is the major authority figure. . . . In short, boys thrive in a patriarchal context, girls in a matriarchal. . . . The most dependent and least dependable adolescents describe family arrangements that are neither patriarchal nor matriarchal, but equalitarian. To state the issue in more provocative form, our data suggest that the democratic family, which for so many years has been held up and aspired to as a model by professionals and enlightened laymen, tends to produce young people who "do not take initiative," "look to others for direction and decision," and "cannot be counted on to fulfill obligations" (Bronfenbrenner, 1960).

In the wake of so sweeping a conclusion, it is important to call attention to the tentative, if not tenuous character of our findings. The results were based on a single study employing crude questionnaire methods and rating scales. Also, our interpretation is limited by the somewhat "attenuated" character of most of the families classified as patriarchal or matriarchal in our sample. Extreme concentrations of power in one or another parent were comparatively rare. Had they been more frequent, we suspect the data would have shown that such extreme asymmetrical patterns of authority were detrimental rather than salutary for effective psychological development, perhaps even more disorganizing than equalitarian forms.

Nevertheless, our findings do find some peripheral support in the work of others. A number of investigations, for example, point to the special importance of the father in the socialization of boys (Bandura and Walters, 1959; Mussen and Distler, 1959). Further corroborative evidence appears in the growing series of studies of effects of paternal absence (Bach, 1946; Sears, Pintler and Sears, 1946; Lynn and Sawrey, 1959; Tiller, 1958). The absence of the father apparently not only affects the behavior of the child directly but also influences the mother in the direction of greater over-protectiveness. The effect of both these tendencies is especially critical for male children; boys from father-absent homes tend to be markedly more submissive and dependent. Studies dealing explicitly with the influence of parental role structure in intact families are few and far between. Papanek (1957), in an unpublished doctoral dissertation, reports greater sex-role differentiation among children from homes in which the parental roles were differentiated. And in a carefully controlled study, Kohn and Clausen (1956) find that "schizophrenic patients more frequently than normal persons report that their mothers played a very strong authority role and the father a very weak authority role." Finally, what might best be called complementary evidence for our inferences regarding trends in family structure and their effects comes from the work of Miller, Swanson, and their associates (1958, 1960) on the differing patterns of behavior exhibited by families from *bureaucratic* and *entrepreneurial* work settings. These investigators argue that the entrepreneurial-bureaucratic dichotomy represents a new cleavage in American social structure that cuts across and overrides social class influences and carries with it its own characteristic patterns of family structure and socialization. Thus one investigation (Gold and Slater, 1958) contrasts the exercise of power in families of husbands employed in two kinds of job situations: a) those working in large organizations with three or more levels of supervision; b) those self-employed or working in small organizations with few levels of supervision. With appropriate controls for social class, equalitarian families were found more frequently in the bureaucratic groups; patriarchal and, to a lesser extent, matriarchal in the entrepreneurial setting. Another study (Miller and Swanson, 1958) shows that, in line with Miller and Swanson's hypotheses, parents from these same two groups tend to favor rather different ends and means of socialization, with entrepreneurial families putting considerably more emphasis on the development of independence and mastery and on the use of "psychological" techniques of discipline. These differences appear at both upper and lower middle class levels but are less pronounced in higher socio-economic strata. It is Miller and Swanson's belief, however, that the trend is toward the bureaucratic way of life, with its less structured patterns of family organization and child rearing. The evidence we have cited on secular changes in family structure and the inferences we have drawn regarding their possible effects on personality development are on the whole consistent with their views.

LOOKING FORWARD

If Miller and Swanson are correct in the prediction that America is moving toward a bureaucratic society that emphasizes, to put it colloquially, "getting along" rather than "getting ahead," then presumably we can look forward to ever increasing numbers of equalitarian families who, in turn, will produce successive generations of ever more adaptable but unaggressive "organization men." But recent signs do not all point in this direction. In our review of secular trends in child rearing practices we detected in the data from the more recent studies a slowing up in the headlong rush toward greater permissiveness and toward reliance on indirect methods of discipline. We pointed out also that if the most recent editions of well-thumbed guidebooks on child care are as reliable harbingers of the future as they have been in the past, we can anticipate something of a return to the more explicit discipline techniques of an earlier era. Perhaps the most important forces, however, acting to redirect both the aims and methods of child rearing in America emanate from behind the Iron Curtain. With the firing of the first Sputnik, Achievement began to replace Adjustment as the highest goal of the American way of life. We have become concerned—perhaps even obsessed—with "education for excellence" and the maximal utilization of our intellectual resources. Already, ability grouping, and the guidance counsellor who is its prophet, have moved down from the junior high to the elementary school, and parents can be counted on to do their part in preparing their youngsters for survival in the new competitive world of applications and achievement tests.

But if a new trend in parental behavior is to develop, it must do so in the context of changes already under way. And if the focus of parental authority is shifting from husband to wife, then perhaps we should anticipate that pressures for achievement will be imposed primarily by mothers rather than fathers. Moreover, the mother's continuing strong emotional investment in the child should provide her with a powerful lever for evoking desired performance. It is noteworthy in this connection that recent studies of the familial origins of need-achievement point to the matriarchy as the optimal context for development of the motive to excel (Strodtbeck, 1958; Rosen and D'Andrade, 1959).

The prospect of a society in which socialization techniques are directed toward maximizing achievement drive is not altogether a pleasant one. As a number of investigators have shown (Baldwin, Kalhorn and Breese, 1945; Baldwin, 1948; Haggard, 1957; Winterbottom, 1958; Rosen and

D'Andrade, 1959), high achievement motivation appears to flourish in a family atmosphere of "cold democracy" in which initial high levels of maternal involvement are followed by pressures for independence and accomplishment.[4] Nor does the product of this process give ground for reassurance. True, children from achievement-oriented homes excel in planfulness and performance, but they are also more aggressive, tense, domineering, and cruel (Baldwin, Kalhorn and Breese, 1945; Baldwin, 1948; Haggard, 1957). It would appear that education for excellence if pursued single-mindedly may entail some sobering social costs.

But by now we are in danger of having stretched our chain of inference beyond the strength of its weakest link. Our speculative analysis has become far more speculative than analytic and to pursue it further would bring us past the bounds of science into the realms of science fiction. In concluding our discussion, we would re-emphasize that speculations should, by their very nature, be held suspect. It is for good reason that, like "damn Yankees," they too carry their almost inseparable sobriquets: speculations are either "idle" or "wild." Given the scientific and social importance of the issues we have raised, we would dismiss the first of these labels out of hand, but the second cannot be disposed of so easily. Like the impetuous child, the "wild" speculation responds best to the sobering influence of friendly but firm discipline, in this instance from the hand of the behavioral scientist. As we look ahead to the next twenty-five years of human socialization, let us hope that the "optimal levels" of involvement and discipline can be achieved not only by the parent who is unavoidably engaged in the process, but also by the scientist who attempts to understand its working, and who—also unavoidably—contributes to shaping its course.

REFERENCES

1. Bach, G. R. "Father-Fantasies and Father-Typing in Father-Separated Children." *Child Develpm.*, 1946, **17,** 63–79.
2. Baldwin, A. L., J. Kalhorn, and F. H. Breese. "The Appraisal of Parent Behavior." *Psychol. Monogr.*, 1945, **58,** no. 3 (whole no. 268).
3. Baldwin, A. L. "Socialization and the Parent-Child Relationship." *Child Develpm.*, 1948, **19,** 127–136.
4. Bandura, A., and R. H. Walters. *Adolescent Aggression.* New York: Ronald, 1959.

[4] Cold democracy under female administration appears to foster the development of achievement not only in the home but in the classroom as well. In a review of research on teaching effectiveness, Ackerman reports that teachers most successful in bringing about gains in achievement score for their pupils were judged "least considerate," while those thought friendly and congenial were least effective. (Ackerman, W. I. "Teacher competence and pupil change," *Harvard educ. Rev.*, **24,** [1954], 273–289.)

5. Bronfenbrenner, U. "Socialization and social class through time and space." in Maccoby, E., Newcomb, T. M., and Hartley, E. L., *Readings in Social Psychology*. New York: Holt, 1958, pp. 400–425.

6. Bronfenbrenner, U. "Some Familial Antecedents of Responsibility and Leadership in Adolescents," in Petrullo, L., and Bass, B. M., *Leadership and Interpersonal Behavior,* New York: Holt, Rinehart and Winston, 1961.

7. Bronson, W. C., E. S. Katten, and N. Livson. "Patterns of Authority and Affection in Two Generations," *J. abnorm. soc. Psychol.,* 1959, **58,** pp. 143–152.

8. Gold, M., and C. Slater. "Office, Factory, Store—and Family: A Study of Integration Setting." *Amer. sociological Rev.,* 1959, **23,** 64–74.

9. Haggard, E. A. "Socialization, Personality, and Academic Achievement in Gifted Children." *The school Rev.,* 1957, **65,** 388–414.

10. Kohn, M. L., and J. A. Clausen. "Parental Authority Behavior and Schizophrenia." *Amer. J. Orthopsychiat.,* 1956, **26,** 297–313.

11. Kohn, M. L. "Social Class and Parental Values." *Amer. J. Sociology,* 1959, **44,** 337–351.

12. Lynn, D. B., and W. L. Sawrey. "The Effects of Father-Absence on Norwegian Boys and Girls." *J. abnorm. Soc. Psychol.,* 1959, **59,** 258–262.

13. Miller D. R., and G. E. Swanson. *The Changing American Parent.* New York: Wiley, 1958.

14. Miller, D. R., and G. E. Swanson. *Inner Conflict and Defense.* New York: Holt, Rinehart and Winston, 1960.

15. Mussen, P., and L. Distler. "Masculinity, Identification, and Father-Son Relationships." *J. abnorm. soc. Psychol.,* 1959, **59,** 350–356.

16. Papanek, M. *Authority and Interpersonal Relations in the Family.* Unpubl. doctoral dissertation on file at the Radcliffe College Library, 1957.

17. Rosen, B. L., and R. D'Andrade. "The Psychosocial Origins of Achievement Motivation." *Sociometry,* 1959, **22,** 185–217.

18. Schachter, S. *The Psychology of Affiliation.* Stanford, California; Stanford University Press, 1959.

19. Sears, R. R., M. H. Pintler, and P. S. Sears. "Effects of Father-Separation on Preschool Children's Doll Play Aggression." *Child Develpm.,* 1946, **17,** 219–243.

20. Sears, R. R., Eleanor Maccoby, and M. Levin. *Patterns of Child Rearing.* Evanston, Ill.: Row, Peterson, 1957.

21. Strodtbeck, F. L. "Family Interaction, Values, and Achievement" in McClelland, D. C., Baldwin, A. L., Bronfenbrenner, U., and Strodtbeck, F. L., *Talent and Society.* Princeton, N.J.: Van Nostrand, 1958, pp. 135–194.

22. Tiller, P. O. "Father-Absence and Personality Development of Children in Sailor Families." *Nordisk Psykologis Monograph Series,* 1958, **9.**

23. Winterbottom, M. R. "The Relation of Need Achievement to Learning Experiences in Independence and Mastery." in Atkinson, J. W., *Motives in Fantasy, Action, and Society.* Princeton, N.J.: Van Nostrand, 1958, pp. 453–494.

chapter two

Motivation and Learning

2.1 *Orientation*

Assuming that developmental progress is affected by variations in environmental experience, many psychologists question the extent to which certain experiences are imperative for normal development and the extent to which the effects of trauma or deprivation can be overcome. For example, can the negative effects on a child of early sensory or emotional deprivation be reduced or eliminated by enriching that child's later environment? If so, it would mean that these negative effects could be *reversed* so that the child's later development progresses as if early deprivation had never occurred. If not, it could be said that the effects of early deprivation are *irreversible;* that is, that such deprivation interferes permanently or irreversibly with future development.

At the heart of the issue of reversibility-irreversibility in human development is the *critical periods hypothesis.* This hypothesis suggests the existence of certain brief periods in the ontogenetic development of an organism during which it is optimally susceptible to particular environmental experiences. The character of these experiences encountered during a critical period affects the quality of the organism's subsequent development. Although striking examples from animal studies support the validity of the critical periods concept (for instance, *imprinting*), psychologists are much more tentative about its application to human development. However, a number of theoretical positions sprinkled throughout the literature on personality development rely heavily upon this concept. A few relevant references are listed in the Recommended Reading.

The attempt by researchers to specify critical periods in development is consistent with an important objective of child study: namely, the identification of conditions that influence growth and development. If one could find a critical period in language development, for example, guidelines for the manipulation of favorable conditions for language learning might be established.

In the Bronson paper, the critical periods hypothesis is applied to emerging motivational systems, an approach also taken by Sontag and Kagan in the third paper reprinted in this chapter. Bronson supports his approach by drawing from the theoretical formulations of Erik Erikson, a widely known psychologist whose psychosocial stage concept of personality development is extremely popular among psychologists and educators. Other points of interest in the Bronson paper include his implications for the stability of behavior over time and the persistent problem of sex differences in motivational development.

RECOMMENDED READING

Caldwell, B. M. "The usefulness of the critical period hypothesis in the study of filiative behavior." *Merrill-Palmer Quart.,* **8** (1962), 229–242.

Denenberg, V. H. "Critical periods, stimulus input, and emotional reactivity: A theory of infantile stimulation." *Psychol. Rev.,* **71** (1964), 335–351.

Scott, J. P. "Critical periods in behavioral development." *Science,* **138** (1962), 949–958.

Stendler, Celia B. "Critical periods in socialization and overdependency." *Child Develpm.,* **23** (1952), 3–12.

2.1 Critical Periods in Human Development

Gordon Bronson, MILLS COLLEGE

One of the most powerful concepts to emerge from psychoanalytic theory is the principle of biologically determined critical periods[1] in the early phases of human development. In its most general terms, the principle recognizes the role of maturational factors in predisposing the organism to acquire certain basic orientations to the world at certain critical stages of its development. The quality of experiences during these early developmental phases, in interaction with the constitutional predisposition of the individual, will affect the fundamental nature of the individual's later involvement with the world; experiences beyond the critical periods act only to influence the modes and the areas in which these orientations will find expression.

Explanation for these processes is found in a theory of emerging motivational systems. At each critical developmental phase the dominant motivation engenders a selective responsiveness to pertinent characteristics of the environment and dictates the significant dimensions of learning. One would also expect significant constitutional differences in the strength of these various motivational systems to first become manifest during the appropriate critical periods.

This paper focuses upon two fundamental aspects of personality hypothesized to be significantly determined by events in the first 3 years: the extent of involvement with other people, and the development of an orientation of independence and competence in coping with problems presented by the environment. The longitudinal data presented here relate the former characteristic to developments during the first year of life, and the latter to influences effective in the third year. These findings are in general accord with the emergence of critical developmental stages described in contemporary clinical theory. Using Erikson's (1959) terms, events during the first year engender a "basic sense of trust," or maladaptively, of distrust. During the dependent orientation of this earliest stage the quality of mothering affects the infant's primary orientation toward the world. In the healthy situation he finds others loving and himself lovable; he develops a basic

[1] This usage of the term "critical period" implies a congruence between the human phenomena and ethological observations; such argument emphasizes the biological necessity, the inflexible chronology, and the irreversible nature of these early developments.

Reprinted from *British Journal of Medical Psychology,* **35** (1962), 127–133. By permission of the author and The British Psychological Society. The author wishes to thank Dr. Nancy Bayley for her generosity in making available to him the data from the Berkeley Growth Study.

attachment to people and a basic optimism regarding social interactions. Under less fortunate circumstances his primary orientation toward others is marked by ambivalence and uncertainty; this insecurity will color his approach to new developmental tasks in later growth periods.

Bowlby has perhaps gone the furthest in stressing the primacy of this early attachment to the mother. While primarily concerned with theoretical issues beyond the scope of this paper, his careful review (1960) of various studies of mother–child separation presents rather clear evidence that this attachment process is strongly developed by at least the second half of the first year of life, although the diverse expressions of this attachment continue to emerge through the early pre-school years.

In brief, among psychoanalytically oriented writers [2] one finds a general agreement that while later events may act to develop further or somewhat alter this basic attachment, the primary social orientation of the individual is to a significant extent determined by experiences during the first year of life.

During the second and third years the maturation of cognitive and motor capacities support the developing impulse toward active exploration and mastery of the environment. Erikson (1959) describes events in this second developmental stage as critical to the acquisition of a basic sense of autonomy, or its opposite, a sense of shame or doubt. A sense of autonomy implies confidence in one's own capacities for mastery: the feeling that one can cope independently, and that impulses can be channelled toward satisfaction without constant referral to others for approval or guidance. The defiant assertions of independence, and the wilful exploration into new frontiers for mastery are obvious expressions of this new motivational orientation. The severe discouragement of such activities, or the chronic disparagement of the achievements, induces in the child a sense of doubt regarding his impulses toward independence, or a sense of shame at his incompetence. Depending on the quality of the limitations imposed, and upon the nature of attachments formed in the preceding stage of development, the result is some admixture of thoughtless and impulsive defiance and/or regression to a position of dependent catering to adult approval.

White (1960) also stresses the importance of this initial stage of zestful curiosity and defiant independence for the development of a basic orienta-

[2] It is to be noted that while Sullivan (1953) described the development of early mother–child interactions with great sensitivity, he was less emphatic regarding the irreversible nature of this earliest learning. Since the interpersonal approach describes developmental stages largely in terms of increasing cognitive complexities rather than emerging motivational systems, relearning through later experience appeared more probable. Granting the relevance of recent studies of imprinting phenomena to human development (see, for example, Scott, 1958), the psychoanalytic principle of motivationally determined critical developmental periods seems more correct.

tion toward active mastery of the environment. While he does not discuss the consequences of environmental pressures which might impede this development, his argument that an autonomous ego drive must motivate this activity implies that it could suffer distortion through parental limitation. White presents a convincing review of the literature in describing the evolution of this capacity into its adult manifestations, subsuming it all under a "sense of competence." This term will be used here in referring to the manifestations of this characteristic at the later ages.

Conclusive documentation of the "critical period" quality of these early developmental phases is difficult since the relative irreversibility of orientations acquired during these stages can be directly established only by cases where marked changes have occurred in the character of the early environment. The present strategy therefore is to study a corollary hypothesis. If the principle of maturationally determined critical periods is correct, then these stages, when the organism is initially and maximally involved in the channeling of newly matured motivational systems, will constitute the most sensitive ages for the prediction of later characteristics. Predictions made from observations of the child before the appropriate period of the most salient learning, will fail to reflect important motivational determinants; predictions made at a later stage will be obscured by the child's involvement in a new developmental task.

This hypothesis will be supported from data on a sample of twenty-four boys taken from a longitudinal study of normal children. A similar sample of twenty-three girls fails to support these predictions. Factors responsible for this sex difference are proposed later in the discussion.

Procedure

The observational data comes from the Berkeley Growth Study (Jones and Bayley, 1941), a longitudinal study of about sixty boys and girls followed from birth to the present age of 33 years. The principal selective factors in recruitment of subjects were the requirements of family cooperation and geographical stability; for present purposes the sample can be considered essentially a normal one. While the principal focus of the study was on mental, motor and physical development, numerous personality ratings were also recorded. It is the latter which are of particular interest here. Subjects were seen at very frequent intervals (monthly up to 15 months, 3-month intervals to 3 years, semi-annually to age 18), which considerably enhances the reliability of ratings when adjacent ages are averaged.

The two rating scales pertinent to the aspects of early development being studied here are "responsiveness to persons" and "responsiveness to toys." These ratings were made by the examiner following sessions for the administration of tests of intellectual development. The ratings reflect (1) the examiner's impression of the extent to which the infant or young child was socially responsive to other people (principally the examiner), and (2) the extent to which he involved himself in exploring and exploiting the problem material presented to him. Judgments were made on these 7-point rating scales monthly from 10 to 15 months, and at 3-month intervals up to age three years.

To test the present hypothesis, these early years are divided into two periods. Ratings within each age span were combined, giving for each subject a mean rating on each of the scales for each of the two age spans. The first age range subsumes the six ratings in the span of 10 to 15 months, and is descriptive of the infant at around the end of his first year. The second group of four ratings covers ages 2 to 3 years. These two age spans correspond to the two critical stages discussed above.

The age range from 9 to 10½ years was selected as a criterion age to assess the predictive value of early orientations. This age is generally recognized as a period of some developmental stability preceding the diverse manifestations of puberty. Semi-annual personality ratings in the form of an adjective check list were available from age 9 on; the four sets of ratings to age 10½ were combined as descriptive of personality in late childhood. These adjective ratings were made by the examiner following sessions spent in the administration of the Stanford–Binet Intelligence Test.[3] The adjectives focus upon two aspects of behavior: (1) The child's orientation toward the examiner, and (2) his approach to the intellectual problems presented by her. Of the thirty-six adjectives in the check list, nineteen are included in the criterion descriptions used here. Twelve were eliminated as rarely marked, and five as not relevant to the present study (i.e. "dexterous," "attack slow," etc.). The remainder are organized into the two relevant dimensions, as shown in Table 1. A child's score for each dimension is the total number of checks over the four testing sessions for adjectives in column A minus the number for column B adjectives. The two dimensions are best described by the adjectives subsumed. They are intended to reflect aspects of personality which are significantly determined by orientations developed in the first two stages of growth. "Involvement with people" measures the extent to which the child presupposes and invites a mutual involvement with other people. "Competence orientation" refers to the degree to which the child actively and purposefully approaches problems calling for independence and mastery, reflected here in his orientation to intellectual tasks.

All subjects for whom ratings were available for more than half of the interviews subsumed in the relevant age groupings were included in the study. For the majority of cases included, complete data were available.

[3] While many of these later ratings were done by the person making the preschool judgments, the finding (below) of marked sex differences in the continuity of personality characteristics over this age span argues against the presence of any significant halo effects in these later ratings.

TABLE 1. Criterion Adjectives

A	B
"Involvement with People"	
Cheerful	Quiet
Talkative	Reserved
Trustful	
"Competence Orientation"	
Alert	Careless
Auto critical	Easily satisfied
Careful	Impulsive
Curious	Suggestible
Problem attitude	Thoughtless
Relevant	
Self-confident	
Self-expressive	
Shows initiative	

Results

Major findings are most clearly presented in tabular form. Product moment correlations of early ratings with characteristics in late childhood are presented in Table 2, relationships among the early ratings are given in Table 3, and relationships of personality ratings to intelligence scores are found in Table 4. The *N*'s which vary slightly due to missing data on some subjects at some ages, are indicated in parentheses.

Correlations between indices of "involvement with people" and "competence orientation" at ages 9–10½ are for boys 0.21 ($N = 24$), and for girls 0.13 ($N = 22$). Neither of these approach significance.

TABLE 2. Correlations of Ratings between Early Years and Late Childhood

	Boys		*Girls*	
"Involvement with People" (9–10½ years)				
"Responsiveness to persons" (10–15 months)	0.73[a]	(24)	−0.33	(20)
"Responsiveness to persons" (2–3 years)	0.24	(23)	0.02	(21)
"Competence orientation" (9–10½ years)				
"Responsiveness to toys" (10–15 months)	0.04	(24)	0.09	(20)
"Responsiveness to toys" (2–3 years)	0.45[b]	(23)	0.11	(21)
"Responsiveness to persons" (10–15 months)	0.18	(24)	−0.05	(20)

[a] $p < 0.01$.
[b] $p < 0.05$.

TABLE 3. Correlations among Ratings within the Early Years

A. Within Age Spans		Boys		Girls	
"Responsiveness to persons" by "Responsiveness to toys"	at 10–15 months	−0.03	(24)	0.17	(23)
	at 2–3 years	−0.35 [a]	(23)	−0.01	(22)
B. Within dimensions					
Ages 10–15 months by 2–3 years	"Responsiveness to persons"	0.27	(23)	0.58 [b]	(19)
	"Responsiveness to toys"	0.32	(23)	0.10	(19)

[a] $p < 0.10$.
[b] $p < 0.01$.

TABLE 4. Correlations of Ratings with Intelligence Scores

	Boys		Girls	
	IQ age 10 years			
"Competence orientation" (9–10½ years)	0.62 [a]	(23)	0.68 [a]	(22)
"Responsiveness to toys" (2–3 years)	0.37 [b]	(22)	0.34	(21)
	IQ age 2½ years			
"Responsiveness to toys" (2–3 years)	0.46 [c]	(23)	0.43 [c]	(21)

[a] $p < 0.01$.
[b] $p < 0.10$.
[c] $p < 0.05$.

DISCUSSION

Consider first the data on the male subjects, where relationships are in accord with theory. "Involvement with people" in late childhood is significantly related to "responsiveness to persons" at about the end of the first year ($r = 0.73$), the age which is considered the critical period for the primary development of social attachments. The predictive value of "responsiveness to persons" at the later age of 2–3 years is markedly attenuated ($r = 0.24$). This supports the concept of critical developmental periods; if one assumes that the early environments of these boys remained relatively stable, it appears that involvement in a new developmental task temporarily obscured ratings of acquisitions from the preceding period;[4] should one assume that marked discontinuities existed in the children's environments one must then recognize the immutable quality of orientations acquired during this first year.

[4] Gesell and Ilg (1949) among others, have repeatedly noted such apparent disruptions of recently acquired characteristics as the child presses into a new stage of development.

Predictions regarding the second developmental phase also find support in the case of male subjects. "Competence orientation," measured here by the degree of confidence and initiative with which the boys approached intellectual problems at ages 9–10½ years is significantly related to the intensity of involvement with new play materials at ages 2–3 years ($r = 0.45$). Prediction from similar ratings during the earlier 10 to 15-month period is negligible ($r = 0.04$). Again the principle of critical periods finds support in the greater predictive efficiency of ratings made during the period when theory predicts maximal involvement in a given developmental process.

The negative correlation during ages 2–3 years between "responsiveness to persons" and "responsiveness to toys" ($r = -0.35$, Table 3)[5] is further indication that boys are coping with a new motivational system during this second period. To the extent that the child gives active expression to impulses toward autonomy and mastery he seems temporarily unable to maintain an orientation of responsiveness to persons. This conflict of motivations is not evidenced at the earlier age ($r = -0.03$).

That ratings of "competence orientation" and "responsiveness to toys" correlate with achievement on intelligence tests (Table 4) is not surprising. The contribution of motivational factors to the child's performance in this area is well recognized.[6] It should be noted that an innate intelligence factor could not be an underlying variable accounting for the predictive value of ratings of "responsiveness to toys" at ages 2–3 years for the later quality of "competence orientation" in boys; although the relationships of these two variables to intelligence are almost identical for boys and girls, the predicted relationship between the two variables is found to be negligible in the female subjects ($r = 0.11$).

These relationships among the various measures for male subjects give support to the thesis that the early periods described constitute critical periods during which new motivational systems first emerge. Although the literature from the fields of both animal studies and clinical psychology stresses the significance of environmental factors as determinants of enduring individual differences, it must be emphasized that because of the design of the present study the consistency in the individual orientations reported here may be due also to constitutional variations in the strengths of these two motivational systems.

Turning to the data on female subjects, it seems improbable that the

[5] While this correlation is of borderline significance, the scatter plot shows a high degree of organization among all but one of the subjects. For an N of 22 the correlation is -0.55.

[6] A more extensive analysis of the relations of ratings of maternal behavior and child's personality to intellectual performance on this same group of children will be found in Bayley and Schaefer (1962).

consistent lack of predicted relationships here represents a failure to replicate.[7] Similar difficulties in locating consistencies in longitudinal data on girls have long been encountered by others working in this area. Assuming these sex differences represent true population differences, two general types of explanation can be offered. The first assumes a difference in the degree to which environmental pressures structure or channel the development of boys and girls in this society. Throughout the late preschool and mid-childhood years boys seem to be accorded less latitude than girls in the diversity of approved behavior. This is particularly true in the area of competence behavior, where boys are encouraged early and consistently toward rather circumscribed expressions of independence and mastery. For girls, on the other hand, competence seems to appear as a more diffusely defined concept, and may include a large component of interpersonal facility as an effective approach for coping with the environment. This line of argument suggests that although the early critical stages discussed here may be the same for both sexes, the arrangement of the criterion adjectives does not accurately reflect the basic motivational orientations of the girls at the late childhood period. For example, adjectives such as "cheerful," "talkative," and "trustful" may in some cases represent effective interpersonal techniques expressive of competence orientation. As such they represent skills acquired in mid-childhood, rather than reflexions of a basic attachment to people. If during the mid-childhood years girls are subject to a more varied and diffuse set of expectations, then the later expressions of basic orientations will be more diverse, obscuring the relationships in small samples such as this one.

The second possible explanation for the different correlational patterns in females proposes a basic biological difference: perhaps the critical periods described here are less characteristic of early female development. If this is the case, girls would be more flexible throughout childhood, in the sense of being more responsive in reflecting at each age the quality of the contemporary environment.

This hypothesis has been offered by Bayley and Schaefer (1962) to account for numerous other differences in the efficacy of long-term predictions between the males and females in this sample of children.[8]

If this is correct, if females do not experience (or experience to a lesser extent) these maturationally determined critical periods, then the early development of girls should be less characterized by marked shifts

[7] A procedural note in support of this: during the analysis of available data there was no attempt at empirical selection aimed at enhancing relationships among the male subjects.

[8] For example, ratings of maternal behavior in the first 3 years were found to be more predictive of later intelligence and personality measures for the male than for the female subjects.

in motivational orientation. Some tentative support for this is found in Table 3. For girls, the degree of "responsiveness to persons" at 10–15 months remains generally undisturbed at the later 2–3 years period ($r = 0.58$), a characteristic less true of males ($r = 0.27$). Furthermore, the conflict between an orientation towards persons and the exploitation of toys evident among the boys at 2–3 years ($r = -0.35$) seems not present in this sample of girls ($r = -0.01$), arguing for a more temperate female approach to issues of mastery and autonomy.

If this second hypothesis regarding observed sex differences has validity, the cultural factors discussed earlier may be in part an accommodation to biological differences in the early motivational structure of human males and females.

SUMMARY

Assuming that critical periods represent developmental stages during which the organism is maximally involved in the initial channelling of a new motivational system, it was predicted that the enduring motivational orientations of an individual could be most sensitively appraised by observations during the appropriate critical periods. Observations made prior to the appropriate developmental stage will fail to reflect the significant motivational determinants; those made at a somewhat later stage will be obscured by the child's involvement in new developmental tasks.

The first year was hypothesized to be a critical stage determining the child's basic orientation towards others; age 2–3 years was predicted to be the critical period for development of a sense of personal competence in coping with problems presented by the environment. Relationships between behavioral observations made during these early age periods and personality ratings at a criterion age of 9–10½ years were examined for two samples of about twenty boys and twenty girls. For the male sample, extent of "involvement with people" at 9–10½ years was predictable only from the first year observations, and the degree of "orientation towards competence and mastery" at 9–10½ years was predictable only from the 2 to 3-year ratings. This selective predictive efficiency was interpreted as evidence of critical periods in early development.

These relationships were not found in the female sample. Both biological and cultural factors were proposed as explanations for this sex difference.

REFERENCES

Bayley, Nancy, and E. S. Schaeffer. Publ. 1962.

Bowley, J. "Grief and mourning in infancy and early childhood." *Psychoanal. Study of the Child,* **15** (1960), 9–52.

Erikson, Erik H. "Identity and the life cycle." *Psychol. Issues,* **1** (1959), no. 1.
Gesell, A., and F. L. Ilg. *Child Development, An Introduction to the Study of Human Growth.* New York: Harper & Brothers, 1949.
Jones, H. E., and Nancy Bayley. "The Berkeley growth study." *Child Develpm.,* **12** (1941), 167–173.
Scott, J. P. "Critical periods in the development of social behaviour in puppies." *Psychosom. Med.,* **20** (1958), 42–54.
Sullivan, H. S. *The Interpersonal Theory of Psychiatry.* New York: Norton, 1953.
White, R. W. Competence and the psychosexual stages of development. In *Nebraska Symposium on Motivation,* M. R. Jones (Ed.) Lincoln: Univ. Nebraska Press, 1960.

2.2 *Orientation*

In its broadest sense, this paper by Bettye M. Caldwell is, like the preceding one, concerned with the critical periods concept. Caldwell's paper is, however, restricted to the first three years of life. This period is viewed by many as being crucial for primary learning and the development of basic social and cognitive skills. Indeed, if the growth curves of children are examined, the most rapid rates of development occurring in many important dimensions of behavior are in the first three years of life. Nowhere is this more apparent than in physical development. By age three, most children have attained roughly 50 percent of their adult height. It is, of course, during the prenatal period and early years that environmental influences, such as nutrition, are felt to be extremely crucial for sound physical development.

Caldwell identifies the general conditions that, by way of inference from the research and clinical data currently available, would constitute an optimal environment for young children's learning. A concept basic to Caldwell's paper is exemplified by Bloom's (1964) hypothesis that the effect of an environmental intrusion on a growth variable is greatest during the period of greatest change for that growth variable. If, as the evidence suggests, rapid social and cognitive development are occurring in the early years, the quality of a child's social and cognitive experiences is critical for both contemporaneous and future development.

An important quality of the Caldwell paper concerns the identification of assumptions underlying certain popular beliefs about children's needs and the nature of their early development. The questions raised by the author relative to the qualifications of child-care workers and the apparent societal resistance to formal social action programs for young children are both timely and stimulating. Data and insights found in this paper converge with Hunt's discussion of the psychological basis for preschool enrichment experiences (Chapter 6) and Harriet Rheingold's discussion of infant social behavior (Chapter 5).

RECOMMENDED READING

Bloom, Benjamin S. *Stability and Change in Human Characteristics.* New York: Wiley, 1964.

Bowlby, J. "The nature of the child's tie to his mother." *Int. J. Psychoanal.,* **39** (1958), 1–23.

Hoffman, M. L., and L. W. Hoffman (Eds.) *Review of Child Development Research.* (vol. 1) New York: Russell Sage, 1964.

2.2 What Is the Optimal Learning Environment for the Young Child?

Bettye M. Caldwell, SYRACUSE UNIVERSITY

A truism in the field of child development is that the milieu in which development occurs influences that development. As a means of validating the principle, considerable scientific effort has gone into the Linnaean task of describing and classifying milieus and examining developmental consequences associated with different types. Thus we know something about what it is like to come of age in New Guinea (29), in a small Midwestern town (4), in villages and cities in Mexico (25), in families of different social-class level in Chicago (12) or Boston (27, 31), in a New York slum (46), in Russian collectives (9), in Israeli kibbutzim (23, 34, 41), in the eastern part of the United States (33), and in a Republican community in Central New York (10). Most of these milieu descriptions have placed great stress on the fact that they were just that and nothing more, i.e., they have expressed the customary scientific viewpoint that to describe is not to judge or criticize. However, in some of the more recent milieu descriptions which have constrasted middle- and lower-class family environments or highlighted conditions in extreme lower-class settings (31, 46), often more than a slight suggestion has crept in that things could be better for the young child from the deprived segment of the culture. Even so, there remains a justifiable wariness about recommending or arranging any

Reprinted from the *American Journal of Orthopsychiatry,* **37** (1967), 8–21.

environment for the very young child other than the type regarded as its natural habitat, *viz.*, within its own family.

Of course, optimizing environments are arranged all the time under one guise or another. For example, for disturbed children whose family environments seem effectively to reinforce rather than extinguish psychopathology, drastic alterations of milieu often are attempted. This may take the form of psychotherapy for one or both parents as well as the disturbed child, or it may involve total removal of the child from the offending environment with temporary or prolonged placement of the child in a milieu presumably more conducive to normal development. Then there is the massive milieu arrangement formalized and legalized as "education" which profoundly affects the lives of all children once they reach the age of five or six. This type of arrangement is not only tolerated but fervently endorsed by our culture as a whole. In fact, any subculture (such as the Amish) which resists the universalization of this pattern of milieu arrangement is regarded as unacceptably deviant and as justifying legal action to enforce conformity.

For very young children, however, there has been a great deal of timidity about conscious and planned arrangement of the developmental milieu, as though the implicit assumption has been made that any environment which sustains life is adequate during this period. This is analogous to suggesting that the intrauterine environment during the period of maximal cellular proliferation is less important than it is later, a suggestion that patently disregards evidence from epidemiology and experimental embryology. The rate of proliferation of new behavioral skills during the first three years of life and the increasing accumulation of data pointing to the relative permanence of deficit acquired when the environment is inadequate during this period make it mandatory that careful attention be given to the preparation of the developmental environment during the first three years of life.

CONCLUSIONS FROM INADEQUATE ENVIRONMENTS

It is, of course, an exaggeration to imply that no one has given attention to the type of environment which can nourish early and sustained growth and development. For a good three decades now infants who are developing in different milieus have been observed and examined, and data relating to their development have made it possible to identify certain strengths and deficiencies of the different types of environments. Of all types described, the one most consistently indicated by the data is the institution. A number of years ago Goldfarb (19) published an excellent series of studies contrasting patterns of intellectual functioning shown by a group of adopted adolescents who had been reared in institutions up to age three and then transferred to foster homes or else placed shortly after birth in foster homes. The development of the group that had spent time in the institution was deficient in many ways compared to the group that had gone directly into foster homes. Provence and Lipton (33) recently published a revealing description of the early social and intellectual development of infants in institutions, contrasting their development with that of home-reared children. On almost every measured variable the institutional infants were found wanting —less socially alert and outgoing, less curious, less responsive, less interested in objects, and generally less advanced. The findings of this study are almost prototypic of the literature in the field, as pointed out in excellent reviews by Yarrow (47) and Ainsworth (1).

Although there are many attributes in combination that comprise the institutional environment, the two most obvious elements are [1] absence of a mother and [2] the presence of a group. These basic characteristics have thus been identified as the major carriers of the institutional influence and have been generalized into an explicit principle guiding our recommendations for optimal environments—learning or otherwise—for young children whenever any type of milieu arrangements is necessary. This principle may be stated simply as: the optimal environment for the young child is one in which the child is cared for in his own home in the context of a warm, continuous emotional relationship with his own mother under conditions of varied sensory input. Implicit in this principle is the conviction that the child's mother is the person best qualified to provide a stable and warm interpersonal relationship as well as the necessary pattern of sensory stimulation. Implicit also is the assumption that socio-emotional development has priority during the first three years and that if this occurs normally, cognitive development, which is of minor importance during this period anyway, will take care of itself. At a still deeper level lurks the assumption that attempts to foster cognitive development will interfere with socio-emotional development. Advocacy of the principle also implies endorsement of the idea that most homes are adequate during this early period and that no formal training (other than possibly some occasional supervisory support) for mothering is necessary. Such an operating principle places quite an onus on mothers and assumes that they will possess or quickly acquire all the talents necessary to create an optimal learning environment. And this author, at least, is convinced that a majority of mothers have such talents or proclivities and that they are willing to try to do all they can to create for their children the proper developmental milieu.

But there are always large numbers of children for whom family resources are not available and for whom some type of substitute milieu arrangement must be made. On the whole, such attempts have followed the entirely logical and perhaps evolutionary approach to milieu development—they have sought to create substitute families. The same is usually true when parents themselves seek to work out an alternate child-care arrangement because of less drastic conditions, such as maternal employment. The most typical maneuver is to try to obtain a motherly person who will "substitute" for her (not supplement her) during her hours away from her young child.

Our nation has become self-consciously concerned with social evolution, and in the past decade a serious attempt has been made to assimilate valid data from the behavioral and social sciences into planning for social action. In this context it would be meaningful to examine and question some of the hidden assumptions upon which our operating principle about the optimal environment for the young child rests.

EXAMINING THE HIDDEN ASSUMPTIONS

1. *Do intermittent, short-term separations of the child from the mother impair the mother-child relationship or the development of the child?* Once having become sensitized to the consequences of institutionalization, and suspicious that the chief missing ingredient was the continued presence of the mother, the scientific and professional community went on the *qui vive* to the possibly deleterious consequences of any type of separation of an infant from its mother. Accordingly, a number of studies (10, 18, 21, 35, 39) investigated the consequences of short-term intermittent separation and were unable to demonstrate in the children the classical syndrome of the "institutional child." In reviewing the literature, Yarrow (47) stressed the point that available data do not support the tendency to assume that maternal deprivation, such as exists in the institutional environment, and maternal separation are the same thing. Apparently short cyclic interruptions culminated by reunions do not have the same effect as prolonged interruptions, even though quantitatively at the end of a designated period the amount of time spent in a mother-absent situation might be equal for the two experiences. Also in this context it is well to be reminded that in the institutional situation there is likely to be no stable mother-child relationship to interrupt. These are often never-mothered rather than ever-mothered children, a fact which must be kept in mind in generalizing from data on institutional groups. Thus until we have data to indicate that such intermittent separation-reunion cycles have similar effects on young children as prolonged separations, we are probably unjustified in assuming that an "uninterrupted" relationship is an essential ingredient of the optimal environment.

2. *Is group upbringing invariably damaging?* In studies done in West European and American settings, social and cognitive deficits associated with continuous group care during infancy have been frequently demonstrated. Enough exceptions have been reported, however, to warrant an intensification of the search for the "true" ingredient in the group situation associated with the observed deficits. For example, Freud and Dann (17) described the adjustment of a group of six children reared in a concentration camp orphanage for approximately three years, where they were cared for by overworked and impersonal inmates of the camp, and then transported to a residence for children in England. The children, who had never known their own mothers but who had been together as a group for approximately three

years, were intensely attached to one another. Although their adjustment to their new environment was slow and differed from the pattern one would expect from home-reared children, it was significant that they eventually did make a reasonably good adjustment. That the children were able to learn a new language while making this emotional transition was offered as evidence that many of the basic cognitive and personality attributes remained unimpaired in spite of the pattern of group upbringing. The accumulation of data showing that kibbutz-reared children (34) do not have cognitive deficits also reinforces the premise that it is not necessarily group care *per se* that produces the frequently reported deficit and that it is possible to retain the advantages of group care while systematically eliminating its negative features. Grounds for reasonable optimism also have been found in retrospective studies by Maas (26) and Beres and Obers (6), although in both cases the authors found evidence of pathology in some members of the follow-up sample. Similarly Dennis and Najarian (14) concluded from their data that the magnitude of the deficit varied as a function of the type of instrument used to measure deficit, and Dennis (13) showed that in institutions featuring better adult-child ratios and a conscious effort to meet the psychological needs of the infants the development of the children was much less retarded than was the case in a group of children residing in institutions with limited and unsophisticated staffs. It is not appropriate to go into details of limitations of methodology in any of these studies; however, from the standpoint of an examination of the validity of a principle, it is important to take note of any exceptions to the generality of that principle.

In this context it is worth considering a point made by Gula (20). He recently has suggested that some of the apparent consistency in studies comparing institutionalized infants with those cared for in their own homes and in foster homes might disappear if it were possible to equate the comparison groups on the variable of environmental adequacy. That is, one could classify all three types of environments as good, marginal, or inadequate on a number of dimensions. Most of the studies have compared children from palpably "inadequate" institutions with children from "good" foster and own homes. He suggests that, merely because most institutions studied have been inadequate in terms of such variables as adult-child ratio, staff turnover, and personal characteristics of some of the caretakers, etc., one is not justified in concluding *ipso facto* that group care is invariably inferior or damaging.

3. *Is healthy socio-emotional development the most important task of the first three years? Do attempts to foster cognitive growth interfere with social and emotional development?* These paired assumptions, which one finds stated in one variety or another in many pamphlets and books dealing with early child development, represent acceptance of a closed system model of human development. They seem to conceptualize development as compartmentalized and with a finite limit. If the child progresses too much

in one area he automatically restricts the amount of development that can occur in another area. Thus one often encounters such expressions as "cognitive development at the *expense* of socio-emotional development." It is perhaps of interest to reflect that, until our children reach somewhere around high school age, we seldom seem to worry that the reverse might occur. But, of course, life is an open system, and on the whole it is accurate to suggest that development feeds upon development. Cognitive and socio-emotional advances tend on the whole to be positively, not negatively, correlated.

The definition of intelligence as *adaptivity* has not been adequately stressed by modern authors. It is, of course, the essence of Piaget's definition (32) as it was earlier of Binet (7). Unfortunately, however, for the last generation or so in America we have been more concerned with how to measure intelligent behavior than how to interpret and understand it. Acceptance of the premise that intelligent behavior is adaptive behavior should help to break the set of many persons in the field of early child development that to encourage cognitive advances is to discourage healthy socio-emotional development. Ample data are available to suggest that quite the reverse is true either for intellectually advanced persons (42, 43) or an unselected sample. In a large sample of young adults from an urban area in Minnesota, Anderson (3) and associates found that the best single predictor of post-high school adjustment contained in a large assessment battery was a humble little group intelligence test. Prediction based on intelligence plus teacher's ratings did somewhat better, but nothing exceeded the intelligence test for single measure efficiency.

It is relevant here to mention White's (45) concept of competence or effectance as a major stabilizing force in personality development. The emotional reinforcement accompanying the old "I can do it myself" declaration should not be undervalued. In Murphy's report (30) of the coping behavior of preschool children one sees evidence of the adjustive supports gained through cognitive advances. In his excellent review of cognitive stimulation in infancy and early childhood, Fowler (16) raises the question of whether there is any justification for the modern anxiety (and, to be sure, it is a modern phenomenon) over whether cognitive stimulation may damage personality development. He suggests that in the past severe and harmful methods may have been the culprits whenever there was damage and that the generalizations have confused methods of stimulation with the process of stimulation *per se*.

4. *Do cognitive experiences of the first few months and years leave no significant residual?* Any assumption that the learnings of infancy are evanescent appears to be a fairly modern idea. In his *Emile,* first published in 1762, Rousseau (38) stressed the point that education should begin while the child is still in the cradle. Perhaps any generalization to the contrary received its major modern impetus from a rather unlikely place—

from longitudinal studies of development covering the span from infancy to adulthood. From findings of poor prediction of subsequent intellectual status (5) one can legitimately infer that the infant tests measure behavior that is somewhat irrelevant to later intellectual performance. Even though these behaviors predictive of later cognitive behavior elude most investigators, one cannot infer that the early months and years are unimportant for cognitive development.

Some support for this assumption has come from experimental studies in which an attempt has been made to produce a durable effect in human subjects by one or another type of intervention offered during infancy. One cogent example is the work of Rheingold (36), in which she provided additional social and personal stimulation to a small group of approximately six-month-old, institutionalized infants for a total of eight weeks. At the end of the experimental period, differences in social responsiveness between her stimulated group and a control group composed of other babies in the institution could be observed. There were also slight but nonsignificant advances in postural and motor behavior on a test of infant development. However, when the babies were followed up approximately a year later, by which time all but one were in either adoptive or boarding homes or in their own natural homes, the increased social responsiveness formerly shown by the stimulated babies was no longer observed. Nor were there differences in level of intellectual functioning. Rheingold and Bayley (37) concluded that the extra mothering provided during the experimental period was enough to produce an effect at the time but not enough to sustain this effect after such a time as the two groups were no longer differentially stimulated. However, in spite of their conservative conclusion, it is worth noting that the experimentally stimulated babies were found to vocalize more during the follow-up assessment than the control babies. Thus there may have been enough of an effect to sustain a developmental advance in at least this one extremely important area.

Some very impressive recent unpublished data obtained by Skeels, offer a profound challenge to the assumption of the unimportance of the first three years for cognitive growth. This investigator has followed up after approximately 25 years most of the subjects described in a paper by Skeels and Dye (40). Thirteen infants had been transferred from an orphanage because of evidence of mental retardation and placed in an institution for the retarded under the care of adolescent retardates who gave them a great deal of loving care and as much cognitive stimulation as they could. The 13 subjects showed a marked acceleration in development after this transfer. In contrast a group of reasonably well matched infants left on the wards of the orphanage continued to develop poorly. In a recent follow-up of these cases, Skeels discovered that the gains made by the transferred infants were sustained into their adult years, whereas all but one of the control subjects developed the classic syndrome of mental retardation.

The fact that development and experience are cumulative makes it difficult ever to isolate any one antecedent period and assert that its influence was or was not influential in a subsequent developmental period. Thus even though it might be difficult to demonstrate an effect of some experience in an adjacent time period, delayed effects may well be of even greater developmental consequence. In a recent review of data from a number of longitudinal studies, Bloom (8) has concluded that during the first three to four years (the noncognitive years, if you will) approximately 50 per cent of the development of intelligence that is ever to occur in the life cycle takes place. During this period a particular environment may be either abundant or deprived in terms of the ingredients essential for providing opportunities for the development of intelligence and problem solving. Bloom (8) states:

> The effects of the environments, especially of the extreme environments, appear to be greatest in the early (and more rapid) periods of intelligence development and least in the later (and less rapid) periods of development. Although there is relatively little evidence of the effects of changing the environment on the changes in intelligence, the evidence so far available suggests that marked changes in the environment in the early years can produce greater changes in intelligence than will equally marked changes in the environment at later periods of development. (pp. 88–89)

5. *Can one expect that, without formal planning, all the necessary learning experiences will occur?* There is an old legend that if you put six chimpanzees in front of six typewriters and leave them there long enough they eventually will produce all the works in the British Museum. One could paraphrase this for early childhood by suggesting that six children with good eyes and ears and hands and brains would, if left alone in nature, arrive at a number system, discover the laws of conservation of matter and energy, comprehend gravity and the motions of the planets, and perhaps arrive at the theory of relativity. All the "facts" necessary to discern these relationships are readily available. Perhaps a more realistic example would be to suggest that, if we surround a group of young children with a carefully selected set of play materials, they would eventually discover for themselves the laws of color mixture, of form and contour, of perspective, of formal rhythm and tonal relationships, and biological growth. And, to be sure, all this *could* occur. But whether this will necessarily occur with any frequency is quite another matter. We also assume that at a still earlier period a child will learn body control, eye-hand coordination, the rudiments of language, and styles of problem solving in an entirely incidental and unplanned way. In an article in a recent issue of a popular woman's magazine, an author (22) fervently urges parents to stop trying to teach their young children in order that the children may learn. And, to be sure, there is always something to be said for this caution; it is all too easy to have planned learning

experiences become didactic and regimented rather than subtle and opportunistic.

As more people gain experience in operating nursery school programs for children with an early history deficient in many categories of experience, the conviction appears to be gaining momentum that such children often are not able to avail themselves of the educational opportunities and must be guided into meaningful learning encounters. In a recent paper dealing with the preschool behavior of a group of 21 children from multiproblem families, Malone (28) describes the inability of the children to carry out self-directed exploratory maneuvers with the toys and equipment as follows:

> When the children first came to nursery school they lacked interest in learning the names and properties of objects. Colors, numbers, sizes, shapes, locations, all seemed interchangeable. Nothing in the room seemed to have meaning for a child apart from the fact that another child had approached or handled it or that the teacher's attention was turned toward it. Even brief play depended on the teacher's involvement and support. (p. 5)

When one reflects on the number of carefully arranged reinforcement contingencies necessary to help a young child learn to decode the simple message, "No," it is difficult to support the position that in early learning, as in anything else, nature should just take its course.

6. *Is formal training for child-care during the first three years unnecessary?* This assumption is obviously quite ridiculous, and yet it is one logical derivative of the hypothesis that the only adequate place for a young child is with his mother or a permanent mother substitute. There is, perhaps unfortunately, no literacy test for motherhood. This again is one of our interesting scientific paradoxes. That is, proclaiming in one breath that mothering is essential for the healthy development of a child, we have in the very next breath implied that just any mothering will do. It is interesting in this connection that from the elementary school level forward we have rigid certification statutes in most states that regulate the training requirements for persons who would qualify as teachers of our children. (The same degree of control over the qualifications and training of a nursery school teacher has not prevailed in the past, but we are moving into an era when it will.) So again, our pattern of social action appears to support the implicit belief in the lack of importance of the first three years of life.

In 1928, John B. Watson (44) wrote a controversial little trade book called *The Psychological Care of Infant and Child*. He included one chapter heretically entitled, "The Dangers of Too Much Mother Love." In this chapter he suggested that child training was too important to be left in the hands of mothers, apparently not because he felt them intellectually inadequate but because of their sentimentality. In his typical "nondirective" style Watson (44) wrote:

> Six months' training in the actual handling of children from two to six under the eye of competent instructors should make a fairly satisfactory child's nurse. To keep them we should let the position of nurse or governess in the home be a respected one. Where the mother herself must be the nurse—which is the case in the vast majority of American homes—she must look upon herself while performing the functions of a nurse as a professional woman and not as a sentimentalist masquerading under the name of "Mother." (p. 149)

At present in this country a number of training programs are currently being formulated which would attempt to give this kind of professional training called for by Watson and many others. It is perhaps not possible to advance on all fronts at the same time, and the pressing health needs of the young child demanded and received top priority in earlier decades. Perhaps it will now be possible to extend our efforts at social intervention to encompass a broader range of health, education, and welfare activities.

7. *Are most homes and most parents adequate for at least the first three years?* Enough has been presented in discussing other implicit assumptions to make it unnecessary to amplify this point at length. The clinical literature, and much of the research literature of the last decade dealing with social-class differences, has made abundantly clear that all parents are not qualified to provide even the basic essentials of physical and psychological care to their children. Such reports as those describing the incidence of battered children (15, 24) capture our attention, but reports concerned with subtler and yet perhaps more long-standing patterns of parental deficit also fill the literature. In her description of the child-rearing environments provided by low lower-class families, Pavenstedt (31) has described them as impulse determined with very little evidence of clear planfulness for activities that would benefit either parent or child. Similarly, Wortis and associates (46) have described the extent to which the problems of the low-income mother so overwhelm her with reactions of depression and inadequacy that behavior toward the child is largely determined by the needs of the moment rather than by any clear plan about how to bring up children and how to train them to engage in the kind of behavior that the parents regard as acceptable or desirable. No social class and no cultural or ethnic group has exclusive rights to the domain of inadequate parentage; all conscientious parents must strive constantly for improvement on this score. However, relatively little attention has been paid to the possibly deleterious consequences of inadequacies during the first three years of life. Parents have been blamed for so many problems of their children in later age periods that a moderate reaction formation appears to have set in. But again, judging by the type of social action taken by the responsible professional community, parental inadequacy during the first three years is seldom considered as a major menace. Perhaps when the various alternatives are weighed, it

appears by comparison to be the least of multiple evils; but parental behavior of the first three years should not be regarded as any more sacrosanct or beyond the domain of social concern than that of the later years.

PLANNING ALTERNATIVES

At this point the exposition of this paper must come to an abrupt halt, for insufficient data about possible alternative models are available to warrant recommendation of any major pattern of change. At present there are no completed research projects that have developed and evaluated alternative approximations of optimal learning environments for young children in our culture. One apparent limitation on ideas for alternative models appears to be the tendency to think in terms of binary choices. That is, we speak of individual care *versus* group care, foster home *versus* institution, foster home *versus* own home, and so on. But environments for the very young child do not need to be any more mutually exclusive than they are for the older children. After all, what is our public education system but a coordination of the efforts of home plus an institution? Most of us probably would agree that the optimal learning environment for the older child is neither of these alone but rather a combination of both. Some of this same pattern of combined effort also may represent the optimal arrangement for the very young child.

A number of programs suggesting alternatives possibly worth considering are currently in the early field trial stage. One such program is the one described by Caldwell and Richmond (11). This program offers educationally oriented day care for culturally deprived children between six months and three years of age. The children spend the better part of five days a week in a group care setting (with an adult-child ratio never lower than 1:4) but return home each evening and maintain primary emotional relationships with their own families. Well child care, social and psychological services, and parent education activities are available for participating families. The educational program is carefully planned to try to help the child develop the personal-social and cognitive attributes conducive to learning and to provide experiences which can partially compensate for inadequacies which may have existed in the home environment. The strategy involved in offering the enrichment experience to children in this very young age group is to maximize their potential and hopefully prevent the deceleration in rate of development which seems to occur in many deprived children around the age of two to three years. It is thus an exercise in circumvention rather than remediation. Effectiveness of the endeavor is being determined by a comparison of the participating children with a control group of children from similar backgrounds who are not enrolled in the enrichment program. Unfortunately at this juncture it is too early for such projects to do more than suggest alternatives. The degree of confidence which comes only from research evidence plus replicated experience will have to wait a little longer.

Effective social action, however, can seldom await definitive data. And in the area of child care the most clamorous demand for innovative action appears to be coming from a rather unlikely source—not from any of the professional groups, not particularly from social planners who try to incorporate research data into plans for social action, but from *mothers*. From mothers themselves is coming the demand that professionals in the field look at some of the alternatives. We need not be reminded here that in America at the present time there are more than three million working mothers with children under six years of age (2). And these mothers are looking for professional leadership to design and provide child-care facilities that help prepare their children for today's achievement-oriented culture. The challenge which has been offered is inevitable. After almost two decades of bombarding women with the importance of their mothering role, we might have predicted the weakening of their defenses and their waving the flag of truce as though to say, "I am not good enough to do all that you are saying I must do."

It is a characteristic of social evolution that an increased recognition of the importance of any role leads to the professionalization of that role, and there can be no doubt but that we are currently witnessing the early stages of professionalization of the mother-substitute role—or, as I would prefer to say, the mother-supplement. It is interesting to note that no one has as yet provided a satisfactory label for this role. The term "baby-sitter" is odious, reminding us of just about all some of the "less well trained" professionals do—sit with babies. If English were a masculine-feminine language, there is little doubt that the word would be used in the feminine gender, for we always speak of this person as a "she" (while emphasizing that young children need more contact with males). We cannot borrow any of the terms from already professionalized roles, such as "nurse" or "teacher," although such persons must be to a great extent both nurse and teacher. Awkward designations such as "child-care worker," or hybridized terms such as "nurse-teacher" do not quite seem to fill the bill; and there appears to be some reluctance to accept an untranslated foreign word like the Hebrew *"metapelet"* or the Russian *"Nyanya."* When such a word does appear, let us hope that it rhymes well and has a strong trochaic rhythm, for it will have to sustain a whole new era of poetry and song. (This author is convinced that the proper verb is *nurture*. It carries the desired connotations, but even to one who is not averse to neologisms such nominative forms as "nurturist," "nurturer," and "nurturizer" sound alien and inadequate.)

Another basis for planning alternatives is becoming available from a less direct but potentially more persuasive source—from increasing knowledge about the process of development. The accumulation of data suggesting that the first few years of life are crucial for the priming of cognitive development call for vigorous and imaginative action programs for those early years. To say that it is premature to try to plan optimal environments because we do not fully understand how learning occurs is unacceptable. Perhaps only by the development of carefully arranged environments will we attain a complete understanding of the learning process. Already a great deal is known which enables us to specify some of the essential ingredients of a growth-fostering milieu. Such an environment must contain warm and responsive people who by their own interests invest objects with value. It must be supportive and as free of disease and pathogenic agents as possibly can be arranged. It also must trace a clear path from where the child is to where he is to go developmentally; objects and events must be similar enough to what the child has experienced to be assimilated by the child and yet novel enough to stimulate and attract. Such an environment must be exquisitely responsive, as a more consistent pattern of response is required to foster the acquisition of new forms of behavior than is required to maintain such behavior once it appears in the child's repertoire. The timing of experiences also must be carefully programmed. The time table for the scheduling of early postnatal events may well be every bit as demanding as that which obtains during the embryological period. For children whose early experiences are known to be deficient and depriving, attempts to program such environments seem mandatory if subsequent learning difficulties are to be circumvented.

SUMMARY

Interpretations of research data and accumulated clinical experience have led over the years to a consensual approximation of an answer to the question: what is the optimal learning environment for the young child? As judged from our scientific and lay literature and from practices in health and welfare agencies, one might infer that the optimal learning environment for the young child is that which exists when [1] a young child is cared for in his own home [2] in the context of a warm and nurturant emotional relationship [3] with his mother (or a reasonable facsimile thereof) under conditions of [4] varied sensory and cognitive input. Undoubtedly until a better hypothesis comes along, this is the best one available. This paper has attempted to generate constructive thinking about whether we are justified in overly vigorous support of [1] when [2], [3] or [4], or any combination thereof, might not obtain. Support for the main hypothesis comes primarily from other hypotheses (implicit assumptions) rather than from research or experimental data. When these assumptions are carefully examined they are found to be difficult if not impossible to verify with existing data.

The conservatism inherent in our present avoidance of carefully designed social action programs for the very young child needs to be re-examined. Such a re-examination conducted in the light of research evidence available about the effects of different patterns of care forces consideration of whether formalized intervention programs should not receive more attention than they have in the past and whether attention should be given to a professional training sequence for child-care workers. The careful preparation of the learning environment calls for a degree of training and commitment and personal control not always to be found in natural caretakers and a degree of richness of experience by no means always available in natural environments.

REFERENCES

1. Ainsworth, Mary. 1962. *Reversible and irreversible effects of maternal deprivation on intellectual development.* Child Welfare League of Amer., pp. 42–62.
2. *American Women.* 1963. Report of the President's Commission on the Status of Women. (Order from Supt. of Documents, Washington, D.C.)
3. Anderson, J. E., *et al.* 1959. A survey of children's adjustment over time. Univ. Minn., Minneapolis.
4. Barker, R. G., and H. F. Wright. 1955. *Midwest and its Children: The Psychological Ecology of an American Town.* New York: Row, Peterson.
5. Bayley, Nancy. 1949. "Consistency and variability in the growth of intelligence from birth to eighteen years." *J. genet. Psychol.,* **75,** 165–196.
6. Beres, D., and S. Obers. 1950. "The effects of extreme deprivation in infancy on psychic structure in adolescence." *Psychoanal. Study of the Child,* **5,** 121–140.
7. Binet, A., and T. Simon. 1916. *The Development of Intelligence in Children,* trans. by Elizabeth S. Kite. Baltimore: Williams & Wilkins.
8. Bloom, B. S. 1964. *Stability and Change in Human Characteristics.* New York: Wiley
9. Bronfenbrenner, Urie. 1962. Soviet studies of personality development and socialization. In *Some Views on Soviet Psychology.* Amer. Psychol. Assoc., pp. 63–85.
10. Caldwell, Bettye M., *et al.* 1963. "Mother-infant interaction in monomatric and polymatric families." *Amer. J. Orthopsychiat.,* **33,** 653–64.
11. Caldwell, Bettye M., and J. B. Richmond. 1964. "Programmed day care for the very young child—a preliminary report." *J. Marriage and the Family,* **26,** 481–488.
12. Davis, A., and R. J. Havighurst. 1946. "Social class and color differences in child-rearing." *Amer. Sociol. Rev.,* **11,** 698–710.
13. Dennis, W. 1960. "Causes of retardation among institutional children." *J. Genet. Psychol.,* **96,** 47–59.
14. Dennis, W., and P. Najarian. 1957. "Infant development under environmental handicap." *Psychol. Monogr.,* **71,** (7 whole no. 536).

15. Elmer, Elizabeth. 1963. "Identification of abused children." *Children,* **10,** 180–184.
16. Fowler, W. 1962. "Cognitive learning in infancy and early childhood." *Psychol. Bull.,* **59,** 116–152.
17. Freud, Anna, and Sophie Dann. 1951. "An experiment in group upbringing." *Psychoanal. Study of the Child,* **6,** 127–168.
18. Gardner, D. B., G. R. Hawkes, and L. G. Burchinal. 1961. "Noncontinuous mothering in infancy and development in later childhood." *Child Develpm.,* **32,** 225–234.
19. Goldfarb, W. 1949. "Rorschach test differences between family-reared, institution-reared and schizophrenic children." *Amer. J. Orthopsychiat.,* **19,** 624–633.
20. Gula, H. January, 1965. Paper given at Conference on Group Care for Children. Children's Bureau.
21. Hoffman, Lois Wladis. 1961. "Effects of maternal employment on the child." *Child Develpm.,* **32,** 187–197.
22. Holt, J. 1965. "How to help babies learn—without teaching them." *Redbook,* **126,** (1), 54–55; 134–137.
23. Irvine, Elizabeth E. 1952. "Observations on the aims and methods of child-rearing in communal settlements in Israel." *Human Relations,* **5,** 247–275.
24. Kempe, C. H., *et al.* 1962. "The battered-child syndrome." *J. Amer. Med. Assn.,* **181,** 17–24.
25. Lewis, O. 1959. *Five Families.* New York: Basic Books.
26. Maas, H. 1963. "Long-term effects of early childhood separation and group care." *Vita Humana,* **6,** 34–56.
27. Maccoby, Eleanor, and Patricia K. Gibbs. 1954. Methods of child-rearing in two social classes. In *Readings in Child Developm.,* W. E. Martin and Celia B. Stendler (Eds.) New York: Harcourt, pp. 380–396.
28. Malone, C. A. 1966. "Safety first: Comments on the influence of external danger in the liver of children of disorganized families." *Amer. J. Orthopsychiat.,* **36,** 3–12.
29. Mead, Margaret. 1953. *Growing Up in New Guinea.* New York: New American Library.
30. Murphy, Lois B., *et al.* 1962. *The Widening World of Childhood.* New York: Basic Books.
31. Pavenstedt, E. 1965. "A comparison of the child-rearing environment of upper-lower and very low-lower class families." *Amer. J. Orthopsychiat.,* **35,** 89–98.
32. Piaget, J. 1952. *The Origins of Intelligence in Children,* trans. by Margaret Cook. New York: International Universities.
33. Provence, Sally, and Rose C. Lipton. 1962. *Infants in Institutions.* New York: International Universities.
34. Rabin, A. I. 1957. "Personality maturity of Kibbutz and non-Kibbutz children as reflected in Rorschach findings." *J.: Proj. Tech.,* pp. 148–253.
35. Radke Yarrow, Marian. 1961. "Maternal employment and child rearing." *Children,* **8,** 223–228.

36. Rheingold, Harriet. 1956. "The modification of social responsiveness in institutional babies." *Monogr. Soc. Res. child Develpm.,* **21,** (63).
37. Rheingold, Harriet L., and Nancy Bayley. 1959. "The later effects of an experimental modification of mothering." *Child Develpm.,* **30,** 363–372.
38. Rousseau, J. J. 1950. Emile (1762). Great Neck, N.Y.: Barron.
39. Siegel, Alberta E., and Miriam B. Hass. 1963. "The working mother: a review of research." *Child Develpm.,* **34,** 513–42.
40. Skeels, H. and H. Dye. 1939. A study of the effects of differential stimulation on mentally retarded children." *Proc. Amer. Assn. on Ment. Def.,* **44,** 114–136.
41. Spiro, M. 1958. *Children of the Kibbutz.* Cambridge, Mass.: Harvard Univ. Press.
42. Terman, L. M., *et al.* 1925. *Genetic Studies or Genius.* (vol. 1) *Mental and Physical Traits of a Thousand Gifted Children.* Stanford, Calif.: Stanford Univ. Press.
43. Terman, L. M., and Melita H. Oden. 1947. *The Gifted Child Grows Up: Twenty-Five Years' Follow-Up of a Superior Group.* Stanford, Calif.: Stanford Univ. Press.
44. Watson, J. B. 1928. *Psychological Care of Infant and Child.* London: G. Allen.
45. White, R. W. 1959. "Motivation reconsidered: the concept of competence." *Psychol. Rev.,* **66,** 297–333.
46. Wortis, H., *et al.* 1963. "Child-rearing practices in a low socio-economic group." *Pediatrics,* **32,** 298–307.
47. Yarrow, L. J. 1961. "Maternal deprivation: Toward an empirical and conceptual re-evaluation." *Psychol. Bull.,* **58,** 459–490.

2.3 *Orientation*

The Fels Research Institute in Yellow Springs, Ohio, has provided a substantive source of longitudinal data on human development. One contribution is a brief report of a facet of longitudinal research by two authorities long associated with this institute's activities. The study of one group of children over a relatively long period of time often permits the derivation of more interpretable data regarding stability and change in human characteristics than does the successive sampling of children of different ages. The behavior documented in this paper concerns the stability of motivation. Test scores and ratings obtained during one stage of development are correlated with similar data obtained on the same subjects at a subsequent stage in development. If the resultant correlations are statistically significant they become the empirical basis for supporting hypotheses concerning the reliability (stability) of the respective behaviors being measured.

This strategy is basically the same as that followed by Bronson in his analysis of Berkeley data presented earlier in this chapter. These Fels data relate to Bronson's study, which is also a statement on motivational behavior associated with certain developmental periods. Taken together the two studies suggest that successive developmental stages are accompanied by particular developmental sensitivities and unique, although common, problems characteristic of each stage. Therefore, different kinds of experiences may become critical in determining or influencing children's emerging capacities. The Fels data discussed in this paper also lend support to the clinical contentions of Erik Erikson (1963): Erikson maintains that the elementary school years are critical for children in developing a sense of industry and satisfaction in work completion versus a sense of inferiority, inadequacy, and work paralysis.

The Kagan and Moss reference below represents a summary of much of the Fels data concerned with personality development.

RECOMMENDED READING

Crandall, Vaughn, *et. al.* "Motivational and ability determinants of young children's intellectual achievement behaviors." *Child Develpm.,* **33** (1963), 643–661.

Erikson, Erik. *Childhood and Society.* (2d ed.) New York: Norton, 1963, pp. 258–261.

Kagan, Jerome, *et. al.* "Personality and IQ change." *J. abnorm. soc. Psychol.,* **56** (1958).

Kagan, Jerome, and Howard Moss. *Birth to Maturity: A Study in Psychological Development.* New York: Wiley, 1962.

Pressey, Sidney F., and Raymond G. Kuhlen. *Psychological Development Through the Life Span.* New York: Harper & Row, 1957. (See chap. 7, "Changing Motivation During the Life Span," pp. 271–321.)

2.3 The Emergence of Intellectual-Achievement Motives

Lester Sontag, FELS RESEARCH INSTITUTE
Jerome Kagan, HARVARD UNIVERSITY

Part of the program of the Fels Research Institute is organized to study the emergence of various behaviors from birth to maturity, and to relate significant aspects of the home and school environment to the child's developing personality.

The longitudinal study of a group of children over a 30-year period makes it possible to assess the relationship between constellations of behaviors displayed at an early age and similar behaviors in adult life. One problem we have studied that is germane to our current theme involves the influence of personality structure on changes in the mental test performance of children over the period from two and one-half to 12 years of age (3). One aspect of personality development is the resolution of the early infantile dependent need for love and nurture and its gradual replacement by independence of action, dependence on self, effective problem-solving and successful competition. The striving for a feeling of competence is present in all adults. The well-adjusted adult is reassured because he feels adequate to deal with environmental crises; he feels socially accepted if he is able to master new tasks and problems, able to function somewhat independently and to compete successfully.

The ways in which he resolves his infantile dependent ties with his parents and, later, others, can often channel the direction of the child's future motivation. He will either learn to anticipate emotional security primarily through contact with and reassurance from people, or learn to achieve this emotional satisfaction through self-reassurance—through confidence in his own autonomy, his ability to solve everyday problems and his successful competition with peers.

Analysis of our mental test data showed conclusively that children who were high in independent problem solving and competitiveness showed large increases in IQ in the period from six to ten years of age. The IQ's of children who looked to parents for emotional comfort and alleviation of anxiety tended to remain constant or declined with age. It is obvious to those who have dealt with psychiatric problems that the independent, confident individual has a much more effective personality, and is less likely to come to grief than the passive, highly dependent one who is vulnerable to perceived rejection and failure.

Reprinted from the *American Journal of Orthopsychiatry,* **37** (1967), 8–21.

Our research indicates that there is a critical period in the development of the motive to master intellectual tasks. This period is between six and ten years of age—the first five years of school (1, 2). It is probably no accident that this is the same period of time when IQ increases or decreases are so intimately associated with the child's over-all personality.

We recently assessed 71 middle-class adult subjects who had been members of the Fels Study since birth. Ratings on behavior were made in nursery school, home, elementary school and day camp from birth through adolescence, at four different age periods. Ratings of adult personality characteristics were made from five-hour interviews at ages 20 to 30 years.

Achievement behavior between the ages of six and ten was highly predictive of adult mastery behavior. For example, the correlation between achievement between six and ten and involvement in intellectual mastery in adulthood was .68 ($p<.001$) for males and .49 ($p<.01$) for females. Achievement between three and six was unrelated to adult behavior for males and moderately associated with adult behavior for females. Achievement during the first three years showed a zero order relation with adult behavior. In summary, behavior during the first five years of school was prognostic of adult mastery strivings.

Moreover, the amount of IQ increase between six and ten was also a good predictor of adult achievement ($r = .49$; $p < .01$). This increase in IQ, which is associated with a competitive and achievement-oriented approach to problems in childhood, was also prognostic of adult mastery behavior. Finally, TAT achievement themes obtained during early adolescence were positively associated with adult achievement behavior ($C = .44$; $p < .01$).

CONCLUSIONS

These findings on IQ change and the development of mastery motivation indicate that the period between six and ten years—the first to the fourth grades—is of vital importance in the development of the desire to meet and master challenging problems. When the child enters school, he is ready to begin severing the close, dependent tie to his parents, and conceptually and physically mature enough to develop skills that will allow him considerable autonomy and independence in problem situations. He has entered a new phase of life so far as the development of his self-reassuring mechanisms are concerned. The next four years will give him an opportunity to develop skills that are self-reassuring, to become more self-confident as a possessor of such skills, and to be free, in part, from the vulnerability that results from strong dependence on parents. These four years are a critical period in his life from the standpoint of the direction in which he will be motivated to seek emotional security. It is his first major opportunity to throw off the family yoke and seek other sources of support in the world.

One of the things a teacher should understand about personality formation is the role played by identification—a child's identification with his teacher. This identification involves the child's perception of the value systems of the teacher, his recognition of his or her strength and knowledge, and his anticipation of her warmth and approval for "being like her." The teacher is a model to the child and identification with her values and motives can act as a spur to academic excellence. The teacher should be aware of the tremendous impact she has as a model upon the impressionable personality of the child. It goes without saying that, insofar as possible, people who are selected for roles in elementary education should be people with strength and warmth to foster such identifications.

ADDITIONAL PROBLEMS

Anxiety over Intellectual Mastery

Even in the first four years of elementary education, a social stigma is often attached to high levels of achievement behavior, to being "too studious." Children at this age, and even at the collegel level, tend to discourage the development of scholastic excellence. The "egg-head" is a derogatory term used for intellectuals in adult life, and a "brain" designates the over-zealous youthful achiever. Social approval for achievement behavior should begin in the first grade. The recent Russian surge in science can probably be accounted for, in part, by the high value Soviet culture places on academic excellence.

Strategies for Studying

Freshman college students who are running into difficulties scholastically often reveal that they are studying "by the hour." I have known them to look at their watches at ten-minute intervals to see when their two or three hours were up. One of the processes of teaching them to survive in college is to induce them to arrange their work not in time blocks, but in problem blocks. The accomplishment of a given task, whether the time involved be long or short, is something over which to feel elated. A problem is something to be mastered, not to be worked at. The obstacle is to be incorporated—not nibbled at. The devising of elementary school curricula to achieve a series of short-term accomplishments, which are in themselves an emotional reward, is an important consideration in the organization of a school program. Some people may master 30 problems in a day, and others only three. Yet there is satisfaction for both if each has accomplished a given objective. Such satisfactions are anxiety-relieving. They help form self-sustaining mechanisms that permit the individual to like himself and feel adequate.

Class Organization

It is desirable whenever possible, but without making either children or parents unduly aware of the fact, to organize classes in groups of somewhat similar ability or achievement level. If children are to experience individually the exhilaration of successful competition, competition must first be encouraged. It is unrealistic to start children in elementary schools with the naïve assumption that they should be shielded from competition. Competition cannot be eliminated; but opportunities for competition should be so organized that everyone can experience success in one area or another, at one time or another. School work can be organized so that every child can be successful on some occasions.

SUMMARY

The period from six to ten years is critical for the crystallization of a desire for task mastery and intellectual competence. High levels of achievement behavior at that age are highly correlated with achievement behavior in adulthood. It is further suggested that the teacher realize the role that she may play as a source of identification to the children she teaches and her power to increase the child's confidence in his ability to deal with problems autonomously.

REFERENCES

1. Kagan, J., and H. A. Moss. "Stability and validity of achievement fantasy." *J. abnorm. soc. Psychol.,* **88** (1959), 357–364.
2. Moss, H. A., and J. Kagan. "The stability of achievement and recognition seeking behaviors." *J. abnorm. soc. Psychol.,* **62** (1961), 504–513.
3. Sontag, L. W., C. T. Baker, and V. L. Nelson. "Mental growth and personality development: A longitudinal study." *Mongr. Soc. Res. child Develpm.,* **23** (1958), 68.

2.4 *Orientation*

The concept of reinforcement is central to any behavioristic discussion of children's learning. Sidney W. Bijou, a leading proponent of descriptive behaviorism (especially as applied to developmental psychology), in this paper examines reinforcement from an *empirical* point of view. Reinforcement is thus defined not by some assumed reward value but by the *effect* of a stimulus event upon the frequency and rate of a child's behavior. This objectivity sets the entire tone for descriptive behaviorism; inferences based upon hypothetical constructs are avoided.

One focal concern of psychologists who deal with the empirical concept of reinforcement is behavior modification. For example, these psychologists are concerned with questions calling for an identification of antecedents that produce variations in the strength and rate of an organism's operant responses.* As compared to a child's reinforcement history, age is considered a less important, if not irrelevant, variable. Theoretical expanation is seen as less pertinent than the precise description of observable events. The basic premise upon which this approach to child development is founded is simply that a child's behavior is modified by the consequences of that behavior.

Descriptive behaviorism carries with it a technical vocabulary that may be unfamiliar to some readers. Such concepts as operant and respondent behavior, positive and negative reinforcement (the latter not to be confused with punishment), and schedules of reinforcement are utilized freely in the Bijou paper. The first Bijou and Baer reference provided below is an excellent source for a study of these concepts. The reader is directed to note specifically the approaches in research emerging from the use of reinforcement principles. These approaches represent a direct contrast to some of the more conventional, and often unfruitful, research strategies used in the study of child development.

RECOMMENDED READING

Bijou, S. W., and D. M. Baer. *A Systematic and Empirical Theory.* vol. 1 of *Child Development.* New York: Appleton-Century-Crofts, 1961.

Bijou, S. W., and D. M. Baer. *Universal Stage of Infancy.* vol. 2 of *Child Development.* New York: Appleton-Century-Crofts, 1965.

Millenson, J. R. *Principles of Behavioral Analysis.* New York: Macmillan, 1967.

Ullman, L. P., and Leonard Krasner (Eds.) *Case Studies in Behavior Modification.* New York: Holt, Rinehart and Winston, 1965.

* An operant response is a volitional, emitted response (e.g., opening a door, tying a shoe). In contrast are involuntary, or reflex, responses (e.g., salivation, eyeblink), which are called respondents.

2.4 An Empirical Concept of Reinforcement and a Functional Analysis of Child Behavior

Sidney W. Bijou, UNIVERSITY OF ILLINOIS

INTRODUCTION

The purpose of this paper is twofold: [1] to discuss the empirical concept of reinforcement in relation to a theory of psychological development, and [2] to present examples of research with children based upon such an orientation.

The meaning of an empirical concept of reinforcement for a theory of child development cannot be appreciated in isolation. Reinforcement is not thought of as a kind of learning theory (such as reinforcement learning theory) or as a miniature behavior theory. It is viewed as a significant statement concerning the temporal relationships between certain classes of stimuli and responses; therefore, this discussion is preambled with an outline of a theory of development that involves an empirical concept of reinforcement (9).

A CONTEXT FOR AN EMPIRICAL CONCEPT OF REINFORCEMENT

Data of psychological development are viewed as progressive changes in behavior (i.e., as differentiations and increases in complexity) that evolve from interactions with the environments of development. The phrase "environments of development" refers to *stimulus events.* Stimulus events include circumstances that *have* interacted with the developing organism (historical) as well as those that *are* interacting with it. Stimulus events may be described by their functional properties *and* by their physical properties. For example, a tone may be characterized by changes in electrical impulses on an oscilloscope and, at the same time, by specific changes in the behavior of an organism. With respect to its relationship with behavior, the onset of the tone may be correlated with an orienting reflex, with a response that has been reinforced in the past, or with an increase in strength of a response that preceded it (as observed in the future occurrences of responses of the same class). Thus the tone may be described by one or by several functional characteristics; it may also be described by its physical dimensions, such as wavelength, amplitude, and composition.

Many stimulus events influence the strength of specific stimulus-response relationships. Such stimulus events are *setting events* or setting factors.

Reprinted from *Genetic Psychology,* **104** (1964), 215–223. By permission of the author and The Journal Press.

> Such setting factors as the hungry or satiated condition of the organism, its age, hygienic or toxic condition, as well as the presence or absence of certain environing objects clearly influence the occurrence or non-occurrence of inter-behavior or facilitate the occurrence of the activities in question in varying degrees (20, p. 95).

Consider the example of hunger or, better still, the deprivation of food as a setting event in the eating behavior of a 10-year-old boy. The training that the boy receives relative to food and to members of the family around the table is in part a function of food deprivation for about four-and-a-half hours prior to coming to the table. Fasting for four-and-one-half hours between meals is a setting event that plays a role in the learning supervised by the boy's parents. When this setting event is changed, the boy's behavior is altered. If we were to observe the boy's eating behavior under conditions of a setting event of only one hour since he last ate, we would be likely to say that his table manners were "poor" or that he exhibited low frequencies of "approved" behaviors and high frequencies of other kinds of behavior. (He spends most of his time "playing with his food.") If we were to watch him under conditions of a setting event of seven hours of food deprivation, we would also be likely to say that his table behaviors were "poor," or that he exhibited low frequencies of "good" behaviors and high frequencies of still other kinds of behavior. (He "devours his food.")

We turn now to an empirical concept of the child as a psychological organism. The developing child may be considered equivalent to a constellation of stimulus and response events. Stimulus events inside the organism are viewed as part of the environments of development and are analyzed in the same manner as external stimuli. No new assumptions are invoked. Because of the frequent inaccessibility of internal stimuli, adherence to an objective conception of them poses special, but not insurmountable, problems for a natural science approach.

The response aspect of the child is analyzed in terms of its physical and functional properties. From the point of view of physical analysis, responses are described by space-time dimensions, such as latency, frequency, and amplitude.[1] From a functional vantage point, responses are described by their relationships to stimuli. To say that a stimulus has a stimulus function is to say that it interacts with a psychological response, a response that involves the organism as a unified system. The response in the interaction is said to have a response function.

Psychological interactions may be divided into two categories on the basis of temporal relationships. One group consists of interactions that vary in strength in accordance with antecedent stimulus action; the other

[1] Data from a particular study will, of course, depend upon the dimension selected (17).

group consists of interactions that vary in accordance with consequent stimulus action. Skinner (34) refers to the first group as respondents; to the second, as operants. Such a classification may be used advantageously to analyze the continual interactions between the developing child and environmental changes divided into stages. An analysis of development in terms of operant and respondent interactions throughout all developmental phases would be in contrast to approaches that view development as changes in motor, linguistic, intellectual, emotional, and social patterns of behavior. The difficulty with schemes of the latter sort is that they are based on shifting and overlapping criteria (physical, social, physiological, etc.), some of which are objectively defined and some of which are not. Furthermore, the specific stimulus functions that are involved (the environmental situations to which they are related) are ignored or minimized.

The other aspects of the systematic and empirical theory of development concern the strengthening and weakening of stimulus-responses relationships, interrelationships between operant and respondent processes, generalization and discrimination, differentiation, chaining, conflict, and self-control.

The aim of the approach is to observe, analyze, and interpret interactions between environmental events and responses so as to extend and refine empirical laws. Accomplishments to date have contributed to an objective theory of development and have provided some principles for educational and child-rearing practices.

AN EMPIRICAL CONCEPT OF REINFORCEMENT

So much for a theoretical frame of reference. We now turn to a discussion of an empirical concept of reinforcement within the context given. At the outset, it should be noted that the concept of reinforcement (empirical and other) is believed to hold only for operant interactions. The concept may be stated as follows:

> [A certain class of behavior is strengthened by certain classes of consequent stimulus events.] The only way to tell whether or not a given event is reinforcing to a given organism under given conditions is to make a direct test. We observe the frequency of a selected response (operant level) then make an event contingent upon it and observe any change in frequency. If there is a change, we classify the event as reinforcing to the organism under the existing conditions (35, p. 73).

One may ask, "Why does a stimulus with reinforcing properties strengthen such behavior?" Some points of view seek an answer in terms of biological or biochemical inferences and data (the reductionistic approaches); some, in terms of hypothetical variables (usually some variation on a drive-reduction notion); still others, in terms of consequent feeling-states. A natural science approach avoids these kinds of attempts at explanation. It accepts the fact of reinforcement.[2] It accepts the fact that a class of objectively defined responses is strengthened by consequent environmental events. It accepts the fact that such events are of two sorts: one sort strengthens on presentation; the other, on withdrawal. Environmental events in the first group are called *positive reinforcers* to emphasize the adding operation; environmental events in the second group are called *negative reinforcers* to emphasize the subtracting operation. A detailed account of the empirical concept of reinforcement involves the procedures for weakening operant behavior (19, 21, 34, 35).

Instead of searching for the correlates of operant strengthening in the neighboring branches of science or of constructing "explanatory interval variables," the empirical approach emphasizes the need for systematic information on the empirical relations between reinforcing stimuli and operants. For example, many investigators are exploring the range of reinforcing stimuli applicable to the young infant (primary reinforcers), the time of the initial appearance of certain operants, the processes and circumstances under which neutral stimuli take on reinforcing functions (acquired reinforcers), and the patterns of interactional contacts between reinforcers and responses (schedules). One of the major tasks in an experimental analysis of child behavior and behavior development is the discovery of stimuli that have positive or negative reinforcing properties for children at different stage levels, and a delineation of their parameters together with their relevant setting events.

In passing, it should be noted that the empirical concept of reinforcement is similar to Hilgard's "neutral definition" of reinforcement (18). There is a difference, however. Hilgard's conception applies to responses that acquire their functions through consequent stimulation (operants) *as well as* through antecedent stimulus action (respondents). Here, the empirical concept of reinforcement does not apply to respondent behavior. It is true that under proper circumstances, operants, as well as respondents, correlate with antecedent stimulation, but these functional relationships are established through different histories. Because each class of interactions has a different history and the stimuli and responses that are involved have different functions, separate analysis is indicated. In the interest of clarity, it is suggested that the empirical concept of reinforcement be restricted to interactions controlled by consequent stimulation

[2] The argument that this position "postulates the problem" is relevant only when one assumes that "causes" in the behavior science must be in terms of variables from biology, biochemistry, etc.

and that, as suggested by MacCorquadale (27), Schlosberg (33), and Skinner (34), a different term be applied to interactions controlled by antecedent stimulation.

EXAMPLES OF RESEARCH WITH CHILDREN

During the past four years, examples of research with children from the point of view of an empirical concept of reinforcement have become more available. Some investigations, as they must in initiating an experimental approach, have been devoted to exploration of the physical features, methods, procedures, and techniques appropriate for the laboratory study of children of all ages. Thus Bijou (5, 6) and Baer (3) have worked on a methodology for normal preschool children. Bijou was concerned with general laboratory techniques; Baer was concerned with specific procedures for analysis of verbal-social stimuli that involved an animated, talking puppet. Long, Hammack, May, and Campbell (23) and Long (22), have concentrated on laboratory methods for preschool children and, particularly, for middle-childhood children. Ellis, Barnett, and Pryer (12) and Orlando, Bijou, Tyler, and Marshall (31) have explored methods appropriate to retarded children in a residential school, and Ferster and DeMyer (13) have made intensive investigations on procedures appropriate for young autistic children in a hospital setting.

Another group of studies, and a rather large group, has been devoted to the specification of reinforcing stimuli for neonates, infants, preschool children, and older children, as well as to the patterns of behavior that are associated with the basic schedules of reinforcement. In a way, this area of inquiry is continuous with methodological investigations because such information is essential to the planning and execution of all studies. In striving to produce reliable relationships, these studies make explicit the reinforcers in operation and the schedule with which they are presented or withdrawn. Some investigators have taken leads from studies on infrahuman subjects; other investigators have explored new contingencies. For example, Bijou (7) has studied the presentation of positive reinforcers by comparing continuous and intermittent schedules on preschool children. Long (22) has studied fixed ratios, fixed intervals, and variable intervals. Ellis, Barnett, and Pryer (12) and Orlando and Bijou (30) have studied basic intermittent schedules with retarded children. Ferster and DeMyer (13) have studied intermittent schedules with autistic children. Examples of studies on the loss of positive reinforcers (withdrawal of short intervals of cartoon movies) include those by Baer (2, 3) on escape and avoidance behavior in norman preschool children, and by Marshall (28) on institutionalized retarded subjects.

A third group of investigations has been concerned with the response functions of normal and deviant children of varying ages. For example,

Brackbill (11) wondered whether the smiling behavior of six-month-old babies has operant properties. Rheingold, Gerwirtz, and Ross (32) asked a similar question about the vocalization of infants. The provocative findings from both of these investigations open the way for a host of new studies. In the same vein, Flanagan, Goldiamond, and Azrin (14, 15) sought to learn whether stuttering can be conditioned according to operant principles. Their encouraging results have new implications for this recalcitrant problem area.

A fourth group of studies has been devoted to setting events; i.e., to circumstances that influence the relationships in a specific psychological interaction. Included in this group are studies by Gewirtz and Baer (16) on the effects of satiation and deprivation of social stimulation on a task reinforced by social stimuli, and by Lovaas (24) on the influence of exposure to symbolic aggression on aggressive behavior in normal preschool children.

A fifth group of investigations centers around problems of discriminative stimuli (stimulus control, cues, perceptual stimuli). Studies on the acquisition and stability of multiple schedules by Bijou (8) on normal children and by Bijou and Orlando (10) on retarded children are of this nature. The influence of verbal behavior on other verbal behavior and on nonverbal behavior, as studied by Lovaas (24, 25), are also pertinent. The laboratory study by Azrin and Lindsley (1) on cooperative behavior also falls in this category. In this last-named study, the cue for the behavior of the "follower" was an objectively defined response by the "leader."

There are several clearly apparent trends in the work of investigators who are following a natural science theory of development that embodies an empirical concept of reinforcement. They may be mentioned briefly. First, the work of such investigators shows a strong interest in adding to an empirical theory of development rather than in testing deductions from a formal theory. Second, there is a preference for laboratory-experimental studies. Third, there is a tendency to study individual children intensively and to seek control of variables through laboratory procedures rather than through psychometric procedures. Experimental design by laboratory control is not indigenous to this approach but is attractive, since many investigators believe that individual analysis is an ultimate objective of a behavioral science. One correlate of this practice is the preference for a standard laboratory situation for all studies, using variations of stimulus or response functions pertinent to the particular study. A second preference is for analysis in free operant situations (rather than under restricted operant conditions as is exemplified in the WGTA) because free operant situations allow for greater control and provide more detailed and continuous information.

SUMMARY

The empirical concept of reinforcement as related to child development has been discussed in the context of a theory from a natural science point of view. The position states that the data of psychological development are progressive changes in behavior (differentiation and increases in complexity) that evolve from interactions with the environment of development. The environments of development consist of stimulus events and of setting events. Stimulus events are stimuli that are described by physical and functional procedures; setting events are operations that affect specific stimulus-response interactions. The developing child is said to be a series of stimulus and response events. The stimulus aspects of the child (internal stimuli) are analyzed in the same way as those in the external environment. The response aspect is also described by its physical properties (frequency, amplitude, latency, etc.) and by its functional properties (whether they are controlled by stimuli that precede or follow them). The former are called respondents, reflexes, or involuntary responses. The latter are designated as operants, instrumental or voluntary responses.

The empirical concept of reinforcement applies only to operant behavior. It states that operant behavior is strengthened by certain consequent stimulus events. Some stimuli strengthen on presentation; some, on withdrawal. The only way to find out whether a stimulus is neutral (no strengthening value), positive (strengthens on presentation), or negative (strengthens on withdrawal) is by empirical test. Research along this line seeks not to "explain" reinforcement with organismic data or with intervening variables, but seeks to delineate the empirical relationships between reinforcing conditions and changes in operant strength.

Samples of research have been grouped into five categories. The first group is devoted to the development of a methodology; the second, to an analysis of the effects of schedules of reinforcing stimuli; the third, to a study of response functions; the fourth, to an investigation of some setting events; the fifth, to discriminative or perceptual stimuli. Some of the predominant characteristics of the work in this area have been pointed out. These include an emphasis on empirical theory building and a preference for laboratory analysis, individual control, and free operant methods.

REFERENCES

1. Azrin, N. H., and O. R. Lindsley. "The reinforcement of cooperation between children." *J. abnorm. soc. Psychol.,* **52** (1956), 100–102.
2. Baer, D. M. "Escape and avoidance response of pre-school children to two

schedules of reinforcement withdrawal." *J. exp. anal. Behav.,* **3** (1960), 155–160.

3. Baer, D. M. "Effects of withdrawal of positive reinforcement on an extinguishing response in young children." *Child Develpm.,* **32** (1961), 67–72.
4. Baer, D. M. "A technique of social reinforcement for the study of child behavior: Behavior avoiding reinforcement withdrawal." *Child Develpm.,* **33** (1962), 847–858.
5. Bijou, Sidney W. "A systematic approach to an experimental analysis of young children." *Child Develpm.,* **26** (1955), 161–168.
6. Bijou, S. W. "Methodology for an experimental analysis of young children." *Psychol. Rep.,* **3** (1957), 243–250.
7. Bijou, S. W. "Patterns of reinforcement and resistance to extinction in young children." *Child Develpm.,* **28** (1957), 47–54.
8. Bijou, S. W. "Discrimination performance as a baseline for individual analysis of young children." *Child Develpm.,* **32** (1961), 163–170.
9. Bijou, S. W., and D. M. Baer. *Child Development: A Systematic and Empirical Theory.* New York: Appleton-Century-Crofts, 1961.
10. Bijou, S. W., and R. Orlando. "Rapid development of multiple-schedule performance with retarded children." *J. exp. anal. Behav.,* **4** (1961), 7–16.
11. Brackbill, Y. "Extinction of the smiling response in infants as a function of reinforcement schedule." *Child Develpm.,* **29** (1958), 115–124.
12. Ellis, N. R., C. D. Barnett, and M. W. Pryer. "Operant behavior in mental defectives: Exploratory studies." *J. exp. anal. Behav.,* **3** (1960), 63–69.
13. Ferster, C. B., and M. K. DeMyer. "The development of performances in autistic children in an automatically controlled environment." *J. chronic. Dis.,* **13** (1961), 312–345.
14. Flanagan, B., I. Goldiamond, and N. Azrin. "Operant stuttering: The control of stuttering through response contingent consequences." *J. exp. anal. Behav.,* **2** (1958), 173–178.
15. Flanagan, B., I. Goldiamond, and N. Azrin. "Instatement of stuttering in normally fluent individuals through operant procedures." *Science,* **130** (1959), 979–981.
16. Gewirtz, J. L., and D. M. Baer. "Deprivation and satiation of social reinforcers as drive conditions." *J. abnorm. soc. Psychol.,* **56** (1958), 165–172.
17. Gilbert, T. F. "Fundamental dimensional properties of the operant." *Psychol., Rev.,* **65** (1958), 272–282.
18. Hilgard, E. R. *Theories of Learning.* (2d ed.) New York: Appleton-Century-Crofts, 1956.
19. Holland, J. G., and B. F. Skinner. *The Analysis of Behavior.* New York: McGraw-Hill, 1961.
20. Kantor, J. R. *Interbehavioral Psychology.* (rev. ed.) Bloomington, Ind.: Principia, 1959.
21. Keller, F. S., and W. N. Schoenfeld. *Principles of Psychology.* New York: Appleton-Century-Crofts, 1950.
22. Long, E. R. The use of operant conditioning techniques in children. In *Child Research in Psychopharmacology,* S. Fisher (Ed.). Springfield, Ill.: Charles C. Thomas, 1959.

23. Long, E. R., J. T. Hammack, F. May, and B. J. Campbell. "Intermittent reinforcement of operant behavior in children." *J. exp. anal. Behav.,* **1** (1958), 315–339.
24. Lovaas, O. I. "Effects of exposure to symbolic aggression on aggressive behavior." *Child Develpm.,* **32** (1961), 37–44.
25. Lovaas, O. I. "Interaction between verbal and non-verbal behavior." *Child Develpm.,* **32** (1961), 329–336.
26. Lovaas, O. I. "Cue properties of words: The control of operant responding by rate and content of verbal operants." *Child Develpm.,* **35** (1964), 245–256.
27. MacCorquadale K. "Learning." *Ann. Rev. Psychol.,* **6** (1955), 29–61.
28. Marshall, D. A. The effects of withdrawal of a positive reinforcer on an extinguishing response in developmentally retarded children. Unpubl. master's thesis. Univ. Wash., Seattle, 1961.
29. Mowrer, O. H. "On the dual nature of learning: A reinterpretation of 'conditioning' and 'problem-solving'." *Harvard educ. Rev.,* **17** (1947), 102–148.
30. Orlando, R., and S. W. Bijou. "Single and multiple schedules of reinforcement in developmentally retarded children." *J. exp. anal. Behav.,* **3** (1960), 339–348.
31. Orlando, R., S. W. Bijou, R. M. Tyler, and D. A. Marshall. "A laboratory for the experimental analysis of developmentally retarded children." *Psychol. Rep.,* **7** (1960), 261–267.
32. Rheingold, H. L., J. L. Gewirtz, and H. W. Ross. "Social conditioning of vocalization in the infant." *J. comp. physiol. Psychol.,* **52** (1959), 68–73.
33. Schlosberg, H. "The relationship between success and the laws of conditioning." *Psychol. Rev.,* **44** (1937), 379–394.
34. Skinner, B. F. *The Behavior of Organisms.* New York: Appleton-Century-Crofts, 1938.
35. Skinner, B. F. *Science and Human Behavior.* New York: Macmillan, 1953.

2.5 *Orientation*

Observations confirm the emphasis placed upon praise and other evaluative comments by parents as they respond to their children's behavior. The study of social reinforcement has evolved into a major category of research on children's learning. Attention is now directed toward the effects that various social "reinforcements" may have on children's subsequent operant behavior.

Zigler and Kanzer concern themselves with two specific types of social reinforcements, praise and correctness, and develop a rationale which postulates that variations in the effect of such reinforcements are related to children's social status. That is, because of significant differences in the learning histories of children in "lower-" and "middle-class" families, differential response frequencies may appear subsequent to the introduction of different classes of verbal reinforcement.

Several aspects of child study are illustrated by this paper. One is the design of the study itself which is commonly referred to as a "two by two" factorial design. In other words, two factors or variables, social class and reinforcement, are each varied in two ways. Socioeconomic status is varied in terms of middle- and lower-class status, while reinforcement is varied in terms of praise and correctness. This type of design permits an assessment of the *interaction* between the variables social class and type of reinforcement, that is, of the differences in behavior that might be due only to the unique combination of these variables as they operate together to produce an effect (influence behavior). Research designs that examine two or more variables in combination are usually termed *multivariate designs* and will be frequently encountered by students of psychological literature. (See the McCoy paper, Chapter 6, for another example of multivariate design.)

Other advantages of the Zigler and Kanzer study include the use of descriptive, objective criterion behavior (dependent variable) and the extension of the findings of practical import for child workers. Most important, the results of the study accentuate the inappropriateness of the assumption that praise is equally effective for all children. A generalization confirmed by many studies is that the effectiveness of verbal comments administered by adults in response to children's behavior depends upon the personal characteristics of the individual child. One of the earliest of these was the Thompson and Hunnicutt study (1944) listed below.

Readers may find the Rosenhan and Greenwald (1965) study provocative. Essentially a replication of the Zigler and Kanzer study, this research failed to support an interaction between social class and the type of verbal reinforcer. Such conflicting results indicate the need for still more carefully controlled experimentation.

RECOMMENDED READING

Allan, S. "The effects of verbal reinforcement on children's performance as a function of type of task." *J. Exp. Child Psychol.,* **3** (1965), 57–73.

Berkowitz, H., and E. Zigler. "Effects of preliminary positive and negative interaction and delay conditions on children's responsiveness to social reinforcement." *J. pers. soc. Psychol.,* **2** (1965), 500–505.

Rosenhan, D., and J. A. Greenwald. "The effects of age, sex, and socioeconomic class on responsiveness to two classes of verbal reinforcement." *J. Pers.,* **33** (1965), 108–121.

Stevenson, H. W. "Social reinforcement of children's behavior." In *Advances in Child Development,* L. P. Lipsitt, and C. C. Spiker (Eds.) Academic Press, New York, **2,** 1965, pp. 97–126.

Thompson, G. G., and C. W. Hunnicutt. "The effect of praise or blame on the work achievement of 'introverts' and 'extroverts'." *J. educ. Psychol.,* **35** (1944), 257–266.

2.5 The Effectiveness of Two Classes of Verbal Reinforcers on the Performance of Middle- and Lower-class Children

Edward Zigler, YALE UNIVERSITY
Paul Kanzer, UNIVERSITY OF CALIFORNIA, BERKELEY

Considerable evidence has been presented to indicate that verbal reinforcers affect performance. Since such reinforcers are usually dispensed by another person, they are included within the rubric of social reinforcement. Although energy continues to be expended in demonstrating that positive social reinforcers heighten or improve performance while negative social reinforcers attenuate performance, little in the way of a careful analysis of the effectiveness of particular reinforcers within these broad reinforcement categories has been carried out. Armed with the knowledge that social reinforcement affects performance, most investigators have been content to conceptualize any particular positive social reinforcer as the functional equivalent of any other positive social reinforcer. This practice of treating social reinforcers as if they were homogeneous pellets dispensed to equally hungry rats was recently called into question by Zigler.[1]

An expanding body of literature has now shown that the effectiveness of a social reinforcer is related to: the type of social reinforcement previously received (Shallenberger and Zigler, 1961; Stevenson and Snyder, 1960); a previously experienced condition of social isolation or social satiation (Gerwitz and Baer, 1958a, 1958b); long-term social deprivation experienced (Stevenson and Fahel, 1961; Zigler, 1961; Zigler, Hodgden, and Stevenson, 1958); anxiety level of the subject (Walters and Ray, 1960); the particular sex of the *E* in relation to the sex of the *S* (Gewirtz and Baer, 1958a; Stevenson, 1961); and the CA or MA of the *S* (Gewirtz and Baer, 1958a; Stevenson, 1961; Zigler, 1958). Of special interest is the finding that verbal reinforcement is more effective in shaping the performance of middle-class than lower-class children (Douvan, 1956; Zigler, 1962).

[1] In a paper presented at SRCD symposium, March, 1961. (The effect of social reinforcement on normal and socially deprived children.)

Reprinted from *Journal of Personality,* **30** (1962), 157–163. By permission of the authors and the Duke University Press.

All of these studies either have evaluated the effectiveness of a particular social reinforcer in *S*s differing in short- or long-term experiences or have evaluated the effectiveness of a particular verbal reinforcer as compared to some tangible reinforcer, e.g., toys, money. While some headway has been made in scaling the reinforcement value of various tangible reinforcers (Clifford, 1959; Witryol and Fischer, 1960), as noted above little effort has been made to evaluate the effectiveness of various verbal reinforcers. Although one could randomly select some verbal reinforcers and empirically assess their relative efficacy, such a procedure would throw little light on why one such reinforcer was more effective than another. A more parsimonious approach would appear to involve the designation of some classificatory principle whereby meaningful subclasses of verbal reinforcers could be constructed.

Optimally, such a classificatory system should eventuate in specific predictions that reinforcers in one class would be more effective across all *S*s than reinforcers in another class or that reinforcers in one class would be more effective with a particular type of *S* than reinforcers in another class. Several of the studies noted above as well as some work done on child-rearing practices (Davis, 1944; Ericson, 1947) suggest that the degree to which a verbal reinforcer emphasizes correctness may constitute such a useful classificatory dimension. A number of investigators have suggested or reported that "being correct" is more reinforcing for middle- than for lower-class children. This has been attributed to the middle-class emphasis on being right for right's sake alone. Obversely, it has been shown (Zigler *et al.,* 1958) that while verbal reinforcers having primarily a praise connotation lengthen the performance of retarded children generally drawn from the lower socio-economic class, they did not lengthen the performance of middle-class children.

Thus the prediction may be generated that reinforcers emphasizing praise will be more effective with lower-class children, while reinforcers emphasizing correctness will be more effective with middle-class children. The problem remains of how to classify verbal reinforcers on the praise–correct dimension. While every verbal reinforcer conveys both an indication of praise and of correctness, it is possible on *a priori* grounds to designate certain verbal reinforcers as primarily having a praise connotation with others having primarily a correctness connotation. In the present study "right" and "correct" were conceptualized as connoting correctness, while "good" and "fine" were conceptualized as connoting praise.

METHOD

Subjects

The *S*s consisted of a group of 20 middle-class and a group of 20 lower-class children matched on the basis of CA. All the *S*s were obtained from second grade classes of public schools in New Haven, Connecticut, and

Harrison, New York. Warner's Index of Social Characteristics (Warner, Meeker, and Eells, 1949) was used to define socio-economic class membership.

Procedure

The experimental game used was quite similar to the one employed by Gewirtz and Baer (1958a). It was a large wooden box having two holes in the side facing the player into which a marble could be dropped and an opening in the bottom through which the marble returned.

The male *E* brought each *S* into a vacant classroom containing two chairs and a table holding the game. The *S* was informed that he was going to play a fun game called Marble-in-the-Hole. He was told that the game was played by picking the marble out of the chute and putting it into either hole. Each *S* played the game for 10 minutes. The first three minutes was a baseline period during which the verbal reinforcers were not dispensed. Following this period in which the preferred hole was noted, the *E* immediately began reinforcing responses made to the hole preferred least during the last minute of the baseline period. The reinforcement schedule employed and its qualifications were identical to those employed by Gewirtz and Baer (1958a). Generally, after the onset of reinforced play every correct response was reinforced until 10 consecutive correct responses had been made. During the next 10 correct responses a reinforcer was delivered after every second correct response. During the next 15 correct responses a reinforcer was delivered after every third correct response. Finally, a reinforcer was given for every fifth correct response until the game ended.

For half of the *S*s in each group the reinforcers dispensed were "good" and "fine." The remaining *S*s were reinforced with "correct" and "right." Each word was used an equal number of times in each reinforcement condition. Care was taken to dispense each of the reinforcers with an equal amount of enthusiasm. Employing these two conditions of reinforcement four groups were formed: middle-class, praise; middle-class, correct; lower-class, praise; lower-class, correct.

The major dependent variable was the reinforcer effectiveness score devised by Gewirtz and Baer (1958a). For each of the 10 minutes of play the percentage of responses to the hole reinforced following the baseline period was computed. The reinforcer effectiveness score employed was the median percentage during the reinforced period minus the percentage during the third minute of the baseline period.

RESULTS AND DISCUSSION

The mean social-effectiveness score and a description of each group are presented in Table 1. A preliminary analysis revealed that the mean reinforcer effectiveness scores under the combined conditions were reliably greater than zero ($t = 4.79$; $p < .001$). As can be seen in Table 1, the onset of verbal reinforcement resulted in all groups increasing the percentage of responses to the reinforced hole. In order to investigate whether the reinforcer effectiveness score was related to the type of *S* or to the particular class of social reinforcers dispensed, a two-by-two analysis of variance was run. Neither the *F* associated with type of subject ($F = 2.40$; $p < .20$) nor with reinforcement condition ($F < 1$) reached the .05 level of significance. However, the interaction effect was significant ($F = 6.21$; $p < .02$). As can be seen in Table 1, this interaction effect reflects the finding that praise reinforcers are more effective for lower- than for middle-class children, while correct reinforcers are more effective for middle- than for lower-class children.

TABLE 1. Composition by Sex, Mean CA, and Social Effectiveness Scores of the Groups

Group				CA (in yr)		Social Effectiveness Scores	
	N	*Boys*	*Girls*	*Mean*	*Range*	*Mean*	*Range*
Middle-class, praise	10	5	5	7.9	7.4–8.6	35.0	13–60
Middle-class, correct	10	5	5	7.8	7.3–8.3	54.6	4–93
Lower-class, praise	10	4	6	7.7	7.3–8.7	42.6	−1–69
Lower-class, correct	10	4	6	7.5	7.2–8.3	22.0	−1–75

This finding would appear to have both practical and theoretical import. It suggests that in experimental work with children care must be taken to employ verbal reinforcers that are optimal for the particular type of child being investigated. As was found with tangible reinforcers (Brackbill and Jack, 1958), such a procedure should decrease the variance in children's performance beneath that found when some particular verbal reinforcer is arbitrarily employed for all children. The findings of this study also suggest that studies which purport to demonstrate cognitive differences between various types of children (e.g., Kounin, 1941) may actually be demonstrating the differential effectiveness of the reinforcer employed. The present findings also appear to be immediately applicable to the everyday problem of motivating middle- and lower-class children and offer support for the view that being right is more rewarding for the middle- than for the lower-class child.

Why being right is more reinforcing than being praised for middle-class seven-year-olds while the reverse is true for lower-class seven-year-olds is not immediately clear. If being praised and being correct are conceptualized as tertiary reinforcers, the possibility presents itself that among middle-class seven-year-olds being right has been more frequently associated with secondary and primary reinforcers, while in lower-class seven-year-olds being praised is more frequently associated with these reinforcers.

The concept of a developmentally changing reinforcer hierarchy may also be applied to the findings of this study. As has been suggested (Beller, 1955; Gewirtz, 1954; Heathers, 1955) the effectiveness of attention and praise as reinforcers diminishes with maturity being replaced by the reinforcement inherent in the information that one is correct. This latter type of reinforcer appears to serve primarily as a cue for the administration of self reinforcement. This process is central in the child's progress from dependency to independence.

This thinking applied to the present study suggests that the lower-class seven-year-old child is developmentally lower than the seven-year-old middle-class child in that he has not made a transition in which reinforcers signifying correct replace praise reinforcers in the reinforcer hierarchy. Some support for this argument may be found in recent work [2] which indicates that social class transcends economic and social considerations and reflects the global level of development attained. Related to this argument is the suggestion (Davis, 1941, 1943; Terrell, Durkin, and Wiesley, 1959) that the lower-class child is less influenced than the middle-class child by abstract, symbolic rewards. Such would be the case if the lower-class child were indeed developmentally lower than the middle-class child of the same CA. Thus, one would expect not only that correct reinforcers would be less effective than praise reinforcers for the lower-class child, but that all verbal reinforcers, due to their abstract quality, would be less reinforcing for lower- than middle-class children of the same CA. Some support for this, albeit not statistically significant, was found in the tendency ($p < .20$) in the present study for all verbal reinforcers to be more effective for middle- than for lower-class children. Other studies (Terrell *et al.*, 1959; Zigler, 1962) have provided statistically significant evidence that abstract reinforcers are less effective with lower- than with middle-class children. The experimental investigation of these ideas would appear to be a fertile area for further research.

SUMMARY

Two types of verbal reinforcers, those emphasizing praise and those emphasizing correctness, were dispensed to groups of middle- and lower-class children equated on CA. A significant interaction was found between the type of reinforcer used and the social class of the *S*. The praise reinforcers were more reinforcing than the correct reinforcers with lower-class children,

[2] Phillips, L. Studies in social competence. Paper read at Eastern Psychol. Assn., New York, April 1960.

while the correct reinforcers were more effective than the praise reinforcers with middle-class children. The practical and theoretical import of this finding was discussed.

REFERENCES

Beller, E. "Dependency and independence in young children." *J. genet. Psychol.,* 1955, **87,** 25–35.

Brackbill, Y. and D. Jack. "Discrimination learning in children as a function of reinforcement value." *Child Develpm.,* 1958, **29,** 185–190.

Clifford, E. "Ordering of phenomena in a paired comparisons procedure." *Child Develpm.,* 1959, **30,** 38–388.

Davis, A. "American status systems and the socialization of the child." *Amer. sociol. Rev.,* 1941, **6,** 345–354.

Davis, A. Child training and social class. In *Child Behavior and Development,* R. G. Barker, J. S. Kounin, and H. F. Wright (Eds.) New York: McGraw-Hill, 1943.

Davis, A. "Socialization and adolescent personality." *Adolescence, (43d Yearbook, pt 1).* Chicago: National Soc. for Study of Educ., 1944.

Douvan, E. "Social status and success striving." *J. abnorm. soc. Psychol.,* 1956, **52,** 219–223.

Ericson, Martha. Social status and child rearing practices. In *Readings in social psychology,* T. M. Newcomb, and E. L. Hartley (Eds.) New York: Holt, 1947.

Gewirtz, J. "Three determinants of attention seeking in young children." *Monogr. Soc. Res. Child Develpm.,* 1954, **19,** no. 2 (serial no. 59).

Gewirtz, J., and D. Baer. "The effect of brief social deprivation on behaviors for a social reinforcer." *J. abnorm. soc. Psychol.,* 1958, **56,** 49–56 (a).

Gewirtz, J., and D. Baer. "Deprivation and satiation of social reinforcers as drive states." *J. abnorm. soc. Psychol.,* 1958, **57,** 165–172 (b).

Heathers, G. "Emotional dependence and independence in nursery school play." *J. genet. Psychol.,* 1955, **87,** 37–57.

Kounin, J. "Experimental studies of rigidity. I. The measurement of rigidity in normal and feebleminded persons." *Charact. and Pers.,* 1941, **9,** 251–273.

Shallenberger, P., and E. Zigler. "Rigidity, negative reaction tendencies, and cosatiation effects in normal and feebleminded children." *J. abnorm. soc. Psychol.,* 1961, **63,** 20–26.

Stevenson, H. "Social reinforcement with children as a function of CA, sex of *E,* and sex of *S.*" *J. abnorm. soc. Psychol.,* 1961, **63,** 147–154.

Stevenson, H., and L. Fahel. "The effect of social reinforcement on the performance of institutionalized and noninstitutionalized normal and feebleminded children." *J. Pers.,* 1961, **29,** 136–147.

Stevenson, H., and L. Snyder. "Performance as a function of the interaction of incentive conditions." *J. Pers.,* 1960, **28,** 1–11.

Terrell, G., Jr., K. Durkin, and M. Wiesley. "Social class and the nature of the incentive in discrimination learning." *J. abnorm. soc. Psychol.,* 1959, **59,** 270–272.

Walters, R., and E. Ray. "Anxiety, isolation, and reinforcer effectiveness." *J. Pers.*, 1960, **28,** 358–367.

Warner, W., M. Meeker, and K. Eells. *Social class in America.* Chicago: Sci. Res. Associates, 1949.

Witryol, S., and W. Fischer. "Scaling children's incentives by the method of paired comparisons." *Psychol. Rep.*, 1960, **7,** 471–474.

Zigler, E. The effect of pre-institutional social deprivation on the performance of feebleminded children. Unpubl. doctoral dissertation. Univ. Tex., 1958.

Zigler, E. "Social deprivation and rigidity in the performance of feebleminded children." *J. abnorm. soc. Psychol.*, 1961, **62,** 413–421.

Zigler, E. Rigidity in the feebleminded. In *Research Readings on the Exceptional Child,* E. P. Trapp and P. Himelstein (Eds.) New York: Appleton-Century-Crofts, 1962.

Zigler, E., L. Hodgden, and H. Stevenson. "The effect of support on the performance of normal and feebleminded children." *J. Pers.*, 1958, **26,** 106–122.

2.6 Orientation

The study of dependency has received increasing research attention in the past several years. Hartup, who has made an extensive study of dependent behavior, has investigated the complex relationship between motivation and learning. In this study of dependency, Hartup bases his theoretical rationale upon a tension-reduction model of learning behavior.

The tension-reduction model of learning behavior proposes that withdrawing nurturance from a child who has previously experienced nurturance will generate anxiety. Anxiety then serves to intensify a child's dependent behavior (nurturance-seeking). If the satisfactory performance of a learning task is then established as a contingency for regaining adult nurturance, the child becomes motivated to perform such responses as will achieve this goal. In the process the child's anxiety is reduced, thus reinforcing the task-oriented behavior necessary for the re-establishment of the nurturant relationship.

Dependency has generally been conceived as a secondary or learned drive. Sears (1965) suggests that it is a child's dependency that gives rise to identification. The current Sears view is that reward for dependency is the source of reinforcement for children's imitative behavior. Identification and imitation are more fully considered later in this volume. Bandura and Walters (1963) prefer to discuss dependency as a set of responses apart from implying any underlying motive or drive. The reader may wish to consider the distinction between dependency as a response and dependency as a drive from the standpoint of measurement problems. For example, how might one measure a dependency motive?

Hartup's findings are particularly interesting with regard to sex differences. The reader may wish to compare his own interpretation of these differences against that of Hartup. Readers will note a relationship between this study and that executed by Zigler and Kanzer, in that nurturance is a type of social reinforcement frequently utilized to induce learning in young children.

Subsequent research has supported the notion that persistent dependency develops from withholding positive reinforcers, such as nurturance, from children whose past experiences have led them to become highly dependent. Thus, according to Hartup's model of learning behavior, if dependency is dominant in a child's response hierarchy, the probability is high that frustration or anxiety will elicit dependent responses.

RECOMMENDED READING

Baer, D. M. "A technique of social reinforcement for the study of child behavior: Behavior avoiding reinforcement withdrawal." *Child Develpm.*, **33** (1962), 847–858.

Bandura, Albert, and R. H. Walters. *Social Learning and Personality Development.* New York: Holt, Rinehart and Winston, Inc., 1963. (See Dependency, pp. 137–148.)

Sears, Robert R., Lucy Rau, and Richard Alpert. *Identification and Child Rearing.* Palo Alto, Calif.: Stanford Univ. Press, 1965.

2.6 Nurturance and Nurturance-Withdrawal in Relation to the Dependency Behavior of Preschool Children

Willard W. Hartup, UNIVERSITY OF MINNESOTA

This investigation is based on the hypothesis that non-nurturance by an adult is more strongly associated with the occurrence of dependency behavior in young children than is nurturance alone. The naturalistic studies of Sears *et al.* (11), Beller (1), and Smith (12) all contain data which show a positive relationship between amount of parental frustrations (non-

Reprinted from *Child Development,* **29** (1958), 191–202. By permission of the author and The Society for Research in Child Development, Inc.

nurturance) and the frequency of dependency behavior observed in young children. Similar results were obtained in the laboratory studies of Gewirtz (5, 6, 7), although Carl's laboratory findings with respect to this hypothesis were inconclusive (2).

The present study was designed to explore the relationship between one specific form of non-nurturance—the withdrawal of nurturance—and young children's acquisition of responses which elicit adult approval. This relationship was studied in the laboratory where some manipulation of the relevant antecedent conditions was possible.

The method of this study has been to provide a comparison in the learning of simple responses which elicit adult approval between a group of children consistently nurtured by an experimenter and another group who were nurtured and then rebuffed (nurturance-withdrawal). It was predicted that children in the presence of an adult female experimenter who withdraws her nurturance in this fashion will learn simple tasks eliciting adult approval in fewer trials and with fewer errors than children in the presence of an experimenter who has been consistently nurturant. This predicton is based, in part, on those aspects of psychoanalytic theory which suggest that attempts by the child to institute closeness and seek affection are most strongly related to the anxiety generated at times of separation from the mother or when the child has experienced loss of the mother's love (4). It is believed that the withdrawal of nurturance by a female experimenter is similar to certain aspects of the caretaker-child relationship. If so, such behavior by the experimenter should generate certain amounts of anxiety in young children which, in turn, should motivate dependency behavior.

Certain aspects of behavior theory are also relevant to the present prediction. Miller (9) and Mowrer (10) suggest that the capacity of a neutral stimulus to evoke anxiety is strengthened through association with increases in drive or delay in primary reinforcement; presumably it is association such as this which results in children becoming anxious when the mother is absent or non-nurturant. If children in our culture commonly do learn to respond in this way to the non-nurturance of adults, if anxiety does motivate behavior, and if adult nurturance has acquired the capacity to reduce anxiety and thereby reinforce behavior for the young child, the experimental prediction formulated for this investigation can be made.

METHOD

Subjects

Subjects used in this investigation were 34 preschool children—15 boys and 19 girls—in attendance at the Harvard University Preschool during the spring of 1954. The subjects ranged in age from three years, ten months, to five years, six months. The mean age of the children in the sample was four years, seven months; the standard deviation was 4.7 months. The preschool population at the time of the experiment was typical of many laboratory nursery schools in that the children were all from academic, professional, or business homes, and were free from severe emotional disturbances and physical handicaps. Two subgroups were drawn from this sample. These subgroups were counterbalanced with respect to sex of child and dependency ratings made by the preschool teachers on scales of the type used by Beller (1). Two young women served as experimenters. Each experimenter worked with a randomly-assigned half of the subjects in each group.

Procedure

Each child was brought individually to the laboratory room for the experimental session. This room was equipped with one-way mirrors for observation and was furnished with a child's table and chairs, an adult-sized table with comfortable chair, and a large bench. The experimental session proceeded as follows:

1. For a period of five minutes, the experimenter interacted nurturantly with the child while the child played with toys. For purposes of this experiment nurturance consisted of adult behavior which rewarded, encouraged, supported, or showed affection to the child; during this five-minute period the experimenter attempted to maximize these qualities in her behavior toward the child. Children in both experimental groups experienced this period of nurturant interaction with the experimenter.
2. Children in the consistent-nurturance group (hereafter called group C) then immediately experienced a second five-minute period like the first.
3. The second five minutes for the nurturance-withdrawal group (group NW) were marked by the experimenter's behaving non-nurturantly toward the child. She ceased to interact with the child, withdrew from his proximity, and did not reward any of the child's supplications beyond telling him that she was "busy." The experience of children in group NW, having first a period of nurturant interaction, then a period of non-nurturance from the experimenter, has been called "nurturance-withdrawal."
4. Children in both experimental groups were then asked by the experimenter to learn two tasks, the reward for which was the verbal approval of the experimenter. Task I consisted of learning a simple *position* concept in an arrangement of two blue and two red one-inch blocks. The task was presented to the child as a guessing game. The experimenter placed the blocks on the floor first in this order (reading from the child's left): red, red, blue, blue. She then said: "I'm thinking of one of the blocks and I want to see if you can guess which one it is. Point with your finger to the one you think is right and I'll tell you if it's the right one." The child's first guess was always unsuccessful, as was his second. The third guess was always successful. This introductory procedure was followed to eliminate chance successes on the first guess. On each succeeding trial the arrangement of the blocks was changed through all the possible order-permutations. The correct block was

always the block in the same position in the row as the one which the child chose on his third guess. The performance criterion was three consecutive correct trials. Task II consisted of copying from memory a row of adjacent blue, red, and yellow one-inch cubes which were shown to the child for five seconds per trial. Six blocks were arranged in the following order: red, yellow, blue, blue, yellow, red. The performance criterion was one perfect reproduction of the arrangement completed by the child from his own supply of blocks. Measures used in the subsequent analysis of the data were: [1] number of errors to criterion on task I; [2] number of trials to criterion on task I; [3] number of errors to criterion on task II; [4] number of trials to criterion on task II. Error- and trial-scores were correlated .93 on task I, .96 on task II.

Measures of the child's tendency to be dependent on adults were from three sources: [1] observation during the period of nurturant interaction in the laboratory; [2] ratings of the child's dependency on adults made by the preschool teachers; and [3] observations of the child's dependency on adults in preschool made by observers.

Behavior categories used for the laboratory observations were as follows:

1. Asks for verbal help and information
2. Asks for material help
3. Seeks reassurance and rewards
4. Seeks positive attention
5. Seeks to be near
6. Seeks physical contact
7. Seeks negative attention
8. Initiates verbal interaction with experimenter

Frequencies in categories 1 through 7 were summed to yield a measure of dependence on the experimenter. Category 8, "verbal interaction," was used independently in the analysis of data.

The following seven-point scales were used for the teacher ratings of the children's dependence on adults in the preschool situation:

1. Seeks recognition
2. Seeks unnecessary help
3. Seeks necessary help
4. Seeks physical contact and proximity
5. Seeks attention

Each child was rated by two of his teachers (reliability coefficients ranged between .73 and .99). The ratings of the two teachers on each scale were pooled; a summary rating score was then obtained by summing the pooled ratings on all five scales. This summary rating score was used to counter-balance the two subgroups as described above and was also used in analyzing the learning scores.

Behavior categories used for the preschool observations of dependency on the teacher were:

1. Seeks recognition and approval
2. Seeks unnecessary help
3. Seeks necessary help
4. Seeks physical contact
5. Seeks to be near
6. Seeks positive attention
7. Seeks negative attention

Frequencies in the seven categories were summed to yield the preschool observation measure of dependence on the teacher which was used in the statistical analysis.

The intercorrelations among the two laboratory scores, the summary teacher rating, and the preschool observation total score are reported in Table 1.

TABLE 1. Intercorrelations among Four Measures of Dependency ($N = 34$)

	1	2	3	4
1. Verbal interaction with experimenter: laboratory	—			
2. Dependence on experimenter: laboratory	.13	—		
3. Dependence on preschool teacher: teacher rating	.03	.40 [a]	—	
4. Dependence on preschool teacher: observer score	.00	.11	.31	—

[a] Significant beyond .05 level.

The data from the learning tasks were studied by a triple-classification analysis of variance technique for unequal cell-entries (13). The three independent variables in this analysis were [1] sex of child; [2] dependency scores as described above and by which the group was separated into two subgroups—high dependency (all cases above the median on the score being used) and low dependency (all cases below the median); [3] experimental treatment, consistent nurturance versus nurturance-withdrawal. Four analyses of variance were completed for each trial- or error-score from the learning tasks: one for each summary dependency score described above. The results of these analyses are summarized in the tables which follow.

RESULTS

Task I—Number of Trials

Table 2 shows that the F ratio for the experimental variable was significant beyond the .01 level in analysis 1 and beyond the .05 level in analysis 2. The means for groups C and NW are reported in Table 3 along with the t ratio for the difference between means. These data show that NW children (who had experienced nurturance-withdrawal) took fewer trials to complete the task than C children (who had experienced consistent nurturance). Table 2 also shows that in two analyses there was a significant interaction between experimental condition and the sex of child. This interaction may be interpreted to indicate that the effects of nurturance-withdrawal by a female adult are dependent on the sex of the child. The data reported in Table 3 show more clearly the effects of this interaction: nurturance-withdrawal was clearly associated with faster learning of the task for girls, but there was no difference between the means for boys in group C and in group NW.

TABLE 2. *F* RATIOS FROM FOUR ANALYSES OF VARIANCE BASED ON NUMBER OF TRIALS ON TASK I ACCORDING TO SEX OF CHILD, DEPENDENCE, AND EXPERIMENTAL CONDITION

Source	Analysis 1 [a]	Analysis 2 [a]	Analysis 3 [a]	Analysis 4 [a]
	(N = 27)	(N = 33)	(N = 32)	(N = 31)
Sex of Child	16.153 [b]	2.618	3.988	2.953
Dependence	7.163 [c]	.002	.527	6.571 [c]
Experimental Condition	13.859 [d]	4.574 [c]	1.759	1.438
Sex × Dependence	3.053	3.630	.028	.015
Sex × Condition	6.744 [c]	2.098	3.549	6.437
Dependence × Condition	2.224	.792	2.249	1.488
Sex × Dependence × Condition	.215	.570	.005	1.186

[a] The measures of dependence used were: analysis 1, frequency of verbal interaction initiated by child in the laboratory session; analysis 2, frequency of dependence on adults observed in the laboratory session; analysis 3, teachers' ratings of dependence; analysis 4, dependence on preschool teachers as recorded by observers.

[b] Significant beyond .001.

[c] Significant between .05 and .01.

[d] Significant between .01 and .001.

TABLE 3. MEAN NUMBER OF TRIALS ON TASK I FOR BOYS AND GIRLS IN TWO EXPERIMENTAL GROUPS

	Group C	N	Group NW	N	t	p
Boys	15.86	7	16.14	7		n.s.
Girls	35.22	9	16.10	10	2.570	$.02 > p > .01$
Boys and Girls	26.77	16	16.11	17	2.041	$.05 > p > .01$

The F ratio for sex of child was significant in one of the analyses reported in Table 2, and the direction of mean differences showed that boys as a group learned the task in fewer trials than girls. This difference is believed to relate to some feature of the task itself rather than the social conditions of the experiment since the same difference was not found in the data for task II; however, the aspect of task I producing the sex difference was not clear from observation of the children in the experiment. The dependency variable was also significant in two analyses; subgroup means showed that the more dependent children (as measured by verbal interaction) learned task I more quickly than the less dependent children, but that more dependent children (as measured by preschool observation) learned task I less quickly than the less dependent children.

Task I—Number of Errors

Since the error-measure was highly correlated with the trials-measure on task I similar results would be expected and were obtained from the analyses of variance. *F* ratios for the experimental variable were significant in analyses 1 and 2 (Table 4). Again, significant interaction between sex of child and experimental condition was found (in analysis 4, Table 4). Table 5 reports the means for the experimental groups according to sex of child, and once more the results show significant differences between the experimental groups for girls but not for boys.

The *F* ratio for sex of child was significant in one analysis indicating that boys learned the task faster than girls. The dependency variable was significant in two analyses, but mean differences were in the same inconsistent directions as in the analysis of trial-scores on task I.

TABLE 4. F Ratios from Four Analyses of Variance Based on Number of Errors on Task I according to Sex of Child, Dependence, and Experimental Condition

Source	Analysis 1 [a] (N = 27)	Analysis 2 [a] (N = 33)	Analysis 3 [a] (N = 32)	Analysis 4 [a] (N = 31)
Sex of Child	9.421 [b]	1.360	2.581	1.385
Dependence	5.060 [c]	.190	1.050	6.577 [c]
Experimental Condition	10.519 [d]	4.640 [c]	1.232	.924
Sex × Dependence	1.943	4.063	.003	.532
Sex × Condition	4.267	1.560	3.262	6.118 [c]
Dependence × Condition	2.458	1.364	1.610	.772
Sex × Dependence × Condition	.074	1.219	.003	1.414

[a] The measures of dependence used were: analysis 1, frequency of verbal interaction initiated by child in the laboratory session; analysis 2, frequency of dependence on adults observed in the laboratory session; analysis 3, teachers' ratings of dependence; analysis 4, dependence on preschool teachers as recorded by observers.

[b] Significant between .01 and .001.

[c] Significant between .05 and .01.

TABLE 5. Mean Number of Errors on Task I for Boys and Girls in Two Experimental Groups

	Group C	N	Group NW	N	t	p
Boys	18.14	7	18.71	7		n.s.
Girls	39.33	9	17.30	10	2.71	$.02 > p > .01$
Boys and Girls	30.06	16	17.88	17	1.90	$.10 > p > .05$

Task II—Number of Trials

The distribution of scores on this measure significantly departed from normality; hence the results are not reported here.

Task II—Number of Errors

The results for errors on task II were consistent with respect to experimental condition with those found on task I, although at a lesser level of significance. Table 6 shows that one F ratio for the conditions variable was significant beyond the .05 level.

The mean number of errors on task II made by the two experimental groups are reported in Table 7. These data are consistent with those for task I and suggest that faster learning was produced under the nurturance-withdrawal condition than under a condition of uninterrupted nuturance. No significant interaction effects were discovered in the analyses of variance.

TABLE 6. F Ratios from Four Analyses of Variance Based on Number of Errors on Task II according to Sex of Child, Dependence, and Experimental Condition

Source	Analysis 1 [a] (N = 24)	Analysis 2 [a] (N = 29)	Analysis 3 [a] (N = 28)	Analysis 4 [a] (N = 28)
Sex of Child	.169	1.567	.170	.056
Dependence	2.146	.493	5.318 [b]	1.359
Experimental Condition	.501	2.788	4.755 [b]	.521
Sex × Dependence	2.332	1.691	2.667	.314
Sex × Condition	.003	.014	.373	1.682
Dependence × Condition	1.155	.037	.311	.167
Sex × Dependence × Condition	.263	.048	.376	1.983

[a] The measures of dependence used were: analysis 1, frequency of verbal interaction initiated by child in the laboratory session; analysis 2, frequency of dependence on adults observed in the laboratory session; analysis 3, teachers' ratings of dependence; analysis 4, dependence on preschool teachers as recorded by observers.

[b] Significant between .05 and .01.

The F ratios for sex of child were not significant in these analyses; the dependency variable (when measured by teacher ratings) yielded a significant F, and the means suggest that more dependent children learned task II faster than less dependent children.

TABLE 7. Mean Number of Errors on Task II for Boys and Girls in Two Experimental Groups

	Group C	N	Group NW	N	t	p
Boys	12.40	5	6.17	6	1.121	$.30 > p > .20$
Girls	8.33	9	4.44	9	1.420	$.20 > p > .10$
Boys and Girls	9.79	14	5.07	15	1.750	$.10 > p > .05$

DISCUSSION

The findings for girls uniformly support the hypothesis that nurturance-withdrawal is associated with more efficient performance on the learning tasks than consistent nurturance. The results for boys, however, showed that there were no differences between the nurturance-withdrawal and the consistent nurturance groups. Actually, the results for boys were not so clearly negative. When the boys' groups were divided according to the measures of dependence, *highly* dependent boys were found to respond much as the girls while *low* dependent boys responded in the reverse fashion. Thus, highly dependent boys (who may be assumed to be generally anxious concerning their relationships with adults) did learn more efficiently when the experimenter withdrew her nurturance. The boys in the low dependency group who were consistently nurtured learned more efficiently than boys in this group who experienced nurturance-withdrawal. Although the number of cases in these subgroups was small, this trend in the data suggests support for the hypothesis concerning the influence of nurturance-withdrawal for highly dependent boys as well as for the girls.

The fact that the findings for boys were so equivocal is an interesting one for further exploration. It may be that boys respond differently from girls to the nurturance-withdrawal of a *female* experimenter. Psychoanalytic theory regarding Oedipal relationships suggests that the punitiveness of a like-sexed adult should be more threatening to a child than the punitiveness of an opposite-sexed adult. It would be comparatively easy to incorporate sex of experimenter as a variable in a study such as this. However, since the results of this study suggest that nurturance-withdrawal fails to motivate only *low* dependent boys, there may be some sort of complex interaction among experimental conditions which this study failed to bring to light. For example, boys of this age who are not overtly dependent on adults may have moved further than highly dependent boys toward identifying with the male sex role, which in our culture contains certain elements of independence and self-reliance. Boys who *are* highly identified with the male role might well respond with greater anxiety to the mothering nurturance of the experimenter than to the condition in which the experimenter ceases to be attentive and leaves the child alone. If this were the case, most efficient learning would then have taken place in the low dependency boys under conditions of consistent nurturance. The experiment contains no measure of identification by which this interpretation can be checked.

The relationship of sex of child and dependence to speed of learning on the experimental tasks are far from being clear-cut in these data. Boys tended to learn task I faster than girls, but not task II. Dependence, as measured either by verbal interaction in the laboratory session or by teacher ratings, was positively associated with speed of learning; however, dependence as rated by observers in the preschool proved to be negatively associated with speed of learning. The sources of these inconsistencies probably lie in the situational and procedural differences involved in the various measures of dependence; the intercorrelations among the dependency measures suggest that the various measures did *not* measure similar behavioral traits. It does not appear possible, therefore, without further study, to suggest the manner in which motivation to be dependent modifies the effects of nurturance-withdrawal on speed of learning in young children.

The general significance of these findings is felt to be clear and in the direction suggested by the hypothesis tested: nurturance-withdrawal stimulates faster learning than nurturance alone on simple cognitive tasks for girls, and probably also for boys. There may be, however, some second- or third-order interaction between nurturance-withdrawal, sex of child, sex of experimenter, and dependence which influences the behavior of boys under conditions like those of this experiment.

SUMMARY

Thirty-four four-year-old preschool children were divided into two experimental groups equated on the basis of sex and teachers' ratings of dependence on adults in preschool. Individual subjects in one group (C) were consistently nurtured by a female experimenter during a 10-minute period of interaction, after which two simple tasks were learned by the child. The subjects in the second group (NW) experienced nurturant interaction with the experimenter during only five minutes, then experienced five minutes of non-nurturant response from the experimenter, and finally were asked to learn the tasks. The data were treated by an analysis of variance technique in which learning scores were divided according to sex of child, dependency ratings, and experimental condition.

Children in group NW took fewer trials to learn task I than children in group C. Although the group findings were significant, analysis according to sex of child showed that nurturance-withdrawal was most clearly associated with faster learning in girls. Children in group NW made fewer errors in learning both task I and task II, although these findings were most significant for girls.

It is felt that these results support the hypothesis that nurturance-withdrawal supplies greater motivation than consistent nurturance for children's behavior which is designed to gain the reassurance of adults.

REFERENCES

1. Beller, E. K. "Dependency and independence in young children." *J. genet. Psychol.,* 1955, **87,** 25–35.
2. Carl, J. An experimental study of the effect of nurturance on pre-school children. Unpubl. doctoral dissertation. State Univ. of Iowa, 1949.
3. Dollard, J., and N. E. Miller. *Personality and Psychotherapy.* New York: McGraw-Hill, 1950.
4. Freud, S. Three contributions to the theory of sex. In *The Basic Writings of Sigmund Freud.* New York: Random House, 1938.
5. Gewirtz, J. L. Succorance in young children. Unpubl. doctoral disseration. State Univ. Iowa, 1948.
6. Gewirtz, J. L. "Three determinants of attention-seeking in young children." *Monogr. Soc. Res. Child Develpm.,* 1954, **19,** no. 2 (ser. no. 59).
7. Gewirtz, J. L. "Does brief social deprivation enhance the effectiveness of a social reinforcer ('approval')?" *Amer. Psychol.,* 1956, **11,** 428 (abstract).
8. Hartup, W. W. Nurturance and nurturance-withdrawal in relation to the dependency behavior of preschool children. Unpubl. doctoral dissertation. Harvard Univ., 1955.
9. Miller, N. E. "Studies of fear as an acquirable drive. I. Fear as motivation and fear-reduction as reinforcement in the learning of new responses." *J. exp. Psychol.,* 1948, **38,** 89–101.
10. Mowrer, O. H. *Learning Theory and Personality Dynamics.* New York: Ronald, 1950.
11. Sears, R. R., *et al.* "Some child-rearing antecedents of dependency and aggression in young children" *Genet. Psychol. Monogr.,* 1953, **47,** 135–234.
12. Smith, H. T. A comparison of interview and observation measures of mother behavior. Unpubl. doctoral dissertation. Harvard Univ., 1953.
13. Walker, H. M., and J. Lev. *Statistical Inference.* New York: Holt, 1953.

2.7 *Orientation*

The study of aggression has also become a major research activity during the past several decades. Scientific understanding of this construct is important in order to control its unconstructive effects. Foremost among the researchers who have studied aggression is Bandura, the senior author of the following paper, who believes that aggressive responses are learned through the process of imitation.

The authors of the paper reprinted here have taken issue with the widely prevalent interpretation of the origin of aggressive behavior: namely, that aggression is the result of frustration. According to these researchers, the frustration-aggression hypothesis is inadequate to account for all forms of aggression; aggression is only one of several possible reactions to frustration. Bandura, Ross, and Ross have preferred to consider as the aggression model a parent, or perhaps an older sibling, whose behavior the child observes and adopts. The present study was designed to validate this point of view. Although children learn in many ways, learning by imitation is one that has broad implications for parents and teachers alike as they set examples in the process of socialization. It should be stressed that this paper assumes that imitation is learned and is not simply an innate response.

Additional points for readers to consider in this paper include the precision with which the experimental procedure is executed, the sex differences revealed in the findings, and the relationship of imitation to the concept of identification (Chapter 5). Additional issues generated by research on aggression are introduced by Mallick and McCandless in Chapter 5.

RECOMMENDED READING

Bandura, Albert, and Richard H. Walters. "Aggression." In *Child Psychology* (62d Yearbook of the National Society for the Study of Educ.). Chicago: Univ. Chicago Press, 1963, pp. 364–415.

Bandura, A., D. Ross, and S. A. Ross. "Vicarious reinforcement and imitative learning." *J. abnorm. soc. Psychol.,* **67** (1963), 601–607.

Baer, D. M., and J. A. Sherman. "Reinforcement control of generalized imitation in young children." *J. exp. child Psychol.,* **1** (1964), 37–49.

Miller, Neal, and John Dollard. *Social Learning and Imitation.* New Haven, Conn.: Yale Univ. Press, 1941.

7 Transmission of Aggression through Imitation of Aggressive Models

'bert Bandura, STANFORD UNIVERSITY
orothea Ross, STANFORD UNIVERSITY
ieila Ross, STANFORD UNIVERSITY

previous study, designed to account for the phenomenon of identifica-on in terms of incidental learning, demonstrated that children readily nitated behavior exhibited by an adult model in the presence of the model Bandura and Huston, 1961). A series of experiments by Blake (1958) nd others (Grosser, Polansky, and Lippitt, 1951; Rosenblith, 1959; chachter and Hall, 1952) have likewise shown that mere observation of esponses of a model has a facilitating effect on subjects' reactions in the nmediate social influence setting.

While these studies provide convincing evidence for the influence and ontrol exerted on others by the behavior of a model, a more crucial test of nitative learning involves the generalization of imitative response patterns new settings in which the model is absent.

In the experiment reported in this paper children were exposed to ag-ressive and nonaggressive adult models and were then tested for amount f imitative learning in a new situation in the absence of the model. ccording to the prediction, subjects exposed to aggressive models would eproduce aggressive acts resembling those of their models and would iffer in this respect both from subjects who observed nonaggressive models nd from those who had no prior exposure to any models. This hypothesis ssumed that subjects had learned imitative habits as a result of prior einforcement, and these tendencies would generalize to some extent to dult experimenters (Miller and Dollard, 1941).

It was further predicted that observation of subdued nonaggressive nodels would have a generalized inhibiting effect on the subjects' subse-uent behavior, and this effect would be reflected in a difference between he nonaggressive and the control groups, with subjects in the latter group isplaying significantly more aggression.

Hypotheses were also advanced concerning the influence of the sex of nodel and sex of subjects on imitation. Fauls and Smith (1956) have hown that preschool children perceive their parents as having distinct references regarding sex appropriate modes of behavior for their chil-lren. Their findings, as well as informal observation, suggest that parents eward imitation of sex appropriate behavior and discourage or punish sex

Reprinted from *Journal of Abnormal and Social Psychology,* **63** (1961), 575–582. By permission of the authors and the American Psychological Association, Inc.

inappropriate imitative responses, e.g., a male child is unlikely to receive much reward for performing female appropriate activities, such as cooking, or for adopting other aspects of the maternal role, but these same behaviors are typically welcomed if performed by females. As a result of differing reinforcement histories, tendencies to imitate male and female models thus acquire differential habit strength. One would expect, on this basis, subjects to imitate the behavior of a same-sex model to a greater degree than a model of the opposite sex.

Since aggression, however, is a highly masculine-typed behavior, boys should be more predisposed than girls toward imitating aggression, the difference being most marked for subjects exposed to the male aggressive model.

METHOD

Subjects

The subjects were 36 boys and 36 girls enrolled in the Stanford University Nursery School. They ranged in age from 37 to 69 months, with a mean age of 52 months.

Two adults, a male and a female, served in the role of model, and one female experimenter conducted the study for all 72 children.

Experimental Design

Subjects were divided into eight experimental groups of six subjects each and a control group consisting of 24 subjects. Half the experimental subjects were exposed to aggressive models and half were exposed to models that were subdued and nonaggressive in their behavior. These groups were further subdivided into male and female subjects. Half the subjects in the aggressive and nonaggressive conditions observed same-sex models, while the remaining subjects in each group viewed models of the opposite sex. The control group had no prior exposure to the adult models and was tested only in the generalization situation.

It seemed reasonable to expect that the subjects' level of aggressiveness would be positively related to the readiness with which they imitated aggressive modes of behavior. Therefore, in order to increase the precision of treatment comparisons, subjects in the experimental and control groups were matched individually on the basis of ratings of their aggressive behavior in social interactions in the nursery school.

The subjects were rated on four five-point rating scales by the experimenter and a nursery school teacher, both of whom were well acquainted with the children. These scales measured the extent to which subjects displayed physical aggression, verbal aggression, aggression toward inanimate objects, and aggressive inhibition. The latter scale, which dealt with the subjects' tendency to inhibit aggressive reactions in the face of high instigation, provided a measure of aggression anxiety.

Fifty-one subjects were rated independently by both judges so as to permit an assessment of interrater agreement. The reliability of the composite aggression score, estimated by means of the Pearson product-moment correlation, was .89.

The composite score was obtained by summing the ratings on the four aggression scales; on the basis of these scores, subjects were arranged in triplets and assigned at random to one of two treatment conditions or to the control group.

Experimental Conditions

In the first step in the procedure subjects were brought individually by the experimenter to the experimental room and the model who was in the hallway outside the room, was invited by the experimenter to come and join in the game. The experimenter then escorted the subject to one corner of the room, which was structured as the subject's play area. After seating the child at a small table, the experimenter demonstrated how the subject could design pictures with potato prints and picture stickers provided. The potato prints included a variety of geometrical forms; the stickers were attractive multicolor pictures of animals, flowers, and western figures to be pasted on a pastoral scene. These activities were selected since they had been established, by previous studies in the nursery school, as having high interest value for the children.

After having settled the subject in his corner, the experimenter escorted the model to the opposite corner of the room which contained a small table and chair, a tinker toy set, a mallet, and a 5-foot inflated Bobo doll. The experimenter explained that these were the materials provided for the model to play with and, after the model was seated, the experimenter left the experimental room.

With subjects in the *nonaggressive condition,* the model assembled the tinker toys in a quiet subdued manner totally ignoring the Bobo doll.

In contrast, with subjects in the *aggressive condition,* the model began by assembling the tinker toys but after approximately a minute had elapsed, the model turned to the Bobo doll and spent the remainder of the period aggressing toward it.

Imitative learning can be clearly demonstrated if a model performs sufficiently novel patterns of responses which are unlikely to occur independently of the observation of the behavior of a model and if a subject reproduces these behaviors in substantially identical form. For this reason, in addition to punching the Bobo doll, a response that is likely to be performed by children independently of a demonstration, the model exhibited distinctive aggressive acts which were to be scored as imitative responses. The model laid Bobo on its side, sat on it and punched it repeatedly in the nose. The model then raised the Bobo doll, picked up the mallet and struck the doll on the head. Following the mallet aggression, the model tossed the doll up in the air aggressively and kicked it about the room. This sequence of physically aggressive acts was repeated approximately three times, interspersed with verbally aggressive responses such as, "Sock him in the nose . . . ," "Hit him down. . . ," "Throw him in the air. . . ," "Kick him. . . ," "Pow. . . ," and two nonaggressive comments, "He keeps coming back for more" and "He sure is a tough fella."

Thus in the exposure situation, subjects were provided with a diverting task which occupied their attention while at the same time insured observation of the model's behavior in the absence of any instructions to observe or to learn the responses in question. Since subjects could not perform the model's aggressive behavior, any learning that occurred was purely on an observational or covert basis.

At the end of 10 minutes, the experimenter entered the room, informed the subject that he would now go to another game room, and bid the model goodbye.

Aggression Arousal

Subjects were tested for the amount of imitative learning in a different experimental room that was set off from the main nursery school building. The two experimental situations were thus clearly differentiated; in fact, many subjects were under the impression that they were no longer on the nursery school grounds.

Prior to the test for imitation, however, all subjects, experimental and control, were subjected to mild aggression arousal to insure that they were under some degree of instigation to aggression. The arousal experience was included for two main reasons. In the first place, observation of aggressive behavior exhibited by others tends to reduce the probability of aggression on the part of the observer (Rosenbaum and deCharms, 1960). Consequently, subjects in the aggressive condition, in relation both to the nonaggressive and control groups, would be under weaker instigation following exposure to the models. Second, if subjects in the nonaggressive condition expressed little aggression in the face of appropriate instigation, the presence of an inhibitory process would seem to be indicated.

Following the exposure experience, therefore, the experimenter brought the subject to an anteroom that contained these relatively attractive toys: a fire engine, a locomotive, a jet fighter plane, a cable car, a colorful spinning top, and a doll set complete with wardrobe, doll carriage, and baby crib. The experimenter explained that the toys were for the subject to play with but, as soon as the subject became sufficiently involved with the play material (usually in about 2 minutes), the experimenter remarked that these were her very best toys, that she did not let just anyone play with them, and that she had decided to reserve these toys for the other children.

However, the subject could play with any of the toys that were in the next room. The experimenter and the subject then entered the adjoining experimental room.

It was necessary for the experimenter to remain in the room during the experimental session; otherwise a number of the children would either refuse to remain alone or would leave before the termination of the session. However, in order to minimize any influence her presence might have on the subject's behavior, the experimenter remained as inconspicuous as possible by busying herself with paper work at a desk in the far corner of the room and avoiding any interaction with the child.

Test for Delayed Imitation

The experimental room contained a variety of toys including some that could be used in imitative or nonimitative aggression, and others that tended to elicit predominantly nonaggressive forms of behavior. The aggressive toys included a 3-foot Bobo doll, a mallet and peg board, two dart guns, and a tether ball with a face painted on it which hung from the ceiling. The nonaggressive toys, on the other hand, included a tea set, crayons and coloring paper, a ball, two dolls, three bears, cars and trucks, and plastic farm animals.

In order to eliminate any variation in behavior due to mere placement of the toys in the room, the play material was arranged in a fixed order for each of the sessions.

The subject spent 20 minutes in this experimental room during which time his behavior was rated in terms of predetermined response categories by judges who observed the session through a one-way mirror in an adjoining observation room. The 20-minute session was divided into 5-second intervals by means of an electric interval timer, thus yielding a total number of 240 response units for each subject.

The male model scored the experimental sessions for all 72 children. Except for the cases in which he served as model, he did not have knowledge of the subjects' group assignments. In order to provide an estimate of interscorer agreement, the performances of half the subjects were also scored independently by a second observer. Thus one or the other of the two observers usually had no knowledge of the conditions to which the subjects were assigned. Since, however, all but two of the subjects in the aggressive condition performed the models' novel aggressive responses while subjects in the other conditions only rarely exhibited such reactions, subjects who were exposed to the aggressive models could be readily identified through their distinctive behavior.

The responses scored involved highly specific concrete classes of behavior and yielded high interscorer reliabilities, the product-moment coefficients being in the .90s.

Response Measures

Three measures of imitation were obtained:

Imitation of physical aggression: This category included acts of striking the Bobo doll with the mallet, sitting on the doll and punching it in the nose, kicking the doll, and tossing it in the air.

Imitative verbal aggression: Subject repeats the phrases, "Sock him," "Hit him down," "Kick him," "Throw him in the air," or "Pow."

Imitative nonaggressive verbal responses: Subject repeats, "He keeps coming back for more," or "He sure is a tough fella."

During the pretest, a number of the subjects imitated the essential components of the model's behavior but did not perform the complete act, or they directed the imitative aggressive response to some object other than the Bobo doll. Two responses of this type were therefore scored and were interpreted as partially imitative behavior.

Mallet aggression: Subject strikes objects other than the Bobo doll aggressively with the mallet.

Sits on Bobo doll: Subject lays the Bobo doll on its side and sits on it, but does not aggress toward it.

The following additional nonimitative aggressive responses were scored:

Punches Bobo doll: Subject strikes, slaps, or pushes the doll aggressively.

Nonimitative physical and verbal aggression: This category included physically aggressive acts directed toward objects other than the Bobo doll and any hostile remarks except for those in the verbal imitation category; e.g., "Shoot the Bobo," "Cut him," "Stupid ball," "Knock over people," "Horses fighting, biting."

Aggressive gun play: Subject shoots darts or aims the guns and fires imaginary shots at objects in the room.

Ratings were also made of the number of behavior units in which subjects played nonaggressively or sat quietly and did not play with any of the material at all.

RESULTS

Complete Imitation of Models' Behavior

Subjects in the aggression condition reproduced a good deal of physical and verbal aggressive behavior resembling that of the models, and their mean scores differed markedly from those of subjects in the nonaggressive and control groups who exhibited virtually no imitative aggression (see Table 1).

TABLE 1. MEAN AGGRESSION SCORES FOR EXPERIMENTAL AND CONTROL SUBJECTS

Response Category	Experimental Groups				Control Groups
	Aggressive		*Nonaggressive*		
	F model	M model	F model	M model	
Imitative physical aggression					
Female subjects	5.5	7.2	2.5	0.0	1.2
Male subjects	12.4	25.8	0.2	1.5	2.0
Imitative verbal aggression					
Female subjects	13.7	2.0	0.3	0.0	0.7
Male subjects	4.3	12.7	1.1	0.0	1.7
Mallet aggression					
Female subjects	17.2	18.7	0.5	0.5	13.1
Male subjects	15.5	28.8	18.7	6.7	13.5
Punches Bobo doll					
Female subjects	6.3	16.5	5.8	4.3	11.7
Male subjects	18.9	11.9	15.6	14.8	15.7
Nonimitative aggression					
Female subjects	21.3	8.4	7.2	1.4	6.1
Male subjects	16.2	36.7	26.1	22.3	24.6
Aggressive gun play					
Female subjects	1.8	4.5	2.6	2.5	3.7
Male subjects	7.3	15.9	8.9	16.7	14.3

Since there were only a few scores for subjects in the nonaggressive and control conditions (approximately 70% of the subjects had zero scores), and the assumption of homogeneity of variance could not be made, the Friedman two-way analysis of variance by ranks was employed to test the significance of the obtained differences.

The prediction that exposure of subjects to aggressive models increases the probability of aggressive behavior is clearly confirmed (see Table 2). The main effect of treatment conditions is highly significant both for physical and verbal imitative aggression. Comparison of pairs of scores by the sign test shows that the obtained over-all differences were due almost entirely to the aggression displayed by subjects who had been exposed to the aggressive models. Their scores were significantly higher than those of either the nonaggressive or control groups, which did not differ from each other (Table 2).

Imitation was not confined to the model's aggressive responses. Approximately one-third of the subjects in the aggressive condition also repeated the model's nonaggressive verbal responses while none of the subjects in either the nonaggressive or control groups made such remarks. This difference, tested by means of the Cochran *Q* test, was significant well beyond the .001 level (Table 2).

TABLE 2. SIGNIFICANCE OF THE DIFFERENCES BETWEEN EXPERIMENTAL AND CONTROL GROUPS IN THE EXPRESSION OF AGGRESSION

Response Category	x^2r	*Q*	p	Comparison of Pairs of Treatment Conditions		
				Aggressive versus Non-aggressive p	*Aggressive versus Control* p	*Nonaggressive versus Control* p
Imitative responses						
Physical aggression	27.17		<.001	<.001	<.001	.09
Verbal aggression	9.17		<.02	.004	.048	.09
Nonaggressive verbal responses		17.50	<.001	.004	.004	*ns*
Partial imitation						
Mallet aggression	11.06		<.01	.026	*ns*	.005
Sits on Bobo		13.44	<.01	.018	.059	*ns*
Nonimitative aggression						
Punches Bobo doll	2.87		*ns*			
Physical and verbal	8.96		<.02	.026	*ns*	*ns*
Aggressive gun play	2.75		*ns*			

Partial Imitation of Models' Behavior

Differences in the predicted direction were also obtained on the two measures of partial imitation.

Analysis of variance of scores based on the subjects' use of the mallet aggressively toward objects other than the Bobo doll reveals that treatment conditions are a statistically significant source of variation (Table 2). In addition, individual sign tests show that both the aggressive and the control groups, relative to subjects in the nonaggressive condition, produced significantly more mallet aggression, the difference being particularly marked with regard to female subjects. Girls who observed nonaggressive models performed a mean number of 0.5 mallet aggression responses as compared to mean values of 18.0 and 13.1 for girls in the aggressive and control groups, respectively.

Although subjects who observed aggressive models performed more mallet aggression ($M = 20.0$) than their controls ($M = 13.3$), the difference was not statistically significant.

With respect to the partially imitative response of sitting on the Bobo doll, the over-all group differences were significant beyond the .01 level (Table 2). Comparison of pairs of scores by the sign test procedure reveals that subjects in the aggressive group reproduced this aspect of the models' behavior to a greater extent than did the nonaggressive ($p = .018$) or the control ($p = .059$) subjects. The latter two groups, on the other hand, did not differ from each other.

Nonimitative Aggression

Analyses of variance of the remaining aggression measures (Table 2) show that treatment conditions did not influence the extent to which subjects engaged in aggressive gun play or punched the Bobo doll. The effect of conditions is highly significant ($x^2_r = 8.96$, $p < .02$), however, in the case of the subjects' expression of nonimitative physical and verbal aggression. Further comparison of treatment pairs reveals that the main source of the over-all difference was the aggressive and nonaggressive groups which differed significantly from each other (Table 2), with subjects exposed to the aggressive models displaying the greater amount of aggression.

Influence of Sex of Model and Sex of Subjects on Imitation

The hypothesis that boys are more prone than girls to imitate aggression exhibited by a model was only partially confirmed; t tests computed for subjects in the aggressive condition reveal that boys reproduced more imitative physical aggression than girls ($t = 2.50$, $p < .01$). The groups do not differ, however, in their imitation of verbal aggression.

The use of nonparametric tests, necessitated by the extremely skewed distributions of scores for subjects in the nonaggressive and control conditions, preclude an over-all test of the influence of sex of model per se, and of the various interactions between the main effects. Inspection of the means presented in Table 1 for subjects in the aggression condition, however, clearly suggests the possibility of a Sex × Model interaction. This interaction effect is much more consistent and pronounced for the male model than for the female model. Male subjects, for example, exhibited more physical ($t = 2.07$, $p < .05$) and verbal imitative aggression ($t = 2.51$, $p < .05$), more nonimitative aggression ($t = 3.15$, $p < .025$), and engaged in significantly more aggressive gun play ($t = 2.12$, $p < .05$) following exposure to the aggressive male model than the female subjects.

In contrast, girls exposed to the female model performed considerably more imitative verbal aggression and more nonimitative aggression than did the boys (Table 1). The variances, however, were equally large and with only a small N in each cell the mean differences did not reach statistical significance.

Data for the nonaggressive and control subjects provide additional suggestive evidence that the behavior of the male model exerted a greater influence than the female model on the subjects' behavior in the generalization situation.

It will be recalled that, except for the greater amount of mallet aggression exhibited by the control subjects, no significant differences were obtained between the nonaggressive and control groups. The data indicate, however, that the absence of significant differences between these two groups was due primarily to the fact that subjects exposed to the nonaggressive female model did not differ from the controls on any of the measures of aggression. With respect to the male model, on the other hand, the differences between the groups are striking. Comparison of the sets of scores by means of the sign test reveals that, in relation to the control group, subjects exposed to the nonaggressive male model performed significantly less imitative physical aggression ($p = .06$), less imitative verbal aggression ($p = .002$), less mallet aggression ($p = .003$), less nonimitative physical and verbal aggression ($p = .03$), and they were less inclined to punch the Bobo doll ($p = .07$).

While the comparison of subgroups, when some of the over-all tests do not reach statistical significance, is likely to capitalize on chance differences, nevertheless the consistency of the findings adds support to the interpretation in terms of influence by the model.

Nonaggressive Behavior

With the exception of expected sex differences, Lindquist (1956) Type III analyses of variance of the nonaggressive response scores yielded few significant differences.

Female subjects spent more time than boys playing with dolls ($p < .001$), with the tea set ($p < .001$), and coloring ($p < .05$). The boys, on the other hand, devoted significantly more time than the girls to exploratory play with the guns ($p < .01$). No sex differences were found in respect to the subjects' use of the other simulus objects, i.e., farm animals, cars, or tether ball.

Treatment conditions did produce significant differences on two measures of nonaggressive behavior that are worth mentioning. Subjects in the nonaggressive condition engaged in significantly more nonaggressive play with dolls than either subjects in the aggressive group ($t = 2.67$, $p < .02$), or in the control group ($t = 2.57$, $p < .02$).

Even more noteworthy is the finding that subjects who observed nonaggressive models spent more than twice as much time as subjects in aggressive condition ($t = 3.07$, $p < .01$) in simply sitting quietly without handling any of the play material.

DISCUSSION

Much current research on social learning is focused on the shaping of new behavior through rewarding and punishing consequences. Unless responses are emitted, however, they cannot be influenced. The results of this study provide strong evidence that observation of cues produced by the behavior of others is one effective means of eliciting certain forms of responses for which the original probability is very low or zero. Indeed, social imitation may hasten or short-cut the acquisition of new behaviors without the necessity of reinforcing successive approximations as suggested by Skinner (1953).

Thus subjects given an opportunity to observe aggressive models later reproduced a good deal of physical and verbal aggression (as well as nonaggressive responses) substantially identical with that of the model. In contrast, subjects who were exposed to nonaggressive models and those who had no previous exposure to any models only rarely performed such responses.

To the extent that observation of adult models displaying aggression communicates permissiveness for aggressive behavior, such exposure may serve to weaken inhibitory responses and thereby to increase the probability of aggressive reactions to subsequent frustrations. The fact, however, that subjects expressed their aggression in ways that clearly resembled the novel patterns exhibited by the models provides striking evidence for the occurrence of learning by imitation.

In the procedure employed by Miller and Dollard (1941) for establishing imitative behavior, adult or peer models performed discrimination responses following which they were consistently rewarded, and the subjects were similarly reinforced whenever they matched the leaders' choice responses. While these experiments have been widely accepted as demonstrations of learning by means of imitation, in fact, they simply involve a special case of discrimination learning in which the behavior of others serves as discriminative stimuli for responses that are already part of the subject's repertoire. Auditory or visual environmental cues could easily have been substituted for the social stimuli to facilitate the discrimination learning. In contrast, the process of imitation studied in the present experiment differed in several important respects from the one investigated by Miller and Dollard in that subjects learned to combine fractional responses into relatively complex novel patterns solely by observing the performance of social models without any opportunity to perform the models' behavior in the exposure setting, and without any reinforcers delivered either to the models or to the observers.

An adequate theory of the mechanisms underlying imitative learning is lacking. The explanations that have been offered (Logan, Olmsted, Rosner, Schwartz, and Stevens, 1955; Maccoby, 1959) assume that the imitator performs the model's responses covertly. If it can be assumed additionally that rewards and punishments are self-administered in conjunction with the covert responses, the process of imitative learning could be accounted for in terms of the same principles that govern instrumental trial-and-error learning. In the early stages of the developmental process, however, the range of component responses in the organism's repertoire is probably increased through a process of classical conditioning (Bandura and Huston, 1961; Mowrer, 1950).

The data provide some evidence that the male model influenced the subjects' behavior outside the exposure setting to a greater extent than was true for the female model. In the analyses of the Sex × Model interactions, for example, only the comparisons involving the male model yielded significant differences. Similarly, subjects exposed to the nonaggressive male model performed less aggressive behavior than the controls, whereas comparisons involving the female model were consistently nonsignificant.

In a study of learning by imitation, Rosenblith (1959) has likewise found male experimenters more effective than females in influencing childrens' behavior. Rosenblith advanced the tentative explanation that the school setting may involve some social deprivation in respect to adult males which, in turn, enhances the male's reward value.

The trends in the data yielded by the present study suggest an alternative explanation. In the case of a highly masculine-typed behavior such as physical aggression, there is a tendency for both male and female subjects to imitate the male model to a greater degree than the female model. On the other hand, in the case of verbal aggression, which is less clearly sex linked, the greatest amount of imitation occurs in relation to the same-sex model. These trends together with the finding that boys in relation to girls are in general more imitative of physical aggression but do not differ in imitation of verbal aggression, suggest that subjects may be differentially affected by the sex of the model but that predictions must take into account the degree to which the behavior in question is sex-typed.

The preceding discussion has assumed that maleness-femaleness rather than some other personal characteristics of the particular models involved, is the significant variable—an assumption that cannot be tested directly with the data at hand. It was clearly evident, however, particularly from boys' spontaneous remarks about the display of aggression by the female model, that some subjects at least were responding in terms of a sex discrimination and their prior learning about what is sex appropriate behavior (e.g., "Who is that lady? That's not the way for a lady to behave. Ladies are supposed to act like ladies. . . ." "You should have seen what that girl did in there. She was just acting like a man. I never saw a girl act like that before. She was punching and fighting but no swearing."). Aggression by the male model, on the other hand, was more likely to be seen as appropriate and approved by both the boys ("Al's a good socker, he beat up Bobo. I want to sock like Al.") and the girls ("That man is a strong fighter, he punched and punched and he could hit Bobo right down to the floor and if Bobo got up he said, 'Punch your nose.' He's a good fighter like Daddy.").

The finding that subjects exposed to the quiet models were more inhibited and unresponsive than subjects in the aggressive condition, together with the obtained difference on the aggression measures, suggests that exposure to inhibited models not only decreases the probability of occurrence of aggressive behavior but also generally restricts the range of behavior emitted by the subjects.

"Identification with aggressor" (Freud, 1946) or "defensive identification" (Mowrer, 1950), whereby a person presumably transforms himself from object to agent of aggression by adopting the attributes of an aggressive threatening model so as to allay anxiety, is widely accepted as an explanation of the imitative learning of aggression.

The development of aggressive modes of response by children of aggressively punitive adults, however, may simply reflect object displacement without involving any such mechanism of defensive identification. In studies of child training antecedents of aggressively antisocial adolescents (Bandura and Walters, 1959) and of young hyperaggressive boys (Bandura, 1960), the parents were found to be nonpermissive and punitive of aggression directed toward themselves. On the other hand, they actively encouraged and reinforced their sons' aggression toward persons outside the home. This pattern of differential reinforcement of aggressive behavior served to inhibit the boys' aggression toward the original instigators and fostered the displacement of aggression toward objects and situations eliciting much weaker inhibitory responses.

Moreover, the findings from an earlier study (Bandura and Huston, 1961), in which children imitated to an equal degree aggression exhibited by a nurturant and a nonnurturant model, together with the results of the present experiment in which subjects readily imitated aggressive models who were more or less neutral figures suggest that mere observation of aggression, regardless of the quality of the model-subject relationship, is a sufficient condition for producing imitative aggression in children. A comparative study of the subjects' imitation of aggressive models who are feared, who are linked and esteemed, or who are essentially neutral figures would throw some light on whether or not a more parsimonious theory than the one involved in "identification with the aggressor" can explain the modeling process.

SUMMARY

Twenty-four preschool children were assigned to each of three conditions. One experimental group observed aggressive adult models; a second observed inhibited nonaggressive models; while subjects in a control group had no prior exposure to the models. Half the subjects in the experimental conditions observed same-sex models and half viewed models of the opposite sex. Subjects were then tested for the amount of imitative as well as nonimitative aggression performed in a new situation in the absence of the models.

Comparison of the subjects' behavior in the generalization situation revealed that subjects exposed to aggressive models reproduced a good deal of aggression resembling that of the models, and that their mean scores differed markedly from those of subjects in the nonaggressive and control groups. Subjects in the aggressive condition also exhibited significantly more partially imitative and nonimitative aggressive behavior and were generally less inhibited in their behavior than subjects in the nonaggressive condition.

Imitation was found to be differentially influenced by the sex of the model with boys showing more aggression than girls following exposure to the male model, the difference being particularly marked on highly masculine-typed behavior.

Subjects who observed the nonaggressive models, especially the subdued male model, were generally less aggressive than their controls.

The implications of the findings based on this experiment and related studies for the psychoanalytic theory of identification with the aggressor were discussed.

REFERENCES

Bandura, A. *Relationship of family patterns to child behavior disorders.* Progress Report, 1960, Stanford Univ., Project no. M-1734, U.S. Public Health Service.

Bandura, A., and Aletha C. Huston. "Identification as a process of incidental learning." *J. abnorm. soc. Psychol.,* 1961, **63,** 311–318.

Bandura, A., and R. H. Walters. *Adolescent Aggression.* New York: Ronald, 1959.

Blake, R. R. The other person in the situation. In *Person Perception and Interpersonal Behavior,* R. Tagiuri and L. Petrullo (Eds.) Stanford, Calif.: Stanford Univ. Press, 1958, pp. 229–242.

Fauls, Lydia B., and W. D. Smith. "Sex-role learning of five-year olds." *J. genet. Psychol.,* 1956, **89,** 105–117.

Freud, Anna. *The Ego and the Mechanisms of Defense.* New York: International Universities, 1946.

Grosser, D., N. Polansky, and R. A. Lippitt. "A laboratory study of behavior contagion." *Hum. Relat.,* 1951, **4,** 115–142.

Lindquist, E. F. *Design and Analysis of Experiments.* Boston: Houghton Mifflin, 1956.

Logan, F., O. L. Olmsted, B. S. Rosner, R. D. Schwartz III, and C. M. Stevens. *Behavior Theory and Sociol Science.* New Haven: Yale Univ. Press, 1955.

Maccoby, Eleanor E. "Role-taking in childhood and its consequences for social learning." *Child Develpm.,* 1959, **30,** 239–252.

Miller, N. E., and J. Dollard. *Social Learning and Imitation.* New Haven: Yale Univ. Press, 1941.

Mowrer, O. H. (Ed.) Identification: A link between learning theory and psychotherapy. In *Learning Theory and Personality Dynamics.* New York: Ronald, 1950, pp. 69–94.

Rosenbaum, M.E., and R. DeCharms. "Direct and vicarious reduction of hostility." *J. abnorm. soc. Psychol.,* 1960, **60,** 105–111.

Rosenblith, Judy F. "Learning by imitation in kindergarten children." *Child Develpm.,* 1959, **30,** 69–80.

Schachter, S., and R. Hall. "Group-derived restraints and audience persuasion." *Hum. Relat.,* 1952, **5,** 397–406.

Skinner, B. F. *Science and Human Behavior.* New York: Macmillan, 1953.

2.8 *Orientation*

Analyses of adult-child interactions reveal marked variations in the patterns of reward and punishment dispensed by adults. Such variations are in part based upon differences in the beliefs adults hold about the nature of learning and what consequences children should receive as a result of performing, or not performing, desired responses. In some cases these beliefs are derived from valid conceptions regarding the conditions under which children learn. In others the beliefs are oversimplified or invalid. Certainly, psychologists have found the experimental analysis of the effects of reward and punishment more complex than it was originally thought to be. The paper by Hermine Marshall interprets a portion of the literature on children's learning, specifically that concerned with punishment as a feedback condition.

Several features of the Marshall paper merit comment: One is the general conclusion that punishment or negative reinforcement facilitates, rather than impedes, children's learning. Another is the question of what concepts are necessary to explain changes in behavior following punishment. This question gives rise to the formulation of a hypothesis with implications depending upon whether *specific responses* or a *general situation* are involved. A third feature is Marshall's reclassification of the research reviewed according to the *timing* and *effect* of reinforcement. This reclassification strategy is executed to support the central hypothesis of the paper.

Although Marshall's interpretation points to the efficacy of appropriately applied punishments, one might address himself to several questions. For example: What are likely to be the cumulative emotional effects of consistent punishment? If punishment indicates failure and a child is unable to avoid failure, how will this affect his performance rate? Finally, it should be re-emphasized that Marshall discusses punishment providing children with knowledge of the results of their actions, not physical punishment.

RECOMMENDED READING

Lazarus, R. S., J. Deese, and S. F. Osler. "The effects of psychological stress upon performance." *Psychol. Bull.,* **49** (1952), 293–317.

Solomon, R. L. "Punishment." *Amer. Psychologist,* **19** (1964), 239–253.

2.8 The Effect of Punishment on Children: A Review of the Literature and a Suggested Hypothesis

Hermine H. Marshall, CALIFORNIA STATE COLLEGE, HAYWARD

INTRODUCTION

The purpose of this paper is to explore the research on the effect on children of punishment or negative reinforcement. An important distinction must first be made between what has been called "punishment training" and "avoidance training." In punishment training, the subject performs a particular act (R) for which he is subsequently "punished" with a negative reinforcer (S). That is, a particular response is followed by the aversive stimulus (R—S). In contrast, in avoidance training, the aversive stimulus occurs first, causing the subject to perform a particular response (S—R). It is on punishment training that this paper focuses. Those punishment situations that have been utilized in research with children include such negative reinforcers as blame, reproof, failure situations, and the word "wrong," as well as the removal of positive reinforcers: e.g., candy and trinkets.

The importance of research findings on the effects of punishment on children for the fields of child rearing, socialization, and education are ob-

Reprinted from *Journal of Genetic Psychology,* **106** (1965), 23–33. By permission of the author and The Journal Press.

vious. The lasting effects of punishment on personality (particularly regarding the oral, dependency, and aggressive aspects of behavior) have been pointed out by Sears (24); by Sears, Maccoby, and Levin (25); and by Whiting and Child (32). The ineffectiveness (over the long run) of punishment as a manner of handling behavior as compared with nonpunitive techniques has been noted in several field studies: e.g. in Sears *et al.* (25); and in Crandall, Orleans, Preston, and Rabson (6). Whiting and Child (32) and Seward (26) have considered the detrimental effect of severe punishment on the process of identification and on the gaining of parental affection. Although all of these field studies emphasize the harmful effects of punishment—particularly of severe punishment—at least one source (25) is inclined to believe that punishment of *specific* acts has the desired effect. What, then, is the consensus of more controlled studies done in the laboratory or in the classroom? That is the question to which we now turn.

EFFECTIVENESS OF PUNISHMENT

Of those studies comparing [1] the effects of administering punishment—either alone or in combination with a reward—with [2] the effects of no punishment or of reward alone, by far the greatest proportion show the former condition to be superior.

In a classroom setting, Hurlock (14) found that those third-, fifth-, and eighth-grade children who had been either praised or reproved improved significantly more than the control group on a group intelligence test. However, reproof was more effective than praise for the fifth grade, for children of superior intelligence, and for those rated superior by their teachers. Brenner's study (4), which utilized the learning and retention of spelling words at the third-grade level, was also carried out in a classroom situation. Brenner concluded that, in learning and recall, blame was a more powerful incentive than praise, and that blame sustained its influence longer than any other incentive. (Although he found "delayed control" to be the most effective condition, the superiority of that condition over blame and praise cannot be analyzed as the study does not make clear just what was said to the control group.) Potter (22) found that reproved groups improved their performance on an arithmetic reasoning test at the sixth-, ninth-, and twelfth-grade levels, as contrasted with the control groups. But the effect of reproof at the higher grades was slight, and it impaired performance at the third-grade level. Although Potter relates this finding to age differences, a more satisfactory explanation might be in terms of task difficulty, which difficulty was not controlled in this experiment. Because the Otis Arithmetic Reasoning Test was constructed for children age 8 and older, one might hypothesize that this test is too difficult for the third grader and too easy for those in grades nine and 12. Therefore, only at the most appropriate age—grade six—was the effect of reproof significant. This hypothesis regarding the importance of task difficulty might also serve to explain the results of the second part of Potter's study in which the reproved group, at the third- and sixth-grade levels, improved more than the control group in a motor task, but the reverse was true at grade nine. The superiority of blame over praise for general performance in the classroom is supported also by Forlano and Axelrod (11), although they used a cancellation test instead of academic materials.

In studies in which the punishment was administered not toward the situation in general but for specific responses, the results also tend to support the beneficial effect of punishment. Stevenson, Weir, and Zigler (30) found that five-year-olds learned a discrimination problem faster if they were penalized for their errors by having to relinquish a reward object than those who were not penalized. These results are substantiated by Brackbill and O'Hara's study (3) in which those kindergarten boys who were rewarded with candy for each correct response and punished by having to return their candy for each incorrect response learned a discrimination problem more rapidly than those who received the reward alone.

Similarly, in those studies utilizing verbal punishment, combinations that included stating the word "wrong" after each incorrect response—whether correct responses were rewarded with "right" or not—led to faster learning than those in which the incorrect response was not thus negatively reinforced (7, 16, 17, 18). Combinations including the word "wrong" were also superior to a condition in which a buzzer followed correct responses and nothing followed incorrect responses (17, 18). In the learning series, no significant difference was found between those groups in which each response was followed appropriately with either "right" or "wrong" and those groups in which only incorrect responses were termed "wrong" and nothing followed correct responses. However, when an extinction series was carried out (17, 18), the nothing-"wrong" group showed little decrement in performance. The explanation that "wrong" is a stronger negative reinforcer than "right" is a positive reinforcer was suggested. However, "nothing" paired with "wrong" acquires the value of a positive reinforcer; and because, in extinction, nothing is said after either a correct or an incorrect response, nothing continues to reinforce positively. This acquired reinforcing value of the "nothing" side of the condition may account satisfactorily for the superiority of the nothing-"wrong" combination over the "right"-"wrong" combination during extinction—without hypothesizing a difference in strength between the reinforcing values of "right" and "wrong."

Although Penney and Lupton's results (19) are in general agreement with the preceding studies concerning the effectiveness of punishment alone and conditions including punishment over reward alone, Penney and Lupton's study with grade-school children showed that the groups who were punished with an intense tone and received no reward learned a discrimination problem faster than those who received a candy reward in addition to the punishing tone. They account for the superiority of the punishment-only group in terms of possible additional frustration received by the punishment-only groups. They hypothesize the source of this frustration to be the unfulfilled expectation of receiving candy, after having seen their peers return with candy. They hypothesize that this frustration increased the motivation level in this group and thereby caused them to perform better.

Using a very small number of six-year-olds, Baer (2) found that the withdrawal of a positive reinforcer (movie) as a punishment led to more rapid extinction and to less spontaneous recovery in the use of a toy "peanut machine" than in the control group the members of which did not receive the punishment. The punished subjects also play more with toys other than the peanut machine than did the control group. Although caution needs to be exercised in applying these findings (due to the small number) they are in the predicted direction.

Despite the large amount of research that shows the superior effect of negative reinforcement, there are a number of studies the results of which are not in complete agreement. Anderson (1) found that performance with a hand dynomometer showed a precipitate drop under failure conditions. In this experiment, "failure" was manipulated by *E* so that each attempt in the series, no matter how successful, was described to the subject as a failure. Hence, these results may not be directly comparable to those in which only incorrect responses were negatively reinforced or with those experiments in which general performance was reproved after the completion of the task and the effect of the reproof was subsequently measured.

Terrell and Kennedy (31) found that those children rewarded with candy learned a discrimination task significantly more rapidly than those punished by reproof. In this experiment, the other conditions in rank order of effectiveness, though at a nonsignificant level, were praise, token to be exchanged for candy, reproof, and control. However, each group (including the control group) was reinforced by a light flash following correct responses. Thus, the candy, praise, and token groups received two sources of positive reinforcement; the reproof group received only one positive reinforcement and one negative reinforcement; and the control group received only one positive reinforcement. The discrepancy between these results and those previously reported might be accounted for by this additional source of reward in all groups but the control group. The double positive reinforcement may have caused better performance. Comparison of the reproved group with the control group, which group received only one source of positive reinforcement, reveals that the reproved group was superior to the control.

The studies by Hurlock (14), by Potter (22), and by Meyer and Seidman (17) did not uniformly support the superior effects of punishment conditions. Hurlock found that eighth graders, children with inferior intellectual ability (*IQ* below 90), and rated average or inferior by their teachers did better following praise than following blame. However, the impaired performance following reproof at the third-grade level (indicated by Potter) has already been noted and explained on the basis of uncontrolled task difficulty. Also, Meyer and Seidman's finding (17) that preschool children performed better under conditions of both "right"-"wrong" and of a buzzer for correct responses and nothing for incorrect responses was not substantiated by their later study (18) and was accounted for by the higher achievement motivation of the children in the former study compared with a more representative sample in the latter.

Thus, the discrepancies in all of the studies that do not completely support the superiority of the effects of punishment (except Hurlock's), can be accounted for, so that basic substantiation of the beneficial effect of negative reinforcement remains. A hypothesis regarding Hurlock's results will be elaborated later.

RELATION OF PUNISHMENT TO OTHER FACTORS

A number of experiments have been concerned not only with the effectiveness of punishment itself, but also with the way other variables contribute to the effect of negative reinforcement. Meyer and Offenbach's study (16) investigated the effect of task complexity by controlling the relevant and irrelevant dimensions in a discrimination problem. Their results, noted earlier, showed that combinations including "wrong" were superior to reward alone for tasks involving at least two irrelevant dimensions. There was no significant difference for tasks involving just one irrelevant dimension. As Postman (20) noted, in most experiments there is only one correct response but several incorrect responses. Therefore, the subject has to learn positively only one item while eliminating several incorrect ones from a rather homogeneous series. When each of the incorrect responses is negatively reinforced, one might expect performance to be better. Meyer and Offenbach's results tend to lend support to this writer's hypothesis accounting for the discrepancy in Potter's results (22) in terms of uncontrolled task difficulty.

Stephens (27, 28) hypothesized that symbolic reward would strengthen weak connections more than symbolic punishment would weaken them, but that symbolic punishment would weaken strong connections more than symbolic reward would strengthen them. Investigations by Stephens and his associates (28, 29) on high-school students confirmed this hypothesis. In addition, it was found that a delay in reinforcement increased the influence of "wrong" on strong connections, but had little effect on weak ones (29). Because the amount of time for review was controlled, they explained that this condition (and that of weak but right) was the only one susceptible to such enhancement. Brenner's investigation (4) of the effect of the delay of reinforcement showed immediate blame and delayed blame to be equally effective with spelling words—when presumably there was no appreciable difference in strength of connections.

Stephens and Baer also showed that wrong associations were avoided more for the group receiving specific instructions regarding the importance of avoiding wrong associations on the retest than the noninstructed group.

The experiment by Stevenson *et al.* (30) investigated the effect of pre-experimental satiation on punishment, by varying the number of reward objects given before the experiment. They found that the amount of pre-experimental satiation made a significant difference in the effectiveness of the penalty of relinquishing reward objects.

Forlano and Axelrod (11) studied the influence of a personality variable on the effectiveness of blame. Using the extraversion inventory from Pintner's Personality Test, they found that introverts who were blamed increased their performance more than the introverts in the control group after both the first and second applications; whereas extroverts increased their performance only after the second time they were blamed.

An elaborate experiment by Schmidt (23) investigated the influence of praise and blame on junior-high and high-school students in a code-substitution test. His results showed that praise was more effective for one tester (a male), and that blame was a better incentive when used by the other tester (a female graduate student); thus pointing to the importance of the experimenter as a variable.

A related conclusion was reached by Kipnis (15) who had a group leader manipulate the atmosphere. In an attempt to induce fifth and sixth graders to change their preferred comic heroes, he found that under the threat of punishment (removal of a promised movie pass) more subjects accepted the leader's influence attempt in the groups to whom the leader lectured; whereas the groups—also under threat of punishment—which participated with the leader in a discussion resisted the attempt and were unwilling to change their standards. Under both participation and lecture leadership, the subjects held a lower affective evaluation of the leader if they had been threatened by punishment than if they had been promised only the reward.

A final dimension investigated is the generalization of preference following negative reinforcement. Starting with N. E. Miller's assumption that the avoidance gradient is steeper than the approach gradient, Gewirtz (12) had first and second graders learn formboard puzzles arranged along a dimension of shape similarity. However, this hypothesis was confirmed only for the group negatively reinforced by failure, reproof, and the withholding of a prize. In accounting for the partial substantiation, she notes that a considerable number of subjects in the positively reinforced group were unaffected by the experimental conditions of success, approval from the experimenter, and a material reward. She attributes this result to the high-achievement motivation of the sample. The negatively reinforced subjects were equally achievement oriented. Nevertheless, Gewirtz suggests that the external motivation from negatively reinforcing conditions was sufficiently more powerful than the positively reinforcing conditions to overshadow the internal achievement motivation, so that the results for this group reveal the effects of this experimental condition. The influence of something akin to achievement motivation or intellectual level has also been noted in the results of the studies by Hurlock (14) and by Meyer and Seidman (17).

That so few studies into the effects of punishment on children have considered and controlled for these additional variables: e.g., task difficulty, achievement orientation, and personality factors is a striking fact. In addition, no experiments considered the relation of ego involvement and level of aspiration. All of these factors might be taken into account to explain variations in experimental results.

LEARNING THEORIES AND EXPLANATIONS OF PUNISHMENT

The research reported in the literature seems to support the contention that punishment or negative reinforcement helps rather than hinders learning in children and that there are a number of other variables related to its effectiveness. We turn now to the question of whether learning theories predict this conclusion and to the explanations that are postulated to explain the conclusion.

Although Thorndike revised his Law of Effect so that it stated that punishment only indirectly weakened S-R connections, Skinner and Estes found that punishment had a temporary or depressing effect upon learning in animals [see (13)]. Baer's conclusion (2) that punishment reduced the number of responses in extinction tends to bear out this effect with children. An important point here, however, is that the punished children played more with other toys. In other words, while punishment reduced the number of nonreinforced responses, it also caused the subjects to shift their activity to something else. It led to more varied behavior. This follows from Thorndike's revised law. As Postman (21) points out, the educative value of this variability of behavior depends upon what the "something else" is that the subjects do.

The main theoretical issue seems to center on this change in behavior: on the question of whether punishment serves as a motivator—instigating and arousing the subject to action—or whether this motivational concept is superfluous and the change in behavior can be explained by referring simply to the cue or to the informative value of the negative reinforcement, or whether both concepts are necessary.

According to Postman (21), Hull regards a punishing state of affairs as an instigator of behavior and the cessation of punishment as reinforcing. Guthrie sees punishment as facilitating learning because it arouses the subject to varied action and provides a multiplicity of cues—thereby utilizing both concepts. Likewise, Tolman includes [1] a "Law of emphasis"—the perceptual impact of cues, [2] a "Law of motivation" to maximize rewards and minimize punishment, and [3] a "Law of disruption." Brown (5) assumes that punishment produces frustration and that this frustration increases drive or motivation. On the other hand, from his work with animals, Dinsmoor (8, 9) criticizes recourse to "acquired drive" in explaining punishment, but accounts for the effect of punishment through the conditioning of discriminative stimuli so that the stimuli that precede the punished response acquire an aversive power and function as would a "warning signal" in avoidance training. Regarding the effect of punishment in terms of discriminative stimuli may be considered analogous to the cue or informative function referred to by Guthrie and Tolman. Farber (10) emphasizes the importance of distinguishing between what he calls the "purely motivational (D) effects" of negative reinforcement and the informative aspects, in addition to its distracting aspects. He also notes that if the negatively reinforcing instructions are applied to performance in general, rather than to specific responses, there is likely to be a decrement in performance.

HYPOTHESIS

By carrying this reasoning further, one might hypothesize that negative reinforcement of *specific* responses has discriminative or informative and therefore beneficial value; whereas negative reinforcement applied to the situation in general may have a motivational function. Whether the increased motivation leads the subject to be more aware of appropriate cues or whether its effect is disruptive may depend on other factors in the situation: e.g., strength of negative reinforcement, task difficulty, achievement orientation. According to this hypothesis, one might predict that reinforcing each response would be informative and hence more beneficial. On the other hand, if negative reinforcement after a series or after the situation serves as a motivator, its beneficial or detrimental effects would be likely to depend on other factors in the situation. For example, the Yerkes-Dodson Law might apply here, so that as motivation increases, subjects would be expected to perform better on simpler tasks. Thus, one might expect less consistent results from experiments where negative reinforcement, administered after the situation, acts as a motivator.

Table 1 classifies the studies reviewed as to [1] whether the punishment was administered after each response or after the situation and [2] whether the punishment improves performance. Of those experiments in which each response was reinforced, only two do not completely support the hypothesis. However, as has been noted, Meyer and Seidman's later study (18) did not substantiate the effectiveness of the buzzer-nothing combination over a combination including the word "wrong." And the discrepant results of the Terrell and Kennedy study have been explained to be the outcome of a double source of positive reinforcement. When negative reinforcement is compared with one source of positive reinforcement, the hypothesis is supported.

TABLE 1. Classification of Studies to Time and Effect of Reinforcement

Reinforcement after Each R	Reinforcement after Situation
Punishment Beneficial	
Stephens and Baer (29)	Hurlock (14)
Brackbill and O'Hara (3)	Brenner (4)
Stevenson *et al.* (30)	Anderson (1)
Curry (7)	Forlano and Axelrod (11)
Meyer and Seidman (17)	Schmidt (23)
Meyer and Seidman (18)	Potter (22)
Penney and Lupton (19)	
Meyer and Offenbach (16)	
Punishment Detrimental	
Terrell and Kennedy (31)	Hurlock (14)
Meyer and Seidman (17)	Brenner (4)
	Anderson (1)
	Schmidt (23)
	Potter (22)

Examination of those experiments in which negative reinforcement was given after the series (or after the situation) indicates that five of the six studies carried out under this condition are listed as evidencing both the helping and the hindering effect of punishment. Hurlock's divergent results fall into this category and are related to grade level, intellectual level, and teacher ratings. Anderson found that a change from success to failure conditions as well as a change from failure to success conditions served to increase performance, but that continued failure led to a drop in performance. Schmidt indicates that whether blame had a beneficial or detrimental effect depended upon the experimenter. Potter's results were related to task difficulty. Brenner showed immediate and delayed blame (though both occurred after the test) to be superior to other conditions except for "delayed control." It was noted that the latter condition was not explained sufficiently to warrant comment. Forlano and Axelrod indicated that blame was even more effective for introverts than for extroverts.

In general, the hypothesis that negative reinforcement of specific responses has an informative and therefore beneficial effect, whereas the effect of negatively reinforcing the situation depends upon the action of other factors, appears to have been supported by the available research. This conclusion is in agreement with the belief expressed by Sears *et al.* (25) regarding the desired effect of parental punishment of specific acts as opposed to the negating effect of general parental "punitiveness."

SUMMARY

A review of the research on the effect of punishment on children reveals that, in general, negative reinforcement tends to improve performance.

Other factors found to influence the effect of punishment include intellectual and achievement level, task complexity, strength of association, delay of reinforcement, pre-experimental satiation, instructions, subjects' personality, experimenter, and atmosphere. The possible effect of ego involvement and level of aspiration have not been considered in the experimental literature.

Suggested and supported by the available research is the hypothesis that negative reinforcement of specific responses has an informative and therefore beneficial effect, while the effect of negatively reinforcing the situation depends upon the action of other factors in the situation.

REFERENCES

1. Anderson, H. H. "Motivation of young children: Further studies in success and failure, praise and blame." *Child Develpm.,* **7** (1936), 125–143.
2. Baer, D. M. "Effect of withdrawal of positive reinforcement on an extinguishing response in young children." *Child Develpm.,* **32** (1961), 67–74.
3. Brackbill, Y., and J. O'Hara. "The relative effectiveness of reward and punishment for discrimination learning in children." *J. comp. physiol. Psychol.,* **51** (1958), 747–751.
4. Brenner, B. "Effect of immediate and delayed praise and blame upon learning and recall." *Teachers Coll. Contrib. Educ.,* 1934 (no. 620).
5. Brown, J. S. *Motivation of Behavior.* New York: McGraw-Hill, 1961.
6. Crandall, V. J., S. Orleans, A. Preston, and A. Rabson. "The development of social compliance in young children." *Child Develpm.,* **29** (1958), 429–443.
7. Curry, C. "Supplementary report: The effect of verbal reinforcement combinations on learning in children." *J. exp. Psychol.,* **59** (1960), 434.
8. Dinsmoor, J. A. "Punishment: I. The avoidance hypothesis." *Psychol. Rev.,* **62** (1955), 96–105.
9. Dinsmoor, J. A. "Punishment: II. An interpretation of empirical findings." *Psychol. Rev.,* **62** (1955), 96–105.
10. Farber, J. E. "The role of motivation in verbal learning and performance." *Psychol. Bull.,* **52** (1955), 311–327.

11. Forlano, G., and H. C. Axelrod. "The effect of repeated praise or blame on the performance of introverts and extroverts." *J. educ. Psychol.,* **28** (1937), 92–100.
12. Gewirtz, H. B. "Generalization of children's preferences as a function of reinforcement and task similarity." *J. abnorm. soc. Psychol.,* **58** (1959), 111–118.
13. Hilgard, E. R. *Theories of Learning.* (2d ed.) New York: Appleton, 1956.
14. Hurlock, E. B. "The value of praise and reproof as incentives for children". *Arch. Psychol. N. Y.,* **11** (1924), no. 71.
15. Kipnis, D. "The effects of leadership style and leadership power upon the inducement of an attitude change." *J. abnorm. soc. Psychol.,* **57** (1958), 173–180.
16. Meyer, W. J., and S. I. Offenbach. "Effectiveness of reward and punishment as a function of task complexity." *J. comp. physiol. Psychol.,* **57** (1962), 532–534.
17. Meyer, W. J., and S. B. Seidman. "Age differences in the effectiveness of different reinforcement combinations on the acquisition and extinction of a simple concept learning problem." *Child Develpm.,* **31** (1961), 419–429.
18. Meyer, W. J., and S. B. Seidman. "Relative effectiveness of different reinforcement combinations on concept learning of children at two developmental levels." *Child Develpm.,* **32** (1961), 117–127.
19. Penney, R. K., and A. A. Lupton. "Children's discrimination learning as a function of reward and punishment." *J. comp. physiol. Psychol.,* **54** (1961), 449–451.
20. Postman, L. "The history and present status of the law of effect." *Psychol. Bull.,* **44** (1947), 489–563.
21. Postman, L. (Ed.) Rewards and punishments in human learning. In *Psychology in the Making.* New York: Knopf, 1962.
22. Potter, E. H. "The effect of reproof in relation to age in school children." *J. genet. Psychol.,* **63** (1943), 247–258.
23. Schmidt, H. O. "The effects of praise and blame as incentives to learning." *Psychol. Monogr.,* **53** (1941), (whole no. 240).
24. Sears, R. R. "Relation of fantasy aggression to interpersonal aggression." *Child Develpm.,* **21** (1950), 3–4.
25. Sears, R., E. E. Maccoby, and H. Levin. *Patterns of Child Rearing.* Evanston, Ill.: Row, Peterson, 1957.
26. Seward, J. P. "Learning theory and identifications: II. The role of punishment." *J. genet. Psychol.,* **84** (1954), 201–210.
27. Stephens, J. M. "Further notes on punishment and reward." *J. genet. Psychol.,* **44** (1934), 464–472.
28. Stephens, J. M. "The influence of symbolic punishment and reward upon weak associations." *J. genet. Psychol.,* **25** (1944), 177–185.
29. Stephens, J. M., and J. A. Baer. "Factors influencing the efficacy of punishment and reward: The opportunity for immediate review and specific instructions regarding the expected role of punishment." *J. genet. Psychol.,* **65** (1944), 53–66.
30. Stevenson, H. W., M. W. Weir, and E. F. Zigler. "Discrimination learning in

children as a function of motive-incentive conditions." *Psychol. Rep.*, 5 (1959), 95–978.

31. Terrell, G., Jr., and W. A. Kennedy. "The discrimination learning and transposition in children as a function of the nature of the reward." *J. exp. Psychol.*, **53** (1957), 257–260.
32. Whiting, J. W. M., and I. L. Child. *Child Training and Personality: A Cross-Cultural Study*. New Haven, Conn.: Yale Univ. Press, 1953.

chapter three

Special Factors in Learning: Expectancies and the Self Concept

3.1 *Orientation*

An increasing amount of research has been directed toward establishing a nomothetic network for the construct labeled *locus of control.* This construct involves the degree to which an individual perceives the consequences of his actions to be a direct function of his own behavior rather than the result of fate or chance circumstances. A person who perceives a direct relationship between his actions and the consequences of his actions perceives reinforcements as being under his personal control. It is important to note that this is a *generalized expectancy* variable in contrast to a motivational variable; however it obviously carries implications for the motivation of behavior. In a recent review of research, Rotter (1966) has pointed to the importance of locus of control for understanding the nature of learning, individual differences in expectancies, the perception of causality, and the acceptance of personal responsibility for one's actions.

The kinds of research problems and issues encountered by psychologists interested in locus of control are essentially the same as those encountered by scientists studying other human characteristics. For example, there is the *measurement* question: How can locus of control be measured? What antecedents are most clearly associated with the development of this characteristic? What are the *behavioral cor-*

relates of this characteristic? The Battle and Rotter study which follows is concerned with these questions, but especially with social-class and ethnic correlates of locus of control. A related study, concerned specifically with children's beliefs about the source of reinforcements for intellectual achievement, follows in this chapter.

RECOMMENDED READING

Lefcourt, Herbert M. "Internal versus external control of reinforcement: A review." *Psychol. Bull.,* **65** (1966), 206–220.

Rotter, Julian B. "Generalized expectancies for internal versus external control of reinforcement." *Psychol. Monogr.* (1966), **80** (I), no. 609, 28 pp.

3.1 Children's Feelings of Personal Control as Related to Social Class and Ethnic Group [1]

Esther S. Battle, FELS RESEARCH INSTITUTE
Julian B. Rotter, UNIVERSITY OF CONNECTICUT

Social class and ethnic group membership are generally accepted as important determinants of personality. This study is devoted to an exploration of the interaction of class and ethnic group with one personality variable: "internal versus external" control of reinforcements.

This construct distributes individuals according to the degree to which they accept personal responsibility for what happens to them, in contrast to the attribution of responsibility to forces outside their control. The external forces might be those of chance, fate, an inability to understand the world, or the influence of other, powerful people. In social learning theory (Rotter, 1954), this construct is considered to describe a generalized expectancy, operating across a large number of situations, which relates to whether or not the individual possesses or lacks power (or personal determination) over what happens to him.

The sense of "powerlessness" has been discussed by Seeman (1959) as one meaning of the sociological variable of "alienation." It is thought to relate to the individual's social circumstances (class and ethnic group status)

[1] This research was supported in part by the United States Air Force under contract No. AF 49 (638)–741, monitored by the Air Force Office of Scientific Research, Office of Aerospace Research.

Reprinted from *Journal of Personality,* **31** (1963), 482–490. By permission of the authors and the Duke University Press.

as well as affecting his social learning. An individual who is thus alienated would hold the expectation that his own behavior cannot determine the outcomes he desires. There is some empirical evidence to support this interpretation. Seeman and Evans (1962) used a form of the forced-choice, adult scale of internal-external control (I-E Scale) developed by Liverant, Rotter, Crowne, and Seeman (Gore and Rotter, 1963), to study the behavior of patients in a tuberculosis hospital. Although the I-E scale makes no reference to disease, they found statistical support for their hypotheses that patients scoring as "internals" would know more about their own condition, would be better informed about T.B. in general, and would be regarded by ward personnel as "better" patients.

In another study, Seeman (1963) studied the effect of such alienation on the learning of prison inmates. He found that the alienated inmate (externally controlled) learned significantly less material relevant to release than those less alienated. It was in the realm of long-range planning and control that the variable was predictive.

The related attitude of "mastery" was discussed by Strodtbeck (1958) as it is affected by religious, national, and social-class orientations perpetuated within the family. He found that Jewish middle- and upper-class *S*s were differentiated from lower-class Italians on the basis of this variable. Most of the variance was attributable to factors of social class. Graves and Jessor adapted the I-E Scale for high school students (Graves, 1961) and studied ethnic differences in an isolated tri-ethnic community. They found whites to be most internal, followed by Spanish Americans. Indians were most external in attitudes. These findings were consistent with their predictions. Although economic factors undoubtedly contributed to differences, Graves felt that "ethnicity" was an important source of variance after other factors were controlled.

The effect of this personality characteristic has been studied by Phares (1957) and James (1957), who were instrumental in the development of the first I-E scales. The latest form of the adult scale has recently been related to the prediction of the type and degree of commitment behavior manifested by Southern Negro students to effect social change in the cause of desegregation (Gore and Rotter, 1963). Crowne and Liverant (1963) showed a relationship between conformity under conditions of high personal involvement and scores on this same scale.

Other approaches to the assessment of this attitude with children have been developed by Crandall, Katkovsky, and Preston (1962), relative to achievement situations, and by Bialer (1961). Bialer's *Locus of Control* questionnaire was developed from the James-Phares (James, 1957) adult scale of internal-external control. Bialer was interested in the developmental aspects of this attitude as well as its relation to the conceptualization of success and failure. He found the more mature child to be more internally controlled and to show greater response to success and failure cues. The Bialer questionnaire was used in the present study.

James (1957) studied the effect of this variable on behavior in angle and line-matching tasks. He demonstrated that externals had more "unusual shifts" in their expectancy for success. That is, they were more likely to expect future success when they had just failed and more likely to expect failure after succeeding. He also found the internals to have a greater increment in expectation for success in a 75 per cent reinforced sequence, substantiating the hypothesis that when one believes he is in control of what happens, positive reinforcement leads to an increasing certainty for future success.

Phares (1957, 1962), James and Rotter (1958), James (1957), Rotter, Liverant, Crowne (1961), Holden and Rotter (1962), and others have shown that the growth and extinction of expectancies for reward vary predictively under different experimental conditions if the tasks are perceived by *S* as chance, luck, or *E*-controlled, rather than as a matter of personal skill.

The present study involves the development of a projective test of the internal-external control attitude to be used with children; the establishment of the relationship between I-E and several sociological and demographic variables (age, sex, class, ethnic group, and IQ); and the replication of some previous findings with adult I-E scales in a performance task.

The behavioral task was an adaptation of James's line-matching task (James, 1957), which allows *E* to control success and failure without *S*'s knowledge. The child is required to match a series of lines which vary in length. Before each trial, he states his expectancy for success on an eleven-point scale. Following a ten-trial training sequence (with a 50 per cent reinforcement schedule), his responses to continuous failure are examined over the 30 extinction trials. This task yields three measures which reflect the effect of the experimental variables: [1] *S*s mean expectancy for success over the ten training trials; [2] the number of "unusual shifts" in expectancy during training (raised expectation for success after failing or lowered expectancy after succeeding); and [3] the number of trials to extinction (two successive trials at zero or one expectancy on a scale of zero to ten.)

The projective task was a "Children's Picture Test of Internal-External Control" originated by Battle. On the six-item cartoon test, the child states "what he would say" in various "lifelike" situations which involve the attribution of responsibility. The reliability of the scoring procedure was established with an independently scored sample of 40 protocols.[2] The result was a Pearsonian $r = .93$ ($p < .001$).

In the development of the test, 29 cartoon items were eliminated because of strong "picture pull" toward one or the other end of the scale. Six items were selected from a remaining eleven on the basis of correlation

[2] Mr. Forest Ward's help in the development of the scoring manual and in rating responses is gratefully acknowledged.

with the total scores with that item removed. Thirty-eight school children were used as pretest *S*s for this analysis. Table 1 gives the six final items (their correlations with total score given in parenthesis). The items are scored along a seven-point scale with three degrees of "internality," three of "externality," and a nondiscriminatory midpoint. The *higher* the score, the more external the orientation.

TABLE 1. Items from the Children's Picture Test of Internal-External Control

1. How come you didn't get what you wanted for Christmas? (.32)
2. Why is she always hurting herself? (.49)
3. When you grow up do you think you could be anything you wanted? (.25)
4. Whenever you're involved something goes wrong! (.22)
5. That's the third game we've lost this year. (.39)
6. Why does her mother always "holler" at her? (.32)

METHOD

*S*s in this study were 80 sixth- and eighth-grade children selected on the basis of sex, social class, and ethnic group membership (Negro-white) from five metropolitan schools.[3] The California Mental Maturity total score was used as a crude measure of "intelligence."

Each child was given the three tasks individually in the same order: [1] line matching, [2] cartoons, and [3] Bialer scale.

The Bialer *Locus of Control* questionnaire was administered to the last 40 *S*s primarily to determine its relationship to the projective test being studied. This is a 23-item "yes" or "no" questionnaire in which *S* attributes the locus of control to himself or others. A *low* score on this scale indicates an external orientation. Since only 40 of the 80 *S*s received the Bialer, some analyses made with the picture test were not repeated with the Bialer scale because of insufficient *N*.

Any child expressing doubt was reassured that there were no punishments or rewards associated with his performance. If the child asked the purpose of the line-matching technique, he was told it was a test to "see how well he could match the length of lines." No child persisted in his questions after this explanation. Each child was thanked and requested not to tell the other children about the tests before a specific day, at which time the testing would be completed. An attempt was made to test all the

[3] Half of the *S*s came from two lower-class, ethnically integrated schools in Columbus, Ohio. The other 40 *S*s were obtained from three Dayton, Ohio, schools. Of the latter *S*s, most of the middle-class Negro children came from the same elementary school. Most middle-class white students came from a second school. Only seven *S*s came from the last school which is situated in a lower-class, ethnically integrated, rooming-house district.

children in one class and school as rapidly as possible to prevent gossip from contaminating the results.

Demographic characteristics were obtained in the following manner: age, sex, and ethnic group were reported on the cumulative record for each child. IQ also was obtained from the cumulative record and was based, in most cases, on the full score of the California Mental Maturity Test most recently attained. Socioeconomic status was determined on the basis of the father or mother's occupation as given on the cumulative record. These occupations were categorized according to Lloyd Warner's classification (Warner, Meeker, and Eels, 1949). For purposes of analysis, classes one, two, three, and four were grouped together and called "middle class" in contrast to the "lower class" of five, six, and seven.

RESULTS

The means and sigmas of the Children's I-E scale scores for each combination of class and ethnic group are given in Table 2.

TABLE 2. Means and Sigmas of Children's I-E Scores by Social Class and Ethnic Group

	Middle Class			Lower Class		
	Mean	*Sigma*	*N*	*Mean*	*Sigma*	*N*
White	15.0	4.4	20	16.4	3.5	21
Negro	15.8	3.5	16	18.3	3.4	23

With an analysis of variance for unequal *N*s (Walker & Lev, 1953), a significant F ratio was found between social classes ($F = 5.13$; $df = 1$ and 72; $p < .05$); the interaction of ethnic group and social class ($F = 72.50$; $df = 1$ and 72; $p < .01$); and the triple interaction of ethnic group, social class, and IQ ($F = 8.12$; $df = 1$ and 72; $p < .01$). The following two-tailed t tests isolate the source of variance for the interaction effects.

A contrast of the middle-class white with the lower-class Negro gives a t of 2.75, $p < .01$. The only other significant comparison was between the lower-class Negro and the middle-class Negro groups ($t = 2.10$, $p < .05$).

It can be seen that the most significant comparison is between the middle-class white as most "internal" and the lower-class Negro as most "external." In addition, it is apparent that it is the lower-class Negro group which differs from all the others.

The means and sigmas of the children's I-E scale scores for each combination of social class, ethnic group, and IQ are given in Table 3.

The significant comparison is between the lower-class Negro with a high IQ (mean I-E score = 19.1) and the middle-class white with a low IQ (mean I-E = 13.8). For the combined N of 11 *S*s the $t = 2.21$, $p < .06$. One interpretation is that it is the externally scoring lower-class Negro whose higher IQ scores reflect a greater need value for academic achieve-

TABLE 3. MEANS AND SIGMAS OF CHILDREN'S I-E SCORES BY SOCIAL CLASS, ETHNIC GROUP, AND IQ

	Negro						White					
	Middle Class			*Lower Class*			*Middle Class*			*Lower Class*		
	mean	*sigma*	*N*	*mean*	*sigma*	*N*	*mean*	*sigma*	*N*	*mean*	*sigma*	*N*
IQ												
High	16.1	2.9	10	19.1	3.2	7	15.4	4.5	16	17.0	.8	4
Low	15.3	5.1	6	18.0	3.8	16	13.8	4.0	4	16.3	4.2	17

ment. When such a person encounters deprivation, due to his class and ethnic group membership, he defends himself with an "external" attitude. The middle-class white with a low IQ may have incorporated his class values of personal responsibility and when faced with the fact of his low ability, he responds characteristically by blaming himself for the failure.

Of the three line-matching measures, only the mean expectancy for success during the ten training trials was found to relate significantly to the children's I-E test ($r = -.31$, $p < .01$). That is, "internals" were "more certain of success" than "externals."

The Bialer questionnaire (1961) was found to relate significantly to the Children's Picture Test ($r = -.42$, $p < .01$). A high score on the Bialer is similar to a low score on the children's I-E scale. Bialer scores were also found to relate to the "number of unusual shifts" in expectancy during the training trials ($r = -.47$, $p < .01$). That is, "external" *S*s raised expectancies after failure and lowered them after success more often than "internals." "Internal control" on the Bialer scale was found to relate significantly to higher social class (r pt. bis. $= .53$, $p < .01$). Since the Bialer scale is a questionnaire test and the children's I-E scale is a projective test, the correlation of these two instruments ($-.42$) lends support to the construct validity of the internal-external control dimension as applied to grade school children.

Neither age (sixth vs. eighth grade) nor sex were found to relate to either children's I-E scale or the Bialer questionnaire.

The most interesting finding in this study is the effect of the interaction of social class and ethnic group on I-E scores. Analysis of the means in Table 2 shows clearly that the combined influence of the two variables is to make the lower-class Negro more external than all other groups. The results suggest that the middle-class Negro in this community might be raised to accept the white cultural beliefs in responsibility and opportunity. These results suggest that one important antecedent of a generalized expectancy that one can control his own destiny is the perception of opportunity to obtain the material rewards offered in a culture. Direct teaching of attitudes of internal vs. external control may also be involved.

SUMMARY

A generalized expectancy for internal vs. external control of reinforcement was examined in 80 Negro and white school children. To assess this characteristic, a newly developed cartoon test was given to all children and a questionnaire scale developed earlier by Bialer was given to half the children. The relationship of test scores to sex, age, social class, ethnic group, and behavior on a line-matching task was investigated. The following findings were obtained:

1. The interaction of social class and ethnic group was highly related to internal-external control attitudes. Lower-class Negroes were significantly more external than middle-class Negroes or whites. Middle-class children, in general, were significantly more internal than lower-class children.
2. Lower-class Negroes with high IQ's were more external than middle-class whites with lower IQ's. Caution must be exercised in interpreting this triple interaction because of the small *N* involved. The findings suggest, however, that brighter lower-class Negroes may develop extreme external attitudes as a defense reaction to perceived reduced choices for cultural or material rewards.
3. Sex was not a determiner of I-E scores in this study nor was age for the two-year difference investigated. California Mental Maturity Test scores did not relate to I-E scores when class and race were undifferentiated.
4. On a line-matching test, higher children's I-E scores were significantly associated with lower mean expectancy for success but not significantly associated with unusual shifts or trials to extinction.
5. The Bialer questionnaire of internal-external control expectancies correlated significantly (−.42) with the projective measure used in this study. The Bialer scale was also significantly related to social class.
6. For the 40 *S*s who had taken the Bialer scale, a significant predicted relationship was found between test scores and number of unusual shifts on the line-matching task; but not with mean expectancy or trials to extinction.
7. The overall findings lend support to the construct validity of the internal-external control variable as a generalized personality dimension and suggest some of the developmental conditions involved in the acquisition of such generalized expectancies.

REFERENCES

Bialer, I. "Conceptualization of success and failure in mentally retarded and normal children." *J. Pers.,* 1961, **29,** 303–320.

Crandall, V. J., W. Katkovsky, and A. Preston. "Motivational and ability determinants of young children's intellectual achievement behaviors." *Child Develpm.*, 1962, **33,** 643–661.

Crowne, D. P., and S. Liverant. "Conformity under varying conditions of personal commitment." *J. abnorm. soc. Psychol.*, 1963, **66,** 547–555.

Gore, M. P., and J. B. Rotter. "A personality correlate of social action." *J. Pers.*, 1963, **31,** 58–64.

Graves, T. D. *Time perspective and the deferred gratification pattern in a tri-ethnic community.* (res. rep. no. 5, Tri-ethnic Res. project) Univ. Colorado, Inst. behav. Sci., 1961.

Holden, K. B., and J. B. Rotter. "A nonverbal measure of extinction in skill and chance situations." *J. exp. Psychol.*, 1962, **63,** 519–520.

James, W. H. Internal vs. external control of reinforcement as a basic variable in learning theory. Unpubl. Ph.D. dissertation. Ohio State Univ., 1957.

James, W. H., and J. B. Rotter. "Partial and 100 per cent reinforcement under chance and skill conditions." *J. exp. Psychol.*, 1958, **55,** 397–403.

Phares, E. J. "Expectancy changes in skill and chance situations." *J. abnorm. soc. Psychol.*, 1957, **54,** 339–342.

Phares, E. J. "Perceptual threshold decrements as a function of skill and chance expectancies." *J. Psychol.*, 1962, **53,** 399–407.

Rotter, J. B. *Social Learning and Clinical Psychology.* Englewood Cliffs, N.J.: Prentice-Hall, 1954.

Rotter, J. B., S. Liverant, and D. P. Crowne. "The growth and extinction of expectancies in chance controlled and skilled tasks." *J. Psychol.*, 1961, **52,** 161–177.

Seeman, M. "On the meaning of alienation." *Amer. sociol. Rev.*, 1959, **24,** 783–791.

Seeman, M. "Alienation and social learning in a reformatory." *Amer. J. Social.* 1963, **69,** 270–284.

Seeman, M., and J. W. Evans. "Alienation and learning in a hospital setting." *Amer. sociol. Rev.*, 1962, **27,** 772–782.

Strodtbeck, F. L. Family interaction, values and achievement. In *Talent and Society,* D. McClelland (Ed.) New York: Van Nostrand, 1958, pp. 138–195.

Walker, H. M., and J. Lev. *Statistical Inference.* New York: Holt, Rinehart and Winston, 1953.

Warner, W. L., M. Meeker, and K. Eels. *Social Class in America.* Sci. Res. Associates, Chicago, 1949, pp. 140–141.

3.2 *Orientation*

Another approach to the measurement of beliefs in internal versus external reinforcement is the work of Crandall, Katkovsky, and Crandall reproduced below. These investigators have developed an intellectual-achievement responsibility scale that is a predictor of intellectual achievement. The study itself demonstrates the necessity for psychologists to establish the validity of psychometric instruments. Furthermore, the study reports normative data, sex differences, and psychosocial correlates of Intellectual Achievement Responsibility. The results provide an interesting comparison to the Battle and Rotter data reported (see preceding selection), for both are broadly concerned with strategies for measuring locus of control. Finally, the normative data relative to the period during which self-responsibility is apparently established provides an interesting relationship to the Sontag and Kagan paper (Chapter 2). Readers will recall that Sontag and Kagan support the period from six to ten years as being critical for the development of intellectual-achievement motives.

RECOMMENDED READING

Crandall, V. J. "Achievement behavior in young children." *Young Child,* **20** (1964), 76–90.

Crandall, V. J., W. Katkovsky, and A. Preston. "Motivational and ability determinants of young children's intellectual achievement behavior." *Child Develpm.,* **33** (1962), 643–661.

Katkovsky, W., V. C. Crandall, and S. Good. "Parental antecedents of children's beliefs in internal-external control of reinforcements in intellectual achievement situations." *Child Develpm.,* **38** (1967), 765–776.

3.2 Children's Beliefs in Their Own Control of Reinforcements in Intellectual-Achievement Situations

Virginia C. Crandall, FELS RESEARCH INSTITUTE
Walter Katkovsky, FORDHAM UNIVERSITY
Vaughn J. Crandall, LATE OF FELS RESEARCH INSTITUTE

Many situations, in the laboratory or in nature, contain cues defining the degree to which reinforcements are contingent on the subject's instrumental acts. Similarly, individuals have been found to differ in the degree to which they believe that they are usually able to influence the outcome of situations. They may believe that their actions produce the reinforcements which follow their efforts, or they may feel that the rewards and

---

Reprinted from *Child Development,* **36** (1965), 91–109. By permission of the authors and The Society for Research in Child Development, Inc. Footnote 1 of the original article omitted by the kind permission of the authors and the Society for Research in Child Development, Inc.

punishments meted out to them are at the discretion of powerful others or are in the hands of luck or fate. In fact, the same reinforcement in the same situation may be perceived by one individual as within his own control and by another as outside his own influence. These personal beliefs could be important determiners of the reinforcing effects of many experiences. If, for example, the individual is convinced that he has little control over the rewards and punishments he receives, then he has little reason to modify his behavior in an attempt to alter the probability that those events will occur. Rewards and punishments, then, will have lost much of their reinforcing value, since they will not be as effective in strengthening or weakening the *S*'s response. A more complete discussion of beliefs in internal (self) versus external (environmental) control and the likely role of these in social learning can be found elsewhere (Rotter, Seeman, and Liverant, 1962).

Recent studies suggest that reinforcement-responsibility beliefs hold promise of being predictive of individual differences in reinforcement sensitivity, in attitudes, and in social behaviors. The original questionnaire constructed to assess this variable was devised by Phares (1955) and revised by James (1957). Research using the I-E (internal vs. external control) scale has found that a belief in external responsibility is positively correlated with defensive and maladaptive level of aspiration behaviors (Phares, 1957; Simmons, 1959), is more prevalent among schizophrenics than among normal subjects (Cromwell, Rosenthal, Shakow, and Kahn, 1961), and is positively associated with high California F-scale scores (Holden, 1958). A newer form of the I-E scale was developed by Liverant, Rotter, Crowne and Seeman (Rotter *et al.,* 1962). Beliefs in internal or self-responsibility on this scale were positively associated with commitments of southern Negro college students to take action toward integration (Gore and Rotter, 1963), with greater attainment of information and understanding of their own disease by tuberculosis patients (Seeman and Evans, 1963), and with realistic and cautious betting behavior (Liverant and Scodel, 1960). In addition, individuals who hold strong convictions of internal responsibility express less conforming attitudes on the Barron Independence of Judgment Scale (Odell, 1959) and display less behavioral conformity to group pressure (Crowne and Liverant, 1963).

The I-E scales mentioned above were constructed for adult *S*s. Recently, two other techniques to measure this construct have been developed for children: the Locus of Control scale devised by Bialer and Cromwell (1961) and the Children's Picture Test of Internal-External Control (Battle and Rotter, 1963). Self-responsibility, as measured by the Locus of Control scale, correlated moderately but positively with chronological age, and to an even greater degree with mental age (Bialer, 1961). Battle and Rotter (1963) found internality on that same scale positively associated with social class and with fewer unusual shifts of expectancy statements on a Level of Aspiration task. In the same study, internal-responsibility beliefs reflected in responses to the Children's Picture Test, like those on the Locus of Control scale, were positively associated with socioeconomic status and were stronger in white than in Negro children. In summary, a belief in reinforcement responsibility is related to a number of demographic variables, attitudes, and behaviors, suggesting that such a variable may be useful in personality and personality-development research.

The Intellectual Achievement Responsibility (IAR) Questionnaire, employed in the present investigation, shares the aim of the above-mentioned scales in that it attempts to measure beliefs in internal versus external reinforcement responsibility. However, it differs from the other measures in several respects. First, the techniques discussed so far contain items describing reinforcements in a number of motivational and behavioral areas such as affiliation, dominance, achievement, and dependency. However, there has been no demonstration so far that such beliefs are consistent across all areas of experience. The IAR, on the other hand, was developed within the context of a larger research program dealing with children's achievement development. Thus, it is aimed at assessing children's beliefs in reinforcement responsibility exclusively in intellectual-academic achievement situations.

The IAR also differs from the other assessment methods in the external environmental forces described. While previous scales include a variety of sources and agents such as luck, fate, impersonal social forces, more-personal "significant others," etc., the IAR limits the source of external control to those persons who most often come in face-to-face contact with a child, his parents, teachers, and peers. This restriction was based on two considerations. The first had to do with the possibility that a child may attribute different amounts of power or control to various external agents. For example, he might attribute a greal deal of control to adults, but discount the influence of luck or fate on his experiences, or vice versa. There is no information yet available to determine whether children have any generality in their belief in the power of various kinds of external forces, although there is some evidence of such generality in adults' beliefs (Rotter *et al.,* 1962). Consequently, at this early stage of investigation, it was thought advisable to restrict the scale to one type of external control. A second reason was that it seemed important from a developmental point of view to focus particularly on children's beliefs in the instrumentality of their own actions compared with that of other people in their immediate environment. The dependence of young children upon others for instrumental help and emotional support is, of course, a necessary condition of early development. However, the resolution of dependence on such caretakers and the concomitant acquisition of independent problem-solving techniques are equally important requisites of normal personality development. It would not be surprising, then, to find that infants and preschool children—if they could report such beliefs—would ascribe reinforcement responsibility to the powerful others in their environment. But with age and experience, most children should begin to feel that their own actions are often instrumental in attaining the reinforcements they receive.

Unlike the other I-E scales, the scale used in this research was constructed to sample an equal number of positive and negative events. It was felt that the dynamics operative in assuming credit for causing good things to happen might be very different from those operative in accepting blame for unpleasant consequences. It is possible that belief in personal responsibility for the two kinds of events may develop at differential rates, or that this may be so for some children but not others. Thus, the IAR was so constructed that, in addition to a total I (internal or self-) responsibility score, separate subscores could be obtained for beliefs in internal responsibility for successes (I+ score) and for failures (I− score).

The aims of the present investigation were both methodological and substantive. It was necessary to determine the strength and the limitations of the IAR for use with children, the best methods of administration at different ages, test-retest reliability, etc. Regarding substantive issues, the study examined relations between children's reinforcement beliefs and a number of demographic variables: age, sex, IQ, socioeconomic status, ordinal position, and size of family.

METHOD

The Intellectual Achievement Responsibility Questionnaire

The children's IAR scale is composed of 34 forced-choice items. Each item stem describes either a positive or a negative achievement experience which routinely occurs in children's daily lives. This stem is followed by one alternative stating that the event was caused by the child and another stating that the event occurred because of the behavior of someone else in the child's immediate environment. The items are presented in Table 1. Internal alternatives are designated by an I. Positive-

TABLE 1. The IAR Scale

Item			
1			If a teacher passes you to the next grade, would it probably be
		______*a*	because she liked you, or
	I +	______*b*	because of the work you did?
2			When you do well on a test at school, is it more likely to be
	I +	______*a*	because you studied for it, or
		______*b*	because the test was especially easy?
3			When you have trouble understanding something in school, is it usually
		______*a*	because the teacher didn't explain it clearly, or
	I −	______*b*	because you didn't listen carefully?

TABLE 1. The IAR Scale—Cont.

Item	Key	Response	Question
4			When you read a story and can't remember much of it, is it usually
		______ *a*	because the story wasn't well written, or
	I −	______ *b*	because you weren't interested in the story?
5			Suppose your parents say you are doing well in school. Is this likely to happen
	I +	______ *a*	because your school work is good, or
		______ *b*	because they are in a good mood?
6			Suppose you did better than usual in a subject at school. Would it probably happen
	I +	______ *a*	because you tried harder, or
		______ *b*	because someone helped you?
7			When you lose at a game of cards or checkers, does it usually happen
		______ *a*	because the other player is good at the game, or
	I −	______ *b*	because you don't play well?
8			Suppose a person doesn't think you are very bright or clever.
	I −	______ *a*	can you make him change his mind if you try to, or
		______ *b*	are there some people who will think you're not very bright no matter what you do?
9			If you solve a puzzle quickly, is it
		______ *a*	because it wasn't a very hard puzzle, or
	I +	______ *b*	because you worked on it carefully?
10			If a boy or girl tells you that you are dumb, is it more likely that they say that
		______ *a*	because they are mad at you, or
	I −	______ *b*	because what you did really wasn't very bright?
11			Suppose you study to become a teacher, scientist, or doctor and you fail. Do you think this would happen
	I −	______ *a*	because you didn't work hard enough, or
		______ *b*	because you needed some help, and other people didn't give it to you?
12			When you learn something quickly in school, is it usually
	I +	______ *a*	because you paid close attention, or
		______ *b*	because the teacher explained it clearly?
13			If a teacher says to you, "Your work is fine," is it
		______ *a*	something teachers usually say to encourage pupils, or
	I +	______ *b*	because you did a good job?
14			When you find it hard to work arithmetic or math problems at school, is it
	I −	______ *a*	because you didn't study well enough before you tried them, or
		______ *b*	because the teacher gave problems that were too hard?
15			When you forget something you heard in class, is it
		______ *a*	because the teacher didn't explain it very well, or
	I −	______ *b*	because you didn't try very hard to remember?
16			Suppose you weren't sure about the answer to a question your teacher asked you, but your answer turned out to be right. Is it likely to happen
		______ *a*	because she wasn't as particular as usual, or
	I +	______ *b*	because you gave the best answer you could think of?

TABLE 1. THE IAR SCALE—Cont.

Item	Scoring	Response	Question
17			When you read a story and remember most of it, is it usually
	I +	_____ *a*	because you were interested in the story, or
		_____ *b*	because the story was well written?
18			If your parents tell you you're acting silly and not thinking clearly, is it more likely to be
	I −	_____ *a*	because of something you did, or
		_____ *b*	because they happen to be feeling cranky?
19			When you don't do well on a test at school, is it
		_____ *a*	because the test was especially hard, or
	I −	_____ *b*	because you didn't study for it?
20			When you win at a game of cards or checkers, does it happen
	I +	_____ *a*	because you play real well, or
		_____ *b*	because the other person doesn't play well?
21			If people think you're bright or clever, is it
		_____ *a*	because they happen to like you, or
	I +	_____ *b*	because you usually act that way?
22			If a teacher didn't pass you to the next grade, would it probably be
		_____ *a*	because she "had it in for you," or
	I −	_____ *b*	because your school work wasn't good enough?
23			Suppose you don't do as well as usual in a subject at school. Would this probably happen
	I −	_____ *a*	because you weren't as careful as usual, or
		_____ *b*	because somebody bothered you and kept you from working?
24			If a boy or girl tells you that you are bright, is it usually
	I +	_____ *a*	because you thought up a good idea, or
		_____ *b*	because they like you?
25			Suppose you become a famous teacher, scientist or doctor. Do you think this would happen
		_____ *a*	because other people helped you when you needed it, or
	I +	_____ *b*	because you worked very hard?
26			Suppose your parents say you aren't doing well in your school work. Is this likely to happen more
	I −	_____ *a*	because your work isn't very good, or
		_____ *b*	because they are feeling cranky?
27			Suppose you are showing a friend how to play a game and he has trouble with it. Would that happen
		_____ *a*	because he wasn't able to understand how to play, or
	I −	_____ *b*	because you couldn't explain it well?
28			When you find it easy to work arithmetic or math problems at school, is it usually
		_____ *a*	because the teacher gave you especially easy problems, or
	I +	_____ *b*	because you studied your book well before you tried them?
29			When you remember something you heard in class, is it usually
	I +	_____ *a*	because you tried hard to remember, or
		_____ *b*	because the teacher explained it well?

TABLE 1. The IAR Scale—Cont.

Item	Scoring	Response	
30			If you can't work a puzzle, is it more likely to happen
	I –	____ *a*	because you are not especially good at working puzzles, or
		____ *b*	because the instructions weren't written clearly enough?
31			If your parents tell you that you are bright or clever, is it more likely
		____ *a*	because they are feeling good, or
	I +	____ *b*	because of something you did?
32			Suppose you are explaining how to play a game to a friend and he learns quickly. Would that happen more often
	I +	____ *a*	because you explained it well, or
		____ *b*	because he was able to understand it?
33			Suppose you're not sure about the answer to a question your teacher asks you and the answer you give turns out to be wrong. Is it likely to happen
		____ *a*	because she was more particular than usual, or
	I –	____ *b*	because you answered too quickly?
34			If a teacher says to you, "Try to do better," would it be
		____ *a*	because this is something she might say to get pupils to try harder, or
	I –	____ *b*	because your work wasn't as good as usual?

event items are indicated by a plus sign, and negative events by a minus sign following the I. A child's I+ score is obtained by summing all positive events for which he assumes credit, and his I– score is the total of all negative events for which he assumes blame. His total I score is the sum of his I+ and his I– subscores.

The Sample

The sample was composed of 923 elementary- and high-school students and was drawn from five different schools so that it would be representative of children in diverse kinds of communities. Included were students from a consolidated country school, a village school, a small-city school, a medium-city school, and a college laboratory school. None came from a large metropolitan school system, however. Subsamples in various grades were: third grade, $N = 102$; fourth grade, $N = 103$; fifth grade, $N = 99$; sixth grade, $N = 166$; eighth grade, $N = 161$; tenth grade, $N = 183$; twelfth grade, $N = 109$.

The socioeconomic status (SES) of the children in grades 6, 8, 10, and 12 was determined by Hollingshead's Two Factor Index of Social Position (Hollingshead, 1957). This index is based on the type of occupation and amount of education of the head of the household, with these two factors weighted and summed. SES information was obtained from a questionnaire administered to the children. Complete information was obtained for all tenth-grade *S*s, but was acquired for only parts of the sixth-, eighth-, and twelfth-grade subsamples. However, *S*s in these grades were in the same schools as the tenth-grade sample, and there was no evidence to suggest that the subsamples on which information was incomplete differed from those with complete information. For grades 3, 4, and 5, an estimate of the children's SES was obtained from their fathers' occupations only, since they were not able to provide information on their fathers' educations. Both SES distributions compare favorably with the normative sample of Hollingshead and Redlich (1958) except that neither is as heavily weighted with children from families on the lower end of the distribution. For the older children the distribution was normal (nonsignificant Fisher g_1 and g_2), and for the younger children the distribution showed some piling up of scores on the lower end of the range (Fisher g_1 significant at the .05 level). However, even the distribution of the younger sample is still not as skewed as Hollingshead and Redlich report is true of their New Haven sample.

The California Test of Mental Maturity, the intelligence test used by all schools for grades 6, 8, 10, and 12 yielded a mean of 103.4 and an SD of 14.15. The intelligence test which all but one of the schools had used for grades 3, 4, and 5 was the Lorge-Thorndike. The mean Lorge-Thorndike score for the *S*s who had had the test was 103.0 with an SD of 12.51.

Administration Procedures

One aim of this study was to investigate children's beliefs in intellectual-academic reinforcement responsibility throughout as broad an age range as possible. Ideally, it would have been desirable to examine these beliefs at least from the time children enter elementary school until they graduate from high school. However, preliminary research indicated that children of average intelligence in the first two elementary grades often had difficulty in responding to the questionnaire, primarily because they could not keep an item and its two alternatives in mind long enough to make meaningful responses. As a result, only children in the third grade and above were used. Interviewing of the subjects used in the preliminary study also indicated that some children in even the third, fourth, and fifth grades were not able to read well enough to take the test in written form. It was decided, therefore, that individual oral presentation of the scale was desirable for children below the sixth grade, and it was administered in this fashion to the third-, fourth-, and fifth-grade samples. The questions were tape recorded so that each child was presented verbal stimuli which had the same inflections, tone, and rate. His oral responses were recorded by the examiner. The older children in grades 6, 8, 10, and 12 were administered the scale in written form in group sessions.

The instructions presented in both the oral and the written administrations requested the *S* to pick the answer "that best describes what happens to you or how you feel." He was told that there were no right or wrong answers and assured that his responses would not be given to anyone at his school.

Data Analyses

Distribution characteristics of IAR scores and all other variables were tested with Fisher *g* statistics, then all non-normal distributions were normalized by McCall T-score transformations. Product-moment correlations were used for measures of association, and tests of difference were *t* test. Two-tailed tests of significance were used to determine all *p* values. Since the *N*s of the subsamples differed, and since some demographic data were not available for all *S*s within a subsample, the *N* for each statistical test is presented separately in the tables.

RESULTS AND DISCUSSION

Descriptive Statistics

Table 2 presents the means and standard deviations for the children's IAR total scores and subscores for each of the grades tested. Since each of the 34 items presents an internal and an external alternative, chance distributions would result in mean total I scores of 17 and mean I+ and I− scores of 8.5 each. In all cases the obtained means exceed the means that would be expected by chance. There is a possibility that some accidental peculiarity in the wording of the IAR items "pulls for" internal responses. However, it may also be that the high means which were obtained indicate that self-responsibility is a characteristic which develops in children as early as the third grade. Common observation would indicate that parents and teachers attempt to promote and encourage a belief in personal responsibility for intellectual-academic success very early in the child's training. Perhaps the genesis of self-responsibility for intellectual activities occurs even earlier than third grade, but a different method of assessing internal responsibility would have to be developed for use with younger subjects since children below that level have difficulty with forced-choice questions.

The high mean scores, the relatively short ranges, and the small amount of variance around means suggest that there are a number of non-discriminating items which elicit an internal response from most children. However, while some of the items are not contributing to the variance, there appear to be sufficient individual differences in children's responses to allow prediction to the achievement performances which are discussed in the final section of this paper.

Reliability

Test-retest reliability The consistency of children's IAR responses over time is moderately high. Forty-seven of the children in grades 3, 4, and 5 were given the test a second time after a 2-month interval. For these

TABLE 2. Means, Standard Deviations and Ranges of IAR Scores

Subjects and Grade		Total I			I+			I−		
	N	*Mean*	*SD*	*Range*	*Mean*	*SD*	*Range*	*Mean*	*SD*	*Range*
Boys:										
3	44	23.16	3.80	16–30	12.32	2.02	8–16	10.84	3.08	4–16
4	59	24.83	3.00	17–30	12.41	2.07	7–16	12.42	2.08	8–17
5	52	24.04	3.69	16–31	12.38	2.52	7–16	11.65	2.46	3–16
6	93	24.74	4.57	12–32	12.99	2.54	6–17	11.75	2.79	5–17
8	68	25.38	3.51	15–32	13.07	1.97	7–17	12.31	2.23	5–16
10	90	25.27	4.62	6–32	13.13	2.60	2–17	12.13	2.83	4–16
12	52	24.38	3.71	14–30	11.85	2.83	5–17	12.54	1.96	8–16
Girls:										
3	58	23.22	4.00	13–31	12.88	2.08	8–16	10.35	3.01	2–15
4	44	24.75	3.81	15–30	12.66	2.20	7–17	12.04	2.65	5–16
5	47	24.36	3.96	15–32	12.47	2.54	6–17	11.85	2.92	1–16
6	73	26.93	3.71	14–33	13.88	2.21	5–17	13.05	2.43	6–16
8	93	26.64	3.86	13–34	13.27	2.35	7–17	13.38	2.27	6–17
10	93	26.50	3.93	16–33	13.29	2.22	6–17	13.22	2.40	5–17
12	57	27.33	2.98	19–32	13.40	2.15	6–17	13.93	1.94	8–17
Total:										
3	102	23.20	3.92	13–31	12.64	2.08	8–16	10.56	3.05	2–16
4	103	24.80	3.37	15–30	12.51	2.13	7–17	12.26	2.35	5–17
5	99	24.19	3.83	15–32	12.42	2.53	6–17	11.75	2.69	1–16
6	166	25.70	4.35	12–33	13.38	2.44	5–17	12.32	2.72	5–17
8	161	26.11	3.77	13–34	13.19	2.20	7–17	12.92	2.31	5–17
10	183	25.90	4.33	6–33	13.21	2.41	2–17	12.68	2.68	4–17
12	109	25.93	3.66	14–32	12.66	2.62	5–17	13.27	2.07	8–17

younger children, the test-retest correlations were .69 for total I, .66 for I+, and .74 for I−. These correlations were all significant at the .001 level. The sixth-, eighth-, tenth-, and twelfth-grade children of the present study were not retested. However, 70 ninth-grade students from one of the same schools used in the present study were given the test after a similar interval of 2 months. The reliability coefficients for these children were .65 for total I, .47 for I+, and .69 for I−. Again, these correlations were all significant at the .001 level. There were no significant sex differences in any of the correlations.

There is some possibility, then, that children's assumptions of responsibility for causing their academic-intellectual failures is a somewhat more stable belief than that for causing their successes. Reasons for such a phenomenon are unknown. However, because several studies (Brackbill and O'Hara, 1958; Sullivan, 1960; Meyer and Offenbach, 1962; Crandall, 1963; and Crandall, Good, and Crandall, 1964) have found negative social reinforcement to be more effective than positive reinforcement, it may possibly be that the greater impact of punishment produces a more durable effect on the internal-external responsibility beliefs surrounding these experiences.

Internal consistency Because the IAR contains two kinds of items, those sampling beliefs in self-responsibility for positive events and those posing negative events, split-half reliabilities were computed separately for the two subscales. Thus, responses to the eight even-numbered items of the I+ subscale were correlated with the nine odd-numbered items of that subscale, and the nine even-numbered I− items were correlated with the eight odd-numbered I−items. For a random sample of 130 of the younger children, the correlation is .54 for I+ and .57 for I− after correction with the Spearman-Brown Prophesy Formula. For a similar random sample of older children, the correlations are .60 for both the I+ and the I− subscales. While the brevity of the subscales militates against high split-half reliabilities, it is apparent that the items within each subscale are somewhat heterogeneous.

Relations between IAR Subscores

Table 3 reports the correlations between the two subscales of the IAR and demonstrates variable, but generally low, relations between I+ and I−. Part of the independence of the subscale scores should, of course, be attributed

TABLE 3. Correlations of IAR Subscale Scores

Grade	N	I + versus I −
3	102	.14
4	103	.11
5	99	.11
6	166	.38 [a]
8	161	.40 [a]
10	183	.43 [a]
12	109	.17

[a] $p < .001$.

to the general heterogeneity of items indicated by the rather low internal consistency of the items within each subscale. However, the obvious independence of the two subscale scores implies that it would be imprudent to assume that I+ and I− scores are measuring the same orientations. Such low interscale correlations may mean that assuming responsibility for successful intellectual-academic experiences may be different from assuming responsibility for failure experiences. In addition, the low correlations between the two subscales raises some doubt about the use of the total I score alone. Since this score combines self-responsibility for success and failure, it may mask important differences between the two in the individual child.

The very low association of subscale scores for the children in the lower grades raises the possibility that self-responsibility for successes and failures may be learned separately, and the young child may assume more responsibility for the one than for the other. Older children in grades 6, 8, and 10 seem to evidence somewhat more generalization of this belief, regardless of the outcome of their efforts. It is difficult to explain the lack of relationship between subscores for grade 12, considering the fact that they were related for the preceding three grades. Since high-school graduation was impending for these children, there is the possibility that anxieties over their vocational or college careers and uncertainty about their ability to control future events in the "big, broad world out there" resulted again in differential responses to the success and failure items.

Age (Grade) and Sex Differences

General tendencies can be noted in Table 2 for positive, negative, and total I scores to increase only slightly with age, and for girls' scores to be somewhat higher than boys', especially from grade 6 upward.

A more definitive examination of age (grade) changes was made by *t*-test comparisons between each two grade levels. No comparison was made between any of the earlier grades and the sixth grade since methods of test administration change at this point. Thus, comparisons were between third and fifth, sixth and eighth, eighth and tenth, and tenth and twelfth grades. Finally, an over-all comparison was made between sixth- and twelfth-grade students in order to observe changes over this broader age span where the test administration was consistent. All analyses were made separately by sex and for the sexes combined.

The *t*-test comparisons revealed that there is indeed no significant change in internality in general (total I) from third grade to fifth, or from sixth grade to twelfth for either of the sexes nor for boys and girls together. Nevertheless, some changes in subscale scores did reach significance over these years. The boys showed a significant decrease in I+ subscale scores between tenth and twelfth grades ($t = 2.80$, $p < .01$) in spite of the fact that the means of earlier grades show a gradual and non-significant growth in the assumption of self-credit. In fact, the decrease between tenth and twelfth grades was so sharp as to cause the over-all test of I+ between grades 6 and 12 to show a drop significant at the .05 level ($t = 2.52$). Two possible reasons for this decrease in I+ from grades 10 to 12 seem worth considering. As mentioned previously, it may be that the imminence of graduation and the necessity of having to find and merit employment or acceptance into college provoked uncertainties in the boys about future success and thus lowered their I+ scores. A very different possibility, however, is that the older boys may have developed an increased sense of modesty, not present at earlier ages, which caused them to respond to the questionnaire as though they were not responsible for their intellectual-academic good fortune.

The girls, on the other hand, did not show a significant increase in their I+ scores, but did significantly increase their internality for negative events from third grade to fifth ($t = 2.89$, $p < .01$), and over the broad span from sixth to twelfth grades ($t = 2.18$, $p < .05$). The means in Table 2 show that the first change actually took place chiefly between third and fourth grades. It is interesting to note that by sixth grade the girls have already assumed a level of responsibility for negative events which is slightly greater than that the boys finally achieve in the twelfth grade. In addition, the girls' I− scores continue to rise even higher during junior and senior high school. This difference in the development of an acceptance of blame in the two sexes is congruent with recent research dealing with sex differences in superego development. In fact, the *t*-test comparisons reported in Table 4 indicate that at any given grade level above the sixth, and for the upper grades combined, girls give significantly more internal responses of both kinds than do boys (except for I+ in grades 8 and 10).

TABLE 4. Sex Differences in IAR Scores

Grade	Total I				I+			I−		
	N	*t*	*p*	*Dir.*	*t*	*p*	*Dir.*	*t*	*p*	*Dir.*
3	102	0.08	ns	$G > B$	1.35	ns	$G > B$	0.81	ns	$B > G$
4	103	0.06	ns	$G > B$	0.69	ns	$G > B$	0.72	ns	$B > G$
5	99	0.42	ns	$G > B$	0.10	ns	$G > B$	0.63	ns	$G > B$
3, 4, 5	304	0.17	ns	$G > B$	1.14	ns	$G > B$	1.16	ns	$B > G$
6	166	3.26	.01	$G > B$	2.27	.05	$G > B$	3.10	.01	$G > B$
8	161	2.20	.05	$G > B$	0.75	ns	$G > B$	3.17	.01	$G > B$
10	183	2.05	.05	$G > B$	0.30	ns	$G > B$	3.08	.01	$G > B$
12	109	4.65	.01	$G > B$	3.11	.01	$G > B$	3.74	.01	$G > B$
6, 8, 10, 12	619	5.80	.001	$G > B$	3.07	.01	$G > B$	6.55	.001	$G > B$

Intelligence and Social Class Influences

Correlations presented in Table 5 indicate that IAR scores relate only moderately to intelligence-test scores and to social status, but reach significance because of the large size of the samples involved.[1] It seems likely

[1] In addition to assessing associations between these variables and total IAR and subscale scores for the sexes pooled among the younger and the older children as reported above. Correlations were run separately for boys and girls at each the grade levels studied. The significant correlations were few and did not form any observable or consistent pattern.

that the moderate relationships found between both self-crediting and self-blaming responses and intelligence are partially accounted for by the greater ability of the bright child to see the casual relationship between the rewards and punishments he receives and his own instrumental behavior. Because the greater adequacy of that instrumental behavior has allowed him to manipulate his environment more successfully than the duller child, he has had more evidence that he can control what happens to him and can achieve success more frequently and with greater competence than the child with less ability. In addition, it may be that he can accept the blame for those failures which he does experience precisely because his generally competent behavior has given him sufficient security to do so.

TABLE 5. Relations of IAR Scores to Intelligence and Social Class

Grades	IQ				Social Class			
	N	*Total I*	*I+*	*I−*	*N*	*Total I*	*I+*	*I−*
3, 4, 5	233	.26 [c]	.22 [c]	.14 [a]	259	.08	.17 [b]	−.04
6, 8, 10, 12	503	.16 [b]	.14 [b]	.14 [b]	346	.11 [a]	.04	.14 [b]

[a] $p < .05$.
[b] $p < .01$.
[c] $p < .001$.

The IAR was originally developed as a predictor to children's intellectual-achievement behaviors. If internality had been found to relate positively, consistently (in each grade), and highly to intelligence-test scores, it might be assumed that internal responses were simply another measure of intelligent behavior, per se. Since this was not the case, however, it may be that an internal or external orientation represents a motivating propensity which will help to account for individual differences in achievement performances.

Social class, as may be seen in Table 5, accounts for only a very small proportion of the variance in IAR scores, although, as has been previously mentioned, it was found to relate to responses on the Locus of Control scale and Children's Picture Test of Internality-Externality. It would seem, as Battle and Rotter (1963) maintain, that there should be a lesser belief in self-responsibility among lower-class individuals than among those of upper classes. Persons from the lower social strata are, by reason of their vocations, lack of education, and little money with which to manipulate their environments, in positions of less power to control the events which influence their lives than are those at high SES levels. It is not surprising, then, that highly significant social-class differences were found in children's responses to the Locus of Control scale and the Children's Picture Test, which sample general social experiences. The IAR, on the other hand, contains a majority of items directly related to school-associated activities. It is our observation that teachers attempt to encourage children of all social classes to achieve an internal orientation toward their academic efforts with such statements as "If you study hard enough you'll pass the test," and "You can be anything you want if you just keep working toward it." It is our conclusion that such precepts (together with direct reinforcement in the form of better grades when the student persists in his study) account for the high mean I scores reported in Table 2. These same school pressures are exerted upon the dull child, as well as the lower-class child, although for the slower child these exhortations may be somewhat attenuated. Thus, it is not surprising that intelligence and SES show little relationship to IAR scores, but that the relationship of intelligence to self-responsibility beliefs should be slightly stronger than that for social class.

It is apparent from Table 5 that the younger children's total I and I− scores, and the older children's I+ scores were predicted by their IQ scores, but not by their social or SES status. For the remaining I scores (younger children's I+ and older childrens' total I and I−), both IQ and SES correlations, though small, were significant. Because of the consistent relationships often reported between social class and intelligence, analyses of variance were computed on these latter scores on the basis of IQ and SES. For the older children's total I scores the one significant effect was that of intelligence ($F = 9.31$, $p < .01$). For their I− scores, however, only the interaction of the two variables was significant ($F = 5.37$, $p < .05$). For the I+ scores of the younger children, social class and the interaction were both significant ($F = 5.79$, $p < .05$, and 8.42, $p < .01$, respectively). Thus, the effects of social class and intelligence, while weak, seem to indicate that intelligence is more often the stronger of the two predictors to internality. In both cases where interaction occurred, t tests revealed that the effects of the two factors are additive, rather than forming a complex interaction.[2]

Ordinal Position and Family Size

An analysis of IAR total and subscale responses by ordinal position was made by dichotomizing the scores of first-born and of later-born children. This analysis yielded no significant differences in the younger group, but indicated that first-born children in the upper grades gave more total I responses ($t = 2.15$, $p < .05$). (Tests of difference on the older children's subscale scores were non-significant.) Responses were also analyzed on the basis of the size of the families from which the children came. Those who came from families of one or two children were considered "small-family" children, those from families of three or more children were designated as coming from large families. Again, no significant differences were found

[2] Results of these analyses are not reported in detail here but may be obtained from the first listed author.

for the younger children, but for the older *S*s total I and I− responses were significantly more prevalent among the children from small families ($t = 2.23$, $p < .05$, and $t = 2.63$, $p < .01$, respectively).

The fact that first-born children accept more self-responsibility than do those born later is predictable from most personality theories and from common observation. Not only are first-born children more often placed in positions of responsibility for household affairs and for their own conduct, but they are often put in charge of younger siblings, as well. Thus, the eldest child comes to observe both the consequences of his actions upon his own successes and failures and also the effect of his actions upon the welfare of his younger siblings and of the total family unit. In contrast, the later-born child is often told that his older brother or sister "will take care of you," allowing him to assume that he is less responsible for his own actions. Probably even more pertinent to the IAR, since it deals with intellectual-academic situations, is the fact that the eldest child must often use school success as his best pathway to parental approval.

Some of the same dynamics probably operate for children in a small-family setting. But, in addition, the child in a one- or two-child family has a greater chance of being recognized as an individual, of having a good deal of attention focused on him, of being required to stand on his own, and of being accountable for his own actions. He cannot be considered just "one of the children." In contrast, the child in a large family is more often involved in larger group activities and is less likely to be able to manipulate the direction of these family affairs or to feel personally responsible for the outcome of family decisions.

Social Desirability

During the last decade, much attention has been focused on the tendency of subjects to give socially desirable answers to self-report instruments. In constructing the IAR, a careful attempt was made to word the internal and external alternatives to avoid discrepancies in the social-desirability "pull" of the two responses. In order to assess the success of those efforts, the children's IAR scores were correlated with their scores on the Children's Social Desirability (CSD) Questionnaire (Crandall, Crandall, and Katkovsky, 1964). This is a scale designed to measure the tendency with which children will dissemble in order to put themselves in a socially desirable light. An absence of relationship between these two measures would suggest that IAR scores are independent of social-desirability tendencies.

Of the six correlations between IAR and CSD scores (CSD with I+, I−, and total I for the younger children, and the same tests of association for the older children), only two were significant. Among the younger children, I−scores related negatively to CSD scores ($r = -.26$, $p < .001$), and among the older subjects I+ scores were positively associated with CSD responses ($r = .15$, $p < .01$). It is apparent, then, that social desirability tendencies do not account for much of the variance in IAR responses, even in the two cases in which the large size of the samples causes these small associations to reach significant levels.

On the other hand, if the tendency to give socially desirable responses is thought of as a personality characteristic, its tendency to be related to reinforcement responsibility beliefs is of some interest. That is, the two small but significant relationships reported above would indicate that there is a trend for the young child who wishes to appear socially acceptable to deny that he is at fault when he fails, and for the older child who seeks social acceptance to claim credit for his successes. These findings are consistent with other research which demonstrated that children with the greatest desire to appear socially acceptable tend to be shy, withdrawn, inhibited, and lacking in self-confidence and a sense of personal worth (Crandall *et al.,* 1964). It may be that children with high social-desirability needs tend to form internal and external responsibility orientations which bolster and defend their uncertain perceptions of their own intellectual-academic adequacy.

The Prediction of Achievement Behavior from Beliefs in Self-responsibility

It will be remembered that the IAR was developed within the context of a larger program of research dealing with children's achievement development. While the intent of the present paper is primarily methodological, the following data are presented in summary fashion as early evidence of the possible predictive utility of the scale. A future paper will present these data in more detail.

IAR scores were correlated with two measures of academic achievement in the present samples. For the younger children, these measures were the Iowa Tests of Basic Skills and their report-card grade averages. Total I scores correlated positively and significantly with almost all achievement-test measures (reading, math, and language subscores and total achievement-test scores) and with report-card grades for grades 3, 4, and 5. However, separate analysis for I+ and I− by sex of child revealed interesting differences in prediction. All achievement-test measures and report-card grades of the girls in grades 3 and 4 were highly related to I+ (all correlations in the .40's and .50's), indicating that the greater the young girl's sense of responsibility for her academic success, the more successful she is likely to be. The I− scores, however (i.e., their self-responsibility for failures), related significantly to all the same measures for the boys at grade 5 (correlations ranging from .34 to .53). In grades 6, 8, 10, and 12, achievement-test scores (California Achievement Tests) were only occasionally related significantly to IAR scores. Whether this difference in prediction is a function of the difference between the Iowa and the California Achievement Tests or the age of the subjects is unknown. However, significant relations in the .20's and .30's between total I and report-card grades were again obtained in each of these upper grades. In a ninth-grade sample used in another study, the achievement-test reading, language, arithmetic, and total test scores of the boys (but not the girls) were predicted from their I+ scores (correlations in the .50's).

Crandall, Katkovsky, and Preston (1962) found IAR scores related to other kinds of achievement behaviors in first-, second-, and third-grade boys. Total I scores (subscale scores were not used) were highly associated with the amount of time the boys chose to spend in intellectual activities during free play (.70) and the intensity with which they were striving in these activities (.66). The correlations between I scores and these variables were not significant for the girls in that study.

In general, the IAR has predicted best to young girls' standardized achievement-test performances and to those of older boys. It has predicted better to young boys' intellectal activities in free play than to those of young girls. Its most consistent prediction has been to report-card grades. The scale, then, predicts differently for the two sexes at different age levels. It seems probable that a belief in self-responsibility constitutes a motivational influence upon achievement performance and thus should predict behavior on tasks where motivational factors account for a relatively large proportion of the variance over and above ability or acquired knowledge. The child who feels responsible for his successes and failures should show greater initiative in seeking rewards and greater persistence in the face of difficulty. This hypothesis seems consistent with the data currently available on the IAR (the data reported above). That is, it may be this motivational factor which accounts for the better prediction found to boys' participation and intensity of striving in intellectual activities of their own choosing than to achievement-test scores. It may also account for the consistent, although low, prediction to report-card grades, since many teachers grade partially on the effort the child seems to display.

In conclusion, the associations found here to demographic variables and achievement behaviors lend some additional support to the construct validity of children's beliefs in their control of reinforcements, as well as providing evidence for the utility of measuring this construct with the present instrument. It is evident, however, from the inconsistencies and small magnitude of many of the relations found that the scale is in need of further refinement. Item analysis would provide a basis for eliminating non-discriminating items and improving the internal consistency of the two subscales. In addition, further research seems warranted relating IAR scores to achievement behaviors such as task persistence and striving, where motivational factors may be primary determinants.

SUMMARY

This study describes a scale for assessing children's beliefs that they, rather than other people, are responsible for their intellectual-academic successes and failures. Subscale scores assessing responsibility for successes and for failures were generally independent of each other. Split-half and test-retest reliabilities were moderately high. Normative data on 923 *S*s in grades 3–12 indicate that self-responsibility is already established by third grade, that older girls give more self-responsible answers than older boys, and that slight but significant age changes occur in subscale scores dependent upon the sex of the child. Responsibility scores were moderately related to intelligence, ordinal position, and size of family, and inconsistently related to social class. Evidence of prediction to intellectual-achievement performance is presented.

REFERENCES

Battle, Esther, and J. Rotter. "Children's feelings of personal control as related to social class and ethnic group." *J. Pers.,* 1963, **31,** 482–490.

Bialer, I. "Conceptualization of success and failure in mentally retarded and normal children." *J. Pers.,* 1961, **29,** 303–320.

Brackbill, Yvonne, and J. O'Hara. "The relative effectiveness of reward and punishment for discrimination learning in children." *J. comp. physiol. Psychol.,* 1958, **51,** 747–751.

Crandall, Virginia C. "The reinforcement effects of adult reactions and non-reactions on children's achievement expectations." *Child Develpm.,* 1963, **34,** 335–354.

Crandall, Virginia C., V. J. Crandall, and W. A. Katkovsky. "Children's social Desirability Questionnaire." *J. consult. Psychol.,* 1964.

Crandall, Virginia C., Suzanne Good, and V. Crandall. "The reinforcement effects of adult reactions and non-reactions on children's achievement expectations: A replication study." *Child Develpm.,* 1964, **35,** 485–497.

Crandall, V., W. Katkovsky, and Anne Preston. "Motivational and ability determinants of young children's intellectual achievement behaviors." *Child Develpm.,* 1962, **33,** 643–661.

Cromwell, R., D. Rosenthal, D. Shakow, and T. Kahn. "Reaction time, locus of control, choice behavior and descriptions of parental behavior in schizophrenic and normal subjects." *J. Pers.,* 1961, **29,** 363–380.

Crowne, D., and S. Liverant. "Conformity under varying conditions of personal commitment." *J. abnorm. soc. Psychol.,* 1963, **66,** 547–555

Gore, Mayo, and J. Rotter. "A personality correlate of social action." *J. Pers.,* 1963, **31,** 58–64.

Holden, K. "Attitude toward external versus internal control of reinforcement and learning of reinforcement sequences." Unpubl. master's thesis. Ohio State Univ., 1958.

Hollingshead, A. *The Two Factor Index of Social Position.* New Haven: Privately printed, 1957.

Hollingshead, A., and F. Redlich. *Social Class and Mental Illness.* New York: Wiley, 1958.

James, W. Internal versus external control of reinforcements as a basic variable in learning theory. Unpubl. doctoral dissertation. Ohio State Univ., 1957.

Liverant, S., and A. Scodel. "Internal and external control as determinants of decision making under conditions of risk." *Psychol. Reps.,* 1960, **7,** 59–67.

Meyer, W. J., and S. I. Offenbach. "Effectiveness of reward and punishment as a function of task complexity." *J. comp. physiol. Psychol.,* 1962, **55,** 532–534.

Odell, Miriam. Personality correlates of independence and conformity. Unpubl. master's thesis. Ohio State Univ., 1959.

Phares, E. Changes in expectancy in skill and chance situations. Unpubl. doctoral dissertation, Ohio State Univ., 1955.

Phares, E. "Expectancy changes in skill and chance situations." *J. abnorm. soc. Psychol.,* 1957, **54,** 339–342.

Rotter, J., M. Seeman, and S. Liverant. Internal versus external control of reinforcement: A major variable in behavior theory. In *Decisions, Values and Groups,* N. F. Washburne (Ed.). (vol. 2) London: Pergamon, 1962.

Seeman, M., and J. Evans. "Alienation and learning in a hospital setting." *Amer. sociol. Rev.,* 1963, **69,** 270–284.

Simmons, W. Personality correlates of the James-Phares scale. Unpubl. master's thesis. Ohio State Univ., 1959.

Sullivan, P. W. "The effects of verbal reward and verbal punishment on concept elicitation in children." *Amer. Psychologist,* 1960, **15,** 401.

3.3 *Orientation*

The study of locus of control involves a different set of expectancies than do studies concerning the self concept. The self concept represents an organized system of expectancies concerning subjective estimates about what one can or cannot do. It is also characterized by a self-evaluative component. The Lipsitt study is one of an earlier series in which a key element was the discrepancy between a person's self rating (actual self) and his evaluation of how he would ideally like to be (ideal self). Some personality theorists view a large discrepancy between actual and ideal ratings as indicative of poor adjustment and suggest that *self-acceptance* is a prerequisite to the acceptance of other people [see McCandless (1967) for a discussion of this position].

As was noted in the Battle and Rotter study of locus of control, difficult problems in measurement are frequently encountered by psychologists. This has indeed been the case with respect to children's self concepts. The Lipsitt study illustrates an attempt to measure the self concept and, in addition, children's manifest anxiety. Test-retest reliability data are reported, and a question is raised concerning the efficacy of utilizing actual self-ideal self discrepancy scores in correlational research. Lipsitt's discussion of the relationship between self disparagement and anxiety based upon conditioning principles kindles once again the motivation-learning issue raised in Chapter 2.

RECOMMENDED READING

Coopersmith, S. "A method for determining types of self-esteem." *J. educ. Psychol.,* **59** (1959), 87–94.

McCandless, B. R. *Children: Behavior and Development.* (2d ed.) New York: Holt, Rinehart and Winston, 1967. (See chap. 6, "The self-concept," pp. 254–292).

Ringness, T. A. "Self-concept of children of low, average, and high intelligence." *Amer. J. ment. Defic.,* **65** (1961), 543–561.

Piers, E. V., and D. B. Harris. "Age and other correlates of self-concept in children." *J. educ. Psychol.,* **55** (1964), 91–95.

3.3 A Self-Concept Scale for Children and Its Relationship to the Children's Form of the Manifest Anxiety Scale

Lewis P. Lipsitt, BROWN UNIVERSITY

The kinds of verbalizations that people "make to themselves," perhaps particularly about themselves, have long been of interest to personality theorists such as Murray, Rogers, Sullivan, and Allport. Such self-talk, as verbal behavior, typically beomes important in personality and clinical appraisals. Self-evaluative behavior, in fact, seems to be involved in the operational definitions of certain personality concepts as ego, superego, ego-ideal, self-concept, ideal-self, and the like. Thus, an individual who verbalizes inadequacy and inferiority is said to have weak ego-strength or a low self-concept. Moreover, persons' verbal representations of themselves are often compared with their concepts of an "ideal self" on the not uncommon assumption that in the conflicted or anxious individual there exists a large discrepancy between his ideal and his conception to himself.

There has arisen, however, some evidence contrary to the assumption

Reprinted from *Child Development,* **29** (1958), 463–473. By permission of the author and The Society for Research in Child Development, Inc.

of a negative relationship between anxiety level and verbal self-estimations. Taylor and Combs (18) presented children with written statements which the authors considered true of all children but which would require self-effacement to admit, finding that those who tended to admit to these statements were those with the highest adjustment scores as measured by the California Test of Personality. Zimmer (19) was unable to find a relationship between a self-acceptance measure and independent measures of conflict derived from a word association task.

Researchers interested in self-concept variables typically utilize discrepancy scores (1, 2, 5, 6, 7, 8, 10, 13, 15, 19) deriving from two test measures, the first involving *S*'s rating himself ("as he really thinks he is") with regard to trait-descriptive adjectives and the second requiring *S* to respond to the same adjectives indicating "how he would like to be." The discrepancy score may consist of the total difference between the two measures, and this discrepancy is considered as reflecting degree of dissatisfaction with oneself.

The present study employs both self-concept and discrepancy measures in fourth, fifth, and sixth grade children and is concerned primarily with [1] the comparative reliabilities of the discrepancy scores and the self-concept scores, and [2] the relationship of each of these two measures to scores on the children's form of the manifest anxiety scale (3, 4, 11, 14).

The self-concept scale contained the following 22 trait-descriptive adjectives, presented here in the order used in the scale: friendly, happy, kind, brave, honest, likeable, trusted, good, proud, *lazy,* loyal, co-operative, cheerful, thoughtful, popular, courteous, *jealous,* obedient, polite, *bashful,* clean, helpful. Each of these adjectives was prefaced by the phrase "I am . . ." and was followed by a five-point rating scale. Nineteen were considered as positive or socially desirable attributes, while three were considered negative (italicized above). The rating categories, scored from 1 to 5, were entitled *not at all, not very often, some of the time, most of the time,* and *all of the time.* A score of 1 was received on an item if *S* checked the first category, a score of 5 if the last category were checked, except in the case of the three negative adjectives which were scored in inverse fashion.[1] A score on the self-concept scale was obtained for each *S* by summing the ratings ascribed to himself on each item. Lower scores were presumed to reflect degree of self-disparagement.

The ideal-self scale contained the same adjectives but here each was prefaced by "I would like to be . . . ." Again, *S* rated himself on each item on similar scales. The discrepancy scores employed in the present

[1] The negative words may provide a detection device for nonreaders and indiscriminate checkers. In the present study, however, no *S*s were eliminated on such a basis.

study consisted of the simple subtraction of the total self-concept score from the total ideal-self score.[2]

Both scales were administered, with the children's manifest anxiety scale (CMAS), to approximately 300 fourth, fifth, and sixth graders on the same day, and again two weeks later. Administration was on a group basis in the classrooms, and *S*s were permitted as much time as needed to complete all the scales. The CMAS was administered first, the self-concept scale next, and the ideal-self scale last.

RELIABILITY OF THE CHILDREN'S FORM OF THE MANIFEST ANXIETY SCALE

A report of the children's form of the manifest anxiety scale (CMAS), published in this journal (3), contained means, standard deviations, and one-week reliability coefficients for a city population of fourth, fifth, and sixth graders. The present study provides additional information concerning the retest reliability of the CMAS for a two-week interval and a different population of same-aged children, and provides some indication of the generality of the originally reported mean scores for these age groups.

Table 1 contains the anxiety means and standard deviations for each grade and sex separately. These statistics may be compared with those describing the original population (3, p. 320). All of the present means fall somewhat below those previously reported. Significant differences between the present and previous means are found for fourth grade girls only ($t = 2.34$, $p = .05$).[3]

TABLE 1. Anxiety Scale Means and Standard Deviations by Grade and by Sex

	Fourth Grade			Fifth Grade			Sixth Grade		
	N	*M*	*SD*	*N*	*M*	*SD*	*N*	*M*	*SD*
Boys	47	13.13	7.38	50	15.16	7.96	41	14.51	8.12
Girls	62	15.61	8.83	61	15.26	7.44	37	16.57	8.16

[2] Seven *S*s who rated themselves higher on the self-concept than the ideal-self scale were eliminated.

[3] Despite the general statistical similarity of these two sets of group means, both of which are derived from presumably normal populations, this one disparity suggests caution in the interpretation of differences found between different test populations (e.g., normal school children vs. clinical samples). That is, significant differences should probably not be taken as necessarily reflecting the presence of population abnormality. It is suggested, furthermore, that the obtained mean for fourth grade girls in the original population may be an overestimate for a population of normal fourth grade girls.

Figure 1 presents a frequency polygon comparable to that of the original group (3, p. 320). The present group provides a somewhat flatter distribution with a tendency for the 20, 50, and 80 percentile positions to be lower by about two score-units (7.18, 14.41, and 22.54, respectively). The present coefficients (Table 2) are generally comparable to those obtained previously (3, p. 321). Each is reliable beyond the .001 level. It should be noted, however, that, whereas the first study provided its lowest reliability coefficient for the fourth grade girls relative to the remaining groups, the present study yielded its highest coefficients for that group.

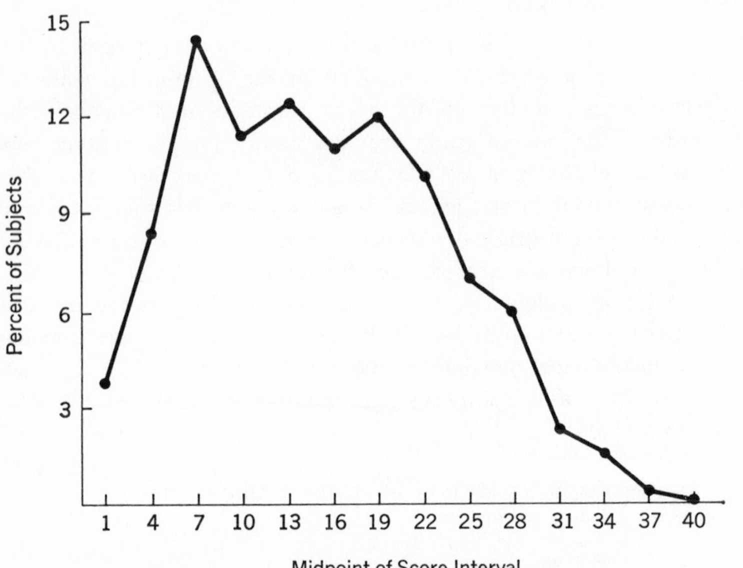

FIGURE 1. Frequency polygon showing the percentage of 298 fourth-, fifth-, and sixth-grade children receiving the indicated scores on the children's form of the manifest anxiety scale.

TABLE 2. Anxiety Scale Test-Retest Correlations by Grade and by Sex

	Fourth Grade		Fifth Grade		Sixth Grade	
	N	*r*	*N*	*r*	*N*	*r*
Boys	44	.89	48	.87	41	.91
Girls	57	.93	52	.89	35	.83

The lie scale means and standard deviations for the present group are reported in Table 3, and may be compared with those of the original population (3, p. 321). All of the present means are greater than those preiously reported. None of the correlations between anxiety and lie scores or each grade and sex separately reaches significance, ranging from −.20 o .16 in the present study. A chi square test indicates that these *r*'s onstitute only chance deviations from a common population value; pooling these *r*'s for all grade-sex combinations yields a composite *r* of −.114, which falls short of significance at the .05 level. Thus, as in the previous study, the tendency to falsify responses on the anxiety scale may result in either a high or low anxiety score.

TABLE 3. Lie Scale Means and Standard Deviations by Grade and by Sex

	Fourth Grade			Fifth Grade			Sixth Grade		
	N	*M*	*SD*	*N*	*M*	*SD*	*N*	*M*	*SD*
Boys	47	4.57	1.95	50	3.84	2.26	41	3.15	2.18
Girls	62	5.58	1.77	61	4.16	2.48	37	3.95	2.63

THE SELF-CONCEPT AND IDEAL-SELF SCALES

Table 4 presents the means and standard deviations for the self-concept scale for each grade and sex separately. An analysis of variance was performed and neither the main effects of grade or sex nor the interaction of these two variables was found significant. The six means were pooled to obtain an estimate of a mean score common to the combined population of fourth, fifth, and sixth graders. This mean is 86.75 with a standard deviation of 8.18.

TABLE 4. Self-Concept Scale Means and Standard Deviations by Grade and by Sex

	Fourth Grade			Fifth Grade			Sixth Grade		
	N	*M*	*SD*	*N*	*M*	*SD*	*N*	*M*	*SD*
Boys	47	85.81	9.75	50	86.24	8.25	41	87.17	6.85
Girls	62	87.39	10.07	61	86.74	8.27	37	87.11	8.76

Figure 2 represents a frequency polygon showing the percentage of *S*s receiving the indicated scores on the self-concept and ideal-self scales. The distribution of scores for the self-concept scale is essentially normal, as contrasted with the distribution for the ideal-self scale, where a J-curve results with most *S*s receiving high scores. Thus, most *S*s rate themselves as being highly desirous of attaining the positive attributes of the scales.

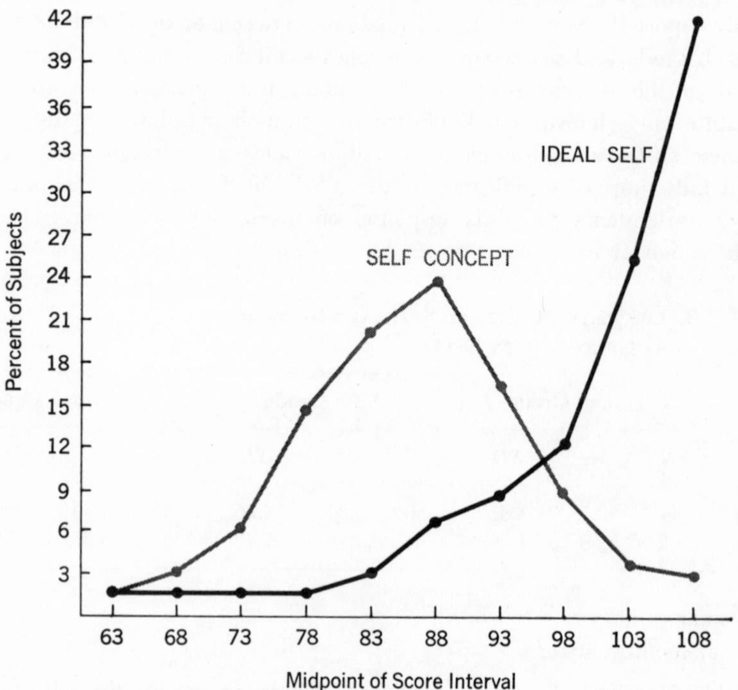

FIGURE 2. Frequency polygon showing the percentage of 298 fourth-, fifth-, and sixth-grade children receiving the indicated scores on the self-concept and ideal-self scales.

Our interest here is in the respective reliabilities of the *self-concept* and *discrepancy* scores. Table 5 depicts the two-week test-retest reliability coefficients for the self-concept measure alone. All of these correlations are significant beyond the .001 level.

Also in Table 5 are the comparable retest correlations for the discrepancy measure. These coefficients are all somewhat below those for the self-concept measure.[4] Four of six attain significance, nevertheless, at the .001 level, and two at the .01 level.

RELATIONSHIPS OF SELF-CONCEPT AND IDEAL-SELF MEASURES WITH SCORES ON THE CHILDREN'S MANIFEST ANXIETY SCALE

Table 6 reveals a negative relationship between the self-concept scores and anxiety scores as measured by the CMAS, for each of the grades and sexes separately. In all cases, these correlations are significant, five at the .01 and one at the .05 level. The magnitude of these correlations may be

[4] The loss of *S*s for the fourth grade in Table 5 was due to the impossibility of administering the ideal-self scale to one of the classes on the second day of testing.

TABLE 5. Test-Retest Correlations for Self-Concept Scale and Discrepancy Scores by Grade and by Sex

	Fourth Grade		Fifth Grade		Sixth Grade	
	N	*r*	*N*	*r*	*N*	*r*
self-concept scale						
Boys	44	.73 [a]	46	.80 [a]	40	.84 [a]
Girls	56	.78 [a]	49	.91 [a]	35	.80 [a]
discrepancy scores						
Boys	28	.57 [b]	44	.72 [a]	38	.56 [a]
Girls	32	.66 [a]	48	.68 [a]	34	.51 [b]

[a] Significant at .001 level.
[b] Significant at .01 level.

compared with those relating anxiety to the discrepancy scores, only four of which attain significance, two at the .01 and two at the .05 level. It would appear, then, that the self-concept score by itself yields a measure that is more reliable than the discrepancy score and that is more highly related to the CMAS score.

TABLE 6. Correlations between Anxiety Scale and Self-Concept Scale and Discrepancy Scores by Grade and by Sex

	Fourth Grade		Fifth Grade		Sixth Grade	
	N	*r*	*N*	*r*	*N*	*r*
anxiety scale and self-concept scale						
Boys	47	−.53 [a]	50	−.40 [a]	41	−.34 [b]
Girls	62	−.63 [a]	61	−.40 [a]	37	−.58 [a]
anxiety scale and discrepancy scores						
Boys	43	.31 [b]	48	.24	40	.20
Girls	55	.51 [a]	60	.39 [a]	36	.39 [b]

[a] Significant at .01 level.
[b] Significant at .05 level.

CONCLUSIONS AND DISCUSSION

The conclusions that may be drawn from these data are: [1] both the self-concept and discrepancy measures, as presented here, provided reliable estimates of an individual difference variable; [2] of these two types of measures, the self-concept score provided a somewhat more reliable measure than the discrepancy score; [3] for the fourth, fifth, and sixth grade *S*s, there were no reliable grade or sex differences in mean self-concept scores; [4] for all six grade-sex combinations, the self-concept measure correlated significantly with performance on the CMAS, while comparable correlations for the discrepancy scores were somewhat less and in some cases not reliable.[5]

The tendency toward self-disparagement, as reflected in responses to the self-concept scale, was found to be significantly related to another independent measure of the degree to which a person admits to possessing symptoms commonly held to reflect anxiety.[6] Several theorists (9, 16) have ascribed drive properties to anxiety; thus, theoretical predictions concerning the role of drive in learning may be applicable here as well.

The tendency toward self-disparagement may be conceived as a phenomenon producing behavioral effects consonant with its status as a drive variable as follows: The conditioning principles presumed to underlie the acquisition of secondary drives assume that neutral stimuli preceding reinforced responses may come through training to elicit those responses themselves in the absence of the original reinforcement. Thus, if a verbal stimulus ("You are naughty") is presented in conjunction with a noxious stimulus (physical punishment) which unconditionally elicits an emotional response (pain), that verbal stimulus may acquire the capacity to elicit (some part of) the emotional response independent of the original noxious stimulus. It is quite conceivable, then, that the conditions (behavior of the child) which originally resulted in the noxious stimulation (punishment) may come to elicit the verbal response and its stimulus counterpart ("I am naughty") which in turn mediates the emotional response. The tendency toward self-disparagement becomes, then, an antecedent condition for general emotional responsiveness (anxiety) or drive.

[5] The lower retest reliabilities of the discrepancy measure may be attributed to the fact that difference scores always involve additional sources of variability to those involved in a single test. The coefficient for the discrepancy measure is a function of the variability of the two tests, since the discrepancy score is derived from the use of both the self-concept and ideal-self scores. McNemar (12, p. 154) points out that the standard error of such difference scores must be lower than for one test alone, and that this tends to depress the reliability estimates of difference scores.

[6] Some may consider this relationship as indicative of the presence of a response set or test-taking attitude which mediates or influences scores on both scales. The view taken here is that whenever two test measures correlate, it may be said that a response set is responsible in that there exists a source of variance common to both measures. When test measures are correlated, they are measuring something in common, response set or whatever.

SUMMARY

The children's form of the manifest anxiety scale and self-concept and ideal-self scales were administered twice to approximately 300 fourth, fifth, and sixth graders at a two-week interval. A discrepancy score, or measure of self-disparagement, was obtained by subtracting *S*s' self-concept ratings from their ideal-self ratings. It was found that the self-concept measure taken by itself was more reliable than the discrepancy measure, and that the self-concept measure was more highly related to CMAS score than was the discrepancy score. Significant correlations were obtained for all grades and sex combinations between CMAS and self-concept scores, with high anxious *S*s producing low self-concept (or high self-disparagement) ratings. The two-week reliability of the CMAS was essentially the same as that for the original population.

REFERENCES

1. Bills, R. E., E. L. Vance, and D. S. McLean. "An index of adjustment and values." *J. consult. Psychol.,* 1951, **15,** 257–261.
2. Block, J., and H. Thomas. "Is satisfaction with self a measure of adjusment?" *J. abnorm. soc. Psychol.,* 1955, **51,** 254–259.
3. Castaneda, A., B. R. McCandless, and D. S. Palermo. "The children's form of the manifest anxiety scale." *Child Develpm.,* 1956, **27,** 317–326.
4. Castaneda, A., D. S. Palermo, and B. R. McCandless. "Complex learning and performance as a function of anxiety in children and task difficulty." *Child Develpm.,* 1956, **27,** 327–332.
5. Chordokoff, B. "Adjustment and the discrepancy between the perceived and ideal self." *J. clin. Psychol.,* 1954, **10,** 266–268.
6. Cowen, E. L., F. Heilizer, and H. S. Axelrod. "Self-concept conflict indicators and learning." *J. abnorm. soc. Psychol.,* 1955, **51,** 242–245.
7. Friedman, I. "Phenomenal, ideal, and projected conceptions of self." *J. abnorm. soc. Psychol.,* 1955, **51,** 611–615.
8. Hanlon, T. E., P. R. Hofstaetter, and J. P. O'Connor. "Congruence of self and ideal self in relation to personality adjustment." *J. consult. Psychol.,* 1954, **18,** 215–218.
9. Hull, C. L. *Principles of Behavior.* New York: D. Appleton-Century, 1943.
10. Levy, L. H. "The meaning and generality of perceived actual-ideal discrepanies." *J. consult. Psychol.,* 1956, **20,** 396–398.
11. McCandless, B. R., and A. Castaneda. "Anxiety in children, school achievement, and intelligence." *Child Develpm.,* 1956, **27,** 379–382.
12. McNemar, Q. *Psychological Statistics.* New York: Wiley, 1955.
13. Miller, K. S., and P. Worchel. "The effects of need-achievement and self-ideal discrepancy on performance under stress." *J. Pers.,* 1956, **25,** 176–190.
14. Palermo, D. S., A. Castaneda, and B. R. McCandless. "The relationship of

anxiety in children to performance in a complex learning task." *Child Devel-pm.,* 1956, **27,** 333–337.

15. Roberts, G. E. "A study of the validity of the index of adjustment and values." *J. consult. Psychol.,* 1952, **16,** 302–304.
16. Spence, K. W. Current interpretations of learning data and some recent developments in stimulus-response theory. In *Kentucky Symposium: Learning Theory, Personality Theory, and Clinical Research.* New York: Wiley, 1954.
17. Spence, K. W. *Behavior Theory and Conditioning.* New Haven: Yale Univ. Press, 1956.
18. Taylor, C., and A. W. Combs. "Self-acceptance and adjustment." *J. consult. Psychol.,* 1952, **16,** 89–91.
19. Zimmer, H. "Self-acceptance and its relation to conflict." *J. consult. Psychol.,* 1954, **18,** 447–449.

3.4 Orientation

Psychologists generally agree that the self concept is learned as the consequence of one's experiences with success and failure, evaluation by others whom one considers significant, and rewards and punishments one receives during the course of socialization. Among the various questions concerning self-concept development is the search for sources of individual differences in self-appraisal. Some children, quite early, appear to utilize autonomous standards for the appraisal of their competence, standards that represent comparative independence in judgment. Other children seem to be more dependent for their self-appraisals upon what other people think or the degree to which approval may be expressed by parent and teachers. Dreyer and Haupt have, in the study reported below, provided insight into the antecedents and correlates of this self-appraisal variable.

The Dreyer and Haupt study is unique in that it deals with the self-evaluative behavior of kindergarten children. A preponderance of self-appraisal and self-concept research has been conducted with older children and adults essentially because these measures require literacy. As an alternative to this strategy, the present study utilizes a projective method to assess children's self-appraisals.

The data obtained are analyzed in relation to an elaborate set of behavior ratings, laboratory measures of the children's level of aspiration and ability to delay gratification, and three measures of maternal behavior. The authors relate the interpretation of their results to motivation theory and speculate upon the influence of child-rearing practices, particularly independence training, on expectancies and self-evaluative tendencies. In this regard, readers will note the relevancy of this study to several companion papers in this volume, notably the Bartlett and Smith study (Chapter 1), which reports a relationship between certain child-rearing practices and the development of independence.

RECOMMENDED READING

Engel, M., and W. J. Raine. "A method for the measurement of the self-concept in children of the third grade." *J. genet. Psychol.,* **102** (1963), 124–137.

Staines, J. W. "Symposium: The development of children's values" (III) "The self-picture as a factor in the classroom." *Brit. J. educ. Psychol.,* **28** (1958), 97–111.

Sears, Pauline, and Vivian S. Sherman. *In Pursuit of Self-Esteem.* Belmont, Calif.: Wadsworth, 1964.

3.4 Self-evaluation in Young Children

Albert S. Dreyer, UNIVERSITY OF CONNECTICUT
Dorothy Haupt, THE MERRILL-PALMER INSTITUTE

INTRODUCTION

The correct or accurate appraisal of reality is considered an important characteristic of mental health by such people as Jahoda (11). Jourard (12), for example, says that the more a person's beliefs depart from reality, the more deviant, ineffective, and unhealthy we might expect his behavior to be. He goes on to state that the criterion against which to compare the person's beliefs may be the opinion of qualified experts.

McCandless (13) has recently dealt with the literature on the "self-concept," which he sees as a set of beliefs or expectancies, plus evaluations of the behaviors with reference to which these expectancies are held. He goes on to point out that there is no way of knowing the "real" self. Our closest approximation, he says, is to compare the statements of a person about himself with judgments of people who know him well. Helper (10) also comments on the widespread agreement that self-evaluation attitudes are believed to arrive rather directly from evaluations made of the individual by others.

A systematic investigation of this problem, however, must contend with

Reprinted from *Journal of Genetic Psychology,* **108** (1966), 185–197. By permission of the authors and The Journal Press.

the paradoxical question of whose reality is more valid—the individual's internal or "subjective" view or another person's external or "objective" view. Sullivan (22) states that the self-structure is made up of "reflected appraisals," appraisals of the individual which were made by parents and significant others. The implication of these comments seems to be that as the parents and significant others defined and evaluated the person, so he would come to define and evaluate himself.

Crandall (6) in his discussion of the development of one of the parameters of achievement standards in children, the *source* of the achievement standards, deals directly with this issue. The standards that children employ to evaluate their competence, he says, may be based on their own subjective standards. Such children less often define the competence of their behavior on the basis of approval or criticism of others. They are said to hold autonomous achievement standards. Other children, in contrast, characteristically tend to look to other persons to define the competence of their performance. They mirror or reflect the standards of others and their standards are designated reflective. He says that developmentally it might be presumed that children who have developed autonomous achievement standards have more readily incorporated the achievement standards which significant others, such as parents, have held for them and have come to accept these standards as their own.

The present paper stems from a larger study dealing with the antecedents and consequences of preschool children's expectations of the demands of school. Within this study we have data pertaining to the child's evaluation of his own competence in meeting the demands of his world and the evaluations of the teachers of the children's capabilities in these matters. The purpose of this paper is to present the differences in behavior between those children who rely on their own standards of evaluation of competence and those who reflect or mirror the evaluative standards of the teacher. We will relate this measure of appraisal of competence, our independent variable, to several dependent variables: school and laboratory behavior, teacher ratings, maternal interview, and questionnaire data concerning achievement demands and sanctions.

METHOD

Subjects

Thirty-two middle-class kindergarten children in the Detroit area, 15 boys and 17 girls, and their mothers and teachers served as subjects.

MEASURES

Appraisal of competence The measure of the child's appraisal of his competence was obtained from a structured-doll-play interview. Five social- and nonsocial-problem situations dealing with such content as competition, independence, and reactions to frustration were presented to the child by the junior author through a combination of verbal instructions and manipulation of the doll figures. The child was asked, using the dolls as a medium, to indicate what he would do to cope with the situation. His verbalizations and behavior were recorded verbatim by the experimenter.

The teachers these children had in nursery school were given these same situations in a questionnaire form and asked to describe how they believed this same child would handle the situations.

The five situations used with the child and teacher are as follows:

Teacher form

1. ______ and another child are playing with the bowling pins and ball. They appear evenly matched in skill and control. Soon, however, child X calls out, "I'm better than you. I knocked down more than you."
2. Child X and ______ are both pulling at a ladder, each screaming loudly, "I had it first."
3. ______ is building a garage. Child X has been annoying him by removing blocks and telling him how silly his garage looks.
4. The teacher brings a collection of boxes of different sizes, shapes, colors, etc., to school and puts them on the table.
5. ______ is dressing up in a costume and having difficulty with some piece of apparel.

Each item was followed by two questions:

What would ______ do in such a situation?
What would *you* do?

Along with other codes, each of the child and teacher story responses were coded for whether the child was expressing competence or incompetence in handling the situation. The definitions of competence and incompetence were as follows:

Competence
Child views self as effectively capable of handling the situation, solving the problem, functioning by his own efforts: example, remains with situational problem, states intended action, or implies he will act.
Incompetence
Child views self as unable or incapable of handling the situation or the problem on his own: example, may leave the room, call for the teacher in a way clearly indicating his own feeling of incapacity, or insist that he cannot do it.

There was also a *no score* category.

Three judges, the junior author and two graduate students in child development, coded a sample of 21 subjects. The per cent of complete agreement between the three sets of coders ranged from 91 to 93 per cent, indicating good agreement for this category.

A competence index for each child and for his teacher was obtained by dividing the sum of competence codes by the competence-plus-incompetence codes. Each competence index was then normalized by using an arc-sign transformation (20).

An "accuracy" of appraisal-of-competence measure was obtained in the following manner. We first ran a discrepancy score by subtracting the child from the teacher-competence index. We disregarded sign—i.e., the direction of the difference—being concerned only with the absolute size of the difference—and formed a distribution of the difference scores between the child- and teacher-competence indices. The distribution was divided at the median.[1] The 16 children whose appraisal of their own competence was highly discrepant from the teacher's evaluation of their competence—i.e., above the median—were termed low accuracy of appraisal of reality or, in Crandall's terminology, the *autonomous* appraisal-of-competence group (AAC); the 16 children whose competence indices were close to their teachers—i.e., below the median—were termed high accuracy of appraisal of reality or, again in Crandall's terms, the *reflective* appraisal-of-competence group (RAC). There were no sex differences in this appraisal-of-competence measure. Boys, that is, did not significantly differ from girls in whether their self-evaluation approximated the teacher's evaluation of them. Each group, then, has both boys and girls within it.

The behavior of these two groups on various dependent measures was then compared.

Classroom observations Observations of these children in their kindergarten settings were made by the authors. There were 11 categories of task and social behaviors (see Table 1) which the observers were interested in assessing. Each of these behaviors was judged on a five-point rating scale. To establish reliability of the categories, six children were observed for a total of 19 joint observations; the per cent of agreement ranged from 74 to 100 per cent over the 11 categories with a median of 84 per cent. Each observer then spent one morning observing the children in our sample in his kindergarten classroom. The child was observed for a 15-minute period and then the child was rated on each category. An observation of the teacher for other purposes followed this child observation and following this, another 15-minute child observation was made. Thus, a rotation of child and teacher observations proceeded throughout the morning so that each child was observed from two to four 15-minute

[1] We originally had planned to analyze all our data using four subgroups in which the child-teacher competence indices were equally high (HH), equally low (LL), child high but teacher low (HL), and child low but teacher high (LH). There were eight children in each subgroup using medial splits of the distributions. A Kruskal-Wallis H test (8) was applied to parts of the data. There were no differences between any of the four subgroups in the observation categories and so we abandoned this method of analysis.

periods. At the end of the morning, the observer then made a final composite rating from his total morning's impressions of the child. The child's score in a given behavior rating scale was the pooled average of all the ratings made.

Laboratory tasks Laboratory measures of the child's level of aspiration and impulse control were obtained. The level of aspiration of each child was measured in a task devised by Sears and Levin (17) and adapted for the present study. Five differently colored rubber balls were hung from an adjustable rod on the ceiling. The easiest to reach was just within fingertip reach of the child, and each of the remaining balls was hung about three inches higher than the preceding one. The child was asked to choose the color of the ball he would try to hit on his jump. There were 10 trials. A weight of 5 was assigned to the highest or hardest ball to reach and a weight of 1 to the lowest or easiest ball to reach. From the child's choices a level-of-aspiration score was derived consisting of the weighted average over the 10 trials. The child's level of aspiration was obtained twice: while he was in nursery school and after he had been in kindergarten at least a month.

A measure of the child's ability to delay immediate gratification was obtained in a task adapted from Block and Martin (3). Each child was given the opportunity to accumulate as much candy as he wished, with the proviso that if he stopped to eat or taste a piece of candy, the game was ended. The candy was placed by the child, one piece at a time, into the cart of a toy known as a "Coke Loader." He cranked the handle which raised the car until it tipped, emptying the candy into a large glass jar. The impulse-control score was simply the number of pieces accumulated in the jar at the time the child chose to eat the candy. The scores ranged from 8 to 50.

Teacher ratings The child's kindergarten teacher rated him on 14 categories of behavior dealing with achievement, independence, and interpersonal behaviors. Most of these were adapted from Winterbottom (25) and the remainder were developed by the authors. Each of these behaviors was judged on a five-point scale; the items were randomized in the list given the teachers. Reliability of the ratings by the teachers using the present form was not feasible to obtain. These ratings, however, are the end result of three preliminary forms of the questionnaire; they represent those reliably rated by teachers with similar training.

Some of the categories listed in Table 3 were clustered into composite scores; the remainder are single-item categories. The composition of the categories used was as follows:

A. *Task or instrumental independence*

1. Overall independence.
2. Ability to do things in school on his own.

3. Ability to entertain himself or keep himself occupied.
4. Ability to look after himself in routines.

B. *Emotional independence*
1. Response to adult authority: obedience—disobedience.

C. *Achievement*
1. Reaction when he does well in something.
2. Overall competitiveness.
3. Reaction to failure or difficulty with a task.
4. Degree to which he wants to do well.

D. *Emotional control*
1. Emotional mood swings.
2. Overall impulsiveness.

E. *Popularity*
1. Degree of popularity with other children.

F. *Assertiveness*
1. Ability to stand up for his rights with other children.

G. *Originality*
1. Degree of conventionality-originality.

Maternal behavior Data on maternal behavior were obtained from three different sources. The first source was a coding of the mothers' reactions to a set of five story-completion situations depicting children's behavior. Each was asked to indicate how she would respond to the situation described and this response was rated on a five-point scale of power-assertive behavior. The power-assertive score used in the present analysis was the mean rating for each mother on these five stories. Power-assertion definitions, reliabilities for the coding, and the stories used can be found in a previous article by the authors (7).

The second source of maternal-behavior data involved a coding of the mother's response to an interview question (18) concerning the handling of dependency behavior on the part of the child: i.e., "How do you generally react if X asks you to help him with something you think he can probably do by himself?" The coding of the mother's behavior was on a five-point scale of unresponsiveness.

The third source of parent data was a questionnaire in which the degree of power-assertion expressed by the mother was measured (19). Following a description of each of 15 adult-child conflict situations, eight multiple-choice responses were presented varying in the degree of control expressed—that is, how much choice is allowed the child. The parent checked the behavior that best fitted her own preferred and usual way of handling the conflict. Five of these situations were achievement or autonomy related so that a parental power-assertion score around achievement was obtained by averaging the mother's weighted responses over these five stories.

Data Analysis

Nonparametric statistics were used since the data were considered to be ordinal in nature. The White test (8) was used for testing the significance of the differences between the two appraisal-of-competence groups. The rank-difference correlation, rho, was used for all measures of association.

The mean scores presented in the tables were not used in the tests of statistical significance but are reported solely for the purpose of communicating to the reader the extent and direction of the differences between the two groups of children.

TABLE 1. Kindergarten Observation Differences between Autonomous and Reflective Appraisal of Competence Groups

Observation Category	Mean Rating	
	RAC	*AAC*
Competence in handling kindergarten	3.81	4.48 [a]
Involvement	3.67	4.00
Friendliness to teacher	3.62	4.10 [a]
Friendliness to other children	3.62	4.18 [a]
Competition	2.50	3.43 [a]
Sharing	3.16	3.63 [a]
Ego control	3.46	3.26
Compliance	1.77	1.95
Interest	3.61	3.94
Persistence	4.18	4.39
Initiation of activities	3.36	4.12 [a]

[a] $p < .05$.

RESULTS

Kindergarten Observations

The observation findings seen in Table 1 indicate that the AAC group were significantly more competent in handling the kindergarten situation; they expressed more friendliness to the teacher and other children; they expressed more competitive behavior; they shared more; and they initiated activities in the kindergarten more than the RAC group. It should be noted, moreover, that all the comparisons, except for the ego-control variable, were in favor of the AAC group. These children, then, whose evaluations of their own competence were very divergent from those of the teachers, are the children whose social and nonsocial interactions are most expansive and most easily expressed. The RAC group, in contrast, those children whose evaluations of their own competence most closely mirror or parallel the teachers' evaluations, are the ones who were rated by the observers as less competent, less friendly to teachers and children, less competitive, less sharing, and who need help more often in initiating activities.

Laboratory Tasks

These differences in kindergarten behavior, especially those concerned with independence behavior, lend support to the notion that the RAC group do need external confirmation of their own capacities, and do not have a stable, internal frame of reference about their performance.

The level-of-aspiration results yield additional data which confirm this supposition. Table 2 indicates that there is no relation between the child's mean level-of-aspiration score on Test 1 (nursery school) plus Test 2 (kindergarten) and whether appraisal of competence is reflective or autonomous. But the greater the reflective-appraisal-of-competence score, the greater is the average shift either up or down in level of aspiration from Test 1 and Test 2. An interpretation of this finding is that the RAC children are uncertain as to the adequacy of their performance without the availability of an outside criterion. Since no external frames of reference are present in the level-of-aspiration situation, they are more unstable in their level-of-aspiration behavior.

That this fluctuation is not necessarily an indication of greater generalized flexibility, moreover, can be found in the correlation of appraisal of competence and impulse control. The more the child's self-evaluation reflects the teacher's evaluation, the greater the impulse-control score (Table 2).

TABLE 2. Relation between Laboratory Tasks and Autonomous-Reflective Appraisal of Competence ($N = 32$)

Laboratory task	Rho
Level of aspiration:	
Mean level of aspiration	.03
Level of aspiration shift	−.66 [a]
Impulse control	−.39 [b]

[a] $p < .01$.
[b] $p < .05$.

Teacher Ratings

Analysis of the differences in behavior between the two groups shows the AAC group to be significantly more achievement oriented (Category C in Table 3). The AAC group is also rated as manifesting significantly more originality (Category G) in their activities in the classroom.

Correlational analysis of the behavior ratings of the teachers are consistent with these and our other findings. The more the child's appraisal of competence is autonomous rather than reflective, the less cautious and more impulsive but also more variable in mood (Category D) he appears to the teacher (rho = .39, $p < .05$). Finally, we also find that the more autonomous the child's appraisal of competence, the more he is rated by the teacher as achievement oriented (Category C, rho = .49, $p < .01$) and original (Category G, rho = .54, $p < .01$).

TABLE 3. Teacher Rating Differences between Autonomous and Reflective Appraisal of Competence Groups

Teacher Rating Category	Mean Rating	
	RAC	*AAC*
A. Task independence	4.01	4.06
B. Emotional independence	2.30	2.44
C. Achievement	3.33	3.96 [a]
D. Emotional control	2.98	2.78
E. Popularity	3.60	3.44
F. Self-assertion	3.56	4.01
G. Originality	3.11	3.80 [a]

[a] $p < .05$.

Maternal Behaviors

What then are the conditions in these children's home environments that relate to these differing modes of appraisal of competence? The maternal data point to high control and low nurturance's being related to reflective appraisal of competence. The more responsive the mother is when the child asks for help in something the mother thinks he can do by himself, the more the child's self-evaluation mirrors the teacher's evaluation of him (rho = .32, $p < .10$). The more power-assertive or controlling the mother is around achievement and autonomy, the more the child again reflects the evaluation of the teacher (rho = .34, $p < .10$). Both these correlations do not reach acceptable levels of statistical significance, but they are in the expected direction. The third source of maternal data is statistically significant and indicates that the more the mother's power-assertion score in the story completions, the more the child's self-evaluation mirrors or reflects the evaluation of the teacher (rho = .40, $p < .05$). Autonomous achievement standards would seem to develop in a home atmosphere where the child's attempts to master his environment are supported by his mother. It would seem that the child needs a learning atmosphere in which he can reduce the gap between what he knows should be done and what he actually can do.

DISCUSSION

Our results indicate that high maternal control and low maternal nurturance tend to be present in the homes of children we have postulated to need external sources for evaluating their own task-oriented, independence behavior. These children, in turn, show less capacity to cope with the demands of their school situation.

Our conceptual framework has grown out of and been consistent with that of McClelland (14) and Atkinson (1) who say that achievement motivation develops out of growing expectations of one's own capacities. The aspect of the theory that is most germane to the present results states that unpleasantness and avoidance motivation results from too large a discrepancy between expectations and event.

Winterbottom (25), in work stemming from these theoretical notions, reported a positive relationship between early independence training and later achievement motivation as McClelland used the term. Chance (4) and Gordon (9), on the other hand, reported that children exposed to early independence-training demands by mothers were not as achievement oriented or as productive as might be expected. There were methodological differences between the studies with Chance concerned with actual achievement and Winterbottom with need for achievement as measured by the TAT. But the findings do suggest that there is an optimum time and climate in which independence behavior is fostered. The lack of maternal responsiveness we found in the mothers of the RAC group interacting with the mother's expectations may serve to increase avoidance motivation in the child and to reduce the degree of coping behavior of the sort expressed in our competence index.

Baumrind has recently reported some data pertinent to this discussion (2). She finds that preschool children highest in observed self-sufficiency and approach tendencies to the world had parents whose behavior was rated highest in control *and* nurturance. She concludes that highly competent child behavior can result from different degrees of control relative to nurturance provided that both are high. She goes on to say that parental control and nurturance are synergic, supporting a point of view about parental behavior we feel needs to be stressed (23). Baumrind explicitly did not study what she termed "covert dynamic forces" with which this paper is dealing and which we believe to be highly important in the study of achievement and independence behavior.

It would seem necessary, then, to carry the problem of the development of self-evaluation in children further by seeing if the children who have reflective appraisals of competence have typically been placed in situations where the expectations of others about their performance were clearly beyond their capacity to confirm. High standards of performance may have very early been specified for them at a time when they were incapable of meeting the standards.

One of the major limitations of these data is that we do not have measures of father's response to dependency demands from the child. The role of the father has been demonstrated to be critical in the development of independence and task-oriented behaviors (15, 21) and we would have liked to include them in our study. Time and personnel limitations made this not possible. The only measure of father behavior we do have is father's response to the five achievement and autonomy questionnaire items scored for degree of power-assertion expressed. These data were collected by Halawi for other purposes (19). It will be recalled that we found a nonsignificant tendency for mother's power-assertion around achievement and autonomy to be related to the child's self-evaluation being more reflective of the teacher's evaluation of him. In contrast, we find a *reverse* but also nonsignificant tendency for the father's power-assertion or control on this measure to be related to the child's self-evaluation being more autonomous of the teacher's evaluation of him (rho $= -.20$, $p > .10$). The difference between the two correlations is, however, not significant (Fisher's $z = .37$, $p = .70$). A number of uncontrolled variables could be operating here like the sex of the child, ordinal position, and sex of siblings which future work should take into account when studying the effects of father's power-assertion on child behavior.

These results confirm some general conclusions reached by Coopersmith (5) in his study of fifth- and sixth-grade children. He secured a high self-esteem but low teacher-esteem group (HL) and a low self-esteem but high teacher-esteem group (LH). These two groups correspond to our AAC group and of them he says that the HL and LH groups ". . . appear to be similar in their refusal to accept the *status quo* and are marked by high achievement motivation, a high level of anxiety . . . and an ideal beyond immediate reach (p. 92)." From these and other findings he questions the usual definitions of adjustment which emphasize the accuracy of perception according to which the HL and LH groups would be considered maladjusted. We concur with Coopersmith that definitions of adjustment defined solely in terms of passivity and acceptance are often inappropriate and inadequate.

The group of children whom we have designated as having an evaluation-of-self autonomous from that of their teachers seems to have made substantial gains in the achievement of competence in the sense that the concept has been used by White (24). Maximum motivation, he and others conclude (16, 24), does not necessarily lead to the most adequate problem solving. We need further work in the parental behaviors fostering this optimum problem-solving orientation and feelings of self-worth.

SUMMARY

Accuracy of self-evaluation of competence was measured in 32 kindergarten children. Two groups were formed on the basis of whether self-evaluation was different from or similar to teacher's evaluation. Level-of-aspiration and impulse-control measures were obtained from the children; kindergarten behavior observations, teacher ratings, and maternal behavior data were also obtained. The children with more autonomous self-evaluations manifested more independence and achievement as well as more affiliative behaviors in kindergarten. Overcontrol of impulse and less stable levels of aspiration characterized the groups with less autonomous self-evaluations. Maternal control was more characteristic of the mothers of the less autonomous group. Implications of these data for the development of self-evaluation is discussed.

REFERENCES

1. Atkinson, J. W. (Ed.) *Motives in Fantasy, Action and Society*. Princeton, N.J.: Van Nostrand, 1958.
2. Baumrind, D. "Child training antecedents of preschool behavior." *Amer. Psychol.*, 1963, **18**, 338 (abstract).
3. Block, J., and B. Martin. "Predicting the behavior of children under frustration." *J. abnorm. soc. Psychol.*, 1955, **51**, 281–285.
4. Chance, J. E. "Independence training and first graders' achievement." *J. consult. Psychol.*, 1961, **25**, 149–154.
5. Coopersmith, S. "A method for determining types of self-esteem." *J. abnorm. soc. Psychol.*, 1959, **59**, 87–94.
6. Crandall, V. J., W. Katkovsky, and A. Preston. "A conceptual formulation for some research on children's achievement development." *Child Develpm.*, 1960, **31**, 787–797.
7. Dreyer, A. S., and D. Haupt. "The assertion of authority: Differences between teachers, student teachers, and mothers of young children." *J. educ. Res.*, 1960, **54**, 63–66.
8. Edwards, A. L. *Statistical Methods for the Behavioral Sciences*. New York: Rinehart, 1956.
9. Gordon, J. E. "Relationships among mothers' *n* achievement, independence training attitudes, and handicapped children's performance." *J. consult. Psychol.*, 1959, **23**, 207–212.

10. Helper, M. "Parental evaluation of children and children's self-evaluation." *J. abnorm. soc. Psychol.,* 1958, **56,** 190–194.
11. Jahoda, M. *Current Concepts of Positive Mental Health.* New York: Basic Books, 1958.
12. Jourard, S. M. *Personal Adjustment.* New York: Macmillan, 1958.
13. McCandless, B. R. *Children and Adolescents.* New York: Holt, Rinehart and Winston, 1961.
14. McClelland, D. C., J. W. Atkinson, R. A. Clark, and E. L. Lowell. *The Achievement Motive.* New York: Appleton-Century-Crofts, 1953.
15. Rosen, B. L., and R. D'Andrade. "The psychosocial origins of achievement motivation." *Sociometry,* 1959, **22,** 185–217.
16. Sarason, S. B., K. S. Davidson, F. K. Lighthall, R. R. Waite, and B. F. Ruebush. *Anxiety in Elementary School Children.* New York: Wiley, 1960.
17. Sears, P. S., and H. Levin. "Levels of aspiration in preschool children." *Child Develpm.,* 1957, **28,** 317–326.
18. Sears, R. R., E. E. Maccoby, and H. Levin. *Patterns of Child Rearing.* Evanston, Ill.: Row, Peterson, 1957.
19. Sigel, I. E., and A. Halawi. Influence technique questionnaire. Unpubl. manuscript, Merrill-Palmer Inst., Detroit, Mich., 1957.
20. Snedecor, G. W. *Statistical Methods.* Ames, Iowa: Iowa State Coll. Press, 1946.
21. Strodtbeck, F. L. Family interaction, values and achievement. In *Talent and Society,* D. C. McClelland, A. L. Baldwin, U. Bronfenbrenner, and F. L. Strodtbeck (Eds.) Princeton, N.J.: Van Nostrand, 1958, pp. 135–194.
22. Sullivan, H. S. *The Interpersonal Theory of Psychiatry.* New York: Norton, 1953.
23. Torgoff, I., and A. S. Dreyer. "Achievement-inducing and independence-granting—Synergistic parental role components: Relation to daughters' 'parental' role orientation and level of aspiration." *Amer. Psychol.,* 1961, **16,** 345 (abstract).
24. White, R. W. "Motivation reconsidered: The concept of competence." *Psychol. Rev.,* 1959, **66,** 297–333.
25. Winterbottom, M. The relation of need for achievement in learning experiences in independence and mastery. In *Motives in Fantasy, Action and Society,* J. W. Atkinson (Ed.) Princeton, N.J.: Van Nostrand, 1958, pp. 453–478.

3.5 *Orientation*

From an examination of two empirically based studies of the self-concept, attention is turned to a theoretical analysis of this psychological construct. Lowe begins with a concise discourse on the history of the self concept as a heuristic construct in research and as a basis for the development of phenomenology in psychology. The basic issue to which Lowe addresses himself is whether the self concept is an objective entity suitable for scientific research or whether it is the metaphysical creation of psychologists to provide an explanatory construct without which certain behavior could not be understood. This is an extremely basic issue which transcends self-concept research and can be examined in relation to many psychological concepts, including some treated in this volume (identification, cognitive style, and catharsis of aggression). Critics of cognitive theory and of self theory frequently point out the extent to which inferences must be made in order to explain the relationship between a stimulus and a response. If a construct remains at the inferential level, that is, cannot be objectively observed, is it scientific to maintain one's dependence upon the construct?

Lowe's exploration of this issue includes a survey of self-concept measures and their validation, an examination of the criterion of consistency in the self concept, and a review of six possible interpretations of the self concept. The variations explained by Lowe provide ample evidence of the theoretical controversies that pervade the behavioral sciences. Such controversies do, however, give impetus to empirical investigation, and without this our horizons of knowledge would remain restricted.

RECOMMENDED READING

Crowne, D. P., and M. W. Stephens. "Self-acceptance and self-evaluative behavior: A critique of methodology." *Psychol. Bull.,* **58** (1961), 104–121.

Wylie, Ruth. *The Self-Concept.* Lincoln, Neb.: Univ. of Nebraska Press, 1961.

3.5 The Self Concept: Fact or Artifact?

C. Marshall Lowe, UNIVERSITY OF CALIFORNIA, BERKELEY

One of the more difficult tasks for psychology is relating the observation of behavior to the study of mental processes. One approach to the problem has been to limit psychology to the study of behavior and to leave to philosophy the task of speculating as to the existence and nature of mind and soul.

Reprinted from *Psychological Bulletin,* **58** (1961), 325–336. By permission of the author and the American Psychological Association, Inc.

There have, however, been psychologists who have sought to make sense out of human action by positing a self or ego, in order that they might understand the coherence and unity which they have thought that they have seen in human behavior. Thus, G. W. Allport (1943) claimed that the concept of ego was made necessary by certain shortcomings in associationism, and he went on to list eight different uses for the concept of the ego. During the 1940s the *Psychological Review* was in fact well-flavored with articles of philosophical taste (Allport, 1943; Bertocci, 1945; Chein, 1944; Lundholm, 1940). These articles were attempts to find the source of human behavior by discussions of concepts, but they failed to make a lasting distinction between the self as subjective knower and the self as object of knowledge. The self as essence defied definition, and the discussions concerning the nature of mind seemed relevant for neither experimental nor applied psychology.

But during the 1940s there was a parallel attempt at construction of a useful concept of the self. While Rogers wrestled with the problem of researching a client centered approach in psychotherapy, one of his students (Raimy, 1943) developed a construct of the self which had a perceptual frame of reference. What Raimy called the self-concept was both a learned perceptual system functioning as an object in the perceptual field, and a complex organizing principle which schematizes ongoing experience. Raimy demonstrated in his dissertation that attitudes toward the self can be found by analyzing counseling protocols, and that these self-perceiving attitudes formed a reliable index for improvement in psychotherapy.

The concept of the self soon formed the theoretical underpinning for a new approach to the study of behavior. Raimy's construct of the self received further development in the book *Individual Behavior* (Snygg and Combs, 1949). The authors stated that behavior was best understood as growing out of the individual subject's frame of reference. Behavior was to be interpreted according to the phenomenal field of the subject rather than be seen in terms of the analytical categories of the observer.

As the self-concept was born with client centered therapy, so congruent were the theory of the self and the practice of psychotherapy that a new self-centered therapy became theoretical for the first time: Rogers (1951) described therapeutic change in a phenomenological frame of reference.

By 1950 the phenomenological view of the self had become the center of a new movement in psychology, having already generated a block of research studies (Rogers, *et al.,* 1949). When Hilgard (1949) postulated in his APA presidential address the need for a self to understand psychoanalytic defense mechanisms, and called for research on the self, psychology listened. To the desert came rain that washed all before it.

The deluge of studies within the last decade has not been contained within any one theoretical channel, so that studies involving the self-concept have spread over into many areas of psychology. Ten years of research efforts have produced a mass of data, reflecting different theoretical assumptions and differing research methods. While the time has now passed for one article to deal adequately with all the studies that have been done, the sheer mass of evidence would suggest that certain questions be asked of theories of the self-concept.

This paper is concerned with the problem as to whether the self is an objective reality which is a fit field for psychological research, or whether it is a somewhat nebulous abstraction useful only to give a theoretical basis to things the psychologist could not otherwise understand. Put in other words, this paper faces the issue as to whether the results of studies of the self are to be accepted at face value, or whether other explanations of results would be more parsimonious or reasonable.

The writer will discuss first attempts to quantify data concerning the self-concept to arrive at an operational definition. We will then assess the validity of measures of the self-concept, and will relate the self-concept to other constructs. We will briefly allude to attempts to establish a relationship between different measures. Finally, the writer will return to certain philosophical and historical considerations in order to reach a conclusion as to whether the self-concept is indeed a fact of nature, or an artifact of men's minds.

MEASURING THE SELF-CONCEPT

Many psychologists have believed that if something exists it can be measured. There have been many investigators who have assumed that the self-concept refers to an existence of some sort and have gone on to measure it.

The most popular type of operational definition has assumed that the self-concept can be defined in terms of the attitudes toward the self, as determined either by the subject's references to himself in psychotherapy or by asking him to mark off certain self-regarding attitudes on a rating scale.

One of the first attempts at attitude measurement was by Sheerer (1949), who extracted from the protocols of cases at the University of Chicago Counseling Center all statements that were relevant either for attitudes to self or to other people. These statements formed the basis for a 101-item rating scale. The Sheerer client statements also formed the basis for rating scales constructed by Phillips (1951) and by Berger (1952).

The only *rating scale* of attitudes towards self that has been published is the Index of Adjustment and Values (Bills, 1958). Bills states that the intent of the index is to measure the phenomenological self view as described by Lecky (1945), Snygg and Combs (1949), and Rogers (1951). This scale is more elaborate in that each item is ranked with three different instructions. First, the subject ranks the item on a scale as to how well it describes himself. Next, he marks the items as to how acceptant he is of his first, or self-rating of the item, and finally he rates the item as to the degree to which he aspires to be like that item.

The scoring of the Bills index also is more elaborate than that traditional for rating scales. There are in fact two different measures, neither one being simply a rating of items in absolute terms, as in the scales previously described. Bills' measures depend instead upon the differences between ratings made under different instructions. A measure of self-acceptance is provided by the degree of similarity between the way the subject sees himself as being, and the way he rates himself as accepting his self-ratings. A measure of self–ideal-self discrepancy is given by comparing the differences in ratings between the way the self is rated as being, and the way the self is rated as wishing to be.

Brownfain (1952) made still another adaptation in the use of the rating scale, deriving a measure of what he termed the stability of the self-concept. Subjects ranked themselves on 25 words and phrases, each describing a different area of personality adjustment. The measure is not of how sure the subject is of himself, but of how sure he is of what he thinks about himself; the subject is instructed to make the ratings twice, first with an optimistic frame of reference, and then with a pessimistic one. The degree of congruence between the two ratings is termed the degree of stability of the self-concept.

A different theoretical approach towards measurement of self-concept involves the use of *Q* technique. Stephenson (1953) describes how one's "inner experiences" can be translated into behavior by means of Q sort, through which the phenomenal field is translated into action. Using this method, two of Stephenson's students at the University of Chicago derived a conceptual self-system in an intensive study of a single subject (Edelson and Jones, 1954).

Others at the University of Chicago have used *Q* sorts as a measure of self-concept, in an attempt to assess changes in self-concept during psychotherapy (Rogers and Dymond, 1954). Statements were taken from counseling protocols, and were sorted both for real self and for ideal self. The degree of congruence between the two sorts is taken as a measure of adjustment.

Attempts to measure the self-concept face three difficulties. First, it must be demonstrated that the operational and philosophic meanings are in fact equivalent. In the case of the self-concept it needs to be shown that the "inner experience" is effectively conveyed by the outward movement of making check marks on lines, or sorting cards. Secondly, an efficient and systematic method must be found for selecting items for the scales and sorts, the problem being that of defining the universe from which items are to be selected. Finally, the different measures imply different operational definitions. Just as one can not multiply apples and pears, so is it impossible to interchange different operational definitions as if they were the same, or to pretend that each means the same thing by the term self-concept.

If something is measured does it exist? If the answer is yes, we must still be aware that we may not fully understand what we are measuring. One must measure, but must then compare and carefully validate.

VALIDATION OF SELF-CONCEPT MEASURES

A psychological construct stands and falls according to how useful it is in understanding human behavior. A term is meaningful only when successful validation studies have found significant relationships with established variables.

It has been popular to validate self-concept scales against tests purporting to measure maladjustment in an attempt to demonstrate that one's phenomenological view of the self is closely related to the degree of adjustment. Positive results abound. Calvin and Holtzman (1953) had college students rank themselves on seven personality traits, and found that self-depreciation was related to high scores on the MMPI. Zuckerman and Manashkin (1957) had neuropsychiatric patients rate themselves on a scale of adjectives, and found that self-ratings correlated positively with the MMPI *K* scale, and negatively with seven of the other scales. Taylor and Combs (1952) tested the hypothesis that sixth grade children found to be well-adjusted on the California personality scale would more often admit statements of self-reference which though unflattering were universally true. They got positive results, the self-depreciation which in other self-concept measures is treated as vice being here treated as virtue. Hanlon, Hofstaetter, and O'Connor (1954) compared the results of high school juniors on the California personality scale with the degree of congruence between ratings of the real and ideal self and found that the more congruence the better the adjustment. Cowen (1954) related low self-ratings on the Brownfain negative self-concept with high scores on the California F Scale. Any doubt about the ability of investigators to find positive results when comparing good adjustment as measured by objective personality inventories with the affirmativeness of self-concept should be dispelled by a study by Smith (1958). He compared congruence between *Q* sorts for self and ideal self with scores on the Edwards PPS, the Cattell factors, and measures of average mood. After making almost 300 correlations, he concluded that having a positive self-concept is indeed related to adjustment.

Other investigators have doubted that the relationship between adjustment and self-satisfaction is such a simple one. Block and Thomas (1955) conceived of maladjustment lying at both ends of the continuum. They felt that too high a degree of self-satisfaction is due to suppressive and repressive mechanisms which cause a person to be rigid, over-controlled, restrained, and aloof. But at the other extreme, the person who is too little satisfied with self will lack ego defenses, and will be able neither to bind tensions nor control emotions. Block and Thomas constructed an ego-control scale from MMPI items. The scale was found to have a correlation of .44 with self-ideal-self *Q* sort congruence, the relationship being curvilinear. Unfortunately, this was the reverse of what Chodorkoff (1954a) had found. Correlating ratings of the self as made from a biographical inventory with the results of projective techniques, he found that maladjustment lies in the middle range of self-satisfaction.

Validating self-concept measures against objective personality tests has generally been successful, but the true significance of these studies is still not made clear. Edwards (1957) demonstrates how more than half the variance in both MMPI scales and in *Q* sorts of self-referent items is accounted for by social desirability. SD can account for significant positive relationships even when other variables are totally unrelated. Edwards' SD robs these studies neither of significance nor of interest, but does suggest that extreme care must be taken in the labeling of constructs.

Attempts have also been made to validate self-concept against projective personality tests. Bills has made several attempts to validate his scale by the Rorschach (Bills, 1953a, 1954; Bills, Vance, and McLean, 1951). The results are a bit ambiguous, and leave two observers (Cowen and Tongas, 1959) extremely dissatisfied. The TAT was used by Friedman (1955) to compare the *Q* sort discrepancy self with the self as projected onto the TAT pictures. The normals were the only group to project positive self-qualities. Neurotics and paranoids both projected negatively.

A different approach to validation has used a word association test. Results show that there is a delayed reaction time for those trait words where there has been a discrepancy in ratings between the self and the ideal self (Bills, 1953b, Roberts, 1952). Delayed associations are assumed to be related to defensiveness about self, which in turn is considered to be related to maladjustment. However, Cowen and Tongas (1959) wondered if defensiveness about trait words does not serve also to raise the original ratings of the actual self.

Cowen chose to validate the self-concept by comparing the absolute self-rating with the learning time for the rated words, and found that there was a higher learning time for words that were presumably threatening. We might however wonder if his and Tongas' criticism of other studies does not apply here also: defensiveness might also cause self-ratings to be raised.

Use was also made of the perceptual New Look. Chodorkof (1954b) presented neutral and threatening words with a tachistoscope, and found that the better the agreement between a self-description and a description of the self by others, the less perceptual threat there will be.

It is unfortunate that the only study of this general type that did not use college students as subjects was negative in its results. Zimmer (1954) presented male mental patients with trait adjectives on which there was a self-rating discrepancy between self and ideal self. A word association test was not found to be significantly related to self-discrepancy.

The results of studies that involve the presentation of "hot" or threatening words seem suggestive, for there seems to be a common element in ability to free associate and learn threatening words. But it is possible that we have in these studies more a measure of ego defenses than of maladjustment, for the fact that the results are positive only with normal groups might suggest that the results are more relevant for a theory of personality than for a theory of psychopathology. In these studies it is indeed likely that we have support for Lecky's theory of self-consistency, and for Snygg and Comb's theory of the maintenance of internal organization. If this is so, then likely it is true as Block and Thomas (1955) suggest that only extremes in ego control are pathological.

A different approach to validation of self-concept measures uses behavior in a social situation as a criterion. The most sweeping results in a study of this type are reported by Turner and Vanderlippe (1958), who report that *Q* sort congruence between the self and the ideal self is greater in those college students who are more active in extracurricular activities, have higher scholastic averages, and are given higher sociometric rankings by fellow students. Holt (1951) found that agreement between self-ratings and ratings by a diagnostic council was positively related to intelligent, active, adventurous living, and a friendly dominant social adjustment. Eastman (1958) found that the degree of acceptance of self-ratings on the Bills index is positively related to ratings for marital happiness. Working in terms of ratings for maladjustment, Chase (1957) found that among maladjusted patients there was greater discrepancy between *Q* sorts for self as compared with sorts for the ideal self and the average other person.

Other attempts to relate self-concept to social behavior have been less successful. Kelman and Parloff (1957) obtained only chance results when they tried to interrelate such variables as congruence between self and ideal self, a symptom disability check list, a discomfort evaluation scale, sociometric ratings, and an ineffective behavior evaluation scale, using 15 neurotic hospital outpatients. Fiedler, Dodge, Jones, and Hutchins (1958) measured the self-concept of college students both by a simple rating scale and by a discrepancy measure. There was a general lack of correlation between these measures and such objective criteria as grade point average, health center visits, army adjustment, the Taylor *MA* scale, and sociometric status. Coopersmith (1959) compared self-esteem as rated by the self with that estimated by observers, using children as subjects. He suggests that there are actually four types of self-esteem: what a person purports to have, what he really has, what he displays, and what others believe he has.

There is no obvious explanation for the discrepancy of results in studies urporting to relate self-concept to behavioral adjustment. Since the basis or selecting items for rating scales and *Q* sorts differs from study to tudy, it is possible that the statements used in the scales of those studies ith positive results had more of a relationship to the criteria than the tatements in studies which were negative.

A different approach to relating self-concept measures to adjustment is hown in a block of psychotherapy research studies at the University of Chicago (Rogers and Dymond, 1954). Change in self-concept was found o occur as a function of improvement during psychotherapy. Butler and Haigh (1954) had clients make *Q* sorts for self and for ideal self both efore therapy and after its completion to test the hypothesis that therapy vill increase satisfaction with the self. Congruence between the two sorts ncreased as a result of psychotherapy, the two sorts moving towards a ommon mean. Rudikoff (1954), using the same subjects, found changes luring periods of time before and after therapy were not nearly as great as those occurring during therapy. Also with the same subjects, Dymond (1954) found that there was closer agreement after therapy between the vay clients sorted the Butler and Haigh *Q* sort cards, and the way two non-Rogerian clinical psychologists sorted the cards between what the vell-adjusted person should say is like him and what is not like him.

The same investigator (Cartwright, 1958) related change in self-concept over therapy to a successful search for identity. She had clients make sortings with Butler and Haigh *Q* sort cards to describe themselves as they saw themselves in relationship to three people of their choice to test the hypothesis that successful therapy increases the consistency of the self-concept which one brings to different social situations. The hypothesis vas confirmed.

Ewing (1954) had counselee college students rate a list of traits for self, ideal self, mother, father, counselor, and a culturally approved figure. There was a regression of the ratings toward a common mean in those clients who were estimated to be the most improved in therapy.

Changes in self-ratings over therapy seem certainly to have occurred. But they seem to take place also without psychotherapy. Taylor (1955) devised a *Q* sort divided between positive and negative statements. After subjects made repeated sortings both for self and for ideal self, he concluded that self-introspection without therapy results in increased positiveness of attitude toward the self; that the self and ideal self will draw closer together; and that repeated self-descriptions are accompanied by increased self-consistency. Engel (1959) studied the stability of self-concept in adolescence, and also found a trend towards more positive *Q* sorting over a 2-year period. And finally Dymond herself (1955) found an increased congruence between *Q* sorts for self and for ideal self among subjects waiting for psychotherapy, although ratings of adjustment based on TAT protocols showed no change over the period.

Dymond attributes increased self–ideal-self congruence without psychotherapy as due to the strengthening of neurotic defenses. It might be charged that similar changes during therapy might have the same basis. Dymond also raises the possibility that the sorts can be influenced by the attitude of the therapist towards the client's self. There is in short no complete assurance that the cognitive self-acceptance as measured by the *Q* sort is related to the deeper level of self-integration that client-centered therapy seeks to achieve.

Indirect evidence of change of the self-concept during counseling is provided by studies showing changes of self-estimates. Several studies show that agreement between self-ratings on interests and the ratings of the self by interest inventories increase as a result of counseling (Berdie, 1954; Froehlich, 1954; Johnson, 1953; Singer and Stefflre, 1954). The first two of these studies show a moderate increase in accuracy in predicting one's intelligence, but very little improvement in rating the self on measures of personality. One might reason that some parts of the self-concept are peripheral to the core of the self (e.g., interests) and are therefore unstable, while other parts (e.g., personality estimates) are central to the self and are therefore extremely resistant to change.

SELF-CONCEPT—SELF-CONSISTENCY

If the self-concept is to have usefulness as a construct it must be shown that it is consistent in a given self. It must be known whether the self-concept is a gestalt that is more than the sum of different self-regarding attitudes, or whether instead the self-concept is an impossible attempt to generalize different feelings toward unique situations.

One answer to this question is provided by Akeret (1959). He intercorrelated self-ratings on academic values, interpersonal relations, sexual adjustment, and emotional adjustment, achieving differentially positive interrelationships. Emotional adjustment was the best indicator, correlating +.61 with a total corrected for part-whole inflation. While Akeret interpreted his results as suggesting that an individual does not accept or reject himself totally, the results might also be interpreted as suggesting that some areas of self-regard are more central to the self-concept than other areas.

Consistency in the self-concept was found by Martire and Hornberger (1957), who found very great similarities between measures of the actual self, the ideal self, and a socially desirable self. But inconsistency was found by McKenna, Hofstaetter, and O'Connor (1956), who found that one's self ideal differed less from one's close friends than the close friends differed from each other. These investigators concluded by rather involved reasoning that the ideal self is sufficiently differentiated to seek different need satisfactions in different people.

The search for consistency in the self led also to comparing scores on different measures of self-concept. Omwake (1954) compared three scales —the Bills, Phillips, and Berger—which measure acceptance both of self and of others. The scales were in closer agreement as to the degree of acceptance of self than they were as to acceptance of others. Brownfain (1952) found that low ratings of self were related on his scale to the discrepancy between optimistic and pessimistic self-ratings, or what Brownfain termed stability of self-concept; and Cowen (1954) found a relationship between the pessimistic Brownfain self-ratings, and the discrepancy between self– and ideal–self-ratings on the Bills index. Bendig and Hoffman (1957) found that Bills' scores on acceptance of self-ratings and on congruence between ratings of self and ideal self related equally well to scales of the Maudsley Personality Inventory. They therefore concluded that the two different Bills index measures are redundant.

But on the negative side, Cowen (1956) found no relation between the so-called stability of self-concept on the Brownfain, and the different measures on the Bills. Hampton (1955) likewise failed to find any significant relationship between ability to make realistic appraisals about oneself and the ability to admit statements that were damaging but probably true.

Different measures of the self-concept have different theoretical and operational bases. Where measures apply similar rationale, significant correlations between measures have been found. But in similar measures such extraneous variables as response set and social desirability will produce similar bias. Measures of self-concept have reliability, and in a certain degree are interchangeable. Whether or not the reasons for similarity are intrinsic to the scales, the notion of the internal frame of reference seems well validated.

DISCUSSION

The scientist can not hold truths to be self-evident. What is known of the self through direct report must be considered suspect due to philosophical considerations, since the nature of the "I" has been seen differently in each ideological epoch. Notions concerning the self are like other human ideas, and are inventions and not discoveries. The task is not that of discovering the "true self," but instead of constructing those notions which increase understanding of human behavior. Just as the number of inventions is potentially unlimited, so there need be no limit on the number of constructions put upon the self. In this discussion we will proceed functionally, and consider the uses to which different selves have been put.

The first self is the knowing self of structural psychology. Its function is to apprehend reality. The rational nature of man has always been in dispute, and the New Look in perception has further undermined this conception. This article has cited studies which throw doubt on the ability of the self to perceive itself correctly in those areas which are of great value to it. It is the change in the self as perceiver of itself that is the aim of client centered therapy. Studies of client centered therapy do not reveal whether therapy brings the client any closer to reality, but they do provide some evidence that the perception of the self is brought closer to social expectancies.

The second construction of the self is that of motivator. This is the self of thinkers who believe that the individual is motivated by a need for self-assertion or self-realization, by realizing those potentialities which inhere within the self. Attempts to validate this construct of the self have been carried on through work on *need achievement*. This construct of the self seems involved also in ratings and *Q* sorts for an ideal self which outdistances the real self. Here, of course, the self whose reach exceeds its grasp is considered to be pathological, for it is shown how psychotherapy helps reduce the disparity between the real and ideal.

The third construct of self is the humanistic, semireligious conception of the self as that which experiences itself. It is the "unique personal experience" of Moustakas (1957) and the experience of feeling in Rogers (1951). The difficulty for the psychologist is that such a conception is more religious than scientific; it becomes a value-orientation, and, as the writer has shown elsewhere (Lowe, 1959), it becomes a highly controversial statement of what is the highest good.

The fourth approach views the self as organizer. This self is the psychoanalytic ego; the internal frame of reference of Snygg and Combs (1949); and the source of construct making in G. A. Kelly (1955). Any operational measure of self-consistency would seem to imply the existence of such a self. It is this self that this article has been most directly concerned with; to the extent that studies have been positive, the self does respond the same way in different situations. Conversely, to the extent that the studies have had negative results there is enough inconsistency in the self that it does not always act according to prediction.

A fifth approach constructs the self as a pacifier. Such a self seems implied in Lewin (1936), who constructed his system of personality in terms of valences or tensions which the organism seeks to keep to a minimum. It seems present also in Angyal (1941) who views life as an oscillation about a position of equilibrium. The self in other words is seen as an adjustment mechanism which seeks to maintain congruence between the self and the nonself. It is the verification of this type of self that seems implied by *Q* sort studies that show increased congruence of real and ideal self as a result of psychotherapy. We must however note that the self as pacifier stands in direct opposition to the self as motivator.

In the sixth view of the self, the self is the subjective voice of the culture, being purely a social agent. It is the self of both sociology and S–R psychology, for it sees behavioral responses solely in terms of social conditions or stimuli inputs. The self as an entity is denied, and behavioral consistency is seen as residing not in the individual but in similar environmental events. If the term self is used, it is seen in terms of ego-involvements with loyalties which are determinative of the self.

From these different conceptions of the self, we can choose the one which best fits our theoretical frame of reference. But which conception is chosen seems to depend more upon faith than upon logic, and the choice of one conception must of necessity deny other constructs. It seems impossible that the self can function as a motivator which constantly tries to change the status quo, and as a pacifier which minimizes the disparity between the real and ideal self. There is a contradiction also between the self as motivator and the self as feeling, for in the latter the self is accepted as it is, but in the former is not. Differences are apparent also between the self as feeling and as pacifier. And finally, the self as agent of society is opposed to all other conceptions.

CONCLUSION

Is the self-concept a fact which, having an objective existence in nature, is observed and measured; or is it an epiphenomenon of deeper reality, invented by man that he might better study his behavior?

The world has sought to be so sure of the self because there is so little else of which it can be certain. The self has become the anchor that man hopes will hold in the ebbtide of social change. But just as a fish could never know it was surrounded by water unless that water were to disappear, it is unlikely that Lecky (1945) would have known about self-consistency had he not lived in a culture which felt inconsistency. In Buberian terminology, the self is an It, which man invents because he can not find a Thou.

The position of this paper must be that the self is an artifact which is invented to explain experience. If the self-concept is a tool, it must be well designed and constructed. We will conclude therefore with that construct of the self which best serves the 1960s. Such a construction combines the self of ego-involvement with the self of feeling. It is a self which is existential not to experience itself, but to mediate encounter between the organism and what is beyond. Such a self is what Pfuetze (1954) calls the "self-other dialogic theory of the self," being interpreted naturalistically through Mead and transcendentally through Buber. It is as an artifact that the self-concept finds meaning.

REFERENCES

Akeret, R. U. "Inter-relationships among various dimensions of the self-concept." *J. counsel. Psychol.,* 1959, **6,** 199–201.

Allport, G. W. "The ego in contemporary psychology." *Psychol. Rev.,* 1943, **50,** 451–478.

Angyal, A. *Foundations for a Science of Personality.* New York: Commonwealth, 1941.

Bendig, A. W., and J. L. Hoffman. "Bills Index of Adjustment and the Maudsley Personality Inventory." *Psychol. Rep.,* 1957, **3,** 507.

Berdie, R. F. "Changes in self-ratings as a method of evaluating counseling." *J. counsel. Psychol.,* 1954, **1,** 49–54.

Berger, E. M. "The relation between expressed acceptance of self and expressed acceptance of others." *J. abnorm. soc. Psychol.,* 1952, **47,** 778–782.

Bertocci, P. A. "The psychological self, the ego, and personality." *Psychol. Rev.,* 1945, **52,** 91–99.

Bills, R. E. "Rorschach characteristics of persons scoring high and low in acceptance of self." *J. consult. Psychol.,* 1953, **17,** 36–38 (a).

Bills, R. E. "A validation of changes in scores for the Index of Adjustment and Values as measures of changes in emotionality." *J. consult. Psychol.,* 1953, **17,** 135–138 (b).

Bills, R. E. "Self-concepts and Rorschach signs of depression." *J. consult. Psychol.,* 1954, **18,** 135–137.

Bills, R. E. *Manual for the Index of Adjustment and Values.* Auburn: Alabama Polytechnic Inst., 1958.

Bills, R. E., E. L. Vance, and O. S. McLean. "An index of adjustment and values." *J. consult. Psychol.,* 1951, **15,** 257–261.

Block, J., and H. Thomas. "Is satisfaction with self a measure of adjustment?" *J. abnorm. soc. Psychol.,* 1955, **51,** 254–259.

Brownfain, J. J. "Stability of the self-concept as a dimension of personality." *J. abnorm. soc. Psychol.,* 1952, **47,** 597–606.

Butler, J. M., and G. V. Haigh. Changes in the relation between self-concepts and ideal concepts consequent upon client-centered counseling. In *Psychotherapy and Personality Change,* C. R. Rogers and R. Dymond (Eds.). Chicago: Univ. Chicago Press, 1954, pp. 55–75.

Calvin, A. D., and W. H. Holtzman. "Adjustment and discrepancy between self-concept and inferred self." *J. consult. Psychol.,* 1953, **17,** 39–44.

Cartwright, R. D. "Effects of psychotherapy on consistency." *J. counsel. Psychol.,* 1958, **4,** 15–21.

Chase, P. H. "Self-concept in adjusted and maladjusted hospital patients." *J. consult. Psychol.,* 1957, **21,** 495–497.

Chein, I. "The awareness of self and the structure of the ego." *Psychol. Rev.,* 1944, **51,** 304–314.

Chodorkoff, B. "Adjustment and the discrepancy between the perceived and ideal self." *J. clin. Psychol.,* 1954, **10,** 266–268 (a).

Chodorkoff, B. "Self-perception, perceptual defense, and adjustment." *J. abnorm. soc. Psychol.,* 1954, **49,** 508–512 (b).

Coopersmith, S. "A method for determining types of self-esteem." *J. abnorm. soc. Psychol.,* 1959, **59,** 87–94.

Cowen, E. L. "The 'negative self-concept' as a personality measure." *J. consult. Psychol.,* 1954, **18,** 138–142.

Cowen, E. L. "Investigation between two measures of self-regarding attitudes." *J. clin. Psychol.,* 1956, **12,** 156–160.

Cowen, E. L., and P. N. Tongas. "The social desirability of trait descriptive terms: Applications to a self-concept inventory." *J. consult. Psychol.,* 1959, **23,** 361–365.

Dymond, R. F. Adjustment changes over therapy from Thematic Apperception Test ratings. In *Psychotherapy and Personality Change,* C. R. Rogers and R. Dymond (Eds.). Chicago: Univ. Chicago Press, 1954, pp. 109–120.

Dymond, R. F. "Adjustment changes in the absence of psychotherapy." *J. consult. Psychol.,* 1955, **19,** 103–107.

Eastman, D. "Self-acceptance and marital adjustment." *J. consult. Psychol.,* 1958, **22,** 95–99.

Edelson, M., and A. E. Jones. "Operational exploration of the conceptual self-system and of the interaction between frames of reference." *Genet. psychol. Monogr.,* 1954, **50,** 43–140.

Edwards, A. L. *Social Desirability Variables in Personality Assessment and Research.* New York: Dresden, 1957.

Engel, M. "The stability of the self-concept in adolesence." *J. abnorm. soc. Psychol.,* 1959, **58,** 211–215.

Ewing, T. N. "Changes in attitude during counseling." *J. counsel. Psychol.,* 1954, **1,** 232–239.

Fiedler, R. E., Joan S. Dodge, R. E. Jones, and E. B. Hutchins. "Interrelations among measures of personality adjustment in non-clinical populations." *J. abnorm. soc. Psychol.,* 1958, **56,** 345–351.

Friedman, I. "Phenomenal, ideal, and projected conceptions of the self." *J. abnorm. soc. Psychol.,* 1955, **51,** 611–615.

Froelich, C. P. "Does test taking change self ratings?" *Calif. J. educ. Res.,* 1954, **5,** 166–169.

Hampton, B. J. An investigation of personality characteristics associated with self-adequacy. Unpubl. doctoral dissertation. New York Univ., 1955.

Hanlon, T. E., P. R. Hofstaetter, and J. P. O'Connor. "Congruence of self and ideal-self in relation to personality adjustment." *J. consult. Psychol.,* 1954, **18,** 215–218.

Hilgard, E. R. "Human motives and the concept of the self." *Amer. Psychologist,* 1949, **4,** 374–382.

Holt, R. R. "Accuracy of self-evaluations." *J. consult. Psychol.,* 1951, **15,** 95–101.

Johnson, D. G. "Effect of vocational counseling on self-knowledge." *Educ. psychol. Measmt.,* 1953, **13,** 330–338.

Kelly, G. A. *Psychology of Personal Constructs.* New York: Norton, 1955.

Kelman, H. C., and M. B. Parloff. "Interrelations among three criteria of improvement in group therapy." *J. abnorm. soc. Psychol.,* 1957, **54,** 281–288.

Lecky, P. *Self-consistency.* New York: Island, 1945.

Lewin, K. *Principles of Topological Psychology.* New York: McGraw-Hill, 1936.

Lowe, C. M. "Value-orientations: An ethical dilemma." *Amer. Psychologist,* 1959, **14,** 687–693.

Lundholm, H. "Reflections on the nature of the psychological self." *Psychol. Rev.,* 1940, **47,** 110–127.

McKenna, H. V., P. R. Hofstaetter, and J. P. O'Connor. "Concepts of ideal self and of the friend." *J. Pers.*, 1956, **24,** 262–279.

Martire, J. G., and R. H. Hornberger. "Self-congruence by sex and between sexes in a 'normal' population." *J. clin. Psychol.*, 1957, **13,** 288–291.

Moustakas, C. *The Self*. New York: Harper, 1957.

Omwake, K. T. "Relation between acceptance of self and acceptance of others shown by three personality inventories." *J. consult. Psychol.*, 1954, **18,** 443–446.

Pfuetze, P. E. *The Social Self*. New York: Bookman, 1954.

Phillips, E. L. "Attitudes toward self and others." *J. consult. Psychol.*, 1951, **15,** 79–81.

Raimy, V. C. The self-concept as a factor in counseling and personality organization. Unpubl. doctoral dissertation. Ohio State Univ., 1943.

Roberts, G. E. "A study of the validity of the Index of Adjustment and Values." *J. consult. Psychol.*, 1952, **16,** 302–304.

Rogers, C. R. *Client-centered Therapy*. Boston: Houghton Mifflin, 1951.

Rogers, C. R., and R. Dymond (Eds.). *Psychotherapy and Personality Change*. Chicago: Univ. Chicago Press, 1954.

Rogers, C. R., *et al.* "A coordinated research in psychotherapy." *J. consult. Psychol.*, 1949, **13,** 149–220.

Rudikoff, E. C. A comparative study of the changes in the concepts of the self, the ordinary person, and the ideal in eight cases. In *Psychotherapy and Personality Change,* C. R. Rogers and R. Dymond (Eds.). Chicago: Univ. Chicago Press, 1954, pp. 85–98.

Sheerer, E. J. "An analysis of the relationship between acceptance of and respect for self and others." *J. consult. Psychol.*, 1949, **13,** 169–175.

Singer, S. L., and B. Stefflre. "Analysis of the self-estimate in the evaluation of counseling." *J. counsel. Psychol.*, 1954, **1,** 252–255.

Smith, G. M. "Six measures of self-concept discrepancy and instability: Their interrelations, reliability, and relations to other personality measures." *J. consult. Psychol.*, 1958, **22,** 101–112.

Snygg, D., and A. Combs. *Individual Behavior*. New York: Harper, 1949.

Stephenson, W. *The study of Behavior*. Chicago: Univ. Chicago Press, 1953.

Taylor, C., and A. Combs. "Self-acceptance and adjustment." *J. consult. Psychol.*, 1952, **16,** 89–91.

Taylor, D. M. "Changes in self-concept with psychotherapy." *J. consult. Psychol.*, 1955, **19,** 205–209.

Turner, R. H., and R. H. Vanderlippe. "Self-ideal congruence as an index of adjustment." *J. abnorm. soc. Psychol.*, 1958, **57,** 202–206.

Zimmer, H. "Self-acceptance and its relation to conflict." *J. consult. Psychol.*, 1954, **18,** 447–449.

Zuckerman, M., and I. Manashkin. "Self-acceptance and psychopathology." *J. consult. Psychol.*, 1957, **21,** 145–148.

chapter four

Cognitive Functioning

4.1 *Orientation*

Our study of cognitive functioning begins with a comprehensive overview of developments in the theory and measurement of intelligence. Aside from very early work in psychophysics, the efforts directed toward the description and explanation of individual differences in intelligence were central to establishing psychology as a scientific discipline. Stott and Ball provide a concise summary of these efforts and trace the important changes that have taken place in the psychologist's conceptualizations of intelligence. Included are the issues of defining intelligence, hereditary and environmental influences, the interaction hypothesis, the nature of the organization of intellectual abilities, and the distinction between quantitative and qualitative developmental changes. The authors moreover comment upon problems of intelligence-measuring which concern psychologists.

Readers are specifically encouraged to note the author's references to two psychologists whose theories of intelligence have generated much of the current work on intelligence: J. P. Guilford of the University of Southern California and Jean Piaget of the University of Geneva. Guilford's three-dimensional structure of the intellect has contributed to the advanced study of intelligence as information-processing and illustrates the use of factor analysis in theory development. Particularly significant has been Guilford's heuristic distinction between convergent and divergent thinking. Piaget's intriguing developmental theory has stimulated many American psychologists to put Piagetian concepts to experimental test. (An original paper by Piaget immediately follows Scott and Ball's review.)

This overview of changing concepts of intelligence was originally conceived to provide the groundwork for a survey, analysis, and evaluation of mental testing as applied to infants and preschool children. The authors conclude that, while advances have been made, more adequate means for appraising the mentality of young children are needed. They find that current intelligence scales for preschool children lack consistency and, in many cases, sound theoretical foundations.

RECOMMENDED READING

Bloom, Benjamin S. *Stability and Change in Human Characteristics.* New York: Wiley, 1964. (chap. 3, "Intelligence," pp. 52–91).

Goodenough, Florence L. The measurement of mental growth in childhood. In *Manual of Child Psychology,* L. Carmichael (Ed.) (2d ed.) New York: Wiley, 1954, pp. 459–491.

4.1 Intelligence: A Changing Concept

Leland H. Stott, THE MERRILL-PALMER INSTITUTE
Rachel S. Ball, ARIZONA STATE UNIVERSITY

A considerable portion of the psychological literature, during the first half of the present century, has been concerned with the problem of "intelligence," its general nature, and its measurement. This problem has long been considered a matter of prime importance to the understanding of human behavior. Children obviously differ tremendously in readiness and ability to learn and in rate of progress in mental development. The nature of the factor or factors underlying these differences has become a matter of theoretical interest; the assessment and equitable social management

Reprinted from *Monographs of the Society for Research in Child Development,* **30** (1965), serial no. 101, 1–45. By permission of the authors and The Society for Research in Child Development, Inc.

of individual differences in mental ability continue to be matters of great practical importance. Before beginning a historical account of the predominant ways in which intellectual ability and its development have been conceived of, a brief review is presented of some of the common, divergent interpretations of the term "intelligence" in use by present-day psychologists.

A WORD WITH MANY MEANINGS

"Intelligence" is one of the many common-parlance terms taken over by psychologists and given "scientific" or "technical" meaning. This alone would make for difficulty in arriving at any degree of consistency or preciseness in its usage. What is even more difficult is the fact that in psychology the term is used with various meanings. Intelligence is often defined as *ability,* i.e., what the subject *can do,* his level of performance (Stoddard, 1943, p. 4).[1] In this sense, intelligence changes; it increases with age as the child develops. The most common symbol indicating the attained level of ability at any point during this developmental period, of course, is the MA (mental age).

Another equally legitimate "technical" use of the term "intelligence" is to let it refer, not to ability or abilities per se, but to the biologically inherited potentiality for the development of those abilities. In this sense, intelligence is fixed by the genes at conception (Freeman, 1940).

Still another very common conception of intelligence is in terms of the child's rate of mental development as measured by the ratio of mental age to chronological age (IQ). The higher the ratio, the brighter or more intelligent the child is said to be. Here again, the focus is not on what the child *can do*—on his abilities as such; nor is IQ a measure of potentiality except in a very indirect way, that is, the very tenuous assumption that the greater the potentiality, the higher the rate of progress toward the achievement of that potentiality. The focus of the IQ, rather, is upon the rate at which the child's mentality is developing.

A number of less frequently used meanings are also attached to the term "intelligence." One is that it is a *function* of a living organism "in much the same sense that maneuverability and speed are functions of an airplane" (Munn, 1946, p. 410). In the view of the present writers, it would be more accurate to say that intelligence is a generalized *attribute* of individual functioning in general, rather than *a* function, just as maneuverability and speed are attributes of the functioning of an airplane. It would seem that this is what Munn really means, as he suggests in his final definition of intelligence. "Intelligence is flexibility and versatility in the use of symbolic processes" (1946, p. 411). The "use of symbolic processes" is a category of functioning, and "flexibility" and "versatility" are descriptive of the overall quality or attribute called "intelligence." In

[1] See the original paper for complete bibliography—Ed.

this sense, intelligence means effectiveness, facility, flexibility, versatility, and general adequacy of functioning in life situations.

Other usages of the term make less sense. For example, to say that intelligence is "native ability" in a strict sense limits its reference only to what a newborn baby can do. "Native," "inborn," "innate," all mean to be born with. As an example of this type of unprecise definition, Burt, Jones, Miller, and Moodie (1934) wrote, "By intelligence, the psychologist understands *inborn,* all-around intellectual ability. . . . It is inherited, or at least innate." Very little, if any, intellectual ability is innate. The child is not born with that ability, only with the potentiality for developing that ability. Undoubtedly these authors meant to refer to the potentiality, rather than ability per se, as being "inborn," "innate."

More recent usages define intelligence, not as ability to do, not as a genetic capacity to develop ability, not as an attribute or quality of functioning, but, rather, in terms of actual processes of central functioning. "Intelligence is conceived of as central operations for the processing of information" (Hunt, 1961, p. 337). These central processes, moreover, are conceived of as "hierarchically arranged within the intrinsic portions of the cerebrum" and as "approximately analogous to the strategies for information processing and action with which electronic computers are programmed" (Hunt, 1961, p. 362).

POINTS OF VIEW ABOUT THE NATURE OF INTELLIGENCE AND ITS DETERMINING FACTORS

Some of the divergence in meanings of the term "intelligence" comes naturally from different broad conceptualizations and points of view concerning the nature of human abilities and their development that have prevailed from time to time in the past.

The Assumption of Inherently Fixed Intelligence

The general idea that intelligence is genetically fixed as a pervading characteristic of the individual has had, perhaps, most general acceptance in the past by both theoretical writers and makers of tests. The idea undoubtedly had its origin in Darwin's (1859) theories of biological evolution and gained impetus from the research and writing of Sir Francis Galton (1869; 1883) on mental inheritance. As a result of his studies of eminent men in Great Britain, Galton became convinced that intellectual genius is inherited; and he set about with energy to devise tests of simple sensory and motor functions, immediate memory, etc., to assess this inherited capacity and to demonstrate individual differences. Many thousands of individuals were given the tests in Galton's laboratory, and, although wide individual differences were demonstrated, the outcome of his project was disappointing in that his measures showed little relation to other criteria of intelligence. Galton's ultimate objective, of course, was to set up a program of race improvement in which the intellectually gifted would be identified early and encouraged to reproduce and, thus, pass on their genius. His simple tests, however, proved not to be an effective means of differentiating high achievers from low achievers.

Alfred Binet began his test-construction project under different motivation and with quite different objectives than Galton. Under a commission from the French Minister of Public Instruction, Binet began the study of the nature of school retardation and the task of devising a means of assessing various degress of mental retardation in children. Binet and his co-worker, Simon, published their first scale of mental ability in 1905. Unlike Galton, they looked for tests of the more complex psychological functions, such as "judgment, otherwise called good sense, practical sense, initiative, the faculty of adapting oneself to circumstances" (1916, p. 42). And, unlike Galton's tests, their scale proved to be effective in differentiating children who achieved success in school from those who did not.

Binet, however, did not hold to the view that intelligence is genetically fixed. On the contrary, he was vehemently opposed to "the deplorable verdict that the intelligence of an individual is a fixed quantity" (Binet, 1909, p. 54). His tests, nevertheless, furnished evidence that was generally interpreted to support the assumption of inherited intelligence.

Certain leading figures in American psychology who played a prominent part in the development of the testing movement also lent strong support to the concept of genetically determined intelligence. H. H. Goddard was the first to introduce and use the Binet-Simon scale in this country. In 1906 a psychological laboratory was set up in the Training School at Vineland, New Jersey, with Goddard as its director. He had seen something of the usefulness of the Binet scale in France as it applied to feeble-minded children and, in 1908, he began using it at Vineland. His first task was to translate the scale into English and to adapt it generally to American conditions. Goddard's work eventuated finally in a restandardization of the scale on two thousand American children. This adaptation was published in 1910 (Goddard, 1910).

Based on his experiences at Vineland, Goddard had little faith in the educability of the feeble-minded. He was strongly oriented in favor of heredity as the basis of individual differences in intelligence and became a strong advocate of the doctrine of fixed intelligence.

Lewis M. Terman is, of course, closely identified with the mental-testing movement in the United States because of his Stanford revisions of the Binet scale, the first one in 1916 (Terman, 1916). The only innovation in his revision, however, was the adoption of the "Intelligence Quotient," a concept previously introduced by Stern (1914) as an index of intelligence.

The concept of IQ, naturally, was a potent reinforcer for the assumption of fixed intelligence. Here was an index of intelligence that showed a wide range of variation in the population, but, at the same time, remained relatively constant from age to age. The IQ, furthermore, showed evidence of validity in that, as a rule, children with IQ's below 85 typically fell behind their age groups in school achievement while those with high IQ's tended to make better-than-average progress and exhibit certain other superior qualities.

Thus, psychologists, generally, and, particularly, those concerned with intelligence and its assessment, came for the most part to assume that intelligence as a universal capacity is genetically determined and remains fixed throughout life.

Predeterminism

Another concept consonant with the assumption of fixed intelligence, but with a different derivation in history and with implications of quite a different sort, is that of predetermination. According to this concept all behavioral development unfolds automatically with the maturation of the anatomical structure of which behavior is a function.

Doctrines of predeterminism, of course, are not of recent origin. The French philosopher, J. J. Rousseau, elaborated his predeterministic theory 200 years ago. He postulated that "all development consists of a series of internally regulated sequential stages which are transformed, one into the other, in conformity with a pre-arranged order and design. According to this conception of development, the only proper role of the environment is avoidance of serious interference with the processes of self-regulation and spontaneous maturation" (Ausubel, 1958, p. 27). To explain the assumed regularity and inevitability with which each individual's predetermined pattern of development proceeds, Rousseau and his followers proposed the idea that the course of individual development parallels or recapitulates the development of the species through the various stages of its evolution.

A hundred years later this doctrine of recapitulation was elaborated and refined by G. Stanley Hall (1904). However, as developmental data accumulated and theoretical constructs regarding the interrelations of the biological and cultural aspects of development were elaborated, Hall's system of parallelisms was no longer accepted. A basic tenet of the doctrine of recapitulation, that maturation is a fundamental process of anatomical development, is still important in developmental theory. As a biological process in organismic development, maturation is well established. However, when maturation is postulated as the sole factor of behavioral, as well as morphological development, we still have predeterminism, albeit lacking the elaborative trimming proposed by Hall.

Arnold Gesell, a student of Hall, has been, perhaps the strongest recent proponent of predetermined development. His great stress on the importance of the "mechanism of maturation" in his model of morphological development has made a strong impact upon current developmental psychology. According to Gesell the "basic configurations, correlations, and successions of behavior patterns are determined by a process of maturation. The tenacity of this process has been demonstrated by developmental studies of both premature and full-term infants and by experimental studies of monozygotic twins" (Gesell, 1954, p. 371).

Clearly, the idea that behavioral development is a product of maturation and, therefore, predetermined, encompasses the concept of fixed intelligence. The assumption is that, not only is the intellectual developmental potential of the individual fixed by his genes, but so also is the course, pattern, and rate of attainment fixed by his potential. Intellectual capacity is attained through the "mechanism of maturation"—a process that is uninfluenced by the individual's encounters with his environment.

It is quite clear, also, that this assumption was rather generally accepted by psychologists during the era of intelligence-test development. The definitions of intelligence that appeared in the psychology text books during the 1920's and 1930's reflect this double assumption of predetermined development and fixed intelligence. Some typical definitions follow:

> By intelligence the psychologist understands inborn, all-around, intellectual ability. It is inherited, or at least innate, not due to teaching or training; it is intellectual, not emotional or moral, and remains uninfluenced by industry or zeal (Burt, *et al.,* 1934, pp. 28–29).
>
> Given equal opportunity and training, two individuals will often be found to differ considerably in the success with which they achieve. There are two factors at work here, namely, native capacity (intelligence) and drive. . . . Intelligence may be broadly defined as the capacity for solving the problems of life (Allport, 1924, p. 104).
>
> Intelligence is the capacity to acquire and perfect new modes of adaptation. Since the intelligence of a person is not his stock of habits but his ability to acquire habits, it would seem to follow that this is a matter, not of practice and experience, but of inborn nature (Dashiell, 1928, p. 306).

Environment as a Factor in Mental Development

Most of, but not all, the textbook writers of the 1920's and 1930's apparently adopted the point of view implied in the above definitions and so strongly urged by Gesell—the point of view that both the upper limit of developmental capacity and its pattern and rate of development are predetermined by heredity. Harvey A. Carr (1926) was one notable exception. In fact, he spelled out in some detail a version of the currently widely accepted "interaction" view of mental development. He wrote:

> All experiences of the individual during life are thus organized into a complex but unitary system of reaction tendencies that determine to a large extent the nature of his subsequent activity. The reactive disposition of the individual, i.e.,

what he does and what he can and cannot do, is a function of his native equipment, of the nature of his previous experiences and of the way in which these have been organized and evaluated (p. 4).

Neither is the ability (intelligence) native in the sense that its development is not dependent upon environment influences. The ability is natively conditioned in that we are born with the *capacity* to develop in this manner (p. 415).

The assumption that all individual, group, and racial differences of IQ are wholly determined by innate differences of constitution must be discarded because of the fact that the IQ is often altered during the course of development (p. 417).

Perhaps the most widely known controversy to be found in the psychological literature was over this very issue. In 1932, Beth L. Wellman (1932a) of the Iowa Child Welfare Research Station published the first in a series of studies reporting marked changes in children's IQ's that were attributed to changes in environment. According to the results, the greatest gains were made by those children whose initial IQ's were below average; the average gain for them was 28 points on their fifth test. The group with average IQ's gained 22 points from their first to seventh test, while the superior group made an average gain of 12 points up to their fifth test.

Wellman's explanation for these findings was that,

Preschool attendance, at least in the laboratories of the Iowa Child Welfare Research Station, causes a rise in IQ, the rise being cumulative from year to year, and sustained throughout the school years when the children are in the environment provided by our University Elementary School. When the same children are home over comparable intervals they fail to gain, although maintaining their higher level (1932a, p. 124).

At the end of her report, however, she admitted that "the question still remains whether these increased IQ's are real or inflated."

In her second report, Wellman (1932b) furnished evidence that the gains in IQ during preschool attendance were not practice effects. She reported that the same children who gained IQ points during the school session failed to make gains in a shorter period between tests during the summer vacation. Her results also indicated that during the preschool season greater gains were shown during a 7- to 8-month interval between tests than during a shorter, 5- to 6-month interval, which would be more likely to show practice effects.

In a study by Crissey (1937), the evidence indicated that children who were rated as "normal or dull-normal" on admission to an orphans' home remained normal or gained slightly in IQ, while those designed as "normal or superior-normal" showed a consistent loss. Children at all levels of ability represented who remained in an institution for the feeble-minded were also found to show a consistent loss in IQ.

During the 7 years following Wellman's initial report, a series of research papers were published by Wellman and her co-workers (Wellman, 1934; 1937; 1938; Wellman and Coffey, 1936; Crissey, 1937; Skeels and

Filmore, 1937; Skeels, 1938; Skeels, Updegraff, Wellman, and Williams, 1938) which supported generally the view that the sort of environmental stimulation young children experience constitutes an important factor in their mental development.

> The concept of intelligence as fixed and unmodified, or only modified within very narrow limits, is fast being replaced by a viewpoint which conceives of intelligence in functional terms. No longer can we say that an early intelligence test rigidly classifies a child for life in terms of mental potentiality (Crissey, 1937, p. 7).

The controversy But the well ingrained idea that intelligence, as represented by the IQ, is an inherited and, therefore, a "fixed" quality that characterizes the individual for life, was not so easily "replaced" by such a radically different viewpoint. Certain students of child development immediately began to look for "erroneous assumptions," flaws in methodology and statistics, and "unwarranted conclusions" in the Iowa findings. Articles extremely critical of Wellman's reports began to appear in the psychological journals. One of the most violent of these attacks was a paper entitled, "The Wandering IQ: Is It Time To Settle Down?" by Simpson (1939). He assumed the role of one who is assigned the bitter task of "exposing" the devious operations of a colleague gone astray as he wrote,

> But to claim miracle working at Iowa that cannot be duplicated in other parts of the country in nursery schools, elementary schools, or high schools, that is much worse than nonsense and ought to be exposed as such, thankless as the task of exposing it may be (p. 366).

In general, Simpson's attack apparently was based more on an emotional reaction to Wellman's point of view than upon a rational and objective evaluation of all the evidence presented. Among his personal thrusts was a change of "statistical incompetence under the influence of wishful thinking."

Another rather strong reaction was voiced by Florence Goodenough, certainly a highly respected authority in the field of intelligence and its evaluation. It should be mentioned, at this point, that in 1928, four years prior to Wellman's initial report, an article by Goodenough appeared in which she reported an "apparent increase" in average IQ in both of two matched groups, one of which had had a year's experience in a nursery school, while the other had not. The results of the study, however, led to her conclusion that the "changes are largely, if not entirely, attributable to irregular standardization of the scale at the early ages and consequently should not be regarded as an indication of actual increase in intelligence" (Goodenough, 1928a, p. 368). No relation between gain in IQ and length of attendance at the nursery school was indicated. In view of her findings in this early study, it is not surprising that Goodenough was highly critical of the Wellman papers.

Dr. Goodenough continued to point out that infant tests had been shown to have no predictive value and that, because of their basic unreliability, a "regressive shift" took place in successive testings of the same groups of children. This meant that those who originally tested highest appeared, as a group, to lose in IQ because many of them, by chance, obtained IQ's that were too high; and those who originally tested at the low end of the scale appeared, as a group, to score higher at the next testing because many of their original scores were, by chance, too low. She was also concerned with an apparent lack of controls over the possibility of examiner bias in the Iowa test results. In general, Goodenough felt that little faith could be put in the results of the studies because of the lack of sufficient substantiating data.

During the following year, Goodenough and Maurer (1940) published a report of a study in which nursery-school children and non-nursery-school children were compared for changes in IQ level after 1, 2, and 3 years of nursery-school experience for the nursery-school group. Interestingly enough, their results were quite different from those of the Iowa studies. At the end of 1 year of nursery-school experience the nursery-school group and the non-nursery-school group showed precisely the same average gain in IQ—4.6 points.

This 1940 paper thus supported the idea of a hereditarily fixed potentiality as well as predetermined development, allowing no place for experience to have "any measurable effect whatever upon the mental development of children" (Goodenough and Maurer, 1940, p. 176).

These conceptions of the nature of intelligence were even more strongly emphasized in Goodenough's review (1940) in which she proposed to answer the question, "What effect, if any, is a specific environmental change likely to have upon the intellectual development of a particular group of children?"

In reviewing the Iowa studies, Goodenough "accounted" for the differential changes shown by their data in terms of such factors as inadequate control groups or control children that were not strictly comparable with respect to age, level of intelligence, and test experience, the failure to take into account and deal with "regressive effects," and other "indefensible" computational and statistical procedures.

After reviewing a number of other studies on this general problem (Kawin and Hoefer, 1931; Peterson, 1937; and Starkweather and Roberts, 1940) Goodenough reached two general conclusions as follows:

1. It is unsafe to assume that attendance at any unspecified nursery school is likely to bring about improvement in the mental ability of the average child, for in most investigations of this matter, no evidence whatever of such an effect has been found. It appears, therefore, that ability to bring about intellectual improve-

ment by this means is at best restricted to a few schools. The precise nature of the difference in the educational regimes of the schools that do, and of those that do not, claim to achieve these results has thus far not been made clear.

2. Analysis of the experimental studies dealing with this problem reveals many possible sources of error in the studies purporting to show a positive effect of nursery school training. Generally speaking, these studies have failed to maintain adequate control of basic variables. Their statistical techniques are also frequently of questionable validity, and in a number of instances, are certainly erroneous (Goodenough, 1940, p. 321).

The particular Iowa studies that were, perhaps, more severely criticized because of extreme statements unjustified by the data, were those of foster children. The reports were largely based upon data on the later development of a group of 154 children who were placed in adoptive homes before they were 6 months of age, and a second group of 65 who were adopted between the ages of 2 and 5½. Certain statements that appeared in these studies were extreme, almost to the point of denying that the biological factor had any bearing at all upon later mental development. One such statement was:

. . . if there is an hereditary constitutional factor which sets the limits of mental development, these limits are extremely broad. Within these, environmental factors can operate to produce changes which for ordinary purposes may represent a shift from one extreme to another of the present distribution of intelligence among children (Skodak, 1939, pp. 131–132).

INVESTIGATIONS AND DISCUSSIONS OF CONTROVERSIAL ISSUES

Considerable discussion in the psychological literature followed the Iowa papers and the criticisms of them. The entire Thirty-ninth Yearbook of the National Society for the Study of Education (1940) consisted of discussions and research findings on the issues. Bayley (1940b) reported a study in which she found that the environmental factors of attendance at nursery school, a child's health record, and his ordinal position in the family, did not influence intelligence ratings. The educational level of parents, however, was found to be significantly related to intelligence ratings at later childhood ages, but was not an important factor under 18 months. Wellman (1940a) considered three possible environmental effects on the child's level of intelligence as reflected in change in IQ: (1) variations in opportunity for utilizing abilities he already possesses; (2) variations in experiences that foster intellectual curiosity; and (3) variations in motivation. The child's inclination to utilize resources at hand, she felt was determined by the nature of the group with which he associated.

Jones and Jorgensen (1940) reported finding no difference in mental growth between children who did and did not attend nursery school. In the same volume, on the other hand, a few investigators other than the Iowa group found some evidence that nursery-school experience elevated the IQ. Frandsen and Barlow (1940) noted a small average gain in IQ for an experimental group who attended a "special nursery school," although the gain was not significantly greater than that made by their matched control group.

McHugh (1943) published a monograph dealing with the relation of preschool experience to IQ changes in a group of 91 children who, after an initial Binet test, were given 30 three-hour sessions of preschool experience and then were again tested. Among McHugh's conclusions were:

1. Children do make significant mean gains in IQ score as a result of such preschool experience.
2. IQ gains from preschool experience are "adjustment gains" rather than growth in intelligence.

Another different approach to the study of environmental influences was made by Bradway (1945a). A group of preschool children, selected as representative of the general population, had been given the Stanford-Binet scale. Ten years later, and with no interaction in the interim, they were re-examined on the same scale, and several environmental factors in the lives of the children who had shown the most significant changes were examined and evaluated. Environmental information was obtained by interviewing the mothers and the children without the interviewer's knowing whether the child's IQ had shown an increase or a decrease. The results are summarized as follows:

1. The mean IQ of the increase group increased 9 points, while the mean of the decrease group decreased 17 points.
2. At the initial testing, the mean IQ's of the two groups were within 6 points of each other. Ten years later, the difference between their mean IQ's was 30 points.

The factors related to these changes were:

3. The mean vocabulary score of the mothers of the increase group was significantly higher than the mean score of the mothers of the decrease group.
4. The mid-parent intelligence scores of the parents of the two groups also differed significantly.

The general conclusion was that the IQ changes that took place between preschool and junior high school were related to environmental factors, but the question of whether the particular factors considered in the study "operated primarily as environmental stimuli or whether they were for the most part merely related to inheritable intelligence which had not been fully realized at the time of the initial examination" could not be answered from the data.

Gesell (1940b) took a position somewhat in line with Bradway's conclusions just cited. Although Gesell generally tended strongly to emphasize the biological influences in his writings, he expressed in this article an "interaction" point of view that is currently rather widely accepted. He wrote,

> In appraising growth characteristics, we must not ignore environmental influences—cultural milieu, siblings, parents, food, illness, trauma, education. But these must always be considered in relation to primary, or constitutional factors, because the latter ultimately determine the degree, and even the mode, of the reaction to so-called "environment." The organism always participated in the creation of its environment, and the growth characteristics of the child are really the end-product expressions of an interaction between intrinsic and extrinsic determiners. Because the interaction is the crux, the distinction between these two sets of determiners should not be drawn too heavily (p. 159).

Studies of Deprivation in Institutionalized Children

In general, the studies so far examined that have been concerned with the evaluation of specific environmental factors in relation to mental development have resulted in inconsistent and contradictory findings. Attempts to isolate and specify particular effects of experience in children reared at home have met with little success. On the other hand, comparisons of infants reared in orphanages with children reared at home, or by mothers, have rather consistently showed wide differences in rate and level of behavioral development favoring the latter group (Goldfarb, 1943; Pasamanick, 1946; Spitz, 1946; 1949).

A common feature of the particular orphanages studied was a minimum of environmental variation for the infant inmates. In a study by Rene Spitz (1949) two groups of infants were compared, one reared in a nursery by their own mothers, the other in a foundling home by an overworked nursing staff of which each nurse cared for 8 to 12 babies. The important difference in the two situations, according to Spitz, was the amount of environmental variation and stimulation, and, especially, conditions allowing for emotional interchange between the infants and those caring for them. Comparisons between the two groups were drawn in terms of developmental quotients (DQ) that represented "six sectors of personality," i.e., level of perception, mastery of bodily functions, social relations, memory and imitation, manipulative ability, and intelligence. The contrasts between the two groups over a 12-month period were striking. At age 2 to 3 months the average DQ of the mother-reared children was 95 as compared with an average of 130 for the foundling-home children. At ages 8 to 10 months the average DQ of the nursery children had risen to 110 while that of the foundling-home group had dropped to around 72. In summary Spitz wrote:

> While the children in "Nursery" developed into normal healthy toddlers, a two-year observation of "Foundlinghome" showed that the emotionally starved children

never learned to speak, to walk, to feed themselves. With one or two exceptions in a total of 91 children, those who survived were human wrecks who behaved either in a manner of agitated or of apathetic idiots (Spitz, 1949, p. 149).

Spitz pointed out that in both institutions the infants received adequate food, the housing was excellent, and medical care was equally adequate.

Similar findings were reported by Goldfarb (1943). He compared the development of children who were placed in an institution during early infancy, remained there until about 3 years of age, and then were placed in foster homes, with other children who had been placed immediately in foster homes. The two groups were from much the same hereditary background. Goldfarb concluded that prolonged residence in the institution during infancy was profoundly detrimental to the children's psychological development. The institutionalized and foster-home children showed percentages of defective speech development of 80 and 15, respectively. Comparable percentages showing mental retardation were 37.5 and 7.5; for the children showing educational difficulties the percentages were 42.5 and 15.0, respectively.

The findings of Spitz and Goldfarb quite convincingly demonstrated the retarding effects of a lack of stimulation and environmental variation upon the behavioral development of young infants. Such findings, however, are open to different interpretations of whether maturation is the sole factor in the development of mental capacity, or whether environment also is a factor of importance. Goldfarb and Spitz, in their above cited works, and Bowlby (1951), and others, assumed that the low ability to perform in an intelligence test, or the defective speech development of institutionalized children is indicative of retarded development of mental capacity. In terms of this assumption, experience in adjusting to environmental variation—coping with an ever changing situation—is essential to the development of intellectual potentiality.

Dennis and Najarian (1957), however, disagreed with the above interpretation. They studied the development of children reared in a Lebanese foundling home in comparison with children brought to the Well Baby Clinic of the American University Hospital of Beirut, Lebanon. Their objective findings were similar to those of Spitz. The average DQ for the institution babies over the age period of from 3 to 12 months was only 63, while that of the Well Baby Clinic group was 101, a highly significant difference. In this age range, all the clinic group tested above the mean of the foundling-home group. Not one of the latter group between the ages of 3 and 12 months had a DQ above 95. In discussing the similarity between Spitz's findings and their own, Dennis and Najarian (1957) wrote:

Spitz's data and ours agree in finding that environmental conditions can depress infant test scores after the second month of life. We disagree with Spitz in regard to the interpretation of the cause of the decline. We believe that Spitz's data, as well as ours, are satisfactorily interpreted in terms of restricted learning opportunities. We suggest that an analysis of the relationship between test items and the conditions prevailing in the Foundling Home would reveal that retardation could readily be explained in terms of restriction of learning opportunities (pp. 10–11).

Dennis and Najarian, then, believed that the unvarying institutional environment does not necessarily interfere with the actual developmental "unfoldment" of mental potential in the child but simply hampers learning, and that life in the institution does not provide the opportunity for the child to learn to perform the tasks, or respond to the kinds of stimuli presented to him in the test situation, to nearly the same degree as does the ordinary home environment. From this point of view, the child may have possessed this capacity to learn these particular tricks, but did not have the opportunity to learn them. This intellectual capacity to learn had been developing all along in spite of stimulus deprivation. Thus, in terms of this theory, the environmental factor is not important in the development of intelligence defined as capacity to learn.

If this latter interpretation were correct—if the retarding effects of a depriving environment were simply the absence of learned responses as a result of the lack of opportunity to learn, rather than a retardation in the development of the capacity to learn—then all that would be needed to correct the condition in a given child would be to place him in an environment rich in opportunity to learn.

In support of this possibility, Pasamanick (1946), in his study of Negro infants in a "depriving" institutional environment, found the usual, progressive behavioral retardation. However, when these infants were given more individual attention, they began to overcome the effects of deprivation.

On the other hand, further findings by Goldfarb (1947) led to the opposite conclusion. In his study of the adjustments of a group of adolescents who had spent the early months and years of their lives in an institution, Goldfarb found that the ill effects of their early environment were still with them. In discussing a particular case, he concluded that

> . . . even after years in a foster home he still demonstrated isolated, infantile impoverished character trends. His intellectual growth potential has been equally frustrated and he reacts to problems on a highly concretistic level that verifies the absence of an intelligent approach to new adjustments (p. 449).

> The investigation was begun in the hope and belief that an understanding of the factors associated with those individual variations in adjustment might help in the formation of a treatment program to counteract the effects of the privation process. The present findings are not encouraging. We have been able to do relatively little once the damage has been wrought (p. 455).

In summary, the evidence seems generally to support the conclusion that experience in coping with a stimulating environment is a factor of importance in mental development. The assumption that mentality is "fixed" and determined in the sense that it is, somehow, derived automatically from the somatic and neutral structures as they develop through the "mechanism of maturation" is hardly tenable. As Baller and Charles (1961) put it, "optimum development of both learning *capacity* and learning *achievement* demand personal involvement of the learner and interaction with a rich environment" (back of p. 245).

The Interaction Point of View

In view of the evidence, then, "fixed intelligence," in the sense that the rate and pattern of its development are predetermined by the genes, is no longer tenable. In another sense, however, intelligence is fixed. In this interpretation, the individual is endowed with a particular intellectual potentiality that is set by the genes, and, surely it is tenable. The idea, of course, is distinct from the idea of predetermined development. There is really no inherent connection between the two concepts. There is no necessity to assume that intellectual development, within the limits set by the genetic factor, is wholly a function of maturation. The degree to which this fixed upper limit is approached by a given individual may be largely determined by the nurture factor—by the nature of his environment and his encounters with it.

Obviously, a child's capacity to function effectively in an everchanging environment increases with age. Intelligence tests from the beginning have been designed to measure these changes, and, in terms of test results, curves of increase in capacity have been plotted. These curves, furthermore, show a leveling off and a gradual cessation of increase as the individual approaches adulthood. Clearly, these are curves of change in capacity to learn or perform adequately in new or difficult situations and, since they do level off with adulthood and, thus, parallel generally the curves of organismic development, they undoubtedly are related to, and reflect generally the course of maturation of the neuro-effector system. It does not necessarily follow, however, that the development of the capacity thus depicted is purely maturational in nature—that it somehow arises automatically from the natural unfolding of an inherently designed anatomical structure uninfluenced by experience. On the contrary, there is increasing evidence that experience is always an important determining factor and that richness of environmental stimulation has much to do, in each case, with the extent to which mental development at any point in time has actually approached the level that the structure at its particular stage of development has made possible. The development of the intellect, like all development, comes about through the interaction of the organism (with its fixed developmental potential) and its environment (Anastasi and Foley, 1948; McCandless, 1952; Escalona and Moriarty, 1961; Hunt, 1961).

As we have seen, this point of view was expressed by Harvey A. Carr back in 1926. A few years later, when the controversy over the effects of environmental change on mental development was at its height, Stoddard and Wellman (1934) proposed the following:

> A theory of mental development for which there is a small amount of supporting evidence and nothing as yet contradictory to it, may be built up along five main lines.
>
> 1. That definite limits to mental development are set by heredity, in increasing order of specificity as we go from species to race, to family, and finally to the individual.
> 2. That inherited mental ability, if allowed to function below its response potentialities, decreases relatively (that is, the intelligence quotient declines).
> 3. That inherited mental ability, in steady combination with stimulation appropriate to its needs, has the appearance of relative increase (that is, the IQ increases).
> 4. That, in certain ways, the nervous system transforms external patterns into adequate internal stimuli and drives whatever mental mechanism is present accordingly.
>
> The mental range, for a given inheritance, runs from flabbiness to athleticism.
>
> 5. That in present day life, there are strong forces definitely subversive to mental development in individuals, in that they are substitutes for thinking, or distractions designed to discourage the process (pp. 178–179).

This interaction theory of Stoddard and Wellman undoubtedly would be more widely accepted today than in 1934 as an explanation for IQ fluctuations and changes.

The current rather widely accepted view of mental development as a process of interaction is quite clearly expressed by Escalona and Moriarty (1961):

> Certainly the authors are not alone with their assumption that intelligence must be viewed as an interaction phenomenon. With apologies to Piaget's and other developmental theories we shall crudely describe intelligence as the result of a continuous stream of transactions between the organism and the surrounding field, which field is the sum total of physical and social environmental conditions. Since the organism brings to each adaptive act certain properties, both those of intrinsic biological nature and those which are the result of the impact of previous experience upon the organism, it is correct to say that intelligence development is at all times dependent upon what the organism is like. Yet, since it requires environmental circumstances to mobilize the organism, and since the kind of transaction which develops depends on the objective content of that to which the organism must adapt, it is equally true to say that the development of intelligence depends at all times on the experience encountered by the growing child (p. 598–599).

Perhaps the strongest recent expositor of interaction in relation to the development of intelligence is J. McV. Hunt (1961). He marshalled the evidence in support of this point of view from research in learning, learning sets, and the effects of early experience, from the programming of electronic computers, and, especially, from the observations of Piaget on the development of logical thinking and intelligence in children. Hunt presented an extensive and systematic review of Piaget's "experiments" and stressed the fact that a basic concept in all of Piaget's theorizing on the growth of intelligence was the concept of interaction between organism and environment that involves the complementary processes of accommodation and assimilation.

> The more new things an infant has seen and the more new things he has heard, the more new things he is interested in seeing and hearing; and the more variation in reality he has coped with, the greater is his capacity for coping. Such relationships derive from the conception that change in circumstances is required during the early sensorimotor stages to force the accommodative modifications in schemata and the assimilation of these modifications that, in combination, constitute development (Hunt, 1961, p. 262).

In his concluding chapter, Hunt pointed out some serious implications of the current, prevailing conceptions and assumptions about the nature of intelligence and how it develops in children in relation to their care and education. He wrote:

> In the light of these considerations it appears that the counsel from experts on child rearing during the third and much of the fourth decades of the twentieth century to let children be while they grow and to avoid excessive stimulation was highly unfortunate. It was suggested in the text above that perhaps the negative correlations found between intelligence test scores for the first two years and the late adolescent level of intelligence may possibly be attributable to such counsel, inasmuch as it would be those educated people at the higher levels of tested intelligence who read and can act in terms of what they read who would have been most likely to follow this advice. The problem for the management of child development is to find out how to govern the encounters that children have with their environments to foster both an optimally rapid rate of intellectual development and a satisfying life (Hunt, 1961, pp. 362–363).

POINTS OF VIEW ON THE "STRUCTURE" OF INTELLIGENCE

Another important area in which theoretical positions have varied and changed over the years is that of the structure or composition of intelligence. As we have already noted, the earliest attempts to measure intelligence were made in terms of separate faculties, processes, or abilities. Out of these early attempts at measurement, and those that followed, however, there gradually developed the concept of "general intelligence," of which the various functions tested were expressions.

The Concept of General Intelligence

Binet, in his writings, gave no single, well formulated definition of intelligence but he did offer a number of descriptions of it, each stressing particular aspects of or functions involved in mental activity. It is clear, however, that underlying these descriptions was the idea of a general intelligence, complex but unified. Intelligence he wrote, is compounded of "judgment, common sense, initiative, and the ability to adapt oneself. . . . To judge well, understand well, reason well—these are the essentials of intelligence" (Binet and Simon, 1916, p. 42). William Stern (1914), on the other hand, offered a definition that clearly differentiated general intelligence from special talents and abilities, and from knowledge and mere information. "Intelligence," he said, "is a general capacity of an individual consciously to adjust his thinking to new requirements. It is general mental adaptability to new problems and conditions of life" (p. 3).

Charles Spearman (1904; 1914; 1927) went further than merely to offer a definiton. Through the application of correlational and other statistical techniques, he developed a theory known as the two-factor theory of intelligence. The first of these factors he referred to as "*g*," or a general factor identified as general intelligence. He conceived of *g* as a "general fund of mental energy." In summarizing his discussion of the nature of *g*, he wrote,

> the facts of general psychology—quite apart from those of individual differences —strongly support the suggestion of mental energy and engines. Moreover, such an energy would seem to be just what is wanted to explain *g* (Spearman, 1927, p. 135).

In his thinking, this general factor was involved in each specific function or performance, although the second factor was the individual's "specific capacity for that particular kind of performance."

Spearman's theory stimulated much interest and discussion. Other workers using Spearman's own formulas often were unable to duplicate his findings and, thus, came to challenge his theory. In opposition to his concept of a general factor was the contemporarily widely accepted view that intelligence consists of many specific abilities not bound together by a common factor (Thorndike, 1914). Spearman's two-factor theory was not generally accepted but the concept of general intelligence has predominated through the years. Some of the most widely used tests of intelligence, such as the Stanford revisions of the Binet scale, were designed and constructed in terms of the concept of general intelligence. The assumption was that all types of mental activity are very largely functions of a single general factor, and that it matters little what particular combination of mental tasks or performance is called for in an intelligence-test scale, since they are all related to and, therefore, tap the same general factor. At least, in part, as a result of this view of the structure of intelligence, many of the scales currently in wide use show little unformity of content one with another; neither do they show any internal uniformity from age level to age level.

Concepts of Multiple Mental Abilities

As indicated above, the alternative view of the structure of intelligence was the concept of specific abilities. Thorndike (1914), an eminent proponent of this view, wrote that

> the mind must be regarded not as a functional unit, nor even as a collection of a few general faculties which work irrespective of particular material, but rather as a multitude of functions each of which involves content as well as form, and so is related closely to only a few of its fellows, to the others with greater and greater degrees of remoteness (p. 366).

Spearman's two-factor theory and his famous tetrad differences technique for demonstrating the presence of a two-factor pattern in a set of correlations, as we have already noted, did give substantial statistical support to the theory of general intelligence. In terms of Spearman's findings, every test item in a scale was thought to be composed of the *g* factor—the universal—plus a specific factor peculiar to it alone. His work also stimulated a great deal of discussion and further research with the use of his technique. In certain of these studies it was found that the intercorrelations between some pairs of tests were too high to be accounted for by their relatively low loadings of *g*. In other words, they involved a common factor in addition to *g*. These additional common factors came to be known as group factors. Spearman himself, and his co-workers, came to recognize a number of such group factors, namely, verbal ability, numerical ability, mental speed, mechanical ability, attention, and imagination. Concurrently, other analytical procedures that were designed to bring out the group factors in a battery of tests, were being experimented with. As a result, a number of methods of multiple-factor analysis were invented. Among the best known were those of Hotelling (1933), Kelley (1935), and Thurstone (1935). Until the advent of the electronic computer, perhaps the most widely used was Thurstone's centroid method of multiple-factor analysis.

In 1938, Thurstone reported a study in which he applied his own technique to the analysis of the intercorrelations among 57 tests that were designed to measure general intelligence. The data were the scores of 240 university students. Without benefit of the modern computer, this was a computational feat of no mean proportions.

The analysis was carried to 13 factors. The first 6 of the first 9 factors accounted for the major portion of the variance; Factors 10, 11, 12 and 13 were finally discarded for having no significant psychological meaning. Thurstone's tentative designations for the 9 meaningful factors were Spacial,

Perceptual, Numerical, Verbal Relations, Memory, Word Fluency, Induction, Restriction, and Deduction.

In a later study, Thurstone and Thurstone (1941) extended their search for primary mental abilities downward to younger ages. On the basis of this study the Thurstones concluded that the following 6 factors met their criteria of primary abilities:

V—Verbal-comprehension	N—Number
W—Word-fluency	M—Memory
S—Space	I—Induction

In other words, general intelligence was found to consist of at least six mental abilities. However,

> none of these factors is considered as fixed, indivisible, or non-combining; each one is dependent for its validity on the nature of the tests and the population examined. But each primary ability behaves as a functional unit that is strongly present in some tests and almost completely absent in many others (Stoddard, 1943, p. 165).

A Three-dimensional Model of Intellect

Two other investigators of note in the use of multiple-factor analysis as applied to the problem of discovering and identifying the components of intelligence were R. B. Cattell (1953) and Guilford (1956; 1957). Guilford and his co-workers, in connection with their "Aptitudes Project" especially, at the University of Southern California (sponsored and financed by the U.S. Office of Naval Research), concentrated particularly on the study of cognitive and thinking abilities.

> The results from the Aptitudes Project that have gained perhaps the most attention have pertained to creative-thinking abilities. These are mostly novel findings. But to me, the most significant outcome has been the development of a unified theory of human intellect, which organizes the known, unique or primary intellectual abilities into a single system called the "structure of intellect" (Guilford, 1959, p. 469).

This model makes room for a large number of factors, each representing a distinct ability. The factors, however, can be identified and ordered in terms of a three-dimensional system of classification. In other words, the model consists of three sets of classification categories. One of these bases of classification is in terms of mental operations. Guilford identified five categories of operations as follows: cognitive processes, memory, covergent thinking, divergent thinking, and evaluation. These categories, in Guilford's conceptualization, constitute the basic kinds of mental processes or "operations" of the intellect.

The second classification indicates the kinds of content that are involved in the intellectual operations. The factors of intelligence so far identified involve the four following kinds of content: *figural,* concrete material actually perceived through the senses; *symbolic,* composed of letters, digits, and other conventional signs, usually organized into general systems such as the alphabet or the number system; *semantic,* in the form of verbal meaning or ideas and *behavioral,* representing the area of interpersonal relationships sometimes called "social intelligence."

The third classification indicates the outcomes or products of the various "operations" as they are applied to any of the three kinds of content. There are six kinds of products. In the words of Guilford (1959),

> When a certain operation is applied to a certain kind of content, as many as six general kinds of products may be involved. There is enough evidence available to suggest that, regardless of the combinations of operations and content, the same six kinds of products may be found associated. The six kinds of products are: units, classes, relations, systems, transformations, and implications. So far as we have determined from factor analysis, these are the only fundamental kinds of products that we can know. As such, they may serve as basic classes into which one might fit all kinds of information psychologically (p. 470).

Guilford's theoretical model of the intellect in terms of its "structure," is thus represented as a solid three-dimensional figure in which the dimensions are the three sets of classification categories—operations, contents, and products. This conceptualization allows for 120 separate factors of intelligence, many of which have already been identified and measured. By dividing the model into vertical layers, or slices, in terms of the five categories of operations, we have five sets of 24 small cubes each. Each of these five sets, then, represents a particular category of mental abilities. Thus, there are the cognitive abilities, memory abilities, divergent-thinking abilities, convergent-thinking abilities, and evaluative abilities. According to the model, each of the 24 cognitive abilities, for example, is an ability to deal with a particular kind of material, such as *symbolic content,* for example. The outcome or *product* of that particular operation would, then, be the *cognition of a symbolic unit,* or a symbolic system, etc.

Since the early days of mental testing, then, we have seen an interesting shift in the nature of the prevailing conceptualizations of the structure of intelligence. As techniques of data analysis have developed, the trend in conceptualization has been away from the original view of intelligence as a unitary, general ability presumed to account for individual differences in any and all sorts of mental functioning, toward greater and greater complexity of conceptualization encompassing a multiplicity of factors. First, in addition to *g,* certain specific, or group factors were postulated to account for the observed correlations among test variables. More refined analysis, however, soon led to the notion of multiple factors, as *g* was broken down into a relatively small number of primary mental abilities. The advent of the electronic computer, of course, has tremendously increased our analytic capacity in sheer number of test variables that can be handled in a single analysis, and in speed of computational operations. This increase has led to the concept of a great variety of relatively independent mental abilities. The job of extracting these factors, identifying them, and testing them is under way. The primary concern of the present project, however, is the problem of the assessment of mental abilities during infancy and early childhood.

THE PROBLEM OF DEVELOPMENTAL CHANGE IN MENTALITY

It has been shown repeatedly (Furfey and Muehlenbein, 1932; Bayley, 1933b, 1955; L. D. Anderson, 1939; J. E. Anderson, 1940; Cavanaugh, Cohen, Dunphy, Ringwell, and Goldberg, 1957) that mental tests administered during the first year of the child's life are of no practical value in predicting later tested intelligence. Furfey and Muehlenbein (1932), for example, set out specifically to determine the predictive value of the Linfert-Hierholzer scale when it was administered during the first 12 months. They found no significant relation between the infant test scores and the Stanford-Binet scores obtained 4 years later. They concluded that since the other published infant scales were very similar to the Linfert-Hierholzer in content and general make-up, their results called into question the predictive value of all infant mental tests.

Bayley (1933b) in her study of mental growth during the first three years, reported her findings on the consistency of mental ratings in terms of correlation coefficients, with different interims between first and later testing. She found that "there is no significant relationship between a child's scores in the first three months and those he makes after nine months." She also found, however, that there was a tendency for the "sigma scores to become more stable as the children grew older" (p. 47).

More recently Bayley (1955) obtained correlations of near zero between scores on the California First Year Mental Scale administered earlier than 1 year of age, and retest scores at 18 months. With retests at later preschool ages the correlations were even negative as high as −.21.

Predictive results with the Cattell Infant Test were found to be very little better (P. Cattell, 1940). Correlations between IQ's at 3, 6, and 9 months, and later 3-year IQ's, were 0.10, 0.34, and 0.18.

A study by L. D. Anderson (1939) produced similar results with infant tests constructed by the usual percentage-of-success method. Zero or insignificant relations were found between scores at 3, 6, 9, or 12 months and Stanford-Binet scores obtained at age 5 years.

Although the tests have been found to be valuable aids in the overall appraisal of health and developmental status of babies, this lack of predictive value has raised serious doubts of their validity as tests of intelligence. J. E. Anderson (1940), for example, was expressing his doubt when he stated that

> the adequacy with which a particular test measures what it purports to measure

> has to be determined in terms of its correlation with tests at later ages. . . . In making the best possible prediction of terminal status, we will also make the best measurement of present status in so far as our concern is with potentiality rather than achievement. . . .
>
> Infant tests as at present constituted measure very little if at all, the function, which is called intelligence at later ages (p. 401).

Anderson, thus, made it clear that he could not accept an appraisal of an infant's mental status as valid unless it reliably foretold future, or terminal mental status. It is interesting to note, in this qualification, that the validity of the criterion (usually the Stanford-Binet scale) in terms of which the infant tests were judged, was generally taken for granted without question, although in some instances the criterion test had been less adequately standardized than the infant test in question (Kawin, 1934).

Because of this concern about predictive validity, some otherwise rather promising tests of infant abilities may have been abandoned. The Linfert-Hierholzer scale, for example, carefully standardized on 300 infants under 1 year of age of which some 50 were tested repeatedly at different ages, has never been used to any extent because it was found not to predict Binet IQ.

Quite obviously, a reliable means of appraising intellectual potential in infants that permits the predicting of future academic ability would be of considerable practical value, particularly to adoption agencies and prospective adoptive parents. The inadequacy of presently available tests for making such early predictions is not only a matter of practical concern but constitutes a theoretical problem of considerable import. It raises the question of the nature of infantile mentality and how it differs from intelligence in later childhood. There have been, in the past, two principal points of view regarding this difference and the nature of mental development. A brief consideration of each of these viewpoints follows.

The Assumption of Quantitative Change

The traditional view is that intelligence is fixed, that it develops naturally with the maturation of the nervous system, and, therefore, that the IQ, when reliably determined, represents a stable characteristic of the individual. This view clearly includes the idea that there is no qualitative change in the nature of intelligence during development but, rather, that the intellect develops through steady and continuous quantitative increments from birth.

Although this viewpoint had its heyday in the early 1930's, it is difficult, nevertheless, to find definite statements by the psychological writers of that period on the nature of infantile mentality or the nature of developmental change in intelligence. The essentially quantitative nature of mental growth was generally assumed without thought or discussion, or without consideration of other possible alternative views. The whole intelligence-testing movement, of course, was based upon this assumption of quantitative change. Inherent in the very concept of measurement was the implication of a scale or system of quantitative units. Thus, if intelligence was to be measured, it had to be in quantitative terms.

Binet on Mental Developmental Change

It is quite clear that Binet approached the task of measuring individual differences in mental capacity among children with the assumption that the differences were essentially quantitative in nature.

As mentioned earlier, although Binet seemed generally to regard intelligence as inherited, he was opposed to the idea of intelligence per se as a fixed quantity. Obviously, when he made that statement he was not applying the term to a genetically determined potentiality but, rather, to a capacity that changes with age. And he was quite specific on the nature of this changing capacity.

> It seems to us that in intelligence there is a fundamental faculty, the alternation or the lack of which is of the utmost importance for practical life. The faculty is *judgment,* otherwise called sense. . . . A person may be a moron or an imbecile if he is lacking in judgment, but with good judgment he can never be either. Indeed the rest of the intellectual faculties seem of little importance in comparison with judgment (Binet and Simon, 1916, pp. 42–43).

Binet, at another point, was more specific on what he meant by "the rest of the intellectual faculties." He indicated that he regarded such processes as sensation and perception as phenomena of intelligence and intellectual manifestations but not essential constituents of intelligence as such. He saw these functions as "distinct from, and independent of judgment" (Binet and Simon, 1916, p. 42).

Binet undoubtedly regarded the *nature* of the *change* in the capacity to judge (intelligence) as largely quantitative. Judgment, from his point of view, is a faculty that grows in a quantitative sense from perhaps a zero amount at birth to varying degrees as children develop.

> It (the development of intelligence) consists in part in the increase of the faculty of comprehension and of judging, at least this is probable. A child understands less and judges with less penetration than an adult; it consists also in the increase of acquisitions of every sort. But these are perhaps secondary characteristics which one may lack without compromising his maturity (Binet and Simon, 1916, p. 257).

On the other hand, although he stressed the quantitative aspect of developmental change, Binet apparently saw in mental development more than the simple addition of quantitative increments. "The child differs from adults," he wrote, "not only in degree and quantity of his intelligence, but also in its form. What this childish form of intelligence is, we do not yet know" (Simon and Binet, 1916, p. 183).

Genetically Endowed Potentiality

Writers following Binet quite obviously were primarily concerned with the measurements of an assumed general quantity called intelligence. Psychologists became preoccupied mainly with the construction and standardization of tests and with the quantitative measurement of growth changes and individual differences. They gave relatively little space in their writings to a consideration of the essential nature of the thing they were trying to appraise, or to the nature of its developmental changes. There was, as we have seen, considerable variation in the usage of the term intelligence. But, in general, there was an implicit, if not stated, assumption that the individual is endowed at conception with a fixed mental developmental potentiality that is his intelligence, and that mental growth, therefore, is an orderly increase in capacity to function within the limits and toward the full realization of that developmental potentiality, which, in itself, does not change.

As we have already noted, the term "intelligence" is often used also to refer specifically to this growing capacity. In that sense, intelligence changes in a quantitative sense but qualitatively remains the same. The child, as he matures, simply gains more of the capacity to sense, learn, solve problems, profit from experience, or judge, but always within the limits of his genetically determined potentiality.

Among those who were quite explicit in their identification with this point of view was Florence Goodenough (1946). She wrote,

> That children reared from infancy in environments where intellectual opportunity is not lacking and where incentive to intellectual achievement is high are likely to reach a higher level of achievement than others of equal original endowment for whom both opportunity and incentives are poor is conceded by practically all who have considered the matter. But this is not equivalent to saying that either opportunity or incentive will bring about changes that go beyond the limitations set by the germ plasm. "Men do not gather grapes from thorns nor figs from thistles." (pp. 485–486).

But the idea of a genetically determined limitation upon the development of mental capacity is by no means peculiar to modern psychologists. Plato, writing 2,000 years ago in *The Republic,* discussed individual differences in mentality in terms of original endowment. "When you spoke of a nature gifted or not gifted in any respect," he inquired, "did you mean to say that one man will acquire a thing easily, another with difficulty? Would not these be the sort of differences which would distinguish the man gifted by nature from the one who is ungifted?"

The concepts of the gifted child and of the mentally defective or retarded child clearly carry the implication of a genetically determined potentiality in which differences are quantitative in nature.

The Theory of Quantitative Change and the Lack of Predictive Value in Infant Tests

The newborn quite obviously lacks the ability on his own to cope with his environment. During the months of early infancy he will not have enough growing time to develop more than a limited degree of functional ability. From the standpoint of quantitative developmental theory, however, that ability (intelligence) would differ only in amount from time to time.

What then, about the fact that the results of infant mental tests and tests administered later at school ages do not correlate significantly? On the theory that there is no qualitative difference in intelligence at these age levels, the general conclusion, of course, has been that the available infant tests do not measure intelligence. On the other hand, in the opinion of many of their users, these tests are valid instruments of measurement and do provide an accurate appraisal of the baby's mental status. If this is true, then intelligence must change in kind or quality as well as in degree.

There are, however, a number of possible alternative explanations for the lack of predictive value of the infant tests. One hypothesis takes account of the profound immaturity of the infant subject. Time is required to establish stimulus-response connections and develop patterns of behavior that constitute adaptive ability. Since intelligence at any level can be tested only in terms of what the subject can do, there is, by virtue of sheer immaturity, an extremely limited basis for testing infant ability or capacity. Not only is the tester limited by what the infant can do but, particularly, he is limited by what he can get the baby to do even within his repertory of possible acts. Resistance to mental testing by 3-year-old children has been found to be an important factor affecting test results (Rust, 1931). Overcoming the resistance that was present at the first testing was found to result in increases in IQ's (Kuhlman-Binet) of approximately 50 per cent of the children, the increases ranging from 15 to 35 IQ points. It is not unreasonable to expect that resistance of similar magnitude and variability occurs among young babies. By the time the infant is 6 months of age he is able to respond to other individuals as individuals. He responds with awareness to strangers. The awareness of a strange person in the tester is more than likely to result in "resistance," affecting his score on the test. This may well be one reason for the lack of correlation between the 6-months and 12-months scores. Level of maturity, as such, may be a factor here, too, in that the baby is relatively immune to verbal persuasion. In his immaturity also he is especially subject to changing bodily conditions and fatigue.

The extent to which infant test performances represent actual ability to perform may also depend upon certain more stable factors in personal makeup. Differences in original temperamental nature, for example, in activity level, characteristic reactivity to stimulation, general alertness, etc., may make for wide differences in performance between two infants with the same capacity level. By the same token, two infants with quite widely different inherent potentialities and capacities may actually exhibit equivalent levels of performance on the test.

Rachel Stutsman (Ball) (1931) was fully cognizant of these factors during the process of developing the Merrill-Palmer Scale. In her discussion of the role of personality factors in the test situation she stated that

> back of every individual response is a group of variables which we have not been able to control and of whose relative strength we are totally uncertain. Self-reliance, initiative, self-consciousness, and persistence are such variables. At present it is impossible for us to isolate the effects produced by these non-intellectual traits from those produced by the intellectual abilities. Even in the most rigidly controlled test situation we are, of course, testing the ability of the individual to do a certain piece of work, and though the results may be called a measure of the individual's intelligence they can certainly be analyzed into causative elements, many of which are not ordinarily implied in that concept (p. 241).

Another area in which individual babies differ fundamentally is in pattern of development. The various aspects of overall development do not keep pace with each other. Each child has an uneven "developmental front" and the pattern of that front is different for each infant. Thus, general expectations of performance at different levels of infancy fit the developmental patterns of different infants with varying degrees of accuracy apart from the question of mental potential. These differences in developmental pattern undoubtedly contribute to the predictive inadequacy of infant tests. Nancy Bayley (1955) took cognizance of this factor of individual differences when she wrote:

> The neonate who is precocious in the developing of the simpler abilities, such as auditory acuity or pupilary reflexes, has an advantage in the slightly more complex behaviors, such as (say) turning toward a sound, or fixating an object held before his eyes. But these more complex acts also involve other functions, such as neuro-muscular coordinations, in which he may not be precocious. The bright one-month-old may be sufficiently slow in developing these later more complex functions so as to lose some or all of his earlier advantage (pp. 807–808).

Other possible causes for the lack of infant test predictivity have been proposed. Escalona (1948; 1950), for example, has suggested that the situation might be improved by interpreting test results and, thus, modifying the scores in terms of clinical observations made at the time of the test. The scores would then be based, not simply on the items passed, but also to some degree on clinical estimates of the child's potential. "The same formal test results," Escalona wrote, "may be interpreted differently in the light of concomitant clinical observations, thus increasing the predictive value of the tests" (1948, p. 281).

It has also been suggested that the inconsistent results of infant tests are caused by their item composition. The tests are said to lack suitable kinds of items. Catalano and McCarthy (1954), for example, studied the prelinguistic vocalizations of a group of infants at an average age of 13 months in relation to the results from an intelligence test administered after an average interval of 31 months. Although their correlations were discouragingly low, the investigators suggested that prelinguistic vocalization might be better predictors of later intelligence than the usual infant-scale items.

The lack of predictive value of infant tests may also be, in part, a function of the amount and quality of stimulation the infant, even very early, has experienced. In terms of the maturation theory, two infants with equivalent mental potentialities would presumably have developed about equal capacities for mental-test performance, but, because of differences in sensory and perceptual experience—experience in coping with environmental stimulation—may not have acquired equally well the response patterns necessary to perform adequately on the test (Dennis and Najarian, 1957).

As is shown in Chapter V, test content, in terms of ability factors and their meaning, is not the same at different age levels in any of the commonly used infant and preschool-age tests. This fact alone may account for much of the lack of predictive validity of early test scores.

A study by Hofstaetter (1954) lends support to the view that age differences in mentality are something more than quantitative in nature. He factor analyzed interage correlations of young children's test scores from the California growth study. At ages under 4 years, he noted two factors, which he called "sensori-motor alertness," that showed up during the first 2 years, and "persistence" between ages 2 and 4. After age 4 he obtained a group factor that he called "manipulation of symbols." It should be noted, however, that Hofstaetter correlated *total* test scores of individuals at different ages in this study. This means that the resulting factors tended strongly to correspond in meaning to the specific tests that went into the analysis in each case.

Development as Qualitative Change

As we have seen, intelligence is often broadly defined as ability or capacity to cope with or adjust to circumstances of living. From this point of view, one naturally thinks of mental development as the elaboration or enlargement of the child's repertory of adjustive behavior patterns. The increase in adaptability is seen as something more than the mere addition of increments to a basic quality or ability. The implication is, rather, that new qualities, new patterns of adaptation, emerge as the child grows and interacts with his environment.

Biologically speaking, the child has been growing through interaction with his environment since the moment of conception. By the time of his birth he has already developed certain simple behavioral, as well as physiological, patterns with which he is able to adapt to the conditions of his new external environment and without which he could not survive. In the sense, then, that intelligence is the capacity to make adaptive responses, the neonate possesses a measure of intelligence. Even with his immaturity and complete dependence at birth, he is equipped with a certain repertory of simple adaptive response patterns.

Generally, these adaptive patterns are standard equipment. They are characteristic of the species at the neonate level. Recent research, furthermore, has led to an increasing acceptance of the view that the young infant is not incompetent. The neonate possesses capacities for sensory discrimination and precision of adaptive response that have only recently been elicited and described (Bronshstein, Antonova, Kamenetskaya, Luppova, and Sytova, 1958; Kessen and Leutzendorff, 1963).

It is largely in relation to these early modes of adaptation that individuality is first expressed. Each infant is unique: he is an individual different from all others in the expression and overall patterning of adaptive behaviors. He displays this individuality in his reactions to stimulation, in the way he nurses, in his crying, in his general activity level, in his patterns of sleeping and waking. Thus, neonatal intelligence expresses itself, to some degree, uniquely in the individuality of each infant. It is an expression of mental development that has previously taken place. In the words of Arnold Gesell (1940a),

> these neonatal expressions of individuality are largely the end products of the primary mental growth which was accomplished in the long period of gestation. From a biological standpoint there are no sharp transitions in the continuum of mental growth. Even birth does not bring about a unique and abrupt transition, because *in utero* the fetus has already anticipated to a great degree the reactions of early neonatal life. He has been prepared; the very arrangement and relationships of his neurons have pointed to the future. In preliminary and provisional form these relationships were laid down by intrinsic patterning prior to and independent of actual experience, this preliminary and prospective kind of patterning is mental maturation. It operates not only *in utero* but throughout the whole cycle of mental growth (pp. 12, 13).

Gesell's View of Developmental Change

Gesell described mind as a process. This process is the organizing, integrating, controlling function of the individual. Mental growth (growth of the mind) for him, therefore, is a process of change, of increase in the effectiveness of the mind. "It is a process of behavior patterning." It is more than the addition of quantitative increments of what is already there. "The child's mind," Gesell (1940a) wrote, "does not grow by a simple linear extension. He has a persisting individuality, but his outlook on life and on himself transforms as he matures. He is not simply becoming more 'intelligent' in a narrow sense of this much misused term. He alters as he grows" (p. 15).

He further identified mind with the functioning of the neuromuscular system and the other involved physical structures, and "mental growth" with the maturation of these structures.

> As the infant grows and as the child grows, these nerve cells become organized into patterns of responsiveness, or into reaction systems. These neuron patterns determine behavior. They are influenced by the constitution of the blood, by endocrine hormones, and by electro-chemical regulators; but in a fundamental sense the patterning of the mind is inseparably connected with the microscopic and ultramicroscopic patterning of nerve cells (Gesell, 1940a, pp. 11–12).

In further emphasizing his view of the great and primary importance of predetermined biological maturation, and of the secondary and limited role played by the environment in mental development, Gesell later (1945) wrote,

> The action system develops as a unitary whole, within which individuation arises, from intrinsic morphogenetic forces. These individuations have a fore-reference; they anticipate subsequent adjustments to the environment with provisional and preparatory arrangements. The environment does *not engender* the arrangements. Experience does not create them. The neural mechanism of walking is laid down before the child can walk. This in turn has been anticipated by pre-neural organizations.
>
> The primary motor attitudes and the basic initiative in psychomotor attitudes are thus endogenous. We apply the term maturation to these intrinsic and prospective aspects of ontogenetic patterning. Environment *inflects* and *specifies* but it does not engender the progressions themselves (p. 163).

Gesell does not claim for his "developmental schedule" that it is primarily a test of infant intelligence but, rather, he regards it as a normative device for appraising developmental status in young children. In fact, he has little use for the term "intelligence." Because of his close identification of mental growth with the maturation of the organism and, thus, with general functional development, the implication is clear that his schedule is designed to be a measure of mental growth. In his rare use of the term "intelligence" he limits its meaning to the adaptive functions of the individual. Thus, in his discussion of the four major fields of behavior covered in his schedule, that is, motor characteristics, adaptive behavior, language, and personal-social behavior, he described the second of these fields, adaptive behavior, as dealing largely with intelligence. "Adaptive behavior," he wrote, "has been described as 'a convenient category for those varied adjustments, perceptual, orientational, manual, and verbal which reflect the child's capacity to initiate new experiences and to profit by past experiences' " (1940a, p. 108).

In summary, it is quite clear that Gesell regarded mental development as the functional aspect of biological maturation—a process of change which is qualitative, as well as quantitative, in nature. A further implication inherent in his viewpoint is that the process in which environment plays only an "inflecting" and "specifying," rather than an "engendering" role, takes place under the control and within the limits of a genetically determined developmental potential.

Piaget's Epigenetic Theory

Jean Piaget and his associates at Geneva, Switzerland, were the first actually to formulate a theory of mental development in which the nature of developmental change as such was a primary concern. Piaget conceived of intelligence in very dynamic terms. He defined it as a process of organization—as "an assimilatory activity whose functional laws are laid down as early as organic life and whose successive structures serving it as organs are elaborated by interaction between itself and the external environment" (Piaget, 1952, p. 359). Three essential elements of his theory are given in this definition. First is the idea that intelligence is not an entity, not a quantity, not a latent potentiality, but a dynamic process, an activity. Second, he indicates the nature of that process. It is a process of organization and adaptation. The third point is that the process—the operation of these "invariant functional laws"—results in many variable structures, or "schemata" which in turn become the "tools" for further interaction with the environment through assimilation and accommodation. Piaget further elaborated on these essential points,

> intelligence constitutes an organizing activity whose functioning extends that of the biological organization, while surpassing it due to the elaboration of new structures . . . if the sequential structures due to intellectual activity differ among themselves qualitatively, they always obey the same functional laws. In this respect, sensorimotor intelligence can be compared to reflective or rational intelligence and this comparison clarifies the analysis of the two extreme terms (1952, p. 407).

In discussing the principles of assimilation and accommodation in their broader application, Piaget wrote,

> it can be said that the living being assimilates to himself the whole universe, at the same time that he accommodates himself to it. . . . It is therefore permissible to conceive assimilation in a general sense as being the incorporation of any external reality whatever to one part or another, of the cycle of organization. In other words, every thing that answers a need of the organism is material for assimilation, the need even being the expression of assimilatory activity as such. . . . The functions of relationship, independently even from psychic life which proceeds from them, are thus doubly the source of assimilation (1952, pp. 407–408).

Although, for Piaget, intellectual developmental changes from birth to maturity constituted a fixed sequence of stages, each characterized by its particular organization of schemata and, thus, qualitatively differing from the one from which it emerged, yet, in his view, there was complete continuity in the course of this development. "Intelligence thus germinates in life itself"; the same invariant processes are at work from the beginning in the organization of new schemata on the basis of the older, more simple ones. He stated that new schemata "whose appearance marks each stage, are always revealed as developing those of the preceding stage" (1952, p. 384).

The concept of need is also basic to Piaget's thinking. The function of the behavior patterns, which he calls "schemata," is the satisfaction of need. This means "that the behavior patterns are from the onset the function of the general organization of the living body. Every living being constitutes a totality which tends to conserve itself and consequently to assimilate to itself the external elements it needs" (1952, p. 389).

As indicated in Piaget's definition of intelligence that is quoted above, the schema is in reality a tool of the process of adaptation (assimilation and accommodation). A schema is a behavior pattern and, thus conceived, it alone constitutes the organizing activity—the functions of assimilation and accommodation. Thus, it is by virtue of the activity of the existing schemata that new schemata are evolved. A schema, then, being a pattern of behavior, is "applied to the diversities of the external environment" and, thus, becomes increasingly generalized through its application to the varied aspects of the environment.

Observed developmental changes in mentality for Piaget, then, are qualitative in nature. Each "stage" of mental development encompasses patterns of behavior (schemata) that are new and different but which, as Piaget puts it, are developments of the old patterns. His theory is truly one of epigenesis. The earliest organic stage gives rise to the next stage by the progressive production of new parts, or schemata, which were previously non-existent, not preformed, and not predetermined.

To both Piaget and Gesell, mental development is qualitative change; for the basis or explanation of that change, however, they are far apart. Gesell placed great emphasis upon the "mechanism of maturation" that brings about these qualitative changes through the natural unfoldment of a predetermined developmental design. Piaget, on the other hand, recognized the important role of the environment. Mental development, for him, is not predetermined, is not a product of biological maturation, but is, rather a result of continuous interaction between the individual and his environment through assimilation and accommodation.

From this point of view, the character and variety of environmental stimulation loom as a matter of vital importance. In the very early weeks of life the infant is incapable of direct, voluntary action on his own initiative. He can simply respond to changes and variations in environmental stimulation. Thus, if he is to develop functionally, his environment must provide changes and variation in conditions for him to cope with. As Hunt (1961) put it,

> The more new things an infant has seen and the more new things he has heard, the more new things he is interested in seeing and hearing; and the more variation in reality he has coped with, the greater is his capacity for coping. Such relationships derive from the conception that change in circumstances is required during the early sensorimotor stages to force the accommodative modifications in schemata and the assimilations that, in combination, constitute development (p. 262).

This emphasis on the importance of stimulus variation for early mental development is appearing more and more frequently in the literature on infant development. A stimulus-rich but carefully ordered environment is a prime condition for optimum mental progress in infants and preschool children in the view of a number of present-day writers and investigators (Moore and Anderson, 1960; Hunt, 1961; Fowler, 962a; 1962b). Discussions of the role of environment in mental development are also leading to some reinterpretation of early studies (Dennis and Najarian, 1957) of the effects of maternal deprivation in institution-reared babies (Ribble, 1943; Goldfarb, 1945; Spitz, 1949; Bowlby, 1951).

Piaget's theory of a developmental sequence of stages in mental development is based primarily upon his carefully recorded observations of his own three children. From these "experiments," as we have seen, he presented a picture of continuous transformations in the organized structures of intelligence. This series of organizations, which are the products as well as the tools of assimilation and accommodation, begins at birth. But, at birth, the organizations consist only of congenital sensorimotor schemata, and these continue to characterize intelligence throughout the first 18 months or 2 years of the child's life. During this period, the sensorimotor period, Piaget distinguished six stages.

The first stage is characterized by the exercise of the ready-made congenital schemata, such as sucking, vocalizing, listening, looking, etc. In the very beginning, as indicated above, there is simply passive release of these schemata by stimulation. There is, then, during this stage, a gradual shift to an active "groping." "The subject does not remain passive but, on the contrary, manifests the behavior pattern emphasized by Jennings: He gropes and abandons himself to a series of 'trials and errors.' That is, according to Claparède, the origin of intelligence" (Piaget, 1952 p. 396). The reflex thus becomes "consolidated and strengthened by virtue of its own functioning." In other words, it is assimilated to the child's needs and functioning. At the same time it becomes adapted or accommodated to the realities of the situation through the groping, trial-and-error process.

The second stage, "primary circular reactions," is characterized by the progressive coordination and assimilation of the ready-made schemata to form motor habits and perceptions. At this stage the "hereditary adaptations are doubled . . . , by adaptations which are not innate to which they are subordinated little by little. In other words, the reflex processes are progressively integrated into cortical activity" (Piaget, 1952, p. 47). Three main developments are recognized during this stage. (1) Variations in schemata appear as a variety of stimuli become assimilated to them. (2) A reciprocal coordination among the schemata takes place. Thus, hand movements, to a degree, become coordinated with sucking, and things looked at become something to be reached for and grasped. (3) Although the child is unable to respond to a vanished object, repeated stimulation by objects leads to perceptual recognition of them. This second period, according to Piaget's observations, extends from about the end of the first month of life to about age 5 months.

Stage three, "secondary circular reactions," extends to about 8 or 9 months of age. Here, again, there is functional continuity with the earlier stages "thus establishing complete continuity between increasingly complex structures." As contrasted with the earlier stage, when the baby's actions are centered on the actions themselves—when he grasps for the sake of grasping—his actions in this third stage become "centered on a result produced in the external environment, and the sole aim of the action is to maintain this result: furthermore, it is more complex, the means beginning to be differentiated from the end, at least after the event" (Piaget, 1952, p. 157). The child now begins to show some anticipation of the consequences of his own acts, the beginning of intentionality.

The fourth stage of the sensorimotor period is characterized by the "coordination of the secondary schemata and their application to new situations" (Piaget, 1952, p. 210). It is during this stage (8-to-9 to 11-to-12 months of age) that the first actually intelligent behavior patterns appear. Schemata, which heretofore were detached, now may be coordinated by the child into a single, more complex act with the aim to attain an end that is not immediately within reach. He thus puts to work, with his intention, schemata coordinated for a new purpose. In this way, the child begins to show behavior in which means are clearly differentiated from ends. In his new relations with his environment, the accommodation aspect of his adaptations is especially apparent as he begins to differentiate the self from the non-self and is able to search to a limited degree for the vanished object. He also shows evidence of an implicit conception of causality and he appears to foresee events that are independent of his own actions.

Stage four, although it evolves from and is a further development of the earlier stage, is clearly marked by qualitatively different behavior features. However, as Piaget points out, the child is still especially limited in the effectiveness of his coping by two conditions:

In the first place, in order to become adapted to the new circumstances in which he finds himself—that is to say, in order to remove the obstacle or discover the requisite intermediate—the child at the fourth stage limits himself to intercoordinating familiar schemata, except for differentiating them through progressive accommodation while adjusting them to each other. In the second place, and through that very fact, the relations which the child establishes between things still depend on completed schemata of which only the *coordination* is new; besides they do not lead to the elaboration of objects entirely independent of the action. . . . In short, the fourth stage, in so far as it is defined by the commencement of the coordination of schemata, appears more as a phase of initiation or of gestation than as a period of realization or accomplishment (Piaget, 1952, pp. 263–264).

The fifth stage, in approximately the second year of life, is, by contrast, primarily the stage of elaboration of the object. It is characterized by the formation of new schemata that are established through a sort of experimentation, a search for something new. These new schemata come about, in other words, through activity directed with more of a purpose to seek novelty for its own sake, rather than simply through the practice of acts that produced chance results, as in the earlier stages.

This stage Piaget (1952) called "tertiary circular reactions." This type of reaction, he says, is quite different:

if it also arises by way of differentiation, from the secondary circular schemata, this differentiation is no longer imposed by the environment but is, so to speak, accepted and even desired in itself . . . the child manifests an unexpected behavior pattern: He tries, through a sort of experimentation, to find out in which respect the objct or the event is new. In other words, he will not only submit to but even provoke new results instead of being satisfied merely to reproduce them once they have been revealed fortuitously (p. 266).

This type of experimentation is seen in the child's deliberately letting an object that he is holding fall to the floor and then watching intently what happens to it. He shakes objects, knocks them, listens to the sounds they make, throws them and watches them bounce or roll. He is constantly experimenting in order to see. In the process of experimentation there is a constant accommodation of patterns (schemata) to the situation, and assimilation of new schemata. This naturally leads to the discovery of new means based on the apprehension of new relations.

Piaget referred to this type of mental activity as "inventive intelligence." In his observations, one of its earliest manifestations was what he called the "behavior pattern of the support." The pattern, based upon perceiving the relation between an object and whatever is supporting it, consists of grasping the underlying support of the object in order to draw it within reach, e.g., the child grasps a cushion and draws it toward him in order to obtain a box placed upon it. A new means of obtaining a desired object is thus discovered and utilized. And, in the opinion of Piaget, such new means can be discovered only through this experimenting-in-order-to-see activity that is characteristic of stage five.

Much groping or trial-and-error behavior is manifested in the child's experimental attempts to obtain desired objects during this stage. Such behavior leads him to an appreciation of spacial and causal relations and temporal sequences. This drive to active exploration and manipulation of objects makes evident the great importance during this stage of an environment rich in appropriate stimulation.

The sixth and last stage of sensorimotor intelligence appears in Piaget's thinking to be, in a sense, a transitional phase between the practical and the systematic or deductive levels of intelligence. In discussing this stage Piaget (1952) takes pains once more to emphasize the fact that the beginning of a new stage "does not abolish in any way the behavior patterns of the preceding stages and that new behavior patterns are simply superimposed on the old ones" (p. 331). The patterns previously described are merely completed behavior patterns of a new type. Something new comes into the picture (qualitative change) without abolishing the old.

"This new type of behavior patterns," wrote Piaget (1952), "characterize[s] systematic intelligence. Now it is the latter which, according to Claparède, is governed by awareness of relationships and no longer by empirical groping" (pp. 331–332). He pointed out further that authoritative writers with different points of view agree that "there exists an essential moment in the development of intelligence: the moment when the awareness of relationships is sufficiently advanced to permit a reasoned pre-vision, that is to say, an *invention* operated by simple mental combination" (p. 332). Unlike the previous stage in which the new means are discovered through groping (pulling the cushion toward one to obtain the object resting on it), new means now may be invented. The child foresees which acts will succeed and which will fail without empirically testing them. The mental process is one of deduction. The resulting procedure is "new" in the sense that "it results from an original *mental* combination and not from a combination of movements actually executed at each stage of the operation" (Piaget, 1952, p. 341).

Along with invention, rather one aspect of it, is representation. Sensorimotor groping gives way to the representation, ideationally, of the various possible acts and how they must be combined to achieve the desired end. "To invent is to combine mental, that is to say, representative, schemata and, in order to become mental, the sensorimotor schemata must be capable of intercombining in every way, that is to say, of being able to give rise to true inventions" (Piaget, 1952, p. 341).

Throughout this whole sequence of early epigenetic stages portrayed by Piaget, the factor of experience plays an extremely important role. Coping with the environment, that is, interaction between the individual and his environment (assimilation and accommodation), constitutes experience. "At every level, experience is necessary to the development of intelligence" (Piaget, 1952, p. 362).

Other Conceptions of Intelligence That Imply Qualitative Change

It is quite clear from the foregoing discussions that any statement on the nature of developmental change in intelligence must be formulated in view of what specifically is meant by the term intelligence. One widely accepted view of the development of behavior in general, at least in its early stages, is that it consists of the differentiation of specific functions and patterns out of mass, undifferentiated, uncoordinated activity. In the words of Jensen (1932), "stimulation of almost any group of receptors by almost any kind of stimulation will lead to a response in almost any part of the organism that is set to respond" (p. 474). As the baby develops, movements become specialized and integrated into patterns that result in the differentiation of specific functional patterns of behavior out of the generalized, undifferentiated activity. Garrett (1946) has advanced the hypothesis that the development of intelligence is likewise a process of differentiation.

For Garrett (1946), intelligence

> includes at least the abilities demanded in the solution of problems which require the comprehension and use of symbols. By symbols I mean words, numbers, diagrams, equations, formulas which represent ideas and relationships ranging from the fairly simple to the very complex. For simplicity we may call the ability to deal with such stimuli *symbol or abstract intelligence* (p. 372).

According to Garrett's hypothesis, the nature of developmental change in intelligence is as follows:

> Abstract or symbol intelligence changes in its organization as age increases, from a fairly unified and general ability to a loosely organized group of abilities or factors. If this hypothesis is true, the measurement of intelligence must perforce change in its methods and objectives with increase in age (Garrett, 1946, p. 373).

Holding strictly to Garrett's definition, intelligence does not exist in early infancy. It gradually emerges as the child begins to invest words and symbols with meaning—lets them represent ideas and relations And, of course, this is the reason, according to his view, why baby tests "show little relationship to language tests of school years and hence with symbol intelligence." The evidence cited by Garrett in support of his differentiation hypothesis thus applies only to school-age-levels when "symbol intelligence" is in evidence, and since intelligence in this sense is nonexistent during infancy, the theory has little direct relevance to the problem of infant mental development. However, Garrett suggests that just as differentiation and specialization of bodily movements take place during infancy, so "this sifting out process is repeated, apparently, in the differentiation of intellectual activities which we encounter later on during the school years" (Garrett, 1946, p. 376). Thus, a process of qualitative change in mental development is clearly implied in Garrett's hypothesis—"intelligence, as I have defined it, changes in its organization with increasing maturity" (Garrett, 1946, p. 373).

At this point, it is instructive to compare Garrett's differentiation hypothesis, insofar as it may apply to early mental development, with Piaget's theory. In Piaget's thinking, there is a process that might be called differentiation but, conceptually, is of a different sort. As we have already seen, for Piaget, intelligent behavior develops from, or is continuous with, the simple, native reflexes, such as the sequence of reflexes involved in sucking. From this point of view, it is not a matter of differentiation of specific patterns from generalized, mass action. There is no mass behavior out of which specialized patterns of behavior are differentiated. The process is rather the coordination of specific, ready-made, sensorimotor schemata (reflexes) that, in the beginning, because they are uncoordinated and disorganized, give the impression of generalized mass action. These ready-made schemata quickly begin to be exercised and coordinated to form motor habits through the invariant operations of accommodation and assimilation. The change process is more a matter of systematization than differentiation.

As has already been noted, Garrett saw the development of intelligence (the comprehension and use of symbols) as separate and apart from, and bearing no relation to the sensorimotor development of early infancy. For Piaget, the reflective intelligence of later ages emerges from and is developmentally continuous with the overt behavioral development beginning at birth.

Another currently common way of defining intelligence is to equate it with the cognitive processes, that is, perceiving, remembering, understanding. In certain respects, this conception of intelligence and its development is similar to that of Garrett. Again, if the term "intelligence" is confined to this meaning, there would be no intelligence in the very early weeks of infancy. As Ausubel (1958) pointed out, although the new baby is able to fixate a light patch and follow it with his eyes, and he can be conditioned to respond differentially to different sizes and shapes as well as to different verbal stimuli, there is no real evidence of genuine perception or memory or understanding of the events and situations represented by these stimuli. There is no clear awareness of the properties of external objects or situations. "Hence it is unwarranted to assume that we are dealing here with psychological processes qualitatively similar to perception and cognition in the older individual" (Ausubel, 1958, p. 544). In other words, these differential reactions to stimulation constitute psychological experience, but of a qualitatively different sort than cognition in which there is, of necessity, some degree of interpretation in terms of an existing ideational residue from experience. If the meaning of the word "intelligence" is limited to perception and the other cognitive processes, then the baby is not born with intelligence. He must acquire it gradually through psychological functioning of a simpler sort. The child gains intelligence only as he acquires the capacity to perceive—not just to react differentially to stimuli, but to know something of external reality as represented in his sensory experiences.

Such representational awareness of the properties of objects, situations, and relations implies symbolization. Hence, verbal symbols are regarded as of great importance. In support of this view, vocalizations have been found to be one of the most valid indicators of emerging intelligence (Catalano & McCarthy, 1954). Gesell (1940a) stressed the fact that consistent language acceleration is one of the most valid signs of superior intelligence in very young children. Illingworth (1960), in discussing the reasons for the view that infant tests have no predictive value, pointed out that most infant tests use purely sensorimotor items, rather than tests of vocalization, along with items designed to elicit such other signs of cognitive superiority as alertness, responsiveness, and interest in surroundings.

Intelligence, as defined in terms of the cognitive processes or cognitive capacity—since this has not yet emerged in the very young infant—obviously cannot be tested directly at that level. But perhaps through more careful study of the precognitive behavior of infants, some indicators of potentiality for cognitive development, such as alertness, responsiveness, or perhaps the frequency and volume of random vocalization, could be established.

Still another recently formulated view of the nature of infantile mentality and its development might be labeled "holistic" (Escalona, 1950). In contrast to the point of view described above, intelligence here is regarded as "a fluctuating function, a delicate interaction of many forces and structural conditions" (p. 117). In measurement, the objective is to assess psychological functioning as a whole rather than intellectual functioning in the narrower sense. Escalona described her "field-theoretical" point of view as follows:

> A behavior even is determined by the structural conditions prevailing within the organism and in the psychological environment on the one hand, and by forces existing within and without the organism *at this moment* in space and time on the other hand. In other words, the object of psychological inquiry (the test response) is not something located within the infant being tested, but a process of interaction between the infant organism and the immediate environment, i.e., the testing situation. In this theory the testing *situation* becomes the object of analysis quite as much as does the infant's behavior as such (p. 118).

Escalona believed that by basing her assessment upon such a comprehensive analysis of the total testing situation the predictive value of the assessment is enhanced. Subtle indicators of mental potentiality are presumably sensed and, thus, constitute, in part, the basis for the appraisal. This view also implies developmental continuity without qualitative invariance.

Escalona's point of view is significant in relation to the theory of the nature of developmental change in mentality discussed earlier in this report, and to the problem of the lack of predictability of infant tests, discussed later. Her view not only allows for qualitative change in mental development, but it also recognizes the importance of environmental variation in relation to the lack of "stability" in early test results.

Simon and Bass (1956) agreed with Escalona in their statement that a serious and very common error in the evaluation of infant mentality is to limit attention and consideration to the numerical values, such as the IQ, as a basis for evaluation. They also insist that the real usefulness of testing hinges upon trained clinicians judging the complete constellation of variables—both intra-organic and extra-organic—that influences intelligence.

Developmental Sequences and the Measurement Problem

Theories of mental development in which qualitative change has been postulated or implied, generally have not been concerned with the lack of correlation between test results in infancy and later school ages. This is particularly true of those conceptions of intelligence that limit the meaning of the term to the reflection of rational processes—the comprehension and use of symbols, cognitive functions, etc. In these instances, the sensorimotor abilities of the infant are regarded as of quite a different order than the intellectual abilities that emerge later.

In every conceptualization of qualitative change that we have reviewed, however, there is inherent in it the idea of a fixed sequence of "stages" or levels of functioning, each, in turn, evolving from or growing out of the previous one. Fundamental to Piaget's theory, for example, is the principle of epigenesis—a continuous sequence of "structures," each qualitatively unique in its organization but developed out of the earlier structure. Gesell's embryological view of behavior patterning stresses the concept of developmental continuity with qualitative change. Developmental sequences, wherever they are observed—whether in the formation of the bones of the hand, or the growth of mental functioning—are conceived in epigenetic terms. Hence, the fact of a difference in kind does not necessarily mean a lack of relation. Developmentally, each qualitatively different level of functioning is related to the one preceding it and the one following it. This being true, one would expect that valid measures of the various functional levels ("stages") would correlate statistically.

A number of possible explanations for the lack of correlations between infant and school-age tests were suggested above. However, under the assumption of qualitative developmental change, perhaps the most logical hypothesis is that since most of the available tests were not conceived or constructed in terms of observed, qualitatively different levels of functioning in a developmental sequence, they frequently missed the mark. Constructed as they were on the theory of a general intelligence factor that grows quantitatively, it would be surprising indeed if two tests at different age levels happened to coincide, in terms of content, with the two qualitatively different, but related, functional levels sufficiently closely to measure individual differences and reveal the actual relation that may exist between those levels.

SUMMARY: Our Present Theoretical Orientation

In this chapter we have been concerned with the various theoretical positions, historical and current, in relation to each of three different aspects of the problem of intelligence. These were, (1) the question of the determining factors of intelligence, (2) its nature and structure, and (3) the nature of mental-developmental change with time. Related to all of these aspects of the problem is the matter of definition. It is important to make clear in each case just what is meant by intelligence. The term is used with a variety of meanings, but in what are perhaps its three most common meanings it refers to (1) the genetically determined mental *potentiality,* (2) the *capacity* one possesses to acquire new and more adequate modes of behavior and new abilities to function at any particular time, and (3) one's present *ability* (or abilities) to function, to do, to perform at a particular time.

On the question of its determining factors, when intelligence is defined as inherent potentiality, it is, by definition, fixed by heredity. The genes determine the possibilities for development. They set the limits beyond which the development of functional capacity cannot go. But even when intelligence is defined as potentiality, its development, nevertheless, occurs always and at all levels through the interaction, or interchange, between organism and environment. Hence, an environment that is not optimum in terms of nutriments, stimulation, or other essentials, may not provide for optimum development. Actually, the full potentiality for the development of mentality at any age level is rarely reached.

When by intelligence is meant the capacity to acquire increased ability, or more adequate ways of functioning within the limits of inherent potentiality, then, obviously, it is not fixed. Intelligence in this sense, changes with age as the child develops. The rate and extent of such change, consequently, are not fixed or predetermined. The ceiling is fixed, but not the level of development below that ceiling.

When by intelligence is meant the ability to perform, its level at any point in time is not only limited by the capacity level so far achieved, but it is also determined, in part, by past environmental opportunity, occasion, or need to acquire that ability. It is always the ability level, of course, that is observed in a test of intelligence. Any appraisal of mental capacity, or potential, therefore, must be arrived at by inference on the basis of what the child was able (or willing) to do. This being true, it is possible that two children of the same chronological age, growing up, one in a stimulating urban home environment, the other in an extremely impoverished rural home, actually are equally endowed with intellectual potentiality. It would, however, probably be impossible to infer such equality on the basis of intelligence tests alone because the performances of the children on the test might differ widely as a result of environmental opportunity to learn to perform the required tasks.

Theories concerning the nature or structure of intelligence generally have reference to mental abilities that are conceived of as the constituents of intelligence. During the 35-year period when most of the currently used tests were developed, the concept of general intelligence, or general mental ability was prevalent. The newer concepts of primary mental abilities and multiple factors of intelligence have come to be dominant during recent years as a result of the development of more effective statistical techniques and electronic computing facilities.

Our present view is that the structure of intellect that is conceived of as a dynamic system of distinct but more or less interrelated abilities in the normal adult is complex indeed, particularly in view of the possible combinations of "operations," "content," and "products" (Guilford, 1959). But this structure requires time to develop through maturation and experience. The baby's functional repertory is limited to relatively simple operations applied largely, it would seem, to content it can sense (figural content). The baby is usually concerned with the exploration, manipulation, and movement of his own body and its parts. He is also sensitive to and reacts differentially to events and objects outside himself. He plays with his toes, rolls from side to side, reaches for and grasps objects. He turns his head in search of the source of sound. He visually explores a new environment. He differentiates between persons. But in this simple sensorimotor activity, mental (central) processes are also involved. He, presumably, has simple cognitive awareness of the situation. Some memory traces from past experiences must also play a role in determining his behavior. Thus, at this early age, a number of specific mental abilities, not just general ability, constitute the structure of mentality.

The quality of one's functioning at any age or stage of development obviously depends upon such specific mental-ability factors. One functions effectively in terms of the realities of a situation only to the extent to which his cognitive abilities make him aware of its various aspects and its complexities, and to the extent that his memory abilities permit him to profit from past experiences, and, also, to the extent that his abilities to "think" —to try out implicitly alternative modes of functioning—facilitate a wise choice of a course of action. In everyday living we see ourselves, or judge others, as bright, clever, intelligent, or dull, dumb, stupid—always in terms of the apparent adequacy, appropriateness, and effectiveness with which a particular life situation or problem is dealt. In the intelligence-test situation, the child is judged as bright, average, or retarded, with an assigned mental age or IQ, in terms of the adequacy with which he performs the tasks and solves the problems presented to him.

We prefer, therefore, to apply the term "intelligence," not to innate mental developmental potential, not to the growing capacity to acquire new and more effective modes of behavior within the limits of that potential, not to one's abilities to perform, but, rather, to the observed, measured, or evaluated *quality* of appropriateness, adequacy, and effectiveness of performance. This quality is, and must always be judged or assessed in terms of what the subject *does* or *can do*.

In devising performance items and constructing scales for appraising this attribute of children's functioning, however, care should be taken, insofar as possible, to include items that will require the child's exercise of all the various abilities that modern research has been able to identify as constituting the complex structure of intellect in children. Tests and scales that have been constructed on the theory of a single, general mental ability may fall far short of the mark.

The question of qualitative versus quantitative change in mental development also involves the problem of the nature (structure) of intelligence. Again, on the theory of a single general-ability factor, development would simply be an increase in amount. A child's intelligence would grow by simple accretion. All his new acquisitions—his increasing ability to solve problems, perform more difficult, abstract, and complex tasks—would be based upon, and come about by virtue of this growing, general-intelligence factor.

As we have seen, it is difficult to explain the lack of correlation between infant and preschool test scores, and scores obtained during later childhood, in terms of the concept of quantitative change. On the other hand, with the assumption of qualitative change, a feasible explanation is that mentality at different levels of development is different in its constituent qualities, as well as amount. Therefore, since the tests were designed on the theory of a constant general-intelligence factor rather than a developmental sequence of qualitatively different levels of functioning, they fail to register adequately the developmental change taking place. It would seem, as a result, that a promising approach to the construction of mental tests for early childhood might be along the lines established by the work of Piaget (1952) and with reference to the findings on structure of mentality as it changes with age (Guilford, 1959). It seems clear that qualitatively different levels of mental functioning occur in the course of development and each level, or stage, although it emerges from and is continuous with the preceding one, has its unique and characteristic structural features. A true developmental sequence of levels of mental functioning, based upon these unique and characteristic features, is needed as a basis for the construction of better infant and preschool-age mental-test scales. The final summation of the mental test would, from this point of view, express the levels of mental functioning for a broad band of abilities, each of which is possibly developing at a different rate depending upon its genetic potentiality and environmental stimulation. Thus, as a diagnostic tool it would be available for a differential analysis of the various aspects of the child's mental life.

4.2 Orientation

During the 1920s a Swiss psychologist named Jean Piaget began studying and testing the reasoning process in children. Among his subjects were his own children, whose development has become immortalized by way of anecdotal material found among Piaget's innumerable publications. From his observations and clinical study of children's cognitive interactions with their environment, Piaget has constructed an elaborate, descriptive developmental-stage theory that during the past decade has generated a massive amount of empirical research.

Piaget conceives of four successive stages or periods in the child's development. The first two years encompass the sensorimotor stage during which time the infant learns to coordinate sensory inputs (stimuli), develops the concept of object permanence, and achieves a gross level of intentional goal-directed activity. The preoperational period, which ranges in time from approximately two to seven years of age, constitutes the second stage of development. The child's reasoning during this rather extended period of transition to higher-level cognitive functioning is heavily dominated by his absolute perceptions of stimulus events. For example, a child may be confronted by two equal lumps of clay one of which is rolled into a sausage, the other into a pancake. The child may then think the pancake has more clay because it looks larger. Children's problem-solving behavior during the latter portion of this stage is said to be intuitive, that is, frequently a problem may be worked through successfully while the child is yet unable to clarify the conceptual strategies or principles he employed.

Between the seventh and eleventh years of age children's thinking becomes stabilized and operational, although it is still stimulus-bound. In a concrete fashion, operations involving such things as reversibility in thought, identity elements, associativity, serial ordering, and class inclusion are internalized. Following this stage of concrete operations, the child develops a facility for the hypothetico-deductive mode of thought. The form of an argument can be examined for logic apart from its content. Propositional thinking, causal thinking, and formal logic can now be applied to events apart from any immediate concrete referent. The transition from concrete to formal operations is said to occur between ages ten to twelve.

The original paper by Piaget reproduced here conveys some of his basic concepts relative to the development of thought. The paper itself is the text of a 1960 address delivered by Piaget to the New York Academy of Sciences' conference on the psychology of thinking. The references listed below will do much to clarify in more detail Piaget's views. It should also be noted that Piaget has studied moral development, which is seen to be intimately fused with cognitive functioning.

RECOMMENDED READING

Berlyne, D. E. "Recent developments in Piaget's work." *Brit. J. educ. Psychol.,* **27** (1957), 1–12.

"Contributions of Piaget to Developmental Psychology: A Symposium." *Merrill-Palmer Quart.,* **9** (1963), 243–285.

Flavell, John H. *The Developmental Psychology of Jean Piaget.* Princeton, N.J.: Van Nostrand, 1963.

Hunt, J. McV. *Intelligence and Experience.* New York: Ronald, 1961. (See chaps. 5, 6, and 7).

4.2 The Genetic Approach to the Psychology of Thought

Jean Piaget, UNIVERSITY OF GENEVA, SWITZERLAND

From a developmental point of view, the essential in the act of thinking is not contemplation—that is to say, that which the Greeks called "theorema" —but the action of the dynamics.

Taking into consideration all that is known, one can distinguish two principal aspects:

Reprinted from *Journal of Educational Psychology,* **52** (1961), no. 6, 275–281. By permission of the author and the American Psychological Association, Inc. Footnote to the original article omitted by the kind permission of the author and the American Psychological Association, Inc.

1. The formal viewpoint which deals with the configuration of the state of things to know—for instance, most perceptions, mental images, imageries.

2. The *dynamic* aspect, which deals with transformations—for instance, to disconnect a motor in order to understand its functioning, to disassociate and vary the components of a physical phenomenon, to understand its causalities, to isolate the elements of a geometrical figure in order to investigate its properties, etc.

The study of the development of thought shows that the dynamic aspect is at the same time more difficult to attain and more important, because only transformations make us understand the state of things. For instance: when a child of 4 to 6 years transfers a liquid from a large and low glass into a narrow and higher glass, he believes in general that the quantity of the liquid has increased, because he is limited to comparing the initial state (low level) to the final state (high level) without concerning himself with the transformation. Toward 7 or 8 years of age, on the other hand, a child discovers the preservation of the liquid, because he will think in terms of transformation. He will say that nothing has been taken away and nothing added, and, if the level of the liquid rises, this is due to a loss of width, etc.

The formal aspect of thought makes way, therefore, more and more in the course of the development to its dynamic aspect, until such time when only transformation gives an understanding of things. To think means, above all, to understand; and to understand means to arrive at the transformations, which furnish the reason for the state of things. All development of thought is resumed in the following manner: a construction of operations which stem from actions and a gradual subordination of formal aspects into dynamic aspects.

The operation, properly speaking, which constitutes the terminal point of this evolution is, therefore, to be conceived as an internalized action reversible (example: addition and subtraction, etc.) bound to other operations, which form with it a structured whole and which is characterized by well defined laws of totality (example: the groups, the lattice, etc.). Dynamic totalities are clearly different from the "gestalt" because those are characterized by their nonadditive composition, consequently irreversible.

So defined, the dynamics intervene in the construction of all thought processes; in the structure of forms and classifications, of relations and serialization of correspondences, of numbers, of space and time, of the causality, etc. One could think at first glance that space and geometry add to the formal aspect of thought. In this way one conceived of the geometric science in the past, considering it impure mathematics, but applicable to perception and intuition. Modern geometry, since *Le Programme d'Erlangen* by F. Klein, has tended, like all other precise disciplines, to subordinate the formal to the dynamic. The geometries are, indeed, understood today as relying all on groups of transformation, so that one can go from one to the other by characterizing one less general "subgroup" as part of a more inclusive group. Thus geometry too rests on a system of dynamics.

Any action of thought consists of combining thought operations and integrating the objects to be understood into systems of dynamic transformation. The psychological criteria of this is the appearance of the notion of conservation or "invariants of groups." Before speech, at the purely sensory-motor stage of a child from 0 to 18 months, it is possible to observe actions which show evidence of such tendencies. For instance: From 4–5 to 18 months, the baby constructs his first invariant, which is the schema of the permanent object (to recover an object which escaped from the field of perception). He succeeds in this by coordinating the positions and the displacements according to a structure, which can be compared to what the geometricians call "group displacements."

When, with the beginning of the symbolic function (language, symbolic play, imagerie, etc.), the representation through thought becomes possible, it is at first a question of reconstructing in thought what the action is already able to realize. The actions actually do not become transformed immediately into operations, and one has to wait until about 7 to 8 years for the child to reach a functioning level. During this preoperative period the child, therefore, only arrives at incomplete structures characterized by a lack in the notion of combinations and, consequently, by a lack of logic (in transitivity, etc.).

In the realm of causality one can especially observe these diverse forms of precausality, which we have previously described in detail. It is true that a certain number of authors—Anglo-Saxon above all—have severely criticized these conclusions, while others have recognized the same facts as we have (animism, etc.). Yet, in an important recent book (which will appear soon) two Canadian authors, M. Laurendeau and A. Pinard, have taken the whole problem up once again by means of thorough statistics. In the main points they have come to a remarkable verification of our views, explaining, moreover, the methodological reasons for the divergencies among the preceding authors.

At about 7 to 8 years the child arrives at his first complete dynamic structures (classes, relations, and numbers), which, however, still remain concrete—in other words, only at the time of a handling of objects (material manipulation or, when possible, directly imagined). It is not before the age of 11 to 12 years or more that operations can be applied to pure hypotheses. At this latter level, a logic of propositions helps complete the concrete structures. This enlarges the structures considerably until their disposition.

The fundamental genetic problem of the psychology of thought is hence to explain the formation of these dynamic structures.

Practically, one would have to rely on three principal factors in order to explain the facts of development: maturation, physical experience, and social interaction. But in this particular case none of these three suffice to furnish us with the desired explanations—not even the three together.

Maturation First of all, none of these dynamic structures are innate, but they form very gradually. (For example: The transitivity of equalities is acquired at approximately 6½ to 7 years, and the ability of linear measure comes about only at 9 years, as does the full understanding of weights, etc.) But progressive construction does not seem to depend on maturation, because the achievements hardly correspond to a particular age. Only the order of succession is constant. However, one witnesses innumerable accelerations or retardations for reasons of education (cultural) or acquired experience. Certainly one cannot deny the inevitable role which maturation plays, but it is determined above all by existing possibility (or limitation). They still remain to be actualized, which brings about other factors. In addition, in the domain of thought, the factors of innateness seem above all limitative. We do not have, for example, an intuition of space in the fourth dimension; nevertheless we can deduce it.

Physical experience Experiencing of objects plays, naturally, a very important role in the establishment of dynamic structures, because the operations originate from actions and the actions bear upon the object. This role manifests itself right from the beginning of sensory-motor explorations, preceding language, and it affirms itself continually in the course of manipulations and activities which are appropriate to the antecedent stages. Necessary as the role of experience may be, it does not sufficiently describe the construction of the dynamic structures—and this for the following three reasons.

First, there exist ideas which cannot possibly be derived from the child's experience—for instance, when one changes the shape of a small ball of clay. The child will declare, at 7 to 8 years, that the quantity of the matter is conserved. It does so before discovering the conservation of weight (9 to 10 years) and that of volume (10 to 11 years). What is the quantity of a matter independently of its weight and its volume? This is an abstract notion corresponding to the "substance" of the pre-Socratic physicists. This notion is neither possible to be perceived nor measurable. It is, therefore, the product of a dynamic deduction and not part of an experience. (The problem would not be solved either by presenting the quantity in the form of a bar of chocolate to be eaten.)

Secondly, the various investigations into the learning of logical structure, which we were able to make at our International Center of Genetic Epistemology, lead to a very unanimous result: One does not "learn" a logical structure as one learns to discover any physical law. For instance, it is easy to bring about the learning of the conservation of weight because of its physical character, but it is difficult to obtain the one of the transitivity of the relationship of the weight:

$$A = C \text{ if } A = B \text{ and } B = C$$

or the one of the relationship of inclusion, etc. The reason for this is that in order to arrive at the learning of a logical structure, one has to build on another more elementary logical (or prelogical) structure. And such structures consequently never stem from experience alone, but suppose always a coordinating activity of the subject.

Thirdly, there exist two types of experiences:

1. The physical experiences show the objects as they are, and the knowledge of them leads to the abstraction directly from the object (example: to discover that a more voluminous matter is more or less heavy than a less voluminous matter).

2. The logicomathematical experience supposes to interrelate by action individual facts into the world of objects, but this refers to the result of these actions rather than to the objects themselves. These interrelations are arrived at by process of abstractions from the actions and their coordinates. For instance, to discover that 10 stones in a line always add up to 10, whether they are counted from left to right or from right to left. Because then the order and the total sum have been presented. The new knowledge consists simply in the discovery that the action of adding a sum is independent of the action of putting them in order. Thus the logicomathematical experience does not stem from the same type of learning as that of the physical experience, but rather from an equilibration of the scheme of actions, as we will see.

Social interaction The educative and social transmission (linguistic, etc.) plays, naturally, an evident role in the formation of dynamic structures, but this factor does not suffice either to entirely explain its development, and this for two reasons:

First, a certain number of structures do not lend themselves to teaching and are prior to all teaching. One can cite, as an example, most concepts of conservation, of which, in general, the pedagogs agree that they are not problematic to the child.

The second, more fundamental reason is that in order to understand the adult and his language, the child needs means of assimilation which are formed through structures preliminary to the social transmission itself—for instance, an ancient experience has shown us that French-speaking children understand very early the expression *"quelques unes de mes fleurs"* [some of my flowers] in contrast to *"toutes mes fleurs"* [all my flowers], and this occurs when they have not yet constructed the relation of inclusion:

$$\text{Some A are part of all B; therefore } A < B$$

In conclusion, it is not exaggerated to maintain that the basic factors invoked before in order to explain mental development do not suffice to explain the formation of the dynamic structures. Though all three of them certainly play a necessary role, they do not constitute in themselves sufficient reason and one has to add to them a fourth factor, which we shall try to describe now.

This fourth factor seems to us to consist of a general progression of equilibration. This factor intervenes, as is to be expected, in the interaction of the preceding factors. Indeed, if the development depends, on one hand, on internal factors (maturation), and on the other hand on external factors (physical or social), it is self-evident that these internal and external factors equilibrate each other. The question is then to know if we are dealing here only with momentary compromises (unstable equilibrium) or if, on the contrary, this equilibrium becomes more and more stable. This shows that all exchange (mental as well as biological) between the organisms and the milieu (physical and social) as composed of two poles: (1) of the *assimilation* of the given external to the previous internal structures, and (2) of the *accommodation* of these structures to the given ones. The equilibrium between the assimilation and the accommodation is proportionately more stable than the assimilative structures which are better differentiated and coordinated.

It is this equilibrium between the assimilation and accommodation that seems to explain to us the functioning of the reversible operations. This occurs, for instance, in the realm of notions of conservation where the invariants of groups do not account for the maturation and the physical experience, nor for the sociolingual transmission. In fact, dynamic reversibility is a compensatory system of which the idea of conservation constitutes precisely the result. The equilibrium (between the assimilation and the accommodation) is to be defined as a compensation of exterior disturbances through activities of the subject orientated in the contrary direction of these disturbances. This leads us directly to the reversibility.

Notice that we do not conceive of the idea of equilibrium in the same manner as the "gestalt theory" does, which makes great use of this idea too, but in the sense of an automatical physical equilibrium. We believe, on the contrary, that the mental equilibrium and even the biological one presumes an activity of the subject, or of the organism. It consists in a sort of matching, orientated towards compensation—with even some overcompensation—resulting from strategies of precaution. One knows, for instance, that the homeostasis does not always lead to an exact balance. But it often leads to overcompensation, in response to exterior disturbances. Such is the case in nearly all occurrences except precisely in the case of occurrences of a superior order, which are the operations of reversible intelligence, the reversible logic of which is characterized by a complete and exact compensation (inverted operation).

The idea of equilibrium is so close to the one of reversibility that G.

Brunner, in a friendly criticism of one of our latest books appearing in the *British Journal of Psychology,* proposes to renounce the idea of equilibrium because the notion of the reversibility seems sufficient to him. We hesitate to accept this suggestion for the following three reasons:

First, reversibility is a logical idea, while the equilibrium is a causal idea which permits the explanation of reforms by means of a probabilistic schema. For instance, in order to explain the formation of the idea of conservation, one can distinguish a certain number of successive stages, of which each is characterized by the "strategy" of a progress of compensation. Now it is possible to show that the first of these strategies (only bearing upon one dimension, to the neglect of others) is the most probable at the point of departure, and further, that the second of these strategies (with the emphasis on a second dimension) *becomes* the most likely—as a function of the result of the first. And, finally, that the third of these strategies (oscillation between the observed modifications upon the different dimensions and the discovery of their solidarity) *becomes* the most likely in the functioning of the results of the preceding, etc. From such a point of view the process of equilibration is, therefore, characterized by a sequential control with increasing probabilities. It furnishes a beginning for causal explanations of the reversibility and does not duplicate the former idea.

Secondly, the tendency of equilibrium is much broader for the operation than the reversibility as such, which leads us to explain the reversibility through the equilibrium and not the reverse. In effect, it is at this level of the obvious regulations and sensory-motor feedbacks that the process of equilibration starts. This in its higher form becomes intelligence. Logical reversibility is therefore conceivable as an end result and not as a beginning and the entire reversibility follows the laws of a semireversibility of various levels.

Thirdly, the tendency to equilibrate does not only explain this final reversibility, but also certain new syntheses between originally distinct operations. One can cite in this regard an example of great importance: the serial of whole numbers. Russell and Whitehead have tried to explain the basic set of numbers through the idea of equivalent classes, without recourse to the serial order. This means that two classes are believed to be equivalent, if one can put their respective elements into a reciprocal arrangement. Only when this relationship relies on the quality of the objects (an A put into relation with an A, a B with a B, etc.) one does not get the quantity. If this relationship is made exclusive of the qualities (an Individual A or B put into relationship with an Individual B or A) then there exists only one way to distinguish the elements from each other. In order not to forget one, or not to count the same twice, one must deal with them in succession and introduce the serial factor as well as the structure of classes. We may then say, psychologically speaking, that the sequence of whole numbers is synthesis between two groupings qualitatively distinct, the fitting of the classes and serialization, and that this synthesis takes place as soon as one excludes the qualities of the elements in question. But how does this synthesis occur? Precisely by a gradual process of equilibration.

On the one hand the child who develops his ideas from numbers is in possession of structures enabling him to fit them into classes (classifications). But if he wants to be exclusive of qualities in order to answer to the question "how many," he becomes unable to distinguish the elements. The disequilibrium which appears, therefore, obliges the child to resort to the idea of order and take recourse to arranging these elements into a lineal row. On the other hand, if the child arranges the elements as 1, 1, 1, etc., how would he know, for instance, how to distinguish the second from the third? This new disequilibrium brings him back to the idea of classification: The "second" is the element which has but one predecessor, and the "third" is one that has two of them. In short, every new problem provokes a disequilibrium (recognizable through types of dominant errors) the solution of which consists in a re-equilibration, which brings about a new original synthesis of two systems, up to the point of independence.

During the discussion of my theories, Brunner has said that I have called disequilibrium what others describe as motivation. This is perfectly true, but the advantage of this language is to clarify that a cognitive or dynamic structure is never independent of motivational factors. The motivation in return is always solidary to structural (therefore cognitive) determined level. The language of the equilibrium presents that activity, that permits us to reunite into one and the same totality those two aspects of behavior which always have a functional solidarity because there exists no structure (cognition) without an energizer (motivation) and vice versa.

4.3 *Orientation*

Harris (1956) has observed that the concept of development when applied to the study of human behavior carries with it two potential limitations. The first springs from the notion that concepts usually depend upon instruments. In other words, the meaning we attach to a phenomenon depends upon the methods of measuring that phenomenon. The less sophisticated or precise the measurement device, the more likely are we to develop concepts that are gross and ill defined; there may be attributes essential to a concept that are not being measured by an instrument that purports to do so. A second related problem is that observations and information may be limited by the concepts around which we choose to develop our theoretical formulations. Both limitations are apparent in the measurement and theories of intelligence. Our understanding of intelligence and its development is contingent upon the methods utilized to measure "intelligent behavior." Further, by looking only for phenomena being measured by conventional instruments a more complete understanding of intelligence may be prevented.

The above theme is well articulated by Irving Sigel who argues that conventional intelligence tests do not provide enough relevant information about the nature of intellectual processes, particularly the process by which an individual arrives at the answer to an intellectual problem. Sigel illustrates how value judgments made by psychologists may contaminate psychological measurements. He also introduces the concept *cognitive style* as useful in understanding how individuals perceive, encode, and decode symbolic material. (Cognitive style has become a popular research variable in recent years.) Individual differences in modes of perceptual organization and conceptual categorization of the external environment are relevant to the study of creativity, which will be reviewed later in this chapter.

Finally, unlike many critics of current measurement practices, Sigel provides several realistic and constructive recommendations for increasing our understanding of the various individual differences in intellectual processes.

RECOMMENDED READING

Harris, D. B. The concept of development. In *Research Readings in Child Psychology,* D. S. Palermo, and L. P. Lipsitt (Eds.) New York: Holt, Rinehart and Winston, 1963.

Witkin, H. A. Origins of cognitive style. In *Cognition: Theory, Research, Promise,* C. Scheerer (Ed.) New York: Harper and Row, 1962, 172–205.

Wohlwill, J. F. "Developmental studies of perception." *Psychol. Bull.,* **57** (1960), 249–288.

Wright, J. C., and J. Kagan. "Basic cognitive processes in children." *Monogr. Soc. Res. child Develpm.,* **28** (1963), ser. no. 86.

4.3 How Intelligence Tests Limit Understanding of Intelligence

Irving E. Sigel, THE MERRILL-PALMER INSTITUTE

The purposes of this paper are (1) to demonstrate how past and present use of intelligence tests continues to restrict our understanding of intellectual function, and (2) to propose alternatives to the current practice of test analyses. Raising these issues is not to deny the usefulness of intelligence tests—they do provide good bases of predicting academic and vocational success. The contention in this paper is that we are not taking advantage of all the information obtained on an intelligence test.

Intelligence tests usually provide a single summative score, expressed in the form of an IQ, MA, or equivalent. The total score represents the number of correct responses to a set of items of varied content. A unidimensional index is therefore implied in the single score. In reality, intelligence tests are multi-dimensional, not unidimensional, because the items represent a variety of areas of knowledge. The Stanford-Binet is a good illustration of the type of heterogeneous scale yielding a single index.

Test constructors, who are aware of the limitations of single score IQ, attempt to solve the problem by providing subtests, each of which is intended to test particular aspects of intellectual ability. A score is obtained for each subtest. Comparisons of subtest scores enable the examiner to study intra-individual variability of performance. In this way, a more detailed and more sensitive assessment of intellectual ability is possible. An example of this type of test is the Wechsler Intelligence Scale for Children (WISC).

Mindful of these characteristics, let us now turn to a discussion of test limitations. A test response indicates "what" the subject can do, but provides no understanding of "how." To assess these underlying processes, it is necessary to make inferences from the subject's responses. A correct answer to an analogies item, for example, may be a function of particular learning, perceptual discrimination, syllogistic reasoning, or any combination of these. There is no way to judge, from the response itself, which of these processes was operating at the time the response was made.

Not only do we have to infer the underlying process, but also the respondent's repertoire of responses. Only one response is usually required and acceptable. Alternative responses other than those indicated by test

---

Reprinted from *Merrill-Palmer Quarterly of Behavior and Development,* 9 (1963), 39–56. By permission of the author and The Merrill-Palmer Institute of Human Development and Family Life.

manuals are not acceptable. The test constructor decides what is the best answer to items he selects as relevant. The psychometric procedures in test making are too well known to need discussion here. What is not sufficiently taken into account is that, for a number of items, alternative responses—although correct at times—are not considered "correct" or "good" or given equal credit, because of cultural conventions.

The most clear-cut illustrations can be found in verbal tests of analogies. For example, in the WISC similarities item, "How are a scissors and a copper pan alike?" the answer, "They are both household utensils," is given a score of one; the answer, "Both are metal," is given two credits. Both responses are class concepts. Yet, from Wechsler's framework, preference is given to a particular system. How does one decide which system is preferable?

The WISC is not the only test which can be looked at in this way. For example, Guilford (1959) employed some items to assess abilities to know classes of units. He asks the respondent to "pick one that does not belong" from the following: clam, tree, oven, and rose. Although Guilford does not provide the answer, perhaps assuming the item is simple enough for the psychologists reading the article, the correct answer probably is *oven*. The remaining three items—clam, tree, and rose—belong to a class of living things, but the same items could also be classified on the basis of function—clam, tree, and oven are related to the preparation of food, thus *rose* does not belong; and on the basis of location,—the *clam* may be picked as not belonging, because it lives in water and the other things belong on land. These would probably be wrong answers.

According to Guilford, Wechsler, and other test constructors, classes as units apparently must be organized on the basis of the common hierarchical logical taxonomy. It is a system by which particular characteristics are selected as the basis for a more extensive classification. The characteristics selected or "abstracted" are those "features which enable us to view that thing as an instance or example of indefinitely repeatable patterns or types of situations" (Cohen and Nagel, 1934, p. 371). The features are selected from among an almost infinite variety of properties. Thus, any attribution of similarity between two items (e.g. horse and cow, because they are animals) does not mean that because a horse is an animal it may not be something else. A particular type of class designation has been identified and valued as correct. Respondents deviating from this conception are "wrong" or "inferior." The conventional class logic is the preferred response.

A word here about "not sharing the conventional class system." The kinds of responses used as illustrations are not bizarre, but bear the reality of consensually agreed attributes of items. Respondents may not share conventional class systems because of different kinds of social and cultural experiences. But non-conventional responses may also reflect the *originality and the novel outlook of respondents.* Aware, as we are, of the obvious cultural and social differences, we still need to be more attentive to differerences which emanate from creative thought. Our tests penalize all deviations, regardless of source.

One can disagree with the above contention, because of the assumption that one of the indices of intelligence is the ability to see things as organized in conventional classes of units. If one agrees with this point of view, then intelligence becomes, in part, synonymous with "conformity" in thinking or reasoning.

If this is true, then we are, in effect, saying that a characteristic of intelligence, as measured, is the ability to organize and to classify materials in a conventional way. Is such a notion really part of our conception of intelligence? If it is, should we not make this criterion articulate? . . .

The exhortation to take into account nonintellective factors points directly at personality-type variables. Thus, intelligence test items are used as "projective" tests. To be sure, there is some value in such consideration. On the other hand, we must be ever mindful that such a mode of analysis overlooks "cognitive process" variables which are of equal significance in understanding *how* an individual arrives at an answer. Such concepts as "cognitive style," for example, provide analytic models by which responses can be assessed. Other kinds of cognitive categories can be found in the literature on thinking, problem solving, and reasoning. The plea here is for an evaluation of conceptual-analytic models which will provide standardized scoring systems, taking into account cognitive variables.

A demonstration of how intelligence tests can be used to enlarge our view of intelligence involves discussion of three problems: (1) the relationship of cognitive style variables to performance on intelligence tests, (2) a model for qualitative analysis of verbal content, and (3) what can be learned from analysis of errors on IQ tests.

First, let us turn to a discussion of cognitive style. "Style" is used as an umbrella term, under which is subsumed a variety of cognitive behaviors. It refers to "modes" an individual employs in perceiving, organizing, and labelling various dimensions of the environment.

Operationally, cognitive styles are apparent in everyday life. From a wide array of stimuli, an individual is provided with many alternatives from which to select a basis of organization and labelling. It is assumed that the characteristic selected—especially when little or no coercion is present—emanates from an acquired predisposition to be attentive to that particular type of cue. If given a number of glass tumblers, for example, some individuals will select color, size, quality, or function of the object materials as the most relevant cue by which to organize and subsequently label the stimuli. Since all cues are equally visible and, to a comparable sample of individuals, equally known, we need to explain the fact that different cues are selected and responded to as organizational bases.

Language provides the individual with a set of labels which refer to various aspects of the environment. These labels may refer to parts or to wholes, to attributes, or to the total. The acquisition of the labels is a function of the individual's socio-cultural experiences. The labels acquired enable him to identify and communicate about his environment.

Language, then, is a manifestation of cognitive style. The underlying reasoning is as follows: As an environmental complex, the world of the child or of the adult can be denoted in various terms (i.e., a glass is a drinking object, a cylindrical object, a three-dimensional round object, a useful object, something you use for drinking). Each of these descriptions or identifiers of the object "drinking glass" is accurate but only represents in language some of the attributes of the object under consideration. Many of these kinds of statements about a glass are known to most literate, verbal people. Chances are that if we reversed the procedure, gave a number of these descriptive statements about a glass to different people, and asked them to select the appropriate class term from a list of words among which was the word "glass," the agreement would be very high. In other words, the fact that individuals know a variety of ways of describing an item, does not necessarily enable prediction of how individuals will organize a set of items.

Previous research has demonstrated that individual differences in labelling behavior do exist (Kagan, Moss, and Sigel, 1962). Children and adults, when faced with sorting and, consequently, labelling figures depicting humans and objects, employ labels which can be classified as descriptive, relational-contextual and categorical-inferential labels (Sigel, 1961).

Descriptive This category includes labels which denote similarity based on manifest objective physical attributes. Subclasses have been identified as, (1) *descriptive part-whole,* labels denoting observable parts of the stimuli; for example, organizing a group of human figures as being similar because "they are all wearing hats" or because "they all have their right arm raised," and (2) *descriptive-global,* labels tending toward denoting the total manifest attributes of the stimuli; for example, identifying a group of uniformed figures as "they are all soldiers" or a group of male figures dressed in identifiable male clothing because "they are men."

Relational-contextual This category includes labels denoting functional or thematic interdependence between two or more elements in an array. The interdependence is particular to that situation and not generalizable beyond the immediate. The meaning of each item in the grouping is defined in terms of its relation to other items in the grouping; for example, from an array of pictures, a horse and a stagecoach are selected because "a horse is used to pull a stagecoach," or, on a thematic basis a man with a cane who is wearing dark glasses and a young boy are selected because "the boy is helping the blind man to cross the street."

Categorical-inferential These labels refer to inferred characteristics of the stimuli and each item in a grouping is representative of the total class or category label. Some subclasses of categorical-inferential are, (1) *functional,* where objects are grouped together on the basis of inferred use, (e.g., referring to a group of tools as "these are things to build with"), (2) *class-naming,* where a taxonomic class label is used (e.g., animals, tools, human beings), and (3) *attribute selection,* where only one particular attribute is inferred (e.g., "they are angry," or "they run by motors").

These styles of categorization are operating for the respondent whenever he is faced with the task of organization of items on the basis of similarity or belongingness. The assumption is that individuals have preferences for particular modes of categorization and these characteristic modes have stylistic properties. The tendency will be to classify on the basis of preferred modes whenever the stimuli allow such behavior to manifest itself.

In this framework, let us look at Wechsler's item, "How are a cat and mouse alike?" Since the task requires a perception of similarity, an individual inclined toward a descriptive part-whole approach may say, "They are alike because both have tails." A categorical-inferential response would be, "Both are animals." Note that these two kinds of responses are both correct, even by Wechsler standards. The descriptive part-whole response is, however, valued lower—it gets one point, while the latter response receives two.

On many tests, the scoring of vocabulary items reflects similar problems. The Stanford-Binet test is an excellent illustration. It does *not* take into account the significance of various types of responses (Terman and Merrill, 1960). Only plus and minus scores are given, thus no credit is given for level of response, or for various types of answers. With the word "scorch," for example, credit is given for using a synonym, such as "singe," or an illustration, to "burn your clothes with an iron." It is apparent that these are qualitatively different, but are treated equally. Here again is a type of test in which no system is provided to examine, in an orderly fashion, the quality of the response.

The lack of precise and systematic scoring methods which take advantage of the multiple contributions of a response is but one way in which current use of psychometric tests restrict our view of intelligence. Another restriction lies in the fact that the tests do not provide for adequate assessment of an individual's repertoire of responses. A single response is all that is required. The first response in a vocabulary or a similarities type item may reflect the preferred mode at which an individual responds, but does not tell the level at which he *can* respond. Thus, when an individual says that a cat and mouse are alike because "they have tails," he may be functioning at a level he finds "preferable." This does not mean, however, that he is *unable* to provide a more "abstract" answer if required to do so. There is no provision for such an opportunity.

To this point, we have discussed how the current use of intelligence tests does limit our understanding of the nature of intellectual functioning because of the ways we test and handle test responses. Still before us is one question of whether it would be any better if we did provide for alternative responses, alternative scoring, or analytic procedures. What evidence is there to support the invocation of the concept of style as a significant variable? To this end, we shall discuss some current research.

Scott (1962) assessed the significance of styles of categorization as a predictor of acquisition of science concepts. He found that—for eleven-year-old boys and girls—the better the performance in a task to measure science concept achievement, the greater the use of categorical-inferential responses in sorting tasks. No significant correlation was found between the IQ test and the use of categorical-inferential labels, or between the IQ test and the science achievement test. In other words, the use of categorical-inferential labels on a sorting task was a better predictor of success in the science test than the IQ measure.[1]

Styles of categorization may be an important intellectual dimension to determine how intelligence operates. An individual's "style" dictates the cues he will use, but not necessarily determines the level on which he performs. The style of categorization sets the direction but not the level on which an individual's intelligence might function.

To illustrate further relationships between cognitive style and intelligence, let us turn to a current investigation of the age changes of styles of categorization among "high," "medium," and "low" text-anxious second and third grade boys and girls (Sigel, 1961). The aims of the study are to determine the relationship between styles of categorization and content to be categorized, as well as the relationship between styles of categorization and IQ, age, and test-anxiety level.

Styles of categorization were assessed by using three sorting tasks: (1) arrays of human figures all familiar to the child, (e.g., fireman, woman, boy), (2) object-animal figures, (e.g., items representing vehicles, animals, food), and (3) geometric forms varying in size and color, (e.g., circles, triangles, squares).

To illustrate, we analyzed the relationship between styles of categorization and performance on the Lorge-Thorndike Primary Form. The Lorge-Thorndike is a three-part, non-verbal intelligence test. We used two of the three parts. The subtests employed for the analysis were as follows: (1) a task requiring the child to identify one item out of four that does not belong, and (2) a task requiring the child to find those items, among four, that go together.

[1] The IQ measure used was the Southend Test of Intelligence, London, England. George Harrup, publisher, 1953.

Because the child is required to discriminate in both tasks, and determine either an irrelevant item or find similar items, he thus has a requirement similar to that in the IQ test. Consequently, we assume that styles of categorization should be related to his performance on the Lorge-Thorndike.

For the high-anxious third grade boys and girls, the use of class-naming labels—a type of categorical-inferential categorization—was related significantly with the total IQ score. For these same children, the more select descriptive-global responses made, the less "able" they were in selecting the item that did not belong in a series of items. Thus, those children who organize material on the basis of global manifest characteristics made errors on tasks requiring perception of structural similarities. In other words, their performance on this test is related to the styles of categorization employed by these children. The success with which children perform on IQ tests is, to some measure, predictable from their styles of categorization. These findings, thus far limited to high test-anxious children, tend to support our contention that performance on an intelligence test measure *is* influenced by a style of categorization.

Another finding relevant to intelligence test performance is that a positive relationship exists between the frequency of use of descriptive part-whole responses and cautiousness. There is some indication that such a preference for categorization tends to call forth a reflective careful approach in making judgments. In fact, Kagan (1962) concludes that reflectiveness is associated with a preference for a descriptive part-whole approach. The concept of reflectiveness or cautiousness as used here can be considered a cognitive set, or approach, and certainly would be manifest in test performance.

How extensive the role of styles of categorization is for all the classes of items employed in intelligence tests is an open question. What can be said at this point is that there is enough evidence from a deductive-analytic basis, as well as an empirical one, to suggest that IQ test scores are influenced by the style of categorization of the individual. The larger task is to determine, with greater specificity, the degree to which such relationships exist, and whether particular styles facilitate or inhibit intellective responses.

Taking this position calls for new ways of scoring our tests, as well as new ways of constructing them. Tests can no longer be scored by the test constructor's convention, nor should there be provision for only one type of response. We shall need to re-examine our testing materials, especially the selection and scoring of items, if we are to assess the relevance of the arguments proposed here.

Styles of categorization provide but *one* approach to the study of IQ responses. Other models for qualitative analysis could be devised. An illustration of this is a study reported by Feifel and Lorge (1950), in which they examined Stanford-Binet vocabulary records to ascertain qualitative changes with age in concept formation. As we shall see, the results of this study show quite dramatically what can be gained from additional scoring systems.

Feifel and Lorge were interested in the successive stages of concept formation, and development of thinking. They studied verbatim reports of nine hundred school children, boys and girls, ranging in age from six to 14. The categories employed were a synonym category, illustration and inferior explanation, and an error category. Their results (1950) were as follows:

> Younger children significantly more often employed use and the description category and illustration demonstration, inferior explanation, and repetition of response; whereas older children significantly used synonyms and explanation type responses (p. 2).

The Feifel and Lorge study provides one kind of framework for setting expectations regarding the age changes in thought. Within this framework, norms can be created which would indicate the child's level of conceptual thought, not possible even from the 1960 revision of the Stanford-Binet. In this way, two types of information can be obtained, how the child thinks and what he knows.

What is of considerable interest, is that current revisions of the Stanford-Binet do not take advantage of what the test really has to offer in the way of understanding intellectual functioning. It certainly would have been a considerable step forward if the test constructors had made substantive improvements incorporating some of the find studies done with this test. In the long run, we would have had better indices of intellectual performance.

One last point on cognitive styles, although tangential, is of cardinal importance. In all our work on styles, a most consistent finding was the phenomena of "sex differences." Not only do boys and girls differ in their styles of categorization, but more important is that the psychological role played by particular styles differs for boys and girls. Personality correlates of styles of categorization differ for the sexes. We find, for example, that the descriptive part-whole approach relates positively with cautiousness for boys, but negatively for girls. The sex difference seems to be basic. Yet, in our intelligence test scores, we do not have separate norms for boys and girls. If we extrapolate from the research on style of categorization, it is reasonable to suppose that sex differences should show up in a host of intellectual operations.

Two kinds of evidence have now been presented to support the contention that intelligence tests, as now viewed, are restrictive. The suggestion has been made persistently that additional scoring systems are necessary in order to extract the meat from the responses, rather than our current approach which is so parsimonious that we lose perhaps more than we gain.

Another area to examine is how the analysis of errors on IQ tests can provide us with useful information. This argument derives from disagreement with the focus on "correct" responses. The assumption is that errors are not random or accidental. They are manifestations of a quality of intellective operations, comparable to the correct response. This is especially the case in those tests where choices are provided, each of which is purposeful, and taps some kind of function.

Errors have been analyzed unsystematically, by clinically oriented examiners, to arrive at a more comprehensive understanding of the particular case. For example, reference is frequently made in reports dealing with the quality of the responses, about the degree to which responses are within the realm of the expected or not. Clinical psychologists, influenced by the Rapaport approach, have been examining Wechsler-Bellevue items from a projective point of view. Thus, errors in the picture arrangement, for example, have been analyzed in personality terms, presumably reflecting intra- or inter-personal conflict.

Such analyses are subject to considerable error because they are not based on a systematic analysis using standardized schema within a comparable conceptual framework. It seems that this is a necessary condition to allow for the exploitation of data in a way that would provide wide comparability. The tragedy is that much data are being overlooked which, if properly used, would add to our knowledge of intellectual functioning.

If the assumption is correct that errors are determined by particular cognitive operations, a systematic analysis of errors should reveal facets of intellectual operations not revealed in the total score of the test. A test which provides such an opportunity is the Raven Progressive Matrices (PM), (Raven, 1938), a non-verbal perceptual-type test made up of a number of designs or matrices, each of which has a piece missing. The respondent examines the matrix and, from a number of choices at the bottom of the page, selects the appropriate one to complete the pattern.

The PM, according to Raven, is a test of "innate educative" ability. It is a test which is supposed to assess the individual's capacity to form comparisons, reason by analogy, and develop logical methods of thinking, regardless of previously acquired information.

If the Raven PM is supposed to measure the intellectual qualities described, then the kinds of errors made should reveal the limitations of the respondents. Further, since the respondents are required to make choices, the kinds of choices made should reveal the quality of intellectual performance. Thus, if variety exists in the choices allowed, only through analysis of all types of choices made can one discover the unique patterns of functioning. If one answers all items correctly, we learn something different about him.

Raven was apparently interested in error analysis; he provides a set of categories in his test manual by which errors can be analyzed (Raven, 1956). No one has systematically done this with large populations of "normal" individuals. Using Raven's system, we analyzed 1,000 records of boys and girls ranging in age from nine to 18. In another study, we compared types of errors of seven-, nine-, and 11-year-old boys to study the positional responses as a source of error.

Each of the sets in the PM is defined as assessing a distinctive process. Set A is described by Raven (1956) as a "simple continuous pattern—completion involving perception of difference, similarity and identity of pattern only" (p. 30). Each choice item reflects some aspect of these factors. The choices as described by Raven (1956, p. 30) are:

Choice 1 The figure is wrongly oriented and is incomplete as far as it goes. This is classified as incomplete correlate.

Choice 2 This figure has similar properties to Choice 1 except that the part corresponding to the correct piece is horizontal.

Choice 3 The figure shown is irrelevant and is classified as a different response.

Choice 4 This figure is contaminated by irrelevancies or distortions and is classified as *inadequate individuation.*

Choice 5 This choice is an instance of *incomplete correlate,* (i.e., figure wrongly oriented).

Choice 6 This is the correct choice and completes the matrix.

With these categories in mind, examination of errors, item by item, should provide us with the specificity of the child's functioning not obtained when just tallying the number of correct responses and referring only to the percentile score. Since it is the rare child who is able to do all the problems correctly, examination of the *kind* of error should provide valuable diagnostic data. In this presentation, we shall focus on some error analyses in order to point up what additional information can be gleaned from such an approach.

To illustrate, look at the responses made to PM Item A-7 (Figure 1). In our analysis, comparisons between boys and girls, as well as two age groups, will be presented to demonstrate the significance of sex as well as age differences.

Table 1 provides the percentage of choices made by nine- and ten-year-old boys and girls. Boys and girls within and between age groups do not differ significantly in the percentage of correct choice. The differences appear in the kinds of errors made. Nine-year-old boys and girls, in erring, selected Choice 4 with greatest frequency. Boys, however, make this error considerably less than the girls.

Girls, in other words, make more of their errors because of difficulty in perceptual discrimination. This finding suggests that more girls at this age are global in their approach than the boys.

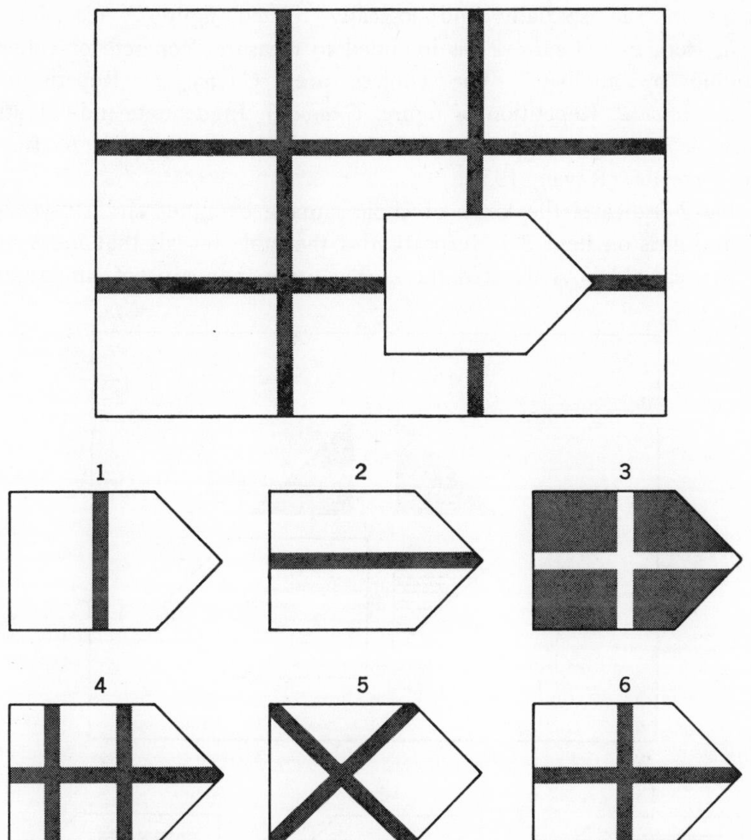

FIGURE 1. Item A-7. (From Raven, J. C. *Progressive Matrices.* London: H. K. Lewis & Co., Ltd.; by permission.)

TABLE 1. PERCENTAGE OF CHOICES MADE BY TWO AGE GROUPS OF BOYS AND GIRLS ON PM ITEM A-7

Choice	Girls 9 yr (N = 42)	Boys 9 yr (N = 34)	Girls 10 yr (N = 53)	Boys 10 yr (N = 49)
1	0	0	3.7	2.4
2	4.8	8.9	1.9	6.1
3	4.8	2.9	3.7	2.0
4	21.4	11.8	20.7	10.2
5	0	0	0	0
6	69.0	76.4	69.8	79.3

Before discussion of the implications of these findings, let us examine one more PM item (Raven, 1956) calling for different intellectual abilities, one from Set B. Set B is presumed to measure "apprehension of analogous changes in [a] spatially and logically related figure." According to Raven, Item B-7 (Figure 2) is intended to measure "concrete or coherent reasoning by analogy." The choices are: *Choice 1.* Repetition of figure. *Choice 2.* Repetition of figure. *Choice 3.* Inadequate individuation. *Choice 4.* Incomplete correlate. *Choice 5.* Is correct. *Choice 6.* Incomplete correlate (Raven, 1956).

Table 2 indicates the kinds of choices made by nine- and ten-year-old boys and girls on item B-7. Inspection of the table reveals that more nine- and ten-year-old boys selected the correct item than girls of similar ages.

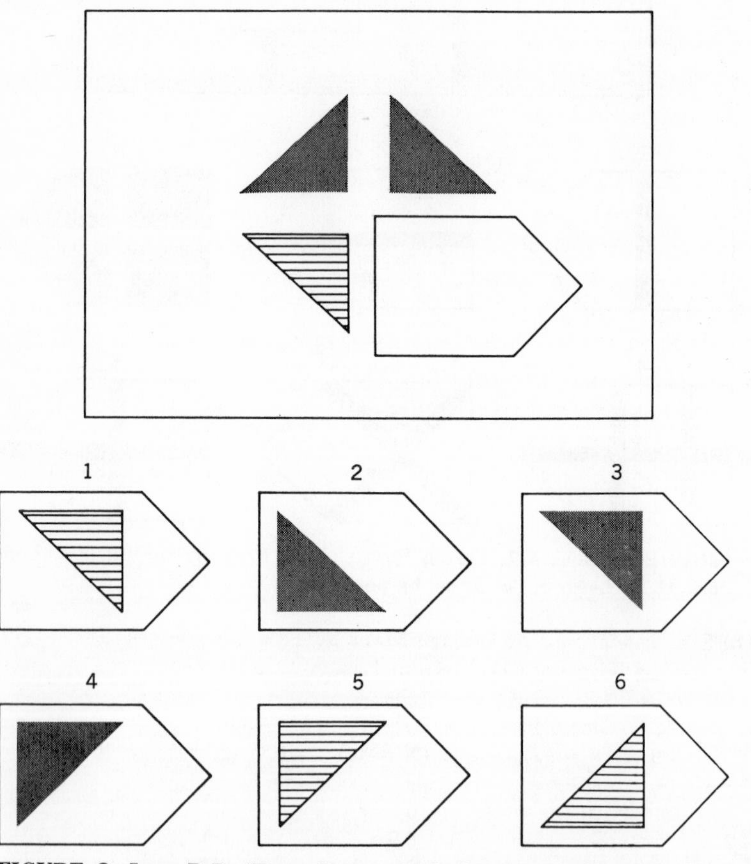

FIGURE 2. Item B-7. (From Raven, J. C. *Progressive Matrices.* London: H. K. Lewis & Co.; by permission.)

When we examine the kinds of errors nine-year-old children make, we find that girls more frequently select Choice 1, a repetition of the figure. The boys select Choice 2, which is also classified by Raven as a repetition of the figure. It is interesting that boys and girls make the same type of error but select a different figure. The difference may be because the girls,

TABLE 2. PERCENTAGE OF CHOICES MADE BY TWO AGE GROUPS OF BOYS AND GIRLS ON PM ITEM B-7

Choice	Girls 9 yr (N = 42)	Boys 9 yr (N = 34)	Girls 10 yr (N = 53)	Boys 10 yr (N = 49)
1	28.6	14.7	26.4	22.5
2	7.1	17.6	16.9	18.4
3	4.8	2.9	0	4.1
4	7.1	0	0	2.0
5	38.1	50.1	47.3	63.3
6	14.3	14.7	9.4	16.3

in reading the pattern from left to right, perseverate and select Choice 1. Boys may perseverate vertically and select Choice 2. If we combine Choices 1 and 2, since both are errors of "repetition of the figure," we find that this type of error is comparable for the nine-year-olds (35.7 per cent of the girls and 35.3 per cent for the boys). At age ten, more children get the correct item, but when errors are made, repetition of figures choices are again the most frequent (43.3 per cent and 40.9 per cent respectively for girls and boys, when Choices 1 and 2 are combined). Other changes occur, somewhat more pronounced for girls in this case. There is a drop in errors of the inadequate individuation kind. The implications of this datum in relation to the discussion of item A-7 need further consideration. We can conclude, however, that for children erring, the perseverative choice increases a year later. It suggests that this factor may be an important symptom of why the children make errors. This occurs in spite of the increases in the number of children making correct responses.

The detailed presentation of item analyses from the PM are illustrative of the kind of information to be gained from examination of errors. For Item A-7, we found that girls tended to have difficulty in perceptual discrimination, while for Item B-7 boys and girls tended to make perseverative errors. In both instances, the trends are similar at age nine and ten for each sex group. Although the age and sex differences as reported here are not statistically significant, they seem to be of sufficient magnitude to warrant further study. Real age and sex differences might be sharpened by conducting experimental studies in which the variables discussed are controlled with a precision not attainable in a test constructed for other purposes.

This kind of information would not be available were we to limit our analysis to the correct response only. Using this procedure for groups or for individuals provides us with information on *how* children are responding to an item. Thus, we may discover the degree to which the child is functioning maturely or not. For example, examination of items like B-7 enables us to assess the degree to which groups or individuals perseverate. Perseveration may be a function of emotional factors, (e.g., anxiety). It could also be interpreted from a cognitive frame of reference. Specifically, from the latter viewpoint, perseveration is an inability to shift one's own framework, and reflects difficulty in judging each choice as a separate. The error is a manifestation of the child's stimulus-boundness and his difficulty in reorienting himself. Of course, the test does not and cannot provide antecedent explanations of these performances. However, the test can and does provide a more comprehensive picture of how children function intellectually in the here and now.

It might be argued that the total score would indicate the degree to which the child is functioning "maturely" or not. Inspection of our data reveals that although children may be consistent within themselves in the errors they make, there seems to be no relationship between type of error and total score. For example, children who err on B-7 by using a perseverative choice (generally considered a less mature response) range from very high to very low total scores on Set B.

In the second study with the PM, the role of position and perseveration of items was studied as a factor in errors. Records of three groups of boys, ages seven, nine, and 11, were examined. The matrix was divided into proximal and distal sections. The proximal field included designs items surrounding the missing piece. The distal field included designs on the periphery. Among the choices are items identical to those in the proximal and distal fields. Figure 3 illustrates the division of the matrix.

The younger children, being more stimulus bound and more perseverative, would be expected, in erring, to select items identical with the matrix items in the proximal field; the older children, to select items identical with the matrix items in the distal field. It was found that significantly more seven-year-olds selected, when erring, the proximal item. The nine-year-olds split about evenly between the proximal and distal choices, and the eleven-year-olds showed a significantly greater selection of the distal choices. We can conclude that errors of younger children are a function of the "principle of proximity," in effect substantiating our predictions.

Not only did the younger children select the items in the proximal field, but, in doing so, tended to select the one identical to the item preceding the missing one. Whether or not the potency of a tendency to perseverate accounts for the high incidence of proximal choices is a question. There are indications that when an identical choice is occasionally available distally, a distal choice is made by seven-year-olds. There are not sufficient items in the test to determine whether identity leads to proximal choices or proximal choices occur because of identity.

In any event, the responses made are functions of more than the child's knowledge. If, as Piaget holds (Inhelder and Piaget, 1958), children of this age are concretistic and do not utilize logical operations, the errors may reflect the quality of intellectual functions. Ironically, we do not know

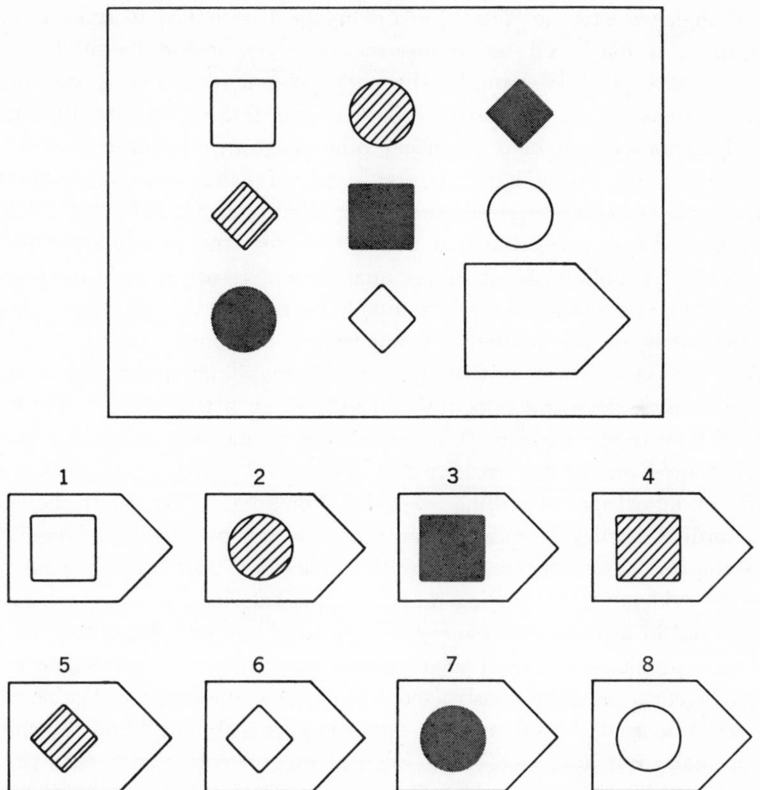

FIGURE 3. Illustration of type of item used to assess proximal or distal choices of young children. (From Raven, J. C. *Progressive Matrices*. London: H. K. Lewis & Co.; by permission.)

what may account for the correct response, but analysis of errors could tell us what kinds of difficulty the child is having.

The type of error analysis discussed provides us with increased specificity of the quality and level of intellectual performance not possible from a consideration of correct responses only. To be sure, the number of correct responses presumably provides us with a measure of what the respondent can do. Analysis of errors should tell us more about the "why not's" of performance.

Another contribution of error analysis, accepting the diagnostic significance of them, is for our understanding of development. Developmental curves based on errors could reveal how children alter their approach with increase in age. To do this would require a conceptualization of errors so that an "erring" response can be identified as having particular significance. The PM provides such a model. No doubt the same could be done with other tests.

Although we have not related errors on the Raven PM to styles of categorization, it may well be that particular styles would be inhibitors to correct responses. For example, the child who tends to be global in his approach may err on the Raven PM item requiring perceptual discrimination, but not on the item requiring other cognitive operations.

Thus far, the focus has been on styles of categorization, qualitative analysis of particular test responses, and, finally, errors. The "style" issue has provided one factor that may account for the kind of response children give. The distribution of qualitative analysis and errors provide methods to increase the information already available on the test as well as to enhance understanding of the individual's intellectual behavior.

Why should new tests not be developed rather than spend time revising the old? Aside from the difficulty of constructing a test, there is the question of how ready are we? It seems we are at the beginning of a period which should enable the creative test constructor to integrate various elements of knowledge regarding cognitive functioning. We must, however, wait until the scientific value of current research in cognitive functioning is established. The concept of cognitive styles is a good case in point. To date the evidence is convincing that individuals do tend to approach classes of material in a consistent manner. If this continues to hold, and if we can show the predictive value of such phenomena, then it is conceivable a test of intelligence could be constructed to tap these dimensions. An item like this could be used: "Rank an item that best goes with cow," and the choices are animal, meat, tail, feet, shoes. Each of these is correct, yet each reflects a different category of response. Perhaps in this way we can get at ability and style.

Resting with our current concepts will not help us understand the "how" of intelligence. Using intelligence tests as we do, limiting our analysis to unsystematic analyses of responses, be they qualitative or quantitative, negates the relevance of other cognitive factors influencing IQ. It may well be that the reason IQ and creativity are not frequently related is just because we have used the IQ in a narrow restricted way. . . . If we broaden our use of IQ tests, we may be in a position to provide a significant test which would not only have broad predictive value, but enlarge our view of how intelligence operates.

In this way, we may avoid such curious contradictions that IQ and creativity are not related. Such findings are essentially artifacts of our test construction. The greater tests reflect theoretical conceptions, the greater our chance of clarifying many of the issues plaguing us.

REFERENCES

Cohen, M. R., and E. Nagel. *Logic and Scientific Method.* New York: Harcourt, 1934.

Feifel, H., and I. Lorge. "Qualitative differences in the vocabulary responses of children." *J. educ. Psychol.,* 1950, **11,** 1–18.

Guilford, J. P. "Three faces of intellect." *Amer. Psychologist,* 1959, **14,** 569–579.

Inhelder, B., and J. Piaget. *The Growth of Logical Thinking from Childhood to Adolescence.* New York: Basic Books, 1958.

Kagan, J., H. A. Moss, and I. E. Sigel. The psychological significance of styles of conceptualization. In *Proceedings of Conference on Cognitive Processes,* J. F. Wright and J. Kagan (Eds.) *Monogr. Soc. Res. child. Develpm.,* 1962.

Raven, J. C. *Progressive Matrices.* London: H. K. Lewis, 1938.

Raven, J. C. *Guide to Using the Coloured Progressive Matrices.* London: H. K. Lewis, 1956.

Scott, N. The relationship of inductive reasoning and cognitive styles and categorization behavior to science concept achievement in elementary school children. Unpubl. doctoral dissertation. Wayne State Univ., 1962.

Sigel, I. E. *Cognitive style and personality dynamics.* Interim progress report for National Inst. of ment. Health, M-2983, 1961.

Terman, L. M., and Maud A. Merrill. *Stanford-Binet Intelligence Scale.* Boston: Houghton Mifflin, 1960.

4.4 Orientation

Since the early 1950s there has been a startling increase of research on creativity—its nature and development. Probably no one psychologist has done more to instigate this research than J. P. Guilford, whose work has been briefly described by Stott and Ball earlier in this chapter. Since creativity can take so many forms and occur on so many different levels, it has been extremely difficult to establish an ordered set of nomothetic statements having broad applicability. The most pressing of the many problems encountered in creativity research has been the criterion problem: What, precisely, is creativity? Is creativity to be viewed from the standpoint of a tangible product? Is there a creative process? How can creativity be objectively measured? Such questions are examined in this critical review of research and theory concerned with the psychological study of creativity.

Although several advances have been made since this review was originally published, most authorities would agree that creativity research is still in an embryonic stage. Guilford and others continue to pursue the psychometric approach in studying creativity. This has enabled psychologists to establish operational definitions of creativity (for example, one's score on a test of divergent thinking). Such tests raise an issue as to whether divergent thinking and creativity are synonymous. Some psychologists have concentrated upon studying the differences between the characteristics of creative people and their less creative peers, however creativity may be assessed (MacKinnon, 1962). Still others have sustained a search for methods that will train children in creativity (Torrance, 1965). This approach seeks to identify the conditions that promote creative outcomes. Readers will observe that Golann believes the investigation of personality factors to be the most fruitful in studying creativity.

From the standpoint of social and educational critics who frequently maintain that society (generally) and the schools (specifically) suppress creativity, the core issue in this area of research involves the conditions under which creativity is manifest. This concern does not obviate the need for a precise definition of creativity, however. Clearly, parents and teachers must know what it is they wish to achieve before they make decisions about how to teach for creativity.

RECOMMENDED READING

MacKinnon, D. W. "The nature and nurture of creative talent." *Amer. Psychologist,* **17** (1962), 484–495.

Torrance, E. P. *Rewarding Creative Behavior: Experiments in Classroom Creativity.* Englewood Cliffs, N. J.: Prentice-Hall, 1965.

Wallach, M. A., and N. A. Kagan. "A new look at the creativity-intelligence distinction." *J. Pers.,* **33** (1965), 348–369.

Yamamoto, Kaoru. "Creative thinking: Some thoughts on research." *Excep. Child.,* **30** (1964), 403–410.

Yamamoto, Kaoru. "Validation of tests of creative thinking: A review of some studies." *Excep. Child,* **31** (1965), 281–290.

4.4 Psychological Study of Creativity

Stuart E. Golann, UNIVERSITY OF MARYLAND

The purpose of the present paper is to review recent theory and research pertaining to the psychological study of creativity so as to highlight the issues and emphases reflected in the literature. Three issues are apparent: (1) What is creativity?—questions of definition and criteria, (2) How does creativity occur?—questions of the process viewed tem-

Reprinted from *Psychological Bulletin,* 1963, **60** (1963), No. 6, 548–565. By permission of the author and the American Psychological Association, Inc.

porally, and, (3) Under what conditions is creativity manifest?—questions of necessary personal and environmental conditions. A striking feature of the literature on creativity is the diversity of interests, motives, and approaches characteristic of the many investigators. Creativity has been viewed as a normally distributed trait, an aptitude trait, an intrapsychic process, and as a style of life. It has been described as that which is seen in all children, but few adults. It has been described as that which leads to innovation in science, performance in fine arts, or new thoughts. Creativity has been described as related to, or equitable with, intelligence, productivity, positive mental health, and originality. It has been described as being caused by self-actualization and by sublimation and restitution of destructive impulses. Clearly there is a need for organization and integration within the psychological study of creativity. What are the many investigators studying? How are they studying it? Four contemporary emphases are apparent: products, process, measurement, and personality. The organization herein will follow this same order. The scope of the paper precludes an exhaustive presentation of all theoretical statements and research reports. The reader is referred to an annotated bibliographical volume prepared by Stein and Heinze (1960). French and Italian bibliographies (Bédard 1959, 1960) are also available.

EMPHASIS ON PRODUCTS

The use of products as criteria of creativity is most frequently encountered in investigations in technological or industrial settings. In such studies creativity is assumed to be a unitary or multifaceted trait which is distributed in the population in a manner comparable to other intellective or personality traits (see Gamble, 1959, p. 292). Several authors believe that creativity can best be studied through products.

In the "Committee Report on Criteria of Creativity" (Gamble, 1959), it was stated that the products of creative behavior should be the first object of study. After the products are judged "creative" the term can be applied to the behavior which produced them, and also the individuals who performed the behavior can be classed as possessing to some degree the trait of creativity.

Several possible product criteria of creativity were proposed by McPherson (1956) who reviewed the problem of determining "inventive level" of patents. Ghiselin (1958) stated that the approach outlined by McPherson would not provide the true criteria of creativity and distinguished two levels of creativity. A higher level of creativity introduces some new element of meaning or some new order of significance while a lower level gives further development to an established body of meaning by initiating some advance in its use.

While the utility of studying creativity through products remains an issue, Harmon (1958), Taylor (1958), and C. Taylor (1959) have studied relationships between criterion variables and determinants of judges' creativity ratings. Harmon reported correlations of .61 and .76 between judged creativity and number of publications. D. Taylor reported a correlation of .69 between ratings of creativity and ratings of productivity given by supervisors of research personnel. In later reports, Taylor (1960, 1961) argued that distinctions among problem solving, decision making, and creative thinking can best be made in terms of the product. A large number of measures were refined by C. Taylor to yield 56 scores on each of a group of research scientists. Included in the refined measures were supervisor, peer, examiner, and self-evaluations; counts of reports and publications; official records; and membership in professional societies. Factor analysis yielded 27 factors. The finding that among the many correlations four out of any five variables were independent of a given criterion was cited as evidence for the "almost overwhelming complexity of the criterion problem."

EMPHASIS ON PROCESS

Creative Process and Illumination

An alternative to the study of creativity through products is to study the process of creativity. Wallas (1926) described the stages of forming a new thought as follows: preparation, incubation, illumination, and verification. While the four stages could be distinguished from one another, Wallas noted that they do not occur in an uninterrupted problem and solution sequence. Controversy has appeared concerning the distinctness of the stages and the relative importance of conscious or other modes of mental activity.

Dashiell (1931) noted at the four stages of the creative process and related inspiration to insight in learning. Recall is dependent on the absence of interfering associations set up by excessive concentration on the recalling. Similarly, Woodworth (1954) stated that incubation implies a theory he prefers not to accept. Illumination, he believed, is the result of laying aside a problem, giving the mind a chance to rest and at the same time to get rid of false sets and directions. Relating the recall of a forgotten name to creative insight, Woodworth stated that the sudden recall of a forgotten name after previous futile attempts suggests that an essential factor in illumination is the absence of interferences which block progress during the preliminary stage.

In addition to considering explanations of unconscious processes and the weakening of erroneous sets, Crutchfield (1961) suggested that incubation may permit, perhaps unaware to the individual, new and better cues from the environment and from ideation to develop while one engages in other activities. An experiment cited suggested that the subject's performance on a former task may facilitate insight on a later task even though they report no awareness of the relevant cue present in the preceding task. Instead of the study of distinct stages, Crutchfield recommended a functional analysis which would seek lawful accounts of the manner in which each step of the creative thinking process was functionally determined by prior steps and in turn governed succeeding steps.

Ghiselin (1956) described insight as the crucial action of the mind in creation. He too preferred to consider the creative process as consisting of fewer discrete steps, and stated that no sort of calculation from known grounds will suffice for creative production. Required for creativity is a fresh formulation, rather than copying with variations or elaborations. Although he believed that concepts of unconscious thoughts are imprecise, he did admit the importance of diversion which is conceptualized as being related to what he terms preconfigurative consciousness.

The illumination controversy could be enlarged upon and conceptually updated. However, the guidelines seem clear in regard to the creative process. Crutchfield's paper is helpful in that he attempted to translate the somewhat literary descriptions of the creative process into better conceptualized psychological variables.

Creative Process: Systematized, Goal Directed, or Plastic

For Harmon (1956) the creative process is any process by which something new is produced: an idea or object, a new form or arrangement of old elements. The essential requirement is that the new creation must contribute to the solution of a problem. The creative process is goal directed. Harris (1959) saw the creative process as consisting of six steps: (1) realizing the need, (2) gathering information, (3) thinking through, (4) imagining solutions, (5) verifying and (6) putting the ideas to work. He stated that the difference between the electrified or illuminated minds of some geniuses and the processes in ordinary people is the speed with which they proceed from Step 1 to Step 4 (see also Arnold, 1959).

Taking a different view, I. Taylor (1959) stated that the rules of logic and scientific method are a psychological straight jacket for creative thought. He proposed five levels of creativity which he identified by the analysis of over 100 definitions of creativity.

Expressive creativity is most fundamental, according to Taylor, involving independent expression where skills, originality, and the quality of the product are unimportant. Spontaneity and freedom are apparent from which later creative talents develop. Individuals proceed from the expressive to the productive level of creativity when skills are developed to produce finished works. The product is creative in that a new level of accomplishment is reached by the person though the product may not be stylistically discernible from the work of others. Inventive creativity is operative when ingenuity is displayed. This level involves flexibility in perceiving new and unusual relationships between previously separate parts. It does not contribute to new ideas but to new uses of old parts. Innovative creativity requires strong abstract conceptualizing skill and is seen when basic foundation principles are sufficiently understood so as to allow improvement through modification. The highest form of creativity is "emergentive creativity," which involves the conception of an entirely new principle at a most fundamental and abstract level. The core of the creative process in Taylor's view is the ability to mold experiences into new and different organizations, the ability to perceive the environment plastically, and to communicate the resulting unique experiences to others.

Stein (1956) stated that creativity is a process of hypothesis formulation, hypothesis testing, and the communication of results which are the resultant of social transaction. Individuals affect and are affected by the environment in which they live. The early childhood family-environment transaction facilitates or inhibits creativity. An empirical definition of manifest creativity is suggested by Stein (1956):

> Creativity is that process which results in a novel work that is accepted as tenable or useful or satisfying by a group at some point in time (p. 172).

Potential creativity is suggested when an individual does not satisfy the requirements of the stated definition, but nevertheless performs on psychological tests like individuals who do manifest creativity. In an earlier paper Stein (1953) elaborated upon his definition of creativity.

EMPHASIS ON MEASUREMENT

Factor Analytic Approach

Since the publication of Chassell's (1916) paper numerous investigators have attempted to devise or adapt tests that would measure creative abilities. Although the types of tests have not changed very much over the past 55 years, the methods of analysis have become more complex. For example, Guilford attempted to define the entire structure of intellect by factor analytic methods. In one of the more recent revisions of his system, he presented a "unified theory of intellect" making use of a cubical model of intellectual abilities in which each dimension represents a mode of variation among the factors (Guilford, 1959a). The lack of psychological knowledge in the area of creativity may be attributable, according to Guilford (1959b) to the inappropriateness of the SR model for the study of higher processes.

Instead, Guilford (1959b) recommended a trait approach for the study of creativity and stated that the most defensible way of discovering dependable trait concepts is factor analysis. He attempted to place his research on creativity within the larger context of the structure of intellect. Noting some 47 known factors of intellect, Guilford suggested that they can be put into a three-way classification according to: the kind of material or content of thought, the varieties of activities or operations performed, and the varieties of resultant products. In this system each primary intellectual ability represents the interaction of a kind of operation applied to a kind of material, vielding a kind of product. Most needed, according to Guilford, was a more thorough understanding of the nature and components of intellect. Accordingly, most of the data reported concern the isolation of a primary factor believed to be of importance for creativity.

The factorial aptitude traits that Guilford currently believes to be related to creativity are described as: ability to see problems, fluency of thinking (the factors of word fluency and ideational fluency), flexibility of thinking (the factors of spontaneous flexibility and adaptive flexibility), originality, redefinition, and elaboration. The types of cognitive abilities Guilford believes to be of importance for creativity are reflected in the measuring devices he has designed or adapted. Very briefly described, his tests require individuals to state defects or deficiencies in common implements or institutions; to produce words containing a specified letter or combination of letters; to produce in a limited time as many synonyms as they can for a stimulus word; to produce phrases or sentences; to name objects with certain properties (for example, objects that are hard, white, and edible); or to give various uses for a common object. Guilford's (1959b) practice in scoring fluency factors is to emphasize sheer quantity —"quality need not be considered so long as responses are appropriate [p. 146]." Other tests employed ask examinees which of a given list of objects could best be adopted to make another object; or to construct a more complex object from one or two simple lines.

Guilford (1959b) presented three ways to measure the trait of originality: counting the number of responses that are judged to be clever, utilizing items calling for remote associations, and weighting the subject's responses in proportion to their infrequency of occurrence in a population of subjects. The first two procedures require a quality criterion.

Much of the research efforts of Guilford and associates has been devoted to the definition of factor traits by isolating patterns of concomitant variation (see Guilford, 1957; Guilford, Kettner, and Christensen, 1954, 1956; Kettner, Guilford, and Christensen, 1959). The studies reviewed herein cluster into two groups: (1) those studies demonstrating a relationship between measures of the factors and criterion variables and (2) those studies suggesting no relationship between measures of the factors and judged creativity.

Correlations of .25 between grades in an astronomy course and performance on a test of experessional fluency, .37 between scores on a test of ideational fluency and a criterion of engineer performance based on pay increases, and .31 between a measure of adaptive flexibility and the pay increase criterion were reported by Guilford (1956). Adaptive flexibility was reported to have consistently shown a relationship to performance in mathematics (average *r* .33). Three Guilford originality tests (Unusual Uses, Consequences, and Plot Titles) were reported by Barron (1956) to correlate in the range of .30–.36 with 10 judges' ratings of originality. Significant multiple correlations were reported by Chorness (1956) between a composite factor score from the Guilford battery and United States Air Force student-instructor characteristics judged to be demonstrative of creative expression. The best single predictor was a test of controlled associations. Statistically removing the effects of intelligence demonstrated that the creativity tests could be employed as predictors of instructor performance since the factor composite predicted the student instructor grades for the phase of the program studied better than an intelligence index which had previously been relied on.

No significant differences between groups rated as creative or not creative on the factors of redefinition, closure, ideational fluency, associational fluency, spontaneous flexibility, sensitivity to problems, and originality were found by Drevdahl (1956). Similarly, Gerry, DeVeau, and Chorness (1957) reported no significant differences on the Guilford battery between awarded and non-awarded employees when the groups had been equated for intelligence, job performance, and education.

Surveying several years of research on creative, effective people, MacKinnon (1961) stated that in all samples studied, the Guilford tests, scored for quantity or quality, did not correlate well with the degree of creativity as judged by experts in the subjects' own fields. Substantiating this, correlations reported by Gough (1961) between criterion ratings of creativity and several of the Guilford tests were: Unusual Uses (quantity −.05, quality .27); Consequences (quantity −.27, quality −.12); Matchsticks (.04); Gestalt Transformations (.27).

Relationship between Measured Creativity and Measured Intelligence

Using an IQ measure (Stanford-Binet, Wechsler Scale for Children, or Henmon-Nelson) and five creativity measures (Word Association, Uses for Things, Hidden Shapes, Fables, and Make-Up Problems), Getzels and Jackson (1959) selected two experimental groups. One group was composed of children who placed in the top 20% on the creativity measures when compared with same-sexed age peers, but below the top 20% in measured IQ. The second group consisted of subjects who placed in the top 20% in IQ, but below the top 20% on the creativity measures. Despite the similarity in mean IQ between the high creative group (IQ = 127) and total population (IQ = 132), and despite the 23-point difference in mean IQ between the two experimental groups in favor of the high intelligence group (IQ = 150), the achievement scores of the two experimental groups on standard subject-matter tests were equally superior to the achievement scores of the remainder of the school population. These data are discussed more fully in a recent volume (Getzels and Jackson, 1962).

The main criticisms of the Getzels-Jackson report have centered around the use of a single atypical school. Torrance studied creative thinking in the early school years (see Torrance, 1958, 1959a, 1959b, 1959c, 1959d, 1959e, 1960a, 1960b, 1960c, 1960d; Torrance, Baker, and Bowers, 1959; Torrance and Radig, 1959) and brought together eight partial replications of the Getzels-Jackson study. Two batteries of creativity tests were used; both consisted of modifications of Guilford-type tests with the exception of the Ask and Guess Test developed by Torrance (Torrance and Radig, 1959). The procedure followed by Torrance (1960c) is similar to Getzels and Jackson in that he selected groups who placed in the upper 20% on either the creativity or IQ measures, but not in the upper 20% on the remaining measure.

In six of Torrance's eight groups, there was no significant difference on measured achievement between the high creative and high intelligence groups. In two of the elementary schools (the small town school and the parochial school) there was a significant difference in measured achievement in favor of the high intelligence group. The question is then raised: Under what conditions do "highly creative" pupils achieve as well as "highly intelligent" ones? Additional data reported by Torrance suggest a tendency for the highly creative groups to be better on reading and language skills than on work-study or arithmetic skills.

Meer and Stein (1955) reported a significant relationship between research chemists scores on the Wechsler-Bellevue, Miller Analogies, and supervisors ratings of creativity. When education was controlled, they concluded that with opportunity held constant, IQ beyond the ninety-fifth percentile is not significant for creative work. Similarly, summarizing several studies, Barron (1961) suggested that a small correlation (about .40) exists between the total ranges of creativity and intelligence. However, beyond an IQ of about 120, measured intelligence is unimportant for creativity. He pointed instead to the importance of motivational and stylistic variables.

Criterion Group Empirical Approach

The Welsh Figure Preference Test (WFPT; Welsh, 1949, 1959a, 1959b) is a different type of psychometric instrument used in the study of creativity. In short, it is a nonlingual test composed of 400 India ink drawings, to each of which the examinee must repond "like" or "don't like." Of primary interest in the present context is an empirical scale derived by contrasting the likes and dislikes of 37 artists and art students with the likes and dislikes of 150 people in general (Barron and Welsh, 1952). This scale has since been revised by Welsh to eliminate any response set and in its present form the Revised Art (RA) scale consists of

30 drawings that artists like more frequently than people do in general, and 30 items that artists dislike more often than people do in general.

Rosen (1955) attempted to use the earlier form of the Art scale (BW) as a predictor of originality and level of ability among artists. He reported a significant difference between artists and art students as contrasted with nonartists, but no evidence that Art scale score increased as a function of level of training of the artist. One art product of each of the students was rated on a 5-point scale of originality by each of the art faculty. The correlation between the Art scale score and the average of the ratings was .40. The correlation between the Art scale score and the grade-point average of the students was .34.

Rank-order correlations of .40 and .35 between scores on the RA scale and creative writing instructor's ratings of originality and creativity of their students were reported by Welsh (1959a). Gough (1961) reported that the BW scale showed the highest single correlation (.41) with criterion judgments of research workers' creativity. Among the many measures which did not correlate well with the criterion judgments were three ability measures, the Allport-Vernon value scales, 56 of the 57 Strong Vocational Inventory scales, Barron's Originality scale, Barron's Preference for Complexity scale, the originality coefficient from Gough's Differential Reaction Schedule, and the six Guilford measures already noted.

Data obtained by MacKinnon (1961) indicated that a group of highly creative architects placed in the same range as artists on the BW scale, while a less creative group obtained lower scores, and a third group not distinguished for its creativity score lowest.

EMPHASIS ON PERSONALITY

Personality is another major emphasis within the psychological study of creativity. It can be subdivided into: (1) the study of motivation of creative behavior and (2) the study of personality characteristics or life styles of creative individuals. Regarding motivation, two divergent viewpoints are apparent. One describes creative behavior as an emergent property which matures as the individual attempts to realize his fullest potentials in his interaction with his environment, while the second treats creativity as a byproduct of repressed or unacceptable impulses.

Among the concepts related to the first viewpoint are Allport's (1937) functional autonomy, Goldstein's (1939), Roger's (1954, 1956), and Yacorzynski's (1954) self-actualization; as well as May's (1959) and Schachtel's (1959) motives for creativity. Individuals are described as being creative because it is satisfying to them since they have a need to relate to the world around them so they may experience their selves in action.

Antithetical to these views are the concepts of psychoanalytic authors who have discussed creativity. Freud (1910, 1924, 1948) originally postulated that all cultural achievements are caused by the diversion of libidinal energy. This displacement, producing higher cultural achievements, he called sublimation (Freud, 1930). Several authors have described creativity as motivated by efforts to defend against unacceptable impulses (see Bergler, 1947; Bychowski, 1951) or as motivated by unconscious restitution for destructive urges (see Fairbairn, 1938; Lee, 1947, 1948, 1950; Rickman, 1957; Sharpe, 1930, 1950). Other reductionistic treatments of creativity can be found in the writings of Abraham (1949), Adler (1927), Bellack (1958), Bischler (1937), Brill (1931), Ehrenzweig (1949), Grotjahn (1957), Kohut (1957), Kris (1952), Levey (1940), Rank (1916), and Sachs (1951). Criticisms of sublimation theory were offered by Bergler (1945), Deri (1939), and Levey (1939).

It is difficult to compare these viewpoints experimentally for several reasons. Creativity has not been defined by either group and it does not seem that they are describing the same types of behaviors. The reductionistic authors most often discuss painting and writing in their attempts to explain creativity. The self-actualizing group seem to describe a much more global style of interacting with one's environment which could lead to products that would be judged as creative. Moreover, such concepts as sublimation and self-actualization are not easily definable or measurable. There are a few experimental studies which have yielded data of varying degrees of consistency or inconsistency with the two views of motivation for creative behavior.

Studies of Motivation for Creativity

Münsterberg and Mussen (1953) attempted to study several hypotheses derived from psychoanalytic formulations of the creative personality. They interpreted the data as supporting the following hypotheses: (1) more artists than nonartists have intense guilt feelings, (2) more artists are introverted and have a richer inner life, (3) more artists than nonartists are unable or unwilling to comply with their parents. No support was reported for the following hypotheses: (1) nonartists are more likely to show overt aggressive tendencies, (2) appreciation of the product supplies basic narcissistic gratification for the artist, (3) the artist interprets appreciation as evidence that others share his guilt. Evidence was reported supporting the single hypothesis which was not derived from psychoanalytic formulations—that more artists than nonartists show a need for creative self-expression.

Myden (1959) defined a highly creative group by choosing 20 subjects from "the top rank" of diverse fields of the arts. Content and formal analysis of the Rorschach suggested that the creative group did utilize primary process significantly more than the noncreative group. Myden stated that in the creative individual the primary process appeared to be integrated with the secondary process and did not seem to arise from, or increase, anxiety. Regression appeared to be a part of the thinking of creative individuals, rather than symptomatic of loss of ego control. No quantitative difference in anxiety was apparent between the two groups. The creative group was reported to employ significantly less repression than did the noncreative group. Myden believed that this may account for the finding that they show a greater amount of psychosexual ambivalence.

One large difference between the two groups, which is not considered in the psychoanalytic literature, was noted to be a significantly stronger sense of psychological role-in-life characteristic of the creative group. Myden (1959) described them as "inner-directed and not easily swayed by outside reactions and opinions [p. 156]."

Golann (1961, 1962) proposed a hypothetical construct—the creativity motive—through which he attempted to express the view that creative products are only one segment of creative behavior which becomes manifest when individuals actively interact with their environment so as to experience their fullest perceptual, cognitive, and expressive potentials. He argued that high creativity motive subjects should prefer stimuli and situations which allowed for idiosyncratic ways of dealing with them. In an attempt to demonstrate this, and in an attempt toward explanation of positive correlations between the Art scales of the WFPT and judged creativity in painting, writing, and research, it was shown that the 30 RA scale items liked by artists were significantly more ambiguous than the RA items artists did not like. A second study revealed the individuals who scored high on the RA scale, subjects who preferred the ambiguous, evocative figures, indicated preference on a questionnaire for activities and situations which allowed more self-expression and utilization of creative capacity, in contrast to low RA subjects who preferred more routine, structured, and assigned activities.

Personality atributes of creative individuals have been treated through experimental study and theoretical descriptive reports. Maslow's (1959) description of self-actualizing creativeness and Roger's (1954) discussion of conditions within the individual that are closely associated with a potentially creative act are highly similar. Both authors placed a great deal of importance on openness to experience rather than premature conceptualization, and on an internal locus of evaluation rather than over concern with the opinions of others. The theme of individuals' desire to fully achieve their potentials through their interaction with the environment is prominent in these writings. Similar or related observations have been made by Fromm (1959), Murphy (1957, 1958), and Mooney (1953a, 1953b).

Studies of Personality Attributes of Creative Individuals

The experimental study of personality attributes of creative individuals tends to contrast criterion groups on either self-descriptions, others' descriptions, test performance, life history material, or work habits. The criterion groups have been selected on the basis of either ratings of creativity, performance on Guilford tests, scores on BW or RA of the WFPT, or nomination of individuals of outstanding creativity by a panel of experts in their field.

The relationship between self-description and degree of creativity has been studied by several investigators. Barron (1952) reported that subjects at the lower extreme on the BW scale described themselves as contented, gentle, conservative, unaffected, patient, and peaceable. In contrast, the high BW subjects characterized themselves as gloomy, loud, unstable, bitter, cool, dissatisfied, pessimistic, emotional, irritable, and pleasure seeking. Similar results were reported by Barron (1958) in a later study. Relating self-descriptions to a productivity criterion VanZelst and Kerr (1954) reported that productive scientists described themselves as more original, imaginative, curious, enthusiastic, and impulsive, and as less contented and conventional. Stein (1956) reported that creative subjects regard themselves as assertive and authoritative, while less creative regard themselves as acquiescent and submissive. Self-descriptions for highly creative and less creative female mathematicians have been reported by Helson (1961) and by MacKinnon (1961) for groups of architects varying in creativeness. MacKinnon reported that the highly creative stress their inventiveness, independence, individuality, enthusiasm, determination, and industry while the less creative stress virtue, good character, rationality, and concern for others. He suggested that the highly creative are able to speak frankly, in a more unusual way about themselves because they are more self-accepting than their less creative colleagues (see also Barron, 1961).

A dimension similar to that apparent in the self-descriptions is reflected in the test performance of subjects varying in creativity. The values of subjects at the extremes on the BW scale were inferred by Barron (1952) from fine arts preferences. He reported that low BW subjects approved of good breeding, formality, religion, and authority and rejected the daring, esoteric, or sensual. In contrast, high BW subjects approved of the modern, experimental, primitive, and sensual while they disliked the aristocratic, traditional, and emotionally controlled.

Barron (1953) equated performance on the BW scale with a bipolar factor of preference for perceiving and dealing with complexity as opposed to preference for simplicity. Positive relationships reported for preference of complexity included: personal tempo, verbal fluency, impulsiveness, expansiveness, originality, sensuality, sentience, esthetic interest, and femininity in men. Negative relationships of preference for complexity included: rigidity, constriction, repressive impulse control, political-economic conservatism, subservience to authority, ethnocentrism, and social conformity. This dimension is discussed more fully in a later report (Barron, 1961).

Studying the relationship between aptitude and nonaptitude factors,

Guilford (1957) stated that the intercorrelations were generally low. Subjects who scored higher on ideational fluency were more impulsive, self-confident, ascendent, more appreciative of originality and somewhat less inclined towards neuroticism. Subjects higher on originality were more interested in esthetic expression, reflective and divergent thinking, more tolerant of ambiguity, and felt less need for orderliness.

Independence as a personality attribute was stressed in several theoretical discussions of creativity. Barron (1953b) reported that subjects who did not yield to the incorrect group consensus in the Asch line judgment situation scored significantly higher on the BW scale than a group of yielders. Barron (1961) also noted that subjects who regularly perform in a creative or original manner on Guilford tests are independent in judgment when put under pressure to conform to a group opinion in conflict with their own.

The suggestion that the real difference between high and low creative individuals might be a function of the lows' defensiveness which inhibits generalization and communication of hypotheses was offered by Stein and Meer (1954). They administered the Rorschach to subjects at exposures ranging from .01 second to full. Their scoring system gave the highest score to a well-integrated response given to a difficult card at the shortest exposure. A biserial correlation of .88 between total weighted score and criterion creativity ratings was reported.

The work style of similarly employed individuals varying in creativity has also been the object of study. Roe (1949) reported that biologists selected for eminence in research were very unaggressive, had little interest in interpersonal relations, were unwilling to go beyond the data presented, and preferred concrete reality to the imaginary. Other data on Rorschach and Thematic Apperception Test performances of groups of eminent scientists are discussed in this and other reports (see Roe, 1946, 1949, 1951, 1952). Bloom (1956) administered projective techniques to outstanding scientists and reported personality and temperamental characteristics similar to those described by Roe. The willingness to work hard seems to be the most general characteristic of the samples studied.

Two research styles were reported by Gough (1961) to correlate with criterion ratings of creativity: the man who is dedicated to research and sees himself as a driving researcher with exceptional mathematical skills; the man with wide interests, analytic in thinking, who prefers research which lends itself to elegant, formal solutions. In a previous paper, Gough (1958) had described eight types of researchers and how these were conceptualized.

Another source of data bearing on creativity and personality is life history material. Roe (1953) reported that social scientists' interaction with their parents involved overprotection while physical and biological scientists developed early a way of life not requiring personal interaction.

A negative relationship between rated creativity and socioeconomic as well as educational status of the parents has been reported by Stein (1956). Creative subjects were more likely to feel that their parents were inconsistent in attitudes towards them. Less creative subjects were more likely to engage in group activities in childhood while the more creative preferred solitary activities. Similar trends were reported in extensive biographical studies by Cattell (1959). MacKinnon (1961) reported relationships between life history material and rated creativity which require and warrant further investigation.

Crutchfield (1961) attempted to describe personality attributes which tend to characterize creative individuals in general. He reported that in cognitive spheres they are more flexible and fluent; their perceptions and cognitions are unique. In approach to problems they are intuitive, empathic, perceptually open, and prefer complexity. In emotional-motivational spheres they demonstrate freedom from excessive impulse control, achieve via independence rather than conformity, are individualistic, and have strong, sustained, intrinsic motivations in their field of work.

Studies with Children

Few studies have been reported on creativity in children despite the great interest in the creativeness of childhood. Mattil (1953) attempted to study the relationship between the creative products of children and their adjustment. The data led Mattil to conclude that elements of adjustment and mental abilities are directly related to creative products.

Limited data on creativity in children is included in a monograph by Adkins and her associates (Adkins, Cobb, Miller, Sanford, Stewart, Aub, Burke, Nathanson, Stuart, and Towne, 1943). Teacher ratings of creativity in school children are reported to correlate positively with independent measures of the following variables: .81 with need for sentience (pleasures); .65 with intraception (imaginative, subjective, human outlook); .65 with the need to produce, organize, or build things; .63 with the need for understanding; .60 with the need to explain, judge, or interpret; .50 with the need to restrive after failure and to overcome weakness; .50 with the enjoying of thought and emotion for its own sake or preoccupation with inner activities. Negative correlations reported for the same teacher ratings include: −.79 with sameness (adherence to places, people, and modes of conduct; rigidity of habits); −.57 with the need of acquisition; and −.54 with the need to reject others.

Reid, King, and Wickwire (1959) reported that creative subjects exhibited superior performance on almost all cognitive variables, indicating that cognitive abilities (as measured by general intelligence, aptitude, and achievement instruments) are related to peer nominations of creativity. While these results can be interpreted as generally consistent with studies on adult populations, the findings that the creative group was significantly higher on *cyclothymia,* while the noncreatives were higher on *schizothymia,* contradicts replicated results with adults who have been described as withdrawn or individualistic and have themselves said they preferred individual pursuits as children.

A recent study by Torrance (1959d), in which he attempted to explore some of the relationships between talkativeness and creative thinking, may help resolve the apparent contradiction. He reported that in the first grade, those children perceived as not speaking out their ideas tend to be more frequently seen as having good ideas, more frequently chosen as friends, higher on a measure of spontaneous flexibility, more intelligent, and higher on a nonverbal measure of creativity. This pattern gradually begins to shift, and by the fourth grade, the highly talkative individuals are more frequently perceived as having good ideas and receive more friendship choices. Thus, highly talkative children tend to earn higher scores on the verbal test of creativity, but not on the nonverbal measure. Torrance's results suggested that a sociometric criterion will select children with well-developed and exercised verbal abilities who are not necessarily more creative than many of their peers. A wide range of issues concerning the development of creativity in children is discussed in a paper by Lowenfeld (1959).

CRITICAL OVERVIEW

What is creativity? Creativity has been viewed as a normally distributed trait; as such its investigation has proceeded in an attempt to find product criteria from which the presence or absence of the trait in an individual could be inferred. Creativity has been viewed as the outcome of a complex of aptitude traits; as such its investigation has proceeded in an attempt to demonstrate the presence of such traits through factor analysis and to develop measuring instruments. Creativity has been viewed as a process culminating in a new thought or insight; as such its investigation has proceeded by introspective reporting, or investigator observation of the temporal sequence. Creativity has been described as a style of life, the personality in action; as such its investigation has been concerned with personality descriptions and assessment of people believed to be creative and investigation of motives for creativity.

All of the possible emphases within the study of creativity require no justification other than noting that each is capable of making important contributions. It would seem, however, that data reported by Taylor, Smith, and Ghiselin (1959), which indicated a very low degree of association among the many possible product criteria, argue against the likelihood of a product approach providing a comprehensive understanding of creativity. Crutchfield's (1961) discussion of the creative process should be helpful to those attempting experimental studies. His explanation of illumination will require careful study in the light of recent reports (see Spielberger, 1962) which suggest that the examiner's awareness of the subject's awareness may be a function of the extent of the postexperimental interview. Difficulty may arise when investigators, working within one area of emphases, with one explicit or implied definition and set of criteria, lose sight of the inherent limitations of their choices. The point can perhaps be illustrated by a reconsideration of the relationship between creativity and intelligence.

The studies by Getzels and Jackson (1959) and Torrance (1959e) indicated that measured intellectual ability and measured creative ability are by no means synonymous. Torrance presented additional data which indicated that in his sample, using only the Wechsler Intelligence Scale for Children, to determine giftedness would have excluded 70% of the children placing in the upper 20% on the creativity measures. The same ratios obtain using other measures of intelligence. Meer and Stein (1955), Barron (1961), and MacKinnon (1961) agree essentially that while there is a correlation over the entire ranges of intelligence and creativity, the magnitude of the correlation varies greatly at different levels of intelligence. Meer and Stein cite the ninety-fifth percentile, Barron an IQ of 120, as the approximate point above which intelligence is unimportant for creativity. The point that needs to be stressed is that these data are in a sense arbitrary: intelligence is not performance on a test; creativity is more than test performance or being judged as creative. What is needed for the understanding of the relationship between creativity and intelligence is not only data at the correlational level, but conceptual reorganization as well. Just as the choice of a series of Guilford tests or judgment procedures implies one definition of creativity, the choice of an intelligence test implies one of many possible definitions of intelligence. I. Taylor (1959), for example, believes intelligence to be an invention of Western culture, which stresses how fast relatively unimportant problems can be solved without making errors. He feels that another culture might choose to measure intelligence in a way more congruent with a high level of creativity.

For these reasons Guilford has attempted to employ a wide variety of criterion measures, grouped by factor analysis, and study relationships among the factors.

One could, however, select criterion measures on the basis of theoretical constructs and still pay careful attention to the predictive efficacy of the criterion and compare its predictive ability with other possible selection criterion. This author agrees with Guilford that what is needed is better understanding of the nature of intellect but does not agree that factor analysis presents the best way of defining one's constructs. The factor analytic approach does not solve the problem of how well the measuring instrument is sensitive to variations in the construct its user believes it to measure. It does not seem that factor analysis will, itself, enrich basic understanding of creative phenomena. Required are not only data at a correlational level, but a developmental understanding as well, and also an understanding of different situations where different correlations are obtained between the same criteria.

If the choice is made to select subjects on conceptual rather than factor analytic bases it would seem that the investigator should attempt in some manner to isolate the contribution of a single criterion choice. The point to be made can perhaps best be seen in the work reported by Barron and MacKinnon. Their studies utilized a compound criterion in the selection of subjects: creative, effective individuals. The criteria of creativity in all cases were judgments clearly the most carefully collected, reliable of all those reported, but judgments nonetheless. The reports by Harmon (1958) and D. Taylor (1958) indicated that judges' ratings of creativity seem heavily determined by the productivity of the individual. Note that the self-descriptions of productive scientists reported by VanZelst and Kerr (1954) are very similar to the self-descriptions of creative individuals reported by Gough, Harmon, and MacKinnon. While it is crucial that creative, productive people be studied as such, it must be kept in mind that the portion of the reported findings attributable to creativity cannot be separated from that portion attributable to that which makes for productivity, and that which leads to being seen by judges as creative. It is possible, and perhaps we are now ready to utilize personality and stylistic modes as criterion variables. In such an approach our criterion variables might be tolerance for or seeking of ambiguity, openness to experience, childlike traits, self-actualization or expression, internal frames of evaluation, or independence of judgment, to name but a few theoretically based descriptive concepts which appear again and again in the literature and deserve further investigation. The important questions would then become: How do these cognitive, stylistic, or motivational modes of interacting with one's environment develop? What are the environmental, interpersonal, and intrapersonal conditions that tend to facilitate or discourage them? How in turn are these factors related at different age levels to behavior which is judged to be creative, effective, and productive? In no sense would this approach solve the problem of using judgments. The argument is not that this approach corrects or circumvents most of the problems inherent in other approaches. However, it is my belief that the use of theoretically derived personality factors as criterion variables has, because of its own inherent difficulties, been neglected, yet holds most promise of providing a functional developmental understanding of creativity.

SUMMARY

In this review of the psychological study of creativity there are 4 emphases; products, process, measurement, and personality. Three main issues concern questions of: definition and criteria, the process viewed temporally, and necessary personal and environmental conditions. The relationship between creativity and intelligence is discussed to illustrate the need for conceptual reorganization as well as correlational data. We should now be able to utilize personality and stylistic modes as criterion variables and to study how these factors are related at different age levels to behavior that is judged to be creative. This approach holds promise for providing a functional, developmental understanding of creativity.

REFERENCES

Abraham, K. The influence of oral erotism on character formation. In *Selected Papers of Karl Abraham,* trans. by D. Bryan and A. Strachey. London: Hogarth, 1949, pp. 393–406.

Adkins, Margaret M., Elizabeth A. Cobb, R. B. Miller, R. W. Sanford, Ann H. Stewart, J. C. Aub, Bertha Burke, I. T. Nathanson, H. C. Stuart, and Lois Towne. "Physique, personality, and scholarship." *Monogr. Soc. Res. child Develpm.,* 1943, **8** (1, ser. no. 34).

Adler, A. *The Practice and Theory of Individual Psychology.* New York: Harcourt, 1927.

Allport, G. W. "The functional autonomy of motives." *Amer. J. Psychol.,* 1937, **50,** 141–156.

Arnold, J. F. Creativity in engineering. In *Creativity,* P. Smith (Ed.) New York: Hastings, 1959, pp. 33–46.

Barron, F. "Personality style and perceptual choice." *J. Pers.,* 1952, **20,** 385–401.

Barron, F. "Complexity-simplicity as a personality dimension." *J. abnorm. soc. Psychol.,* 1953, **48,** 162–172 (a).

Barron, F. "Some personality correlates of independence of judgment." *J. Pers.,* 1953, **21,** 287–297 (b).

Barron, F. The disposition towards originality. In *The 1955 University of Utah Research Conference on the Identification of Creative Scientific Talent,* C. Taylor (Ed.) Salt Lake City: Univ. Utah Press, 1956, pp. 156–170.

Barron, F. The needs for order and for disorder as motives in creative activity. In *The 1957 University of Utah Research Conference on the Identification of Creative Scientific Talent,* C. Taylor (Ed.) Salt Lake City: Univ. Utah Press, 1958, pp. 119–128.

Barron, F. Creative vision and expression in writing and painting. In *Conference on the Creative Person.* Berkeley: Univ. Calif. Inst. pers. Assessment and *Res.,* 1961 (chap. 2).

Barron, F., and G. S. Welsh. "Artistic perception as a possible factor in personality style: Its measurement by a figure preference test." *J. Psychol.,* 1952, **33,** 199–203.

Bédard, R. J. *Creativity in the arts, literature, science, and engineering: A bibliography of French contributions.* (Creativity Res. exch. bull. no. 10.) Princeton, N.J.: Educ. testing Serv., 1959.

Bédard, R. J. *Creativity in the arts, literature, science, and engineering: A bibliography of Italian contributions* (Creativity Res. exch. bull. no. 9.) Princeton, N.J.: Educ. testing Serv., 1960.

Bellack, L. "Creativity: Some random notes to a systematic consideration." *J. proj. Tech.,* 1958, **22,** 363–380.

Bergler, E. "On a five-layer structure in sublimation." *Psychoanal. Quart.,* 1945, **14,** 76–97.

Bergler, E. Psychoanalysis of writers and of literary productivity. In *Psychoanalysis and the Social Sciences,* G. Roheim (Ed.) (vol. 1). New York: International Universities, 1947, pp. 247–296.

Bischler, W. "Intelligence and higher mental functions." *Psychoanal. Quart.,* 1937, **6,** 277–307.

Bloom, B. S. Report on creativity research at the University of Chicago. In *The 1955 University of Utah Research Conference on the Identification of Creative Scientific Talent,* C. Taylor (Ed.) Salt Lake City: Univ. Utah Press, 1956, pp. 182–194.

Brill, A. A. "Poetry as an oral outlet." *Psychoanal. Rev.,* 1931, **18,** 357–378.

Bychowski, G. "Metapsychology of artistic creation." *Psychoanal. Quart.,* 1951, **20,** 592–602.

Cattell, R. B. The personality and motivation of the researcher from measurements of contemporaries and from bibliography. In *The 1959 University of Utah Research Conference on the Identification of Creative Scientific Talent,* C. Taylor (Ed.) Salt Lake City: Univ. Utah Press, 1959, pp. 77–93.

Chassell, L. M. "Tests for originality." *J. educ. Psychol.,* 1916, **7,** 317–329.

Chorness, M. H. An interim report on creativity research. In *The 1955 University of Utah Research Conference on the Identification of Creative Scientific Talent,* C. Taylor (Ed.) Salt Lake City: Univ. Utah Press, 1956, pp. 132–153.

Crutchfield, R. The creative process. In *Conference on the Creative Person.* Berkeley: Univ. Calif., Inst. pers. Assessment and Res., 1961 (chap. 6).

Dashiell, J. F. *Fundamentals of General Psychology.* New York: Houghton Mifflin, 1931.

Deri, F. "On sublimation." *Psychoanal. Quart.,* 1939, **8,** 325–334.

Drevdahl, J. E. "Factors of importance for creativity." *J. clin. Psychol.,* 1956, **12,** 21-26.

Ehrenzweig, A. "The origin of the scientific and heroic urge." *Int. J. Psychoanal.,* 1949, **30,** 108–123.

Fairbairn, W. R. D. "Prolegomena to a psychology of art." *Brit. J. Psychol.,* 1938, **28,** 288–303.

Freud, S. *Three Contributions to the Theory of Sex.* New York: Nervous & Mental Disease Publishing Company, 1910.

Freud, S. "Civilized" sexual morality and modern nervousness. (Orig. publ. 1908) In *Collected Papers.* (vol. 2) (Trans. by J. Riviere) London: Hogarth, 1924, pp. 76–99.

Freud, S. *Civilization and Its Discontents,* trans. by J. Riviere. New York: Cope & Smith, 1930.

Freud, S. The relation of the poet to daydreaming. (Orig. publ. 1908) In *Col-*

lected Papers. (vol. 4.) (Trans. by J. Riviere) London: Hogarth, 1948, pp. 173–183.

Fromm, E. The creative attitude. In *Creativity and Its Cultivation,* H. Anderson (Ed.) New York: Harper, 1959, pp. 44–54.

Gamble, A. O. Suggestions for future research. In *The 1959 University of Utah Research Conference on the Identification of Creative Scientific Talent,* C. Taylor (Ed.) Salt Lake City: Univ. Utah Press, 1959, pp. 292–297.

Gerry, R., L. DeVeau, and M. Chorness. *A review of some recent research in the field of creativity and the examination of an experimental creativity workshop.* (Proj. No. 56–24) Lackland Air Force Base, Tex.: Train. Anal. and Develpm. Div., 1957.

Getzels, J. W., and P. W. Jackson. The highly intelligent and the highly creative adolescent: A summary of some research findings. In *The 1959 University of Utah Research Conference on the Identification of Creative Scientific Talent,* C. Taylor (Ed.) Salt Lake City: Univ. Utah Press, 1959, pp. 46–57.

Getzels, J. W., and P. W. Jackson. *Creativity and Intelligence: Explorations with Gifted Children.* New York: Wiley, 1962.

Ghiselin, B. The creative process and its relation to the identification of creative talent. In *The 1955 University of Utah Research Conference on the Identification of Creative Scientific Talent,* C. Taylor (Ed.) Salt Lake City: Univ. Utah Press, 1956, pp. 195–203.

Ghiselin, B. Ultimate criteria for two levels of creativity. In *The 1957 University of Utah Research Conference on the Identification of Creative Scientific Talent,* C. Taylor (Ed.) Salt Lake City: Univ. Utah Press, 1958, pp. 141–155.

Golann, S. E. The creativity motive. Unpubl. doctoral dissertation. Univ. North Carolina, 1961.

Golann, S. E. "The creativity motive." *J. Pers.,* 1962, **30,** 588–600.

Goldstein, K. *The Organism.* New York: American Book, 1939.

Gough, H. G. Stylistic variations in the self-views and work attitudes of a sample of professional research scientists. Paper read at Western Psychol. Assn., Monterey, Calif., April 1958.

Gough, H. G. Techniques for identifying the creative research scientist. In *Conference on the Creative Person.* Berkeley: Univ. Calif. Inst. pers. Assessment and Res., 1961 (chap. 3).

Grotjahn, M. *Beyond Laughter.* New York: McGraw-Hill, 1957.

Guilford, J. P. The relation of intellectual factors to creative thinking in science. In *The 1955 University of Utah Research Conference on the Identification of Creative Scientific Talent,* C. Taylor (Ed.) Salt Lake City: Univ. Utah Press, 1956, pp. 69–95.

Guilford, J. P. "Creative abilities in the arts." *Psychol. Rev.,* 1957, **64,** 110–118.

Guilford, J. P. Intellectual resources and their values as seen by scientists. In *The 1959 University of Utah Research Conference on the Identification of Creative Scientific Talent,* C. Taylor (Ed.) Salt Lake City: Univ. Utah Press, 1959, pp. 128–149 (a).

Guilford, J. P. Traits of creativity. In *Creativity and Its Cultivation,* H. Anderson (Ed.) New York: Harper, 1959, pp. 142–161 (b).

Guilford, J. P., N. W. Kettner, and P. R. Christensen. *A factor-analytic study across the domains of reasoning, creativity, and evaluation: I. Hypotheses and description of tests.* U. Sth. Calif. Psychol. Lab. Rep., 1954, no. 11.

Guilford, J. P., N. W. Kettner, and P. R. Christensen. *A factor analytic study across the domains of reasoning, creativity and evaluation: II. Administration of tests and analysis of results.* U. Sth. Calif. Psychol. Lab. Rep., 1956, no. 16.

Hadamard, J. *An Essay on the Psychology of Invention in the Mathematical Field.* Princeton: Princeton Univ. Press, 1945.

Harmon, L. R. Social and technological determiners of creativity. In *The 1955 University of Utah Research Conference on the Identification of Creative Scientific Talent,* C. Taylor (Ed.) Salt Lake City: Univ. Utah Press, 1956, pp. 42–52.

Harmon, L. R. The development of a criterion of scientific competence. In *The 1957 University of Utah Conference on the Identification of Creative Scientific Talent,* C. Taylor (Ed.) Salt Lake City: Univ. Utah Press, 1958, pp. 82–97.

Harris, R. A. Creativity in marketing. In *Creativity,* P. Smith (Ed.) New York: Hastings, 1959, pp. 143–166.

Helson, Ravenna. Creativity, sex, and mathematics. In *Conference on the Creative Person.* Berkeley: Univ. Calif. Inst. pers. Assessment and Res., 1961 (chap. 4).

Kettner, N. W., J. P. Guilford, and P. R. Christensen. "A factor analytic study across the domains of reasoning, creativity, and evaluation." *Psychol. Monogr.,* 1959, **73** (9, whole no. 479).

Kohut, H. "Observations on the psychological functions of music. *J. Amer. Psychoanal. Assn.,* 1957, **5,** 389–407.

Kris, E. *Psychoanalytic Explorations in Art.* New York: International Universities, 1952.

Lee, H. B. "On the esthetic states of mind." *Psychiatry,* 1947, **10,** 281–306.

Lee, H. B. "Spirituality and beauty in artistic experience." *Psychoanal. Quart.,* 1948, **17,** 507–523.

Lee, H. B. The values of order and vitality in art. In *Psychoanalysis and the Social Sciences,* G. Roheim (Ed.) (vol. 2) New York: International Universities, 1950, pp. 231–274.

Levey, H. B. "A critique of the theory of sublimation." *Psychiat.,* 1939, **2,** 239–270.

Levey, H. B. "A theory concerning free creation in the inventive arts." *Psychiat.,* 1940, **3,** 229–293.

Lowenfeld, V. *Educational implications of creativity research in the arts.* (Creativity Res. exch. bull. no. 8) Princeton, N.J.: Educ. testing Serv., 1959.

MacKinnon, D. W. The study of creativity and creativity in architects. In *Conference on the Creative Person.* Berkeley: Univ. Calif., Inst. pers. Assessment and Res., 1961 (chaps. 1 and 5).

McPherson, J. H. A proposal for establishing ultimate criteria for measuring creative output. In *The 1955 University of Utah Research Conference on the Identification of Creative Scientific Talent,* C. Taylor (Ed.) Salt Lake City: Univ. Utah Press, 1956, pp. 62–68.

Maslow, A. H. Creativity in self-actualizing people. In *Creativity and Its Cultivation,* H. Anderson (Ed.) New York: Harper, 1959, pp. 83–95.

Mattil, E. L. A study to determine the relationship between the creative products of children, aged 11–14, and their adjustments. Unpubl. doctoral dissertation. Penna. State Univ., 1953.

May, R. The nature of creativity. In *Creativity and its Cultivation,* H. Anderson (Ed.) New York: Harper, 1959, pp. 55–68.

Meer, B., and M. I. Stein. "Measures of intelligence and creativity." *J. Psychol.,* 1955, **39,** 117–126.

Mooney, R. L. *Classification of items in "A preliminary listing of indices of creative behavior."* Columbus: Ohio State Univ., Bureau of educ. Res., 1953 (a).

Mooney, R. L. *A preliminary listing of indices of creative behavior.* Columbus: Ohio State Univ., Bureau of Educ. Res., 1953 (b).

Münsterberg, Elizabeth, and P. H. Mussen. "The personality structures of art students." *J. Pers.,* 1953, **21,** 457–466.

Murphy, G. *Personality: A Biosocial Approach to Origins and Structure.* New York: Harper, 1947.

Murphy, G. *Human Potentialities.* New York: Basic Books, 1958.

Myden, W. "Interpretation and evaluation of certain personality characteristics involved in creative production." *Percept. mot. Skills,* 1959, **9,** 139–158.

Rank, O., and H. Sachs. *The Significance of Psychoanalysis for the Mental Sciences.* Washington, D.C.: Nervous & Mental Disease Publishing Company, 1916.

Reid, J. B., F. J. King, and Pat Wickwire. "Cognitive and other personality characteristics of creative children." *Psychol. Rep.,* 1959, **5,** 729–737.

Rickman, J. On the nature of ugliness and the creative impulse. (Orig. publ. 1940) In *Selected Contributions to Psychoanalysis,* W. Clifford and M. Scott (Eds.) London: Hogarth, 1957, pp. 68–89.

Roe, Anne. "Artists and their work." *J. Pers.,* 1946, **15,** 1–40.

Roe, Anne. "Psychological examinations of eminent biologists." *J. consult. Psychol.,* 1949, **13,** 225–246.

Roe, Anne. "A psychological study of eminent biologists." *Psychol. Monogr.,* 1951, **65** (14, whole no. 331).

Roe, Anne. *The Making of a Scientist.* New York: Dodd-Mead, 1952.

Roe, Anne. "A psychological study of eminent psychologists and anthropologists and a comparison with biological and physical scientists." *Psychol. Monogr.,* 1953, **67** (2, whole no. 352).

Rogers, C. R. "Toward a theory of creativity." *Etc.,* 1954, **11,** 249–260.

Rogers, C. R. What it means to become a person. In *The Self,* C. Moustakas (Ed.) New York: Harper, 1956, pp. 195–211.

Rosen, J. C. "The Barron-Welsh art scale as a predictor of originality and level of ability among artists." *J. appl. Psychol.,* 1955, **39,** 366–367.

Sachs, H. *The Creative Unconscious.* (2d ed.) Cambridge, Mass.: Science-Art Publishers, 1951.

Schachtel, E. G. *Metamorphosis.* New York: Basic Books, 1959.

Sharpe, Ella F. Certain aspects of sublimation and delusion." *Int. J. Psychoanal.,* 1930, **11,** 12–23.

Sharpe, Ella F. Similar and divergent unconscious determinants underlying the sublimations of pure art and pure science. In *Collected Papers on Psychoanalysis,* M. Brierly (Ed.) London: Hogarth, 1950, pp. 137–154.

Spielberger, C. D. "The role of awareness in verbal conditioning." *J. Pers.,* 1962, **30,** 73–101.

Stein, M. I. "Creativity and culture." *J. Psychol.,* 1953, **36,** 311–322.

Stein, M. I. A transactional approach to creativity. In *The 1955 University of Utah Research Conference on the Identification of Creative Scientific Talent,* C. Taylor (Ed.) Salt Lake City: Univ. Utah Press, 1956, pp. 171–181.

Stein, M., and Shirley Heinze. *Creativity and the Individual.* Glencoe, Ill.: Free Press, 1960.

Stein, M. I., and B. Meer. "Perceptual organization in a study of creativity." *J. Psychol.,* 1954, **37,** 39–43.

Taylor, C. (Ed.) *The 1959 University of Utah Research Conference on the Identification of Creative Scientific Talent.* Salt Lake City: Univ. Utah Press, 1959.

Taylor, C. W., W. R. Smith, and B. Ghiselin. Analysis of multiple criteria of creativity and productivity of scientists. In *The 1959 University of Utah Research Conference on the Identification of Creative Scientific Talent,* C. Taylor (Ed.) Salt Lake City: Univ. Utah Press, 1959, pp. 5–28.

Taylor, D. W. Variables related to creativity and productivity among men in two research laboratories. In *The 1957 University of Utah Research Conference on the Identification of Creative Scientific Talent,* C. Taylor (Ed.) Salt Lake City: Univ. Utah Press, 1958, pp. 20–54.

Taylor, D. W. "Thinking and creativity." *Ann. N.Y. Acad. Sci.,* 1960, **91,** 108–127.

Taylor, D. W. Environment and creativity. In *Conference on the Creative Person.* Berkeley: Univ. Calif., Inst. pers. Assessment and Res., 1961 (chap. 8).

Taylor, I. A. The nature of the creative process. In *Creativity,* P. Smith (Ed.) New York: Hastings, 1959, pp. 51–82.

Torrance, E. P. *Sex-role Identification and Creative Thinking.* Minneapolis: Univ. of Minn., Bureau of educ. Res., 1958.

Torrance, E. P. *Explorations in creative thinking in the early school years:* II. *An experiment in training and motivation.* Minneapolis: Univ. Minn., Bureau of educ. Res., 1959 (a).

Torrance, E. P. *Explorations in creative thinking in the early school years:* V. *An experimental study of peer sanctions against highly creative children.* Minneapolis: Univ. Minn., Bureau of educ., Res. 1959 (b).

Torrance, E. P. *Explorations in creative thinking in the early school years:* VI. *Highly intelligent and highly creative children in a laboratory school.* Minneapolis: Univ. Minn., Bureau of educ. Res., 1959 (c).

Torrance, E. P. *Explorations in creative thinking in the early school years:* VII. *Talkativeness and creative thinking.* Minneapolis: Univ. Minn., Bureau of educ. Res., 1959 (d).

Torrance, E. P. Explorations in creative thinking in the early school years: A progress report. In *The 1959 University of Utah Research Conference on the Identification of Creative Scientific Talent,* C. Taylor (Ed.) Salt Lake City: Univ. Utah Press, 1959, pp. 58–71 (e).

Torrance, E. P. *Changing reactions of girls in grades four through six to tasks requiring creative scientific thinking.* Minneapolis: Univ. Minn., Bureau of educ. Res., 1960 (a).

Torrance, E. P. *A collection of ideas for developing the creative thinking abilities through the language arts.* Minneapolis: Univ. Minn., Bureau of educ. Res., 1960 (b).

Torrance, E. P. *Educational achievement of the highly intelligent and the highly creative: Eight partial replications of the Getzels-Jackson study.* Minneapolis: Univ. Minn., Bureau of educ. Res., 1960 (c).

Torrance, E. P. *Social Stress in Homogeneous and Heterogeneous Groups.* Minneapolis: Univ. Minn., Bureau of educ. Res., 1960 (d).

Torrance, E. P., F. B. Baker, and J. E. Bowers. *Explorations in creative thinking in the early school years:* IV. *Manipulation of objects and inventiveness.* Minneapolis: Univ. Minn., Bureau of educ. Res., 1959.

Torrance, E. P., and H. J. Radig. *The Ask and Guess Test: Scoring manual and rationale.* Minneapolis: Univ. Minn., Bureau of educ. Res., 1959.

VanZelst, R. H., and W. A. Kerr. "Personality self-assessment of scientific and technical personnel." *J. appl. Psychol.,* 1954, **38,** 145–147.

Wallas, G. *The art of Thought.* New York: Harcourt, Brace, 1926.

Welsh, G. S. A projective figure-preference test for diagnosis of psychopathology: I. A preliminary investigation. Unpubl. doctoral dissertation. Univ. Minn., 1949.

Welsh, G. S. *Preliminary manual: Welsh Figure Preference Test.* (Res. ed.) Palo Alto, Calif.: Consulting Psychologists Press, 1959 (a).

Welsh, G. S. *Welsh Figure Preference Test.* (Res. ed.) Palo Alto, Calif.: Consulting Psychologists Press, 1959 (b).

Woodworth, R. S., and H. Schlossberg. *Experimental Psychology.* (2d ed.) New York: Holt, 1954.

Yacorzynski, G. K. The nature of man. In *Aspects of Culture and Personality,* F. L. K. Hsu (Ed.) New York: Abelard-Schuman, 1954, pp. 173–186.

4.5 Orientation

One characteristic of exploratory research is that it frequently leads to the identification of relationships somewhat removed from an investigator's original objectives. Such has been the case in this study of the relationship between somatotype and conceptual behavior among children. Kagan and his colleagues several years ago began studying children's cognitive styles. Their research led them to describe a dimension involving the tendency to analyze and differentiate the stimulus field as opposed to the strategy of categorizing percepts which is based upon the stimulus field as a whole. Eventually instruments were devised which measured individual differences in the extent to which children make analytic responses to stimulus material. An analytic response mode is said to be characterized by a *reflective,* as opposed to a more *impulsive,* attitude. It is with this latter element of conceptual behavior that Kagan's paper deals.

Somatotype theory, to which Kagan refers in establishing correlates of conceptual behavior, maintains that certain bodily conformations are associated with specific personality characteristics; it is perhaps one of the most controversial theoretical positions in psychology. Originally developed in European psychological circles, its utilization has been less widespread in America.

The Davidson *et al.* (1957) and Hanley (1951) papers listed below are examples of studies that apply somatotype theory to children's behavior.

RECOMMENDED READING

Davidson, M. A., R. G. McInness, and R. W. Parnell. "The distribution of personality traits in seven-year-old children: A combined psychological, psychiatric, and somatotype study." *Brit. J. educ. Psychol.,* **127** (1957), 48–61.

Hanley, C. "Physique and reputation of junior high boys." *Child Develpm.,* **22** (1951), 247–60.

Kagan, J. "Reflection—impulsivity and reading ability in primary grade children." *Child Develpm.,* **36** (1965), 609–628.

Kagan, J. "Individual differences in the resolution of response uncertainty." *J. pers. soc. Psychol.,* **2** (1965), 154–60.

Kagan, J. *et al.* "Information processing in the child: significance of analytic and reflective attitudes." *Psychol. Monogr.,* **78** (1964), 1–37.

4.5 Body-Build and Conceptual Impulsivity in Children

Jerome Kagan, HARVARD UNIVERSITY

Interest in the psychological correlates of physique variables has a long and episodic history. Ever since Hippocrates postulated the *habitus phthisicus* and the *habitus apoplecticus,* man has displayed temporary spurts of in-

Reprinted from *Journal of Personality,* **34** (1966), 118–128. By permission of the author and the Duke University Press.

quiry into a possible relation between the shape of a person's body and his behavior. In contemporary social science, the decade between 1917 and 1927 produced considerable work on this provocative problem, for it was during this period that Kretschmer postulated the asthenic, athletic, and pyknic body types (Kretschmer, 1925).

A generation later Sheldon (1942) published an essay on physique and temperament, substituting ectomorph, endomorph, and mesomorph for Kretschmer's trio. There was little interest in this area during and immediately after the war, but recently, a generation after Sheldon's work, investigators have once again revealed their basic attraction to this problem. The hardiness of this class of empirical inquiry suggests that the relationship between body shape and behavior is probably not artifactual. In general, the data are more consistent than inconsistent, although associations are often tentative and fragile. The focus of unrest derives from the interpretation of the findings rather than from the raw data. No systematic review of the enormous literature on this problem will be attempted. The reader is referred to Eysenck (1947), Sheldon (1942), and Sanford, Adkins, Miller, and Cobb (1943).

Although there is considerable and heated disagreement over the significance of an association between physique and behavior, the evidence suggests slight positive associations between a build that is short and broad with traits resembling friendliness, moodiness, aggression, and impulsivity, or between a build that is tall and narrow with the traits of introversion, inhibition, and obsession.

Rationale

We did not initially intend to study body build as part of our inquiry into the significance of conceptual reflection—impulsivity, but we were led to it by informal observations that suggested that boys with short-wide body builds tended to be more impulsive on tests with response uncertainty than tall-thin boys. We speculated that the impulsive child might perceive himself as *shorter* than his actual height, and the anxiety created by this belief might have led him to a tendency toward impulsivity. This paper summarizes three independent attempts to assess the relation between conceptual impulsivity, on the one hand, and body build on the other.

Masurements of Reflection-Impulsivity

The reflection-impulsivity dimension describes the degree to which a child reflects upon the differential validity of alternative solution hypotheses in situations where many response possibilities are available simultaneously (Kagan, Rosman, Day, Albert, and Phillips, 1964). In these problem situations the children with fast tempos impulsively report the first hypothesis that occurs to them, and this response is typically incorrect. The reflective child, on the other hand, delays a long time before reporting a solution hypothesis and is usually correct. The reflective child considers the alternatives available to him and evaluates their differential validity. The most sensitive test for this variable is a device called Matching Familiar Figures. In this test the child is shown a picture of a familiar object (the standard) and six similar stimuli, only one of which is identical to the standard. Figure 1 illustrates two sample items.

The *S* is asked to select the one stimulus that is identical to the standard. The standard and six variations are always available to the *S*. The major variables scored are number of errors and the average response time to the first selection for the 12 test items. There is typically a negative correlation (in the sixties) between response time and number of errors. Children who delay before offering their first answer make fewer errors. Moreover, with age, there is a linear increase in response time and a decrease in errors. A child is classified as impulsive if he is above the median on errors and below the median on response time for a large group of children his own age and grade. A reflective child is one whose response times are above the median and his error score below the median.

STUDY I

Method

A large group of third-grade children was administered the MFF, together with other tests, in a single session by a male or female examiner. Each *S*'s height and chest girth (in inches) were also measured. Three measures of each bodily dimension were taken and the average of the three was the score used in the analyses. *S*s came from two different schools in the same city, with a population of about 50,000. All *S*s were Caucasian and there were no special minority or ethnic groups present in the population. The distributions of height and girth were split at the median for *each sex* and *each school population* separately (four different distributions in all). Each *S* was then categorized as falling into one of four cells: tall and broad, tall and narrow, short and broad, short and narrow.

Perception of body image Each *S* was shown an array of nine silhouettes that represented nine basic body builds of *S*s between nine and 10 years of age. The silhouettes were of three heights (43, 50, and 58 inches) and three chest girths (10, 13, and 16 inches). Each height was matched with each girth, yielding a total of nine silhouettes. The *S* was placed 18 inches from the nine randomly arranged silhouettes and asked to select the one that was *most like his own body*.

Each child was classified as reflective or impulsive based on his performance on the Matching Familiar Figures test. The distributions for speed and errors were split at the median; *S*s who were above the median on *speed* and *errors* were classified as impulsive, and *S*s who were below the

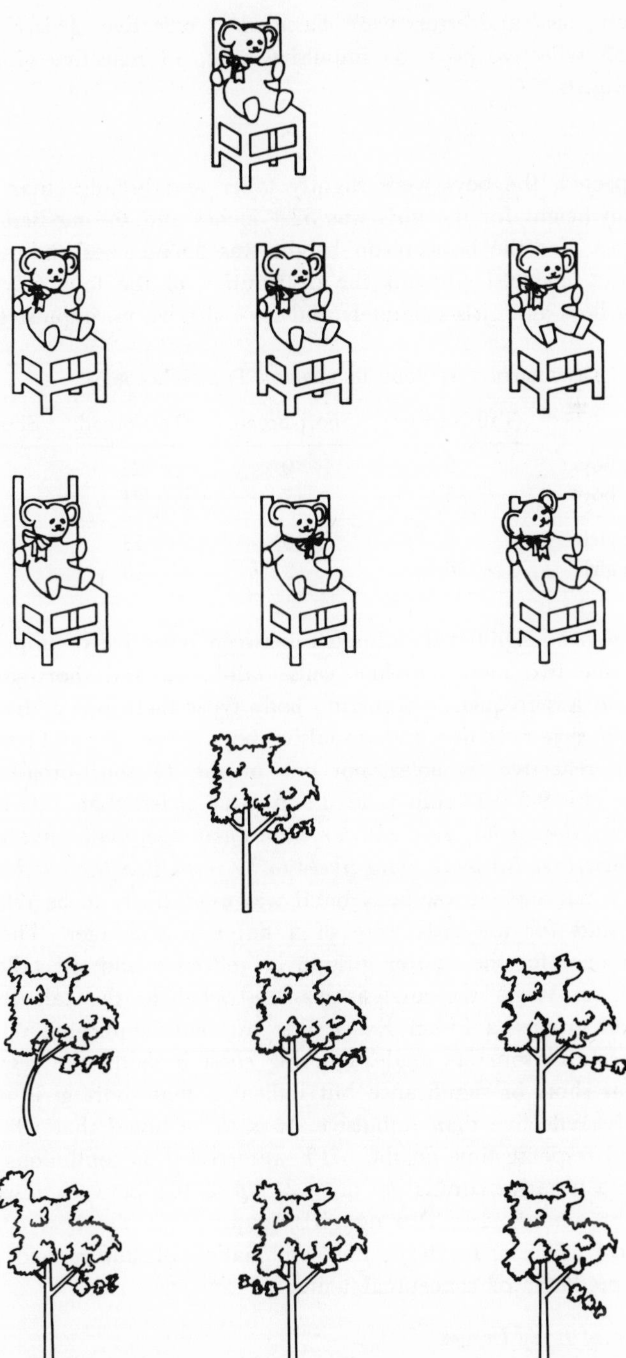

FIGURE 1. Sample items from Matching Familiar Figures (MFF) test.

median on *speed* and *errors* were classified as reflective. This classification yielded 53 reflective boys, 63 impulsive boys, 43 reflective girls, and 39 impulsive girls.

Results

As expected, the boys were slightly taller and broader than the girls. The mean height for the girls was 52.4 inches and the median girth was 13.1 inches. For the boys, mean height was 53.3 inches and mean girth 13.3 inches. Table 1 presents the distribution of the four types of body builds for boys and girls separately and for reflective vs. impulsive children.

TABLE 1. Distribution of Body Builds for Third-Grade *S*s.

	Tall-Narrow	Short-Broad	Tall-Broad	Short-Narrow
Reflective boys	9	0	22	22
Impulsive boys	5	17	21	20
Reflective girls	6	10	13	17
Impulsive girls	6	2	18	13

There was no significant difference between reflective or impulsive children for the two most populous cells—tall-broad and short-narrow. But for the two less frequently occurring body types there was a dramatic difference between reflective and impulsive boys. Nine of the 14 tall-narrow boys were reflective; whereas, not one of the 17 short-broad boys was reflective. This 9-5-0-17 split yielded a p value of less than .001 by Fisher's Exact Test. *Boys who were shorter than their age mates but of slightly greater chest breadth were more likely to be impulsive than reflective.* The boy with a tall and narrow body build was more likely to be reflective.

The results for the girls were of a different character. There was a slight tendency for the shorter girls to be reflective and the taller girls to be impulsive. When the analysis was restricted to the tall-narrow and short-broad groups, a Fisher Exact Test was not significant. When a tall vs. short comparison was made, ignoring chest breadth, the resulting chi-square was short of significance but indicated that short girls were more likely to be reflective than impulsive. It is to be noted that when the *S*'s height and response time on the MFF were coded as continuous variables, there was a negative correlation of $-.21$ ($p < .10$) between response time and height among girls. Among girls, stature was the best correlate of impulsivity; whereas, for boys, the combination of stature and girth was the best predictor of conceptual tempo.

Perception of Body Image

In general, *S*s were relatively accurate in selecting the silhouette that matched their height and girth; the mean differences between actual stature and stature of silhouette hovered around one inch. In order to assess the degree of distortion, each *S*'s actual height and girth were subtracted from the height and girth of the silhouette the *S* chose to represent himself. The mean discrepancies for reflective and impulsive children were compared for each of the four categories of body build.

The impulsive boys were prone to perceive themselves as shorter than reflective boys of similar stature, but the differences in discrepancy scores between reflective and impulsive boys were not significant. In a second analysis the frequency of selection of a silhouette that was five or more inches shorter than the *S*'s actual height or three or more inches taller than *S*'s actual height was tallied. These criterion values represented the top and bottom 10 per cent of the distribution of discrepancy scores. Eleven reflective *S*s and 14 impulsive *S*s (from a total of 109 cases) met one of these criteria. Of the 11 reflectives, seven selected silhouettes taller than themselves and four selected silhouettes shorter. Of the 14 impulsives, only three selected taller silhouettes, while 11 selected shorter silhouettes. This 4-11-7-3 distribution yielded a probability value of less than .05 using Fisher's Exact Test. Thus, when the analysis was limited to extreme distortions in selection of silhouettes, the impulsives perceived themselves as shorter and the reflective boys as taller than their actual statures.

The results for the girls were equivocal. The tall, reflective girls picked silhouettes that were shorter than they were; the short, reflective girls picked silhouettes taller than they were. It appears that the reflective girls selected forms less extreme than their actual statures.

The favored interpretation of these data rests on the assumption that the 10-year-old child is aware of the desirability of specific body types appropriate to his sex. Boys should be tall, girls should be small. The boy who is shorter than his peers is apt to develop feelings of impotence and inadequacy as a result of two related sets of experiences. First, the daily comparison between his height and that of his peers will lead to a negative self-evaluation. The short boy will not be able to reach as high or throw as far as his peers, and these skills are critical for the preadolescent boy. Second, it is likely that the shorter boy will be defeated in fights with age mates and suffer the humiliation and anxiety over potency that are the sequellae of such defeats. However, impulsivity is more characteristic of the short boy with a broad chest breadth rather than the short boy with a narrow girth. How can this difference be explained? It is suggested that the two fundamental reactions to anxiety are retreat or retaliation. An impulsive orientation is basically retaliative. The impulsive child does not withdraw from the risks of failure, and he tends to minimize the potential danger associated with risky responses. It is possible that the extra muscle mass possessed by the short-broad boy, in contrast to the short-narrow boy, facilitated the attainment of instrumental successes that the short boy of more fragile build did not attain. At a more speculative level, it is possible that the extra muscle mass is responsible directly for promptings to action that form one base for impulsivity.

The notion that impulsivity springs, in part, from anxiety over adequacy, with body image being an essential component of personal adequacy, is supported by the girls' data. Among girls of this age there is a growing awareness that girls are supposed to be small rather than large. Thus, one might expect impulsive girls to be taller and larger than reflective girls, and the data support this prediction. More of the short girls were reflective, while more impulsive girls were tall and broad.

This argument assumes that boys wish to be tall and girls wish to be small, and additional data support this position. Three to five months after the children were seen for the session in which they selected the silhouettes that best represented them, they were again shown the nine silhouettes and asked to pick the *one they would most like to be.* There was minimal variability in their choices, and there were no differences between reflective and impulsive children. Some 79 per cent of the boys chose the tallest figure, and 21 per cent chose the figure of medium height. Not one boy chose the short silhouettes. This finding supports the previous interpretation that boys value height and place a negative evaluation on short stature. Among the girls there was also a general tendency to value height, for 64 per cent chose the tallest figure, 28 per cent the figure of medium height, and 8 per cent the short figure. There was no difference between impulsive or reflective girls on the silhouette chosen to represent their ideal. Although the girls' modal choice seems to indicate that girls also value height, it is to be noted that there was a significant sex difference in choice of the short and medium figures. Only 21 per cent of the boys chose one of the two shorter figures in contrast to 37 per cent of the girls (chi square = 7.03; $p < .05$), suggesting a stronger tendency among girls than boys to view small stature as an ideal attribute.

STUDY II

Replication on Actual Body Build

Additional data support the relation between body build and the reflection-impulsivity dimension. A second study included a group of fourth- and fifth-grade children who had been given the MFF and classified as reflective or impulsive on the basis of their response times and errors. Table 2 shows the distribution of body builds for the reflective and impulsive children.

Once again, the short-broad boys were impulsive and the tall-thin boys reflective. The 4-2-1-5 distribution yielded an exact probability of .12. However when the girth dimension was collapsed and only height considered, 70 per cent of the impulsives were short, whereas only 25 per cent of the reflectives were short ($p < .05$ by exact test). The data for the girls supported the earlier findings. The reflective girls were shorter than the impulsives, but these results were not significant.

TABLE 2. Distribution of Body Builds for Fourth-Grade and Fifth-Grade Children

	Tall-Narrow	Short-Broad	Tall-Broad	Short-Narrow
Reflective boys	4	1	5	2
Impulsive boys	2	5	3	6
Reflective girls	2	4	5	5
Impulsive girls	4	1	2	2

STUDY III

Replication on First-Grade Ss

The interpretation of the relation between body size and impulsivity rests primarily on the notion that preadolescent boys have learned anxieties over potency as a result of direct encounters with peers and knowledge of the ideal male physique as presented by the culture. This set of assumptions suggests that this relation may not obtain for younger children (say, ages six to seven), for the six year old is probably not yet aware of the positive value placed on size for males. This assumption was put to test in a final study.

Method

Each of the 155 first-grade children from four different public schools in Newton, Massachusetts, was given the MFF by one of three female examiners. In addition, the height and chest girth of each child was assessed. *S*s were classified as impulsive or reflective using the criteria described earlier. The impulsive child was above the median on errors and below the median on response time, while the reflective child was below the median on errors and above the median on response time. Children were classified into the four basic body types.

Results

Table 3 presents the distribution of body types for reflective and impulsive children, keeping sexes separate. There was no significant association between height or height-girth and reflection-impulsivity for boys. The data for girls were unusual. The reflectives were tall and broad and the impulsives short and narrow, this being the first time such an association occurred.

TABLE 3. Distribution of Body Builds for First-Grade Children

	Tall-Narrow	Short-Broad	Tall-Broad	Short-Narrow
Reflective boys	3	5	14	15
Impulsive boys	7	4	8	12
Reflective girls	5	5	16	6
Impulsive girls	4	5	9	15

SUMMARY AND DISCUSSION

The most reliable finding was that boys in the third, fourth, or fifth grades who were shorter and broader than their age mates were more likely to be impulsive than reflective. Moreover, impulsive boys in the third grade tended to perceive themselves as shorter than reflective boys of similar bodily proportions.

The suggested interpretation of these data is that the typical boy of ages eight through 10 places a strong positive value upon height, and the boy who is shorter than his peers is more anxious over his strength and potency (e.g., his ability to defend himself, his ability to compete successfully in gross motor games and skills) than the taller, larger boy of similar social class or mental ability. This anxiety is probably chronic, for a discrepant height is omnipresent during every part of the child's waking day. It was assumed, further, that the boy's defensive reaction to this anxiety depended, in part, on the degree to which he experienced occasional success as a result of attempts to be successful in peer-valued tasks. The short-narrow boy with minimal muscle mass is likely to be least successful, and as a result he is likely to withdraw from this competition. The short-broad boy with more muscle mass is likely to experience occasional success in peer-valued skills, and these reinforcements should help to establish a habit of attempted competitive involvement. The assumptions above lead to the prediction that the short-broad boy is anxious over his potency but predisposed to act in a way that denies or attenuates this anxiety. An impulsive orientation in problems with high response uncertainty is a reasonable reaction to expect from such a boy. The boy is threatened by not being able to supply an answer immediately and is not able to tolerate the time required to select the best possible answer. He must act, for action has been a successful method of gaining success.

The less dramatic and less consistent results for girls agree with the general assumption that body size is not as salient an attribute for the young girl as it is for the boy. However, the older girls' data argue for the importance of congruence between sex-typed body build and reflection. The lack of a relation between body build and reflection among first-grade boys is congruent with the hypothesis that the negative evaluation attached to sex-role standards for stature has not been acquired this early in development.

Alternative Interpretations

It is possible to argue that the relationship between a short-broad build and impulsivity has strong biological correlates over and above the psychodynamic interpretation outlined above. Recent work at the Gesell Clinic by Walker (1962) indicates that preschool children with mesomorphic body builds tend to be more aggressive and more active than children with tall-linear builds. It is not likely that children this age would have learned the sex-role association between stature and potency. Thus, the Walker data argue for the possibility of biological variables influencing the association between build and behavior.

In sum, this report presents still another instance of a relation between body build and behavioral variables. Although the author favors an interpretation based on the assumption of the establishment of attitudes toward the self as a function of body build, it is not possible to rule out completely the possible influence of complex physiological factors that are antecedent to both body build and the behavioral variables.

REFERENCES

Eysenck, H. J. *Dimensions of Personality.* London: Kegan Paul, 1947.

Kagan, J., B. C. Rosman, J. Albert, and W. Phillips. "Information processing in the child: Significance of analytic reflective attitudes." *Psychol. Monogr.*, **78** (1964), no. 578.

Kretschmer, E. *Physique and Character.* New York: Harcourt, Brace, 1925.

Sanford, R. W., M. M. Adkins, R. B. Muller, and E. Cobb. "Physique, personality and scholarship." *Monogr. Soc. Res. child Develpm.*, **7** (1943), no. 34.

Sheldon, W. H. *The Varieties of Temperament.* New York: Harper, 1942.

Walker, R. N. "Body build and behavior in young children." *Monogr. Soc. Res. child Develpm.*, **27** (1962), no. 84.

4.6 Orientation

Judging from recent research reports, developmental psychologists have maintained a strong interest in the relationship between the motor behavior and intelligence of children. These reports have yielded conflicting results, however, primarily because of lack of experimental controls, differences in tasks, and measurement techniques used. The authors of the following study have utilized previous and sometimes conflicting research findings to develop a hypothesis concerning intelligence, motor activity, and response inhibition during problem solving. Their results suggest that successful problem solving among four- and five-year-olds depends in large part upon their ability to inhibit expressive movement and that this inhibition is specific as to duration and situation.

The above finding is significant when compared with a recent analysis of developmental changes in learning, perception, spatial orientation, and intellectual functioning (White, 1965). White's review of developmental data in these four areas and his synthesis of theoretical formulations on cognition led him to suggest that children in the five-to-seven age period are shifting from an associative level of mental functioning to a higher level cognitive mode. A major distinction between the two levels is that more advanced cognitive functioning is predicated, at least in part, upon the child's ability to inhibit impulsive, and frequently maladaptive, responses. Such responses are often termed *first-available responses* and are considered to be the product of a long history of associative learning.

In addition to the results, the Maccoby *et al.* study reported here describes the use of the actometer, an extremely useful instrument for measuring the motor activity of school children. It also describes a set of unique tasks developed for this study, tasks that call for the slow emission of motor responses. Other advantages of the study are the authors' cautionary interpretation of their results and the suggestions they advance for further research. This paper, taken with Kagan's study on body-build and conceptual impulsivity lends support to the general principle that *all aspects of development interact.*

RECOMMENDED READING

White, Sheldon. Evidence for a hierarchal arrangement of learning processes. In *Advances in Child Development and Behavior,* Lewis P. Lipsitt and Charles C. Spiker (Eds.) (vol. 2) New York: Academic Press, 1965, pp. 187–220.

4.6 Activity Level and Intellectual Functioning in Normal Preschool Children

Eleanor E. Maccoby, STANFORD UNIVERSITY
Edith M. Dowley, STANFORD UNIVERSITY
John W. Hagen, STANFORD UNIVERSITY
Richard Degerman, JOHN HOPKINS UNIVERSITY

It would be reasonable to expect that the child who is most active in exploring his environment during the early years when certain basic perceptual and motor skills are laid down would be the child who shows the most rapid intellectual development. He ought to have a larger store of appropriate learning sets for transfer to new learning situations and ought to have become sensitized to a greater variety of perceptual distinctions which will be relevant to a number of intellectual functions.

Several studies with animals indicate that depriving animals of the opportunity for active exploration during their early developmental period results in lowered performance on animal "intelligence tests" (Forgays and Forgays, 1952; Hunt, 1961, pp. 100–102, 315, 316). Among preschool children, Lois Murphy (1962) reports positive correlations between activity and measures of the "capacity to cope with the environment." Witkin, Dyk, Faterson, Goodenough, and Karp (1962) have found one aspect of activity—"assertiveness, striving, an interest in being active"—to be correlated with "field independence," a facet of intellectual performance that has been found to be positively correlated with WISC measures of performance IQ (though not with verbal IQ). Sontag, Baker, and Nelson (1958), in a longitudinal study, found passivity to be associated with declining IQ. These investigators did not have a direct measure of activity level, but they did find that aggressiveness, competitiveness, independence, and self-initiation (all "active" traits) were positively correlated with gains in IQ.

In contrast, several studies in which activity level was directly measured have found *negative* correlations between activity and measures of intellectual ability. Grinsted (1939) studied children in grades 1-7 and 11. Using a time-sampling technique, he observed children in the classroom, recording whether a child was or was not moving during each of the moments when an observation was taken. Grinsted reports a correlation of $-.52$ between the amount of movement and IQ, and when age was partialled out, this correlation rose to $-.81$. A number of investigators have studied activity level among retardates on the hypothesis that hyperactivity is a

Reprinted from *Child Devlopment,* **36** (1965), 761–770. By permission of the authors and The Society for Research in Child Development, Inc.

symptom of brain damage. Cromwell, Palk and Foshee (1961) measured activity level with a ballistograph during a conditioning session for a group of extremely retarded subjects (mean IQ was 34.6) and found a correlation of −.57 between IQ and the amount of movement during the conditioning session. In an earlier study with retardates, Foshee (1958) also found the more active subjects to have lower IQ's.

Schulman, Kasper, and Throne (1965) failed to find any relation between activity and IQ among a group of retarded boys whose IQ's ranged from 36 to 77. In this study, activity was measured with "actometers" (described below), which were worn by the subjects through a full day of normal activity.

Kagan, Moss, and Sigel (1963) studied "analytic style"—again, an aspect of intellectual functioning which is correlated more consistently with performance than with verbal IQ. Case studies of children who later proved to be analytic in their mode of dealing with stimulus materials revealed that during early childhood these children tended to be quiet, contemplative, willing to play alone for extended periods, and likely to approach new situations cautiously rather than impulsively. They were not especially active children, in comparison with the children who later proved to be non-analytic in their perceptions.

It may be seen, then, that the literature provides some instances in which the more active children are brighter and more competent and other instances in which it is the *less* active children who have higher IQ's or perform better on certain kinds of tasks which relate to a component of intelligence. The relation between activity and intellectual performance evidently depends upon the situation in which activity is measured and what kind of activity is being recorded. General bodily activity is sometimes functional for the achievement of the individual's goals (e.g., in Murphy's observations, 1962); sometimes it is not (Cromwell *et al.*, 1961; Grinsted, 1939)—indeed such movement would probably interfere directly with the performance of certain tasks. In this connection it is interesting to note that restless movement has a consistent relation to the course of problem solving. Grinsted studied a group of subjects who were seated in a chair that recorded bodily movements while they solved mental problems. He found that least movement occurred just at the point when a solution to the problem was being reached. Movement was high after successful solution or when the subject gave up his attempts to solve a problem that proved too difficult. Belazs (1938) also reports increased movement when difficulty is encountered during the problem-solving process. Of course, we do not know whether the increase in restless activity during problem-solving difficulties is a result or a cause of the difficulties—perhaps it is both to some degree. But at least these findings would be consistent with the hypothesis that the inhibition of certain kinds of movement is a necessary condition for the solution of problems that do not themselves call for physical activity.

Does this imply that the child who is skillful in solving intellectual problems will have a lower general activity level in a variety of situations? There is a suggestion in the work of psychoanalytic writers that this should be the case. Escalona and Heider (1959, p. 237), for example, argue that a high general activity level tends to reflect either an unusual intensity of impulse or unusually weak mechanisms of impulse control and modulation and that either of these is inimical to the development of abstract thought.

We suggest that the inhibition of expressive movement which must occur for successful problem-solving may be highly specific both as to situation and duration. Periods of inhibition of movement are very likely to be followed by periods of expressive activity—perhaps they *must* be, for the sake of releasing muscular tensions which are built up during periods of inactivity (Johnson, 1931). The successful problem solver, then, probably does not engage in less total bodily activity over an extended period of time; he merely modulates, or regulates, his activity, so that expressive activity is inhibited during crucial points of problem-solving where it might constitute an interference and so that it occurs at other moments when it is not incompatible with other on-going activity. It is likely, of course, that brighter children will spend more of their time engaged in organized, instrumental sequences of behavior than will less bright children; hence, time-sampling of activity ought to show that a higher proportion of the activity of the more intelligent children is instrumental rather than purely expressive. But this does not mean that their total activity would be less. Indeed, as noted earlier, it is reasonable to expect that exploratory behavior and motor trial-and-error are positive factors for intellectual development, so that the brighter children should be *more* active on measures of total activity, while at the same time being able to inhibit movement when engaged in a task that requires such inhibition.

This analysis would resolve an apparent contradiction in previously cited findings: namely, that studies that measured activity during problem-solving (Cromwell *et al.,* 1961; Grinsted, 1939) obtained negative correlations between activity and IQ, while no such correlation was obtained in a study measuring total activity level throughout a day that presumably involved both problem-solving and free-play situations (Schulman *et al.,* 1965).

In the present study, both total activity during a half-day nursery-school session and the ability to inhibit movement under a task set that requires it have been measured with nursery-school subjects. These activity measures have been related to two measures of intellectual ability. On the basis of an assumption that, in the "permissive" nursery school where the research was done, the proportion of time when inhibition of gross motor activity would be required for school routine is relatively small, it is predicted that total gross motor activity will be *positively* related to intellectual proficiency. Further, it is predicted that the ability to inhibit motor activity when required wll also be positively related to ability scores. These predictions imply, then, that the most intelligent children will be those with the greatest discrepancies between their free-play activity scores (which will be high) and their inhibition test scores (where their amount of movement will be low).

Work by Sigel (1963) has indicated that the sexes may differ in the way impulsive movement is related to performance on an intellectual task. We have therefore analyzed the data for the two sexes separately.

METHOD

Subjects

The subjects were 21 boys and 20 girls attending the Stanford Village Nursery school. Many of the *S*s were children of Stanford graduate students, although there was an admixture of children from the "town." We selected a fairly narrow age range—all *S*s were between their fourth and fifth birthdays. Their average IQ was 135; the range of IQ's was from 95 to 154, with an SD of 13.7. Thus, although the average intelligence of the *S* population was high, the range was not unduly restricted.

Ability Tests

The Stanford-Binet intelligence test was administered to all *S*s. Since some of the work cited above had suggested a relation between the activity-passivity dimension and nonverbal functions such as field-independent perceiving (Witkin *et al.*, 1962) and analytic ability (Kagan, *et al.*, 1963; Sigel, 1963) we administered the Children's Embedded Figures Test (CEFT) to determine whether this specific area of function was especially closely related to activity or to its inhibition. The CEFT, developed by Karp and Kornstadt (1963), is a children's version of the Embedded Figures Test employed by Witkin and his colleagues (1962). The CEFT was individually administered to our *S*s.

General Activity Level

We used the actometer, a device for measuring activity, which was developed by Schulman and his colleagues (1959). The actometer is a self-winding calendar watch with the timing mechanism removed. The hands on the dial reflect the amount of movement of the part of the body to which the watch is attached. One actometer was strapped onto the *S*'s wrist, another onto his ankle. The measurements, then, do not reflect head movements or finger movements, but only movements in which the arms and legs are involved. Each *S* wore his actometers on a single occasion for approximately two hours, through most of a regular nursery-school session. Two pairs of watches were used, and measures were taken on two children per session. Watches were set to zero at the beginning of the measurement period. "Clock" time was also recorded at the beginning and end of the period, and the activity scores were the amount of actometer time per unit clock time. The variability of actometer scores was high: for example, the raw arm scores for girls ranged from 32.6 to 206.3 "hours" of actometer time.

For reliability measures, 15 boys and 13 girls (a subgroup of the primary sample) wore the actometers during two different nursery-school sessions, 7–14 days apart.

Test-retest reliabilities were lower for boys than for girls, with the boys' scores yielding a reliability of only .31 for arm measurements and .22 for leg measurements, while the comparable girls' reliabilities were .76 and .44. Inspection of the scatter plots indicated that one male *S* who had been one of the most active *S*s during one session was one of the least active in the other—perhaps because of illness or some other temporary condition. With this one case eliminated, the reliabilities of the boys' scores were .65 and .53 for the arm and leg scores, respectively. It is a curious fact that the arm and leg scores were more closely related for boys than for girls—among boys, the two scores correlated .92, and for girls, .66. Standard scores were computed for leg and arm measures separately, and these scores were added to provide a total activity score for each *S*.

Inhibition of Movement

Out of four inhibition of movement tests (devised by Hagen and Degerman) which were pretested, three were chosen.

1. The "Draw a Line Slowly" Test: This test consisted of a picture of two telephone poles with three wires between them and a fourth wire conspicuously missing. *S*s were first given practice at drawing straight lines with a ruler and pencil on a blank sheet of paper. Then the *S* was shown the picture and told what it was if he failed to recognize it; the missing wire was pointed out, and the *S* was told to draw in the missing wire using the ruler. The time taken to draw the line was recorded. The task was administered a second time, this time with the following instructions: "Here is another picture of the telephone poles with the broken wire. This time I want you to fix the missing wire, but I want you to draw it in just as slowly as you can. Remember, draw it *very slowly*." A subsample of 10 children was retested on another occasion under the "slowly" instructions, and the test-retest reliability of this measure was .77.

2. The "Walk Slowly" Test: A 6 ft. walkway 5 in. wide was marked off on the floor with two strips of masking tape. The *S* was told to pretend that the walkway was a sidewalk and that he and the *E* would play a game to see if they could walk down it without stepping on the sides. The *S* went first, and then the *E* walked down the walkway, deliberately stepping on a line once and verbalizing his error. On the second administration of

this task, the *S* was told to walk "just as slowly as you can." A few *S*s had difficulty keeping their balance during this task; all seemed very concerned to avoid stepping on the lines. Time scores were recorded for both instructions. The test-retest reliability of the scores under the "slowly" instructions was .81.

3. The "Truck" Test: A toy tow truck with an adapted winch that wound easily and a toy jeep that could be hooked on to the string of the truck winch were used. The sidewalk from test 2 was used as the road in this test, and *S*'s task was to wind up the winch and bring the jeep up to the tow truck. The truck and the jeep were placed on the "road" 30 in. apart, and the winch string was attached to the jeep. The tow truck had its wheels blocked so that it would not move. The jeep moved when the *S* wound the winch. If the jeep crossed the edge of the taped roadway, the *E* put it back on course, but this seldom occurred. This test was also administered twice, the second time under "slowly" instructions. Again, time scores were obtained, and a test-retest reliability of .89 was obtained for the "slowly" condition.

The three tests were administered in the same order to all *S*s; the three tests were given first under instructions that did not involve reference to speed of performance, and then all three tests were given a second time under "slowly" instructions. The *S*s' level of interest in these tests remained high throughout the testing session, and they seemed well adapted to the age level of the *S*s; each subtest yielded a good dispersion of scores, and all *S*s were able to complete all the tests.

The intercorrelations of the three inhibition tests under "slowly" instructions may be seen in Table 1. The intercorrelations among these tests when the *S*s were not under "slowly" instructions were considerably lower and not significant.

Total scores on inhibition of movement were obtained by adding standard scores from the three tests. Girls were somewhat more consistent from task to task in their performance; hence, their total inhibition scores are more reliable.

RESULTS

The measure of general activity level and the scores on inhibition of

TABLE 1. INTERCORRELATIONS AMONG THE SUBTESTS FOR INHIBITION OF MOVEMENT

Test	Boys	Girls
Draw a line slowly versus walk slowly	.51	.69
Draw a line slowly versus truck test	.39	.53
Walk slowly versus truck test	.42	.71

movement proved to be independent for boys ($r = -.06$), and somewhat negatively related for girls ($r = -.38$, $p < .10$). That is, the more active girls in a free nursery-school situation have somewhat more difficulty than inactive girls in inhibiting motor movement when a task demands it, while this is not true for boys (see Table 2).

TABLE 2. Intercorrelations among Activity and Intellectual Measures, by Sex

Measures	Intercorrelations	
	Boys	*Girls*
Activity and inhibition scores	−.06	−.38
IQ and CEFT	.50	.18

As Table 3 shows, for both sexes, the ability to inhibit movement is positively related to Stanford-Binet IQ ($r = .44$, $p < .01$ for the sexes combined). There is a tendency toward positive correlation between inhibition and CEFT as well, although this correlation is not quite significant. The prediction that ability scores should be positively related to general activity level in nursery school was not borne out. For both sexes, this relation is essentially zero.

TABLE 3. Correlations between Activity Measures and Mental Abilities

Mental Measures	Activity Measures			
	Boys		*Girls*	
	actometer scores	*inhibition of movement*	*actometer scores*	*inhibition of movement*
Stanford Binet IQ	.02	.38	−.06	.50
CEFT	−.28	.23	.07	.34

DISCUSSION

Our results indicate that the ability to inhibit movement is related to intellectual ability among nursery-school children but that the more intelligent children are not characterized by any generalized inhibition of movement throughout their daily activities. Rather, they are able to inhibit movement in a situation that requires them to do so, but they are fully as active as the children who score lower on IQ tests during free-play situations. We expected that the high-IQ children would be exploratory and that this should be reflected in a high total activity level; we can only suppose that they may indeed be exploratory but that, while some of their exploratory activity involves a good deal of gross motor activity, much does not. Sedentary play (drawing, working puzzles, constructing with blocks) may be fully as functional for intellectual growth as more kinetic play, but our findings do suggest that sedentary play is not necessarily the *more* functional of the two.

It is always possible, of course, that a different relationship between activity and IQ would obtain among a group of children from different socioeconomic levels or with lower average IQ scores than those characterizing our *S*s. Data on other *S* populations would be helpful.

Do our results, then, support the psychoanalytic position concerning the importance of impulse control for intellectual functioning? To a degree they do, if one specifies that the inhibition need not be general but is specific as to duration and situation. The problem for research using activity level as an index of impulse control would appear to be that, while all impulsive children are probably highly active, not all highly active children are impulsive. There may well be differences among highly active children in the degree to which their activity is directed, organized, and sequential. It would be useful in future research to devise a means of breaking down total activity scores into measures that would distinguish instrumental from expressive, or scattered from organized, activity. One of these forms of activity should be an indicator of lack of impulse control, the other should not, and hence they should correlate differently with measures of intellectual ability.

There is a further reservation concerning the relevance of our results for the concept of impulse control. It is true that our high-IQ children were more capable of inhibiting movement when instructed to do so. Is this because they have better impulse control or because they are more able to follow *any* instructions than their low-IQ counterparts? If we had asked them to do the tasks as *rapidly* as possible, would they also have excelled at the tasks under these instructions? We did not run this control condition, and we are not sure it is the proper control condition to answer the question we have raised, for the ability to do something fast under instructions to do so may not reveal impulsiveness but a high degree of motor control and coordination. In any case, the degree to which the ability to inhibit movement may be properly interpreted as "impulse control" requires further study.

SUMMARY

In this study, the ability to inhibit motor movement is distinguished from a more generalized low activity level. It is argued that the former should be functional for problem-solving while the latter should not. With a sample of 42 nursery-school children, measures were taken of activity level during free play, of inhibition of motor movement, of IQ, and of performance on the Children's Embedded Figures Test. Scores on inhibition of movement proved to be positively correlated with the measures of intellectual ability, while general activity scores were not.

REFERENCES

Balazs, M. D. "Agondvekodas soran fellepo babralasrol." *Psychol. stud. univ. Bp.,* 1938, **2,** 182–183. (*Psychol. Abstr.,* 1939, **13,** 1875)

Cromwell, R. L., B. F. Palk, and J. G. Foshee. "Studies in activity level: V. The relationship among eyelid conditioning, intelligence, activity level, and age." *Amer. J. ment. Def.,* 1961, **65,** 744–748.

Escalona, S., and G. M. Heider. *Prediction and Outcome.* New York: Basic Books, 1959.

Forgays, D. G., and J. W. Forgays. "The nature of the effect of free environmental experience in the rat." *J. comp. physiol. Psychol.,* 1952, **45,** 322–328.

Foshee, J. G. "Studies in activity level: I. Simple and complex task performance in defectives." *Amer. J. ment. Def.,* 1958, **62,** 882–886.

Grinsted, A. D. Studies in gross bodily movement. Unpubl. doctoral dissertation. Louisiana State Univ., 1939.

Hunt, J. M. *Intelligence and Experience.* New York: Ronald, 1961.

Johnson, H. M. Sleep. In *Readings in Experimental Psychology,* W. L. Valentine (Ed.) New York: Harper, 1931, pp. 241–291.

Kagan, J., H. Moss, and I. Sigel. "Psychological significance of styles of conceptualization." *Monogr. Soc. Res. child Develpm.,* 1963, **28,** no. 2. (serial no. 86).

Karp, S. A., and Norma L. Konstadt. *Manual for the Children's Embedded Figures Test.* Brooklyn, N.Y.: Cognitive Tests, 1963.

Murphy, Lois. *The Widening World of Childhood.* New York: Basic Books, 1962.

Schulman, J. L., and J. M. Reisman. "An objective measure of hyperactivity." *Amer. J. ment. Def.,* 1959, **64,** 455–456.

Schulman, J. L., J. C. Kasper, and R. M. Throne. *Brain Damage and Behavior.* Springfield, Ill.; Charles C Thomas, 1965.

Sigel, I. Styles of categorization and their perceptual, intellectual and personality correlates in young children. Unpubl. manuscript, Merrill-Palmer Inst., 1963.

Sontag, L. W., C. T. Baker, and V. L. Nelson. "Mental growth and personality development: a longitudinal study." *Monogr. Soc. Res. Child Develpm.,* 1958, **23,** no. 2.

Witkin, H. A., R. B. Dyk, H. F. Faterson, D. R. Goodenough, and S. A. Karp. *Psychological Differentiation.* New York: Wiley, 1962.

chapter five

Social Development, Identification, and Emotional Behavior

5.1 Orientation

Much empirical research in developmental psychology uses the nomothetic approach, which attempts to formulate "laws" of behavior having general applicability to human learning and development. In contrast, the idiographic approach involves the study of the individual. Although the two approaches are complementary, principles of behavior and development are frequently based upon nomothetic study. A combination of factors, including the comparative youth of psychology as a science and the complexity of human behavior, has made it difficult to develop general principles having direct application in individual children. Progress toward this goal is constantly being made, however.

This paper by Harriet Rheingold, an internationally recognized authority on infancy and maternal care, is based upon four principles the author believes to apply especially to infant social behavior. To support the principles that provide the nucleus of her paper, Rheingold cites a number of studies, including some relevant investigations with animals on a phylogenetic scale lower than man.

The amount of research on infant behavior and the effects of early experiences has drastically increased in the past several years. The augmented interest in the study of infancy can be documented by examining the chapters on developmental psychology published in the *Annual Review of Psychology.* Of the total number of articles mentioned in the 1962 *Review,* roughly 15 percent directly involved infant behavior and the effects of early experiences in infancy. By contrast, over 25 percent of the studies reviewed in the 1966 edition cover the same topics. If one adds the research pertinent to the early experiences of animals to the articles involving human infants, the figure rises to nearly 50 percent of the total 1966 references on developmental psychology!

Readers interested in parent-child relationships are especially encouraged to note Rheingold's fourth principle. This proposition relates to a long-overlooked research issue, namely, the effect of the infant's behavior on his parents. Child-rearing research has in the past been directed almost exclusively to the effects of parents' behavior on that of their children. Such a "one-way" conception of parent-child interaction is inadequate to advance our understanding of personality development.

RECOMMENDED READING

Hoffman, M. L., and L. W. Hoffman. *Review of Child Development Research.* (vol. 1) New York: Russell Sage, 1964. (See chaps. 1, 6, and 7.)

5.1 The Development of Social Behavior in the Human Infant

Harriet L. Rheingold, UNIVERSITY OF NORTH CAROLINA

The assignment to write a paper often forces one to search for some system by which to organize what one thinks important on the given topic. Thus, in a recent paper (Rheingold, in press) I proposed four general principles of behavior under which the facts and current theories about human infancy could be organized. The principles were (1) that the infant is responsive to stimulation; (2) that the infant is an active organism; (3) that the infant's behavior is modifiable; and (4) that the infant in turn

Reprinted from *Monographs of the Society for Research in Child Development,* **31** (1966), Serial no. 107, 1–17. By permission of the author and The Society for Research in Child Development, Inc.

modifies the environment, particularly the social environment. The principles, it is obvious, apply to the behavior of older as well as younger organisms and to the behavior of one species as well as another. That they also apply to the behavior of the infant testifies to their generality. As a consequence, developmental psychology may be integrated with a more comprehensive science of behavior.

In the present paper, the same four principles will be used but now applied to the development of *social* behavior in the infant. Although the development of social behavior in the human infant will be the primary focus of attention, some data on the development of social behavior in a few other mammalian species will be included. A complete comparative psychology of the development of social behavior will not result, but the form it could take will be suggested.

The advantages of a comparative approach are several: It provides a wider and more objective theater for viewing the behavior of the human infant. It supplies a corrective for inexact generalizations from animal to man. It serves, also, to bring knowledge about man's behavior into closer association with knowledge about the behavior of his mammalian relatives.

A few definitions at this point may remove some later ambiguities. *Infancy* is a period of time in the life of an organism; its origin is plain, but its termination is without firm criteria. In the human infant, I have elsewhere proposed (Rheingold, in press) that the use of words to indicate simple wants could serve as such a criterion. In many mammals, the time when the infant leaves its mother suggests itself as a possible criterion but, obviously, not an appropriate one for the ungulates.

The term "development" will cause us no trouble. For me, it is a descriptive, not an explanatory, concept, and as such I find most definitions acceptable. A particularly congenial definition, however, is Nagel's (1957), given 10 years ago at the thirtieth anniversary of the Institute: "The connotation of *development* thus involves two essential components: the notion of a system possessing a definite structure and a definite set of pre-existing capacities; and the notion of a sequential set of changes in the system, yielding relatively permanent but novel increments not only in its structure but in its modes of operation as well" (p. 17).

We will not tarry long, either, over a definition of social behavior. It is behavior that is evoked, maintained, and modified by the presence or bebehavior of another organism, usually by a member of one's own species. Social stimuli, those provided by these organisms, differ from inanimate stimuli in more than origin; they are often more responsive and more unpredictable (Krech and Crutchfield, 1948, p. 9), more variable, more flexible, and more likely to be intermittent (Skinner, 1953, p. 299).

To conclude this introduction, it needs only to be remarked that all mammalian infants, by virtue of their means of obtaining nourishment, are born into a social enivronment.

The four principles stated earlier, revised for the present purpose, may now be presented as follows:

1. The infant is responsive to stimuli arising from social objects.
2. The infant is active in initiating social contacts.
3. The infant's social behavior is modified by the responses of others (social objects) to him.
4. The infant's social responses modify the behavior of others in his group.

THE INFANT IS RESPONSIVE TO SOCIAL STIMULI

The infant's sensitivities determine the stimuli arising from social objects to which he can respond; his capabilities determine the responses he can make to these stimuli. The task here is to enumerate both the sensory systems of the infant that are stimulated by the presence and behavior of other members of his group, and the responses he gives to the stimulation.

The human infant, from birth, is responsive to a wide range of external stimulation. He possesses almost all the sensory systems he will have as an adult, and every sense he does possess functions, at least to some extent. In this respect he differs from the young of other mammals, such as the rodents and carnivores, which with few exceptions are functionally blind and deaf at birth. As a consequence, the human infant, from the beginning, lives in a broader environment.

We now ask, to what stimuli arising from social objects is the human infant responsive? Certainly the visual stimuli presented by people, that is, the sight of social objects, evoke responses in him almost from the day of birth. He not only sees them, but, as he grows older, he actively looks at them and subjects them to considerable visual exploration (Wolff, 1963). He smiles and vocalizes and, on occasion, also cries at their appearance. As his motor skills mature, he first reaches out, then grasps, and finally holds on to people. Somewhat later, he crawls and creeps to them on visual cues (e.g., Bayley, 1933; Cattell, 1940; Griffiths, 1954). During the first month, he also attends to the voices of social objects (Bayley, 1933), quiets at the sound, and then may smile and vocalize (Griffiths, 1954; Wolff, 1963). But he is 4 months of age before he can turn his head in the direction of a voice (Cattell, 1940). Furthermore, he appears sensitive to the tone of the voice and, by 8 months of age, to what the voice says.

The human infant is also responsive to the tactile and kinesthetic stimulation provided by social objects. During the first month of life, he quiets when picked up (e.g., Bayley, 1933) and smiles if his hands are rhythmically moved (Wolff, 1963). Much more of a definitive nature cannot be said; his responses to tactile and kinesthetic stimulation from the social object, in the absence of accompanying visual and auditory stimulation, have not yet been systematically studied.

Attractive as the possibility may be to some, there is at present no evidence that the infant responds to olfactory stimuli presented by social objects.

Quite different from the human infant's are the sensitivities and responses of other mammalian infants to stimuli arising from members of their own species. (For a review of the sensory and motor development of many young mammals, see Cruikshank, 1954.) For example, 8 minutes after birth, the newborn kitten, on its own, makes contact with its mother's body. It cannot be sensitive to the visual stimuli presented by the mother because its eyes do not open until the seventh day. No, it is sensitive to the thermal and auditory stimuli she presents (Tilney and Casamajor, 1924); it is these stimuli that give direction to its head movements. Prominent, too, in the newborn kitten's environment, are its littermates. They also offer thermal and tactile stimuli to which the kitten responds, for kittens, like rodent and dog pups, pile up on each other in the mother's absence, become quiet, and sleep. (Bolles and Woods, 1964; Rheingold, 1963; Scott and Marston, 1950). During the first 2 weeks of life, the rodent and carnivore infants' chief social responses are effecting and maintaining contact with mother and littermates. In the third week, tactile and thermal stimuli are no longer dominant; now the kitten and the pup respond to visual, auditory, and olfactory stimuli emanating from social objects. Especially the sight of others stimulates approach and play behavior.

The rhesus infant, however, contrasts with the human, on the one hand, and with the rodent and carnivore infants, on the other. He sees and hears,[1] but his primary responses to social stimuli—aside from nursing, which characterizes all mammalian infants and is not separately discussed—are grasping and clinging (Harlow, 1960), responses that secure thermal, tactile, and kinesthetic stimulation.

In contrast to the human infant, the early responsiveness of other mammals, for example, the rodent, carnivore, and subhuman primate families, appears to depend on different sensitivities—thermal, tactile, and kinesthetic. Associated with these sensitivities are capabilities for locomotion and grasping, which bridge the distance between these infants and others, and effect, instead of visual ties, ties of contact.

The most physically helpless infant, the human, who can neither cling nor locomote, seems, nevertheless, effective in bridging the distance—the distance he cannot travel—between himself and members of *his* group

[1] Animals may possess good sensory perception in several modalities but, nevertheless, predominantly use only a few. To possess a sense does not mean that it is characteristically utilized. Thus, the rhesus infant sees but responds to social objects primarily by grasping.

primarily by the use of vision and hearing and by responses such as looking, smiling, and vocalizing, which hold them at his side. Thus, Ainsworth (1964), Rheingold (1961), and Walters and Parke (1965) have pointed to the role of distance receptors in the genesis and maintenance of social responsiveness in the human infant.

The sensitivities and capabilities of still other mammalian infants should at some time be considered. What can we make of the ungulate infant that not only sees *and* locomotes almost from birth, but also uses visual cues to guide his locomotion?

In focusing our attention on the immature mammal's social behavior, we are likely to ignore that very early in life he tends to give the same responses to nonsocial as to social objects. Thus, the human infant looks at a variety of visual arrays and often smiles and vocalizes to them as well (Piaget, 1952; Preyer, 1893; Rheingold, 1961; Salzen, 1963). When a few months older, he reaches out to them, and in another few months crawls to them. Other young mammals, once they have left their mothers, also approach, manipulate, and play with both inanimate and animate objects, (Bolles and Woods, 1964; Harlow, 1962). This observation will be discussed later.

The analysis of the infant's sensitivity to social stimuli has glossed over too lightly the complexity of the social object. Social objects are indeed complex stimulus objects, and often stimulate more than one sense. Their dimensions, nevertheless, are assumed to be specifiable. To discover the effective dimensions, the investigator reduces the complexity of the social object by the experimental manipulation of its structure and behavior. Thus, Rosenblatt and Lehrman (1963), in measuring maternal behavior, used as a standard stimulus for rat mothers any living infant rat 5 to 10 days of age. Replicas and models have also been used; well known are Schneirla and Rosenblatt's (1961) brooder for kittens, Harlow's (1958) terry-cloth cylinder for rhesus infants, and Igel and Calvin's (1960) surrogate mother for dogs. Still farther removed from the real-life social object are the replicas of human faces and parts of faces used to study smiling in human infants (e.g., Ahrens, 1954; Spitz and Wolf, 1946). At an even more abstract level of analysis, Welker (1959), in an attempt to identify the stimuli that facilitate huddling in a litter of pups, measured the effect of contact upon the pup's locomotion under varying room temperatures.

This partial account suggests the diversity of avenues through which the social stimuli of one's own species come to the infant, and the diversity of responses he gives them. It goes without saying that infants of different species differ in their sensory apparatuses, in the state of maturity of each apparatus at birth, and in the rate of development of each subsequent to birth. They differ as well in their capabilities, that is, in the response classes activated by stimulation from social objects. Diverse though their sensory apparatuses and capabilities may be, however, infants of every mammalian species do sense members of their own group—most often, of course, the mother—and do respond to them.

THE INFANT INITIATES SOCIAL BEHAVIOR

The infant not only responds to social stimuli, he also initiates social contacts. No one will dispute the statement. Yet here, in the absence of evidence from controlled studies, we will often have to rely on everyday and naturalistic observation. Still, observation is clear on this point: The infant is no more passive in his social behavior than he is in other kinds of behavior.

Human infants frequently look at people before they are looked at, smile before they are smiled to, vocalize before they are spoken to, and cry. As a consequence, they attract the attention of individuals and draw them closer. They expose themselves, thus, to social stimulation and, by their own efforts, increase the amount of stimulation in their environments.

What of other mammalian infants? Infant rats on the thirteenth day of life begin to groom each other. A day later, when their eyes start to open, they "play" with each other, "running into one another, jumping, climbing, burrowing, chasing, wrestling" (Bolles and Woods, 1964, p. 433).

Puppy dogs, too, make physical contacts with their mothers and littermates, not waiting to be contacted. In the third week of life, as vision guides their responses, they mouth and bite, first the mouths of littermates, then other parts of their littermates' and the mothers' bodies. In the fourth week, they paw, box, tumble, tussle, and chase each other; in brief, they play. At this age, too, pups go to the mother's head, instead of her belly, whine and cry, raise a paw to her, and lick her face (Rheingold, 1963; Scott and Marston, 1950).

Kittens, too, when 3 weeks of age, leave the home site and approach the female to nurse. They also romp around her, pounce on her, paw her, and toy with her tail. They respond the same way to their littermates. When 4 weeks of age, they initiate almost all the contacts they have with the mother, while she now tries to avoid them (Schneirla, Rosenblatt, and Tobach, 1963).

Rhesus infants, while still very young, approach other infants (Rowell, Hinde, and Spencer-Booth, 1964). Harlow (1962), in reporting his playroom and playpen studies of the infant rhesus, gave details of the infant's initiation of social contacts with other infants. He identified three components: "One of these is a visual-exploration component, in which the animal orients closely to, and peers intently at . . . the other animal. A second is oral exploration, a gentle mouthing response, and the third pattern is that of tactual exploration" (p. 216). These behaviors were characteristic of surrogate-raised infants and were labeled "presocial." Rough-and-tumble play followed, in which both partners participated in pushing, pulling, mauling, and biting each other. The persistent initiation of contact by rhesus infants—with mothers who reject them—is by now well known (Harlow, Harlow, and Hansen, 1963).

Similarly, infant langur monkeys, observed in the wild, climb on adult females during the first 3 months of life. At 5 months of age, they chase and wrestle with other young. They initiate play with adult females by jumping on them, racing around them, pulling their fur, and pushing up against them; later they initiate playful contact even with adult males (Jay, 1963).

In general, the principle of infant initiation of social behavior is important because it assigns a measure, a rather large measure, of responsibility to the infant for the genesis of his own social behavior. The brevity of treatment accorded this principle here should not be taken as a measure of its importance.

THE INFANT'S SOCIAL BEHAVIOR IS MODIFIABLE

The third principle states that the infant's social behavior is modifiable, that it is maintained and altered by the responses of social objects to his behavior. The position taken here is that behavior in the immature organism is not fixed but flexible. Nevertheless, I do not wish to set in opposition the processes of maturation and learning; rather, I take the now accepted position that any behavior, no matter how simple or how early its appearance, is already the result of an interaction of genetic material and environmental condition. To claim that the infant's behavior is modifiable, claims nothing about the origin of the behavior, whether innate or learned, for it is always possible to begin the study of learning with any behavior or response the organism already possesses. The purpose here is to examine some social responses of the immature organism that appear to be modifiable by the behavior of social objects in his environment.

The composition of the social group into which the infant is born determines the potential evoking and reinforcing agents of his social behavior and the agents who will provide discriminative stimuli for subsequent social responses. Every member of the group, and seldom is the mother the only member, is potentially a caretaker, if we do not limit the term "caretaker" too narrowly. They are the organisms toward whom he will display social behavior and who will display social behavior toward him; they are the organisms to whose behavior he will respond and the organisms who will respond to his behavior. It is clear, then, that an account of the nature of the infant's social group would have been as appropriate to the discussion of the first two principles as to this principle.

What of the social group into which the human infant most commonly is born in our culture? His is usually a single birth. In this respect, he is different from the rodent and carnivore infant, which is one of many and will have almost constant contact with many littermates. He is also different from the ungulate and primate infants, which early associate with other infants both about the same time. The human infant usually joins a small group composed of mother, father, and perhaps a few older siblings. These few members contrast with the packs and troops that some other mammals form. The primate group, for example, is often composed of several males of varying orders of dominance, several females with young, and many juveniles of all ages. The human infant's, therefore, is a smaller world as far as day-by-day experiences go. Yet, on occasion, his social environment becomes more varied and more extensive; he has relatives of all ages, and babysitters, and, sometimes he is transported to environments rich in both physical and social stimulation.

No recital of how the infant's social behavior is modified can be complete without taking into account the sensitivities and capabilities of the social objects in the infant's environment, factors raised here for the first time, but important for the whole discussion. Social objects do not respond to all the infant's behavior; presumably some of these lacks can be traced to varying degrees of sensitivity to the infant's behavior. The nature of the response, it is evident, depends upon what the social objects can do, that is, their capabilities. Needless to say, adequacy of care for any specific species is not here at issue; by hypothesis, all the behavior of present species must be equally adaptive. But one may still ask, what is the nature of the response the members of the group give the infant? In passing, I cannot refrain from calling attention to the numerous and ingenious tools and artifacts man has devised to supplement and sometimes supplant the responses he can make to the infant.

We turn now to the major topics of this section: (1) the infant's social behavior is modified by the responses of social objects to his social behavior, and (2) the processes by which modification is effected. It has previously been stated that the infant past the neonatal stage often gives similar responses to both the animate and inanimate objects in his environment. It is now proposed that he learns to discriminate between social objects—that is, members of his own group—and nonsocial objects by the different nature of the responses he receives from both classes.

Let us consider the case for the human infant and use his smiling as an example of responsiveness to social objects. The choice is dictated by the early appearance of smiling and by the attention it has received from developmental psychologists. During the first few weeks of life, the literature reports smiles that are evoked only by stimuli arising from social objects, their voices and their appearances (see Ambrose, 1960; and Gewirtz, 1965, for reviews), and by rhythmic movements of the infant's arms, when these are initiated by a person (Wolff, 1963). There is one exception: Ahrens's (1954) report of an infant smiling at patterns of dots during the second month of life.

I pass over without comment the next few weeks, during which the smile appears more quickly and more frequently, to make a few observations that seem not to have received the attention they deserve. The first is that sometime during the third month, and still more apparent during the fourth month, the smile becomes one component in a chain of responses evoked primarily by visual stimuli. In this chain, the first response is intent regard accompanied by a reduction or even a cessation of physical activity. The next response is facial brightening, and then smiling. The smile is followed by an increase in physical activity. Then, as the infant kicks, waves his arms, or arches his back, he vocalizes (Gesell and Thompson, 1934, p. 261; Washburn, 1929).

This sequence of responses I have labeled "the smiling response." It seems important to make the point, first, because it relates intent visual regard and vocalizing with the smile and, second, because at this period of time the response is given not only to social objects but also to such disparate objects as toys (Piaget, 1952; Rheingold, 1961), the infant's own hand (Piaget, 1952), and a swinging lamp (Preyer, 1893). In *The Origins of Intelligence in Children,* Piaget (1952) reported a number of observations on the development of vision in his son, Laurent. From these observations—and you must remember that smiling was not their focus—I tallied every instance in which Piaget reported a smile *and* the object that evoked it. In eight reports, from 1 month 15 days to 2 months 4 days, the stimulus object was a person. At 2 months 11 days, we find the first reports of smiling to nonsocial objects. On that day, the infant smiled to a handkerchief, a rattle, and other toys, both in motion and motionless. In the next 23 reports of smiles, at ages up to 4 months when the section on vision ended, in only six was the stimulus a social object. In 17 of the 23 smiling episodes in the third and fourth months, the stimulus was a nonsocial object. The smiling response, therefore, cannot be equated with the social response; the nature of the stimulating object must define whether the response is social or nonsocial.

The evidence suggests that, during a stage in the development of the *seeing* human infant, smiles are primarily evoked by visual arrays possessing certain, as yet unspecified, stimulus properties, whether presented by social or nonsocial objects. Schneirla (1959) pointed to low intensity as the effective stimulus property (p. 33), Bowlby (1958), to "certain inherently interesting stimulus patterns" (p. 361), and Salzen (1963), to any contrast or change in brightness. The role of learning in the development of the smiling response at this stage is not yet clear (Gewirtz, 1965). Some of the reinforcing effects of sensory feedback may be unconditioned (Skinner,

1953), although they soon do become conditioned. At any rate, I am less concerned with the origin of the smiling response than with an analysis of the stimulus properties that evoke it.

In the next stage of development, beginning sometime after 4 months of age, the smiling response is evoked more and more often by animate objects, less and less often by inanimate objects; it is evoked by people, seldom by things. These stages, of course, are not precisely fixed in time or mutually exclusive. It must be admitted, further, that in delineating this stage I am predicting what seems reasonable; the studies have not yet been performed.

Two processes can account for the developing discrimination. First, the social object, being animate, possesses, and therefore more regularly presents, the set of effective stimuli. Second, the social object, being animate *and* human, that is, a member of one's own species, is *responsive* to the infant's smiling. The infant's smiling evokes responses from persons much of the time, from things not at all. A smile is often met with a smile, and sometimes also with words and touches. At the least, the human observer will move closer, stay longer, and pay attention. It is upon this characteristic of human interchange that Bowlby (1958) based his statement on the adaptive value of the infant's smile for his own survival.

Controlled studies have shown that, when these naturally occurring interactions between infant and adult are experimentally programmed, the social responses of infants can in fact be modified by responses from social objects. For example, the number of vocalizations 3-month-old infants give to the sight of a person has been systematically increased (Rheingold, Gewirtz, and Ross, 1959; Weisberg, 1963), as well as the number of smiles in 4-month-old infants (Brackbill, 1958).

These studies suggest that instrumental conditioning may be the process by which the discrimination between people and things is learned, that is, the events contingent upon the infant's response increased the subsequent occurrence of the response. While in general I believe the evidence supports this conclusion, other mechanisms may also be operating. As long as infants are fed and made warm and dry by human hands, we cannot rule out the possibility that social objects are discriminated on the basis of secondary reward value (Keller and Schoenfeld, 1950). Recently, Sears (1963) wrote, "One apparent result of this mutually satisfying relationship is the creation of secondary rewards or reinforcers for both members of the pair. That is, the mother's talking, patting, smiling, her gestures of affection or concern, are constantly being presented to the baby in context with primary reinforcing stimulations such as those involved in eating, fondling, and caressing" (p. 30). Multicausality is not rare in behavior theory, and important responses may well be overdetermined.

One final word on the discrimination between people and things: Exploratory behavior has been defined (Berlyne, 1960, p. 78) as a response that increases the organism's exposure to his environment. Social behavior, specifically the smiling response, increases the infant's exposure to the sight and sound of persons because of their response to it. The smiling response, like exploratory behavior, maximizes the inflow of stimulation and, thus, of information from the object in question. Although it is possible to simplify too much, still, some more powerful and general principles of behavior may result from categorizing at least some classes of social behavior as exploratory. Exploratory behavior could describe the larger class; social behavior, the class in which the object is not a thing but another living organism.

In the next stage of the smiling response—and here, as elsewhere, the stages are characterized by extensive temporal overlapping—the infant discriminates between familiar and strange social objects. As early as the third month, an infant may sober upon the appearance of a strange person (Gesell and Thompson, 1934). In speaking of this discrimination, I do not refer solely to distress responses. Observation and experimental evidence do not consistently support the conclusion that infants at a certain age are afraid of strangers. First, in my experience, distress responses are not typical of the majority of infants; they occur in some infants for short periods of time, and only a few infants for longer periods of time. In our laboratory, 9-month-old infants smile easily to the entire staff. In spite of the amount of attention paid the phenomenon, we still do not have, even at this late date, normative data on a representative sample of infants. Second, as for evidence: Morgan (1965) found that when the stranger did not touch the infant but smiled, talked, and moved his head as if playing peekaboo, infants 4 to 12 months of age tended to react positively. Gewirtz (1965), measuring the occurrence and frequency of smiles to a relatively strange person presenting an expressionless face, found no abrupt decline in a large sample of children from 1 to 18 months of age; those living in environments in which they had considerable contact with a smaller number of adults, a condition often thought to be correlated with fear of strangers, declined the least.

The distress response aside, it seems likely that most infants give the smiling response to strange persons more slowly and less fully than to familiar ones. We expect the response to be sensitive to such variables as the familiarity of the surrounding environment, the distance from the mother, the brusqueness of the stranger's approach, and the intrusiveness of his behavior. In most instances, whatever the complex set of stimuli that constitutes strangeness may be, its effect wears off fairly quickly. It is interesting to note, in passing, that we tend to call the stimulus "novel" when it evokes approach behavior and "strange" when it evokes withdrawal and distress behavior.

A preference for the familiar—often overlooked these days in our concern with the control exerted over behavior by the novel—is under certain, as yet unknown, conditions characteristic of all animals of all ages; it is a component of the pattern of behavior known as "wildness." In part, the preference for the familiar can be labeled "perceptual learning," previous exposure being required for the discrimination (Kimble, 1961); in part, it would appear to be a matter of the known reinforcers being more reinforcing.

In the next developmental stage, the infant discriminates between one familiar person and another. His social responses—here, specifically, the smiling response—may occur more quickly and more frequently and in greater intensity to persons other than the mother, to perhaps the father or a sibling, as Ainsworth (1964) noted. The same observation was made by Schaffer and Emerson (1964) in recording the infant's response to the departure of known persons. The very constancy of the mother's presence, the fact that her flow of stimuli is often not contingent upon acts of the infant, as well as the aversive nature of some of the necessary caretaking activities, may operate against maximum social interchange. In contrast, the responses of fathers and siblings are intermittent, are more often—we can surmise—contingent on the infant's behavior, and are more often playful, that is, offering stimulation for its own sake, characteristics that should make for more powerful reinforcement. The appearance of these other persons, then, would possess discriminative stimuli for future reinforcement; they provide cues for the occurrence of interesting stimulation.

The development of the smiling response has been presented in detail as an example of the principle that the infant's social behavior is modified by the responses of people to *his* social behavior. What of the modification of other classes of social behavior in other mammals?

For the infant mammal, too, it is obvious that its behavior toward members of its group must be modified by the responses the social objects give in turn. After the period of close physical attachment to the mother in the rodent, carnivore, and primate young, the infant approaches and contacts both animate and inanimate objects in its environment (Bolles and Woods, 1964; Harlow, 1962; Rheingold, 1963). In time, his responses to them became differentiated, as do his responses to littermates, juveniles, and adults. The infant mammal, too, like the human infant, discriminates early between strange and familiar organisms, and then between different familiar organisms.

The social behavior of animal infants has also been modified in laboratory studies. Rhesus infants raised on surrogate mothers do not develop normal social behavior (Harlow, 1963); rhesus infants raised in bare cages cling to each other (Harlow, 1963); kittens raised on brooder mothers are inept in making contact with their own mothers (Schneirla *et al.*, 1963). Deprivation of normal experiences appears then to markedly affect the development of social behavior in infants.

Suggestive also are the results of some studies of the social responsiveness of dog to man. Puppies ran more often and faster to a passive human being than to one who patted and made a fuss over them. This behavior was modified by deprivation of social contact and, further, occurred in animals reared in isolation which therefore had no history of receiving food at the hands of people. A passive person thus appears to be a primary reinforcer of social approach behavior in the puppy (Bacon and Stanley, 1963; Stanley, 1965; Stanley and Elliot, 1962; Stanley, Morris and Trattner, 1965).

In the analysis of this principle, no reference has been made to some concepts that occur from time to time in treatments of early social behavior; I refer to such concepts as social bond, social attachment, and critical periods. These are higher-order concepts which go beyond this elementary presentation. Omitted also, but only because of time and space exigencies, is a consideration of sex differences in early social behavior.

THE INFANT MODIFIES THE BEHAVIOR OF OTHERS

The fourth principle states that the infant, by his appearance and behavior, modifies the behavior of other social objects. He not only evokes responses from them but maintains and shapes their responses by reinforcing some and not others. From our individual experiences, we know how effective he can be! He is so effective because he is relatively helpless yet active and because he is so attractive to his beholders. The amount of attention and the number of responses directed to the infant are enormous —out of all proportion to his age, size, and accomplishments. Under ordinary circumstances, in any human group containing an infant, the attention directed toward him is usually considerable. Although I have no data to cite for the human group, the facts in primate groups have been well documented (e.g., DeVore, 1963; Jay, 1963; Rowell *et al.,* 1964). For the langur monkey, Jay (1963) has reported, "From birth the newborn is a focal point of interest for all adult and subadult females in the troop. Females gather around the mother as soon as they notice the newborn. . . . A group of from four to ten females quickly surrounds and grooms the mother. . . . Each time she sits, three or four females crowd in front of her to touch, smell, and lick the newborn. . . . An infant may be held by as many as eight or ten females and carried as far as 75 feet from its mother in the first two days of life" (pp. 288–289). Similarly, for the baboon, DeVore (1963) wrote:

> The birth of a new infant absorbs the attention of the entire troop. From the moment the birth is discovered, the mother is continuously surrounded by the other baboons, who walk beside her and sit as close as possible when she rests. . . . After a week or 10 days, older juveniles and females who sit beside the mother and groom her quietly for several minutes may be allowed to reach over and touch the infant lightly. Young juveniles and older infants sit near the mother and

watch her newborn intently, but are seldom able to approach the mother because of the older troop members around her. . . . Older juvenile or subadult females appear to be most highly motivated toward the newborn infant, and the moment a mother sits one or more of these females is likely to stop whatever she is doing and join the mother. . . . Juvenile and young adult males express only perfunctory interest in the infant, but older males in the central hierarchy frequently come and touch the infant (pp. 313–314).

Appearance aside, the helplessness of most mammalian infants, of course, demands caretaking responses. The nature and frequency of caretaking have been documented for many mammals (e.g., Rheingold, 1963), including the human infant (e.g., Rheingold, 1960). Rosenblatt and Lehrman (1963) have shown that the maintenance of maternal responses, although partly dependent on the mother's physiological condition, is also partly dependent on stimulation by the young. And Harlow *et al.* (1963) have shown how some rhesus infants, by their repeated efforts to attach themselves to rejecting rhesus mothers, eventually made the mothers passably accepting of them. The infant also evokes nurturant behavior in others than the mother. Noirot (1964) has shown how maternal or caretaking behavior was increased in both male and female mice by brief contact with an infant mouse. The above passages from Jay and DeVore make the same points.

Further, the infant's positive social responses evoke responsiveness in kind from others in his environment. The human infant's smiles, for example, are met by smiles; his vocalizations, by vocalizations; his playful overtures, by play. Here, too, may be mentioned the distress cries of the infants; surely they modify the behavior of others. Generally, they exert a powerful effect upon the members of almost all mammalian groups. So aversive, especially to humans, is the crying of the infant that there is almost no effort we will not expend, no device we will not employ, to change a crying baby into a smiling one—or just a quiet one.

Although the mechanisms have not yet been specified, there seem to be strong reinforcing effects in caring for the needs of the helpless and dependent. Caretakers appear to find satisfying the operations of feeding, bathing, and putting the infant to sleep. We have long paid attention to how the infant's behavior is modified by the behavior of his caretakers; only now are we beginning to ponder on how the infant's behavior may modify the behavior of his caretakers.

CONCLUSION

The four principles, in summary, provide a framework for classifying and organizing knowledge of the development of social behavior in the human and other mammalian infants. They may also provide the distance required to gain a fresh perspective on the development of social behavior.

They bypass controversies, especially the troublesome one of innate versus learned behavior. They are not, of course, explanatory principles, but they do leave the door open for an analysis of the processes by which behavior is modified. The four principles, furthermore, do not represent four stages in development; rather, they exist together and are intimately related. Within each principle, however, there are stages of development, here only hinted at. Finally, they take cognizance of species-characteristic behavior in their dependence upon the sensitivities, capabilities, and social organization of each animal.

The principles, in addition, may serve to correct for premature and incautious generalizations from one species to another. More and more rarely now do we make the error of construing the behavior of animals in human terms; we must guard as carefully, in the absence of supporting evidence, against the error of construing the behavior of humans in animal terms.

In this presentation, it has been assumed that no extra theories, laws, or constructs are necessary to account for the behavior of the infant as distinct from the behavior of older organisms, to account for social behavior as distinct from other classes of behavior, or to account for the behavior of one species as distinct from the behavior of other species. Much can be gained, I believe, by an integration of all mammalian behavior into a science of behavior.

We find ourselves, then, in a dilemma. On the one hand, we find attractive the idea that if stimuli, responses, and reinforcers are selected to be appropriate for the species under investigation, the laws of learning may be similar (Skinner, 1957). We find congenial too, Hull's (1945) assumption that "all behavior of the individuals of a given species and that of all species of mammals, including man, occurs according to the same set of primary laws" (p. 56). On the other hand, we are always conscious, and must always be, of the differences. Hull proposed that the forms of the equations representing the behavioral laws of both individuals and species are identical, and that the differences between individuals and species will be found in the empirical constants of the equations. The behavorial scientist has faith in the set of primary laws; his task is to find both them and the constants. Perhaps the dilemma will be resolved when we restrict the objectives of the science of behavior and seek not to explain *behavior* but to explain only the *regularities* in behavior.

REFERENCES

Ahrens, R. "Beitrag zur Entwicklung des Physiognomie und Mimikerkennens." *Zeitschrift für experimentalle und angewandte Psychologie,* 1954, **2,** 412–454.

Ainsworth, Mary D. "Patterns of attachment behavior shown by the infant in interaction with his mother." *Merrill-Palmer Quart.,* 1964, **10,** 51–58.

Ambrose, J. A. The smiling and related responses in early human infancy: an experimental and theoretical study of their course and significance. Unpubl. doctoral dissertation. Univ. London, 1960.

Bacon, W. E., and W. C. Stanley. "Effect of deprivation level in puppies on performance maintained by a passive person reinforcer." *J. comp. physiol. Psychol.,* 1963, **56,** 783–785.

Bayley, Nancy. *The California First-Year Mental Scale.* (Univ. Calif. Syllabus Series, no. 243.) Berkeley: Univ. Calif. Press, 1933.

Berlyne, D. E. *Conflict, Arousal, and Curiosity.* New York: McGraw-Hill, 1960.

Bolles, R. C., and P. J. Woods. "The ontogeny of behaviour in the albino rat." *Animal Behav.,* 1964, **12,** 427–441.

Bowlby, J. "The nature of the child's tie to his mother." *Int. J. Psycho-analysis,* 1958, **39,** 350–373.

Brackbill, Yvonne. "Extinction of the smiling response in infants as a function of reinforcement schedule." *Child Develpm.,* 1958, **29,** 115–124.

Cattell, Psyche. *The measurement of intelligence of infants and young children.* New York: Psychol. Corp., 1940.

Cruikshank, Ruth M. Animal infancy. In *Manual of Child Psychology,* L. Carmichael (Ed.) (2d ed.) New York: Wiley, 1954, pp. 186–214.

DeVore, I. Mother-infant relations in free-ranging baboons. In *Maternal Behavior in Mammals,* Harriet L. Rheingold (Ed.) New York: Wiley, 1963, pp. 305–335.

Gesell, A., and Helen Thompson. *Infant Behavior: Its Genesis and Growth.* New York: McGraw-Hill, 1934.

Gewirtz, J. L. The course of smiling by groups of Israeli infants in the first 18 months of life. In *Studies in psychology: Scripta Hierosolymitana,* **14,** Jerusalem: Hebrew Univ. Press, in press.

Griffiths, Ruth. *The Abilities of Babies.* New York: McGraw-Hill, 1954.

Harlow, H. F. "The nature of love." *Amer. Psychologist,* 1958, **13,** 673–685.

Harlow, H. F. "Primary affectional patterns in primates." *Amer. J. Orthopsychiat.,* 1960, **30,** 676–684.

Harlow, H. F. Development of the second and third affectional systems in macaque monkeys. In *Research Approaches to Psychiatric Problems: A Symposium,* T. T. Tourlentes, S. L. Pollack, and H. E. Himwich (Eds.) New York: Grune and Stratton, 1962, pp. 209–238.

Harlow, H. F. The maternal affectional systems. In *Determinants of Infant Behavior II,* B. M. Foss (Ed.) London: Methuen, 1963, pp. 3–29.

Harlow, H. F., Margaret K. Harlow, and E. W. Hansen. The maternal affectional system of rhesus monkeys. In *Maternal Behavior in Mammals,* Harriet L. Rheingold (Ed.) New York: Wiley, 1963, pp. 254–281.

Hull, C. L. "The place of innate individual and species differences in a natural-science theory of behavior." *Psychol. Rev.,* 1945, **52,** 55–60.

Igel, G. J., and A. D. Calvin. "The development of affectional responses in infant dogs." *J. comp. physiol. Psychol.,* 1960, **53,** 302–305.

Jay, Phyllis. Mother-infant relations in langurs. In *Maternal Behavior in Mammals,* Harriet L. Reingold (Ed.) New York: Wiley, 1963, pp. 282–304.

Keller, F. S., and W. N. Schoenfeld. *Principles of Psychology.* New York: Appleton-Century-Crofts, 1950.

Kimble, G. A. *Hilgard and Marquis' Conditioning and Learning.* New York: Appleton-Century-Crofts, 1961.

Krech, D., and R. S. Crutchfield. *Theory and Problems of Social Psychology.* New York: McGraw-Hill, 1948.

Morgan, G. A. Some determinants of infants' responses to strangers during the first year of life. Unpubl. doctoral dissertation. Cornell Univ., 1965.

Nagel, E. Determinism and development. In *The Concept of Development,* D. B. Harris (Ed.). Minneapolis: Univ. of Minn. Press, 1957, pp. 15–24.

Noirot, Eliane. "Changes in responsiveness to young in the adult mouse. IV. The effect of an initial contact with a strong stimulus." *Animal Behav.,* 1964, **12,** 442–445.

Piaget, J. *The Origins of Intelligence in Children,* trans. by Margaret Cook. New York: International Universities, 1952.

Preyer, W. *The Senses and the Will,* trans. by H. W. Brown. New York: Appleton, 1893.

Rheingold, Harriet L. "The measurement of maternal care." *Child Develpm.,* 1960, **31,** 565–575.

Rheingold, Harriet L. The effect of environmental stimulation upon social and exploratory behaviour in the human infant. In *Determinants of Infant Behavior,* B. M. Foss (Ed.) London: Methuen, 1961, pp. 143–177.

Rhiengold, Harriet L. Maternal behavior in the dog. In *Maternal Behavior in Mammals,* Harriet L. Rheingold (Ed.) New York: Wiley, 1963, pp. 169–202.

Rheingold, Harriet L. Infancy. In *The International Encyclopedia of the Social Sciences.* New York: Crowell-Collier, 1967.

Rheingold, Harriet L., J. L. Gewirtz, and Helen W. Ross. "Social conditioning of vocalizations in the infant." *J. comp. physiol. Psychol.,* 1959, **52,** 68–73.

Rosenblatt, J. S., and D. S. Lehrman. Maternal behavior in the laboratory rat. In *Maternal Behavior in Mammals,* Harriet L. Rheingold (Ed.) New York: Wiley, 1963, pp. 8–57.

Rowell, T. E., R. A. Hinde, and Y. Spencer-Booth. " 'Aunt'-infant interactions in captive rhesus monkeys." *Animal Behav.,* 1964, **12,** 219–226.

Salzen, E. A. "Visual stimuli eliciting the smiling response in the human infant." *J. genet. Psychol.,* 1963, **102,** 51–54.

Schaffer, H. R., and Peggy E. Emerson. "The development of social attachments in infancy." *Monogr. Soc. Res. child Develpm.,* 1964, **29,** no. 3 (serial no. 94).

Schneirla, T. C. An evolutionary and developmental theory of biphasic processes underlying approach and withdrawal. In *Nebraska Symposium on Motivation.* Lincoln: Univ. Nebraska Press, 1959, pp. 1–42.

Schneirla, T. C., and J. S. Rosenblatt. "Behavioral organization and genesis of the social bond in insects and mammals." *Amer. J. Orthopsychiat.,* 1961, **31,** 223–253.

Schneirla, T. C., J. S. Rosenblatt, and Ethel Tobach. Maternal behavior in the cat. In *Maternal Behavior in Mammals,* Harriet L. Rheingold (Ed.) New York: Wiley, 1963, pp. 122–168.

Scott, J. P., and Mary-'Vesta Marston. "Critical periods affecting the development of normal and mal-adjustive social behavior of puppies." *J. genet. Psychol.*, 1950, **77**, 25–60.

Sears, R. R. Dependency motivation. In *Nebraska Symposium on Motivation*, M. R. Jones (Ed.) Lincoln: Univ. Nebraska Press, 1963, pp. 25–64.

Skinner, B. F. *Science and Human Behavior*. New York: Macmillan, 1953.

Skinner, B. F., "The experimental analysis of behavior." *Amer. Scientist*, 1957, **45**, 343–371.

Spitz, R. A., and Katherine M. Wolf. "The smiling response: A contribution to the ontogenesis of social relations." *Genet. Psychol. Monogr.*, 1946, **34**, 57–125.

Stanley, W. C. "The passive person as a reinforcer in isolated beagle puppies." *Psychonomic Sci.*, 1965, **2**, 21–22.

Stanley, W. C., and O. Elliot. "Differential human handling as reinforcing events and as treatments influencing later social behavior in Basenji puppies." *Psychol. Rep.*, 1962, **10**, 775–788.

Stanley, W. C., D. D. Morris, and Alice Trattner. "Conditioning with a passive person reinforcer and extinction in Shetland sheep dog puppies." *Psychonomic Sci.*, 1965, **2**, 19–20.

Tilney, F., and L. Casamajor. "Myelinogeny as applied to the study of behavior." *Arch. Neurology Psychiat.*, 1924, **12**, 1–66.

Walters, R. H., and R. D. Parke. The role of the distance receptors in the development of social responsiveness. In *Advances in Child Development and Behavior*, L. P. Lipsitt and C. C. Spiker (Eds.) (vol. 2) New York: Academic Press, 1965, pp. 59–96.

Washburn, R. W. "A study of the smiling and laughing of infants in the first year of life." *Genet. Psychol. Monogr.*, 1929, **6**, 396–537.

Weisberg, P. "Social and nonsocial conditioning of infant vocalizations." *Child Develpm.*, 1963, **34**, 377–388.

Welker, W. I. "Factors influencing aggregation of neonatal puppies." *J. comp. physiol. Psychol.*, 1959, **52**, 376–380.

Wolff, P. H. Observations on the early development of smiling. In *Determinants of Infant Behavior II*, B. M. Foss (Ed.) London: Methuen, 1963, pp. 113–134.

5.2 *Orientation*

A number of the studies in this volume have demonstrated the prevalence of sex differences in children's behavior and personality development. The nature and process of sex-role and parental identifications are hypothesized to be a major source of such differences by David Lynn in this insightful paper. Although identification theory serves as the broad context for Lynn's discussion, his concern is more the outcomes of identification, specifically those related to learning style and interpersonal relationships, than it is the motive(s) that may initially give rise to identification. Substantial theoretical issues exist regarding the motivation of identification behavior. Various interpretations include identification based upon fear, parental power, status envy, positive reinforcement, and incidental learning. Readers are referred to the references below for information and summaries on this topic.

The concept of identification as a process has figured heavily in the study of character development, conscience, and psychopathology in children and adults. This concept also suggests implications for the behavior enacted by parents and teachers in the socialization of children. Lynn's paper classifies the distinction between sex-role identification and parental identification and establishes five hypotheses concerning sex difference in the process of identification. Of particular relevance is Lynn's suggestion that identification behavior is related to broad differences in children's cognitive style, a concept discussed in Chapter 4. Cognitive-style research has revealed that girls tend to make fewer analytic responses and tend toward greater field dependence than boys. This evidence supports Lynn's contention concerning the nature of identification for girls in contrast with that for boys.

RECOMMENDED READING

Bandura, Albert, and Aletha Huston. "Identification as a process of incidental learning." *J. abnorm. soc. Psychol.,* **43** (1961), 311–318.

Bronfenbrenner, Urie. "Freudian theories of identification and their derivatives." *Child Develpm.,* **31** (1960), 15–40.

Kohlberg, Laurence. "Moral development and identification." In *Child Psychol.* (62d yearbook) Publ. of the National Soc. for the Study of Educ. Chicago: Univ. Chicago Press, 1963, pp. 277–332.

Stoke, Stuart. "An inquiry into the concept of identification." *J. genet. Psychol.,* **76** (1950), 163–189.

Sears, R. R. Dependency motivation. In *Nebraska Symposium on Motivation,* M. R. Jones (Ed.) Univ. Nebraska Press, 1963, pp. 25–64.

5.2 Sex-Role and Parental Identification

David B. Lynn, COLLEGE OF SAN MATEO, CALIFORNIA

It is doubtful that psychological theories have fully posed, much less resolved, the question of the extent of sex differences in personality development. In this connection Sarason *et al.* comment: "No one to our

Reprinted from *Child Development,* **33** (1962), 555–564. By permission of the author and The Society for Research in Child Development, Inc.

knowledge has denied they [such sex differences] are pervasive, and yet the problem of degree of pervasiveness has not been critically examined despite its implications for theory, methodology, and the direction of future research" (23, p. 260).

A perusal of the journals shows that many studies, which include both male and female *S*s in the sample, do not make provisions for sex differences in the hypotheses. Where sex differences are found they are, consequently, rationalized *post facto*. Moreover, often no statistical analysis of sex differences is performed, despite their importance in psychological processes.

This paper presents a theoretical formulation which postulates basic sex differences in the *nature* of sex-role and parental identification, as well as basic differences in the *process of achieving* such identification. The developmental processes described are considered neither inevitable nor universal. If they are appropriate to the U.S. culture today, they may, nevertheless, be inappropriate for many other cultures and for a significantly altered U.S. culture of the future. This formulation refers to the "typical" pattern, although recognizing that a "typical" pattern, if not a myth, is at least an exception. Research findings considered relevant to this formulation are reviewed.

Before developing this formulation, let us briefly define identification as it is used here. *Sex-role identification* refers to the internalization of the role considered appropriate to a given sex and to the unconscious reactions characteristic of that role. *Parental identification* refers to the internalization of personality characteristics of one's own parent and to unconscious reactions similar to that parent. Thus, theoretically, an individual might be well identified with the appropriate sex-role generally and yet poorly identified with his same-sex parent specifically. This differentiation also allows for the converse circumstances wherein a person is well identified with his same-sex parent specifically and yet poorly identified with the appropriate sex-role generally. In such an instance the parent with whom the individual is well identified is himself poorly identified with the appropriate sex-role. An example might be a girl who is well identified with her own mother, but the mother is identified with the masculine rather than the feminine role. Such a girl, therefore, through her identification with her mother, is poorly identified with the feminine role.

In a previous paper (17) the author differentiated the concept of *sex-role identification* from *sex-role preference* and *sex-role adoption*. The present formulation is a departure from that previous paper and also shares various features in common with others (2, 3, 11, 24).

This formulation uses a hypothesis from the previous paper as a postulate from which to deduce a number of new hypotheses. Hopefully, this formulation will offer a unified theoretical framework consistent with a number of varied findings concerning sex differences.

The aspects of the previous formulation pertinent to the present one are summarized as follows:

Both male and female infants were hypothesized to learn to identify with the mother. Boys, but not girls, must shift from this initial identification with the mother to masculine identification. The girl has the same-sex parental model for identification (the mother) with her more than the boy has the same-sex model (the father) with him. Much incidental learning takes place from the girl's contact with her mother and which she can apply directly in her life.

However, despite the shortage of male models, a somewhat stereotyped and conventional masculine role is nonetheless spelled out for the boys, e.g., by his mother and women teachers in the absence of his father and male teachers. In this connection a study by Sherriffs and Jarrett (28) indicated that men and women share the same stereotypes about the two sexes. Through the reinforcement of the culture's highly developed system of rewards for indications of masculinity and punishment for signs of femininity, the boy's early learned identification with the mother eventually weakens and becomes more or less replaced by the later learned identification with a culturally defined, somewhat stereotyped masculine role. "*Consequently, males tend to identify with a cultural stereotype of the masculine role, whereas females tend to identify with aspects of their own mothers' role specifically*" (17, p. 130). This hypothesis was generally supported by the research findings reviewed (9, 16).

This hypothesis is not meant to minimize the role of the father in the development of males. Studies of father-absence suggest that the presence of the father in the home is of great importance for boys (1, 18, 25). It is beyond the scope of this paper to elaborate on the role of the father, but it is our position that it has a very different place in the development of the boy's masculine-role identification than does the mother in the girl's mother identification. The father, as a model for the boy, may be thought of as analogous to a map showing the major outline but lacking most details, whereas the mother, as a model for the girls, might be thought of as a detailed map. The father, of course, serves many other functions besides that of model for the boy's masculine-role identification. He may, for example, reinforce the boy's masculine strivings and stimulate his drive to achieve masculine-role identification. Because fathers typically do spend so much time away from home and, even when home, usually do not participate in as many intimate activities with the child as does the mother (e.g., preparation for bed), it is probably true that the time spent with the father takes on much importance in the boy's identification development.

Although recognizing the contribution of the father in the identification of males and the general cultural influences in the identification of females, it nevertheless seems meaningful, for simplicity in developing this formulation, to refer to *masculine-role identification* in males as distinguished from *mother identification* in females.

It is postulated that the task of achieving these separate kinds of identification for each sex requires separate methods of learning. These separate identification tasks seem to parallel the two kinds of learning tasks differentiated by Woodworth and Schlosberg: the *problem* and the *lesson.* "With a problem to master the learner must explore the situation and find the goal before his task is fully presented. In the case of a lesson, the problem-solving phase is omitted or at least minimized, as we see when the human subject is instructed to memorize this poem or that list of nonsense syllables, to examine these pictures with a view to recognizing them later. . . ." (36, p. 529). The task of achieving mother identification for the female is considered roughly parallel to the learning *lesson,* and the task of achieving masculine-role identification for the male is considered roughly parallel to the learning *problem.*

It is assumed that finding the goal does not constitute a major problem for the girl in learning her mother identification lesson. Since the girl, unlike the boy, need not shift from the initial mother identification and since she typically has the mother with her a relatively large proportion of the time, it is postulated that the question of the object of identification (the mother) for the girl seldom arises. She learns the mother identification lesson in the context of an intimate personal relationship with the mother, partly by imitation, which as used here includes covert practice of the actions characteristic of the mother (19). She also learns the mother identification lesson through the mother's selective reinforcement of mother-similar tendencies in the girl. Hartup (12) did a relevant study concerning parental imitation in children aged 3 to 5 in which he correlated sex-role preference in the Brown It Scale (2) with the degree to which the *S*'s doll play showed the child doll imitating the same-sex parental doll. The results suggested to Hartup that girls become feminine partly as a result of a tendency to imitate their mothers more than their fathers and that the acquisition of masculinity by boys appears to be independent of the tendency to imitate the father more than the mother.

Similarly, abstracting principles defining mother identification is not considered a concern for the girls. Any bit of behavior on the mother's part may be of potential importance in learning the mother identification lesson, and therefore the girl need not abstract principles defining the feminine role. It is not principles defining the feminine role that the girl need learn, but rather an identification with her specific mother.

It is assumed, on the other hand, that finding the goal *does* constitute a major problem for the boy in solving the masculine-role identification problem. There is evidence to indicate that between two-thirds and three-fourths of children by the age of 3 are able to make the basic distinction between sexes (6, 7, 26). When the boy begins to be aware that he does not belong in the same sex-category as the mother, he must then find the proper sex-role identification goal. Hartley says, of the identification problem that faces the boy, ". . . the desired behavior is rarely defined positively as something the child *should* do, but rather negatively as something he should *not* do or be—anything, that is, that the parent or other people regard as 'sissy.' Thus, very early in life the boy must either stumble on the right path or bear repeated punishment without warning when he accidentally enters into the wrong ones" (11, p. 458). From these largely negative admonishings, often made by women and often without the benefit of the presence of a male model during most of his waking hours, the boy must learn to set the masculine role as his goal. He must also restructure the admonishings, often negatively made and given in many contexts, in order to abstract the principles defining the masculine role.

One of the basic steps in this formulation can now be taken. It is assumed that, in learning the appropriate identification, each sex is thereby acquiring separate methods of learning which are subsequently applied to learning tasks generally. The little girl acquires a learning method which primarily involves: [1] a personal relationship and [2] imitation rather than restructuring the field and abstracting principles. On the other hand, the little boy acquires a different learning method which primarily involves: [1] defining the goal; [2] restructuring the field; and [3] abstracting principles.

HYPOTHESES

The following hypotheses are considered to follow from the above formulation:

1. It is in the context of a close personal relationship with the mother that the little girl learns the mother identification lesson. She is reinforced by appropriate rewards for signs that she is learning this lesson. Since the little girl is rewarded in the context of the personal relationship with her mother, maintaining the rewarding relationship with her mother should acquire strong secondary-drive characteristics. By generalization, the need for affiliation in other situations should also have strong secondary-drive characteristics for the girl.

The boy, relative to the girl, has little opportunity to receive rewards for modeling an adult male in a close personal relationship. He receives his rewards for learning the appropriate principles of masculine-role identification as they are abstracted from many contexts. Therefore, the need for affiliation in general should not acquire as much strength as a secondary drive for males as for females. *Consequently, females will tend to demonstrate greater need for affiliation than males.*

2. In learning to identify with the mother, any bit of behavior on the mother's part might be of potential importance in the girl's perception of

her. The mother identification lesson does not require that the girl deviate from the given, but rather that she learn the lesson as presented.

For the boys, solving the problem of masculine-role identification must be accomplished without adequate exposure to adult male models. It must be solved by using the admonishings, such as "don't be a sissy," which, occurring in many contexts, serve as guides in defining the masculine role. To solve the masculine-role identification problem the boy must restructure the field. Therefore, the masculine learning method *does* include restructuring the field as a learning principle. *Consequently, females tend to be more dependent than males on the external context of a perceptual situation and hesitate to deviate from the given.*

3. In the process of solving the masculine-role identification problem, the male acquires a method of learning which should be applicable in solving other problems. On the other hand, the feminine learning method, emerging from the process of learning the mother identification lesson, is not well geared to problem solving. *Consequently, males tend to surpass females in problem-solving skills.*

4. The masculine learning method is postulated to include abstracting principles, whereas the feminine one is not. The tendency to abstract principles should generalize to other problems in addition to the problem of achieving masculine-role identification. It should, for example, generalize to the acquisition of moral standards. If one is very responsive to the moral standards of others, it is relatively unnecessary to internalize standards. If one, on the other hand, tends to learn moral standards by abstracting moral principles rather than being highly responsive to the standards of others, then one *does* need to internalize one's standards. If one is to stick by one's principles, they had better be internalized. It is postulated that males more than females will tend to learn moral standards by abstracting moral principles. *Consequently, males tend to be more concerned with internalized moral standards than females.*

5. Conversely, the feminine learning method indicates that one learns by imitation through a relationship whereas the masculine learning method does not. The little girl, it was assumed, tends to learn the lesson as given, without restructuring. Such a learning method should generalize to the acquisition of standards. *Consequently, females tend to be more receptive to the standards of others than males.*

RELEVANT FINDINGS

Let us now see how consistently these hypotheses correspond to previous findings and whether this formulation helps clarify and unify the data.

Hypothesis 1, predicting that females will demonstrate greater need for affiliation than males, is supported by a study by Edwards (4) which showed that women have significantly higher means than men on affiliation on the Edwards Personal Preference Schedule (EPPS).

McClelland, Atkinson, Clark, and Lowell (20) found that college women did not show an increase in achievement motive scores as a result of the arousal instruction, based on reference to leadership and intelligence, effective for male college students. Women did obtain higher scores, however, when the dimension of "achievement" was social acceptability.

Lansky, Crandall, Kagan, and Baker (15), in a study of children aged 13 to 18, used the French Insight Test (5) to measure affiliation. The French test, as used in this study, consisted of 20 items describing a characteristic behavior of a boy (girl), e.g., "Tom never joins clubs or social groups." For each item the *S* answers these three questions: [1] what is the boy (girl) like? [2] what does he (she) want to have or do? and [3] what are the results of his (her) behavior apt to be? Girls were significantly higher than boys on preoccupation with *affiliation,* which was scored when the goal is to be liked or accepted by others or to be part of a group.

When Harris (10) repeated Symonds' 1935 studies (30, 31) of having adolescents rank interests, he found that girls persist in their greater interest in social relations than boys. When Winkler (34) analyzed the replies of children aged 7 to 16, he found that girls seemed more interested than boys in social relationships, especially face-to-face contacts. The girl's early preoccupation with affiliation was noted by Goodenough (8) who found that nursery school girls drew more pictures of persons and mentioned persons more often than boys.

Thus, these data are consistent with hypothesis 1 that females will demonstrate greater need for affiliation than males.

Evidence concerning hypothesis 2, predicting that females tend to be more dependent than males on the external context of a perceptual situation and will hesitate to deviate from the given, is furnished by Witkin, Lewis, Hertzman, Machover, Meissner, and Wapner (35). They found that female *S*s were more readily influenced by misleading cues than were male *S*s and thus were higher in "perceptual-field dependence."

Additional evidence concerning this hypothesis is found in a study by Wallach and Caron (33) with sixth-grade school children. These children were given a concept attainment session in which to establish crtieria concerning geometric forms with certain characteristics. A test session followed in which the *S*s judged whether figures of varying deviation from the standard were similar to it. It was found that girls tolerated less deviation than males by every index, thus agreeing with the hypothesis that females more than males hesitate to "move away" from the given. Both studies are in agreement with hypothesis 2.

Studies reported by Sweeney (29) are relevant to hypothesis 3 that males generally surpass females in problem-solving skills. Most of the studies reported by Sweeney support this hypothesis. Moreover, he reported experiments of his own which demonstrate that men solve certain classes of problems with greater facility than do women, even when differences in intellectual aptitude, special knowledge or training, and special abilities are controlled. Sweeney obtained scores on the College Board Scholastic Aptitude test for 130 men and 139 women to whom McNemar (21) had given four tests of logical reasoning: False Premises, Essential Operations, Syllogisms, and Problem Solving. Significant differences favoring the men were found on all four of these tests for 100 pairs who had been matched in verbal aptitude scores. For 90 pairs matched in mathematical aptitude and 69 pairs matched both in verbal and mathematical aptitude, a difference was obtained only for Problem Solving, a test which essentially involves arithmetic reasoning. In Sweeney's most elaborate experiment, large samples of men and women were given a wide variety of problems. Significant sex differences were obtained for groups matched in general intelligence, spatial ability, mechanical comprehension, mathematics, achievement, or the amount of training in mathematics. In general, the results confirmed the hypothesis that sex differences favoring men will occur in problems which involve difficulties in restructuring, but not in similar problems which involve no such difficulties.

Milton's study (22) with college students is pertinent to hypothesis 3 concerning sex differences in problem-solving skills. In this study the Terman-Miles M-F test (32) was the primary index of sex-role typing, although other M-F questionnaires were also employed. Two types of problem-solving skill, restructuring and straightforward solution, were employed, half requiring numerical solutions and half non-numerical. In general, the results indicate that there is a positive relation between the degree of masculine sex-role typing and problem-solving skill both across sexes and within a sex. When this relation is accounted for, the difference between men and women in problem-solving performance is diminished.

Thus, these studies are consistent with hypothesis 3 that males generally surpass females in problem-solving skills. Moreover, Milton's study also suggests that these differences are accounted for in the typical sex-role development of each sex.

Hypothesis 4, suggesting that males tend to be more concerned with internalized moral standards than females, is consistent with findings in the previously mentioned study of children aged 13 to 18 by Lansky, Crandall, Kagan, and Baker (15). The *S*s were given a story completion test which was designed to elicit responses regarding severity of moral standards and defenses against guilt following transgression of such standards. *Severity of moral standards* was rated for the degree to which the hero (heroine) punished himself, consciously or unconsciously, for his actions. The boys scored higher than girls on this variable. This finding is considered to support hypothesis 4 in that the *severity of moral standards* was scored when the hero (heroine) punished himself, thus implying that the standards are internalized.

Data from two national sample interview studies of adolescents, reported by Douvan (3), have relevance here. In answer to two questions to detect self-awareness, boys showed greater concern with establishing satisfactory internal standards and personal control than girls.

Findings in Douvan's studies are also in agreement with hypothesis 5 that females will be more receptive to the standards of others than males. Douvan found that girls are more likely to show an unquestioned acceptance of parental regulation. Koch (13, 14), along with Sheehy (27), found girls to be more obedient and amenable to social controls than boys. Thus, these studies seem consistent with hypothesis 5.

In general, the hypotheses that were generated by the theoretical formulation seem consistent with the data. Thus, by postulating that separate learning methods for the two sexes are derived in the process of acquiring appropriate identification, one can formulate hypotheses which are consistent with very diverse findings ranging from the males' superior problem-solving skill to the females' greater need for affiliation. It is not assumed that this formulation, in and of itself, adequately accounts for these diverse findings even though it is generally consistent with them. It is beyond the scope of this paper to attempt to integrate motivation into the formulation, or the psychological implications of anatomical and physiological differences, or adequately to place the role of the father in the development of identification in each sex. These steps, and others, would be necessary adequately to account for these findings. However, it is felt that a formulation along the lines presented here may prove to have a place in more elaborate theories of identification development and may prove helpful in making more sensitive hypotheses concerning psychological sex differences.

SUMMARY

The purpose of this paper is to present a theoretical formulation which postulates basic sex differences in the *nature* of sex-role and parental identification, as well as basic differences in the *process of achieving* such identification. There was a differentiation made between *sex-role identification* and *parental identification*.

The theoretical formulation in this paper used a hypothesis from a previous one (17) as a postulate from which to derive a number of new hypotheses. That hypothesis suggested that males tend to identify with a cultural stereotype of the masculine role, whereas females tend to identify with aspects of their own mothers' role specifically. For simplicity this paper refers to *masculine-role identification* in males as distinguished from *mother identification* in females.

This formulation adopted the distinction made by Woodworth and Schlosberg (36) between two kinds of learning tasks, viz., the problem and the lesson. This distinction was used in describing the separate task assigned each sex in learning the appropriate identification. It was further assumed that, in learning the appropriate identification, each sex acquires separate methods of learning which are subsequently applied to learning tasks generally. In learning the mother identification lesson, the little girl acquires a learning method which primarily involves: [1] a personal relationship and [2] imitation rather than restructuring the field and abstracting principles. In solving the masculine-role identification problem, the boy acquires a learning method which primarily involves: [1] finding the goal; [2] restructuring the field; and [3] abstracting principles.

By assuming that these learning methods are applicable to learning tasks generally, the following hypotheses were derived:

1. Females will demonstrate greater need for affiliation than males.
2. Females are more dependent than males on the external context of a perceptual situation and will hesitate to deviate from the given.
3. Males generally surpass females in problem-solving skills.
4. Males tend to be more concerned with internalized moral standards than females.
5. Females tend to be more receptive to the standards of others than males.

These hypotheses were in general agreement with the research findings which were reviewed.

REFERENCES

1. Bach G. R. "Father-fantasies and father-typing in father-separated children." *Child Develpm.*, 1946, **17,** 63–80.
2. Brown, D. G. "Sex-role preference in young children." *Psychol. Monogr.*, 1956, **70,** no. 14 (whole no. 421).
3. Douvan, E. "Independence and identity in adolescence." *Children,* 1957, **4,** 186–190.
4. Edwards, A. L. *Edwards Personal Preference Schedule.* Psychological Corp., 1959.
5. French, E. G. Development of a measure of complex motivation. In *Motives in Fantasy, Action, and Society: A Method of Assessment and Study,* J. Atkinson (Ed.) Van Nostrand, 1958, pp. 242–248.
6. Gesell, A., *et al. The First Five Years of Life.* Harper, 1940.
7. Gesell, A., F. L. Ilg, *et al. Infant and Child in the Culture of Today.* Harper, 1943.

8. Goodenough, E. W. "Interest in persons as an aspect of sex differences in the early years." *Genet. Psychol. Monogr.*, 1957, **55,** 287–323.
9. Gray, S. W., and R. Klaus. "The assessment of parental identification." *Genet. Psychol. Monogr.*,1956, **54,** 87–109.
10. Harris, D. B. "Sex differences in the life problems and interests of adolescents, 1935 and 1957," *Child Develpm.*, 1959, **30,** 453–459.
11. Hartley, R. E. "Sex-role pressures and the socialization of the male child." *Psychol. Rep.*, 1959, **5,** 457–468.
12. Hartup, W. W. "Some correlates of parental imitation in young children." *Child Develpm.*, 1962, **33,** 85–96.
13. Koch, H. L. "Some personality correlates of sex, sibling position, and sex of sibling among five- and six-year old children." *Genet. Psychol. Monogr.* 1955, **52,** 3–51.
14. Koch, H. L. "The relation of certain family constellation characteristics and attitudes of children toward adults." *Child Develpm.*, 1955, **26,** 13–40.
15. Lansky, L. M., V. J. Crandall, J. Kagan, and C. T. Baker. "Sex differences in aggression and its correlates in middle-class adolescents." *Child Develpm.*, 1961, **32,** 45–58.
16. Lazowick, L. M. "On the nature of identification." *J. abnorm. soc. Psychol.*, 1955, **51,** 175–183.
17. Lynn, D. B. "A note on sex differences in the development of masculine and feminine identification." *Psychol. Rev.*, 1959, **66,** 126–135.
18. Lynn, D. B., and W. L. Sawrey. "The effects of father-absence on Norwegian boys and girls." *J. abnorm. soc. Psychol.*, 1959, **59,** 258–261.
19. Maccoby, E. E. "Role-taking in childhood and its consequences for social learning." *Child Develpm.*, 1959, **30,** 239–252.
20. McClelland, D. C., J. W. Atkinson, R. A. Clark, and E. L. Lowell. *The Achievement Motive.* Appleton-Century-Crofts, 1953.
21. McNemar, O. W. *Word association, methods of deduction and induction, and reactions to set in good and poor reasoners.* Stanford Univ. Depart. of Psychol., Tech. Rep. No. 2, 1954.
22. Milton, G. A. "The effects of sex-role identification upon problem-solving skill." *J. abnorm. soc. Psychol.*, 1957, **55,** 208–212.
23. Sarason, S. B., K. S. Davidson, F. F. Lighthall, R. R. Waite, and B. F. Ruebush. *Anxiety in Elementary School Children.* Wiley, 1960.
24. Sears, R. R., E. E. Maccoby, and H. Levin. *Patterns of Child Rearing.* Row, Peterson, 1957.
25. Sears, R. R., M. H. Pintler, and P. S. Sears. "Effect of father separation on pre-school children's doll play aggression." *Child Develpm.*, 1946, **17,** 219–243.
26. Seward, G. H. *Sex and the Social Order.* McGraw-Hill, 1946.
27. Sheehy, L. M. *A study of preadolescents by means of a personality inventory.* Catholic Univ. of America, 1938.
28. Sherriffs, A. C., and R. F. Jarrett. "Sex differences in attitudes about sex differences." *J. Psychol.*, 1953, **35,** 161–168.
29. Sweeney, E. J. *Sex differences in problem solving.* Stanford Univ. Depart. of Psychol., Tech. Rep. No. 1, 1953.

30. Symonds, P. M. "Life interests and problems of adolescents." *Sch. Rev.,* 1936, **44,** 506–518.
31. Symonds, P. M. "Sex differences in the life problems and interests of adolescents." *Sch. and Soc.,* 1936, **43,** 751–752.
32. Terman, L. M., and C. C. Miles. *Sex and Personality.* McGraw-Hill, 1936.
33. Wallach, M. A., and A. J. Caron. "Attribute criteriality and sex-linked conservatism as deteminants of psychological similarity." *J. abnorm. soc. Psychol.,* 1959, **59,** 43–50.
34. Winkler, J. B. "Age trends and sex differences in the wishes, identifications, activities and fears of children." *Child Develpm.,* 1949, **20,** 191–200.
35. Witkin, H. A., H. B. Lewis, M. Hertzman, K. Machover, P. B. Meissner, and S. Wapner. *Personality through Perception.* Harper, 1954.
36. Woodworth, R. S., and H. Schlesberg. *Experimental Psychology.* Holt, 1954.

5.3 *Orientation*

The study of identification dramatizes the lack of reliable and valid measures for this concept. In fact, the lack of consensus on appropriate measurement methods is probably a major reason for the controversial nature of identification theory. Attempts to resolve this controversy have relied heavily upon the psychometric and projective methods.

The psychometric method frequently involves the use of correlational techniques to establish the degree of relationship in attitudes and interests between the responses of parents and their children. An interesting variation of the psychometric approach is reported by Heilbrun (1965), whose Identification Scale is a self-report form composed of two measures: an adjective check list based upon manifest needs and a rating of the extent to which an individual perceives himself as similar to father or mother.

A second approach to the measurement of sex-role identification is provided by the use of projective techniques. These techniques include doll play, projective drawing tests, and the "It Test." McCandless (1967) provides a review of these methods, all of which assume that an individual will project his perceptions and feelings into the "test" situations.

A third identification measurement strategy, one designed to assess expressive behavior and autonomic reactivity, is explained in the following study by Kagan and Phillips. The ingenious methodology conceived by these researchers is sufficient to make this a significant contribution to the study of identification. However, their paper is important in advancing the distinction between imitation and identification. Vicarous affective experience is postulated to be a requisite of identification, whereas a child may imitate in a variety of situations without this type of emotional involvement. In addition to the experimental conditions established for this study, readers are directed to note the three assumptions underlying the experiment which are made explicit by the authors.

RECOMMENDED READING

Heilbrun, A. B., Jr. "The measurement of identification." *Child Develpm.*, **36** (1965), 111–127.

McCandless, B. R. *Children: Behavior and Development.* (2d ed.) New York: Holt, Rinehart and Winston, 1967. (See chap. 10.)

5.3 Measurement of Identification: A Methodological Note

Jerome Kagan, HARVARD UNIVERSITY
William Phillips, FELS RESEARCH INSTITUTE

In an earlier theoretical paper (Kagan, 1958) identification was defined as the belief that some of the characteristics of a model belonged to the subject. A major implication of this definition was that if a subject was identified with a model he would behave as if events occurring to the model were occurring to him. This conception of identification leads one to look for situations in which subjects might show vicarious involvement in the experiences of models, and to use degree of such involvement as an index of identification. This operational definition of identification differs from more popular indexes that rely on similarity in behavior between a subject and a model. Since such similarities can arise through a variety of mechanisms (i.e., reward and punishment sequences) they are, at best, imperfect measures of degree of identification. The data to be presented in this brief report summarize a preliminary attempt to assess whether children would show signs of greater involvement in the performance of the same-sex parent than in the performance of a stranger. The indexes used were both behavioral and autonomic. The assumptions behind the experiment follow.

Reprinted from *Journal of Abnormal and Social Psychology,* **69** (1964), no. 4, 442–444. By permission of the authors and the American Psychological Association, Inc.

1. The child is more highly identified with the parent of the same sex than with a stranger of the same sex.

2. If a child is identified with a model, the child should behave as if events occurring to the model were occurring to him (i.e., vicarious involvement with the model).

3. Differences in degree of vicarious involvement should be manifested in differential signs of joy or sadness, and hopefully in differential degrees of cardiac reactivity to experiences occurring to the model.

In the experiment the child was told that he was going to watch a contest between his parent and a stranger. Both parent and stranger had been prerehearsed to fail and pass specific items on a test and it was expected that the child would behave differentially in this situation.

METHOD

Subjects

The subjects were 16 children (7 boys and 9 girls) and their same-sex parent. The subjects ranged in age from 5–6 to 8–7.

Procedure

The subject was told that he was going to watch a contest between his parent and (Mr. or Mrs.) ———, and that his muscles would be measured while he watched this contest. Electrodes for measuring heart rate were then attached to the subject's right arm and left leg and a transducer was placed around his chest to record respiration. The child was seated between the stranger and the parent and all three individuals sat facing a screen. From this point on all communications were directed to the adults and the child was ignored. The adults were told that pictures would be projected on the screen in front of them. Their task was to detect the differences between two similar pictures (4 parents were given this instruction) or to classify a picture that was initially blurred and was gradually brought into focus (12 parents were given this instruction). The adults were told that the winner would receive a valuable prize.

The parent and stranger were first given two practice pictures followed by eight test pictures. The adults alternated in solving the perceptual problem. The parent and stranger each passed and failed four of the test items according to a prearranged schedule. The examiner praised the adult when he passed and censured him when he failed. Neither parent nor stranger looked at the child throughout the 60-minute experiment. When one adult was performing the other sat with hands folded looking down at his lap. In addition to the monitoring of heart rate and respiration, an observer viewed the subject through a one-way vision screen and coded his behavior every 10 seconds during the experiment. The categories of child behavior were: looks at parent, looks at stranger, looks at picture on screen, smiles, looks away from screen and adult, and restless movement.

The child's behavior and cardiac reactions were studied during the time when the parent or stranger was trying to solve the perceptual task, and after the examiner announced whether the adult had passed or failed the test item.

RESULTS

Behavioral Observations

Occurrence of smiling after the examiner announced the success or failure of the adult was the only behavior to differentiate the child's reactions to parent versus stranger. The mean number of smiles after a parent success was 3.2; whereas the corresponding value following stranger's success was only 1.1. When parent success and stranger failure were pooled and contrasted with parent failure and stranger success, the means were 5.0 versus 2.1 ($t = 2.71$, $p < .02$, two-tailed). Thus, the child behaved as though he were elated by the success of his parent or the failure of the stranger—a reasonable indication of vicarious involvement with the parent.

Other aspects of the child's behavior during the time that the adult was studying the pictures were in a predicted direction but not statistically significant. The child looked more at the parent than at the stranger, and was slightly less distractible and less restless when the parent was attempting to solve the problem than when the stranger was performing.

Cardiac Reactions

The child's heart rate during the times when the parent was solving the problem did not differ from his heart rate when the stranger was studying the stimulus. However, the amount of cardiac acceleration following the examiner's statement regarding the success or failure of parent or stranger indicated greater involvement with the parent. In this analysis the first 15 heartbeats immediately following the examiner's statement of praise or failure were divided into 3 groups of 5 each. The mean of the first 5 beats was then subtracted from the mean of the second or third set of 5 beats, whichever was higher. The larger this difference the greater the acceleration to the examiner's communication of praise or failure. The mean acceleration following parent success and stranger failure was significantly larger than the acceleration following parent failure and stranger success ($t = 1.83$, $p < .10$, two-tailed).

DISCUSSION

These data offer tentative support for the feasibility of measuring degree of identification with the model—in vivo—in a laboratory situation. The greater number of smiles and larger cardiac accelerations to events that were "good" for the parent (i.e., parent success or stranger failure) suggest that the child was vicariously sharing in the positive experiences of the parental model and was behaving as if events that occurred to the model were occurring to him. This association between psychological involvement in the situation and cardiac acceleration agrees with conclusions reached in another investigation (Kagan and Moss, 1962).

It is acknowledged that interpretation of these results does not require introduction of the concept of identification. One could argue that these findings would occur with any pair of social objects with whom the child was differentially familiar (e.g., sibling versus strange peer; opposite-sex parent versus stranger). Or one could argue that these results are the result of differential empathy. It is not an easy task to decide which of these interpretations is most valid, for identification is more likely to occur with social objects with whom the child is familiar and with whom he feels empathic. Thus, empathy, familiarity, and identification tend to covary. The phenomena described here are not regarded as unambiguous evidence of the authors' definition of identification, but are predicted by that definition.

The major purpose of this note is to communicate to others the feasibility of measuring affective involvement in a laboratory setting and to stimulate other investigators to develop measures of identification that rely on vicarious involvement with a model.

SUMMARY

Each of 16 children (age 5–8 years) watched his same-sex parent and a stranger of the same sex compete in a perceptual recognition task. Stranger and parent were prerehearsed to pass and fail specific items during the competition, and each was praised or censured following success or failure. The child's overt behavior and heart rate were recorded during the session. The children smiled more after the parent succeeded and the stranger failed than after parent failure and stranger success. Degree of cardiac acceleration following parent success and stranger failure was larger than under the opposite conditions. The data suggest the feasibility of assessing vicarious involvement with the model as an index of identification.

REFERENCES

Kagan, J. "The concept of identification." *Psychol. Rev.*, **65** (1958), 296–305.

Kagan, J., and H. A. Moss. *Birth to Maturity: A Study of Psychological Development.* New York: Wiley, 1962.

5.4 *Orientation*

One of the first, and most difficult, tasks facing those who are beginning their study of a scientific discipline is to learn the technical vocabulary. This is patently true of psychology. Students' difficulties notwithstanding, a specific technical vocabulary is imperative if psychologists and other behavioral scientists are to communicate clearly with one another. The basic problem is that this technical vocabulary has not in all instances been standardized or agreed upon by all specialists in child study.

The issue of overlapping concepts is central to the following paper by Winfred Hill. His specific concern is with the process of value acquisition, a process popularly explained by way of the identification phenomenon. Acknowledging the multifarious ways in which the terms *identification, internalization,* and *introjection* are used, Hill proposes an application of the principle of parsimony to help resolve this issue. In other words, he suggests that we may more clearly and accurately explain the acquisition of values and the development of character by using the consensual vocabulary of learning theory without resorting to these other concepts. Readers will recall that in the preceding paper, Kagan and Phillips question whether it is necessary to introduce the concept of identification to explain their findings on vicarious involvement. The issue reduces to one fundamental question: Is the concept of identification superfluous if one accepts basic conditioning principles?

Hill's paper provides a succinct review of many principles of learning which are sprinkled throughout this volume, especially in Chapter 2. Readers may wish to consider Hill's viewpoint in relation to that expressed by Lowe in his discussion of the self concept (Chapter 3), for both men dissect a psychological concept for the purpose of evaluating its validity. Finally, readers are encouraged to question the extent to which present learning theory adequately explains character development.

RECOMMENDED READING

Eysenck, H. J. "Symposium: The development of moral values in children (VII) The contribution of learning theory." *Brit. J. educ. Psychol.,* **30** (1960), 11–21.

5.4 Learning Theory and the Acquisition of Values

Winfred F. Hill, NORTHWESTERN UNIVERSITY

The processes by which a child acquires the values of his culture and his various overlapping subcultures is, as a recent review of the subject points out (Dukes, 1955), still rather obscure. This obscurity is certainly not due to lack of interest in the topic. Psychologists, psychiatrists, anthropologists, sociologists, pediatricians, and educators have all given attention to the question of how children come to share the attitudes, ideals, and ethical standards of those around them. Nor is this interest undeserved, for few topics are of greater practical importance.

Perhaps this very convergence of interest from many directions is partly responsible for the difficulties involved in studying the topic. This area of research has become a battleground for conflicting terminologies, with one term often having a multiplicity of half-distinct meanings, and with what appears to be the same meaning often bearing different labels. Although many terms contribute to this confusion, three are of particular interest here: *identification, introjection,* and *internalization.* All involve some relation between an individual, hereinafter designated the subject (*S*), and another person or personalized entity, the model or *M,* such that *S*'s behavior is in some way patterned after *M*'s. However, these terms may refer either to a state of affairs or to the process which brought it about (Lazowick, 1955); the *M* may be a person, a group, or an idea (Glaser, 1958); and the relation may involve specific responses, broad meanings, or emotional reactions.

Some of the confusion as to the meaning of the term identification may be seen in the following uses. Lazowick (1955) distinguishes three main uses of the term identification in the literature: pseudoidentity, imitation, and personality change. He suggests that the term should be used only with regard to broad meanings, with imitation being the corresponding term for specific acts. Freud (1950) contrasts a boy's identification with his father, which forms the basis of his ego ideal, and his identification with his mother as an abandoned object cathexis. Davis and Havighurst (1947) maintain that a child will identify with his parents only if he loves them, but Anna Freud (1946) emphasizes identification with the aggressor. Lynn (1959) contrasts sex-role identification, which is "reserved to refer to the actual incorporation of the role of a given sex, and to the unconscious reactions characteristic of that role" (p. 127), with sex-role preference and

Reprinted from *Psychological Review,* **67** (1960), no. 5, 317–331. By permission of the author and the American Psychological Association, Inc.

sex-role adoption. He regards figure drawing as a measure of identification and choice of dolls for play as a measure of preference. Sears, Maccoby, and Levin (1957), however, use children's choices of dolls as a measure of identification. Sanford (1955), discouraged by such confusions of meaning, considers the possibility of abandoning the term identification altogether, but decides to retain it to describe a defense mechanism involving extreme adoption of *M*'s behavior by *S*, a mechanism which is not important in normal personality development. Finally, this collection of meanings, diverse as it is, still omits those cases where identification is used as a synonym for loyalty or for empathy.

There is similar confusion concerning the meaning of introjection and internalization. Both carry the implication of values being incorporated into the personality. Hence, particularly with introjection, there is the suggestion of some relation with orality (Freud, 1950). However, Freud in the same discussion also uses introjection synonymously with identification. Parsons (1955), on the other hand, treats identification and internalization as synonyms.

The many discussions of these three terms in the literature seem to indicate that there are several processes involved but no generally accepted conventions for labeling them. A number of writers, including several already cited, have expressed discouragement at this state of affairs, but the usual result of such discouragement seems to be a redefinition of terms, which may clarify the particular exposition but which only serves further to confuse the field as a whole. Whereas Lynn (1959) believes that a term as widespread as identification must have potential usefulness, the present writer believes that clarity would be served by abolishing not only identification but also introjection and internalization from the technical vocabulary of personality development.

What, then, should be substituted? The topics to which the above terms have been applied certainly deserve discussion, and if the redefinition of the old terms is unsatisfactory, the introduction of new terms would be even worse. An answer may be found, however, in a sort of reductionism. Since the processes involved are learning processes, the existing vocabulary of learning is the obvious candidate for the job of describing them. It is quite possible, of course, that the existing vocabulary of learning theory will be inadequate for the complexities of value acquisition. However, if its use is carried as far as possible, the successes of this application should clarify our thinking about personality development, while any gaps which result should point to possible extensions of learning theory.

This approach involves treating human learning in a sociocultural environment in the same terms, at least for a first approximation, as animal learning in the environment of laboratory apparatus. For this purpose, the social rewards and punishments applied to humans may be treated as equivalent to the food pellets and electric shocks used with rats. Similarly, social roles are the equivalents of mazes which must be learned in order to obtain the rewards and avoid the punishments. Human beings of course constitute a far more variable environment than laboratory hardware, and one on which *S* can exercise greater influence. However, since most of the theory in this area is concerned with the adaptation of *S* to a relatively constant human environment (whether it be called culture, social system, or the personalities of the parents), this should not prove a serious stumbling block. There is ample precedent for such an approach in the writings of Dollard and Miller (1950), Mowrer (1950), Whiting and Child (1953), and others.

In addition, this approach treats values as nothing more than inferences from overt behavior. In principle this assumption should cause no difficulty. Few behavioral scientists would regard values (in the empirical, not the transcendental sense) as fundamentally different from such behavioristic constructs as Hull's (1943) habit strength or Tolman's (1949) equivalence beliefs. In practice, however, some theorists might take issue with this view on at least two bases.

For one thing, the measurement of values (including attitudes, ideals, and ethical standards) is commonly by verbal methods (see the review by Dukes, 1955). This leads to the suspicion that any measurement of values by nonverbal means must be inadequate, that only verbal measures can get at the significance of an act for an individual. However, verbal responses are part of the total behavior of the human organism and may be studied like other responses. The processes of unconscious motivation, semiconscious hypocrisy, and deliberate concealment all indicate that it would be unwise to treat verbal and nonverbal measures of values as equivalent. Rather than treat either verbal or nonverbal behavior as the true indicator of values and the other as a side issue, it seems more useful to study both and to ascertain empirically to what extent they lead to the same generalizations about a given *S*.

Another possible objection involves the distinction between specific acts and broad meanings, as in Lazowick's (1955) contrasting definitions of imitation and identification, noted above. This distinction between specific acts and broad meanings may refer either to the presence of mediating responses (see Osgood, 1953) or to the generality of the stimuli and responses involved. Neither of these distinctions, however, is dichotomous. Hull (1952) has indicated how a mediator, the fractional antedating goal response, may function in animal behavior, and Russell and Storms (1955) have demonstrated mediational processes in rote learning. Thus the mediation mechanism is by no means restricted to the "higher mental processes" of humans. As for the generality of the behavior and of the stimuli which guide it, this presumably represents a continuum from the most specific to the most inclusive categories. If, for example, washing the hands before meals is an example of imitation and cleanliness an example of identification, where would wearing clean clothes be classified? So, although the distinction between specific acts and broad meanings is a legitimate one, there are no sharp breaks on the continuum and there is no reason to assume that basically different laws are involved.

In view of the above considerations, an attempt to study the acquisition of values as a branch of learning theory appears justified.

KINDS OF REINFORCEMENT

The concept of reinforcement is basic to learning theory. While theorists are by no means unanimously agreed on the value of reinforcement terminology, there is little question that an empirical law of effect holds, that the consequences of an act influence its subsequent occurrence. A classification of kinds of reinforcers will be used here as the basis for analyzing the learning of values.

Primary Reinforcement

For the present purpose, three kinds of reinforcement may be distinguished: *"primary," secondary,* and *vicarious.* Placing "primary" in quotes indicates that it refers to the effects not only of innate physiological reinforcers but also of those social reinforcers which play a primary role in human motivation. Presumably the positively reinforcing effects of attention and praise and the negatively reinforcing effects of criticism, ridicule, and rejection are at least partly learned, but the nature of the learning process is obscure, and at the present level of analysis it seems preferable to treat praise for a human as comparable to food for a rat. The distinction between "primary" and secondary reinforcement is thus one of convenience between that which we take as given and that for which we can find a specific learned basis. Though arbitrary, this distinction is perhaps no more so than the decision as to whether food in the mouth should be considered a primary or a secondary reinforcer.

One particular kind of learning by "primary" reinforcement is the acquisition of a generalized tendency to imitate others. Miller and Dollard (1941) have indicated how a generalized tendency to imitate the behavior of others may be learned in the same way as any other class of responses. Although their demonstrations of imitation involved *S*'s patterning his behavior after a leader who was present, Church (1957) has shown that rats can also learn to respond appropriately to the same cues to which the leader rat is responding. In spite of some negative animal evidence (Solomon and Coles, 1954), there is little doubt that humans can learn to pattern their behavior after that of other people, not only when the *M* is present, but also in *M*'s absence by utilizing the appropriate environmental cues. As the child is repeatedly rewarded for imitative behavior in a variety of otherwise different situations, and as his capacity for abstraction increases, it seems plausible that a generalized imitative tendency would develop. It would be desirable, however, if the widespread anecdotal support for this deduction could be bolstered by experimental data.

The same process presumably applies to verbal instructions. The child is typically reinforced (though with some striking exceptions) for doing what others tell him to do. Hence (common parental impressions to the contrary notwithstanding), a generalized tendency toward conformity to verbal instructions may be expected to develop. With increasing intellectual development, this tendency should come to include conformity to fictional examples or to abstract ethical exhortations.

Secondary Reinforcement

Although no basic distinction is made here between primary and secondary reinforcement, there is one case frequently discussed in the literature where the acquisition of reinforcing properties by certain stimuli may be analyzed in detail. These stimuli are those which are connected with care of the child by adults, i.e., the non-essential aspects of nurturance. These include patterns of speech, facial expressions, gestures, and the like. Since these occur with those nurturant behaviors which are primary reinforcers, such as feeding and cuddling, they may become secondary reinforcers. By stimulus generalization, these behaviors should also be rewarding to the child (although less so) when produced by himself. As the child grows older and the parents expect him to take greater care of his own needs, he is more and more forced to provide not only his own primary reinforcers, but his own secondary reinforcers as well. Hence he may be expected to show some of the same mannerisms as his parents showed when caring for him.

This kind of learning appears to be one of those processes which Freud (1950) includes under the heading of identification or introjection, that in which abandoned object cathexes become incorporated into the ego. However, in the view presented here, the coincidence of abandonment and incorporation into the ego refers only to performance, not to learning. The secondary reinforcing value of the parental mannerisms is built up during the period of nurturance, but becomes evident in the child's behavior as nurturance begins to be withdrawn. This learning process has been discussed by Mowrer (1950, Ch. 24) in connection with the learning of language, and by Lindemann (1944) as a reaction to the death of a loved one. Although this process appears better adapted to the learning of rather trivial mannerisms, it is capable at least in principle of being adapted to more general and significant values as well.

Vicarious Reinforcement

Vicarious reinforcement does not have the same dignified status in learning theory as do primary and secondary reinforcement, but some such process appears necessary in order to explain some important human learning.

Vicarious reinforcement involves the generalization of reinforcing effects from others to oneself, hence learning from the reinforcers which others receive. A given act is reinforced for *S* as a result of the act being performed by *M,* followed by reinforcement to *M*. For example, if *S* observes *M* trying to solve a problem by certain techniques and succeeding, *S* is more likely to use the same techniques when faced by a similar problem than if *M* had failed to solve the problem. Although most of the evidence for such learning is anecdotal, Lewis and Duncan (1958) have provided some evidence of it in a human gambling situation, and Darby and Riopelle (1959) have demonstrated it in discrimination learning by monkeys.

Although vicarious reinforcement involves selective imitation, it differs from the selectivity of imitation, described by Miller and Dollard (1941), in which *S* imitates some *M*s and not others because of differential reinforcement received by *S* for imitating the two *M*s. Vicarious reinforcement does not involve any reinforcers delivered directly to *S;* the discrimination of *M*s to be imitated or not is made entirely on the basis of *S*'s observation of *M*'s experience. This distinction is emphasized by Campbell (in press). In Hullian terms, vicarious reinforcement involves the acquisition of *K* by observation.

This type of learning need not be restricted to the effect of particular reinforcers administered to *M* under specific conditions. Stimulus generalization should occur not only from *M*'s behavior to *S*'s but also from one act of *M*'s to another. As a result, if *M* is frequently reinforced, *S* should find it rewarding to resemble *M* in general, including imitation of some of *M*'s behaviors which *S* has never seen rewarded. Thus a beginning salesman (*S*) might treat a customer with extreme politeness because he had observed another salesman (*M*) making a large sale while using such behavior, and he might also smoke a cigar because he had observed his highly successful salesmanager (*M*) doing so. In the former case *M*'s behavior (politeness) and *M*'s reinforcement (a large sale) were paired, whereas in the latter case the reinforcement (business success) was a perennial experience of *M,* but not paired with the particular behavior (smoking cigars) in question. Both, however, are examples of vicarious reinforcement.

Vicarious reinforcement corresponds to identification as defined by Masserman (1946) and to that aspect of identification referred to by Kagan (1958) as "the motivation to command or experience desired goal states of a model" (p. 298). Freud's (1946) identification with the aggressor also fits under this heading if successful aggression is assumed to be reinforcing to the aggressor. Sanford's (1955) concept of identification also involves the adoption as *M* of someone perceived by *S* as successful.

Conflicting Sources of Reinforcement

Traditionally the terms identification, introjection, and internalization might be applied to any or all of the learning processes described above or to their end product, similarity between *S* and some *M*. Since for the most part these processes involve learning by imitation, require some kind of reinforcement, and result in similarity between *S* and *M*, it may be asked why detailed analysis of the rather subtle differences among them is called for.

The answer is apparent when the possibility of conflict is considered. Conditions for a given *S* may be such that one of these processes tends to produce one kind of behavior while another tends to produce quite different or even opposite behavior. Such a conflictful situation might be expected in a child reared by a nurturant mother, whose mannerisms would become secondarily reinforcing, and a domineering father, who would be perceived as successful in mastering the environment. Freud (1950) recognized the frequent occurrence of just such a conflict, but did not consider it necessary to use different words for the two learning processes. Another common conflict is between the tendency to imitate *M*s whom *S* is directly reinforced for imitating (e.g., well behaved children) and the tendency to imitate *M*s whom *S* perceives as successful (e.g., tough kids). Such conflict is inevitable to a certain extent in children, since they are not permitted to imitate their (presumably more successful) elders in all respects, but it is particularly prominent in members of low-status social categories, (e.g., Negroes) who are often conspicuously not reinforced for imitating high-status *M*s. In the broadest sense, any situation where there is discrepancy among what *S* is told to do, what he is rewarded for doing, and what he sees others doing is a potential conflict situation, and one in which the use of any single inclusive term such as "identification" obscures the relevant variables.

The occurrence of conflict among the various reinforcement processes makes possible a finer analysis of the acquisition of values than could be made otherwise. If there is perfect agreement among what *S* is told to do, what those who nurture him do, what those around him conspicuously master the environment by doing, and what he himself is directly rewarded for doing, there is little basis for judging how much each of these factors contributed to *S*'s adoption of the values of those around him. By observing situations in which they conflict, greater knowledge of the efficacy of each kind of reinforcement may be obtained. Research in conflict situations might answer such theoretically and practically important questions as: "Does dominance or nurturance on *M*'s part do more to make *M* effective in modifying *S*'s values?"; "Do words and examples completely lose their efficacy if the appropriate behaviors, when elicited, are not reinforced?"; and "To what extent is behavior influenced by *M*s presented verbally (e.g., in literature)?"

There is of course no special merit to the classificatory scheme presented here. Except for the concept of vicarious reinforcement, the writer has avoided attaching distinctive labels to the learning processes described. The purpose of this discussion was to show how the terminology of learning theory can be applied to processes of value acquisition which have been described by personality theorists. This not only serves as a step toward the integration of these two areas of study, but also suggests the probable usefulness of employing such independent variables as number, percentage, magnitude and delay of reinforcement, distribution of practice, and discriminability of stimuli in the study of value acquisition. As both learning theory and personality theory develop further, it is to be expected that any schema developed now will be at least partially replaced by newer concepts. Rather than developing in further detail the ideas suggested above, the remainder of this discussion will therefore concentrate on the application of this kind of thinking to a narrower area, the development of conscience.

CONSCIENCE

Negative values, or conscience, have received much more attention than positive values. Educators seeking to improve children's characters, psychoanalysts concerned with the tyranny of the superego, anthropologists trying to distinguish between shame and guilt cultures, and experimental psychologists noting the persistence of avoidance responses have shared this emphasis on values of the "Thou shalt not" variety. Because of this widespread interest in conscience, it is a particularly appropriate topic with which to illustrate the possibilities of the learning theory approach to the study of values. Sears, Maccoby, and Levin (1957), in their challenging book *Patterns of Child Rearing,* devote a chapter to the development of conscience in preschool children. Their treatment of the topic will serve as a starting point for the present analysis.

Criteria for Conscience

Sears, Maccoby, and Levin give three criteria for recognizing the operation of conscience in young children: *resistance to temptation, self-instructions* to obey the rules, and *evidence of guilt* when transgression occurs. These three criteria are treated jointly as defining conscience, and no attempt is made to analyze their separate developments. Although the authors mention that the aspects of conscience do not necessarily all appear at once, they regard conscience as representing an internalization of control which is fundamentally different from external control, whether by force, fear of punishment, or hope of material reward. This treatment of conscience as essentially a single variable seems premature in our present state of knowledge; certainly the learning theory approach to personality advocated here would involve separate analyses of these diverse response patterns.

The first criterion, *resistance to temptation,* may be viewed simply as avoidance learning. Although this kind of learning is still a focus of theoretical controversy, much experimental data are available concerning it (Solomon and Brush, 1956). Sidman's (1953) studies of avoidance behavior without a warning signal and Dinsmoor's (1954) analysis of punishment show how feedback from an individual's own acts can become a cue for avoidance, and how persistent such avoidance may be. Although children can presumably learn to respond to more abstract characteristics of cues than can animals, there is no reason to regard a child's learning to avoid certain behaviors as fundamentally different from a rat's learning to do so. The fact that the child avoids the forbidden acts even in the absence of the parents is presumably due to the parents' having in the past discovered and punished (in the broadest sense of that word) transgressions committed in their absence.

This relating of conscience to avoidance learning suggests that independent variables known to be effective in animal avoidance learning would be among the most appropriate ones for study in connection with the development of conscience in children. Within certain limits, the greater the intensity of the punishments (Brush, 1957; Miller, 1951) and the shorter the delay between transgression and punishment, (Mowrer and Ullman, 1945; Solomon and Brush, 1956) the greater should be the resulting inhibition. Though the data are somewhat ambiguous, greater certainty of punishment might be expected to produce inhibition which would be more complete in the short run but also less persistent once punishment was permanently withdrawn (Grant, Schipper and Ross, 1952; Jenkins and Stanley, 1950; Reynolds, 1958). This prediction suggests that even this one criterion of conscience may not be unitary, that different laws may apply depending on whether one asks how completely the child obeys the prohibitions or how long he continues to obey them after leaving the parental home. If partial reinforcement should turn out to be a crucial variable in the human situation, these two criteria might even be inversely related. The prediction also suggests that the question, "Is inconsistent discipline bad?" is far too simple; one must at least ask, "Bad for what?"

It must also be kept in mind that punishment is not restricted to physical chastisement or even to noxious stimuli in general, including scolding and ridicule. Withdrawal of positive reinforcers may be very effective as a punishment, a fact which complicates the analysis. As this is a much discussed topic in personality theory, it will be considered below.

Sears, Maccoby, and Levin's second criterion of conscience, *self-instruction,* obviously makes the human case different from the animal case, but it does not introduce any new motivational principle. One of the advantages of membership in the human species is the possibility of using verbal symbolization in dealing with one's problems. It is natural that a person learning an avoidance, like a person learning any other difficult response pattern, should give himself verbal instructions, especially since verbal coaching by others is so important in the learning of social prohibitions. Moreover, such self-instruction is an imitative act which might be learned according to any of the reinforcement paradigms discussed above. Presumably the learning of prohibitions proceeds differently in verbal and nonverbal organisms, but observations of the relation between moral statements and moral behavior (Hurlock, 1956, pp. 406, 411–412) argue against the assumption that there is a high correlation between verbal and other criteria of conscience, except as both are influenced by the values represented in the social environment.

The third criterion of conscience, *guilt* at violations of the prohibitions, is itself complex, with many verbal, autonomic, and gross behavioral aspects. However, the striking paradox about guilt, which has seemed to some students to set it apart from the ordinary laws of learning, is that it often involves the seeking of punishment. The person who has transgressed, rather than trying to avoid punishment, or even waiting passively for it to come, actively seeks out the authorities, confesses, and receives his punishment with apparent relief. He may also, or instead, go to great lengths to make restitution. Were it not for these phenomena of punishment-seeking and self-sacrificing restitution, it would be easy to dismiss guilt as merely the kind of fear associated with anticipation of certain sorts of punishment. As it is, the existence of guilt serves as an argument for regarding conscience as something more than the sum of all those avoidances which have moral significance in one's culture.

However, the attempt to distinguish between guilt-controlled and other behaviors has not been very successful. Though the distinction between guilt cultures and shame cultures has had a considerable vogue in anthropology (e.g., Benedict, 1946; Havighurst and Neugarten, 1955; Mead, 1950), the inadequacies of the distinction have been pointed out by Ausubel (1955) and by Singer (1953). Moreover, the relation between conformity to a standard and guilt when the standard has been violated is open to question. Shaw (1948) suggests that confession may even be so satisfying to some people that it constitutes a reinforcement for sinning. So, although the phenomena of guilt may raise difficulties for learning theory, these difficulties probably cannot be solved by using guilt to define a distinctive kind of learning.

The above considerations should suffice to indicate that conscience cannot be assumed *a priori* to be unitary. The extent to which short-run conformity, long-run conformity, self-instructions to conform, certain kinds of distress at having failed to conform, and voluntary confession of nonconformity are intercorrelated is a matter to be empirically determined. Moreover, even if high positive intercorrelations are found, it is possible that they may reflect correlations in the environment rather than any fundamental unity of process. If environmental pressures toward conformity vary markedly, artificially high correlations among the criteria of conscience are to be expected. However, even when this artifact is removed, an analysis of separate learning processes for different behaviors may still lead to the prediction of high correlations among the behaviors. Such an analysis is presented below.

Learning of Conscience

Sears, Maccoby, and Levin found that the development of conscience, as defined jointly by their three criteria, was greater in those children whose parents used love-oriented forms of discipline (praise, isolation, and withdrawal of love) than in those whose parents used "materialistic" forms of discipline (material rewards, deprivation of privileges, and physical punishment). A similar finding, though not highly reliable statistically, is reported by Whiting and Child (1953, Ch. 11) in a cross-cultural study of guilt as measured by attitudes toward illness. This is consistent with the widely held view that the acquisition of parental values occurs most fully in an atmosphere of love (e.g., Ausubel, 1955; Davis and Havighurst, 1947). It is possible, however, that this finding may be due, not to love-oriented discipline as such, but to other characteristics of discipline which are correlated with it. The effect of this kind of discipline may be to accentuate the learning of several different responses, all of which contribute to the overall diagnosis of high conscience.

The various kinds of punishments commonly applied to children probably differ markedly in the temporal relations and the reinforcement contingencies involved. Physical punishment is likely to occur all at once and be over quickly, while punishment by deprivation of objects or privileges is likely to be either for a fixed period of time or for as long as the disciplinarian finds convenient. Discipline by withdrawal of love, on the other hand, probably much more often lasts until the child makes some symbolic renunciation of his wrongdoing, as by apologizing, making restitution, or promising not to do it again. The child is deprived of his parents' love (or, the parents would claim, of the outward manifestations of it!) for as much or as little time as is necessary to get him to make such a symbolic renunciation. When he has made it, he is restored to his parents' favor. If the normal relation between the parents and child is one of warmth, such discipline strongly motivates the child to make the renunciation quickly. On repeated occasions of transgression, punishment by withdrawal of love, and symbolic renunciation, the child may be expected not only to learn the renunciation response as an escape from parental disfavor but eventually to use it as an avoidance rather than merely an escape response. Thus if the wrongdoing is not immediately discovered, the child may anticipate his parents' impending disfavor by confessing in advance and making the symbolic renunciation.

The result of this hypothesized sequence of events is that the child makes a verbal response which is in effect an instruction to himself not to repeat his wrongdoing. The next time temptation comes, he is more likely to make this verbal response before transgressing. Although this does not guarantee that he will not transgress, it is likely to reduce the probability. If he succumbs to temptation, he is more likely to confess before being caught and thereby avoid the temporary loss of his parents' love. Thus if the above reasoning is correct, all three criteria of conscience should be present to a greater degree in the child who has been disciplined in this fashion than in other children. According to the present hypothesis, however, this will be due to the fact that punishment continues until the child makes a symbolic renunciation, rather than to the fact that the punishment involves withdrawal of love. If physical chastisement or loss of privileges are used in the same way, the same outcome is predicted.

A possible weakness of this hypothesis is that children might learn a discrimination between the symbolic and the actual avoidances, so that they would develop a pattern of violating parental standards, immediately confessing and apologizing, and then transgressing again at the next hint of temptation. If forgiveness is offered freely and uncritically enough, such a pattern presumably does develop. In this case the correlation among the criteria of conscience would be expected to drop, actual avoidance of wrongdoing no longer being associated with the other criteria. (For this reason, Sears, Maccoby, and Levin might have found smaller relations if they had studied older children.) However, if the parents' discrimination keeps up with the child's so that the child cannot count on removing all the parents' disfavor with a perfunctory apology, the efficacy of this kind of discipline should be at least partially maintained.

If this explanation of greater conscience in children disciplined by withdrawal of love is correct, why was greater conscience also found with the other kinds of love-oriented control? Since these were all found to be intercorrelated, and since their relations to the degree of conscience were uniformly low, interpretations either of separate techniques or of love orientation as a general trait are necessarily somewhat dubious. As an example of the difficulties involved, it may be noted that reasoning with the child is counted as a love-oriented technique solely on the grounds of its correlation with the other such techniques. Nevertheless, it shows a higher relation to conscience than do two of the three clearly love-oriented techniques. In view of such complexities, it seems legitimate to suggest that the crucial factor in those techniques associated with conscience may not be love orientation as such, but something else correlated with it.

To test this hypothesis, it would be necessary to have further detailed information of the sort that Sears, Maccoby, and Levin used, so that disciplinary methods could be classified according to the time relations discussed above. It is predicted that the parents' tendency to make termination of punishment contingent on symbolic renunciation would be correlated with love-oriented discipline. However, if each were varied with the other held constant, conscience should be more closely related to response contingency than to love orientation.

Along with this overall analysis of conscience, more detailed analyses could be made of the various components of conscience. According to the present view, intercorrelations among these criteria would be moderate for the entire sample and low when method of discipline was held constant.

The learning sequence discussed above is only one of several possible explanations of the Sears, Maccoby, and Levin finding. By suggesting that the crucial causal factor is not the distinction between materialistic orientation and love orientation, but another distinction correlated with it, the present hypothesis gains an advantage in objectivity and in practical applicability. Whether it also has the advantage of correctness must be empirically determined. The chief purpose of the present example is to point to the availability of such reductionist hypotheses in the study of values and to argue that they deserve priority in the schedule of scientific investigation.

Permanence of Conscience

It would be particularly desirable to have a follow-up study to compare evidences of conscience in kindergarten with those of the same people later in life, when they were no longer primarily under the direct influence of their parents. Such a follow-up would help to clarify the relation between short-run and long-run conformity discussed above. Is the child who thoroughly obeys all his parents' prohibitions also the one who sticks to these standards when his parents are no longer around and his new associates have different standards? Anecdotal evidence can be cited on both sides, though the bulk is probably in the affirmative. To the extent that current and later conformity are independent, what variables influence one more than the other?

Predictions from learning theory on this topic are by no means unambiguous. Nevertheless, two lines of reasoning may be suggested concerning the type of discipline likely to result in the most persistent avoidances. (Persistence here refers, not to absolute level of avoidance, but to relative lack of decrement in the strength of avoidance with time.)

The first line of reasoning is from the differences in the slopes of *generalization gradients* for different kinds of learning (Dollard and Miller, 1950). In most cases the contrast in slope is between approach (or excitatory) and avoidance (or inhibitory) tendencies. It appears, however, that the basic distinction is between response tendencies activated by innate and by learned (generally fear) drives (Miller and Murray, 1952). When stimulus conditions change, the resultant removal of cues for fear produces a greater weakening of response tendencies based on fear than of response tendencies based on other drives. Hence, the generalization gradient of responses and inhibitions based on fear is steeper than that of other responses and inhibitions. This implies that discipline based on fear should lose its efficacy more quickly than discipline based on rewards as distance from the disciplinarian or any other change in conditions increases. Since this difference in slope is found on continua both of distance (Miller, 1944) and of similarity (Miller and Kraeling, 1952; Murray and Miller, 1952), it seems reasonable to predict that it also applies to that complex continuum along which an individual makes the transition away from parental apron strings. It would follow from this analysis that of two inhibitions learned in childhood, equal in age and original strength, one learned from the threat of losing rewards would be more effective later in life than one learned from the fear-provoking threat of punishment.

In this analysis, the advantages of discipline by manipulation (including withdrawal) of reward would apply to any kind of reward, material or social, not merely to parental love. However, the desire to continue receiving love from the parents may persist after the child has outgrown the need for other parental rewards, such as gifts and privileges. Discipline by withdrawal of love, in an atmosphere of warmth, might therefore be even more effective than other forms of discipline by denial of reward in producing persistent avoidances.

The other line of reasoning, involving the *partial reinforcement effect,* argues for the persistence of conscience learned by the process outlined above, in which a symbolic renunciation of wrongdoing terminates punishment. Although the greater resistance to extinction of responses which have received less than 100% reinforcement has been demonstrated primarily with positive reinforcement, it applies to negative as well (Humphreys, 1939, 1940; Grant, Schipper, and Ross, 1952). Partial reinforcement is of course present with all kinds of discipline, since punishment depends on the parents' moods and on the social situation, as well as on the child's being caught. However, the above analysis of the kind of punishment which terminates when the child makes a symbolic renunciation of wrongdoing suggests that such discipline may involve an additional source of partial reinforcement. As was indicated above, the child may learn that he can avoid punishment by confessing and apologizing. When this happens, the avoidance starts to extinguish. However, the discerning parent then learns not to accept the apology, and the child is punished anyway. The child must then make a more vigorous and convincing symbolic renunciation than before in order to terminate the punishment. In addition, the discrimination he has made between the symbolic renunciation and the actual avoidance is broken down; punishment can only be prevented by actual avoidance of wrongdoing. If, however, after a period of obedience he once more transgresses and then confesses, he is likely again not to be punished. This starts the cycle of extinction and reconditioning of the avoidance response going again, thus continuing to provide a reinforcement schedule in which only part of the child's transgressions are punished.

To predict that such partial reinforcement will retard extinction is admittedly problematic, both because of the complexity of the avoidance paradigm and because the unpunished transgressions are assumed to occur in blocks rather than randomly. Nevertheless, the hypothesis deserves consideration, not only as a prediction from learning principles to personality, but also as a case where the needs of personality theory might guide research in learning.

Although these two lines of reasoning agree in predicting maximally persistent conformity to parental prohibitions by children reared in an atmosphere of parental warmth and disciplined by withdrawal of love, they differ in their other predictions. To test these various hypotheses separately would require both short-run and long-run analyses of the effects of a variety of parental discipline patterns. The following hypotheses might be tested: (1) that discipline by deprivations (whether of things, privileges, or love) has more persistent effects than discipline by noxious stimulation (whether physical or social); (2) that where the child is taught to confess and apologize for his transgressions, avoidance behavior will go through cycles of extinction and reconditioning; and (3) that punishing only part of a child's transgressions results in more persistent obedience than does punishing all of them.

SUMMARY AND CONCLUSIONS

It is suggested that the terms identification, introjection, and internalization be replaced by detailed analyses in learning-theory terms of the acquisition of values. A reinforcement framework for such analyses is outlined, and examples are presented dealing with the concept of conscience and the factors influencing its development. It is argued that this would simplify terminology, encourage more precise study, and further the integration of learning and personality theories.

This analysis, like all attempts to integrate the harder-headed and the softer-hearted portions of behavioral science, is open to attack from both sides. On the one hand it may be objected that the present treatment is too cavalier with the interpersonal and intrapsychic complexities of personality development, that the internalization of values and the identification of one person with another cannot be treated as though they were nothing but the simple learning of a rat in a maze. The answer to this objection is that no "nothing but-ism" is intended; it is an empirical matter both to determine how far the principles of learning (not necessarily simple) can go in explaining personality development and to decide how much the additional principles suggested by some writers actually contribute to our understanding of the phenomena in question. The attempt to catch too much complexity at a single stroke may retard rather than advance our understanding.

On the other hand it may be objected that the interpretations given here are untestable, that the variables involve such diverse and subtle behaviors over such long periods of time as to defy adequate measurement. Admittedly the questionnaire, interview, and brief-observation techniques used in this area leave much to be desired. However, as long as applied behavioral scientists are called upon to deal with questions of personality development, poor data to guide their decisions are better than none. Study of learning of values by humans, guided by the principles of learning based on both animal and human studies, has the potential to make vital contributions to many theoretical and applied areas of knowledge. It is hoped that the present discussion may contribute something to that goal.

REFERENCES

Ausubel, D. P. "Relationships between shame and guilt in the socializing process." *Psychol. Rev.,* 1955, **62,** 378–390.

Benedict, Ruth. *The Chrysanthemum and the Sword.* Boston: Houghton Mifflin, 1946.

Brush, F. R. "The effects of shock intensity on the acquisition and extinction of an avoidance response in dogs." *J. comp. physiol. Psychol.,* 1957, **50**, 547–552.

Campbell, D. T. Social attitudes and other acquired behavioral dispositions. In *Investigations of Man as Socius: Their Place in Psychology and the Social Sciences,* vol. 6 of *Psychology: A Study of a Science,* S. Koch (Ed.) New York: McGraw-Hill, 1963.

Church, R. M. "Transmission of learned behavior between rats." *J. abnorm. soc. Psychol.,* 1957, **54,** 163–165.

Darby, C. L., and A. J. Riopelle. "Observational learning in the rhesus monkey." *J. comp. physiol. Psychol.,* 1959, **52,** 94–98.

Davis, W. A., and R. J. Havighurst. *Father of the Man.* Boston: Houghton Mifflin, 1947.

Dinsmoor, J. A. "Punishment: I. The avoidance hypothesis." *Psychol. Rev.,* 1954, **61,** 34–46.

Dollard, J., and N. E. Miller. *Personality and Psychotherapy.* New York: McGraw-Hill, 1950.

Dukes, W. F. "The psychological study of values." *Psychol. Bull.,* 1955, **52,** 24–50.

Freud, Anna. *The Ego and the Mechanisms of Defense.* New York: International Universities, 1946.

Freud, S. *The Ego and the Id.* London: Hogarth, 1950.

Glaser, D. "Dynamics of ethnic identification." *Amer. sociol. Rev.,* 1958, **23,** 31–40.

Grant, D. A., L. M. Schipper, and B. M. Ross. "Effect of intertrial interval during acquisition on extinction of the conditioned eyelid response following partial reinforcemet." *J. exp. Psychol.,* 1952, **44,** 203–210.

Havighurst, R. J., and Bernice L. Neugarten. *American Indian and White Children.* Chicago: Univ. Chicago Press, 1955.

Hull, C. L. *Principles of Behavior.* New York: Appleton-Century, 1943.

Hull, C. L. *A Behavior System.* New Haven: Yale Univ. Press, 1952.

Humphreys, L. G. "The effect of random alternation of reinforcement on the acquisition and extinction of conditioned eyelid reactions." *J. exp. Psychol.,* 1939, **25,** 141–158.

Humphreys, L. G. "Psychogalvanic responses following two conditions of reinforcement." *J. exp. Psychol.,* 1940, **27,** 71–75.

Hurlock, Elizabeth B. *Child Development* (3d ed.) New York: McGraw-Hill, 1956.

Jenkins, W. O., and J. C. Stanley. "Partial reinforcement: A review and critique." *Psychol. Bull.,* 1950, **47,** 193–234.

Kagan, J. "The concept of identification." *Psychol. Rev.,* 1958, **65,** 296–305.

Lazowick, L. "On the nature of identification." *J. abnorm. soc. Psychol.,* 1955, **51,** 175–183.

Lewis, D. J., and C. P. Duncan. "Vicarious experience and partial reinforcement." *J. abnorm. soc. Psychol.,* 1958, **57,** 321–326.

Lindemann, E. "Symptomatology and management of acute grief." *Amer. J. Psychiat.,* 1944, **101,** 141–148.

Lynn, D. B. "A note on sex differences in the development of masculine and feminine identification." *Psychol. Rev.,* 1959, **66,** 126–135.

Masserman, J. H. *Principles of Dynamic Psychiatry.* Philadelphia: Saunders, 1946.

Mead, Margaret. Some anthropological considerations concerning guilt. In *Feelings and Emotions: The Mooseheart Symposium,* M. L. Reymert (Ed.) New York: McGraw-Hill, 1950.

Miller, N. E. Experimental studies of conflict. In *Personality and the Behavior Disorders,* J. McV. Hunt (Ed.). New York: Ronald, 1944, pp. 431–465.

Miller, N. E. Learnable drives and rewards. In *Handbook of Experimental Psychology,* S. S. Stevens (Ed.). New York: Wiley, 1951, pp. 435–472.

Miller, N. E., and J. Dollard. *Social Learning and Imitation.* New Haven: Yale Univ. Press, 1941.

Miller, N. E., and Doris Kraeling. "Displacement: Greater generalization of approach than avoidance in a generalized approach-avoidance conflict." *J. exp. Psychol.,* 1952, **43,** 217–221.

Miller, N. E., and E. J. Murray. "Displacement and conflict: Learnable drive as a basis for the steeper gradient of avoidance than of approach." *J. exp. Psychol.,*1952, **43,** 227–231.

Mowrer, O. H. *Learning Theory and Personality Dynamics.* New York: Ronald, 1950.

Mowrer, O. H., and A. D. Ullman. "Time as a determinant in integrative learning." *Psychol. Rev.,* 1945, **52,** 61–90.

Murray, E. J., and N. E. Miller. "Displacement: Steeper gradient of generalization of avoidance than of approach with age of habit controlled." *J. exp. Psychol.,* 1952, **43,** 222–226.

Osgood, C. E. *Method and Theory in Experimental Psychology.* New York: Oxford Univ. Press, 1953.

Parsons, T. Family structure and the socialization of the child. In *Family, Sociali-*

zation and Interaction Process, T. Parsons and R. F. Bales (Eds.) Glencoe, Ill.: Free Press, 1955.

Reynolds, W. F. "Acquisition and extinction of the conditioned eyelid response following partial and continuous reinforcement." *J. exp. Psychol.,* 1958, **55,** 335–341.

Russell, W. A., and L. H. Storms. "Implicit verbal chaining in paired-associate learning." *J. exp. Psychol.,* 1955, **49,** 287–293.

Sanford, N. "The dynamics of identification." *Psychol. Rev.,* 1955, **62,** 106–118.

Sears, R. R., Eleanor E. Maccoby, and H. Levin. *Patterns of Child Rearing.* Evanston, Ill.: Row, Peterson, 1957.

Shaw, G. B. Preface to *Androcles and the Lion. In Nine Plays.* New York: Dodd, Mead, 1948.

Sidman, M. "Two temporal parameters of the maintenance of avoidance behavior by the white rat." *J. comp. physiol. Psychol.,* 1953, **46,** 235–261.

Singer, M. B. Shame cultures and guilt cultures. In *Shame and Guilt,* G. Piers and M. B. Singer (Eds.) Springfield, Ill.: Charles C. Thomas, 1953.

Solomon, R. L., and Eleanor S. Brush. Experimentally derived conceptions of anxiety and aversion. In *Nebraska Symposium on Motivation IV.* Lincoln: Univ. Nebraska Press, 1956.

Solomon, R. L. and M. R. Coles. "A case of failure of generalization of imitation across drives and across situations." *J. abnorm. soc. Psychol.,* 1954, **49,** 7–13.

Tolman, E. C. "There is more than one kind of learning." *Psychol. Rev.,* 1949, **56,** 144–155.

Whiting, J. W. M., and I. L. Child. *Child Training and Personality.* New Haven: Yale Univ. Press, 1953.

5.5 *Orientation*

In parental discussions of children's behavior and problems one of the most frequently discussed topics is that of children's fears. A cursory examination of popular parent-education literature reveals that questions concerning the nature of children's fears and "how to handle" these fears are among those most frequently asked by parents. For reasons both practical and theoretical, the study of fear (including its physiological basis, its various stages, its effect on learning, and its modification) has a long history in psychology. Extensive efforts have also been directed to classify fear reactions; one general result has been a distinction between fear and anxiety. For example, Freud distinguished three general emotional reactions based upon fear and anxiety: fear of the external world (reality anxiety), fear of one's own impulses (neurotic anxiety), and guilt (moral anxiety). The following research by Adah Maurer introduces some of the major theoretical positions on fear and proceeds to discuss these in relation to the fears reported by a large number of children ranging from five to fourteen years.

The Maurer paper, aside from its focus upon fear in children, illustrates two points, one methodological and the other related to the type of data obtained. Methodologically, the study utilizes the cross-sectional research design: The responses elicited from samples of children of different ages are compared at approximately the same point in time. This procedure enables the researcher to examine data for apparent trends and differences that may be attributable to, or associated with, age changes. The data obtained, being age-based, are normative, that is, descriptive. Normative data, involving frequencies or the statistics derived from them, are not explanatory in and of themselves. However, psychologists often utilize normative data to aid in developing and testing theories of growth as has Maurer. Readers will find her speculations on the relation of fear to children's learning and intellectual functioning particularly provocative. Her position, in general, is that the kind and intensity of fears held by children may impede the maximum utilization of their intellectual powers.

RECOMMENDED READING

Hebb, D. O. "On the nature of fear." *Psychol. Rev.,* **53** (1946), 259–276.

Hurlock, E. B. *Child Development.* (4th ed.) New York: McGraw-Hill, 1964. (See "Emotional Development," chap. 7.)

Jersild, A. T. Emotional development. In *Manual of Child Psychology,* Leonard Carmichael (Ed.) (2d ed.) New York: Wiley, 1954, pp. 833–917.

5.5 What Children Fear

Adah Maurer, UNIVERSITY OF CALIFORNIA, DAVIS

INTRODUCTION

Children do not fear the atomic bomb (1, 11). They do not even fear the things they have been taught to be careful about: street traffic and germs. The strange truth is that they fear an unrealistic source of danger in our urban civilization: wild animals. Almost all 5- and 6-year-olds and more

Reprinted from *Journal of Genetic Psychology,* **106** (1965), 265–277. By permission of the author and The Journal Press.

than one-half of 7-to-12-year-olds claim that the things to be afraid of are mammals and reptiles (most frequently): snakes, lions, and tigers. Not until age 12 or more do most children recognize actual sources of danger and, when they do, these dangers are almost always highly personal rather than politically or socially determined (2).

One 12-year-old boy said that the things to be afraid of are "Wild animals, fierce dogs and cats, and snakes." Another of same age answered "Not being able to get a job." Both boys had earned intelligence scores within the normal range (low 90s) on the Wechsler Intelligence Scale for Children; both had mild learning problems, but there the similarity ended. After an assessment that included achievement tests, the school history, parent interviews, and a study of the family dynamics, a marked difference became apparent. The first boy had been overprotected and lacked opportunity to care for himself and to make decisions. He was the youngest of a large family and had been babied and restricted in experiences. The second boy had been overwhelmed with excessive demands from his parents. His irresponsible father had drifted from one menial job to another and was unemployed at the time of the study. The boy, the eldest of his siblings, had borne the brunt of his father's disgust at the latter's incompetence and had been belittled and criticized to an excessive degree. Compared to that of the first boy, the conversation of the second boy seemed mature.

Did the answers these boys gave to the question about fears reflect in some measure the underlying problem? In the second case, it would seem that it did, yet without knowing the kinds of answers one might expect from normal children, it would be easy to jump to unwarranted conclusions. Was the first boy's fear of animals due to some traumatic experience? Had he lived in a primitive area where wild animals actually were a threat to his safety? Or had his father been a pioneer and entertained the boy with tales of the dangers of the woods? And if any of these suppositions had been true (which they were not) did they relate in any way to his learning problem? To answer questions such as these and to determine the etiology of fear in children became the purpose of a year-long study of normal children.

A 5-year-old boy, referred because of excessive aggressiveness, answered the question thus: "Dogs!" He was encouraged to go on. "And what else?" He grimaced and said, "Dog, dog, two dogs!" In the silence that followed he screamed, *"DOGS!"* Again he was asked, "Anything else?" More quietly, but still firmly he said, "Ten dogs." He proved to be a very fearful child, uncertain of the stability of his home and of his place in it. His belligerence in school seemed to stem from a psychological need to defend himself.

Children's fears have been explained by several diverse theories. The first, a folklore, denies that children fear by calling the emotion "stubbornness." The parents of the boy who feared dogs, dogs, ten dogs said, "We've told him that dogs won't hurt him but he won't listen!" The attempted cure had been repeated spankings for this and much else, and spankings again for passing the punishment on to his contemporaries.

The Freudian considers fear as a displacement of the son's fear of the father who, so the child believes, will retaliate for the son's incestuous desire for his mother by castrating the son. The Freudian postulates that, during the oral stage characterized by sucking, the child fears being eaten because he feels guilt about his desire to eat (or bite) his mother's breast (3). Psychoanalytic therapy has consisted of an effort to resolve an oedipal triangle, thus permitting the child to enter the genital phase of his development. The American Academy of Child Psychiatry has re-evaluated this formulation, as have many of the neo-Freudians; but the emphasis remains firmly rooted in the dynamics of the child's emotional involvement with his parents (5, 9).

The behaviorist finds that fears are conditioned responses based upon associational ties with one or another of the fears present at birth. John B. Watson, the earliest behaviorist to apply the theory to child rearing, was certain that the fear of dogs proceeded from a traumatic experience in which the loud barking of a dog had triggered the original fear of loud sounds. His recommended cure consisted of unconditioning the fear by the introduction of a dog or a toy dog at some pleasant time, such as during a meal, and gradually bringing it closer until it could be tolerated on the tray (12). This theory, too, has undergone considerable modification; but the emphasis remains upon the learning, unlearning, and modification of fear through environmental experiences.

A follower of Jung's early theories (6) would explain a fear of animals as an expression of the collective unconscious. In more primitive times, the boy's ancestors feared the rampaging wolf, the stealthy poisonous snake, and other natural enemies. Although the boy lives in the midst of the trappings of civilization, and the descendants of the wolf have been tamed to family pets; yet deeply submerged is the tribal fear, built in perhaps to the neutral network present but dormant at birth. Thus the child goes through a stage that he outgrows as he matures into succeeding phases of the ontogenetic recapitulation of the history of his race. This theory has been muddied by mysticism and has been neglected in the ongoing debate between the psychoanalysts and the experimentalists. Animal ecologists (7), however, have demonstrated the specificity of fears in animals, notably in the giraffe which animal, though born in captivity and raised on a bottle, nevertheless startles and shies away from the mock-up of a lion, the traditional enemy of his species; but approaches and sniffs at the mock-up of a giraffe. Humans, however, generally are considered to have lost their instincts and to have become dependent upon learning.

Gesell (4) and the maturation theorists have demonstrated the primacy of growth in physical and mental functions, yet for the most part they have omitted similar studies of the maturation of the emotions, especially of fear. It may be that they have thought of fear as an abnormal manifestation or a malfunctioning rather than as an aspect of normal growth.

The eclectic finds it difficult to choose among the theories for they have little in common. Psychoanalysts have been concerned chiefly with the abnormal, and their preemption of the subject of fear has colored general thinking along these lines. The behaviorists have dealt with fear largely as a means to eliminate unwanted responses. Their use of punishment is empirical, with no discussion of fear it arouses since fear is a subjective phenomenon. Yet it should be obvious that a judicious, rational fearfulness is life preservative and therefore an inescapable aspect of the normal child (8). Excessive, irrational fears are widely known to be intimately connected with learning difficulties, delinquency, and withdrawal. Preventive methodology requires more knowledge of the normal fears of normal children thus defining, highlighting, and permitting evaluation of the unique and the aberrant.

Based upon the results of this study, each of the major theories appears to contain some part of the truth. It also becomes clear that the amount, depth, and kind of fear as well as its objects is ascertainable and definitely of diagnostic value.

METHOD

Over a period of a year, each child who was given the Wechsler Intelligence Scale for Children was asked an additional question. At the conclusion of the comprehension subtest, in the same neutral tone used for other questions, the examiner said, "What are the things to be afraid of?" Each answer was recorded as nearly verbatim as possible, as were all answers for all subtests. Silent approval and recognition that the fears were legitimate was given by a sympathetic nod. When the child stopped speaking he was encouraged to go on. "And what else?" and then, "Anything else?" Four children replied "Nothing." One answered "You shouldn't be afraid of anything." In these cases, to provide the ease of replying by projection, the question was rephrased. "Some children are afraid of some things some of the time, aren't they?" All nodded or said "Yes." The examiner continued: "What are these children sometimes afraid of?" In all cases this brought a satisfactory reply.

The direct question "What are you afraid of?" was not used because children might interpret this as critical and tend to reply defensively. Since the question necessarily came after four failures (except for the brightest who scored very high in comprehension) most of the children seemed relieved by an "easy" one and, with some exceptions, the answers flowed smoothly and without shock. For severely disturbed children, the question was omitted.

SUBJECTS

The subjects of the study consisted of 130 children of whom 91 were boys and 39 were girls. In age they ranged from 5 years and 5 months to 14 years and 6 months. All of them were in regular attendance at elementary schools in middle- or lower-middle-class suburbs. Eighteen of them proved to be mentally retarded (nine boys, nine girls), two of them severely (one boy, one girl). Since the study was for the purpose of tabulating the fears of normal children, these 18 were eliminated from all calculations except one. In this one calculation, the attempt was made to determine whether replies conformed to a chronological or mental-age pattern and the retarded were included in the group of their mental-age mates. In all other tabulations and discussions, the subjects are the 112 students whose *IQ*s fell between 80 and 144 (see Tables 1 and 2).

TABLE 1. Subjects in the Study by Age and Sex

Age	Boys	Girls	Total
5 and 6	13	7	20
7 and 8	20	9	29
9 and 10	21	10	31
11 and 12	18	1	19
13 and 14	10	3	13
Total	82	30	112

TABLE 2. Subjects in the Study by IQ Scores[a]

Age	Intelligence Quotient		
	Slow 80-89	*Average 90-110*	*Bright 111-144*
5 and 6	2	14	4
7 and 8	8	12	9
9 and 10	7	18	6
11 and 12	4	12	3
13 and 14	8	5	0
Total	29	61	22

[a] The distribution approaches the normal probability of 22, 68, 22 per cent in the three divisions, respectively, closely enough to consider this a fair sample of school children.

Each of the children had been referred to the school psychologist and to that extent was perhaps atypical. The reasons for referral covered a wide range. For some, testing was requested to help determine the advisability of retention or double promotion. Some had speech defects or verbal infantilisms. Some had reading problems. A few merely needed glasses. Some were noisy, defiant, failed to do their homework, or to conform in some way to the demands of teachers. A few were shy and apparently friendless, while others were the center of playground disputes. Some were the entirely normal siblings of disturbed or retarded children. None was so severely disturbed that referral for psychiatric care was deemed mandatory, thus all could be considered within the normal range. If the somewhat unexpected results were a function of atypicality, the study nevertheless is of value because [1] the technique proved to be an important diagnostic clue and [2] the need for additional studies along this line is clearly indicated.

The number of responses ranged from a single answer followed by "That's all!" to a spontaneous 18 responses, which number was unique in that the next largest number was nine. Boys averaged slightly higher than girls (4.23 *v.* 4.00), but the difference is not significant. There was very little difference between the age groups perhaps because of the technique used, and there was no observable tendency for the younger or older children to give more or fewer replies. The more fluent children tended to elaborate or modify their answers or go on to relate personal experiences. The shy children and those with speech difficulties tended to be slower and more patience was required in drawing them out, but they averaged as many responses as the others.

RESULTS

Of the 467 responses, 233 or 50 per cent, consisted of a single category: animals. Seventy-two of the 112 children, or 64 per cent, replied solely or partly by naming animals in general or one or more specific animals including: alligator, ape, bat, bear, bee, bird, black widow, bobcat, buffalo, bull, cat, centipede, cow, crocodile, deer, dinosaur, dog, eel, elephant, fox, gorilla, hawk, hippopotamus, horse, insect, leopard, lion, lizard, mosquito, mountain lion, parakeet, pinchbug, rat, reptile, rhinoceros, scorpion, shark, snake, spider, spit-monkey, tarantula, tiger, turtle, wildcat, whale and wolf.

The most unpopular animal is the snake. Thirty-three of the subjects, 23 boys and 10 girls (28 per cent and 33 per cent respectively) mentioned them. Next in order came lions, mentioned 28 times; tigers, 14 times; and bears, nine times.

The most striking fact that emerged from the study, besides the near universality of fear of animals, is that fear of animals decreases sharply with age (from 80 per cent of the 5- and 6-year-olds to 23 per cent of those 13 and 14 years old). The older children also tended to qualify their responses. Rather than simply "Lion, tiger," they said "Wild animals if you are in a jungle without arms," "Dogs with rabies," "A cow that might kick you," or "A parakeet that's infected."

Fear of the dark seems to disappear after age 7, with only two stragglers who admitted to it after that age, both of them qualifying their responses: "Little kids are afraid of the dark," and "Highways at night." Similarly, fears of nonexistent entities, such as monsters, the boogie man, ghosts, witches, and animated skeletons, are left behind after age 10. Thus the questions about the effect of television dramas highlighting horror becomes a matter of age. Fright films would seem to be traumatic before the child thoroughly understands that they are only imaginary; after that age, the possibility of their being therapeutic may enter. Age nine to 10 appears to be the dividing line.

Unique and individual responses rise from zero at 5 and 6 years to 46 per cent as children reach early adolescence. The subject matter becomes more realistic and more closely tied to learned or experienced objects and situations (see Table 3).

TABLE 3. Subject Matter of Fears

	Percent[a]						
Age	*Animals*	*People*	*Dark*	*Spooks*	*Natural hazards*	*Machinery*	*Miscellaneous*
5 and 6	80	20	20	33	0	20	0
7 and 8	73	17	3	17	34	34	14
9 and 10	61	42	3	10	35	35	16
11 and 12	68	42	0	0	26	42	26
13 and 14	23	39	0	0	31	46	46

[a] In each age group, the per cent of subjects who replied that things to be afraid of were such as to be classifiable under the categories. "People" includes "bad men," "kidnappers," "people who . . . ," "if somebody . . . ," as well as members of the family and playmates mentioned by name. "Spooks" includes "monsters," "ghosts," "witches," "man made of iron," "Frankenstein," etc. "Natural hazards" includes storms, fire, water, waves, flood, volcano, etc. "Machinery" includes all man-made gadgets and inventions, such as weapons, cars, electricity, trains, etc.

The question arises: Is this maturational trend a function of chronological age or does intelligence play a part? Two severely retarded children, whose replies were not tabulated with the above, gave immature replies. The boy (age 14:8, *IQ* 44, *MA* 6:8) said, "Cow, horse, goat, snake." The girl (age 15:6, *IQ* 46, *MA* 7:5) said, "Bears, lions, train if you go in front of it, and alligators." On the other hand, an exceptionally bright boy (age 9:6, *IQ* 134, *MA* 14:2) answered the same question, "Things you can't overcome." Asked to explain, he added, "Well, if you are afraid of water, for example, you probably will never overcome it." His home life showed an excessive responsibility for his mother who lived under the constant tension of having her husband away from home for long stretches on cruise as a Lieutenant Commander in the Navy.

To determine if these children typified dull and bright intelligences, the replies of all of the children in the study, plus those of the 18 mentally retarded children, were evaluated on the basis of mental age (see Table 4). On this basis, the sharp dropping away of fear of the dark and of spooks is even more marked. The fear of animals maintained a high level through age 12, but only one child with a mental age of 13 or more admitted to it. There were only nine cases in this most mature group, and thus it is difficult to determine whether this is a universal phenomenon. Each of the nine gave a unique answer. One boy (age 13:5, *IQ* 110) said, "Getting killed, parents getting a divorce, falling off a bike. The world is full of fears." Another (age 13:0, *IQ* 96) shrugged and said, "Trouble, the principal, spankings, going home if you lose money."

TABLE 4. Responses Tabulated by Mental Age

Mental Age	Percent [a]						
	Animals	*People*	*Dark*	*Spooks*	*Natural hazards*	*Machinery*	*Miscellaneous*
4 to 6	75	21	11	39	11	7	3
7 and 8	59	25	7	12	19	12	12
9 and 10	57	30	0	5	27	35	15
11 and 12	54	37	0	0	42	54	17
13 to 15	11	44	0	0	22	11	55

[a] The figures refer to the per cent of the responses (not per cent of the children) of 130 children, including 112 normals and 18 mentally retarded children. The sharp drop in fear of the dark and of spooks after age 8 and of animals after age 12 is even more marked when mental age rather than chronological age is considered.

But it was also true that the younger children often gave personal clues in their replies. A boy (6:6, *IQ* 104) said, "Spiders, pinchbugs, a big boy beating you up." Thus, *IQ* alone does not tell the whole story. A precocious sense of danger in the specifics of living may be found in nonacademic children. A girl (8:9, *IQ* 84) gasped and rattled off a long story that was caught only in part as "Falling down and getting hurt. You might go to a hospital. . . . If you get stitches in your eye, you might have an operation and you might die." She was a member of a large, dependent family, whose troubles constantly recurred. At the time of the test, her mother was in the hospital but for what purpose could not be determined.

Nor does a high *IQ* necessarily move a 6-year-old to considerations of a realistic assessment of the world of dangers he lives in, perhaps because his home and environment were particularly safe, congenial, and supportive. Such a boy (age 6:5, *IQ* 144, *MA* 9:2) said without concern, "Lion, tiger, rat, buffalo and bull." He read words on the fifth-grade reading list without hesitation; in class he was so bright and well adjusted that his teacher had recommended double promotion. He was tall for his age, handsome, and in excellent health. Nothing about him suggested "immaturity" as that word is used by educators to characterize the egocentric crybaby.

Educators long have been dissatisfied with the *IQ* as the sole index of expected achievement. Motivational and emotional factors, it is generally agreed, play a strong part in determining progress, but attempted measurement of these has fallen short of usefulness. Personality type and preferences have proved less than predictive. It is strongly suggested by this study that the kind and level of fearfulness may act as a brake on usable intelligence, and that its measurement by a highly polished tool may prove as enlightening as the studies on creativity, which have uncovered another additional dimension.

Fear of fire is the traditional example used to prove that children learn by experience. "A burnt child fears the fire" seems to imply that the unburnt child does not or that only by experience does the child learn to fear or learn what to fear. The folk saying is older than central heating and seems to have little specific pertinence in today's world. Among our 20 children of 5 and 6 years (who gave a total of 91 replies), 54 replies were of animals, only one was fire. Four per cent of the 7- and 8-year-olds, five per cent of the 9- and 10-year-olds, 16 per cent of the 11- and 12-year-olds and nine per cent of the oldest group included fire (forest fire, burning house, etc.) among the things to be feared. In no case, however, could it be ascertained that this response sprang from a personal experience. The one child known to have suffered extensive burns, a girl (age 11:6, *IQ* 60, *MA* 6:9) replied with a standard "Lion, tiger, dog, cat, snakes, rattlers, spiders." Her scars, which extended from neck to buttocks on her back, had been covered with grafts from her thighs. They had come to be her one claim upon her contemporaries for awed attention and upon adults for sympathy. Accordingly, she valued them and was quick to lift her skirts for strangers, a habit that tended to be misinterpreted. Asked directly if she feared fire, she looked puzzled and then smiled happily, "I guess so."

Other natural hazards mentioned by this group of children included storms, deep water, waves, earthquake, volcano, hurricane, tornado, quicksand, sharp rocks, cliffs, a tunnel cave-in, avalanche ("snow falling down from the hill"), poison oak, and the desert. No one of them was mentioned often enough to have any general significance. Individually, some seemed merely to represent the most recent subject of adventure stories read or viewed; others proved to have deep personal significance in the light of subsequent parent interviews. As a group, natural hazards (including fires) supplied one of the responses of the 5- and 6-year-olds, but from one-fourth to one-third of the responses of the 7- to 12-year-olds. The age of adventure thus begins at 7.

Machinery is perhaps an inadequate title for a category that includes cars, trucks, trains, construction, buildings, airplanes, guns, knives, electricity, a trapdoor, explosions, a submarine, helicopter, firecrackers, rusty nails, bicycles, a tractor, a crane, a hatchet, electric chair, gas, falling bricks, trolley car and a stairwell. What was intended was a grouping of those hazards that are man made and that are elements of an industrial civilization. Here it is obvious that learning has taken place. There is no possibility that a collective unconscious could have suggested to a boy that tractors are dangerous because "you might move the wrong lever and it would start up." The amazing discovery lies in the fact that teaching has had so little effect.

Surely every kindergartner and first grader listens to lengthy lessons about the dangers inherent in highways, traffic, cars, and trucks. Yet when asked what are the things to be afraid of, not one gave evidence of having learned his lesson. Among older children—7 to 14—only 15 per cent of the replies referred in any way to the Number 1 threat to life in America today. Automobile accidents account for more deaths and disabilities among school-age children than any disease and far more than all the dangers that children fear put together. Perhaps this is just as well. We would not want our children to be terrified of crossing a street in the same unreasoning sense that some of them are terrified of dogs. Establishing the habit of stop, look, and listen before you cross is apparently enough; to add warnings of peril is ineffective because, for whatever reason, it is not learned.

Trains, usually qualified, were mentioned 11 times; weapons only seven times. All the others were unique replies. Many of them were qualified or explained. Some children went on to tell of personal experiences that gave important clues to their life style. The boy who replied "Walking down the highway at night you might be hit by a car" had indeed been doing just that. His wanderings in search (it would seem) of a lost father helped to explain his listlessness in school. Another who listed "Big cranes, big trucks, when you're tearing down a house" was describing his father's occupation and admitting inadvertently both his fear of his father and his fear that his father would leave.

The category "people" was also revealing of underlying difficulties. Forty-five replies involved "people who . . . (come with guns, hit you, try to give you trouble," etc.) or specific persons. Alas for learning, only five mentioned "Somebody who tells you to get in his car." All children should have been warned against child enticers; perhaps most had been, but spooks, monsters, and ghosts remained frightening to more children than kidnappers. One boy blurted out "My brother! He comes up behind me in the dark and says, 'Boo!' " Another, a girl, replied "People who might try to make you nervous or give you a heart attack." She was describing, not her own, but her mother's palpitations. Five children said, "If your parents get a divorce." This should perhaps be a separate category since it indicated not a fear of people but a resurgence of the separation anxiety of infancy. In these cases there was little need to hunt further for the cause of poor school work. A family break up, almost without exception, causes at least a temporary emotional upheaval in the children that is often reflected in an inability to concentrate.

Miscellaneous responses included: war, 5; the atom bomb, 2; punishment, 4; disease, 4; separation ("if you're all alone," "if you get lost," etc.), 4; breaking the moral code, 2; death, 6; unemployment, 1; and Hell, 1. Some of these seemed to be thoughtful assessments of dangers in the abstract. Others were obviously specific to the particular life situation of the child. A few were so strange as to be baffling. One boy replied "My little brother sleeps with me" possibly implying that otherwise he would be afraid of the dark or that there was danger in this arrangement either for the brother or himself. It could not be determined, and was not necessary. The parents, with very little persuasion, agreed to provide bunk beds. Another changed the subject: "We planted some flowers in our garden," and would say no more. There is a farfetched possibility that the "flowers" might have been marijuana and that the girl sensed her parents' concern about being caught or that a body was buried in the garden and camouflaged, but such speculations were considered out of bounds and the matter was not pursued.

CONCLUSIONS

The question, "What are the things to be afraid of?" asked routinely in the course of the Wechsler test proved to be an important clue to the emotional dynamics of the child being tested.

Eighty per cent of children of 5 and 6 reply to the question by naming one or more wild animals, with snake, lion, tiger, and bear predominating. Sixty per cent or more of children between the ages of 7 and 12 answer similarly but, after mental age 12, it is rare.

One-third of children under 7 admit to fear of imaginary beings (monsters mainly), and a fifth of them fear the dark. Both of these replies drop off sharply after age 7.

The things that children are taught to fear (traffic, germs, and kidnappers) are rarely mentioned. Punishment, war, and the atom bomb are also scarce replies at any age although it is likely that children would answer "yes" if they were asked directly "Do you fear . . . any of these"?

As children mature, the kinds of things they regard as frightening become diverse, unique, and are often tied directly or indirectly to their central concern.

Refusals to answer, replies of "Nothing," long pauses, changes of volume or pitch of the voice, and facial expressions (while not common) provide clues to the intensity of the fear.

An "immature" reply may characterize the well-protected child and in some cases the mentally retarded. The child who has been burdened with excessive responsibility or hardship is more likely than others to give a unique, "mature" reply, as is also the bright child with a mental age of 12 or more.

Much caution is needed in interpretation, for recent events and the child's mood during the examination may be the fleeting cause of any particular answer.

All four of the major theories of childhood (psychoanalysis, behaviorism, the collective unconscious, and maturation) contribute, albeit incompletely, to an understanding of childhood fears.

A strong maturational factor, partly influenced by intelligence and partly influenced by the amount of responsibility thrust upon the child, seems to be at work upon an archaic instinctual base. The child is born with the capacity to fear, apparently more than is necessary to preserve his life. Although he feels fear, the child does not know with the same certainty as the smaller-brained mammals just what objects or situations are to be feared. Much infant questioning (10), especially that relating to life and death, is prompted by a curiosity about the missing information and by a desire to locate accurately the causative objects of the amorphous sense of possible danger. If archaic instincts to avoid specific hazards are lacking, it may be that the fear of being eaten by wild animals or poisoned by snakes retains a certain ease of arousal. Among the uneducated, the folk habit of enforcing obedience by supplying incorrect information to children for the purpose of controlling them ("The wizard man will eat you if you stray!") is enormously effective, but also, by rousing archaic fears, it may be a limiting factor to the full use of mental powers.

As the child matures, the emotion of fear fastens upon more and more realistic objects depending upon experience learning rather than upon instruction.

The intensity of the child's fear depends for the most part upon the family relationships.

REFERENCES

1. Escalona, S. "Children's responses to nuclear threat." *Children,* **10** (1963), 137–142.
2. Freud, A., and D. Burlingame. *War and Children.* New York: Willard, 1943.
3. Freud, S, Analysis of a phobia in a five year old boy. In *Collected Papers.* (vol. 3) London: Hogarth and the Inst. of Psycho-analysis, 1925, pp 149–288.

4. Gesell, A., and C. Amatruda. *Developmental Diagnosis.* New York: Harper, 1941.
5. Josselyn, I. "Concepts related to child development: The oral stage." *J. child Psychiat.,* **1** (1962), 209–224.
6. Jung, C. G. The Archtypes and the Collective Unconscious. *Collected Works —Bollinger Series.* New York: Pantheon, 1962.
7. Masserman, J. Ethology, comparative biodynamics and psychoanalytic research. In *Theories of the Mind,* M. D. Scher (Ed.) New York: Free Press, 1962, pp. 15–64.
8. Maurer, A. "The child's knowledge of non-existence." *J. exist. Psychiat.,* **2** (1961), 193–212.
9. Maurer, A. "Did little Hans really want to marry his mother?" *J. humi. Psychol.,* **4** (1964), 139–148.
10. Piaget, J. *Language and Thought of the Child.* New York: Meridian, 1955, pp. 171–240.
11. Schwebel, M. Nuclear cold war: Student opinions. Unpubl. manuscript read at the convention of the Amer. Orthopsychiat. Assn., March 1963.
12. Watson, J. B. *Behaviorism.* Chicago: Univ. Chicago Press, 1959.

5.6 *Orientation*

Two concepts regarding children's aggression seem to be firmly entrenched in the popular parent-education literature. One of these springs from the psychoanalytic view of motivation frequently referred to as the "hydraulic" model of personality adjustment. This model, based on the pleasure-pain principle, assumes that the individual continually strives to reduce the tension that accumulates from the inevitable conflicts and frustrations of social living. The ideal affective state is therefore tension-free; a homeostatic process operates to minimize tension. Because frustration is seen to produce tension it is further assumed in this model that acting-out behavior will serve to reduce the tension. Thus aggression is assumed to have a cathartic value; catharsis is considered essential for the purpose of maintaining mental health. The "hydraulic" notion applies in the sense that if the direct expression of aggression is thwarted, or is seen by the individual to be socially inappropriate, indirect modes of aggression-expression will prevail. Hopefully, from the viewpoint of parents and teachers, children learn constructive, or at least non-destructive, modes of expressing aggressive feelings. Since aggression may be expressed in some way as long as there is a tension-load, children are encouraged to reduce their tensions and frustrations through play, finger-painting, and assorted physical activities.

A second popular belief in our culture is that boys not only are more overtly aggressive than girls, but also experience more intensive aggressive feelings. This notion is reflected in many ways, including the "sugar and spice and everything nice" concept of what little girls are made of.

Both of the above views have been investigated by psychologists. An elaborate theoretical controversy has been generated as to whether the expression of aggression is in any way cathartic. Issues related to this point of contention and the belief about sex differences provide the basis for the Mallick and McCandless paper reproduced here. Although these issues are sufficient in themselves to create a paper with high interest value, readers will find the methodology of this well-controlled study highly original. Aside from its relationship to the Bandura, Ross, and Ross paper (Chapter 2), which deals with the antecedents of aggressions, the study suggests implications for general human-relations training and the counseling strategies utilized with children. The foremost among these suggestions involves interpreting for children the reasons for their aggressive feelings and the reasons for the aggressive behavior of others, by the adults responsible for the socialization of children.

RECOMMENDED READING

Kenny, K. T. An experimental test of the catharsis theory of aggression. Unpubl. doctoral dissertation. Seattle: Univ. Wash., 1952.

Lawson, Reed, and Melvin Marx. "Frustration: Theory and experiment." *Genet. Psychol. Monogr.*, **42** (1958), 393–464.

Rosembaum, M. E., and R. de Charms. "Direct and vicarious reduction of hostility." *J. abnorm. soc. Psychol.*, **40** (1960), 105–11.

5.6 A Study of Catharsis of Aggression

Shahbaz Khan Mallick, PURDUE UNIVERSITY, MICHIGAN CITY CAMPUS
Boyd R. McCandless, EMORY UNIVERSITY

BACKGROUND TO THE PROBLEM

Many of those interested, theoretically or practically, in personality theory, therapy, or general social psychology, for that matter, believe that aggressive acting-out behavior reduces aggression and hostility. Most theory

Reprinted from *Journal of Personality and Social Psychology,* **4** (1966), no. 6, 591–596. By permission of the authors and the American Psychological Association, Inc.

of play therapy is still based on this hydraulic notion: the frustrated, angry, hostile child behaves aggressively, and this aggressive behavior reduces his level of hostility and aggression. Many parents and teachers accept the dictum that it is well to allow their children to blow off steam. Boxing, wrestling, and other intramural athletics are considered by some to provide catharsis for hostile aggression (Miller, Moyer, and Patrick, 1956). Freud spoke of Thanatos or a death instinct constantly working to return the organism "to the quiescence of the inorganic world [Freud, 1959, p. 108]." Libido interacts with the death instinct, neutralizing its effects on the person, by directing it outward as destruction, mastery, and will to power, concepts which may be subsumed under the general term *catharsis*.

Dollard, Doob, Miller, Mowrer, and Sears (1939) considered that inhibiting aggression is frustrating, and that aggressive behavior reduces the instigation to aggression (is cathartic in its effects). Buss (1961) also believes that violent aggression (and perhaps any violent activity) diminishes anger level following frustration and results in feelings of satisfaction about the acting-out behavior. Similarly, Berkowitz (1962) argues that a person whose anger has been aroused will tend to express it and that this expression will give him feelings of satisfaction similar to those obtained upon completing any motivated task.

The research evidence about some form of counteraggression or catharsis as an aggression-reducing behavior is neither voluminous nor convincing. Thibaut and Coules (1952) find that subjects prevented from responding to the experimenters' confederate reduced friendly expressions toward the confederate significantly less than for subjects who were allowed to respond, and that those who were delayed in response increased in hostile responses more than those allowed to respond immediately.

Feshbach's (1955) well-known study using college students as subjects suggests that fantasy aggression may be cathartic. Hornberger (1959), in a partial replication of Feshbach's study, failed to obtain similar results. In another paper, Feshbach (1956) used children as subjects, and failed to find that aggressive free play reduced aggression: indeed, the boys (but not the girls) in his study who were initially low in aggressive behavior showed a significant increase in overt hostility after a series of permissive free-play experiences.

Hokanson (1961), like Feshbach (1955) and Hornberger (1959), used college students as subjects. His 80 male subjects were studied according to whether they were high or low in "test hostility," threatened or not threatened by the experimenter with retaliation, and frustrated or not frustrated. A variety of measures were employed, of which number and vigor of aggressive *behavioral* responses made toward the experimenter and *ratings* of hostility toward the experimenter are most relevant for the present study.

Hokanson's subjects gave both more and more vigorous "shocks" to the experimenter following frustration, but the more vigorous the shocks given, the less hostility they rated themselves as holding toward the experimenter following their "punishing" him. Hokanson thus finds that frustration increases *behavioral* aggression, using at least one measure similar to the one employed in the present study, and has a subfinding suggesting that behavioral expressions of aggression to the frustrator reduce or are at least associated with less intense verbal ratings of hostility toward him.

HYPOTHESES

Their interest in frustration-aggression-catharsis theory led the authors to set up and test the following five hypotheses, using children as subjects:

1. Angry aggression directed toward an inanimate object is not cathartic.
2. Aggression, unmotivated by anger or hostility, has no cathartic effect but may, instead, lead to an increase in aggressive responses, particularly in a socially permissive atmosphere.
3. Positive and reasonable verbal interpretation of a frustrating situation to the subject who has been frustrated has cathartic value in that it reduces hostility toward the frustrator.
4. Verbal aggression against a frustrator of the same sex does not reduce the hostility toward him (does not serve as catharsis).
5. United States girls, presumably because of cultural forces, will show less open aggression than boys. (*a*) However, in a permissive situation where privacy is assured, sex differences in open expression of aggression will be reduced.

Three experimental studies, the first a pilot study, the third an almost exact replication of the second, were conducted to test these hypotheses.

STUDY I

Methods and Results

In the first study, 30 male and 18 female children from two third-grade classes in a middle- and lower-middle-class public school were selected randomly from the total third-grade population and assigned randomly, 5 boys and 3 girls to each of 6 treatment conditions. Their ages ranged from 8 years, 4 months, to 9 years, 5 months, with a mean of 9 years.

Two sixth-grade children, one boy and one girl, were selected as confederates by nomination by class teachers and the school principal as "the most cooperative and dependable children in their grade." They were taken into the experimenter's full confidence.

The study followed a $2 \times 3 \times 2$ factorial design. There were 2 treatments—frustration and nonfrustration—and 3 types of interpolated activities—shooting a play gun at different targets on which were drawn figures either of a boy, girl, man, woman, cat, or dog; shooting at targets blank except for a bull's-eye; and solving simple arithmetic problems. The boy-girl dimension formed the third facet of the design.

The first phase of the study lasted for 5 minutes. In the frustration condition, the sixth-grade confederate "inadvertently and clumsily" prevented the subject from completing any of five moderately simple block construction tasks. The experimenter had promised the subject a nickel for each task completed within a time limit. The confederate also interspersed his interference with a predetermined set of six sarcastic remarks, such as "Ha! I see! You really need money. Let's see how you get it." No subject was allowed to complete any task.

In the nonfrustration condition, the confederate (always the same sex as the subject) helped subjects to complete their tasks (all subjects were allowed to complete all tasks), and no reward was promised or given, other than the experimenter's verbal comment, "Very good," at the end of each task.

The second, or activity interpolation phase, immediately followed the treatment phase and lasted for 8 minutes.

In the third phase, each subject was shown his partner (the same-sex confederate), who was sitting outside the experimental room with his hands in contact with electric wires which were apparently attached to a shock apparatus installed in the experimental room. The experimenter casually reminded each subject in the frustration condition of the confederate's uncooperative behavior, and told him that he could "get even" by pushing a button, thus administering shocks (which would not hurt the frustrator very much, but would make him uncomfortable). They were further told that the frustrator would not know who was shocking him. No limit was set on the number of "shocks" that could be administered. The number of shocks ostensibly given to the confederate was taken as a measure of his hostility.

Subjects in the nonfrustration treatment were also shown the confederate, no mention of noncooperation was made, but they were told they could administer shocks if they wanted to and that the confederate would not know who had shocked him.

At the end of the study, the nature of the experiment was discussed with all subjects. Without exception they thought it funny.

A large number of subjects made a response of one shock only, but only a few gave a large number. The distribution of scores was thus extremely skewed, and a log $(X + 1)$ transformation of scores was used.

The analysis of variance of the transformed aggression scores is shown in Table 1. Frustrated subjects manifested greater hostility than nonfrustrated subjects, but neither the sex of the subject nor the type of interpolated activity resulted in differences in amount of hostility.

TABLE 1. Analysis of Variance of the Transformed Aggression Scores in Study I (Five Boys and Three Girls in Each Condition)

Source	df	MS	F
Frustration (F)	1	1.15566	15.10[a]
Activities (A)	2	.16679	2.18
Sex (S)	1	.00153	<1
F × A	2	.07398	<1
F × S	1	.00306	<1
A × S	2	.24056	3.14
F × A × S	2	.12031	1.57
Error *MS*	36	(.07651)	

[a] $p < .01$.

STUDY II

Method

Thirty male and 30 female third graders from a school with a principally middle- and upper-class population were randomly selected from four third-grade classes and randomly assigned to five experimental conditions, six boys and six girls to each condition. Confederates were six boys and six girls, nominated as cooperative and dependable by their teachers and principal. Each worked with five subjects of the same sex, completing one unit of the five experimental conditions. As in Study I, they enjoyed the experimenter's full confidence.

The experimental tasks and the subjects' frustration or nonfrustration by the same-sex confederate were similar to those in Study I, except that subjects were given five nickels in advance. One nickel was taken from him after he had "failed" each of the five tasks, so that he ended the 8-minute frustration period penniless. At the end of this phase, each subject was asked to check a simple 5-step "like-dislike" scale ranging from 1, "I like him/her very much," to 5, "I really don't like him/her [the confederate] at all."

The second 8-minute experimental phase for one group each of frustrated and nonfrustrated subjects consisted of shooting guns at a target on which was placed a picture of an 11-year-old child of the same sex. The second pair of groups (one frustrated, one nonfrustrated) engaged in social talk (moderately standard for all subjects) with the experimenter for 8 minutes. The third frustration group was administered social talk plus interpretation (beginning in the third minute of conversation) to the effect that the frustrator was sleepy, upset, and would probably have been more cooperative if the subject had offered him two of the five nickels. At the end of the second phase, each subject was again asked to check the 5-point like-dislike rating of his/her confederate.

Phase 3 of Study II lasted for 2 minutes. Each subject was shown a "response box." He was told that the experimenter would go to an adjoining room and ask the confederate to do the same set of block-building tasks the subject had done. The subject could slow the older sixth grader's work by pushing one button, or help him by pushing the other. He could not push the button more than 20 times, although he need not count, as the experimenter would flash a signal light after the twentieth push. The experimenter then left the room, presumably to work with the confederate. The hostility criterion (aggression score) was the number of times the "slowing" button was pushed.

Upon completion of Study II, all subjects were told the nature of the experiment and, like the subjects in Study I, thought it great fun.

Table 2 is a schematic representation of Study II.

TABLE 2. Schematic Presentation of the Design of Study II

1st phase (8 min)	2d phase (8 min)						3d phase (2 min)
Initial Treatment	*Play with Guns and Targets*		*Social Talk*		*Reinterpretation*		*Measure of Residual Hostility*
	boys	*girls*	*boys*	*girls*	*boys*	*girls*	
Frustration	6	6	6	6	6	6	
Nonfrustration	6	6	6	6	0	0	

Results

Table 3 summarizes the analysis of variance of the aggression scores (number of pushes of the slowing button). Scores were transformed into log scores, using a log $(X + 2)$ transformation. Only the treatments effect was significant.

Multiple comparisons were made among the total aggression scores of subjects in the different treatments, using Duncan's multiple-range test. The results of these comparisons are given in Table 4. Mean aggression scores for the aggressive play and social talk treatments did not differ significantly from each other either for the frustrated or nonfrustrated subjects. However, for each of these treatments, frustrated subjects had significantly higher mean aggression scores than comparable treatment groups of nonfrustrated subjects. These results are in line with those of Study I, where the frustration effect was highly significant, but the effect of interpolated activities was not.

Comparisons involving the interpretation group reveal that subjects to whom interpretation of the confederate was given produced significantly fewer aggression responses than subjects in the other two frustration groups (*p*'s for each of the two comparisons are less than .001), but this frustration group did not differ significantly from either of the two nonfrustration groups.

Like-dislike ratings, collected at the end of the first and second phases of Study II, are available for only 50 subjects. The first of these ratings was intended to reveal hostility engendered by frustration as opposed to nonfrustration, while it was hoped that the second rating would reflect the influence of the interpolated activity on attitude toward the confederate. The authors are doubtful about the success of their methods, since the correlation between the post-treatment and the postinterpolation rating was .90. For this reason, detailed tabular presentations of the two ratings and changes from the first to the second are not given. However, the following findings appeared:

For the first rating, *F* for the frustration treatment was highly significant. (The three frustration groups disliked their same-sex confederates much more than the two nonfrustration groups, but there were no differences among the three frustration or the two nonfrustration groups.) *F*s for sex and Frustration × Sex were also significant at the .05 level of confidence. Girls admitted to less dislike than boys, but only in the frustration condition.

The pattern was the same (as would be expected from the high correlation between the two ratings) for the rating following the interpolated activity. However, when change scores were computed, *F* was highly significant for treatments, but not for sex or Treatments × Sex. Subjects in the social talk and aggressive play interpolated condition did not reduce their dislike of their same-sex confederate, while those in the interpretation condition did (*p* for each comparison was less than .005). This finding is even more striking when the high correlation between the two ratings is considered.

As has been mentioned, the authors hoped the second like-dislike rating would reflect residual hostility affected by different interpolated treatments following frustration. As such, these ratings should be correlated with the behavioral aggression score (number of times the slowing button was pushed). This proved to be the case, as the second like-dislike rating and the aggression score correlated .51.

However, it is possible that the way in which the like-dislike ratings were introduced affected the behavioral expression of aggression. Study III was run to introduce the attitudinal measures as an independent variable.

TABLE 3. Analysis of Variance of Aggression Scores among the Experimental Conditions of Study II

Source	df	MS	F
Treatments (T)	4	1.11387	9.49[a]
Sex (S)	1	.03049	<1
T × S	4	.02982	<1
Error *MS*	50	(.11739)	

[a] $p < .01$.

TABLE 4. Multiple Comparisons among Total Aggression Scores of the Experimental Treatments of Second Study II[a]

Treatments	Frustration-Reinterpretation	Nonfrustration-Social Talk	Nonfrustration-Aggressive Play	Frustration-Aggressive Play	Frustration-Social Talk
Mean Aggression Scores	6.37391	6.52881	8.14602	13.40896	13.72438
Order	a	b	c	d	e

Multiple Comparisons

	a	*b*	*c*	*d*	*e*
a	—	*ns*	*ns*	b	b
b		—	*ns*	b	b
c			—	c	c
d				—	*ns*
e					—

[a] $N = 6$ per cell in each treatment.
[b] $p < .001$.
[c] $p = .005$.

STUDY III

Study III is an exact replication of Study II in terms of procedures and number, sex, and social classes of subjects except that like-dislike ratings were administered to only half the subjects in each treatment condition and omitted for the other half.

As in Study II, raw aggression scores (slowing button pushing) were transformed into log scores using log $(X + 2)$ transformation. A $2 \times 2 \times 5$ analysis of variance was performed (treatments—frustration, nonfrustration—*replications—where Replication 1 did* not *include like-dislike ratings, and Replication 2 included the ratings as described for Study II* —and interpolated activities—as in Study II).

Table 5 summarizes this analysis of variance.

TABLE 5. Analysis of Variance of Aggression Scores among the Experimental Conditions in Study III

Source	df	MS	F
Treatments (T)	4	1.0292	16.44[a]
Sex (S)	1	.1986	3.17
Replications (R)	1	.3640	5.81
T × S	4	.0679	1.08
T × R	4	.1753	2.80
S × R	1	.0002	<1
T × S × R	4	.2297	3.67
Error	40	.0626	

[a] $p < .01$.

*F*s for treatments, replications, the Treatments × Replications interaction, and the triple-order interaction of Treatments × Sex × Replications were all significant. Total aggression scores for subjects who had been administered the like-dislike ratings were significantly greater than those of subjects who had *not* been given the ratings, suggesting that the *x* variable of being "asked to consider your enemy" may actually intensify the expression of aggression toward him. Main effects of sex and interactions of treatments and sex, and sex and replication condition were not significant.

Comparison of the broad pattern of findings of Study II with Study III reveals no significant differences in any dimension, despite the larger number of significant *F*s in Study III. Hence, conclusions drawn from Study III may be considered to agree closely with those of Study II (or vice versa).

An interesting difference between the correlations of the second like-dislike ratings and the aggression scores for the two studies appears, however. For Study II, this r was .51, but for Study III it was $-.01$ (where $N = 30$). Of course, this may well be a chance variation. As in Study II, correlation between the first and second like-dislike ratings was high (.85 in Study III).

DISCUSSION

One of the hypotheses toward which the three studies reported in the main body of this paper were directed questioned the value of expression of aggression as a catharsis serving to reduce (in this case, frustration-produced) aggression or hostility. This doubt appears to have been justified, at least when expression of aggression is toward inanimate objects.

Another hypothesis suggested was that aggression without anger lacks cathartic value, but that aggressive play in the presence of a permissive adult may lead to increase in aggression. All three of the studies reported above support this hypothesis. Actually, nonfrustration-aggressive play subjects consistently showed higher aggression scores (as manifested by "shocking" or "slowing down" a same-sex confederate) than nonfrustration-social talk subjects. (The difference, however, was significant only when the behavioral expression of aggression was preceded by like-dislike ratings of the experimenter's confederates.)

Taken together, the findings suggest that aggressive play, with or without previous frustration, has no cathartic value.

A major thesis of the present paper is that reasonable, positive interpretation of the frustrating situation has a cathartic effect. Studies II and III, where the hypothesis was tested, strongly support it. Behavioral expressions of aggression were lower for frustrated subjects to whom interpretations had been given, and greater reductions in "dislike" ratings occurred following interpretation.

Verbal expression of aggression (like-dislike ratings) seems to have no cathartic effect on aggression directed toward a frustrator. If anything, such an expression by rating appears to have the opposite effect. This finding, if repeated in other contexts and for other populations, has rather startling implications: Verbal expressions of hostility (in this case, ratings) may actually lead to an increase of aggressive behavior toward the subject of the hostile expression—malicious gossip may induce action? expression of hostile feelings in therapy may lead to aggressive behavior in real life?

There were, somewhat to the authors' surprise and despite their hypothesis, no significant sex differences in behavioral expression of aggression toward frustrators. In other words, in a permissive situation where they are assured they cannot be detected, girls behave just as aggressively as boys. However, girl subjects gave more favorable like-dislike ratings of their frustrators than boys. (This finding was statistically significant in Study II, but not in Study III.) This is contrary to the general conviction that girls *talk* (in this case, *rate*), while boys *act*. The finding may, of course, be due to the ages of the subjects, most of whom were 8- or 9-year-olds. Cultural stereotypes of what is sex appropriate may not be well established by these ages, although there is considerable literature suggesting the contrary.

SUMMARY

Sixth-grade confederates of the same sex as the 3rd-grade Ss either frustrated (interfered with) or did not frustrate a total of 168 8- and 9-year-old children, about ½ of whom were boys, ½ girls. Treatments following either frustration or nonfrustration included aggressive play, social talk, and reasonable interpretation of the frustrator's behavior. Aggression was measured behaviorally (responses were allowed that presumably punished the confederate, whether he had or had not been a frustrator) and by like-dislike ratings. Data from the 3 studies reported are consonant in direction when the designs permit direct comparisons, and lead to the following conclusions: Frustration leads to heightened aggressive feelings, but subsequent aggressive behavior does not reduce the aggression. Aggression in the absence of anger is without cathartic value. Reasonable interpretation of a frustrator's behavior is strikingly effective in reducing both behavioral and verbal (rating) aggression toward him. Verbal aggression toward the frustrator does not reduce aggression directed toward him, but may actually increase it. In a permissive, confidential situation, girls *behave* as aggressively as boys, although their like-dislike ratings of frustrating confederates reveal less hostility than boys'.

REFERENCES

Berkowitz, L. *Aggression: A Social Psychological Analysis.* New York: McGraw-Hill, 1962.

Buss, A. G. *The Psychology of Aggression.* New York: Wiley, 1961.

Dollard, J., L. W. Doob, N. E. Miller, O. H. Mowrer, and R. R. Sears. *Frustration and Aggression.* New Haven, Conn.: Yale Univ. Press, 1939.

Feshback S. "The drive reducing function of fantasy behavior." *J. abnorm. soc. Psychol.* **50** (1955), 3–11.

Feshbach, S. "The catharsis hypothesis and some consequence of interaction with aggressive and neutral play objects." *J. Pers.* **24** (1956), 449–462.

Freud, S. *Beyond the Pleasure Principle.* New York: Bantam Books, 1959.

Hokanson, J. E. "The effects of frustration and anxiety on overt aggression." *J. abnorm. soc. Psychol.* **62** (1961), 346–351.

Hornberger, R. H. The differential reduction of aggressive responses as a function of interpolated activities. Paper read at Amer. Psychol. Assn., Cincinnati, Ohio, September 4, 1959.

Miller, F. A., J. H. Moyer, and R. B. Patrick. *Planning Student Activities.* Englewood Cliffs, N.J.: Prentice-Hall, 1956.

Thibaut, J. W., and J. Coules. "The role of communication in the reduction of interpersonal hostility." *J. abnorm. soc. Psychol.,* **47** (1952), 770–777.

chapter six

Child Development and Childhood Education

6.1 Orientation

For many persons the value of data from developmental psychology is to be determined by the extent of the data's relevance, or useful application, to practical problems of child rearing and childhood education. But, from a scientific point of view, the embryonic state of knowledge and understanding of human behavior and developmental processes is such that direct practical applications are, at best, extremely tenuous. This is the "cautionary" thesis developed by David P. Ausubel as he elaborates his views, as a developmental psychologist, physician, and educator on curriculum development. At the same time, Ausubel provides a psychological rationale for the execution of educational practices which he believes can be based upon basic developmental research.

Four issues comprise the bulk of Ausubel's paper: confusion of the concepts *maturation* and *readiness,* the structure of the curriculum (breadth versus depth), curriculum design based upon children's expressed interests, and the organization of learning experiences made problematic by naïve concepts of children's cognitive functioning. Ausubel highlights as inappropriate the practice of borrowing concepts from other fields of study and supports the strategy of developing concepts from within the context of psychology. Also apparent in his discussion is the plea for more sophisticated experimental research, especially that related to cognitive development.

Since the publication of this paper in its original form, Ausubel has written extensively on teaching strategies and the learning process. Much of this writing is based upon concepts of cognition advanced by Piaget (Chapter 4). Piaget's influence can be detected in Ausubel's comments on secondary-school pedagogy. His proposition concerning proactive and retroactive inhibition has also been subjected to experimental test. These and other of Ausubel's views on school learning have been summarized in his *The Psychology of Meaningful Verbal Learning* (see the Recommended Reading). Additional commentaries on "what shall the school teach?" may be obtained by referring to the journal in which this paper initially appeared. Included are viewpoints on curriculum issues from the disciplines of contemporary philosophy, sociology, and learning theory.

RECOMMENDED READING

Ausubel, D. P. *The Psychology of Meaningful Verbal Learning.* New York: Greene and Stratton, 1963.

Bugelski, B. R. *The Psychology of Learning Applied to Teaching.* Indianapolis: Bobbs-Merrill, 1964. (See "Early and late learning," chap. 6, pp. 129–45.)

Meyer, W. J. *Developmental Psychology.* New York: The Center for appl. Res. in Educ., 1964.

Siegel, Lawrence (Ed.) *Instruction: Some Contemporary Issues.* San Francisco: Chandler, 1967. (See "Formulations emphasizing learner behavior," pt. III, pp. 141–260.)

Taba, Hilda. *Curriculum Development: Theory and Practice.* New York: Harcourt, 1962. (See "The concept of development," chap. 7, pp. 88–99.)

Travers, R. M. W. *Essentials of Learning.* (2d ed.) New York: Macmillan, 1967. (See "Developmental processes in relation to learning," chap. 9, pp. 265–298.)

6.1 Viewpoints from Related Disciplines: Human Growth and Development

David P. Ausubel, UNIVERSITY OF TORONTO

CHILD DEVELOPMENT AND EDUCATIONAL PRACTICE

What light can the field of human growth and development throw on the issue "What shall the schools teach?" I only wish it were possible for me to list and discuss a dozen or more instances in which developmental principles have been validly utilized in providing definitive answers to questions dealing with the content and organization of the curriculum. Unfortunately, however, it must be admitted that at present our discipline can offer only a limited number of very crude generalizations and highly tentative suggestions bearing on this issue. In a very general sense, of course, it is undeniable that concern with child development has had a salutary effect on the educational enterprise. It alerted school administrators to the fact that certain minimal levels of intellectual maturity were necessary before various subjects could be taught with a reasonable degree of efficiency and hope of success; and it encouraged teachers in presenting their subject matter to make use of the existing interests of pupils, to consider their point of view, and to take into account prevailing limitations in command of language and grasp of concepts. On the other hand, premature and wholesale extension of developmental principles to educational theory and practice has caused incalculable harm. It will take at least a generation for teachers to unlearn some of the more fallacious and dangerous of these overgeneralized and unwarranted applications.

Much of the aforementioned difficulty proceeds from failure to appreciate that human growth and development is a pure rather than an applied science. As a pure science it is concerned with the discovery of general laws about the nature and regulation of human development *as an end in itself.* Ultimately, of course, these laws have self-evident implications for the realization of practical goals in such fields as education, child rearing, and guidance. In a very general sense they indicate the effects of different interpersonal and social climates on personality development and the kinds of methods and subject-matter content that are most compatible with developmental capacity and mode of functioning at a given stage of growth. Thus, because it offers important insights about the changing intellectual and emotional capacities of children as developing human beings, child development may legitimately be considered one of the basic sciences un-

Reprinted from Teacher's College Record, **60** (1959), 245–254. By permission of the author and the Bureau of Publications, Teacher's College, Columbia University.

derlying education and guidance and as part of the necessary professional preparation of teachers—in much the same sense that anatomy and bacteriology are basic sciences for medicine and surgery.

Actual application to practical problems of teaching and curriculum, however, is quite another matter. Before the educational implications of developmental findings can become explicitly useful in everyday school situations, much *additional* research at the engineering level of operations is necessary. Knowledge about nuclear fission, for example, does not tell us how to make an atomic bomb or an atomic-powered submarine, antibiotic reactions that take place in petri dishes do not necessarily take place in living systems, and methods of learning employed by animals in mazes do not necessarily correspond to methods of learning that children use in grappling with verbal materials in classrooms. Many of the better-known generalizations in child development—the principle of readiness, the cephalocaudal trend, the abstract to concrete trend in conceptualizing the environment, and others—fit these analogies perfectly. They are interesting and potentially useful ideas to curriculum specialists but will have little practical utility in designing a social studies or physical education curriculum unless they are rendered more specific in terms of the actual operations involved in teaching these subjects. This lack of fruitful particularization, although unfortunate and regrettable, does not in itself give rise to damaging consequences except insofar as many beginning teachers tend to nurture vague illusions about the current usefulness of these principles, and subsequently, after undergoing acute disillusionment, lose the confidence they may have felt in the value of a developmental approach to educational problems.

Much more detrimental in their effects on pupils and teachers have been the consequences of far-fetched and uncritical application to educational practice of developmental generalizations that either have not been adequately validated or only apply to a very restricted age segment of the total span of children's development. Two illustrations of the latter category of highly limited generalizations—the "internal ripening" theory of maturation and the principle of self-selection—will be given later in this discussion. A widely accepted but inadequately validated developmental principle frequently cited to justify general or over-all ability grouping of pupils is that a child's growth and achievement show a "going-togetherness." Actually, except for a spuriously high correlation during infancy, the relationship between physical status and motor ability on the one hand, and intelligence and intellectual achievement on the other is negligible and declines consistently with increasing age. Even among the different subtests of intelligence and among the different areas of intellectual achievement, the weight of the evidence indicates that as a child grows older his component rates of growth in these various functions tend increasingly to diverge.

Keeping these qualifications about the relevance of child development for educational practice in mind, I propose briefly to consider from the standpoint of developmental psychology the following aspects of the issue under discussion: (1) readiness as a criterion for curricular placement; (2) developmental factors affecting breadth of the curriculum; (3) the child's voice in determining the curriculum; and (4) the content and goals of instruction in relation to the organization and growth of the intellect.

READINESS AND GRADE PLACEMENT

There is little disagreement about the fact that readiness always crucially influences the efficiency of the learning process and often determines whether a given intellectual skill or type of school material is learnable at all at a particular stage of development. Most educators implicitly accept also the proposition that an *optimal* age exists for every kind of learning. Postponement of learning experience beyond the age of optimal readiness wastes valuable and often unsuspected learning opportunities, thereby unnecessarily reducing the amount and complexity of subject matter content that can be mastered in a designated period of schooling. It is also conceivable that beyond a certain critical age the learning of various intellectual skills becomes more difficult for an older than for a younger child. On the other hand, when a pupil is prematurely exposed to a learning task before he is ready for it, he not only fails to learn the task in question but even learns from the experience of failure to fear, dislike, and avoid it.

Up to this point, the principle of readiness—the idea that attained capacity limits and influences an individual's ability to profit from current experience or practice—is empirically demonstrable and conceptually unambiguous. Difficulty first arises when it is confused with the concept of *maturation* and when the latter concept in turn is equated with a process of "internal ripening." The concept of readiness simply refers to the adequacy of existing capacity in relation to the demands of a given learning task. No specification is made as to *how* this capacity is achieved—whether through prior practice of a specific nature (learning), through incidental experience, through genically regulated structural and functional changes occurring independently of environmental influences, or through various combinations of these factors. Maturation, on the other hand, has a different and much more restricted meaning. It encompasses those increments in capacity that take place in the demonstrable absence of specific practice experience—those that are attributable to genic influences and/or incidental experience. Maturation, therefore, is not the same as readiness but is merely one of the two principal factors (the other being learning) that contribute to or determine the organism's readiness to cope with new experience. Whether or not readiness exists, in other words, does not necessarily depend on maturation alone but in many instances is solely a function of prior learning experience and most typically depends on varying proportions of maturation and learning.

To equate the principles of readiness and maturation not only muddies the conceptual waters but also makes it difficult for the school to appreciate that insufficient readiness may reflect inadequate prior learning on the part of pupils because of inappropriate or inefficient instructional methods. Lack of maturation can thus become a convenient scapegoat whenever children manifest insufficient readiness to learn, and the school, which is thereby automatically absolved of all responsibility in the matter, consequently fails to subject its instructional practices to the degree of self-critical scrutiny necessary for continued educational progress. In short, while it is important to appreciate that the current readiness of pupils determines the school's current choice of instructional methods and materials, it is equally important to bear in mind that this readiness itself is partly determined by the appropriateness and efficiency of the previous instructional practices to which they have been subjected.

The conceptual confusion is further compounded when maturation is interpreted as a process of "internal ripening" essentially independent of *all* environmental influences, that is, of both specific practice and incidental experience. Readiness then becomes a matter of simple genic regulation unfolding in accordance with a predetermined and immutable timetable; and the school, by definition, becomes powerless to influence readiness either through its particular way of arranging specific learning experiences or through a more general program of providing incidental or nonspecific background experience preparatory to the introduction of more formal academic activities.

Actually, the embryological model of development implicit in the "internal ripening" thesis fits quite well when applied to human sensorimotor and neuromuscular sequences taking place during the prenatal period and early infancy. In the acquisition of simple behavioral functions (for example, locomotion, prehension) that characterize all members of the human species irrespective of cultural or other environmental differences, it is reasonable to suppose that for all practical purposes genic factors alone determine the direction of development. Environmental factors only enter the picture if they are extremely deviant, and then serve more to disrupt or arrest the ongoing course of development than to generate distinctive developmental progressions of their own. Thus, the only truly objectionable aspect of this point of view is its unwarranted extrapolation to those more complex and variable components of later cognitive and behavioral development where unique factors of individual experience and cultural environment make important contributions to the direction, patterning and sequential order of all developmental changes.

It is hardly surprising, therefore, in view of the tremendous influence on professional and lay opinion wielded by Gesell and his colleagues, that many people conceive of readiness in absolute and immutable terms, and thus fail to appreciate that except for such traits as walking and grasping, the mean ages of readiness can never be specified apart from relevant environmental conditions. Although the modal child in contemporary America may first be ready to read at the age of six and one-half, the age of reading readiness is always influenced by cultural, subcultural, and individual differences in background experience, and in any case varies with the method of instruction employed and the child's IQ. Middle-class children, for example, are ready to read at an earlier age than lower-class children because of the greater availability of books in the home and because they are read to and taken places more frequently.

The need for particularizing developmental generalizations before they can become useful in educational practice is nowhere more glaringly evident than in the field of readiness. At present we can only speculate what curricular sequences might conceivably be if they took into account precise and detailed (but currently unavailable) research findings on the emergence of readiness for different subject-matter areas, for different subareas and levels of difficulty within an area, and for different techniques of teaching the same material. Because of the unpredictable specificity of readiness as shown, for example, by the fact that four- and five-year-olds can profit from training in pitch but not in rhythm, valid answers to such questions cannot be derived from logical extrapolation but require meticulous empirical research in a school setting. The next step would involve the development of appropriate teaching methods and materials to take optimal advantage of existing degrees of readiness and to increase readiness wherever necessary and desirable. But since we generally do not have this type of research data available, except perhaps in the field of reading, we can only pay lip service to the principle of readiness in curriculum planning.

BREADTH OF CURRICULUM

One of the chief complaints of the critics of public education, both in the United States and in New Zealand, is that modern children fail to learn the fundamentals because of the broadening of the elementary school curriculum to include such subjects as social studies, art, science, music, and manual arts in addition to the traditional three R's. This, of course, would be a very serious charge if it were true, because the wisdom of expanding a child's intellectual horizons at the expense of making him a cripple in the basic intellectual skills is highly questionable to say the least. Fortunately, however, the benefits of an expanded curriculum have thus far not been accompanied by a corresponding deterioration in the standard of the three R's. Evidently the decreased amount of time spent on the latter subjects has been more than compensated for by the development of more efficient methods of teaching and by the incidental learning of the fundamentals in the course of studying these other subjects. Nevertheless, the issue of breadth versus depth still remains because there *is* obviously a point beyond which increased breadth could only be attained by sacrificing mastery of the fundamental skills; and even if we agreed to maintain or improve the present standard of the three R's, we would still have to choose between breadth and depth in relation to other components of the curriculum, particularly at the junior and senior high school levels. It is at these points of choice that developmental criteria can be profitably applied.

Generally speaking, maximal breadth of the curriculum consistent with adequate mastery of its constituent parts is developmentally desirable at all ages because of the tremendously wide scope of human abilities. The wider the range of intellectual stimulation to which pupils are exposed, the greater are the chances that all of the diverse potentialities both within a group of children and within a single child will be brought to fruition. By the same token, a broad curriculum makes it possible for more pupils to experience success in the performance of school activities and thus to develop the necessary self-confidence and motivation for continued academic striving and achievement. The very fact that elementary school children are able to make significant progress in science and social studies also indicates that myopic concentration on the three R's would waste much available readiness for these types of learnings and thus compel junior and senior high schools to devote much of their instructional time to materials that are easily learnable in the lower grades. In fact, one of the major failings of the secondary school curriculum today is that because it still has not adequately adjusted to the expansion of the elementary school syllabus, entering pupils are subjected to much stultifying repetition and fail to break the new ground for which they are obviously ready.

The relationship between breadth and depth must also take into account the progressive differentiation of intelligence, interests, and personality structure with increasing age. The elementary school child is a "generalist" because both his intellect and his personality are still relatively unstable and uncrystallized and lack impressive internal consistency. Thus, many different varieties of subject matter are equally compatible with his interest and ability patterns. Furthermore, unless he has experience with many different fields of knowledge and gives each a provisional try, he is in no position to judge which kinds of intellectual pursuits are most congruent with his major ability and value systems. Hence, quite apart from the future life adjustment values of a broad educational background, it is appropriate on developmental grounds for elementary and early high school curricula to stress breadth rather than depth.

Toward the latter portion of the high school period, however, precisely the opposite kind of situation begins to emerge. Interests have crystallized and abilities have undergone differentiation to the point where greater depth and specialization are possible and desirable. Many students at this stage of intellectual development are ready to sink their teeth into more serious and solid academic fare, but unfortunately suitable instructional programs geared at an advanced level of critical and independent thinking are rarely available. The changes that have taken place in secondary school curricula since the academy days have been primarily characterized by the belated and half-hearted addition of more up-to-date and topical information. Very little has been done in the way of providing the student with a meaningful, integrated, systematic view of the major ideas in a given field of knowledge.

THE CHILD'S VOICE IN CURRICULUM PLANNING

One extreme point of view associated with the child-centered approach to education is the notion that children are innately equipped in some mysterious fashion for knowing precisely what is best for them. This idea is obviously an outgrowth of predeterministic theories (for example, those of Rousseau and Gesell) that conceive of development as a series of internally regulated sequential steps that unfold in accordance with a prearranged design. According to these theorists, the environment facilitates development best by providing a maximally permissive field that does not interfere with the predetermined processes of spontaneous maturation. From these assumptions it is but a short step to the claim that the child himself must be in the most strategic position to *know* and *select* those components of the environment that correspond most closely with his current developmental needs and hence are most conducive to optimal growth. Empirical "proof" of this proposition is adduced from the fact that nutrition is adequately maintained and existing deficiency conditions are spontaneously corrected when infants are permitted to select their own diets. If the child can successfully choose his diet, he must certainly know what is best for him in all areas of growth and should therefore be permitted to select everything, including his curriculum.

In the first place, and refuting this theory, even if development were primarily a matter of internal ripening, there would still be no good reason for supposing that the child is therefore implicitly conversant with the current direction and facilitating conditions of development and hence axiomatically equipped to make the most appropriate choices. Because the individual is sensitive in early childhood to internal cues of physiological need we cannot conclude that he is similarly sensitive to cues reflective of psychological and other developmental needs; even in the area of nutrition, selection is a reliable criterion of need only during early infancy.

Second, unless one assigns a sacrosanct status to endogenous motivations, there is little warrant for believing either that they alone are truly reflective of the child's *genuine* developmental requirements or that environmentally derived needs are "imposed," authoritarian in spirit, and inevitably fated to thwart the actualization of his developmental potentialities. Actually, most needs originate from without and are internalized in the course of the child's interaction and identification with significant persons in his family and cultural environments.

Third, one can never assume that the child's *spontaneously* expressed interests and activities are completely reflective of *all* of his important needs and capacities. Just because capacities can potentially provide their own motivation does not mean that they always or necessarily do so. It is not the possession of capacities that is motivating, but the anticipation of future satisfactions once they have been successfully exercised. But because of such factors as inertia, lack of opportunity, lack of appreciation, and preoccupation with other activities, many capacities may never be exercised in the first place. Thus, children typically develop only *some* of their potential capacities, and their expressed interests cannot be considered coextensive with the potential range of interests they are capable of developing with appropriate stimulation.

In conclusion, therefore, the current interests and spontaneous desires of immature pupils can hardly be considered reliable guideposts and adequate substitutes for specialized knowledge and seasoned judgment in designing a curriculum. Recognition of the role of pupil needs in school learning does not mean that the scope of the syllabus should be restricted to the existing concerns and spontaneously expressed interests that happen to be present in a group of children growing up under particular conditions of intellectual and social class stimulation. In fact, one of the primary functions of education should be to stimulate the development of motivations that are currently nonexistent. It is true that academic achievement is greatest when pupils manifest felt needs to acquire knowledge as an end in itself. Such needs, however, are not endogenous but acquired—and largely through exposure to provocative, meaningful, developmentally appropriate instruction. Hence, while it is reasonable to consider the views of pupils and even, under certain circumstances, to solicit their participation in the planning of the curriculum, it makes little developmental or administrative sense to entrust them with responsibility for significant policy or operational decisions.

ORGANIZATION AND COGNITIVE DEVELOPMENT

The curriculum specialist is concerned with more than the appropriate grade placement of different subjects and subject-matter content in accordance with such criteria as readiness and relative significance for intellecutal, vocational, or current adjustment purposes. More important than what pupils know at the end of the sixth, eighth, and twelfth grades is the extent of their knowledge at the ages of twenty-five, forty and sixty as well as their ability and desire both to learn more and to apply their knowledge fruitfully in adult life. In light of these latter criteria, in comparing, for example, the quantity and quality of our national research output in the pure and applied sciences with those of European countries, the American educational system stands up relatively well even though our school children apparently absorb less academic material. We are dealing here with the ultimate intellectual objectives of schooling, namely, with the long-term acquisition of stable and usable bodies of knowledge and intellectual skills and with the development of ability to think creatively, systematically, independently, and with depth in particular fields of inquiry. Instruction obviously influences the outcome of these objectives—not so much in the substantive content of subject matter but in the organization, sequence, and manner of presenting learning experiences, their degree of meaningfulness, and the relative balance between conceptual and factual materials.

But obviously, before we could ever hope to structure effectively such instructional variables for the optimal realization of these designated objectives, we would have to know a great deal more about the organizational and developmental principles whereby human beings acquire and retain stable bodies of knowledge and develop the power of critical and productive thinking. This type of knowledge, however, will forever elude us unless we abandon the untenable assumption that there is no real distinction either between the logic of a proposition and how the mind apprehends it or between the logical structure of subject-matter organization and the actual series of cognitive processes through which an immature and developing individual incorporates facts and concepts into a stable body of knowledge. It is perfectly logical from the standpoint of a mature scholar, for example, to write a textbook in which topically homogeneous materials are segregated into discrete chapters and treated throughout at a uniform level of conceptualization. But how closely does this approach correspond with highly suggestive findings that one of the major cognitive processes involved in the learning of any new subject is progressive differentiation of an originally undifferentiated field? Once we learn more about cognitive development than the crude generalizations that developmental psychology can currently offer, it will be possible to employ organizational and sequential principles in the presentation of subject matter that actually parallel developmental changes in the growth and organization of the intellect. In the meantime let us examine briefly how such generalizations as the concrete-to-abstract trend, the importance of meaningfulness, and the principle of retroactive inhibition have been used and abused in educational practice.

Many features of the activity program are based on the premise that the elementary school child perceives the world in relatively specific and concrete terms and requires considerable firsthand experience with diverse concrete instances of a given set of relationships before he can abstract genuinely meaningful concepts. Thus, an attempt is made to teach factual information and intellectual skills in the real-life functional contexts in which they are customarily encountered rather than through the medium of verbal exposition supplemented by artificially contrived drills and exercises. This approach has real merit, if a fetish is not made of naturalism and incidental learning, if drills and exercises are provided in instances where opportunities for acquiring skills do not occur frequently and repetitively enough in more natural settings, and if deliberate or guided effort is not regarded as incompatible with incidental learning. Even more important, however, is the realization that in older children, once a sufficient number of basic concepts are consolidated, new concepts are primarily abstracted from verbal rather than from concrete experience. Hence in secondary school it may be desirable to reverse both the sequence and the relative balance between abstract concepts and supportive data. There is good reason for believing, therefore, that much of the time presently spent in cook-book laboratory exercises in the sciences could be much more advantageously employed in formulating precise definitions, making explicit verbal distinctions between concepts, generalizing from hypothetical situations, and in other ways.

Another underlying assumption of activity and project methods is that concepts and factual data are retained much longer when they are meaningful, genuinely understood, and taught as larger units of interrelated materials than when they are presented as fragmented bits of isolated information and committed to rote memory. This, of course, does not preclude the advisability of rote learning for certain kinds of learning (for example, multiplication tables) *after* a functional understanding of the underlying concepts has been acquired. Unfortunately, however, these principles have made relatively few inroads on the high school instructional program, where they are still applicable. The teaching of mathematics and science, for example, still relies heavily on rote learning of formulas and procedural steps, on recognition of traditional "type problems," and on mechanical manipulation of symbols. In the absence of clear and stable concepts which serve as anchoring points and organizing foci for the assimilation of new material, secondary school students are trapped in a morass of confusion and seldom retain rotely memorized materials much beyond final exam time.

This brings us finally to a consideration of the mechanisms of accretion and long-term retention of large bodies of ideational material. Why do high school and university students tend to forget so readily previous day-to-day learnings as they are exposed to new lessons? The traditional answer of educational psychology, based upon studies of short-term rote learning in animal and human subjects, has been that subsequent learning experiences which are similar to but not identical with previously learned materials exert a retroactively inhibitory effect on the retention of the latter. But wouldn't it be reasonable to suppose that all of the existing, cumulatively established ideational systems which an individual brings with him to any learning situation have more of an interfering effect on the retention of new learning material (proactive inhibition) than brief exposure to subsequently introduced materials of a similar nature (retroactive inhibition)? Because it is cognitively most economical and least burdensome for an individual to subsume as much new experience as possible under existing concepts that are inclusive and stable, the import of many specific illustrative items in later experience is assimilated by the generalized meaning of these more firmly established and highly conceptualized subsuming foci. When this happens the latter items lose their identity and are said to be "forgotten." Hence, if proactive rather than retroactive inhibition turned out to be the principal mechanism affecting the longevity with which school materials were retained, it would behoove us to identify those factors that counteract it and to employ such measures in our instructional procedures.

6.2 *Orientation*

One of the foremost historical figures in American child psychology is the late Arnold Gesell. Dr. Gesell in 1911 founded the Clinic of Child Development of Yale University; it was there that an extensive longitudinal study of children's development from birth to adolescence provided a wealth of normative data and insights into the sequence of growth. A prolific writer, Gesell has communicated his philosophy of growth to millions of American parents. Devoted to the assessment of infant behavior and development, he devised diagnostic techniques that have been extensively used to determine developmental and psychological problems. Since Gesell's death in 1961, his work has been continued by two colleagues, both of whom participated in the Yale institute research activity for many years. Louise Ames and Frances Ilg have, most recently, immersed themselves in the study of school readiness. The study reprinted here preceded the publication of a major volume that examines in detail the problems of assessing developmental readiness.

This paper by Ames and Ilg is an exemplar of prediction studies concerned with a major practical problem in education. The authors have incorporated into their prediction strategy the assessment of visual-motor behaviors believed to be more relevant to subsequent school performance than global measures of intelligence. Broadly conceived, their approach is consistent with an emerging trend in psychology which endeavors to achieve specificity in defining patterns of cognitive and affective behavior required for various levels of academic performance. It has long been recognized that chronological age, per se, is inadequate as a criterion for readiness.

The practical question stimulated by the Ames and Ilg paper is whether tests such as the Gesell behavior tests, rather than chronological age, should be used to select children for school admission. Ausubel's position (see preceding paper) on readiness suggests that our problem is more one of adjusting teaching methods and materials so as to develop readiness and learning efficiency than it is a problem of selecting children who are most likely to profit from conventional educational programs. This, however, increases rather than obviates the need for precise assessment techniques.

RECOMMENDED READING

Gesell, Arnold, and Frances Ilg. *The Child From Five to Ten.* New York: Harper & Row, 1946.

Gesell, Arnold, and C. S. Amatruda. *Developmental Diagnosis.* New York: Hoeber, 1947.

Ilg, Frances, and Louise Ames. *School Readiness.* New York: Harper & Row, 1964.

Simon, Maria D. "Body configuration and school readiness." *Child Develpm.,* **30** (1959), 493–512.

Tyler, Fred T. "Issues related to readiness to learn." *Theories of Learning and Instruction.* (63d Yearbook) Publ. of the National Soc. for the Study of Educ. Chicago: Univ. Chicago Press, 1964, pp. 210–239.

6.2 Gesell Behavior Tests as Predictive of Later Grade Placement

Louise Bates Ames, GESELL INSTITUTE OF CHILD DEVELOPMENT
Frances L. Ilg, GESELL INSTITUTE OF CHILD DEVELOPMENT

The thesis of the current Gesell work on school readiness (1, 2) is that the time of starting school should be determined by the child's behavior age rather than by his age in years or by his IQ. That is, if—as in the case in most communities—a child is considered to be ready for kindergarten

Reprinted with permission of author and publisher: Ames, L. B., and Ilg, F. L. "Gesell Behavior tests as predicative of later grade placement." *Percep. Mot. Skills.* **19** (1964), 719–722.

when he is five, then he should be *behaving like* a 5-year-old before he begins kindergarten and not merely have reached his fifth birthday.

Behavior level can be determined on the basis of the Gesell battery of developmental tests, largely a series of visual and motor tests which require a child to perceive and then reproduce various simple stimulus situations.

The present paper compares actual school performance of a group of sixth graders with our predictions as to their readiness or non-readiness at the time of entering kindergarten.

METHOD

*S*s were 52 of an original group of 80 kindergarten boys and girls from the Hurlbutt School in Weston, Connecticut, who were still in the school in sixth grade. All *S*s were given a behavior examination, two projective tests (the Rorschach and the Mosaic tests) and a visual examination, in the Fall of 1957. Readiness for kindergarten was determined on the basis of these three sets of tests. Children were judged ready (for kindergarten) by all three examiners, ready by two of the three examiners, questionably ready, or unready.

These evaluations, which in themselves constitute predictions as to how well the children would do in the grades to which they had been arbitrarily assigned on the basis of age, were checked against actual school performance as measured by the grade or section of the grade to which the children were assigned by the school in the Fall of 1963. Of the 52 students who remained in this school, 2 had been doubly promoted and were in the seventh grade, 2 had failed a grade and were only in fifth grade. The rest were in Grade 6, distributed among four divisions, 1, 2, 3, and 4, 1 being the highest. Class groups were made up on the basis of general school performance.

RESULTS

General Results

As Table 1 shows, there is a product-moment correlation of .74 between prediction made at the time of school entrance and school performance at the beginning of sixth grade. Sixty-seven per cent of *S*s judged ready by all three examiners in 1957 were, in 1963, either in the top section of the class or had been doubly promoted and were in the class above. Seventy-eight per cent were either in Group 1 or 2. Of those judged ready by two of the three examiners, 87% were in either Group or Group 2, the largest number being in Group 2. Of those judged questionable in 1957, 82% were in either Group 2 or Group 3. All children judged unready for kindergarten in 1957 were, in 1963, in either Group 3 or 4 failed the grade entirely and were in fifth grade.

TABLE 1. Outcome of Weston Kindergarten Predictions, Made in 1957 When Checked with Actual School Performance in 1964

Classification	N	Percentage Distribution				
		Grade 7 & Grade 6-1	*Grade 6-2*	*Grade 6-3*	*Grade 6-4 & Grade 5*	Σ
		13	*16*	*14*	*9*	
Ready: 3 judges	9	67	11	22	0	100
Ready: 2 judges	15	40	47	13	0	100
Questionable	17	6	47	35	12	100
Unready	11	0	0	36	64	100

IQ and Readiness

A second check was made to determine whether or not those children with the highest IQs at the age of five were on the average in the highest divisions of Grade 6, six years later. Table 2 shows a correlation of kindergarten IQ and later grade placement of .56. To a large extent, as the table shows, children with the higher IQs were in the higher groups. Table 2 shows that, for all *S*s, grouped by IQ and ungrouped, the relation between prediction on early behavior examination and later grade placement is higher than that between early IQ and later grade placement.

TABLE 2. Distribution (Per cent) by IQ and Placement and Correlations of Kindergarten IQ with Sixth-Grade Placement

IQ	Grade 7 & Grade 6-1	Grade 6-2	Grade 6-3	Grade 6-4 & Grade 5
125 up	75%	13%	13%	0%
115-124	19	44	19	19
105-114	33	42	25	0
Below 105	0	15	46	38

	Full Range	Grouped by IQ
Grade versus Prediction	.74	.70
Grade versus IQ	.56	.49

Table 3 shows that mean IQ decreases steadily from Group 1 (or better), down through Group 4 or lower. However, as the table shows, range in IQ for each group is wide. Thus, a child with an IQ as low as 109 may be in Group 1; a child with an IQ as high as 123 may be in Group 4.

TABLE 3. IQ AND SCHOOL READINESS AND PERFORMANCE

	Mean IQ and Range of IQ for the Several Sixth-Grade Groups			
	Group 1	*Group 2*	*Group 3*	*Group 4*
Mean IQ	122	114	108	106
Range of IQ	109-143	93-131	91-119	89-123
N	11	16	14	7
	Mean IQ and Range of IQ for *S*s Judged Ready and Not-ready			
	Ready by 3	*Ready by 2*	*Questionable*	*Unready*
Mean IQ	121	114	112	106
Range of IQ	96-134	93-131	97-130	89-123
N	7	15	17	9

The same is true when mean kindergarten IQ and range of IQ are determined for those 5-year-old *S*s considered ready by all three examiners, ready by two, questionable, and not ready, on the basis of behavior tests. Mean IQ decreases gradually (see Table 3) from the most to the least ready group, but range of IQ is wide and overlapping. Thus, *S* with as low an IQ as 96 might be in the fully ready group; one with an IQ as high as 123 could be in the unready group.

Age and Readiness

In general mean age at the time of kindergarten entrance of sixth grade Group 1 *S*s was slightly higher than that of children in other groups. The mean age of Group 1, Grade 6 *S*s at the time of kindergarten entrance was 5 years, 5 months (range of 5,0 to 5,8); mean age of Group 2 *S*s was 5,2 (range of 4,9 to 5,8); mean age of Group 3 was 5,4 (range 4,10 to 5,7); and mean age of Group 4 was 5,2 (range 4,9 to 5,9).

SUMMARY

The present study tests the hypothesis that behavioral age is a more effective criterion for determining optimal time of school entrance than is chronological age or intelligence quotient. Fifty-two public school kindergarten pupils (judged ready for school entrance on the basis of their chronological age) were evaluated as to actual readiness on the basis of a battery of Gesell developmental tests, two projective techniques, and a battery of visual tests. *S*s were divided into four groups on the basis of performance: those ready by all three tests, those ready on two tests, those whose readiness for kindergarten was questionable, and those clearly unready. Predictions, made in the fall of 1957, were checked against actual school performance when the children reached sixth grade and were divided into four groups (1 to 4) on the basis of the excellence of their school work. Children judged ready (either by two or by all three judges) in kindergarten were with few exceptions in Groups 1 or 2 in sixth grade. Those judged unready were without exception in the lower groups, 3 or 4. Correlation between sixth grade school performance and prediction of readiness based on behavior tests was .74. Correlation between sixth grade school performance and kindergarten IQ was .56. Children who were chronologically older at the time of school entrance appeared slightly more likely to be in Group 1 in sixth grade.

REFERENCES

Ilg, F. L., and L. B. Ames. *School Readiness: Behavior Tests Used at the Gesell Institute*. New York: Harper & Row, 1964.

Ilg., F. L., L. B. Ames, and R. J. Apell. "School readiness as evaluated by Gesell, developmental, visual and projective tests." *Genet. Psychol. Monogr.*, 1964.

6.3 Orientation

The past few years have been characterized by unparalleled support for preschool education. This support is particularly strong as regards children who, by virtue of their early experiences, may enter the conventional school system unprepared to cope with the verbal and conceptual tasks associated with formal academic training. The federally financed Head Start Program, essentially an attempt to compensate for social and educational disadvantages among some children, is a prime example of the current commitment to the "preschool education" concept. In the following paper, the psychological underpinnings for the design of enriched preschool experiences are discussed by J. McVicker Hunt.

A major theme of this paper involves a specification of significant changes in psychological thinking which, according to Hunt's analysis, have taken place during the past thirty years. The author believes it is these changes that have fostered a greater receptivity to the procedures of compensatory education during the early years of childhood. The student is encouraged to consider Hunt's paper in relation to the Stott and Ball analysis of changing concepts of intelligence (Chapter 4), for their view essentially substantiates Hunt's position. Readers may also observe that the apparent psychological soundness of appropriate compensatory educational experiences during the early phases of children's development implies the "critical period" concept introduced in Chapter Two.

Hunt's paper is an outgrowth of the Arden House Conference on Pre-school Enrichment of Socially Disadvantaged Children held in December 1962.

RECOMMENDED READING

Deutsch, Martin. "Facilitating development in the pre-school child: social and psychological perspectives." *Merrill-Palmer Quart.*, **10** (1964) (3), 249–263.

Hechinger, F. M. (Ed.) *Pre-School Education Today.* New York: Doubleday, 1966.

Hess, R. D. (Ed.) *Early Education: Current Theory, Research, and Practice.* Chicago: Aldine, 1967.

Montessori in Perspective. Washington, D.C.: National Assn. for the Educ. of Young Children, 1966.

Passow, A. H. (Ed.) *Education of the Disadvantaged.* New York: Holt, Rinehart and Winston, 1967.

6.3 The Psychological Basis for Using Pre-School Enrichment as an Antidote for Cultural Deprivation

J. McVicker Hunt, UNIVERSITY OF ILLINOIS

It is very interesting, and very exciting for me, to encounter people who are generally considered sensible, planning to utilize pre-school experiences as an antidote for what we are now calling cultural deprivation and social disadvantage. The group at the Child Welfare Research Station in Iowa,

---

Reprinted from *Merrill-Palmer Quarterly of Behavior and Development,* **10** (1964), 209–248. By permission of the author and the Merrill-Palmer Institute of Human Development and Family Life.

under George D. Stoddard (see Stoddard and Wellman, 1940), described effects of nursery school which they considered evidence that would justify just such a use of nursery schools. This was about 25 years ago. Their work, however, was picked to pieces by critics and in the process lost much of the suggestive value it was justified in having. Many of you will recall the ridicule that was heaped upon the "wandering I.Q." (Simpson, 1939) and the way in which such people as Florence Goodenough (1939) derided in print the idea of a group of 13 "feeble-minded" infants being brought within the range of normal mentality through training by moron nurse-maids in an institution for the feebleminded (referring to the work of Skeels and Dye, 1939, to which we shall return). The fact that just such a use of pre-school experience is now being seriously planned by sensible people with widespread approval means that something has changed.

The change, of course, is not in the nature of man or in the nature of his development; it is rather in our conceptions of man's nature and of his development. Some of our most important beliefs about man and his development have changed or are in the process of changing. It is these changes in belief which have freed us to try as demonstrative experiments what only as recently as World War II would have been considered a stupid waste of effort and time. It is also these changes in theoretical belief about man and his development which provide my topic, namely, the psychological basis for using pre-school enrichment as an antidote for cultural deprivation.

I number these changed or changing beliefs as six. Let me state them in their pre-change form; in the form, in other words, that has so much hampered the sort of enterprise in which this group is about to engage:

1. a belief in fixed intelligence;
2. a belief in predetermined development;
3. a belief in the fixed and static, telephone-switchboard nature of brain function;
4. a belief that experience during the early years, and particularly before the development of speech, is unimportant;
5. a belief that whatever experience does affect later development is a matter of emotional reactions based on the fate of instinctual needs;
6. a belief that learning must be motivated by homeostatic need, by painful stimulation, or by acquired drives based on these.

Let me discuss the evidential and conceptual bases for the change which has been taking place since World War II in these hampering beliefs, one by one. Then I shall close by trying to justify the sort of enterprise you propose, and by indicating how the largely forgotten work of Maria Montessori may well contain practical suggestions concerning the way to go about the enterprise.

THE BELIEF IN FIXED INTELLIGENCE

Almost every idea has roots in a communicated conceptual history and in observed evidence. The notion of fixed intelligence has conceptual roots in Darwin's (1859) theory of evolution and in the intense emotional controversy that surrounded it. You will recall that Darwin believed that evolution took place, not by changes wrought through use or disuse as Lamarck (1809) had thought, but by changes resulting from variations in the progeny of every species or strain which are then selected by the conditions under which they live. Their selection is a matter of which variations survive to reproduce so that the variations are passed on into the successive generations. The change is conceived thus to be one that comes via the survival of a variation in a strain through reproduction. Implicit in this notion was the assumption that the characteristics of any organism are predetermined by the genetic constitution with which the organism comes into being as a fertilized ovum. Probably this implicit assumption would never have caught on with anywhere near the force it did, had it not been for two outstanding figures in the history of relatively recent thought. The first of these is Sir Francis Galton, Charles Darwin's younger cousin. You will remember that it was Galton who made the assumption of the hereditary determination of adult characteristics explicit. Galton reasoned, furthermore, that if his cousin were correct, it would mean that the hope of improving the lot of man does not lie in *euthenics,* or in trying to change him through education; rather, such hope lies in *eugenics,* or in the selection of those superior persons who should survive. Secondly, he saw that if decisions were to be made as to which human beings were to survive and reproduce, it would be necessary to have some criteria for survival. So he founded his anthropometric laboratory for the measurement of man, with the hope that by means of tests he could determine those individuals who should survive. Note that he was not deciding merely who should be selected for jobs in a given industry, but who should survive to reproduce. This was his concern. Because of the abhorrence which such a plan met, Galton talked and wrote relatively little about it. However, the combination of the context of his life-work with the few remarks he did make on the subject gives these remarks convincing significance (see Hunt, 1961).

Galton had a pupil who was very influential in bringing such conceptions into the stream of American thought. This was J. McKeen Cattell, who brought Galton's tests to America and, beginning in 1890, gave them to college students, first at the University of Pennsylvania and then at Columbia University. Because Cattell was also an influential teacher at both Penn and Columbia, his influence spread through the many students he had before World War I—when his sympathies with Germany led to a painful separation from Columbia.

A second psychologist who was almost equally influential in bringing the stream of thought supporting fixed intelligence into American thought is G. Stanley Hall. Hall did not personally know Galton; neither did he personally know Darwin, but he read about evolution while still a college student, and as he has written in his autobiography, "it struck me like a light; this was the thing for me." Hall's importance lies in that he communicated a strong attachment to the notion of fixed intelligence to his students at Clark University, of which he was the first President, and these students became leaders of the new psychology in America (see Boring, 1929, p. 534). Among them were three of the most illustrious leaders of the testing movement. One was Henry H. Goddard, who first translated the Binet tests into English for use at the Vineland Training School and also wrote the story of the Kallikak family (1912). Another was F. Kuhlmann, who was also an earlier translator and reviser of the Binet tests and who, with Rose G. Anderson, adapted them for use with pre-school children. The third was Lewis Terman, who is the author of the Stanford-Binet revision, the most widely known version of the Binet tests in America. These three communicated their faith in fixed intelligence to a major share of those who spread the testing movement in America.

So much for the conceptual roots of the belief in fixed intelligence that come by way of communication in the history of thought.

The assumption of fixed intelligence also had an empirical basis. Not only did test-retest reliabilities show that the positions of individuals in a group remained farly constant, but also the tests showed some capacity to predict such criterion performances as school success, success as officers in World War I, etc. All such evidence concerned children of school age for whom the experience to which they are exposed is at least to some degree standardized (see Hunt, 1961). When investigators began to examine the constancy of the D.Q. (developmental quotient) or I.Q. in pre-school children, the degree of constancy proved to be very much lower. You will recall some of the very interesting interpretations of this lack of constancy in the pre-school D.Q. (see Hunt, 1961, p. 311ff). Anderson argued that since the tests at successive ages involved different functions, constancy could not be expected. But an epigenesis of man's intellectual functions is inherent in the nature of his development, and the implications of this fact were apparently missed by these critics of the findings from the infant tests. While they knew that the basic structure of intelligence changes in its early phases of development just as the structures of the body change in the embryological phase of morphological development, they appear not to have noted that it is thus inevitable that the infant tests must involve differing content and functions at successive ages.

It was Woodworth (1941) who argued, after examining the evidence from the studies of twins, that there might be some difference in I.Q. due to the environment but that which exists among individuals in our culture is largely due to the genes. In the context of cultural deprivation, I believe Woodworth asked the wrong question. He might better have asked: What would be the difference in the I.Q. of a pair of identical twins at age six if one were reared as Myrtle McGraw (1935) reared the trained twin, Johnny (so that he was swimming at four months, roller-skating at eleven months, and developing various such skills at about one-half to one-fourth the age that people usually develop them), and if the other twin were reared in an orphanage, like the one described by Wayne Dennis (1960) in Teheran, where 60% of the infants two years of age are still not sitting up alone and where 85% of those four years of age are still not walking alone? While observations of this kind come from varied sources and lack the force of controlled experimentation, they suggest strongly that lack of constancy is the rule for either I.Q. or D.Q. during the pre-school years and that the I.Q. is not at all fixed unless the culture or the school fixes the program of environmental encounters. Cross-sectional validity may be substantial, with predictive validity being little above zero (see Hunt, 1961). In fact, trying to predict what the I.Q. of an individual child will be at age 18 from the D.Q. obtained during his first or second year is much like trying to predict how fast a feather might fall in a hurricane. The law of falling bodies holds only under the specified and controlled conditions of a vacuum. Similarly, any laws concerning the rate of intellectual growth must take into account the series of environmental encounters which constitute the conditions of that growth.

THE BELIEF IN PREDETERMINED DEVELOPMENT

The belief in predetermined development has been no less hampering, for a serious consideration of pre-school enrichment as an antidote for cultural deprivation than that in fixed intelligence. This belief also has historical roots in Darwin's theory of evolution. It got communicated into the main stream of psychological thought about development by G. Stanley Hall (see Pruette, 1926). Hall gave special emphasis to the belief in predetermined development by making central in his version of the theory of evolution the conception of recapitulation. This is the notion that the development of an individual shows in summary form the development of the species. Hall managed to communicate many valuable points about psychological development by means of his parables based on the concept of biological recapitulation. One of the most famous of these is his parable of the tadpole's tail. To Hall also goes a very large share of the responsibility for the shape of investigation in child and developmental psychology during the first half of this century. This shape was the study of normative development, or the description of what is typical or average. It was, moreover, as you all know, Arnold Gesell (see, e.g., 1945, 1954), another student of G. Stanley Hall, whose life's work concerned the normative description of children's behavioral development. Gesell took over Hall's faith in predetermined development in his own notion that development is governed by what he has termed "intrinsic growth." It should be noted that once one believes in "intrinsic growth," the normative picture of development is not only a description of the process but an explanation of it as well. Thus, whenever little Johnny does something "bad," the behavior can be explained by noting that it is just a stage he is going through. Moreover, following Hall's parable of the tadpole's tail—in which the hind legs fail to develop if the tail is amputated—Johnny's unwanted behavior must not be hampered else some desirable future characteristic will fail to appear.

This notion of predetermined development also has an empirical basis, for the evidence from various early studies of behavioral development in both lower animals and children was readily seen as consonant with it. Among these are Coghill's (1929) studies of behavioral development in amblystoma. These demonstrated that behavioral development, like anatomical development, starts at the head-end and proceeds tailward, starts from the inside and proceeds outward, and consists of a progressive differentiation of more specific units from general units. From such evidence Coghill and others inferred the special additional notion that behavior unfolds automatically as the anatomical basis for behavior matures. From such a background came the differentiation of the process of learning from the process of maturation.

Among the early studies of behavioral development are those of Carmichael (1926, 1927, 1928), also with amblystoma and frogs, which appeared to show that the circumstances in which development takes place are of little consequence. You will recall that Carmichael divided batches of amblystoma and frog eggs. One of these batches he chloretoned to inhibit their activity; another batch he kept in tap water on an ordinary table; and a third group he kept in tap water on a work bench, where they received extra stimulation. Those kept in tap water on an ordinary table swam as early as did those that got the extra stimulation from the work bench. Moreover, even though those that were chloretoned had been prevented from activity through five days, they appeared to be as adept at swimming within a half an hour after the chloretone was washed out as were either of the two batches reared in tap water. Although Carmichael himself was very careful in interpreting these results, they have commonly been interpreted to mean that development is almost entirely a function of maturation and that learning, as represented in practice, is of little consequence.

Such an interpretation got further support from early studies of the effects of practice. In one such study of a pair of identical twins by Gesell and Thompson (1929), the untrained twin became as adept at tower-building and stair-climbing after a week of practice as was the trained twin who had been given practice in tower-building and stair-climbing over many weeks. In another such study by Josephine Hilgard (1932), a group of 10 pre-school children were given practice cutting with scissors, climbing a ladder, and buttoning over a period of 12 weeks; yet they retained their superiority over the control group, which had received no special practice, for only a very short time. One week of practice in those skills by the control group brought their performance up to a level which was no longer significantly inferior to that of the experimental group from a statistical standpoint. Later work by two other investigators appeared to lend further support. Dennis and Dennis (1940) found that the children of Hopi Indians raised on cradleboards, which inhibited the movements of their legs and arms during waking hours, walked at the same age as did Hopi children reared freely, in the typical white-man's manner. Moreover, Dennis and Dennis (1935, 1938, 1941) found the usual sequence of autogenic behavior items in a pair of fraternal twins reared under conditions of "restricted practice and minimal social stimulation." Many such studies appeared to yield results which could be readily seen as consonant with the notion that practice has little effect on the rate of development, and that the amount of effect to be got from practice is a function of the level of maturation present when the practice occurs.

It was just such a notion and just such evidence that led Watson (1928) to argue in his book, *The Psychological Care of the Infant and Child,* that experience is unimportant during the pre-school years because nothing useful can be learned until the child has matured sufficiently. Thus, he advised that the best thing possible is to leave the child alone to grow. Then, when the child has "lain and grown," when the response repertoire has properly matured, those in charge of his care can introduce learning. He conceived that learning could "get in its licks" tying these responses to proper stimuli, via the conditioning principle, and by linking them together in chains to produce complex skills. I suspect that the use of B. F. Skinner's baby-box, with controlled temperature, humidity, etc., may be based upon just such assumptions of predetermined development and of an automatic unfolding of a basic behavioral repertoire with anatomical maturation.

It should be noted that the animal evidence cited here comes from amblystoma and frogs, which are well down the phylogenetic scale. They have brains in which the ratio of those portions concerned with association or intrinsic processes to the portons concerned directly with input and output is small; i.e., the A/S ratio, as formulated by Hebb (1949), is small. When organisms with higher A/S ratios were studied, in somewhat the fashion in which Coghill and Carmichael studied the behavioral development of amblystoma and frogs, the evidence yielded has been highly dissonant with the implications of predetermined development. When Cruze (1935, 1938) found that the number of pecking errors per 25 trials decreased through the first five days, even though the chicks were kept in the dark—a result consonant with the notion of predeterminism—he also found facts pointing in a contrary direction. For instance, chicks kept in the dark for 20 consecutive days, and given an opportunity to see light and have pecking-experience only during the daily tests, *failed* to attain a high level of accuracy in pecking and exhibited almost no improvement in the striking-seizing-swallowing sequence.

Smilarly, Kuo's (see Hunt, 1961) wonderful behavioral observations on the embryological development of chicks in the egg indicate that the responses comprising the pecking and locomotor patterns have been "well-practiced" long before hatching. The "practice" for pecking seems to start with head-bobbing, which is among the first embryonic movements to be observed. The practice for the locomotor patterns begins with vibratory motions of the wing-buds and leg-buds; these movements become flexion and extension as the limbs lengthen and joints appear. At about the 11th day of incubation, the yolk sac characteristically moves over to the ventral side of the embryo. This movement of the yolk sac forces the legs to fold on the breast and to be held there. From this point on, the legs cannot be fully extended. They are forced henceforth to hatching to remain in this folded position with extensive thrusts only against the yolk sac. Kuo argues that this condition establishes a fixed resting posture for the legs, and prepares them for lifting of the chick's body in standing and locomotion. Moreover, his interpretation gets some support from "an experiment of nature." In the 7,000 embryos that he observed, nearly 200 crippled chicks appeared. These crippled chicks could neither stand nor walk after hatching. Neither could they sit in the roosting position, because their legs were deformed. Over 80% of those with deformed legs occurred in those instances in which the yolk sac failed for some reason, still unknown, to move over to the ventral side of the embryo.

Such observations suggest that the mammalian advent of increasingly long uterine control of embryological and fetal environment in phylogeny reflects the fact that environmental circumstances more and more become important for early development, as the central nervous system control becomes more predominant. It should be noted, moreover, that as central nervous sytem control become more predominant, capacity for regeneration decreases. Perhaps this implies a waning of the relative potency of the chemical predeterminers of development as one goes up the phylogenetic scale.

Perhaps even more exciting in this connection is the work of Austin Riesen (see 1958), Brattgård (1952), and others. Riesen undertook the rearing of chimpanzees in darkness in order to test some of Hebb's (1949) hypotheses of the importance of primary learning in the development of perception. What he appears to have discovered—along with Brattgård (1952); Liberman (1962); Rasch, Swift, Riesen, and Chow (1961); and

Weiskrantz (1958)—is that even certain anatomical structures of the retina require light stimulation for proper development. The chimpanzee babies who were kept in the dark for a year-and-a-half have atypical retinas; and, even after they are brought into the light, the subsequent development of their retinas goes awry and they become permanently blind. The result of such prolonged stimulus deprivation during infancy appears to be an irreversible process that does not occur when the chimpanzee infant is kept in darkness for only something like seven months. Inasmuch as Weiskrantz (1958) has found a scarcity of Müller fibers in the retinas of kittens reared in the dark, and since other investigators (especially Brattgård, 1952) have found the retinal-ganglion cells of animals reared in the dark to be deficient in the production of ribonucleic acid (RNA), these studies of rearing under conditions of sensory deprivation appear to be lending support to Hydén's (1959, 1960) hypothesis. This reasons that the effects of experience may be stored as RNA within the glial component of retinal tissue and, perhaps, of brain tissue as well.

For our present purposes, it is enough to note that such studies are bringing evidence that even the anatomical structures of the central nervous system are affected in their development by experience. This lends credence to Piaget's (1936) aphorism that "use is the aliment of a schema."

Consider another study of the effects of early experience. This is a study by Thompson and Heron (1954), comparing the adult problem-solving ability of Scotty pups which were reared as pets in human homes from the time of weaning until they were eight months of age with that of their litter-mates reared in isolation in laboratory cages for the same period. The adult tests were made when the animals were 18 months old, after they had been together in the dog pasture for a period of 10 months. Adult problem-solving was measured by means of the Hebb-Williams (1946) test of animal intelligence. In one of these tests, the dog is brought into a room while hungry. After being allowed to smell and see a bowl of food, the dog is permitted to watch as this food is removed and put behind a screen in one of the opposite corners of the room. Both pet-reared and cage-reared dogs go immediately to the spot where the food disappeared. After the same procedure has been repeated several times, the food is then placed, while the animal watches, behind a screen in another opposite corner of the room. In order to see this clearly, think of the first screen being in the corner to the dog's right, the second in the corner to the dog's left. Now, when the dog is released, if he is pet-reared he goes immediately to the screen in the left corner for food. But, if he was cage-reared, he is more likely to go to the screen in the right corner where he had previously found food. In his tests of object permanence, Piaget (1936) describes behavior of children about 9 months old resembling that of the cage-reared pups, and of children about 14 months old resembling that of the pet-reared pups.

It is interesting to compare the results of this study by Thompson and Heron (1954), in which dogs were the subjects, with the results of various studies of the effects of early experiences on adult problem-solving in which rats were subjects (see Hebb, 1947; Gauron and Becker, 1959; Wolf, 1943). Whereas the effects of early experience on the problem-solving of dogs appear to be both large and persistent, they appear to be both less marked and less permanent in the rat. Such a comparison lends further credence to the proposition that the importance of the effects of early experience increases as the associative or intrinsic portions of the cerebrum increase in proportion, as reflected in Hebb's notion of the A/S ratio.

But what about the fact that practice appears to have little or not effect on the development of a skill in young children? How can one square the absence of the effects of practice with the tremendous apathy and retardation commonly to be found in children reared in orphanages? In the case of the orphanage in Teheran reported on by Dennis (1960), the retardation in locomotor function is so great, as I have already noted, that 60% fail to sit up alone at two years of age, even though nearly all children ordinarily sit up at 10 months of age; and 85% still fail to walk alone at four years of age, even though children typically walk at about 14 or 15 months of age and nearly all are walking before they are two years of age. I believe the two sets of results can be squared by taking into account the epigenesis in the structure of behavior that occurs during the earliest years. The investigators of the effects of practice neglected this epigenesis. They sought the effects of experience only in practice of the function or schema to be observed and measured. The existence of an epigenesis of intellectual function implies that the experiential roots of a given schema will lie in antecedent activities quite different in structure from the schema to be observed and measured. Thus, antecedent practice at tower-building and buttoning may be relatively unimportant for the development of skill in these activities; but an unhampered antecedent opportunity to throw objects and to manipulate them in a variety of situations, and an even earlier opportunity to have seen a variety of sights and to have heard a variety of sounds, may be of tremendous importance in determining both the age at which tower-building and buttoning will occur and the degree of skill that the child will manifest. I shall return to this topic.

BRAIN FUNCTION CONCEIVED AS A STATIC SWITCHBOARD

One can not blame Darwin for the conception of brain function as static, like that in a telephone switchboard. The origin of the ferment leading to these conceptions, however, does derive from Darwin's (1872) shift of attention from the evolution of the body to the evolution of mind. This he began in his book, *The Expressions of the Emotions in Man and Animals.* It was thus Darwin who provided the stimulus for what was later to be called *comparative psychology*. The original purpose was to show that there is a gradual transition from the lower animals to man in the various faculties of mind. It was Romanes (1882, 1883) who took up this task in an attempt to show the manner in which intelligence has evolved. Romanes's method was to show through anecdotes that animals are capable of intelligent behavior, albeit at a level of complexity inferior to man's. It was C. Lloyd Morgan (1894) who saw that it was reasoning by very loose analogy to impute to dogs, cats, and the like, the same kind of conscious processes and faculties that man can report. It was Morgan who applied Ockham's "razor of parsimony" to the various mental faculties. Then, shortly, Thorndike and Woodworth (1901) knocked out such old-fashioned faculties as memory with their studies showing that such forms of practice as daily memorizing poetry does not improve a person's capacity to memorize other types of material, and that being taught mathematics and Latin does not improve performance on reasoning tests.

It was still obvious, however, that animals do learn and that they do solve problems. Morgan (1894) saw this occurring by a process of trial-and-error. According to this conception, as Hull (1943) later elaborated it, an organism comes to any given situation with a ready-made hierarchy of responses. When those at the top of the hierarchy fail to achieve satisfaction, they are supposed to be weakened (extinguished). Other responses lower in the hierarchy then take their places and become connected with stimuli from the situation. Or, as Thorndike (1913) put it earlier, new S-R bonds are established. Complex behavior was explained by assuming that one response can be the stimulus for another, so that S-R chains could be formed. The role of the brain in such learning also needed explanation. Here the telephone was the dramatic new invention supplying a mechanical model for a conception of the brain's role. Inasmuch as the reflex arc was conceived to be both the anatomical and the functional unit of the nervous system, the role of the brain in learning could readily be conceived to be analogous to that of a telephone switchboard. Thus, the head was emptied of active functions, and the brain, which filled it, came to be viewed as the focus of a variety of static connections.

All this led to what I think is a basic confusion in psychological thought, one which has been prominent for at least the last 35 or 40 years. This is a confusion between S-R methodology, on the one hand, and S-R theory on the other. We cannot escape S-R methodology. The best one can possibly do empirically is to note the situations in which organisms behave and to observe what they do there. But there is no reason why one should not relate the S-R relationships, the empirical relationships one observes between stimulus and response, to whatever the neurophysiologist can tell us about inner brain function and to whatever the endocrinologist can tell us. The broader one makes his nomological net, the better, in that the more nearly his resulting conceptions will approach those of imaginary, all-seeing eye of Diety.

Stimulus-Response (S-R) methodology appeared at first to imply the notion of the empty organism. It is interesting to recall, however, that very shortly after the mental faculties had been removed by C. Lloyd Morgan with Ockham's razor of parsimony, Walter Hunter (1912, 1918) discovered that various animals could delay their responses to stimuli and also learn double alternation. Both achievements implied that there must be some kind of representative or symbolic process intervening between stimulus and response. It was to explain just such behavior, moreover, that Hull (1931) promulgated the notion of the pure-stimulus act. This became in turn the response-produced cues and the response-produced drives of Miller and Dollard. When Miller and Dollard (1941, p. 59) began conceiving of the responses which serve as stimuli occurring within the brain, traditional S-R theory with its implicit peripherality of both stimulus and response began to fade. The demise of peripheral S-R theory became nearly complete when Osgood (1953) turned these response-produced cues and drives into central mediating process. It is interesting to note in this connection that it is precisely observations from S-R methodology which have undone traditional peripheral S-R theory, and it is these observations which are now demanding that brain function be conceived in terms of active processes.

The theoretical need for active brain processes, however, has been both stimulated by and got much of its form from cybernetics (Wiener, 1948). Such investigators as Newell, Shaw, and Simon (1958), in the process of programming computers to solve problems, and especially logical problems, have been clarifying the general nature of what is required for solving such problems. They have described three major kinds of requirements: (1) memories or information stored somewhere, and presumably in the brain; (2) operations of a logical sort which are of the order of actions that deal with the information in the memories; and (3) hierarchial arrangements of these operations and memories in programs. Thus, the electronic computer has been replacing the telephone as the mechanical model for brain function.

Such a notion of memories and, even more, the notion of operations of a logical sort as actions, and the notion of hierarchical arrangements of these operations—these notions differ markedly from the notion of reflexes being hitched to each other. Moreover, ablation studies have been showing that it is not communication across the cortex from sensory-input regions to motor-output regions that is important for behavior. The cortex can be diced into very small parts without serious damage to behavioral function; but if the fibers, composed of white matter, under an area of the gray matter cortex are cut, behavior is damaged seriously. Thus, the notion of transcortical association gives way to communication back-and-forth from the center to the periphery of the brain (see Pribram, 1960). With such changes in conception of brain function being dictated by their own observations, when neuropsychologists become familiar with what is required in programming computers to solve logical problems, it is not surprising that they ask themselves where one might find a locus for the various requirements of computer function—*i.e.,* for the memories, the operations, and the hierarchical arrangements of them. Carl Pribram (1960) has reviewed the clinical and experimental findings concerning the functional consequences of injuring various portions of the brain, and he has come up with a provisional answer. The brain appears to be divided into intrinsic portions and extrinsic portions. This is the terminology of Rose and Woolsey (1949), and here the term *intrinsic* is used because this portion has no direct connections with either incoming sensory fibers or outgoing motor fibers. The extrinsic portion is so called because it does have such direct peripheral connections. What Pribram suggests is that these components of what is required for the various kinds of information processing and of decision-making may well reside in these intrinsic portions of the brain.

There are two intrinsic portions: one is the frontal portion of the cortex, with its connections to the dorsal frontal nuclei of the thalamus; the other, the nonsensory portions of the parietal, occipital, and temporal lobes with their connections with the pulvenar or the posterior dorsal nucleus of the thalamus. Injury to the frontal system disrupts executive functions and thereby suggests that it is the locus of the central, neural mechanism for plans. Injury to the posterior intrinsic system results in damage to recognitive functions, which suggests that it may be the locus of central, neural mechanisms for information processing *per se*. The intrinsic portions of the cerebrum appear to become relatively larger and larger as one samples organisms up the phylogenetic scale. Perhaps what Hebb (1949) has called the A/S ratio might better be called tht I/E ratio—for "Intrinsic/Extrinsic."

From such studies, one can readily conceive the function of early experience to be one of "programming" these intrinsic portions of the cerebrum so that they can later function effectively in learning and problem-solving.

PREVERBAL EXPERIENCE UNIMPORTANT

Early experience, particularly preverbal experience, however, has historically been considered to be relatively unimportant. It has been argued that such experience can hardly have any effect on adult behavior, because it is not remembered. There have been, of course, a few relatively isolated thinkers who have given at least lip service to the importance of early experience in the development of the personality. Plato is one who thought that the rearing and education of children was too important a function to be carried out by mere amateur parents. But when he described the rearing that children should have in his *Republic,* he described only experiences for youngsters already talking. Rousseau (1762) gave somewhat more than lip service in *Emile* to the importance of early experience. Moreover, at least implicitly, he attributed importance to preverbal experience with his prescription that the child, Emile, should very early be exposed to pain and cold in order that he might be toughened.

An even earlier example is to me somewhat embarrassing. I thought that I had invented the notion of split-litter technique for determining the effects of infant feeding-frustration in rats—but later I found, in reading Plutarch's *Lives,* that Lycurgus, the Law-Giver of the Spartans, took puppies from the same litter and reared them in diverse ways, so that some became greedy and mischievious curs while others became followers of the scent and hunters. He exhibited these pups before his contemporaries, saying, "Men of Sparta, of a truth, habit and training and teaching and guidance in living are a great influence toward engendering excellence, and I will make this evident to you at once." Thereupon he produced the dogs with diverse rearing. Perhaps it is from the stories of the Spartans that Rousseau got his notion that Emile should be toughened. Such followers of Rousseau as Pestalozzi and Froebel certainly saw childhood experience as important, but as educators they were concerned with the experiences of children who had already learned to verbalize. So far as I can tell, the notion that preverbal experience is seriously important for adult personal characteristics comes from Freud (1905) and his theory of psychosexual development.

Unimportance of Psychosexual Development

Freud not only attributed importance to preverbal experience; he also proposed an hypothesis concerning the nature of the kinds of experience important for later development. These were the experiences driving from the fate of instinctive impulses arising out of homoestatic need, painful stimulation, and, especially, the pleasure-striving which he saw as sexual in nature (Freud, 1905). If one examines the objective studies of the effects of the various kinds of factors deemed to be important from the standpoint of their theory of psychosexual development, one has a very hard time finding clear evidence that they are important (see Hunt, 1945, 1956; Orlansky, 1949). For every study that appears to show an effect of some given psychosexual factor in early infancy, there is another study to be matched with it that fails to show an effect. Furthermore, the more carefully the various studies appear to be controlled, the more nearly the results tend to be consonant with the null hypothesis. The upshot of all this is that it looks very much as if the kinds of factors to which Freud attributed importance in his theory of psychosexual development are not very important.

It was commonly believed before World War II that early experience was important for emotional development and for the development of personality characteristics, but unimportant for the development of intellect or intelligence. Some of the animal studies of early experience were widely quoted to support this belief. One of these was my own study of the effects of infant feeding frustration upon adult hoarding in rats (Hunt, 1941). Actually, the effects of the infantile feeding frustration were exhibited in both eating rate and hoarding, and exhibited in the eating rate more regularly than in the hoarding. Rats do not always hoard as a consequence of infantile feeding frustration, although they do regularly eat faster than littermates without such experience. Yet, the feeding or drinking frustration need not occur in infancy to get the effect of speeded eating or speeded drinking (Freedman, 1957). In the case of the work of my colleagues and myself, much of it still unpublished, various kinds of effects that should, theoretically, have followed did not occur. The upshot of all this, I now believe, is that our theoretical expectations were wrong. I also believe that the general notion that the emotional characteristics of persons are most influenced by early experienced while the intellectual characteristics are not influenced is also quite wrong.

Importance of Preverbal Experience for Intellect

I am prompted to change my belief because the approach to the study of the effects of early experience suggested by Donald Hebb's theorizing about cerebral functioning has regularly yielded results confirming his hypothesis. According to Hebb's (1949) theory, firing systems, which he terms "cell assemblies" and "phase sequences," must be built into the cerebrum through what he has termed "primary learning." This may be seen as another way of expressing the idea that the intrinsic regions of the cerebrum must be properly programmed by pre-verbal experience if the mammalian organism is later to function effectively as a problem-solver. Most of this "primary learning" Hebb (1949) presumed, moreover, to be based upon early perceptual experience. It is in this presumption that he broke most radically with the traditional emphasis on the response side in learning (a point to which I shall return).

It was this conception which led Hebb (1947) early to compare the problem-solving ability in adulthood of those rats which had their perceptual experience limited by cage-rearing, with that of rats that had their perceptual experience enriched by pet-rearing. As I have already noted in connection with my comments on the notion of predetermined development, the problem-solving ability of the cage-reared rats was inferior to that of the pet-reared rats. The theory, as encouraged by these exploratory results, led then to a series of studies in which various kinds of early perceptual experiences were provided for one sample of rats and not for an otherwise comparable sample. Thus, the difference between the groups in later problem-solving, or maze-learning provided an index of both the presence and the degree of effect. Such studies have regularly yielded substantial effects for various kinds of early perceptual experience. These studies, moreover, appear to be clearly reproducible (Hunt and Luria, 1956). Furthermore, as I have already noted in connection with my remarks on predetermined development, these effects of early perceptual experience on adult problem-solving appear to become more and more marked up the phylogenetic scale as the intrinsic portions come to constitute a higher and higher proportion of the cerebrum. It looks now as though early experience may be even more important for the perceptual, cognitive, and intellective functions than it is for the emotional and temperamental functions.

Change in the Conception of Trauma

The investigations of the effects of early experience in animals appear to be calling for still further changes in our conception of the nature of the most important kinds of early experience. Freud (1900, 1915, 1926) had various theories of anxiety. But in his later theorizing about it he not only relied upon the notion of association but also conceived of painful stimulation, either through excessive homeostatic need or an overflow of excitement, as a basis for trauma. He also presumed that organisms which had experienced high levels of such traumatic excitement during infancy were made more prone to be anxious and neurotic later in life.

With the goal of demonstrating just such effects, Levine, Chevalier, and Korchin (1956) undertook the experiment in which they shocked rats daily for two minutes, keeping them squealing frantically throughout this period, on each of the first 20 days of their lives. A second sample of rats were picked up and brought to the grid-box, where they were put down without being shocked. Those of a third group were left unmolested in the maternal nest. One of the adult tests (at 60 days of age) involved defecation and urination in an unfamiliar situation. This is the test of so-called emotionality invented by Hall (1934). Those animals that had been shocked during infancy did not defecate and urinate more than those handled or than those left unmolested in the nest, as would be expected from trauma theory. On the contrary, the shocked animals defecated less on the average. The difference in this experiment fell short of statistical significance; but various subsequent experiments by both Levine and Denenberg (see Denenberg, 1962) yielded results showing that rats shocked in infancy defecated and urinated significantly less than those left unmolested in the maternal nest. Levine, Chevalier, and Korchin (1956) also found that the animals shocked in infancy and the animals handled in infancy both learned to avoid shock, by learning to respond to a signal before the onset of shock, in fewer trials than did those animals which had remained unmolested in the maternal nest. Confirming results have been obtained by Denenberg (1962).

Other evidence has come from the work of my own students. Goldman (1963) has shown that the intensity of shock required to move a rat over a barrier, from one end of a runway to the other end, is greater for rats that have been shocked during their pre-weaning stage of infancy than it is for those which have been left unmolested in the warm maternal nest. Salama (Salama and Hunt, 1964) has repeated the Farber (1948) study, in which rats shocked just past the choice point in a T-maze became "rigid" about giving up the place where they had got food, even after food has ceased to appear there. Salama compared the number of trials required to bring about such a shift in goal-box by animals shocked in infancy, by animals merely picked up in infancy, by animals petted in infancy, and by animals left unmolested in the maternal nest. While animals shocked in infancy require more trials (nine, on the average) to make the shift from the "fixated" arm and goal-box to the other arm of the T-maze than do animals which have not been shocked at the choice point (an average of 2.8 trials), they require substantially fewer than do animals handled or left unmolested in the maternal nest before weaning (an average of 20.7) or than do those petted (an average of 21.4 trials). Thus, the experience of having been shocked regularly before weaning appears actually to diminish the capacity of shock either to motivate behavior or to fixate a response.

Such evidence appears to call for a revision of the trauma theory. I find this evidence from animal studies especially interesting, moreover, because there is a study of human children with results which are consonant. This is a study by Holmes (1935) in which fear scores for children of a day-care center proved to be much lower than those for children of a nursery school. These results have seldom been cited in the secondary literature, perhaps because they were troublesomely dissonant with the dominant theoretical expectations. The dominant expectation would be that the opposite should have prevailed, because the children of daycare centers came from the lower class where painful experience and hunger (i.e., traumatizing experiences) were common; whereas the children of the nursery schools came from the upper class where such presumably traumatizing experiences are relatively rare. I believe this is an item of evidence from human subjects to indicate that children, as well as infant animals, who have been through a great many painful circumstances are not as fearful in strange or unfamiliar situations as are children who have not experienced such painful circumstances. This evidence lends support to the recommendations that Rousseau made for Emile, and it helps to clarify how the Spartan culture could have survived for something like 500 years even though it practiced what has sometimes been seen as "infant torture."

It now looks as if there may be two quite different kinds of effect of early infantile experience. One is that just described, in which the effect of painful experience is one of reducing the aversiveness of later painful or strange circumstances. Although the evidence is not clear yet, that from Salama's experiment indicates that such other kinds of early experience as mere picking up or petting do not have this effect. The other kind of effect is one increasing the capacity of an organism to learn. I have already mentioned that both the shocked rats and the handled rats in the study by Levine, Chevalier, and Korchin (1956) learned to respond to a signal to avoid shock more rapidly than did the rats that remained unmolested in the maternal nest. This is adaptive. Denenberg (see 1962) has shown that even shocking animals once on the second day of life will decrease the number of trials they require to learn an avoidance response, as compared with those left unmolested in the maternal nest. This kind of effect appears to result not only from shock during the pre-weaning phase of development but also from handling and petting. It looks very much as if any increase in the variation of circumstances encountered during those first three weeks of life will facilitate later learning, not only in the avoidance situation but also in such problem-solving situations as those to be found in the Hebb-Williams (1946) tests of animal intelligence.

Change in Conception of the Relative Importance of the Sensory and the Motor

Yet another belief about what is important in early experience appears to need correction. G. Stanley Hall was fond of the aphorism that "the mind of man is handmade." (Pruette, 1926). Watson (1919) and the other behaviorists have believed that it is the motor side, rather than the sensory side, that is important in learning. Dewey (1902) gave emphasis to the motor side also in his belief that the child learns chiefly by doing. Dewey went even further to emphasize that the things that the child should be encouraged to do are the things that he would later be called upon to do in taking his place in society. More recently, Osgood (1952) has conceived that the central processes which mediate meanings are the residues of past responses. I am simply trying to document my assertion that in the dominant theory of the origin of mind or of central mediating processes, these have been conceived to be based upon the residues from past responses.

Hebb's (1949) theorizing, as I have already noted, took sharp issue with this dominant theoretical position. He has conceived the basis for primary learning to be chiefly on the sensory side. Riesen (1958) began his experiments on the effects of rearing chimpanzees in darkness with what he called S-S, or stimulus-stimulus relations. Piaget (1936), although he has emphasized "activity as the aliment of a schema," has conceived of *looking* and *listening,* both of which are typically viewed as sensory input channels, as existing among the schemata ready-made at birth. Moreover, it is looking and listening to which he attributes key importance during the first phases of intellectual development. This emphasis is registered in his aphorism that, "the more a child has seen and heard, the more he wants to see and hear" (Piaget, 1936, p. 276).

Evidence requiring this correction of belief comes from more than just the studies of the effects of early perceptual experience on the later problem-solving capacity of animals. It also comes from comparing the effects of the cradling practice on the age of onset of walking in Hopi children, with the effects of the homogeneous auditory and visual stimulation on the age of onset of walking in the children in a Teheran orphanage. The cradling practice inhibits actions of an infant's legs and arms during his walking hours through most of the first year of his life. Yet, the mean and standard deviation of the age of walking for those cradled proved to be the same as that for those Hopi children reared with free use of their legs and arms (Dennis and Dennis, 1940). Contrariwise, 85% of the children in the Teheran orphanage were still not walking alone at four years of age—and here the factor in which the circumstances of these children most differ from those of most young infants was probably the continuous homogeneity of auditory and visual experience (Dennis, 1960). The children of the Teheran orphanage had full use of the motor function of their legs and arms. The Hopi children reared with the cradling practice did not have free use of their legs and arms—but they were exposed, by virtue of their being carried around on their mothers' backs, to a very rich variety of auditory and visual inputs.

Perhaps this emphasis on the motor side is erroneous only as another example of failure to take into account the epigenesis of behavioral and intellectual functions. While it may be true that education by doing is best for children of kindergarten and primary-school age, it appears that having a variety of things to listen to and look at may be most important for development during the first year of life (see also Fiske and Madde, 1961).

ALL BEHAVIOR AND ALL LEARNING ARE MOTIVATED BY PAINFUL STIMULATION OR HOMEOSTATIC NEED

The fact that both apathy and retardation have been regularly noted in orphanage-reared children who typically live under conditions of homogeneous circumstances (especially marked of the children observed by Dennis in the Teheran orphanage) suggests that homogeneous stimulation somehow reduces motivation. This suggestion brings me to yet another major change of theoretical belief.

It is common to state that "all behavior is motivated." But to make this statement specific, it must be completed with the complex phrase, "by homeostatic need, painful stimulation, or by innocuous stimuli which have previously been associated with these." This has been the dominant conception of motivation for most of the last half-century—dominant because it has been held both by academic behavior theorists (e.g., Dashiell, 1928;

Freeman, 1934; Guthrie, 1938; Holt, 1931; Hull, 1943; Melton, 1941; Miller and Dollard, 1941; Mowrer, 1960) and by psychoanalysts (e.g., Fenichel, 1945; Freud, 1915).

This notion implies that organisms should become quiescent in the absence of painful stimulation, homeostatic need, or the acquired drives based upon them. Since World War II, evidence has accumulated to indicate quite clearly that neither animals nor children actually do become quiescent in the absence of such motivating conditions (see Hunt, 1963a). Bühler (1928) noted earlier that the playful activity of children is most evident in the absence of such motivating conditions, and Beach (1945) has reviewed evidence to show that animals are most likely to show playful activity when they are well-fed, well-watered, and in comfortable circumstances. Harlow, Harlow, and Meyer (1950) have found that monkeys learn to disassemble puzzles with no other motivation than the privilege of disassembling them. Similarly, Harlow (1950) found that two monkeys worked repeatedly at disassembling a six-device puzzle for 10 continuous hours even though they were quite free of painful stimulation and homeostatic need. Moreover, as he notes, at the tenth hour of testing they were still "showing enthusiasm for their work."

In an important series of studies beginning in 1950, Berlyne (see 1960) found that comfortable and satiated rats will explore areas new to them if only given an opportunity, and that the more varied the objects in the region to be explored, the more persistent are the rats' explorations. In a similar vein, Montgomery (1952) has found that the spontaneous tendency for rats to go alternately to the opposite goal-boxes in a T- or Y-maze is no matter of fatigue for the most recently given response, as Hull (1943) contended, but it is one of avoiding the place which the animals have most recently experienced. The choice of place is for the one of lesser familiarity (Montgomery, 1953), and rats learn merely in order to get an opportunity to explore an unfamiliar area (Montgomery, 1955; Montgomery and Segall, 1955). In this same vein, Butler (1953) has observed that monkeys will learn discriminations merely to obtain the privilege of peeking through a window in the walls of their cages, or (Butler, 1958) of listening to sounds from a tape recorder. All of these activities appear to be most evident in the absence of painful stimulation, homeostatic need, and cues which have previously been associated with such motivating stimuli. It is these findings which call for a change in the traditionally dominant theoretical conception of motivation.

Some of the directions of change in belief show in the modes of theoretical significance given to such evidence. One of these ways is drive-naming. Thus, in recent years, we have been hearing of a manipulatory drive, an exploratory drive, a curiosity drive, etc. This form of theoretical recognition, which is logically circular, appears to be revisiting McDougall's (1908) theory of instincts.

A second mode of theoretical recognition is naming what appears to be the telic significance of an activity. This is what Ives Hendrick (1943) has done in conceiving of the delight which children take in their new-found accomplishments as evidence of an "urge to mastery." This is also what White (1959) has done in his excellent review of such evidence by attributing the various activities observed to "competence motivation." Such terms of telic significance may be helpful as classificatory and mnemonic devices, but they provide few implications of antecedent-consequent relationships to be investigated.

A third mode of theoretical recognition has consisted in postulating *spontaneous activity.* I have been guilty of this (Hunt, 1960) and so also have Hebb (1949), Miller, Galanter, and Pribram (1960), and Taylor (1960). When my good colleague, Lawrence I. O'Kelly, pointed out that the notion of spontaneous activity may be just as malevolently circular as drive- and instinct-naming, however, I could readily see the force of his argument. But I could also see that I had begun to discern at least the outlines of a mechanism of what I have termed "intrinsic motivation" or "motivation inherent in information processing and action" (Hunt, 1963a).

Intrinsic Motivation

The outlines of the nature of this mechanism of intrinsic motivation are to be discerned from the evidence which has called for a change in the conception of the functional unit of the nervous system from that of the reflex arc to that of the feedback loop. The concept of the reflex was first formulated by Hall (1843). However, it was developed and popularized by Sherrington (1906) who clearly recognized, in spite of the anatomical evidence for the reflex arc, that the reflex was a logical construct rather than an obvious and palpable reality. It must be noted that the anatomical evidence for the notion of a reflex arc is based on an overgeneralization of the Bell-Magendie Law, which states that the dorsal roots of the spinal nerve are composed entirely of incoming sensory fibers and that the ventral roots are composed entirely of outgoing motor fibers. The statement is untrue. It is clear from recent neurophysiological investigation that the dorsal roots contain motor as well as sensory fibers and that the ventral roots contain sensory as well as motor fibers (see Hunt, 1963a). Illustrative evidence for the first portion of this new statement comes from such observations as the cessation of the firing associated with the onset of a tone or a buzzer in the cochlear nucleus of a cat when the cat is shown a mouse in a bell jar (Hernandez-Peon, Scherrer, and Jouvet, 1956). Evidence for the second portion may be illustrated by the observation that eye-movements can be elicited by electrical stimulation of any portion of the visual receptive area in the occipital lobes of monkeys (Walker and Weaver, 1940). Such evidence makes way and calls for the concept of the feedback loop.

The notion of the feedback loop provides, in turn, the basis for a new answer to the motivational question concerning what starts and stops behavior. So long as the reflex served as the conception of the functional unit of neural function, any given kind of behavior was presumed to be started by the onset of a drive stimulus and to be stopped by its cessation. As the feedback loop takes the place of the reflex, the onset of behavior becomes a matter of incongruity between the input from a set of circumstances and some standard within the organism. Miller, Galanter, and Pribram (1960) have termed this the Test-Operate-Test-Exit (TOTE) unit (see Fig. 1).

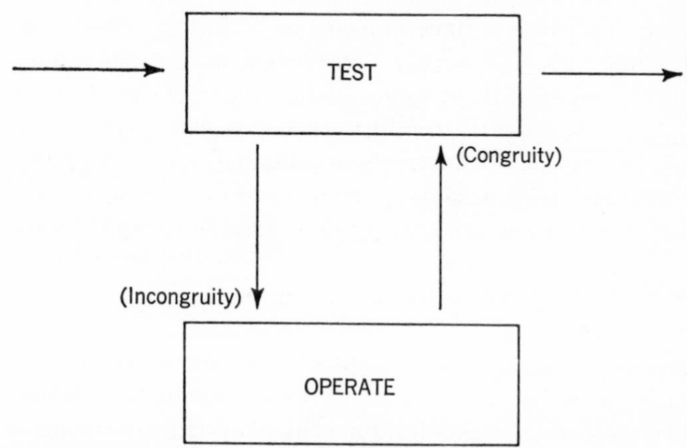

FIGURE 1. Diagram of the TOTE Unit. [After Miller, Galanter, and Pribram (1960, p. 26).]

This TOTE unit is, in principle, not unlike the thermostat which controls the temperature of a room. In such a case, the standard is the temperature at which the thermostat is set. When the temperature falls below this standard, the "test" yields an incongruity which sets the furnace into operation (see the arrow connecting the "test" to the "operate"). The furnace continues to operate until the temperature in the room has been raised to the standard. This congruity stops the operation, and this particular motive system can be said to "exit."

One can base a taxonomy of incongruities upon the various kinds of standards existing within organisms. One class of incongruities may be based on the "comfort standard." While no one would have invented the TOTE unit to account for pain avoidance, conceiving of a "comfort standard" brings the facts of pain avoidance into a consonant relationship with the notion of the TOTE unit. A second class of incongruities may be conceived to be based on what Pribram (1960) has termed the "biased homeostats of the hypothalamus." Organisms have standards, for the most part innately established, for such things as the concentrations of blood-sugar or of sodium ions in the blood stream. When, for instance, the blood-sugar concentration falls below a certain level, the receptors along the third ventricle are activated. At one level of incongruity they serve to release glycogen from the liver; but at a higher level, they prime the receptors to respond to the signs of food, the organism follows them with avid excitement, and the hunger motive is said to be activated. It is not easy to make the sex system consonant with such a scheme.

On the other hand, a variety of standards can be found within an organism's informational interaction with its circumstances. Perhaps the most primitive of such informational standards is the ongoing input of the moment. Whenever there is change from this standard, an organism exhibits what the Russians have termed the "orienting reflex" (see Berlyne, 1960; Razran, 1961). The operation elicited by such incongruity consists of an orientation toward the source of the change in input and arousal, as registered by the classical expressive indicators of emotion or by the electroencephalogram. A second kind of informational incongruity is based upon a standard of expectations, where the expectations are based on information stored in the course of previous encounters with the same object, person, or place. Such systems of expectations as the self-concept appear to take on special importance in motivation. Aesthetic standards appear to be another variation of expectations.

Another category of standards appears to be comprised of ends or goals. These are what Miller, Galanter, and Pribram (1960) have termed "plans." Some plans are tied to painful stimulation or to homeostatic needs, but others are quite independent of these. Piaget (1936) has described how an infant will make holding onto an interesting input, or regaining it, a goal. Typically, inputs have become interesting through repeated encounters by becoming recognizable. It would appear that emerging recognition can make objects, persons, and place attractive. Later it is novelty which is attractive. The full range of the various kinds of standards that emerge in the course of a child's informational interaction with his circumstances during the process of psychological development has never been described. At adolescence, however, an important variety of standards consists of ideals. This kind of standards appears to emerge with the development of what Piaget (1947) has termed "formal operations." With the emergence of these operations, the adolescent can imagine a world more desirable than the one he encounters, and the incongruity between the world observed and the imagined ideal can instigate plans for social reforms. These same formal operations enable the adolescent to formulate "theories" of how various aspects of the world operate, and incongruities between observed realities and these theoretical creations instigate inquiry. Thus, one may view scientific work as but a professionalization of a form of cognitive motivation inherent in the human organism's informational interaction with circumstances.

Incongruity and the Direction-Hedonic Question

The concept of incongruity also provides a tentative, hypothetical answer to the puzzling direction-hedonic question—the question of what it is that determines whether an organism will approach or withdraw from the source of incongruous or novel information (see also Schneirla, 1959). This is also an answer to the hedonic question, because approach presumably indicates a positive hedonic value in the source of stimulation, and withdrawal presumably indicates a negative hedonic value.

The evidence that incongruous or novel information will instigate approach to its source and that it has positive hedonic value derives from several sources. In an early study by Nissen (1930)—which has never got into the textbooks, apparently because it was far too dissonant with the dominant beliefs—it was shown that rats will suffer the pain of electric shocks from a Warden obstruction apparatus in order to get from empty cages into a Dashiell maze filled with novel objects. Once the animals have discovered the fact that such a maze exists at the end of the runway beyond the obstruction apparatus, they will endure the pain of the crossing in order to achieve the opportunity to explore this "interesting place" and to manipulate the "interesting objects." The behavior of the rats in this study of Nissen's resembles in many ways that of Butler's (1953) monkeys, which would undertake the learning of discriminations in order to peek through the window at students passing the hall beyond. In fact, most of the evidence cited to show that animals and children do not become quiescent in the absence of homeostatic need and painful stimulation may be arranged to support the notion that a certain degree of incongruity is appealing, and that too little is boring and unappealing.

Perhaps even more convincing are the results from the studies of so-called "stimulus deprivation" in the McGill laboratory by Bexton, Heron, and Scott, (1954). You will recall that the McGill students who served as subjects in these experiments were paid $20 a day to lie on a cot in a room with temperature and humidity controlled to provide an optimum of comfort, with translucent glasses on that provided for light to reach the eyes but did not permit pattern vision, with sound variation attenuated as much as possible, and with movement inhibited by the padded cardboard sleeves for arms and legs. Yet they could seldom endure such homogeneous circumstances for longer than two or three days, even for such a liberal monetary reward. The strength of the tendency to withdraw from such homogeneity of circumstances and to approach any source of stimulation that would provide some variety is dramatized by the word-of-mouth story of a student with "high-brow" musical tastes who, several times an hour, pressed a key that brought the playing of a scratchy, well-worn recording of "country-music." This makes it look as if it were a case of, to paraphrase the seaman's aphorism, "any port of relative incongruity in a storm of homogeneous circumstances."

Withdrawal from the source of incongruous information also occurs, this when the degree of incongruity between the incoming information and that already stored in the memory from previous experience is too great. Here the evidence comes largely from the work of Hebb (1946). His studies of fear in chimpanzees were designed to call into question Watson's notion that emotional reactions to innocuous stimuli are based upon their having been associated with earlier painful stimulation (see Watson and Rayner, 1920). Ths traditional conception of fear met with sharply dissonant evidence, when Hebb and Riesen (1943) noted that fear of strangers does not appear in chimpanzee infants reared in the nursery of the Yerkes Primate Laboratory until these infants approach about four months of age. The fact that the histories of these infants were fully recorded made it possible to know with certainty that these strangers had not been associated with previous painful stimulation. Later, Hebb (1946) found that even intense panic reactions could be induced in adult chimpanzees reared in this laboratory merely by showing them the sculptured head of a chimp or human being, or by showing them an anesthetized infant chimpanzee. Such figures were clearly familiar but definitely without previous association with painful or other fearful stimuli. The fact that an infant chimpanzee, which had been a pet, withdrew in fear upon seeing its beloved experimenter-master in a Halloween mask or even in the coat of an equally familiar "keeper" suggested that the basis for the fearful withdrawal resided in seeing "a familiar figure in an unfamiliar guise." Thus, the absence of the expected remainder of the body in the case of the sculptured head of a chimpanzee or human being, and the absence of the expected motions and customary postures in the case of the anesthetized infant chimpanzee, provide "the unfamiliarity of guise"—or the discrepancy between what is expected on the basis of past experience and what is observed, that I am calling incongruity.

Puzzling emotional disturbances in children and pets become readily understandable in these terms. It was, for instance, fear of the dark and fear of solitude in the human child that puzzled Freud (1926) and made him unhappy with even his later theory of anxiety, and it was such behavior in the chimpanzee that puzzled Köhler (1925, p. 251). These can be readily seen as incongruity which results from the presence of unaccustomed receptor inputs or from the absence of accustomed receptor inputs within any given context. Still other examples are that of the child who became disturbed when a familiar nursery rhyme was altered in the reading; that of the pet dog that barks excitedly and whines when he observes his young master walking on his hands; and that of the cat that runs frantically to hide at the sight of his child-mistress being hoisted onto the shoulders of a familiar neighbor. Although Piaget (1936) was without special concern about the point, he noted in his observations that his children showed emotional distress in seeing altered versions of things with which they had become familiar.

The fact that incongruous information can elicit both an approach to its source and a withdrawal from its source may be puzzling, until one notes that this implies that there is an optimum of incongruity (see Hunt, 1963a). Hebb (1949) first gave at least implicit recognition to the notion of an optimum of incongruity in his theory of the nature of pleasure. In this theory he noted that organisms tend to be preoccupied with "what is new but not too new" in any situation. This suggests that controlling intrinsic motivation is a matter of providing an organism with circumstances that provide a proper level of incongruity—that is, incongruity with the residues of previous encounters with such circumstances that the organism has stored in his memory. This is what I find myself calling "the problem of the match" between the incoming information and that already stored (Hunt, 1961, p. 267ff).

Relevant experiments in this area are difficult to find; but one by Dember, Earl, and Paradise (1957) is particularly interesting. Incongruity can be a matter of the discrepancy between the level of complexity encountered and the level of complexity with which an organism has become accustomed. The efforts to keep an optimum of incongruity, or discrepancy and complexity, provides a kind of explanation for the sort of "growth motivation" which Froebel (1826) postulated and which Dewey (1900) later appears to have borrowed from Froebel. What Dember, Earl, and Paradise (1957) did in their experiment was to present rats placed in a figure-8 maze with a choice between two levels of complexity. In the two mazes used, the walls of one loop were painted in a solid color and those of the other loop in black-and-white horizontal stripes, or the walls of one loop had horizontal stripes and the other had vertical stripes. On the basis of theorizing similar to that presented here, these experimenters made no attempt to predict which loop would be preferred immediately by any given rat because they had no knowledge concerning the degree of incongruity to which the rats had become accustomed. They did, however, predict that any animal registering a change of choice of loop between his first and second exposures to this choice would make a change toward the more complex loop. This would mean that they would expect no changes of preference from the striped loop to the one painted a solid color, but would rather expect all changes to occur in the opposite direction. This prediction was confirmed. In a total of 13 animals making such spontaneous changes of choice, 12 were clearly in the predicted direction. Such experiments need to be repeated and elaborated. In the light of such considerations, the problem for a teacher endeavoring to keep children interested in intellectual growth is one of providing circumstances so matched, or mismatched, to those with which her pupils are already familiar that an interesting and attractive challenge is continually provided.

Epigenesis of Intrinsic Motivation

In the traditionally dominant theory of motivation, the basic structure of the motivational system is essentially preformed. Learning is conceived to operate only by way of the conditioning principle, wherein previously innocuous circumstances acquire motivational significance by virtue of being associated with either painful stimuli or homeostatic needs. The fact that Piaget's observations indicate so clearly that there is an epigenesis in the structure of intelligence and in the construction of such aspects of reality as the object, causality, space, and time suggests that there may also be a hitherto unnoted epigenesis in the structure of what I am calling "intrinsic motivation." Piaget has been unconcerned with motivation; he has narrowed his field of concern largely to intelligence and to the development of knowledge about the world. Nevertheless, many of his observations and certain of his aphorisms have implications which provide at least a hypothetical picture of an epigenesis of intrinsic motivation (see Hunt, 1963b). Such is the case with the aphorism that "the more a child has seen and heard, the more he wants to see and hear" (Piaget, 1936, p. 276).

Three phases appear to characterize this epigenesis of intrinsic motivation. These phases, or stages, may well characterize the organism's progressive relationships to any completely new set of circumstances (Harvey, Hunt, and Schroeder, 1961). They may appear as phases of infantile development only because the infant is encountering various sets of completely new circumstances almost simultaneously during his first two years of life.

During the first phase, the child is, of course, motivated by homeostatic need and painful stimulation, as O. C. Irwin's (1930) classic studies have shown. Studies of the Russian investigators (see Berlyne, 1960; Razran, 1961) have shown that the orienting reaction is also ready-made at birth in all mammals including the human being. During this first phase, which lasts from birth to something like four or five or six months of age, the child is chiefly a responsive organism, responding to the short-term incongruities of change in characteristics of the ongoing input. Thus, the relatively sudden dimming of a light or the sudden disappearance of a sound which has been present for some time will instigate a young infant's orienting response or attention to bring about physiological evidences of arousal. During this first phase, the ready-made schemata of sucking, of looking, of listening, of vocalizing, or grasping, and of wiggling each change by something like the traditional conditioning process, in which various new kinds of change in stimulation acquire the capacity to evoke the schemata consistently. Thus, something heard becomes something to look at, something to look at becomes something to grasp, and something to grasp becomes something to suck. This phase terminates with a "landmark of transition" in which the child comes gradually to try actively to retain situations or circumstances or forms of input which he has encountered repeatedly (see Hunt, 1963b; Piaget, 1936).

The second phase begins with this "landmark of transition" in which the infant manifests intentional interest in what may be characterized as the newly familiar. The newly familiar is, of course, some circumstance or situation which has been encountered repeatedly. Presumably, this course of encounters has gradually constructed and stored somewhere within the intrinsic system of the cerebrum some kind of template which provides a basis of recognition for the circumstance when it recurs. One evidence for such recognition comes in the infant's smile. Rene Spitz (1946) has conceived of this smiling response as social in nature. But Piaget's (1936) observations indicate that recognition of the parental face is but a special case of a more general tendency to smile in the presence of a variety of repeatedly encountered situations—which include the toys over an infant's crib, Piaget's newspaper laid repeatedly on the hood over his son's bassinette, and the child's own hands and feet. Such behavior may properly be described as intentional, because it occurs when the situation disappears and the child's efforts clearly imply an anticipation of the circumstance or spectacle to be regained. Moreover, inability to get the newly recognized circumstance or spectacle to return commonly brings on frustrative distress. Separation anxiety and separation grief appear to be special cases of the emotional distress that follows inability to restore the recognized circumstance or spectacle. This consideration suggests that the process of repeated encounters leading to recognition may in itself be a source of emotional gratification and pleasure which may be at least one basis for the reinforcement important in the early emotional attachments or cathexes—which Freud (1904) attributed to the libido, and which Hull (1943) and Miller and Dollard (1941) have attributed to drive reduction, and which Harlow (1958) has recently attributed to the softness of the surrogate mothers of the infant chimpanzees in his experiments. This second phase in the epigensis of motivation terminates when repeated encounters with familiar objects have led gradually to something like the boredom that comes with too little incongruity, and when this boredom provides the basis for an interest in novel variations in the familiar.

This interest in the newly familiar may well account for such autogenic activities as the repetitious babbling commonly appearing in the second, third, and fourth months, and the persistent hand-watching and foot-watching commonly beginning in the latter part of the fourth month and possibly persisting well into the sixth month. It would appear to be in the process of babbling that the infant brings his vocalizing schema under the control of his listening schema. It would appear to be in the course of hand-watching, and sometimes foot-watching, that the infant establishes his eye-hand, and eye-foot, coordinations. This second phase terminates when, with repeated encounters with various situations, boredom ensues and the infant come to be interested in what is new and novel within the familiar situation (see Hunt, 1963b).

The third phase begins with the appearance of this interest in novelty. Typically, this begins at about the end of the first year of life, or perhaps somewhat earlier. Piaget (1936) describes its beginnings with the appearance of the throwing schema. In the course of this throwing, the child's attention shifts from the act of throwing to observing the trajectory of the object thrown. It shows also in an interest not only in familiar ways of achieving ends but also in the development of new means through a process of groping. It shows in the child's attempts to imitate not only those schemata, vocal and otherwise, which he has already developed, but also new schemata. This development of interest in the novel is accompanied by a marked increase in the variety of the infant's interests and actions. He learns in this way new phones within the vocalization schema, and these become symbols for the images he has already developed, and pseudo-words make their appearance (see Hunt, 1961, 1963b; Piaget, 1945).

With the development of interest in novelty, the child has achieved the basis for the "growth motivation" already illustrated in the intriguing experiment by Dember, Earl, and Paradise (1956).

APPLICATIONS OF SUCH THEORIZING FOR THE DEVELOPMENT OF AN ANTIDOTE FOR CULTURAL DEPRIVATION

It remains for me to examine some applications of the theoretical fabric that I have been weaving to the development of a pre-school enrichment program for the culturally deprived. First of all, cultural deprivation may be seen as a failure to provide an opportunity for infants and young children to have the experiences required for adequate development of those semi-autonomous central processes demanded for acquiring skill in the use of linguistic and mathematical symbols and for the analysis of causal relationships. The difference between the culturally deprived and the culturally privileged is, for children, analogous to the difference between cage-reared and pet-reared rats and dogs. At the present time, this notion of cultural deprivation or of social disadvantage is gross and undifferentiated, indeed. On the basis of the evidence and conceptions I have summarized, however, I believe the concept points in a very promising direction. It should be possible to arrange institutional settings where children now culturally deprived by the accident of the social class of their parents can be supplied with a set of encounters with circumstances which will provide an antidote for what they may have missed.

The important study of Skeels and Dye (1939), that met with such a derisive reception when it first appeared, is highly relevant in this context.

You will recall that it was based on a "clinical surprise." Two infants, one aged 13 months with a Kuhlman I.Q. of 46 and the other aged 16 months with an I.Q. of 35, after residence in the relatively homegeneous circumstances of a state orphange, were committed to a state institution for the feebleminded. Some six months later, a psychologist visiting the wards noted with surprise that these two infants had shown a remarkable degree of development. No longer did they show either the apathy or the locomotor retardation that had characterized them when they were committed. When they were again tested with the Kuhlman scale, moreover, the younger had an I.Q. of 77 and the older an I.Q. of 87—improvements of 31 and 52 points respectively, and within half a year. You will also remember that in the experiment which followed this clinical surprise, every one of a group of 13 children showed a substantial gain in I.Q. upon being transferred from the orphange to the institution for the feebleminded. These gains ranged between 7 points and 58 points of I.Q. On the other hand, 12 other youngsters, within the same age-range but with a somewhat higher mean I.Q., were left in the orphanage. When these children were retested after periods varying between 21 and 43 months, all had shown a substantial decrease in I.Q., ranging between 8 and 45 points of I.Q., with five of these decreases exceeding 35 points.

In the last year-and-a-half, Harold Skeels has been engaged in a following-up study of the individuals involved in these two groups. With about three fourths of the individuals found, he has yet to find one of the group transferred from the orphange to the institution for the feebleminded who is not now maintaining himself effectively in society. Contrariwise, he had not yet found any one of the group remaining in the orphanage who is not now living with institutional support (personal communication). Although the question of the permanence of the effects of experiential deprivation during infancy is far from answered, such evidence as I have been able to find, and as I have summarized here, would indicate that if the experiential deprivation does not persist too long, it is reversible to a substantial degree. If this be true, the idea of enriching the cognitive fare in day-care centers and in nursery schools for the culturally deprived looks very promising.

Probable Nature of the Deficit from Cultural Deprivation

The fact that cultural deprivation is such a global and undifferentiated conception at present invites at least speculative attempts to construe the nature of the deficit and to see wherein and when the infant of the poor and lower-class parents is most likely to be experientially deprived.

One of the important features of lower-class life in poverty is crowding. Many persons live in little space. Crowding, however, may be no handicap for a human infant during most of his first year of life. Although there is no certainty of this, it is conceivable that being a young infant among a large number of people living within a room may actually serve to provide such wide variations of visual and auditory inputs that it will facilitate development more than will the conditions typical of the culturally privileged during most of the first year.

During the second year, on the other hand, living under crowded conditions could well be highly hampering. As the infant begins to throw things and as he begins to develop his own methods of locomotion, he is likely to find himself getting in the way of adults already made ill-tempered by their own discomforts and by the fact that they are getting in each other's way. Such considerations are dramatized in Lewis's (1961) *The Children of Sanchez,* an anthropological study of life in poverty. In such a crowded atmosphere, the activities in which the child must indulge for the development of his own interests and skills must almost inevitably be sharply curbed.

Beginning in the third year, moreover, imitation of novel patterns should presumably be well-established, and should supply a mechanism for learning vocal language. The variety of linguistic patterns available for imitation in the models provided by lower-class adults is both highly limited and wrong for the standards of later schooling. Furthermore, when the infant has developed a number of pseudo-words and has achieved the "learning set" that "things have names" and begins asking "what's that?", he is all too unlikely to get answers. Or, the answers he gets are all too likely to be so punishing that they inhibit such questioning. The fact that his parents are preoccupied with the problems associated with their poverty and their crowded living conditions leaves them with little capacity to be concerned with what they conceive to be the senseless questions of a prattling infant. With things to play with and room to play in highly limited, the circumstances of the crowded lower-class offer little opportunity for the kinds of environmental encounters required to keep a two-year-old youngster developing at all, and certainly not at an optimal rate and not in the direction demanded for adaptation in highly technological culture.

If this armchair analysis has any validity, it suggests that the infant developing in the crowded circumstances of lower-class poverty may develop well through the first year; begin to show retardation during the second year; and show even more retardation during the third, fourth, and fifth years. Presumably, that retardation which occurs during the second year, and even that during the third year, can probably be reversed to a considerable degree by supplying proper circumstances in either a nursery school or a day-care center for children of four and five—but I suspect it would be preferable to start with children at three years of age. The analysis made here, which is based largely upon what I have learned from Piaget (1936) and from my own observations of development during the pre-school years, could be tested. You may be interested to know that Dr.

Ina Uzgiris and I are attempting to develop a way of using the sensorimotor and early symbolic schemata which Piaget has described for the first two, and hopefully three, years of the child's life, to provide a method of assessing intellectual and motivational development. If our effort is successful, it should provide a tool with which to determine when and how the conditions of development within the crowded circumstances of poverty begin to result in retardation and/or apathy.

Pre-school Enrichment and the Problem of the Match

Our traditional emphasis in education upon arithmetic and language skills can well lead us astray in the attempt to develop a program of pre-school enrichment. If Piaget's (1945) observations are correct, spoken language—that is to say the motor side of the language skill—comes only after images, or the central processes representing objects and events, have been developed out of repeated encounters with those objects and events. The fact that chimpanzees show clearly the capacity to dissemble their own purposes even though they lack language (Hebb and Thompson, 1954) lends support from phylogenetic comparisons to this notion of Piaget's. You have undoubtedly heard that O. K. Moore, of Yale, has been teaching pre-school children to read with the aid of an electric typewriter hooked up to an electronic system of storing and retrieving information. The fact that, once children have learned to recognize letters by pressing the proper keys of a typewriter, they are then enabled to discover spontaneously that they can draw these letters with chalk on a blackboard, lends further support to the image-primacy thesis. Moreover, Moore has observed that the muscular control of such four-year-olds as have presumably acquired solid imagery of the letters in the course of their experience with those letters at the electric typwriter corresponds to that typical of seven- or eight-year-olds (personal communication).

What appears to be important for a pre-school enrichment program is an opportunity to encounter circumstances which will foster the development of these semi-autonomous central processes that can serve as imagery representative of objects and events and which can become the referents for the spoken symbols required in the phonemic combinations of spoken or written language. Moore's results also suggest to me that these semi-autonomous central processes, if adequately developed, can serve as the basis for motor control. Such considerations suggest that a proper pre-school enrichment program should provide children with an opportunity to encounter a wide variety of objects and circumstances. They suggest that the children should also have an opportunity to imitate a wide variety of models of action and of motor language. The danger of attempting to prescribe materials and models at this stage of knowledge, however, is that the prescriptions may well fail to provide a proper match with what the child already has in his storage. The fact that most teachers have their expectations based on experience with culturally-privileged children makes this problem of the match especially dangerous and vexing in work with the culturally deprived.

Revisiting Montessori's Contribution

In view of the dangers of attempting prescriptions of enrichments for pre-school children, it may be well to re-examine the educational contributions of Maria Montessori. Her contributions have been largely forgotten in America. In fact, until this past August (1962), I could have identified Maria Montessori only by saying that she had developed some kind of kindergarten and was an educational faddist who had made quite a splash about the turn of the century. I was, thus, really introduced to her work by Dr. Jan Smedslund, a Norwegian psychologist, who remarked to me, during a conference at the University of Colorado, that Maria Montessori had provided a practical answer to what I have called "the problem of the match" (Hunt, 1961, p. 276ff).

When I examined the library for materials on Maria Montessori, I discovered that the novelist, Dorothy Canfield Fisher, had spent the winter of 1910–1911 at the Casa de Bambini in Rome and that she had returned to write a book on Montessori's work. This book, entitled *A Montessori Mother* (1912), may still be the best initial introduction to Montessori's work. Books by E. M. Standing (1957) and Nancy Rambusch (1962) have brought the record up to date, and the book by Rambusch contains a bibliography of the materials in the English language concerning Montessori's work assembled by Gilbert E. Donahue.

Montessori's contribution is especially interesting to me because she based her methods of teaching upon the spontaneous interest of children in learning, i.e., upon which I am calling "intrinsic motivation." Moreover, she put great stress upon teachers observing the children under their care to discover what kinds of things foster their individual interests and growth. Furthermore, she put great stress on the training of what she called sensory processes, but what we might more appropriately call information processes today. The fact that she placed strong emphasis upon the training of sensory processes may well be one of the major reasons why her work dropped out of the main stream of educational thought and practice in America before World War I. This emphasis was too dissonant with the dominant American emphasis in learning upon the motor response, rather than upon the sensory input or information processes. It was Montessori's concern to observe carefully what interested a child that led her to discover a wide variety of materials in which she found children showing strong spontaneous interest.

Secondly, Montessori broke the lock-step in the education of young children. Her schools made no effort to keep all the children doing the same thing at the same time. Rather, each child was free to examine and to work with whatever happened to interest him. This meant that he was free to persist in a given concern as long as he cared to, and also free to change from one concern to another whenever a change appeared appropriate to him. In this connection, one of the very interesting observations made by Dorothy Canfield Fisher concerns the prolonged duration that children remain interested in given activities under such circumstances. Whereas the lore about pre-schoolers holds that the nature of the activity in a nursery school must be changed every 10 or 15 minutes, Mrs. Fisher described children typically remaining engrossed in such activities as the buttoning and unbuttoning of a row of buttons for two or more hours at a time.

Thirdly, Montessori's method consisted in having children aged from three to six years old together. As I see it, from taking into account the epigenesis of intellectual development, such a scheme has the advantage of providing the younger children with a wide variety of models for imitation. Moreover, it supplies the older children with an opportunity to help and teach the younger. Helping and teaching contain many of their own rewards.

Perhaps the chief advantage of Montessori's method lies in the fact that it gives the individual child an opportunity to find the circumstances which match his own particular interests and stage of development. This carries with it the corollary advantage of making learning fun.

There may be yet another advantage, one in which those financing pre-school enrichment will be heartily concerned. Montessori's first teacher was a teenage girl, the daughter of the superintendent of the apartment house in the slums of Rome where the first of the Case dei Bambini was established in 1907. In that school this one young woman successfully taught, or should we say, set the stage for the learning of, between fifty and sixty children ranging in age from three to six years old. I say "successfully" because, as Dorothy Canfield Fisher (1912) reports, a substantial proportion of these children learned to read by the time they were five years old. Moreover, they had learned it spontaneously through their own intrinsic motivation, and they appeared to enjoy the process. This observation hints that Montessori's contribution may also contain suggestions of importance economically.

SUMMARY

I began by saying that it was very exciting for me to encounter people, who are generally considered sensible, to be in the process of planning to utilize pre-school experience as an antidote for the effects of cultural deprivation. I have tried to summarize the basis in psychological theory and in the evidence from psychological research for such a use of pre-school enrichment. I have tried to summarize the evidence showing: (1) that the belief in fixed intelligence is no longer tenable; (2) that development is far from completely predetermined; (3) that what goes on between the ears is much less like the static switchboard of the telephone than it is like the active information processes programmed into electronic computers to enable them to solve problems; (4) that experience is the programmer of the human brain-computer, and thus Freud was correct about the importance of the experience which comes before the advent of language; (5) that, nonetheless, Freud was wrong about the nature of the experience which is important, since an opportunity to see and hear a variety of things appears to be more important than the fate of instinctual needs and impulses; and, finally, (6) that learning need not be motivated by painful stimulation, homeostatic need, or the acquired drives based upon these, for there is a kind of intrinsic motivation which is inherent in information processing and action.

In applying these various lines of evidence and these various changes in conception, I have viewed the effects of cultural deprivation as analogous to the experimentally found effects of experiential deprivation in infancy. I have pointed out the importance and the dangers of deriving from "the problem of the match" in attempting to prescribe from existing knowledge a program of circumstantial encounters for the purpose of enriching the experience of culturally deprived pre-school children. In this connection, I have suggested that we re-examine the work of Maria Montessori for suggestions about how to proceed. For she successfully based her teaching method on the spontaneous interest of children in learning, and answered the problem of the match with careful observation of what interests children and by giving them individual freedom to choose which of the various circumstances made available they would encounter at any given time.

REFERENCES

Beach, F. A. "Current concepts of play in animals." *Amer. Natur.*, 1945, **79,** 523–541.

Berlyne, D. E. *Conflict, Arousal, and Curiosity*. New York: McGraw-Hill, 1960.

Bexton, W. H., W. Heron, and T. H. Scott. "Effects of decreased variation in the sensory environment." *Canad. J. Psychol.*, 1954, **8,** 70–76.

Boring, E. G. *A History of Experimental Psychology*. New York: Century, 1929.

Brattgard, S. O. "The importance of adequate stimulation for the chemical composition of retinal ganglion cells during early postnatal development." *Acta Radiol.*, Stockholm, 1952, suppl. 96.

Bühler, K. Displeasure and pleasure in relation to activity. In *Feelings and Emotions: The Wittenberg Symposium,* M. L. Reymert (Ed.) Worcester, Mass.: Clark Univ. Press, 1928 (chap. 14).

Butler, R. A. "Discrimination learning by rhesus monkeys to visual exploration motivation." *J. comp. physiol. Psychol.,* 1953, **46,** 95–98.

Butler, R. A. "The differential effect of visual and auditory incentives on the performance of monkeys." *Amer. J. Psychol.,* 1958, **71,** 591–593.

Carmichael, L. "The development of behavior in vertebrates experimentally removed from influence of external stimulation." *Psychol. Rev.,* 1926, **33,** 51–58.

Carmichael L. "A further study of the development of behavior in vertebrates experimentally removed from the influence of external stimulation." *Psychol. Rev.,* 1927, **34,** 34–47.

Carmichael, L. "A further study of the development of behavior." *Psychol. Rev.,* 1928, **35,** 253–260.

Cattell, J. McK. "Mental tests and measurements." *Mind,* 1890, **15,** 373–381.

Coghill, G. E. *Anatomy and the Problem of Behavior.* Cambridge: Cambridge Univ. Press, 1929.

Cruze, W. W. "Maturation and learning in chicks." *J. comp. Psychol.,* 1935, **19,** 371–409.

Cruze, W. W. "Maturation and learning ability." *Psychol. Monogr.,* 1938, **50,** no. 5.

Darwin, C. *Origin of the Species.* London: Murray, 1859.

Darwin, C. *The Expressions of the Emotions in Man and Animals.* New York: Appleton, 1873 (orig. publ. London: Murray, 1872).

Dashiell, J. F. *Fundamentals of Objective Psychology.* New York: Houghton Mifflin, 1928.

Dember, W. N., R. W. Earl, and N. Paradise. "Response by rats to differential stimulus complexity." *J. comp. physiol. Psychol.,* 1957, **50,** 514–518.

Denenberg, V. H. "The effects of early experience." In *The Behaviour of Domestic Animals,* E. S. E. Hafez (Ed.) London: Ballière, 1962.

Dennis, W. "Causes of retardation among institutional children." *J. genet. Psychol.,* 1960, **96,** 47–59.

Dennis, W., and Marsena G. Dennis. "The effect of restricted practice upon the reaching, sitting and standing of two infants." *J. genet. Psychol.,* 1935, **47,** 21–29.

Dennis, W., and Marsena G. Dennis. "Infant development under conditions of restricted practice and minimum social stimulation: a preliminary report." *J. genet. Psychol.,* 1938, **53,** 151–156.

Dennis, W., and Marsena G. Dennis. "The effect of chadling practice upon the onset of walking in Hopi children." *J. genet. Psychol.,* 1940, **56,** 77–86.

Dennis, W., and Marsena G. Dennis. "Infant development under conditions of restricted practice and minimum social stimulation." *Genet. Psychol. Monogr.,* 1941, **23,** 149–155.

Dewey, J. *The School and Society.* Chicago: Univ. Chicago Press, Phoenix Books, P3, 1960 (first publ. 1900).

Dewey, J. *The Child and the Curriculum.* Chicago: Univ. Chicago Press, Phoenix Books, P3, 1960 (first publ. 1902).

Farber, I. E. "Response fixation under anxiety and non-anxiety conditions." *J. exp. Psychol.,* 1948, **38,** 111–131.

Fenichel, O. *The Psychoanalytic Theory of Neurosis.* New York: Norton, 1945.

Fisher, Dorothy Canfield. *A Montessori Mother.* New York: Holt, 1912.

Fiske, D. W., and S. R. Maddi. *Functions of Varied Experience.* Homewood, Ill.: Dorsey Press, 1961.

Freedman, A. Drive conditioning in water deprivation. Unpubl. doctoral dissertation. Univ. Ill., 1957.

Freeman, G. L. *Introduction to Physiological Psychology.* New York: Ronald, 1934.

Freud, S. The interpretation of dreams. In *The Basic Writings of Sigmund Freud,* A. A. Brill (Trans. and Ed.). New York: Modern Library, 1938. (*The Interpretation of Dreams,* orig. publ. 1900).

Freud, S. The psychopathology of everyday life. In *The Basic Writings of Sigmund Freud,* A. A. Brill (Trans. and Ed.). New York: Modern Library, 1938. (*Three Contributions to the Theory of Sex,* orig. publ. 1905).

Freud, S. Instincts and their vicissitudes. *Collected Papers,* **4,** 60–83. London: Hogarth, 1927. (*Instincts and Their Vicissitudes,* orig. publ. 1915).

Freud, S. *The Problem of Anxiety,* H. A. Bunker (Trans.). New York: Norton, 1936. (*Hemmung, Sympton und Angst,* orig. publ. 1926).

Froebel, F. *The Education of Man,* W. N. Hailmann (Trans.). New York: Appleton, 1896. (*Die Menschenerziehung,* orig. publ. 1826).

Galton, F. *Hereditary Genius: an Inquiry into its Laws and Consequences.* London: Macmillan, 1869.

Gauron, E. F., and W. C. Becker. "The effects of early sensory deprivation on adult rat behavior under competition stress: an attempt at replication of a study by Alexander Wolf." *J. comp. physiol. Psychol.,* 1959, **52,** 689–693.

Gesell, A. *The Embryology of Human Behavior: the Beginnings of the Human Mind.* New York: Harpers, 1945.

Gesell, A. The ontogenesis of infant behavior. In *Manual of Child Psychology,* L. Carmichael (Ed.) New York: Wiley, 1954 (chap. 6).

Gesell, A., and Helen Thompson. "Learning and growth in identical twin infants." *Genet. Psychol. Monogr.,* 1929, **6,** 1–124.

Goddard, H. H. *The Kallikak Family: a Study in the Heredity of Feeble-mindedness.* New York: Macmillan, 1912.

Goldman, Jacquelin R. "The effects of handling and shocking in infancy upon adult behavior in the albino rat." *J. genet. Psychol.,* 1964, **102,** 301–310.

Goodenough, Florence. "A critique of experiments on raising the I.Q." *Educ. Meth.,* 1939, **19,** 73–79.

Guthrie, E. R. *The Psychology of Human Conflict: the Clash of Motives within the Individual.* New York: Harper, 1938.

Hall, C. S. "Emotional behavior in the rat: I. Defecation and urination as measures of individual differences in emotionality." *J. comp. Psychol.,* 1934, **18,** 385–403.

Hall, M. *New Memoire on the Nervous System.* London: Proc. Royal Acad., 1843.

Harlow, H. F. "Learning and satiation of response in intrinsically motivated complex puzzle performance by monkeys." *J. comp. physiol. Psychol.,* 1950, **43,** 289–294.

Harlow, H. F. "The nature of love." *Amer. Psychologist,* 1958, **13,** 673–685.

Harlow, H. F., M. K. Harlow, and D. R. Meyer. "Learning motivated by a manipulation drive." *J. exp. Psychol.,* 1950, **40,** 228–234.

Harvey, O. J., D. E. Hunt, and H. M. Schroeder. *Conceptual Systems and Personality Organization.* New York: Wiley, 1961.

Hebb, D. O. "On the nature of fear." *Psychol. Rev.,* 1946, **53,** 259–276.

Hebb, D. O., "The effects of early experience on problem-solving at maturity." *Amer. Psychologist,* 1947, **2,** 306–307.

Hebb, D. O. *The Organization of Behavior.* New York: Wiley, 1949.

Hebb, D. O., and A. H. Riesen. "The genesis of irrational fears." *Bull. Canad. Psychol. Assn.,* 1943, **3,** 49–50.

Hebb, D. O., and W. R. Thompson. The social significance of animal studies. In *Handbook of Social Psychology,* G. Lindzey (Ed.) Cambridge, Mass.: Addison-Wesley, 1954, (chap. 15).

Hebb, D. O., and K. Williams. "A method of rating animal intelligence." *J. gen. Psychol.,* 1946, **34,** 59–65.

Hendrick, I. "The discussion of the 'instinct to master'." *Psychoanal. Quart.,* 1943, **12,** 561–565.

Hernandez-Peon, R., H. Scherrer, and M. Jouvet. "Modification of electric activity in cochlear nucleus during 'attention' in unanesthetized cats." *Sci.,* 1956, **123,** 331–332.

Hilgard, Joseph R. "Learning and maturation in pre-school children. *J. genet. Psychol.,* 1932, **41,** 36–56.

Holmes, Frances, B. An experimental study of children's fears. In *Children's Fears,* A. T. Jersild and Frances B. Holmes (Eds.) New York: Teachers Coll., Columbia Univ. (*Child Develpm. Monogr.,* **20**), 1935.

Holt, E. B. *Animal Drive and the Learning Process.* New York: Holt, 1931.

Hull, C. L. "Goal attraction and directing ideas conceived as habit phenomena." *Psychol. Rev.,* 1931, **38,** 487–506.

Hull, C. L. *Principles of Behavior.* New York: Appleton-Century, 1943.

Hunt, J. McV. "The effects of infant feeding-frustration upon adult hoarding in the albino rat." *J. abnorm. soc. Psychol.,* 1941, **36,** 338–360.

Hunt, J. McV. Experimental psychoanalysis. In *Encyclopedia of Psychology,* P. L. Harriman (Ed.) New York: Philosophical Library, 1945.

Hunt, J. McV. Psychosexual development: the infant disciplines. Unpubl. manuscript of a chapter written for *Behavioral Science and Child Rearing,* 1956.

Hunt, J. McV. "Experience and the development of motivation: some reinterpretations." *Child Develpm.,* 1960, **31,** 489–504.

Hunt, J. McV. *Intelligence and Experience.* New York: Ronald, 1961.

Hunt, J. McV. Motivation inherent in information processing and action. In *Cognitive Factors in Motivation and Social Organization,* O. J. Harvey (Ed.) New York: Ronald, 1963 (a).

Hunt, J. McV. "Piaget's observations as a source of hypotheses concerning motivation." *Merrill-Palmer Quart.,* 1963, **9,** 263–275 (b).

Hunt, J. McV., and Zella Luria. Investigations of the effects of early experience in sub-human animals. Unpubl. manuscript of a chapter written for *Behavioral Science and Child Rearing,* 1956.

Hunter, W. S. "The delayed reaction in animals and children." *Behav. Monogr.,* 1912, **2,** no. 1, 1–85.

Hunter, W. S. "The temporal maze and kinaesthetic sensory processes in the white rat." *Psychobiol.,* 1918, **2,** 339–351.

Hydén, H. The neuron. In *The Cell: Biochemistry, Physiology, Morphology,* IV. In *Proc. 4th Internat. Congr. Biochem., III. Biochemistry of the central nervous system,* F. Brücke (Ed.). London: Pergamon, 1959.

Hydén, H. The neuron. In *The Cell: Biochemistry, Physiology, Morphology, IV. Specialized Cells,* J. Brachet and A. E. Mirsky (Eds.) New York: Academic Press, 1960, pp. 215–323.

Irwin, O. C. "The amount and nature of activities of new-born infants under constant external stimulating conditions during the first 10 days of life." *Genet. Psychol. Monogr.,* 1930, **8,** 192.

Kohler, W. *The mentality of Apes.* New York: Harcourt, 1925.

Lamarck, J. Chevalier de. *Zoological Philosophy,* (trans. of *Philosophie Zoologique,* by H. Elliot). London: Macmillan, 1914 (orig. publ., 1809).

Levine, S., J. A. Chevalier, and S. J. Korchin. "The effects of early shock and handling on later avoidance learning." *J. Pers.,* 1956, **24,** 475–493.

Lewis, O. *The Children of Sanchez.* New York: Random House-Knopf, 1961.

Liberman, R. "Retinal cholinesterase and glycolysis in rats raised in darkness." *Sci.,* 1962, **135,** 372–373.

McDougall, W. *An Introduction to Social Psychology.* Boston: Luce, 1908.

McGraw, Myrtle B. *Growth: A Study of Johnny and Jimmy.* New York: Appleton-Century, 1935.

Melton, A. W. Learning. In *Encylopedia of Educational Research,* W. S. Munroe (Ed.) New York: Macmillan, 1941.

Miller, G. A., E. H. Galanter, and K. H. Pribram. *Plans and the Structure of Behavior.* New York: Holt, 1960.

Miller, N. E. and J. Dollard. *Social Learning and Imitation.* New Haven: Yale Univ. Press, 1941.

Montgomery, K. C. "A test of two explanations of spontaneous alternation." *J. comp. physiol. Psychol.,* 1952, **45,** 287–293.

Montgomery, K. C. "Exploratory behavior as a function of 'similarity' of stimulus situations." *J. comp. physiol. Psychol.,* 1953, **46,** 129–133.

Montgomery, K. C. "The relation between fear induced by novel stimulation and exploratory behavior." *J. comp. physiol. Psychol.,* 1955, **48,** 254–260.

Montgomery, K. C., and M. Segall. "Discrimination learning based upon the exploratory drive." *J. comp. physiol. Psychol.,* 1955, **48,** 225–228.

Morgan, C. L. *An Introduction to Comparative Psychology* (2d ed.) London: Scott, 1909 (orig. publ., 1894).

Mowrer, O. H. *Learning Theory and Behavior.* New York: Wiley, 1960.

Newell, A., J. C. Shaw, and H. A. Simon. "Elements of a theory of human problem solving." *Psychol. Rev.,* 1958, **65,** 151–166.

Nissen, H. W. "A study of exploratory behavior in the white rat by means of the obstruction method." *J. genet. Psychol.,* 1930, **37,** 361–376.

Orlansky, H. "Infant care and personality." *Psychol. Bull.,* 1949, **46,** 1–48.

Osgood, C. E. "The nature and measurement of meaning." *Psychol. Bull.,* 1952, **49,** 192–237.

Piaget, J. *The Origins of Intelligence in Children,* Margaret Cook (Trans.) New York: International Universities, 1952 (orig. publ., 1936).

Piaget, J. *Play, Dreams, and Imitation in Childhood,* C. Gattegno and F. M. Hodgson (Trans.) New York: Norton, 1951 (orig. publ. as *La formation du symbole chez l'enfant,* 1945).

Piaget, J. *The Psychology of Intelligence,* M. Piercy and D. E. Berlyne (Trans.) London: Routledge, 1947.

Pribram, K. H. "A review of theory in physiological psychology." *Annu. Rev. Psychol.,* 1960, **11,** 1–40.

Pruette, Lorine. *G. Stanley Hall: a Biography of a Mind.* New York: Appleton, 1926.

Rambusch, Nancy M. *Learning How to Learn: an American Approach to Montessori.* Baltimore: Helicon Press, 1962.

Rasch, E., H. Swift, A. H. Riesen, and K. L. Chos. "Altered structure and composition of retinal cells in dark-reared mammals." *Exp. cell. Res.,* 1961, **25,** 348–363.

Razran, G. "The observable unconscious and the inferable conscious in current Soviet psychophysiology: interoceptive conditioning, semantic conditioning, and the orienting reflex." *Psychol. Rev.,* 1961, **68,** 81–147.

Riesen, A. H. Plasticity of behavior: psychological aspects. In *Biological and Biochemical Bases of Behavior,* H. F. Harlow and C. N. Woosley (Eds.) Madison: Univ. Wis. Press, 1958, pp. 425–450.

Romanes, G. J. *Animal Intelligence.* New York: Appleton, 1883 (1882).

Romanes, G. J. *Mental Evolution in Animals.* New York: Appleton, 1884 (1883).

Rose, J. E., and C. N. Woosley. "The relations of thalamic connections, cellular structure and evocable electrical activity in the auditory region of the cat." *J. comp. Neurol.,* 1949, **91,** 441–466.

Rousseau, J. J. *Emile,* Barbara Foxley (Trans.) New York: Everyman's Library, 1916 (orig. publ., 1762).

Salama, A. A., and J. McV. Hunt. " 'Fixation' in the rat as a function of infantile shocking, handling, and gentling." *J. genet. Psychol.,* 1964, **100** (in press).

Schneirla, T. C. An evolutionary and developmental theory of biphasic processes underlying approach and withdrawal. In *Nebraska Symposium on Motivation,* M. R. Jones (Ed.). Lincoln: Univ. Nebraska Press, 1959, pp. 1–43.

Sherrington, C. S. *The Integrative Action of the Nervous System.* New York: Scribners, 1906.

Simpson, B. R. "The wandering IQ." *J. Psychol.,* 1939, **7,** 351–367.

Skeels, H. M., and A. B. Dye. "A study of the effects of differential stimulation on mentally retarded children." *Proc. Amer. Assoc. Ment. Def.,* 1939, **44,** 114–136.

Spitz, R. A. "The smiling response: a contribution to the ontogenesis of social relations." *Genet. Psychol. Monogr.,* 1946, **34,** 67–125.

Standing, E. M. *Maria Montessori: Her Life and Work*. Fresno, Calif.: Academy Library Guild, 1957.

Stoddard, G. D., and Beth L. Wellman. "Environment and the IQ." *Yearb. Nat. Soc. Stud. Educ.,* 1940, **39** (I), 405–442.

Taylor, D. W. Toward an information processing theory of motivation. In *Nebraska Symposium on Motivation,* M. R. Jones (Ed.) London: Univ. Nebraska Press, 1960, pp. 51–79.

Thompson, W. R., and W. Heron. "The effects of restricting early experience on the problem-solving capacity of dogs." *Canad. J. Psychol.,* 1954, **8,** 17–31.

Thorndike, E. L. *Educational Psychology.* Vol. II. *The Psychology of Learning.* New York: Columbia Univ. Press, 1913.

Thorndike, E. L., and R. S. Woodworth. "The influence of improvement in one mental function upon the efficiency of other function." *Psychol. Rev.,* 1901, **8,** 247–261; 384–395; 553–564.

Walker, A. E., and T. A. Weaver, Jr. "Ocular movements from the occipital lobe in the monkey." *J. Neurophysiol.,* 1940, **3,** 353–357.

Watson, J. B. *Psychology from the Standpoint of a Behaviorist.* Philadelphia: Lippincott, 1919.

Watson, J. B. *Psychological Care of Infant and Child.* New York: Norton, 1928.

Watson, J. B., and R. Rayner. "Conditioned emotional reactions." *J. exp. Psychol.,* 1920, **3,** 1–14.

Weiskrantz, L. "Sensory deprivation and the cat's optic nervous system." *Nature,* 1958, **181,** (3), 47–1050.

White, R. W. "Motivation reconsidered: the concept of competence." *Psychol. Rev.,* 1959, **66,** 297–333.

Wiener, N. *Cybernetics.* New York: Wiley, 1948.

Wolf, A. "The dynamics of the selective inhibition of specific functions in neuroses." *Psychosom. Med.,* 1943, **5,** 27–38.

Woodworth, R. S. "Heredity and environment: A critical study of recently published material on twins and foster children." *Soc. Sci. Res. Coun. Bull.,* 1941, no. 47.

6.4 Orientation

The nature of evaluation procedures in education has, in part, instigated speculation among psychologists about two related problems: (1) What are the effects of such evaluation procedures upon children's cognitive and emotional behavior? (2) What are the effects of children's emotional responses upon their academic test performance? An example of research related to these problems is that concerned with test anxiety. As anxiety scales suitable for use with children have been developed (see Lipsitt, Chapter 3) an enormous amount of research has accumulated. Of immediate concern is the relationship of test anxiety, generally considered a situational emotional response, to children's performance of tasks under conditions similar to those in most classrooms where testing is carried out in the presence of an evaluative adult. The author of this study, Norma McCoy, manipulates three independent variables in a "2 × 2 × 2" factorial design: anxiety level, type of task, and nature of instructions. Children's task performance is the dependent variable.

For her theoretical rationale, McCoy draws upon the influential work of Sarason *et al.* (1960). Within this framework, anticipatory failure is seen to be the stimulus condition for anxiety arousal, regardless of how realistic such anticipation may be. Where the child perceives failure to be highly probable, his anxiety level increases. This increase in turn serves to interfere with test performance, thus is self-defeating. Sarason and his colleagues have engaged in extensive longitudinal research on the relationship of test anxiety to school performance, with the general conclusion that such a relationship increases in magnitude as children progress through the elementary grades. Further, it has been observed that some children manifest marked increases in anxiety from the first to the fifth grade while others show marked decreases. These changes are reported to be accompanied by opposite-direction changes in IQ and achievement-test performance. In other words, children whose anxiety level increases over time have successively lower IQ and achievement-test scores. Children whose anxiety level decreases throughout the elementary grades manifest progressively higher academic test scores. It is difficult to determine in this case which is cause and which is effect; however, the relationship is firmly documented (Sarason, Hill, and Zimbardo, 1964).

The theoretical rationale, methodology, and findings combine to make the McCoy study a highly appropriate current example of research on anxiety. Readers should consider (1) the implications of the findings for a teacher's behavior in relation to high-anxiety children and (2) the relationship of McCoy's findings on children's verbalizations and the use of materials under test conditions to a study performed by Cox (1966). Cox found that the response rate of high-anxiety children decreases in the presence of an observing adult while low-anxiety children tend to increase their rate of response under this condition.

RECOMMENDED READING

Cox, F. N. "Some effects of test anxiety and presence or absence of other persons on boy's performance on a repetitive motor task." *J. exp. child Psychol.,* **3** (1966), 100–112.

Levitt, E. E. *The Psychology of Anxiety.* Indianapolis: Bobbs-Merrill, 1967.

Ruebush, B. E. "Anxiety." *Child Psychology.* (2d Yearbook) Publ. of the Soc. Study Educ. Chicago: Univ. Chicago Press, 1963, pp. 460–516.

Sarason, S. B. *et al. Anxiety in Elementary School Children.* New York: Wiley, 1960.

Sarason, S. B., K. T. Hill, and P. G. Zimbardo. "A longitudinal study of the relation of test anxiety to performance on intelligence and achievement tests." *Monogr. Soc. Res. child Develpm.,* **29** (1964), ser. no. 98, 51 pp.

6.4 Effects of Test Anxiety on Children's Performance as a Function of Type of Instructions and Type of Task

Norma McCoy, SAN FRANCISCO STATE COLLEGE

Research supporting the theory of test anxiety developed by the workers at Yale (Sarason, Davidson, Lighthall, Waite, and Ruebush, 1960) indicates that test anxiety in children interferes with performance on testlike tasks (Lighthall, Ruebusch, Sarason, and Zweibelson, 1959; Sarason *et al.,* 1960; Zweibelson, 1956) and on relatively unstructured or creative tasks (Fox, Davidson, Lighthall, Waite, and Sarason, 1958; Sarason, Davidson, Lighthall, and Waite, 1958b). However, facilitation of performance has been demonstrated on gamelike tasks (Lighthall *et al.,* 1959; Sarason *et al.,* 1960; Zweibelson, 1956) and on tasks which reward cautious dependent behavior (Ruebush, 1960b; Waite, 1959).

In the present study, two major questions were raised. The first question was whether the test-anxious child discriminates between formal test and nontest situations or responds to all performance situations, in which an adult is present, as test situations. According to the theory (Sarason *et al.,* 1960), test anxiety has its origins in early evaluative situations in the home which for the most part antedate the beginning of formal schooling. Generally, these situations involve repeated devaluation of the child's performance by the parent. The end result is that the child in the school test situation has strong needs to avoid failure because of the highly threatening consequences he perceives it to have (loss of love, etc.). If test anxiety truly originates in early nonschool situations with the parents, then all

Reprinted from *Journal of Personality and Social Psychology,* **2** (1965), no. 5, 634–641. By permission of the author and the American Psychological Association, Inc.

situations which involve performance for an observing adult—not only formal test situations—should become "test" situations for the text-anxious child.

To investigate this prediction, a simple gamelike task involving perceptual-motor skill (the tracing task) was administered to both high test-anxious (HA) and low test-anxious (LA) subjects with either test or game instructions. It was expected that given the presence of an observing adult, the LA child would respond to a noncompetitive game as a "game" while the HA child would respond to a noncompetitive game as a "test." Therefore, it was predicted that although LA subjects given test (evaluative) instructions would perform significantly better than those given game (nonevaluative) instructions, HA subjects under test and game instructions would perform similarly. Because of the simple, gamelike nature of the task and the consequent unlikelihood that HA subjects would show interference under test instructions (Lighthall *et al.,* 1959; Sarason *et al.,* 1960; Zweilbelson, 1956), it was predicted that under test instructions the performance of LA and HA subjects would not differ significantly. Under game instructions, however, it was predicted that HA subjects would perform at a significantly higher level than LA subjects because of their perception of the situation as an evaluative one.

The second question raised concerns the extent to which fear of failure is basic to the arousal of the test-anxious reaction. According to the theory (Sarason *et al.,* 1960), the HA child anticipates failure in the test situation and views the consequences of failure, in terms of the reactions from others, as highly threatening. It is this anticipation of failure and the fear of its consequences which arouses anxiety and results in interference in performance. Thus, in a situation in which the task is structured and "easy"—one in which the probability of failure is low—the HA child should not evidence interference in performance due to test anxiety (Lighthall *et al.,* 1959; Sarason *et al.,* 1960; Zweibelson, 1956). However, in a performance situation in which the HA child feels that failure is inevitable, test anxiety should be aroused and should result in marked interference in performance.

Because previous studies have not demonstrated a differential effect of failure and success instructions with either HA adults or HA children (Mandler and Sarason, 1952; Waite, Sarason, Lighthall, and Davidson, 1958), a different approach to the creation of a failure situation was used in the present study. A gamelike task (the drawing task) with two parts was administered along with the tracing task discussed above. Each subject received the same kind of instructions (test or game) with the drawing task as he did with the tracing task. In each part of the drawing task the subject was asked to make a drawing for which paper and an array of art materials were provided. In one part the child was asked to make a picture (free drawing), while in the other part he was asked to make a picture of a POSKON. Because the child was in no way informed that POSKON was a nonsense syllable, it was assumed that the majority of subjects would anticipate failure on this task. The reasoning was that if anticipation of failure is basic to the arousal of test anxiety, then the POSKON subtask would arouse anxiety in the HA child which would be reflected in performance. Although the free drawing subtask of the drawing task was somewhat unstructured and might have been expected to result in impaired performance by the HA child (Fox *et al.,* 1958; Sarason *et al.,* 1958b), it was predicted that HA and LA subjects would differ most in performance of the POSKON subtask.

Assuming, as in the first major hypothesis, that both situations (test or game) would be perceived as evaluative by the HA child, it was expected that anxiety would be reflected in the performance of the HA child on the POSKON subtask under both test and game instructions. Such anxiety would result in constricted behavior (Fox *et al.,* 1958) as reflected by smaller drawings, the use of fewer types of art materials and with the exception of questions, fewer verbalizations. Questions were excluded in this prediction because previous findings (Sarason *et al.,* 1958a, 1958b) suggest that the HA child would ask more questions than the LA child as a reflection of high dependency needs.

METHOD

Subjects and Design

Four hundred and sixteen fourth-grade boys from six elementary schools in a predominantly middle-class suburb of Minneapolis, were pretested on the Test Anxiety Scale for Children (TASC; Sarason *et al.,* 1960) and the Defensiveness Scale for Children (DSC; Ruebusch, 1960a). After discarding those who had repeated a grade, those for whom a verbal score from the Lorge-Thorndike Intelligence Test, Form 3A, was not available, and those who were left-handed (the tracing task apparatus was designed for right-handed persons), 28 HA and 28 LA subjects were selected from those below the median on defensiveness (DSC). The HA subject had scores $\geqq 17$ (eighty-second percentile) and the LA subject had scores $\leqq 7$ (thirty-sixth percentile). Defensiveness was controlled because recent evidence indicates that the defensiveness is an important variable in investigations of anxiety in children (Ruebusch, 1960a, 1963). One half of each anxiety group was randomly assigned to the test condition, the other to the game condition. Within each of the groups the order of the two experimental tasks was counterbalanced; half received the tracing task first (order TD) and half receiving the drawing task first (order DT). This resulted in a 2 (anxiety levels) $\times$ 2 (conditions) $\times$ 2 (orders) factorial arrangement with seven subjects in a cell.

The characteristics of the four Anxiety $\times$ Condition groups in the final sample with regard to age, verbal scores, and IQs, TASC scores, and DSC scores are presented in Table 1. It can be seen that the LA and HA subjects differed on mean Lorge-Thorndike verbal scores ($t = 2.18$, $df = 54$, $p < .05$). However, because the present study involved simple perceptual-motor tasks, a difference at this level was judged not crucial. This was substantiated in later analysis.

TABLE 1. CA, Lorge-Thorndike Verbal Score, TASC, and DSC Means and Standard Deviations

Group	CA in Months	Verbal Score	Verbal IQ	TASC Score	DSC Score
HA-test					
M	118.5	45.4	106.9	20.2	9.6
SD	3.6	11.0	10.8	3.3	4.0
HA-game					
M	117.4	43.9	106.7	19.9	9.6
SD	3.3	13.7	10.6	3.5	2.8
LA-test					
M	120.1	53.8	112.4	5.1	11.0
SD	3.7	11.3	10.9	1.8	2.6
LA-game					
M	119.6	53.9	112.6	4.0	11.5
SD	3.3	10.9	7.5	2.5	2.5

Tracing-Task Apparatus

The appratus consisted of a sloping wooden panel with an elevation of 4.5 inches in the rear and 2.5 inches at the front. The panel was 18 inches wide and 14 inches deep. Centered on its horizontal face was a thin translucent white Lucite screen, 10.5 inches wide and 12.5 inches deep. The screen was enclosed by a grooved frame at the bottom and two sides which was designed to accommodate 11 × 12 inch copper-laminated plates, each bearing a picture drawn with black oil paint.

Each picture contained figures of a parent and of a boy. A strip of copper 3⁄16 inch wide was removed from around the outline of the boy, exposing the phenolic inner core. The outline of the figure was illuminated from below with six 6-watt, 110-volt pilot lamps placed under the panel and beneath the Lucite screen. On each of the copper plates, removal of the copper from around the figure of the boy was terminated .25 inch from where removal was begun to provide a pathway with a beginning and an end. The beginning of the pathway on each plate was indicated at the foot of the boy by a large yellow plastic tape arrow.

A standard pin jack which served as a receptacle for a metal-tipped stylus was placed on the right side of the panel.

Six pictures, two with neutral content (Pictures 1 and 2), two with dependency content (Pictures 3 and 4), and two with aggressive content (Pictures 5 and 6) were presented to the subject in the apparatus described above.

Drawing-Task Materials

Five different types of art materials were provided for the drawing task, crayons of 8 different colors, round stick pastels of 12 different colors, 12 square stick pieces of charcoal, pencils of 12 different colors, and felt-tip markers of 6 different colors. All sets of materials were aligned in a wooden tray and presented in a different random order for each subject. Two sheets of 12 × 18 inch white drawing paper were used with each subject.

Procedure

All subjects were tested individually in a small room at their school by one female experimenter who did not know the anxiety level of any of the subjects. After seating the subject at the table with the apparatus for the first task, the experimenter asked three standard questions dealing with baseball, summer vacation, and favorite school subjects to establish good rapport. After completion of the first task, the experimenter and the subject moved to another table where the second task was administered. Then the subject returned to his classroom with the experimenter.

Each subject received instructions according to the condition and the order to which he had been assigned. The instructions were as follows:

> [Test condition] My name is Miss ______ and I am in the schools today giving some tests. I have two tests to give you and I want you to do your very best. I will give you a score on each test and your scores will be compared with the scores of the other boys. It is very important that you do your best. These tests are hard, but I'm sure you'll do well.
>
> The *first* [second] test is the *Construction* [Psychomotor Dexterity] Test. Listen carefully to the instructions and then you can begin. As I said before, your scores will be compared with those of the other boys so it is very important that you do your best.
>
> [Game condition] My name is Miss ______ and I have some games to show you. These games are games which I have made and I want to find out how boys your age play with them and like them. They are not tests and have nothing to do with how well you're doing in school. They're fun games and I think you'll like them.
>
> The *first* [second] game is the Drawing [Tracing] game. First I'll tell you how it goes and then you can play it. It's a fun game and I think you'll like it.

For the tracing task, the experimenter explained that the idea was to trace the outline of the boy in each of the six pictures, to pick up the stylus when the picture was exposed, to start at the yellow arrow, and do it as quickly as possible without removing the stylus and without touching the sides of the pathway. When the buzzer sounded it meant the sides had been touched. The set of six pictures was presented once to each subject in random order with the restrictions that Picture 1 always be first and that no two pictures with the same content be presented consecutively. Picture 1 served as a practice picture although it was not designated as such to the subject.

For each picture the experimenter said, "Ready? Begin," and then removed the cover. When the subject had reached the end of the path, the experimenter then removed the picture and asked the subject to replace the stylus in the receptacle.

The drawing task consisted of two parts presented in counterbalanced order. The subject was presented with paper and the tray of art materials and asked to make "a picture" (Subtask A) and to make a picture of a POSKON (Subtask P). The nonsense name, POSKON, was printed on an 8 × 5 inch card which the experimenter presented to the subject as the experimenter pronounced the word. In neither condition did the experimenter intimate that POSKON was not a real word. In each subtask the subject was allowed to work 4 minutes from the time he began to draw No mention of a time limit was made to the subject and 4 minutes appeared to be ample time for the majority of subjects.

To maintain the unstructured nature of the task all questions from subjects were answered uninformatively but pleasantly with replies such as, "Do as you think," "Draw whatever you think it is," "It is up to you to decide," etc.

Response Measures

Tracing task Two latency measures were used: the time in seconds that elapsed between exposure of a picture and removal of the stylus from the receptacle by the subject and the time in seconds that elapsed between removal of the stylus and the point at which the subject began to trace. These latencies were obtained in order to test predictions about the effects of picture content. As picture content will not be discussed in this report, the analysis of these data will not be presented but are available elsewhere (McCoy, 1962). The number of occasions that the subject contacted the copper (errors) and the time taken to trace each picture (time score) were recorded automatically.

Drawing task The time in seconds between the end of each set of instructions and the point at which the subject began to draw was measured by a manually operated clock. Because of skewed distributions and heterogeneity of variance, the latencies were changed to log scores [log $(X + 1)$].

All remarks that the subjects made were recorded by the experimenter and later categorized as questions, exclamations, statements of inadequacy to the task, self-depreciatory statements, general statements, and sentence fragments. Questions were defined as interrogatory sentences; exclamations, as interjections or emotional ejaculations; statements of inadequacy to the task, as expressions of inability to perform as requested; self-depreciatory statements, as devaluation of own attempts or accomplishments; general statements, as comments or any word or words expressing a thought that was not included in the other categories; and sentence fragments, as interrupted or unfinished sentences. Agreement was 95.6% when protocols of eight subjects were categorized by an independent rater.

Other measures included number of different colors and materials used by each subject as well as the area covered by each drawing. Area utilized in the drawings was estimated by applying a 12 × 18 inch grid with 216 1-in squares to each drawing. The number of squares which contained a part of the drawing constituted an area score for that drawing. Because of skewed distributions these scores were also transformed to logarithms.

RESULTS

Tracing Task

Analysis of time and error scores In order to investigate the importance of intelligence level in performance of the tracing task, time and error scores were each plotted against Lorge-Thorndike verbal scores. Since there was no evidence of nonlinearity, Pearson r's were computed. Neither the r of .04 between errors and verbal scores nor the r of −.26 between time and verbal scores was significant; thus the findings are not attributable to the difference between the two groups in verbal scores.

Because each subject was instructed to trace as "quickly and carefully" as possible, success in the tracing task involved both the number of errors made and the time taken in making them. Computation of a product-moment correlation revealed an r of −.54 ($t = 4.01$, $p < .01$) between total error scores and total time scores indicating that subjects who traced rapidly tended to make more errors than subjects who traced slowly. In order to determine differences in performance between groups with time held constant, an analysis of covariance was performed for errors with time as the covariate. The rationale for this use of analysis of covariance is presented by Lindquist (1953). The results are presented in Table 2.

As can be seen in Table 2, the main effect of Condition was significant indicating that subjects in the game condition (adjusted $M = 66.0$) made more errors than subjects in the test condition (adjusted $M = 45.4$). The interaction of Anxiety × Condition which was predicted was also significant. The adjusted means for this interaction are plotted in Figure 1. It can be seen that the prediction that the difference between the performance of LA subjects in the test condition and the game condition would be significantly greater than the difference between the performance of the HA subjects in the two conditions was supported.

TABLE 2. Analysis of Variance and Analysis of Covariance of Error Scores with Time as the Covariate

Source	Analysis of Variance			Analysis of Covariance		
	df	*MS*	*F*	*df*	*MS*	*F*
Anxiety (A)	1	90.0		1	56.6	
Condition (C)	1	4131.4	4.88[a]	1	5916.0	10.67[b]
A × C	1	1794.4	2.12	1	2646.9	4.77[a]
Order (O)	1	795.0		1	529.1	
A × O	1	2900.2		1	953.5	
C × O	1	920.2		1	4.9	
A × C × O	1	1794.4		1	745.3	
Error (within)	48	846.5		47	554.3	
Total	55			54		

[a] $p < .05$.
[b] $p < .005$.

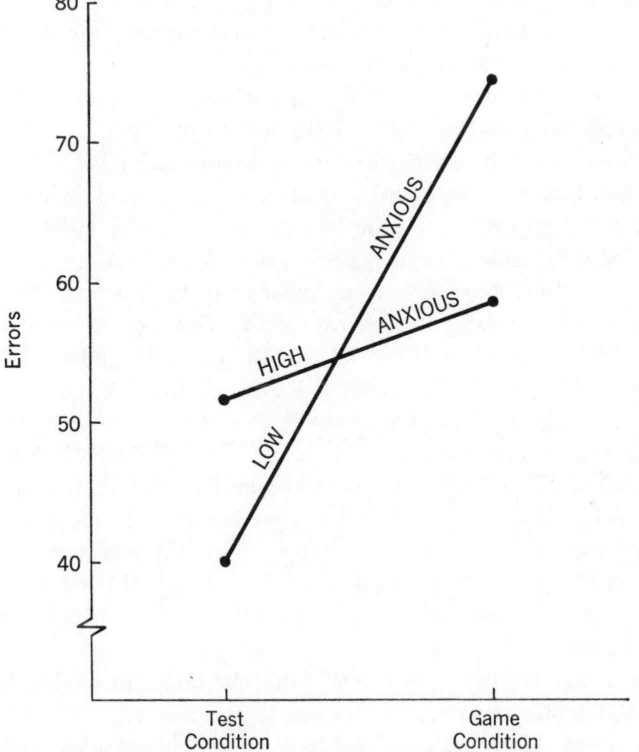

FIGURE 1. Adjusted mean errors for high- and low-anxious subjects in the test and game conditions.

Employing the error variance of the difference between two adjusted means (Lindquist, 1953), t ratios were computed. The LA subjects made significantly fewer errors in the test condition (adjusted $M = 39.5$) than in the game condition (adjusted $M = 74.0$) ($t = 3.84$, $p < .01$), while the HA subjects did not differ in the two conditions (test: adjusted $M = 51.2$; game: adjusted $M = 58.1$, $t < 1$). Although the HA subjects in the game condition performed considerably better than the LA subjects in the game condition, this difference only reached borderline significance ($t = 1.78$, $p < .10$). The difference between adjusted means of HA-T and LA-T subjects was not significant ($t = 1.32$).

Drawing Task

Analysis of verbalizations Because of the low frequency of verbalizations in all but the questions category, data for exclamations, statements of inadequacy to the task, self-depreciatory statements, general statements, and sentence fragments were submitted to chi-square analysis using 2 × 2 contingency tables. The HA and LA subjects were divided as to whether each made a particular type of verbalization or not. Calculation of chi-square using the Yates correction for continuity revealed one category in which there was a significant difference between anxiety groups. Regardless of subtask or condition significantly more LA subjects (20) made general statements, that is, "I think I'll use blue," "Maybe I'll draw a dog," than HA subjects (10) ($\chi^2 = 7.22$, $df = 1$, $p < .01$).

As a further means of getting at the differences in verbal behavior between the two anxiety groups, analyses of variance for each subtask of the drawing task were performed using scores based on the number of verbalizations or communications a subject made. Verbalizations in all categories except sentence fragments were included in these scores. The results of the two analyses revealed a significant main effect of condition for Subtask A (freedrawing) ($F = 10.52$, $df = 1/48$, $p < .001$) and for Subtask P (POSKON) ($F = 18.60$, $df = 1/48$, $p < .001$), both reflecting more verbalizations in the game condition (Subtask A: $M = 4.7$; Subtask P: $M = 6.5$) than in the test condition (Subtask A: $M = 2.1$; Subtask P: $M = 2.8$). The main effect of anxiety was significant in the analysis for Subtask P only ($F = 4.56$, $df = 1/48$, $p < .05$), indicating that HA subjects made significantly fewer verbalizations ($M = 3.8$) than LA subjects ($M = 5.6$) while drawing a POSKON. Thus, the prediction that HA subjects would make fewer verbalizations than LA subjects in Subtask P but not in Subtask A was supported.

In order to test the hypothesis concerning questions, an analysis of variance for each subtask was performed employing the number of questions the subject asked during each subtask as a score. The analysis for Subtask P revealed a significant main effect of condition, indicating that subjects asked fewer questions in the test ($M = 1.4$) than in the game condition

($M = 2.9$) ($F = 11.41$, $df = 1/48$, $p < .005$). The prediction that HA subjects would ask more questions than LA subjects regardless of condition was not supported.

Analysis of drawing behavior For each subtask, analyses of log latencies for elapsed time before the subject began to draw revealed no significant differences.

As one means of discovering how the groups differed in their use of the art materials, the number of HA and LA subjects using more than one of the five types of art materials was analyzed for each subtask and for each condition separately using 2 × 2 contingency tables. Subjects were divided according to whether they used one, or more than one, type of art material. Of the four analyses, the only significant difference between groups was the difference between the LA subjects and the HA subjects in the game condition in the free-drawing situation (Subtask A) (Fischer exact probability = .028). Whereas 10 LA subjects in the game condition utilized more than one type of art material, only 4 HA subjects in the game condition did so.

In a further analysis of the use of the art materials, a color score was given to each subject for each subtask by totaling the number of different colors used in making each drawing. Analyses of color scores were performed for the two subtasks separately and revealed no significant findings for Subtask A. For Subtask P, however, there was a significant main effect of order ($F = 7.29$, $df = 1/48$, $p < .05$) indicating that more colors were used in order TD ($M = 2.46$), on the average, than in order DT ($M = 1.61$). The Anxiety × Condition interaction was significant for Subtask P ($F = 9.92$, $df = 1/48$, $p < .005$) indicating that HA subjects used more colors ($M = 2.36$) in the test condition than in the game condition ($M = 1.57$), while LA subjects used more different colors in the game condition ($M = 1.50$) than in the test condition ($M = 2.71$). The Anxiety × Condition = Order interaction was also significant for Subtask P ($F = 4.10$, $df = 1/48$, $p < .05$) and indicates that the differences reflected by the Anxiety × Condition interaction were more pronounced in order TD.

The analysis of switching scores or scores obtained by counting the number of times a subject switched from one color and/or material to another for each of the subtasks revealed the same significant effects and interactions and reflected trends identical to those in the analysis of color scores discussed above.

As a means of analyzing the drawings themselves, log-area scores were obtained and an analysis of variance of these scores was performed for the drawings in each subtask separately. In the analysis for Subtask A, the main effect of order was significant ($F = 7.01$, $df = 1/48$, $p < .05$) indicating that the drawings tended to cover more area in order DT (M log $= 2.35$) than in order TD (M log $= 1.74$). In the analysis for Subtask P, there was a significant main effect of anxiety ($F = 4.73$, $df = 1/48$, $p < .05$) indicating that regardless of condition, HA subjects used significantly less area (M log = 1.20) in drawing a POSKON than did LA subjects (M log = 1.42).

DISCUSSION

The findings for the tracing task suggest that although LA subjects in the test condition responded to the experimental situation in a manner entirely different from that of LA subjects in the game condition, this was not true for HA subjects. While both LA and HA subjects performed well in the test condition, the HA subjects, in contrast to the LA subjects, performed just as well in the game condition, as was predicted. The explanation that seems most likely is that although HA subjects attended to the instructions, the fact that the HA child was required to perform for an observing adult made the game situation evaluative and testlike. An alternate explanation for the findings is that HA subjects, in contrast to LA subjects, did not attend to external cues, that is, instructions. However, it seems unlikely that, if questioned, HA subjects in the game condition would have stated that they had been asked to take a test rather than to play a game, and particularly unlikely in light of the simple, game-like, perceptual-motor task employed.

Although these results need substantiation in further research, they certainly suggest that although the classroom teacher may be rewarded for instructing the LA child that he is being tested and should do his very best, such admonishing is unnecessary in the case of the HA child.

With regard to the second major hypothesis, it was expected that the HA boys would show less freedom and spontaneity than the LA boys in the POSKON subtask because of its failure implications, and that the anxiety aroused would be reflected in fewer verbalizations and restricted use of the art materials. Analyses of the results for the two subtasks in the drawing task revealed no significant effects of anxiety for Subtask A (free drawing), but for the POSKON task HA boys made significantly fewer verbalizations and covered significantly less area with their drawings than LA boys, as was predicted. Contrary to prediction, however, it was found that HA boys in the test condition used more colors and "switched" back and forth among colors and materials more frequently than did LA boys, and, unlike LA boys, did not exhibit such behavior in the game condition. It was in the game condition, where exploratory use of the art materials would seem entirely appropriate, that the HA boys used fewer colors. Also pertinent is the finding that the HA boys used fewer different types of art materials in the least anxiety-arousing subtask (free drawing) and condition (game) —only 4 HA boys as compared with 10 LA boys used more than one type of art material in Subtask A in the game condition. Such findings suggest that in an unstructured game situation in which the HA child cannot determine what is desired of him, his fear that his response will receive negative evaluation leads him to avoid performing or to respond as little as possible. When the unstructured task is presented as a test, the HA boy is forced to perform because of the certainty of failure if he does not. He is then choosing the lesser of two evils. This explanation is consistent with the theory, but remains, nevertheless, a post hoc one.

The finding that only 10 of the 28 HA boys made conversational remarks (general statements) during performance of the drawing task, whereas 20 LA boys made such remarks, is an interesting one. It adds further support to the hypothesis that the HA child experiences anxiety in situations in which he must perform for an adult regardless of how the adult represents the situation, that is, game or test, or whether or not interference in performance occurs.

It must be noted here that the differences reflected by the Anxiety × Condition interaction in the analyses of color scores and switching scores were present in order TD only. Although the tasks in the present study were counterbalanced in keeping with principles of good experimental design, it was not expected that order of task administration would affect the results. Others who have investigated test anxiety have also been plagued with unexpected order effects (Doris and Sarason, 1955; Doris, Sarason and Berkowitz, 1963; Mandler and Sarason, 1952) and no adequate explanations have as yet been offered which can incorporate all of the findings. Results involving order in the present study suggest the possibility that LA subjects may become less interested and motivated the longer they are kept in the task situation, while the HA subjects become more anxious with time. If this were true it would explain why significant differences appeared in drawing performance when the drawng task was administered last but not when it was administered first. This and other likely hypotheses have not, as yet, been adequately investigated.

The expectation that HA subjects would ask more questions than LA subjects as a reflection of high dependency needs was not supported. Further consideration of the experimental situation in this and in previous studies suggests an explanation of this finding. Previous studies (Ruebush, 1960b; Sarason *et al.,* 1958a, 1958b) which have demonstrated dependency behavior in HA children have employed situations in which such behaviors were reinforced. In both subtasks of the drawing task, however, the only information provided in reply to questions was that the procedure was up to the child. Thus, in the drawing-task situation, asking questions did not result in task-relevant information and served only to emphasize the unstructured nature of the task and the fact that no further information would be provided. It is suggested, therefore, that the HA boy will continue to express his dependency by question asking only when he is reinforced for such behavior. Attempts to investigate differences in dependency behavior in HA children must utilize experimental situations in which reinforcement of such behavior is varied systematically.

SUMMARY

Two tasks were administered to 28 high test-anxious (HA) and 28 low test-anxious (LA) 4th-grade boys. One half of each group received test instructions and one half received game instructions. The first hypothesis was that HA Ss perform as if being tested regardless of instructions. On a simple gamelike tracing task, LA Ss in the test condition made fewer errors than LA Ss in the game condition, while HA Ss in the 2 conditions did not differ. The second hypothesis was that fear of failure is basic to the arousal of test anxiety. On a 2-part drawing task Ss were required to make "a picture" and to draw a "poskon." No anxiety group differences were found for the free drawing; in drawing a "poskon"—the failure task—HA Ss made smaller drawings and verbalized less. In addition, HA Ss tended to switch colors and materials more in the test than in the game condition while the reverse was true for LA Ss.

REFERENCES

Doris, J., and S. B. Sarason. "Test anxiety and blame assignment in a failure situation." *J. abnorm. soc. Psychol.,* **50** (1955), 335–338.

Doris, J., S. B. Sarason, and L. Berkowitz, "Test anxiety and performance on projective tests." *Child Develpm.,* **4** (1963), 751–766.

Fox, Cynthia, K. S. Davidson, F. F. Lighthall, R. R. Waite, and S. B. Sarason. "Human figure drawings of high and low anxious children." *Child Develpm.,* **29** (1958), 297–301.

Lighthall, F. F., B. Ruebush, S. Sarason, and I. Zweibelson. "Change in mental ability as a function of test anxiety and type of mental test." *J. consult. Psychol.,* **23** (1959), 34–38.

Lindquist, E. F. *Design and Analysis of Experiments in Psychology and Education.* Boston: Houghton Mifflin, 1953.

Mandler, D., and S. B. Sarason. "A study of anxiety and learning." *J. abnorm. soc. Psychol.,* **47** (1952), 166–173.

McCoy, Norma. Effects of test anxiety on children's performance as a function of instructions and type of task. Unpubl. doctoral dissertation. Univ. Minn., 1962.

Ruebush, B. K. Children's behavior as a function of anxiety and defensiveness. Unpubl. doctoral dissertation. Yale Univ., 1960 (a).

Ruebush, B. K. "Interfering and facilitating effects of test anxiety." *J. abnorm. soc. Psychol.,* **60** (1960), 205–212 (b).

Ruebush, B. K. Anxiety. In *Child Psychology: The 62 Yearbook of the National*

Society for the Study of Education, H. W. Stevenson (Ed.) (pt. 1). Chicago: Univ. Chicago Press, 1963, pp. 460–516.

Sarason, S. B., K. S. Davidson, F. F. Lighthall, and R. R. Waite. "Classroom observations of high and low anxious children." *Child Develpm.,* **29** (1958), 287–295 (a).

Sarason, S. B., K. S. Davidson, F. F. Lighthall, and R. R. Waite. "Rorschach behavior and performance of high and low anxious children." *Child Develpm.,* **29** (1958), 277–285 (b).

Sarason, S. B., B. K. Davidson, F. F. Lighthall, R. R. Waite, and B. K. Ruebush. *Anxiety in Elementary School Children.* New York: Wiley, 1960.

Waite, R. R. Test performance as a function of anxiety and type of task. Unpubl. doctoral dissertation. Yale Univ., 1959.

Waite, R. R., S B. Sarason, F. F. Lighthall, and K. S. Davidson. "A study of anxiety and learning in children." *J. abnorm. soc. Psychol.,* **57** (1958), 267–270.

Zweibelson, I. "Test anxiety and intelligence test performance." *J. consult. Psychol.,* **20** (1956), 479–481.

6.5 Orientation

From an empirical study we now turn to a more clinical and philosophical treatment of issues involved in the psychology of teacher-pupil relationships. Discipline, or training in self-control, is noted as the major problem faced by teachers. Certainly, no aspect of classroom management provokes more apprehension among preservice teachers than that of discipline. To stimulate thinking and discussion on discipline and its ramifications, the following paper by Hirsch Silverman has been included. Silverman directs attention to at least three major considerations: the issue of punishment, sources of recalcitrant behavior, and principles thought to be imperative for a discipline based on a sound educational psychology.

A review of the research on classroom discipline can be characterized by two conditions. First, there is the paucity of meaningful research. Ausubel (1965) has correctly observed that concepts of discipline are much more a matter of opinion than research. Unfortunately, even the "opinion" approach to discipline is geared to such an abstract, general, and sometimes idealistic level that it provides little value to parents and teachers. Perhaps even more unfortunate is the frequent tendency to discuss discipline apart from principles of learning, motivation, and development. Although some persons have developed techniques of behavioral modification based on principles of learning, others are unable or unwilling to incorporate them into a consistent discipline. A second major weakness in the literature on discipline is the tendency to rationalize the beginning teacher's concerns about discipline by saying that "Experience will solve your problems for you," or "Good teachers do not have discipline problems." While there is a certain amount of validity to both points, they do little to prepare the prospective teacher for handling inevitable problems. However, it must be recognized that the operation of multiple variables, organismic and situational, makes the definition of specific techniques designed to "guarantee" success highly improbable.

The literature on discipline can be summarized as follows. First, there seems to be agreement that the goal of all discipline is the development and maintenance of self-control rather than externally imposed control. Second, there has been a growing emphasis upon the relationship of discipline to mental health. This emphasis has culminated in a much more democratically based concept of discipline than was characteristic during early periods of American education. Critics, however, frequently charge that a distortion of the democratic approach has resulted from overpermissiveness that leads to classroom anarchy and the lack of self-control. A third, and more positive, trend is the recognition that consistent antisocial behavior is frequently symptomatic of social and emotional disturbances. Although some encouraging trends in classroom management and discipline (Long and Newman, 1961) have emerged, the road to more satisfactory solutions to these problems appears to be a long and complex one.

RECOMMENDED READING

Ausubel, D. P. "A new look at classroom discipline." In *Mental Health and Achievement,* E. P. Torrance, and R. D. Strom (Eds.) New York: Wiley, 1965.

Long, N. J., and Newman, R. G. "The teacher's handling of children in conflict." *Bull. Sch. Educ., Indiana Univ.,* **37** (1961), 62 pp.

Mowrer, O. H. "Discipline and mental health." *The Harvard educ. Rev.* **17** (1947), 284–296.

Phillips, E. G., D. V. Weiner, and N. G. Haring. *Discipline, Achievement and Mental Health.* Englewood Cliffs, N.J.: Prentice-Hall, 1966.

6.5 Discipline: Its Psychological and Educational Aspects

Hirsch L. Silverman, SETON HALL UNIVERSITY

The director of the National Education Association's research division sums up the matter of discipline in these words: "Any assumption that most of today's children and youth are going to the dogs is a serious mistake" (1). This conclusion by Dr. Lambert is based on the responses to a questionnaire mailed by the NEA to a stratified sampling of classroom teachers, in which teacher opinion on the topic of discipline was asked. But much that is psychological, scientific, objective and technical in the area of discipline certainly needs expression, analysis, integration and ultimately implementation.

We know that in dealing with the administration of pupil personnel boards of education have the authority, either expressed or implied, to make and enforce any rule or regulation governing the conduct of pupils which is not unreasonable (2). It should be pointed out also that the authority of the school board extends to the pupil while off the school grounds if the act in question is such as to affect directly the discipline and good order of the school. It is well established that a board of education may discipline a pupil to the point of suspension or expulsion for disobedience of reasonable rules and regulations.

But parents, adults everywhere, and even teachers and school administrators are now deeply concerned over the kind of generation of children our schools are producing. Pronouncements in the press, in magazines, in books, and by parents themselves are often strongly critical of the schools and their effect on modern young people. The great confusion existing in the minds of parents and critics alike is owing in part to the change in the very nature of discipline itself. Because the so-called rod is ceasing to be the symbol of authority, and punishment is no longer the basis or impetus of school-boy effort, many people assume that discipline is disappearing.

A school of psychologists believes that perhaps America needs more than anything else at this time a generation of parents who accept as fact that their most important business in the world is the raising of children with proper and appropriate discipline. Our life today is far more complex, more demanding and more mobile than ever before, and parents often unwittingly rush their children into the obligations and doings that are in-

---

Reprinted from *Mental Hygiene,* **42** (1958), 274–284. By permission of the author and The National Association for Mental Health.

appropriate for them, simply to satisfy the whim and wish of the parents themselves. This too causes lack of discipline and lack of control in the pupils later in life.

Let us examine the area, problems, factors and ramifications of the field of discipline.

What is discipline? Educationally and psychologically, Smith's (3) definition is rather appropriate here, since its application is direct in most of our democratic classrooms: "School discipline is merely social control within the school group; it includes all the forces that mold attitudes and inspire conduct of pupils. Its essence is that subtle thing called school spirit. Thus in every phase of school work, the problem of discipline or social control must enter as part of the educative program, not incidentally."

In part, earlier concepts of discipline aimed to teach conformity and obedience. A pupil who questioned the word of a teacher was regarded as an upstart who deserved immediate and harsh punishment. The teacher's word was law, and failure to conform was punished by use of the hickory stick.

Both the method and the aim of discipline in today's school are different from those of former years. Today the aim is to secure good order and socially oriented self-direction. Order which stems from purposeful activity will not always be "pin-drop" silence, but it will persist without adult control. When given an opportunity, children continually surprise adults with their ability to be intelligently self-directive.

Let us examine the matter objectively and in psychological terms. One important aspect of discipline in the schools today is that punishment is largely directed toward the symptoms of misbehavior instead of being useful as a means of getting at the causes. The present view in psychological thinking leans in the direction of mental hygiene, *i.e.,* that causes must be determined before an attack on symptoms can be very successful. Authoritarian discipline often gets the desired result of conformity, but in far too many cases the tension takes some other form of expression. A teacher may get silence in the classroom upon demand, but the suppressed tension of the student finds vent in varied ways, *e.g.,* in writing on the hallway walls or in defacing the desks.

Psychologists feel that before an individual pupil's behavior is condemned harshly the causative factors in the social climate and the standards of the group should be analyzed. Behavior patterns are acquired during the total learning situation and consequently an individual's conduct cannot be judged apart from his social environment. Discipline, instruction and environmental factors are interactive; in this, educators are in agreement with psychologists. If the child is to acquire rational behavior, he must have, as in other types of learning, the satisfaction of right responses and the related annoyance of incorrect responses. The type of activities from which a child derives his satisfactions certainly is an important consideration in guiding his behavior. The child who finds his greatest satisfaction from self-centered activities displays a lack of social maturity.

Misbehavior requires treatment and control no less than physical illness. However, treatment that breaks down self-confidence in a child and makes him overly fearful of rebuke can seriously retard his educational and emotional growth. Disciplining by parents or teachers that creates constant fears and anxiety will inhibit children by stifling their natural tendencies to explore and to experiment. Certainly punishment at times is warranted, but if punishment is inflicted it should have a corrective value as well as provide the child with a sense of having learned something that will guide him in the future. Punishment should not be inflicted for its own sake, nor merely as a quick emotional flare-up in response to a particular act of bad conduct.

Also, acquiring proper patterns of behavior involves self-activity on the part of the learner. For children to be able to grow in self-discipline, they must have ample opportunity to secure this growth. Where children are working cooperatively under the guidance of a teacher to achieve goals they have planned to work towards, there is no thought of conduct except to determine the best method of achieving the group's objectives. Discipline here is inseparable from teaching. Wholesome growth in discipline takes place as children gradually assume more and more responsibility (4).

The teacher may well be concerned with the sum total of temperament, outlook and habitual choice which involves the personality of the child. Children should be given the tools of analysis and should be given the opportunity to pass judgment on conduct just as they are given a basis for passing judgment on the merit of a piece of literature. Growth in proper behavior must be based upon the insights and understandings of how individuals may become better judges of good and evil (5).

If it is to be effective, discipline must be predicated on certain basic rules of conduct. If our future society is to be strong and sound mentally, emotionally, physically and educationally, parents and teachers would do well to acquire fundamental knowledge and sound habits in the training of children. Regular hours of rest and sleep, coupled with wholesome food, are requirements not only of the home but of the school in its indoctrination of children. Parents must be consistent in their handling of children, loving them yet being firm and must give of their time to explain the responsibilities of daily living. Discipline is also based on proper home environment, a home in which religion is made the cornerstone, not merely given lip service. This must, of course, include parents who truly love each other and live together in mutual respect. Discipline of children also requires a father who feels his responsibility for participating in the training of the child, in all possible ways.

In diagnosing children's behavior the teacher must come to recognize the part that emotional factors play in determining human conduct. Many of the important decisions made by our pupils, particularly by the more immature among them, are largely on an emotional basis. Fundamentally, the function of education is to lead the child toward greater mental maturity and thereby assist him in making more of his decisions on a rational basis. Yet one who takes a realistic view of human behavior cannot fail to recognize the critical impact of the emotions upon conduct.

The child needs practice in learning to behave appropriately in various situations. It is no more reasonable to assume that errors in behavior may be eliminated by verbal instruction alone than it is to expect that errors in grammar may be eradicated so easily. Only as the child is presented with numerous opportunities for correct action, together with an understanding of its real meaning, does he learn to behave in a better manner. He then must practice continuously so that acceptable behavior becomes more or less automatic and habitual, even involuntary.

Another important psychological principle is this: Only when the individual understands the implications of his acts do they become significant and aid in his character development. When the teacher acts merely as a censor for outward mannerisms, she thwarts the child's growth in accepting moral responsibility for his actions. The teacher should play the role of stimulator to right behavior, rather than critic. Certainly learning to behave properly is among the most complex of all learnings. It is achieved only by constant effort. Children need guidance, not dictation, in establishing habits of good conduct.

Many factors and conditions influence child behavior. In order to understand and direct a child's behavior in an intelligent manner, the teacher should recognize that individual behavior is in part the result of many forces in the community. Some of these forces are economic; others derive from the standards of conduct of other children and adults. Particularly significant in the thinking of the child and his overt behavior are the standards of values held by the children of the group with whom he associates. Where a community sets wealth as a standard of personal value, a child's acceptance by various social levels or units may be mainly (and unfortunately) on an economic basis. Even if he has a sound personality, possesses qualities of leadership and is able to gain admittance into the so-called exclusive circles, he may still be confused in his thinking and even be handicapped in his activities. The point we are making is, nevertheless, that the teacher has the responsibility of assisting pupils in the developing of a sound set of values.

Studies of children enrolled in schools reveal that too many are handicapped by serious defects or illnesses. Many more have minor defects. It is to be remembered that problems of behavior may often be traced directly to the child's physical handicaps. Even feelings of physical inadequacy result in social maladjustment and acts of misbehavior. This is particularly true if the handicap is serious enough to prevent the child from taking part in gym work or sports.

Many factors account for restlessness in children. Malnutrition, poor vision and defective hearing contribute to poor achievement and the child then is irritated with the school situation. The teacher should not be too quick to punish, and should be able to recognize signs of malnutrition and of possible mental and physical fatigue.

Just as the teacher should understand child behavior, she should recognize the basic needs of her pupils. Every child needs to have feelings of security, a sense of belonging and a growing realization of adequacy or success. If he does not satisfy these needs in some part at least, his need for satisfaction may manifest itself in negative behavior, at school and in the home. Emotional blocks may even develop in a school situation in which the child is subjected to strongly rigid requirements of conduct.

Essentially, the so-called "problem child" may often be the product of heredity rather than environment. New findings in human genetics may in time nullify the prevailing tendency to blame all defects in personality on a child's early environment and conditioning. According to some teachers and other adults who work with delinquent and seriously undisciplined children, too heavy a burden of blame and responsibility is often placed on the parents of children who were supposedly "just born that way." There is mounting evidence that heredity produces degrees of susceptibility or resistance to innumerable traits and characteristics which often are regarded as purely environmental. These children who are delinquent may have been born with tendencies which incline them much more than other children to abnormal behavior or functioning. In fact, psychological thinking would prevail upon teachers, parents and adults to avoid calling everything "environmental" or "psychosomatic" or "conditioned." Needless to say, then, the greatest and most immediate hope of the field of education should be in reducing human defectiveness in whatever area and also in improving environmental factors.

The seriousness of behavior difficulties is often determined by the mental maturity of the individual. A child of low intelligence is often susceptible to the suggestions of other persons and might find himself in a behavior situation without discriminating as to the seriousness of the difficulty or its implications. But many problems requiring discipline often arise among children of high intelligence, too. If the school situation fails to present a challenge for the bright child to exercise his mental abilities, boredom and restlessness may cause him to misbehave.

Parents can learn a lot about dealing with their children's behavior by becoming familiar with disciplinary lessons that every teacher is expected to know. The object of discipline is to help an individual to do what is expected of him; and if a child is to do what is expected of him, he must first be helped to understand real goals and limitations. Children need the security that comes from feeling there is a guide, a protective authority that will watch over them. Basic to good discipline also is the function of helping the child develop a feeling of personal worth. The good teacher and the good parent should provide the kind of discipline all children need; that includes, among other things, giving the child a limited area in which to experiment and make mistakes, helping him understand his mistakes, and showing how the problems of living call for certain kinds of behavior.

Let us not overlook this fact, namely, that a child's behavior is greatly influenced by his home environment. The standards of conduct of his parents are usually reflected in the child's acceptance or rejection of their behavior patterns. Discord in the family resulting from parental differences over the severity or the methods of punishment often results in confused and inconsistent child behavior. Bickering and arguments in the home are conducive to emotional disturbances in the child. The presence in the home of a more talented or a more gifted brother or sister, or a favorite child, may cause deep resentments on the part of the child less fortunate or less favored. The child of an immigrant or foreign-born family which may have been subjected even inadvertently to acts of discrimination in the community may be unable to make a satisfactory adjustment to school life. The rather important point here is that, even if it may be necessary at times to correct a pupil's actions immediately, the teacher has the responsibility to search for and, if possible, to find the causal factors of misbehavior.

Estes (6) states: "After punishment is administered the effect on the organism is to produce an inhibition of behavior." Although a teacher may prevent a pupil from sucking his thumb by shaming him, the teacher may not notice that the pupil's insecurity may now show itself in his withdrawal from the groups in which the teacher works. Repressions may serve the needs of teachers at times, but does not help the child to become more self-directing.

Study of the psychology of the school group reveals many factors contributing to anti-social or unsocial conduct of individual pupils. In an analysis of the structure of the school group, Sheviakov and Redl (7) suggest six factors which may cause undesirable individual conduct. The following is an adaptation of their viewpoint:

Dissatisfaction in the work process The subject matter may be too easy to challenge the abilities of the students, thereby causing them to seek other outlets; or the subject matter may be too difficult and produce student indifference or irritation. Also, assignments may be poorly planned.

Emotional unrest in interpersonal relations Tensions growing out of strong friendships or animosities among pupils may supersede work interests. Competing cliques may become emotional disturbances. Clashes of personality between pupils and teachers often result in serious maladjustment.

Disturbances in group climate By the term "group climate" Sheviakov and Redl mean the basic feeling tone which underlies the life of a group, the sum total of everybody's emotions toward each other, toward work and toward the organization.

They give the following examples of different types of group climate:

Punitive climate: One in which pupils are accepted or rejected on the basis of the teacher's behavior code.

Emotional blackmail climate: In this situation the children develop a strong emotional dependence upon the teacher and there is strong rivalry between the children who conform and those who are not close to the teacher.

Hostile competition climate: Everybody is whipped into competition with everybody else. The result is extreme uncooperativeness among members of the group.

Group pride climate: In its extreme form, feelings of group vanity and conceit may result. The individual who does not meet all the requirements of group loyalty may be made an outcast subject to group persecution.

Mistakes in organization and group leadership During the period of adolescence there is need for the gradual emancipation of the child from adult domination. Some of the features of the school organization which disregard this need of youth are too much autocratic pressure, too much organization, and group organization out of focus with the age, maturity, background and special needs of the group.

Emotional strain and sudden change A member of a group may become unduly excited about examinations, athletic contests or community events. Sudden changes in behavior requirements, techniques and leadership frequently result in emotional upsets of both individuals and group.

The composition of the group Frictions and discipline problems may develop unless children are grouped on the basis of criteria relevant to group life.

Parents and teachers sometimes place too much faith in the rational process in trying to get across to children the importance of certain rules of behavior. There are times when the adults should simply say to children that a rule must be insisted upon only because the adult knows better what is good for the child. The democratic way is, of course, vital in working with children, but we must not make the mistake of thinking that children will follow rules and regulations just because they have been carefully explained and discussed. Discipline cannot be totally permissive; yet ruling children haphazardly through fear and punishment can be damaging. Within a framework of adult-set limitations and controls, the child must still have freedom to make mistakes and to experiment, for only in this way can he develop the inner controls necessary for self-discipline.

To be sure, the amount of freedom suitable for a child depends upon the child's age and maturity. The ideal situation in terms of discipline is one in which areas of freedom are inconsistently widened over the years. Also, an atmosphere of love and acceptance is the first essential for helping children grow in self-discipline. Along with conditions stimulating to free action, there is a need for careful organization of the child's life at school; as children grow and mature, they should take increasing responsibility for helping to establish their own limitation and rules. In many situations in a child's life, however, the teacher, the parent, the adult generally, must assume final responsibility; and in such situations, vagueness or confusion make for poor discipline.

We feel that all pupils should not be disciplined in the same manner. The shy pupil may well be treated kindly while the deliberately mischievous child may require more vigorous methods of control. There is certainly need at times for placing restraints upon the activities of individuals and groups of children but the manner in which the restraints are imposed is especially significant. There are a few basic considerations which teachers may find helpful in preventing individual violations of good behavior. Bernard (8) lists several of these, again keeping in mind that mental hygiene is the basis of good discipline.

Teachers must understand the nature of children It should be remembered that growth takes place on uneven fronts; because pupils may have gained independence in one area does not necessarily mean that they can reasonably be expected to be independent in all activities. The degree of pupil control usually varies with the situation. It is natural for children to desire freedom of movement; to restrict this freedom unnecessarily or injudiciously is to ignore one of their innate drives. The teacher should recognize the individuality of each child. Every child is unique and the teacher should understand this just as she understands that every pupil's learning interest varies. All pupils cannot be forced into any one particular kind of mold, intellectually, academically, emotionally.

Strict domination should be avoided While there must be order underlying productive work, the lock-step procedures all too often used in classrooms do not bring about continuously productive activity. Work done under compulsion develops a distaste in the pupil.

Discipline should be appropriate and consistent Appropriate discipline takes into account the individual, the time, the total situation, and the degree to which the behavior differs from the individual's typical responses. As to consistency, one should not overlook a given response at one time and deal with it decisively and abruptly at another time.

Shaming, sarcasm, and ridicule should be avoided Any procedures which belittle another person may tend either to undermine his own sense of worth or to stimulate resentments that are destructive to a cheerful classroom atmosphere. When sarcasm and ridicule are used, it is not likely that the child will get the security needed from the feeling of companionship with his teacher, his school and his fellow students. Any words or actions which undermine his feeling of personal worth must be strongly condemned from the standpoint of good discipline.

Pupils should be kept busy with interesting tasks If the child is interested in his work there will be less need for imposed discipline. Busy and interested pupils have no time for acts that could keep them from reaching their objective.

A good adult example should be set Much behavior is learned by direct imitation and much by unconscious imitation or suggestion. Pupils try to imitate their admired teachers. Especially in high school, boys and girls consciously aim to pattern their behavior after teachers whom they have selected as heroes. Because of this, a teacher's attitude toward aspects of discipline (lying, cheating, work habits, etc.) has direct influence on the conduct of his students. Not only the words he speaks but the attitudes he reveals may be taken as models by the pupils.

Friendliness, fair-mindedness and respect for others—or suspicion, jealousy and bigotry—are learned from one's intimates. This does not mean that a teacher has to be perfect. If a teacher cannot always be a sound example of self-discipline, he or she can at least make a consistent effort to grow better toward self-control.

Seek the cause of misbehavior At times a student does something just because he can get away with it, but usually misbehavior is generated by some tension or deprivation felt by the child.

Have confidence in self and pupils Autocratic procedures by the teacher are likely to grow out of personal feelings of insecurity. The teacher may demand strict conformity because of the fear that things will get out of hand; he must be confident that the pupils are capable of assuming responsibility. Children enjoy living up to expectations. If they know mature conduct is expected, they will strive for it; but if they know the teacher suspects them of incompetence, it will not likely hurt their feelings to show the teacher that he or she is right.

Use reasoning Understanding is necessary to self-discipline. The teacher has the responsibility of explaining to erring students the reasons for rules and regulations in general and the reason for a specific requirement in a specific case. This reasoning should take place when the teacher is emotionally calm. If reasoning is attempted at a time of emotional stress, there is too great a likelihood that what is said will degenerate into wrangling, even nagging. Teachers should not expect youngsters, even of high school age, to understand their own motivation; it is therefore not very practical to try to reason with them by asking, "What makes you do this?" Too often, the pupil honestly does not know the answer to such a question. It is better psychology to try to have the pupil place himself in the situation of another. Try to get him to see how he would feel on the receiving-end of the very behavior in which he has been indulging.

Authority must be positive In many schools pupils participate in the making of disciplinary policy and share in carrying out the policy. However, the teacher is accountable for classroom conduct. Specialization carries with it authority that can be and should be used constructively.

Provide for substitute behavior Instead of forbidding the child to interrupt what another is presenting in class, the teacher may ask him to wait his own turn and then make some thought-out contribution (9). Instead of telling him only that he must study, the teacher should make an attempt to discover why he is not interested in the project and help him find some aspect of it that will challenge him. Providing substitute activities is not being educationally or psychologically "soft." Rather it is recognition of the fact that behavior is caused; that the ultimate aim of discipline is self-direction; that growth is an individual process; and that a mature individual must get along wthout constant supervision.

Discipline should be democratic Democratic discipline has a triple advantage. It is in accord with the objectives and principles of our society, and thus provides preparation for more effective adulthood. It tends to capitalize on individual assets, and thus provides a means of stimulating growth toward independence and self-direction. And it lessens the chances of generating habits and tensions that are harmful to mental health.

Wholesome discipline can be developed when the teacher's direction is not only positive but also cooperative, fair, consistent and attentive to individual differences. Such discipline depends on teachers who have a thorough knowledge of growth principles in general and an appreciation of the specific causes of behavior in terms of the school and out-of-school backgrounds of individuals.

Too often discipline is thought of in the school only. Essentially, discipline must have its impetus and origin in the home. Only those children with parents or guardians who are themselves well disciplined may be expected to be soundly disciplined as individuals. No greater mistake can ever be made by parents than to attempt to discipline children by temper and by screaming at them, or by pushing children around in a bullying fashion. Parents actually set the example through their own personal conduct of the standards they profess to want for their children; there are too many parents who preach one thing and do another, however. Discipline of children requires parents who are honestly interested in their children's activities; who try to find out what the natural interests and activities of their children are; who encourage their children to discuss problems with them; and who try to help their children to find opportunities for development of those aptitudes and interests that the children too, at the time, feel to be important in their lives. Basically and fundamentally, disciplined parents will have disciplined children if they encourage their children to accept responsibility and allow them to share consistently and intelligently in family planning within the family group.

Those of us concerned with the entire field of discipline and its psychological implications should realize that there are at least a number of aims of education that we should strive for in the foreseeable future. Not only psychologists but teachers working directly with pupils of all ages may well give much thought and planning to teaching children to be critical observers and listeners. Children should learn to live and work together harmoniously. They should be taught functioning skills in such academic subjects as reading, writing and arithmetic, to help decrease the possibility of delinquent action and behavior in later years. They should be taught how to seek facts and to find answers. They should understand human geography; they should develop a thorough understanding of the peoples and cultures of the world, however different and varied they may be from their own. Children should be taught to adjust to change without fear. They should learn to express themselves clearly in order to communicate with others. They should learn to respect leadership and learn to regard authority not with defiance but with sufficient respect for the experience, the training and the knowledge that proper leadership requires. They should be encouraged to meet their fullest potential; they should not just learn to read, for example, but learn to read as well as they are capable of reading. Finally, they should be taught by parents, teachers, and other adults to develop a sense of responsibility to each other in their roles as citizens of the community.

REFERENCES

1. Lambert, Sam M. "What a national survey of teachers reveals about pupil behavior." *NEA J.* **45** (September 1956), 339.
2. Monroe, Walter S. (Ed.) School law. In *Encyclopedia of Education Research.* New York: Macmillan, 1950, pp. 1093–1098.
3. Smith, W. R. *Constructive and School Discipline.* New York: American Book, 1936, p. 45.
4. See Hockett, J. A., and E. W. Jacobsen. *Modern Practices in Elementary Schools.* New York: Ginn, 1941.
5. For a sound argument in this regard, see Mehl, Marie A., Hubert H. Mills, and Harl R. Douglass. *Teaching in the Elementary School.* New York: Ronald, 1950.
6. Estes, W. K. "An experimental study of punishment," *Psychol. Mongr.,* **57** (3, 1944), 36.
7. Redl, Fritz, and George V. Sheviakov. *Discipline for Today's Children and Youth.* Washington: Assn. for Supervis. and curriculum Develpm., National educ. Assn., 1944, pp. 44–56.
8. Bernard, Harold W. *Mental Hygiene for Classroom Teachers.* New York: McGraw-Hill, 1952, pp. 180–181.
9. For a review of the administrative aspects of discipline, see Elsbree, Williard S., and Harold J. McNally. *Elementary School Administration and Supervision.* New York: American Book, 1951.

6.6 Orientation

This volume concludes with a discourse on the nature of discipline and mental health with provocative philosophical overtones. In a broad sense, Ausubel's paper may be construed as a critique of our society's value system. In this regard the author is not alone, for such intellectuals as Paul Goodman, Edgar Friedenberg, and David Reisman all share the belief that society not only holds a restricted concept of "normal" or "healthy" behavior, but moreover has too long stressed a definition of mental health based upon ideals of conformity and adjustment to societal norms.

Ausubel introduces the reader to at least two issues. One involves the criteria for the selection and evaluation of teachers. The matter of basic teaching competence, Ausubel stresses, should outweigh personality characteristics, which rarely—if ever—are objectively measured. Further, many of these personal qualities may be irrelevant to the process of education. On this point there is much disagreement among educators. The second issue discussed in this paper is that generated by the conflicting concepts of authoritarianism and democratic values. Ausubel seems less concerned with making a value judgment about authoritarianism per se than he is with the maladaptive effects of authoritarianism within the context of social discontinuities or shifts in societal expectations and reward patterns that occur for children as they increase in age. In some cases, these shifts represent complete reversals as is apparent for New Zealand adolescents as they confront the transition from the secondary school to occupational life. An additional point of interest in this paper is Ausubel's concern for the mental health of teachers. Teachers are frequent targets of misguided criticism in our society. Their task is even more frequently unappreciated by people who have absolutely no concept of what it is like to confront daily, large numbers of students characterized by broad individual differences.

Finally, readers are urged to consider thoughtfully Ausubel's four proposals for placing into perspective the mental health-discipline issue in educational practice.

RECOMMENDED READING

Kounin, J. S., P. V. Gump, and J. J. Ryan III. "Explorations in classroom management." *J. teach. Educ.,* **12** (1961), 235–246.

Symonds, P. M. "Classroom discipline." *Teachers Coll. Rec.,* **51** (1949), 147–158.

Woodruff, A. D. "Discipline." In *Encyclopedia of Educational Research.* New York: Macmillan, 1960, pp. 381–84.

6.6 Some Misconceptions Regarding Mental Health Functions and Practices in the School

David P. Ausubel, UNIVERSITY OF TORONTO

Most reasonable persons would agree today that the legitimate functions of the school extend beyond the development of intellectual skills and the transmission of subject-matter knowledge. The school also has undeniable responsibilities with respect to mental health and personality development, simply because it is a place where children spend a good part of

Reprinted from *Psychology in the Schools,* **2** (1965), 99–105. By permission of the author and Psychology Press, Inc.

their waking hours, perform much of their purposeful activity, obtain a large share of their status, and interact significantly with adults, age-mates, and the demands of society. Hence, as long as the organizational, administrative, disciplinary, and interpersonal aspects of the school environment inevitably affect the mental health and personality development of its future citizens, it obviously behooves society to arrange these matters as appropriately and constructively as possible. Nevertheless, because the mental hygiene role of the school has been oversold and misrepresented so frequently by educational theorists, I would like to consider in this article what I believe to be some of the more serious misconceptions about mental health functions and practices in the school setting.

THE PRIMARY RESPONSIBILITY OF THE SCHOOL

To begin with, I think we need to recognize that the primary and distinctive function of the school in our society is not to promote mental health and personality development but to foster intellectual growth and the assimilation of knowledge. The school admittedly has important responsibilities with regard to the social, emotional, and moral aspects of the pupil's development, but certainly not the primary responsibility; the school's role in intellectual development, however, is incontrovertibly primary. Furthermore, much of the school's legitimate concern with interpersonal relations in the classroom does not stem merely from interest in enhancing healthful personality development as an end in itself. It also reflects appreciation of the negative effects which an unfavorable social and emotional school climate has on academic achievement, on motivation to learn, and on desirable attitudes toward intellectual inquiry. For example, if pupils feel unhappy and resentful about the discipline and social environment of the school, they will neither learn very much while they are in school nor remain much longer than they have to. And if they are goaded by fear to accept uncritically the views of their teachers and to memorize materials they do not really understand, they neither learn how to think for themselves nor build the foundations of a stable and usable body of knowledge.

THE SELECTION AND EVALUATION OF TEACHERS

Over the past three decades, in selecting and appraising school personnel, educators have tended to overvalue the personality attirubutes of the teacher and the mental health implications of teacher-pupil relationships, and to undervalue the teacher's intellectual functions and capabilities. But although teacher training institutions and teachers themselves over-emphasize the importance of personality and interpersonal factors in the classroom, there is some evidence that pupils are primarily concerned with their teachers' pedagogic competence or ability to teach, and not with their role as kindly, sympathetic, and cheerful adults (Taylor, 1962). Despite the recent trend in such fields as government and business administration to place ability in getting along with people ahead of professional competence, it is self-evidently a dangerous state of affairs when professional personnel in any field of endeavor are judged mainly on the basis of personal qualities. It is obvious that because teachers deal with impressionable children and affect their personality development, they should not have unstable or destructive personalities. Nevertheless, the principle criterion in selecting and evaluating teachers should not be the extent to which their personality characteristics conform to the theoretical ideal promoting healthful personality development, but rather their ability to organize and present subject matter effectively, to explain ideas clearly, and to stimulate and competently direct pupil learning activity.

THE LIMITS OF NORMALITY

As was long true in the area of physical hygiene, some educators also tend to exaggerate the seriousness and permanence of the effects on mental health of minor deviations from the norm of desirable hygienic practice. There is every reason to believe, however, that a wide margin of safety is the rule both in physical and mental health. Within fairly broad limits, many different kinds of teacher personality structure and ways of relating to children are compatible with normal mental health and personality development in pupils. This principle applies when either mildly undesirable classroom practices prevail over an extended period of time, or when more serious deviations from optimal standards occur occasionally. In general, children are not nearly as fragile as we profess to believe, and do not develop permanent personality disabilities from temporary exposure to interpersonal practices that fall short of what the experts currently regard as appropriate.

THE CULT OF EXTROVERSION

In education, as in many other vocational fields, we have succumbed to the cult of the warm, outgoing, amiable, and extroverted personality, and have tended to regard any deviation from this standard as axiomatically undesirable from a mental hygiene standpoint. Formerly a pupil would be referred to the school psychologist if he was boisterous, aggressive, and refractory to discipline. Now it is the child who is reserved, contemplative, and unconcerned about the opinion of his peers who arouses the clinical concern of the child guidance specialist. Similarly, many excellent teachers who happen to be shy and introverted are viewed with alarm by their psychologically oriented superiors. Yet there is absolutely no evidence that they impair their pupils' mental health, even though they may conceivably be less popular as individuals than their extroverted colleagues; and as far as pupils are concerned, it has been definitely established that popularity may be a grossly misleading index of social adjustment. An ostensibly popular individual may be little more than a "stranger in his group" in terms of the depth of his attachments, or may be popular simply because he is docile, conforming, and willing to be directed and "used" by others (Wittenberg and Berg, 1952). Contrariwise, the pupil who is unpopular because of temperamental shyness or strong intellectual interests is not necessarily socially maladjusted or inevitably fated to become so (Morris, Soroker, and Buruss, 1954).

THE EFFECTS OF AUTHORITARIANISM

Many educators have uncritically accepted the ethnocentric psychological dictum that only democratic teacher-pupil relationships are compatible with normal mental health and personality development. Yet there are many examples of authoritarian western cultures (e.g., Germany, Italy, Switzerland) in which all of the indices of mental health and mature personality development compare very favorably with those prevailing in the United States. Hence, it is obviously not authoritarianism per se that has damaging mental health consequences, but rather the existence of authoritarian practices in home and school that are incongruous with the general pattern of interpersonal relations in the culture at large. Children *are* able satisfactorily to internalize adult personality traits and mature attitudes toward authority, even in an authoritarian home and school environment, providing that (1) personal, social, and working relationships among adults are similarly authoritarian, and (2) that adults generally make as stringent demands on themselves as they do on young people. In countries like Germany and Switzerland these latter conditions prevail, and therefore authoritarianism in home and school has few adverse effects on mental health and personality development. In New Zealand, on the other hand, authoritarianism in the home and secondary school has more serious effects because it contrasts sharply with the egalitarian and generally relaxed character of vocational and social life in the adult world.

Older children and adolescents do not satisfactorily internalize values that are indoctrinated in an authoritarian fashion if the adult culture itself is organized along democratic and egalitarian lines. Under these circumstances they feel unjustly treated and discriminated against; and not only do they tend to resent the authoritarian discipline that is imposed upon them, but also to conform to adult standards only under threat of external compulsion. This is particularly true if they perceive that many adults do not honor these standards but nevertheless presume to punish them whenever they are guilty of lapses. Hence, when adults preach the virtue of hard work, ambition, responsibility, and self-denial, but do not practice these virtues themselves in occupational life, children tend to emulate their example rather than their precepts. They become habituated to striving and working hard under external pressure but fail adequately to internalize these values. Thus when they finally enter the adult vocational world and the customary authoritarian demands for conscientious effort are lifted, the tenuous structure of their disciplined work habits tends to collapse in the absence of genuinely internalized needs for vocational achievement.

Furthermore, when a teen-ager in New Zealand obtains a job he dresses as an adult, is treated as an adult, and, from the age of eighteen, is paid on an adult wage scale. Even in the armed forces where working relationships are traditionally authoritarian, he is treated no differently than anyone else. Neither a shop foreman nor an army sergeant would ever think of using a cane on a seventeen-year-old factory hand or recruit who broke one of the rules or failed to do his work neatly. Yet in the secondary school this same teen-ager is treated very much as a child, wears short pants, and is growled at or caned for similar lapses. Hence, when he perceives the vastly more egalitarian treatment accorded his contemporaries in occupational life and in the military services, it is small wonder that he often feels resentful and sometimes manifests anti-adult and anti-social tendencies.

It also seems reasonable to suppose that as children enter adolescence, disciplinary practices should be progressively liberalized to meet increasing needs for self-determination and growing capacities for self-discipline. Quite paradoxically, however, since the primary school in New Zealand has always been much less authoritarian than the secondary school, and especially so over the past two decades, discipline tends to become stricter, more rigorous, and more explicit as children pass from the former to the latter. It is entirely understandable, therefore, that when the adolescent is unexpectedly subjected to a more restrictive discipline than he was in primary school—despite his greater physical, intellectual, emotional, and social maturity—he tends to become bewildered, dismayed, and resentful.

Attributable in part to the incongruous authoritarianism of the secondary school in New Zealand are many immature attitudes toward authority. First, in public situations, New Zealanders tend to defer excessively to the opinions of authority figures and to overconform to their dictates. Second, coexistent with this exaggerated public deference to authority, particularly among university students, is a puerile species of defiance, and an irresistible impulse to reject traditional values out-of-hand, to take outrageously extreme positions, and to shock the sensibilities of conventional folk with sacrilege, profanity, and the desecration of revered symbols. Third, because of resentment toward a discriminatory type of authoritarianism and overhabituation to external controls, many secondary school pupils fail adequately to internalize recognized social norms and individual restraints. Hence they feel quite justified in violating rules and asserting themselves when authority turns its back. Finally, the distinctive feature of adolescent misbehavior in New Zealand is simply a more exaggerated and generalized expression of anti-adult feeling and puerile defiance of adult authority. In its most extreme form, bodgieism, it is basically a cult of exhibitionistic nonconformity, out-of-bounds loutishness, and of studiously labored rejection of adult respectability. Among its multiple causes must certainly be counted widespread adolescent resentment of an inappropriately authoritarian type of discipline and subordination relative to other age groups in New Zealand society. It bears some relation to the beatnik movement in the United States, but occurs in a younger age group, is less intellectual in its manifestations, and is more directly aggressive rather than philosophical in its protest.

DISTORTIONS OF DEMOCRATIC DISCIPLINE

Proponents of democratic classroom discipline believe in imposing the minimal degree of external control necessary for socialization, personality maturation, conscience development, and the emotional security of the child. Discipline and obedience are not regarded as ends in themselves but only as means to these latter ends. They are not striven for deliberately, but are expected to follow naturally in the wake of friendly and realistic teacher-pupil relationships. Explicit limits are not set routinely or as ways of showing "who is boss," but only as the need arises, i.e., when they are not implicitly understood or accepted by pupils.

Democratic discipline is as rational, nonarbitrary and bilateral as possible. It provides explanations, permits discussion, and invites the participation of children in the setting of standards whenever they are qualified to do so. Above all it implies respect for the dignity of the individual, and avoids exaggerated emphasis on status differences and barriers between free communication. Hence it repudiates harsh, abusive, and vindictive forms of punishment, and the use of sarcasm, ridicule, and intimidation.

The aforementioned attributes of democratic classroom discipline are obviously appropriate in cultures where social relationships tend to be egalitarian. This type of discipline also becomes increasingly more feasible as children become older, more responsible, and more capable of understanding and formulating rules of conduct based on concepts of equity and reciprocal obligation. But contrary to what the extreme permissivists would have us believe, democratic school discipline does not imply freedom from all external constraints, standards, and direction, or freedom from discipline as an end in itself. And under no circumstances does it presuppose the eradication of all distinctions between pupil and teacher roles, or require that teachers abdicate responsibility for making the final decisions in the classroom.

Many educational theorists have misinterpreted and distorted the ideal of democratic discipline by equating it with an extreme form of permissiveness. These distortions are most commonly encountered in the United States, but have also found acceptance in some New Zealand primary school circles. They have been dogmatically expressed in various psychologically unsound and unrealistic propositions that are considered sacrosanct in many teachers' colleges. Fortunately, however, most classroom teachers have accepted them only for examination purposes—while still in training—and have discarded them in actual practice as thoroughly unworkable.

According to one widely held doctrine, only "positive" forms of discipline are constructive and democratic. It is asserted that children must only be guided by reward and approval; that reproof and punishment are authoritarian, repressive, and reactionary expressions of adult hostility which leave permanent emotional scars on children's personalities. What these theorists conveniently choose to ignore, however, is the fact that it is impossible for children to learn what is *not* approved and tolerated, simply by generalizing in reverse from the approval they receive for behavior that *is* acceptable. Even adults are manifestly incapable of learning and respecting the limits of acceptable conduct unless the distinction between what is proscribed and approved is reinforced by punishment as well as by reward. Furthermore, there is good reason to believe that acknowledgment of wrongdoing and acceptance of punishment are part and parcel of learning moral accountability and developing a sound conscience. Few if any children are quite that fragile that they cannot take deserved reproof and punishment in stride.

A second widespread distortion of democratic discipline is reflected in the popular notion that there are no culpably misbehaving children in the classroom, but only culpably aggressive, unsympathetic, and punitive teachers. If children misbehave, according to this point of view, one can implicitly assume that they must have been provoked beyond endurance by repressive and authoritarian classroom discipline. Similarly, if they are disrespectful, then the teacher, by definition, must not have been deserving of respect. It is true, of course, that much pupil misconduct *is* instigated by harsh and abusive school discipline; but there are also innumerable reasons for out-of-bounds behavior that are completely independent of the teacher's attitudes and disciplinary practices. Pupils are also influenced by factors originating in the home, the neighborhood, the peer group, and the mass-media. Some children are emotionally disturbed, others are brain-damaged, and still others are aggressive by temperament; and there are times when even the best behaved children from the nicest homes develop an irresistible impulse—without any provocation whatsoever—to test the limits of a teacher's forbearance.

Both of the aforementioned distortions of classroom democracy are used to justify the commonly held belief among educators that pupils should not be reproved or punished for disorderly or discourteous conduct. I have, for example, observed classrooms where everybody talks at once; where pupils turn their backs on the teacher and engage in private conversation while the latter is endeavoring to instruct them; and where pupils verbally abuse teachers for exercising their rightful disciplinary prerogatives. Some educators contend that all of this is compatible with wholesome, democratic teacher-pupil relationships. Other educators deplore this type of pupil behavior but insist, nevertheless, that punishment is unwarranted under these circumstances. In the first place, they assert, reproof or punishment constitutes a "negative" and hence axiomatically undesirable approach to classroom management; and, secondly, the misbehavior would assuredly have never occurred to begin with, if the teacher's attitudes had been less autocratic or antagonistic. I have already answered the second group of educators, and to the first group I can only say that I am still sufficiently old-fashioned to believe that rudeness and unruliness are not normally desirable classroom behavior in any culture.

When such misconduct occurs, I believe pupils have to be unambiguously informed that it will not be tolerated and that any repetition of the same behavior will be punished. This action does not preclude in any way either an earnest attempt to discover why the misbehavior occurred, or suitable preventive measures aimed at correcting the underlying causes. But, by the same token, the mere fact that a pupil has a valid psychological reason for misbehaving does not mean that he is thereby absolved from moral accountability or rendered no longer subject to punishment.

Still another related distortion of democratic discipline is reflected in the proposition that it is repressive and authoritarian to request pupils to apologize for discourteous behavior or offensive language. However, if we take seriously the idea that the dignity of the human being is important, we must be willing to protect it from affront; and apology is the most civilized and effective means mankind has yet evolved for accomplishing this goal. In a democratic society nobody is that important that he is above apolgizing to those persons whom he wrongfully offends. Everybody's dignity is important—the teacher's as well as the pupil's. It is no less wrong for a pupil to abuse a teacher than for a teacher to abuse a pupil.

If apologies are to have any real significance in moral training, however, it is obvious that, even though they are explicitly requested, they must be made voluntarily, and must be reflective of genuine appreciation of wrongdoing and of sincere regret and remorse. Purely formal and mechanical statements of apology made under coercion are less than worthless. Apologies are also without real ethical import unless their basis is reciprocal, i.e., unless it is fully understood that under comparable circumstances the teacher would be willing to apologize to his pupils.

In seeking to correct these undesirable permissive distortions of classroom democracy, it would be foolhardy to return to the equally undesirable opposite extreme of authoritarianism that flourished in the United States up to a quarter century ago, and still prevails in many western nations. Democratic school discipline is still an appropriate and realistic goal for education in a democratic society; hence there is no need to throw away the baby with the bath water. It is only necessary to discard the aforementioned permissivist doctrines masquerading under the banners of democracy and behavioral science, and to restore certain other traditional values that have been neglected in the enthusiasm of extending democracy to home and school.

More specifically, we first have to clear up the semantic confusion. We should stop equating permissiveness with democratic discipline, and realistic adult control and guidance with authoritarianism. Permissiveness, by definition, is the absence of discipline, democratic or otherwise. We should cease instructing teachers that it is repressive and reactionary to reprove or punish pupils for misconduct, or to request them to apologize for offensive and discourteous behavior.

Second, we should stop misinterpreting what little reputable evidence we have about discipline, and refrain from misrepresenting our personal biases on the subject as the indisputable established findings of scientific research. The available evidence merely suggests that in a democratic cultural setting, authoritarian discipline has certain undesirable effects—*not* that the consequences of *laissez-faire* permissiveness are desirable. As a matter of fact, research studies (Cunningham, 1951) show that the effects of extreme permissiveness are just as unwholesome as are those of authoritarianism. In the school situation a *laissez-faire* policy leads to confusion, insecurity, and competition for power among pupils. Assertive pupils tend to become aggressive and ruthless, whereas retiring pupils tend to withdraw further from classroom participation. The child who is handled too permissively at home tends to regard himself as a specially privileged person. He fails to learn the normative standards and expectations of society, to set realistic goals for himself, and to make reasonable demands on others. In his dealings with adults and other children he is domineering, aggressive, petulant, and capricious.

Third, we should stop making teachers feel guilty and personally responsible for all instances of misconduct and disrespect in the classroom. We do this whenever we take for granted, without any actual supporting evidence, that these behavior problems would never have arisen in the first place if the teachers involved were truly deserving of respect and had been administering genuinely wholesome and democratic discipline.

Finally, teachers' colleges should terminate the prevailing conspiracy of silence they maintain about the existence of disciplinary problems in the schools. Although discipline is the one aspect of teaching that the beginning teacher is most worried about, he receives little or no practical instruction in handling this problem. Many teacher training institutions, as pointed out above, rationalize their inadequacies in this regard by pretending that disciplinary problems are relatively rare occurrences involving the disturbed child, or more typically the disturbed teacher. Due respect for the facts of life, however, suggests that prospective teachers today not only need to be taught more realistic propositions about the nature and purposes of democratic discipline, but also require adequately supervised, down-to-earth experience in coping with classroom discipline.

REFERENCES

Cunningham, Ruth. *Understanding Group Behavior of Boys and Girls.* New York: Teachers College, Columbia Univ., 1951.

Morris, D. P., E. Soroker, and G. Buruss. "Follow-up studies of shy, withdrawn children. I. Evaluation of later adjustments." *Amer. J. Orthopsychiat.*, **24** (1954), 743–754.

Taylor, P. H. "Children's evaluations of the characteristics of the good teacher." *Brit. J. educ. Psychol.*, **32** (1962), 258–266.

Wittenberg, R. M., and J. Berg. "The stranger in the group." *Amer. J. Orthopsychiat.*, **22** (1952), 89–97.

In Retrospect

Ellis D. Evans, UNIVERSITY OF WASHINGTON, SEATTLE

Readers who have proceeded systematically in their study of this volume have been exposed to a broad sampling of research and theory in child development. Undoubtedly it has been recognized that questions concerning children's behavior and development greatly outnumber the answers. Inevitably, research activities designed to answer specific questions result in the formulation of still further questions. Progress is therefore laborious, and the practical application of research findings is limited.

Aside from the ubiquitous issues of research design and data analysis, three interrelated problems face child-development researchers. The first is one of definition. How is a behavioral construct to be defined? By no means is there universal agreement among psychologists in defining such basic constructs as intelligence, aggression, anxiety, and the self concept. A second basic problem is measurement. How shall behavior be measured? The quality of research is always influenced by the validity and reliability of its measurement procedures. In empirical research it should be noted that a concept or construct is actually defined by the technique utilized to measure the behavior; therefore definition and measurement actually become synonymous. A third problem is created by the diverse theoretical interpretations of research findings. As reflected in the present set of readings, three major theoretical positions have dominated child-development research: psychoanalytic theory, self theory, and learning theory. A fourth view, based upon the psychology of cognition, has been progressively influential in generating research problems. Underlying each theoretical position are assumptions and postulates which frequently give rise to different predictions and explanations of behavior. The purpose of this volume has not been to elaborate upon the major theoretical positions, although a broad familiarity with each is a virtual prerequisite to the ordering and relating of research findings. Several encapsulated reviews of theoretical positions are ideal for this purpose.*

The goals of a scientific study of children are typically formulated in terms of the explanation of behavior, the prediction of behavior, and the appropriate control of variables known to influence growth, development, and learning. If anything is certain at this point in time it is that these goals remain elusive.

*See Baldwin, Alfred L., *Theories of Child Development* (New York: Wiley, 1967) and Hall, Calvin and Gardner Lindzey. ***Theories of Personality*** (New York: Wiley, 1957).

Author Index

Subject Index